THIRD EDITION

Community Organizing and Development

Herbert J. Rubin

Northern Illinois University

Irene S. Rubin

Northern Illinois University

Allyn and Bacon

Boston ■ London ■ Toronto ■ Sydney ■ Tokyo ■ Singapore

Editor-in-chief: *Karen Hanson*
Series editorial assistant: *Alyssa Pratt*
Manufacturing buyer: *Jacqueline Aaron*
Composition and prepress buyer: *Linda Cox*
Cover administrator: *Linda Knowles*
Editorial-production service: *Modern Graphics, Inc.*
Electronic composition: *Modern Graphics, Inc.*

Library of Congress Cataloging-in-Publication Data
Rubin, Herbert J.
  Community organizing and development / Herbert J. Rubin, Irene S. Rubin.—3rd ed.
    p. cm.
  Includes bibliographical references and index.
    ISBN 0-205-26116-7 (pbk.)
  1. Community development—United States 2. Community organization—United States. 3. Social action—United States. 4. Community power—United States. I. Rubin, Irene. II. Title.

HN90.C6 R73 2000
307.1′4′0973—dc21

00-041619

Printed in the United States of America

10 9 8 7 6 5 4 3 2   05 04 03 02

CONTENTS

PREFACE

Community organizing involves mobilizing people to work together to solve shared problems. As part of the mobilization effort, people learn that individual problems have social causes and that collectively fighting back is a more reasonable, dignified approach than passive acceptance or personal alienation. Development comes about as people increase their capacity to pressure government and businesses, obtain needed goods and services, and build and sustain democratic organizations. Through organizing and development people gain the confidence and tools to collectively resolve societal problems.

This book is for organizers working in community or in social change organizations who propose to spend their energy in mobilizing and coordinating others to solve shared problems. Though the craft of organizing is learned from firsthand experience, a text such as this places such experience in context by introducing a variety of models, suggesting skills organizers need, and alerting activists to dilemmas they face.

Because community organizing is difficult work and sometimes frustrating, why would someone choose to become an organizer? Some people become organizers because they are angry enough to fight back. Maybe their family and neighbors have been made ill by a chemical dump; perhaps their handicapped child has been denied access to needed services. Some individuals are outraged by injustice, watching the treatment of gays in the military, or seeing people sleep in doorways and huddle over subway grates to get a little warmth. Or maybe organizers are motivated by the unkept promises of a society to guarantee that all people are equal before the law, are free to practice their religion and speak their minds, vote, travel, and have access to jobs and housing. Organizers fight to make those promises a reality. Or maybe people become organizers just because they do not like to see anyone bullied or humiliated and, in response, spend their lives teaching others how to fight back.

This book introduces activists to ways of bringing about needed changes. We discuss theories of organizing and present hundreds of examples, while describing techniques and tactics. The book explains what has been tried, what has worked in the past and what is likely to work in the present. Throughout the text we integrate the experiences of organizers and activists with academic knowledge about communities, the political system, organizations, and social mobilization. We call attention to the choices—the tradeoffs—organizers and activists must make to bring about needed changes.

We balance descriptions of stirring protest actions and visible projects with the behind-the-scenes routines that make such work possible. Action campaigns are the dramatic, visible side of community organizing. Protesters chain themselves to bulldozers to protect a neighborhood from an unneeded highway. Civil rights activists confront police who push them back with fire hoses and bare-fanged dogs. Community groups replace old buildings used as crack houses with clean, safe, affordable housing. But the work of organizing involves much more than demonstrations or proudly cutting the ribbon of a new building. These visible and newsworthy events are the culmination of many months of steady effort in mobilizing people, creating and sustaining an organization, finding money, and mastering a changing and often hostile political environment.

To succeed at their work, organizers need management and budgeting skills, they have to know how to run meetings, and they have to be patient as people slowly reach decisions in a democratic manner. Protests and projects succeed or fail based on the details. In a protest rally, have the media been notified? Is the sound system working? In refurbishing a neighborhood, organizers need to know about mortgages, subsidies, tax breaks, and the nitty-gritty of construction. The organizer's motivation may be anger or empathy, but the tools he or she needs for success include knowledge of the environment and a variety of technical skills.

Reflections on the Third Edition

The core philosophy in the third edition carries on the ideas in earlier editions.

> Organizing is about empowering people, individually and collectively.
> **Bringing about change is not enough unless change is brought about democratically. Solving problems is important, but even more important, people need to learn to solve their own problems, to develop the knowledge, skills, and self-confidence to sustain the effort.**

We have also made some important modifications:

We have changed certain concepts. A goal of activism is to build capacity, a process we label as "development," while when talking about providing goods and services to the community or restoring the physical neighborhood we use the phrase *social production. Development* then means empowering individuals to learn skills and gain the confidence to try new approaches. We have expanded the concept of *community* beyond that of a geographic place and the bonds between people by exploring the idea of social capital, the psychological and material linkages that enable people to help one another.

We continue to point out tensions organizers face but emphasize how they can be resolved. We explicitly recognize that those involved in direct actions—protests— are often in dispute with activists who emphasize social production. We argue, though, that these models are complementary, each involving a different configuration of needed skills and worthwhile goals. We note a change toward more multicultural neighborhoods and an increasing competition between ethnic groups contending for the same area. Today, organizers need the ability to work with a variety of ethnic, racial, and cultural communities.

We have added some new material and different slants. We emphasize that problems are intentionally *framed* to communicate what participants want others to understand about a situation or action. We argue that perceptions are important, and that battles are fought less often about the facts of the matter than about the interpretation of those facts. In this edition, we discuss how to get expertise and resources from an emerging support sector and what materials are now easily available on the Internet. The material on social production organizations has been bolstered with new interviews with practitioners.

Throughout the text, the references to the literature have been updated and descriptions of the political and social environment have been altered to reflect the current situation.

The Contents of the Book

This book contains seven parts. The first sets the stage, presenting a synthesis of several approaches to organizing. In Part Two, we discuss problems that communities face and the half-hearted responses of government. Then we provide a brief history of organizing, showing how people, by working together, have solved and continue to address many community problems.

Part Three focuses on two core concepts. First, we examine what is meant by *empowerment,* both individually and collectively. Then we explore several meanings of *community:* the place where organizing occurs; the social integration toward which organizers build; and, the social capital on which people build as they work together.

Part Four deals with how people get involved and stay involved in community work. We first describe the role of the organizer, the person who catalyzes the entire process, then examine different models of how people are mobilized into action. We talk about documenting problems and building democratic organizations. This section of the book ends with a discussion about the meetings that get people fired up and help them decide what to do and how to do it.

The remaining two sections present complementary approaches to community work. In Part Five, we focus on the social action model, first by providing an overview of principles then offering details about how to pressure government. We examine ways of aggressively protesting social injustices and then conclude by presenting a variety of techniques for extending power by building coalitions, effectively using the media, and successfully negotiating a conclusion to a campaign.

In Part Six, we detail the social production model. We first describe the wide variety of social production activities from day care to housing construction. Then we trace how projects are planned, funded, implemented, and managed, drawing heavily on projects done by community-based, community-controlled renewal organizations. The final chapter of Part Six describes the support sector of larger organizations that help community and social-change groups.

In the Epilogue, we review our model for organizing and discuss our concerns about the future of community work. We present our belief that community organizing must adapt by monitoring and responding to the changing needs of people in an evolving society.

Acknowledgments

We would like to thank the reviewers who commented on this edition: Michael Reisch, University of Pennsylvania, and William Cloud, University of Denver.

Community Organizing and Development

PART ONE

Organizing for Empowerment

Community organizing is a search for social power, for both the individuals and the communities in which they live. Organizing is the antidote to the sense of helplessness people feel as they confront shared problems. In this section, we describe how people effectively combat a sense of powerlessness to bring about community improvement and needed social changes.

CHAPTER

1 Organizing for Collective Empowerment

Community activists join with labor organizers to picket sweatshops; grandmothers, mothers, and daughters march on Washington to defend abortion rights; neighbors work together to protect their homes and health from the menace of toxic wastes. Community-based development organizations partner with city hall to build affordable housing; community members contest industries that remove jobs from their cities; neighbors support a community health clinic. Through collective actions people call attention to social, political, and economic injustice and then work together to combat these problems. Community organizing is about creating a democratic instrument to bring about sustained social change.

Community organizations have reduced overcrowding in schools, provided access to health care, increased the amount of affordable housing, and eased tensions between ethnic and cultural groups. Grassroots efforts have secured legal rights for minorities, workers, feminists, and gays. Organizing helps people learn technical skills, increases personal competence, and achieves the empowerment to make government and businesses accountable to citizens.

Community organizing involves bringing people together to combat shared problems and to increase peoples' say about decisions that affect their lives. *Community development* occurs when people strengthen the bonds within their neighborhoods, build social networks, and form their own organizations to provide a long-term capacity for problem solving. When many people and many organizations join together to combat injustice and inequality they create a *social movement*.

People, Problems, and Feelings of Powerlessness

People fight back to eliminate a variety of socially caused problems. Urban redevelopment programs destroy needed housing. Housing discrimination concentrates the poor, minorities, and new immigrant groups in high-crime neighborhoods served by inadequate school systems. These neighborhoods contain health hazards, from lead-based paint to toxic fumes from incinerators. Health-care costs keep going up, while more than 40 million individuals, many of them children, have no health insurance. The combined burdens of child rearing and earning a living are falling increasingly on women, but women have difficulty getting jobs that pay enough to support a family. Employment in manufacturing industries is decreasing as international conglomerates move jobs abroad, while white collar workers fear layoffs when their companies downsize. In general, the rich get richer and the poor fall further behind.

Why People Feel Helpless

Even when people experience problems, they often do not think about the possibility of fighting back. To complain to corporations seems futile. Government appears as a collection of bumbling, indifferent bureaucrats who are allied with the business interests that are causing some of the problems. Further, many of the problems people routinely encounter are complex; people have no idea how to solve them.

Whom do you fight when a city development agency, working with national real estate promoters, destroys neighborhood housing to build a shopping mall made accessible by a highway funded by a state agency? What happens if a waste removal company wants to set up an incinerator near a town's supply of clean water, or if a public hospital is deluged with victims of drug-resistant tuberculosis, or if the economically dispossessed mix with the mentally handicapped to form a highly visible group of homeless people that no one wants to shelter? Feeling helpless is natural when faced with such overwhelming problems.

Sometimes people feel helpless because they blame themselves for problems they experience, even though they are not at fault. When a plant is shut down, some of the unemployed assume they are responsible for their misfortunes: "If only I were more deserving or worked elsewhere or had stayed in school longer, this would not have happened." By looking inward they fail to recognize that the problem was caused, in part, by the incentives that government provided to businesses that helped them move. Battered women and victims of rape often react in a similar way: "If I had been a better wife, prepared tastier foods, or looked prettier, perhaps he would not have hit me." Or, "Maybe my clothes were too provocative; the police said I shouldn't have been walking by that park at night." Such self-blame distracts from the organizing needed to pressure the police to arrest abusers and rapists. Until individuals understand that they are not at fault, and that the problems occur because of broader economic or social forces, they cannot respond constructively.

Fear of retaliation is another reason why many people do not raise their voices in protest. Retaliation may include arrests of those provoked into violence, disseminating false rumors to ruin a person's reputation, or actual physical harm. People who marched for civil rights faced hostile police who dispersed them with water cannons and set dogs to attack them. Their homes were bombed and their lives threatened. Bosses sometimes fire people who are identified as troublemakers and then blackball them— that is, circulate lists of their names to employers to prevent the person from being hired elsewhere. The impact of such actions is not lost on those who remain.

In part, people fail to protest because they have been taught and accept the idea that those in authority are right and that questioning authority is wrong. As Piven and Cloward describe:

> An elaborate system of beliefs and ritual behaviors . . . defines for people what is right and what is wrong and why; what is possible and what is impossible. . . . Because this superstructure of beliefs and rituals is evolved in the context of unequal power, it is inevitable that the beliefs and rituals reinforce inequality, by rendering the powerful divine and the challengers evil (Piven & Cloward, 1977, p. 1).

People in positions of wealth or political power shape the ideas through which the rest of us interpret the world. In doing so, they exercise a subtle dominance over the society. Antonio Gramsci calls this ability of those in power to frame how others think about key issues, an *intellectual hegemony* (Gramsci, 1973). Workers are taught and believe that business people have a right to do with their firms as they please, regardless of whether employees get hurt. Wives often accept the idea that their husbands should make the important family decisions, regardless of the consequences for themselves and their children. As part of this imposed framing, people accept the idea that those in power are there legitimately and should not be opposed, even when what they are doing is harmful to others.

Even when people earnestly want to fight against the conditions under which they live, they don't know how. Poor people have little way of discovering how to set up community-based development organizations to rebuild their own neighborhoods. People have little experience with organizing a rally or demonstration, or persuading others to join in the battle, or pressuring politicians. The traditions of protest are ignored in schools and colleges so as to avoid threatening "the superstructure of beliefs and rituals" that support those in power.

A further reason why people feel helpless is that they are financially or socially dependent on precisely those that are causing them harm. Citizens understand that their families are being poisoned by dirty air, undrinkable water, and tainted food and worry about the effects of industrial wastes on their health but are unwilling to antagonize the companies that provide their jobs. Wives who are abused stay in a marriage because they cannot figure out how to support themselves and their children without their husbands' income.

Finally, people feel vulnerable when they think they are alone in facing a problem and recognize that an isolated individual who complains is easy for the opposition to pick off, defuse, or ignore. Sometimes isolation comes about because of geographic separation as among the handicapped, or environmentalists, or even housewives. More often, people are isolated because they occupy separate social space. Social distance makes it hard for poor African American women and middle-class White women to interact; blue-collar and white-collar workers are separated at work and home; those educated at universities and those educated by life face distinct worlds, as do gays and straights, and people of different ages or ethnicity.

Though keenly aware of the many problems they face, people often feel powerless and do not act. This failure to take charge of their lives and to protest against injustice may be misconstrued by those in power as consent or approval for the status quo.

Organizing is About Obtaining Collective Power for Ordinary People

Through organizing and fighting back, people reduce this sense of powerlessness. As people join together, they learn from one another that the causes of problems are social or economic, not personal, and that problems are shared. Collectively people forge a shared sense of legitimacy and purpose that challenges the myth that decision makers are right because they are in formal positions of power. Organizing builds the confidence necessary for democracy, while addressing a wide range of social and economic problems.

People build organizations that can gather and focus information, pressure government agencies, conduct successful protests, or create new forms of ownership. Initial successes give ordinary people more confidence that they can solve future problems, and, by joining together in an organization, individuals reduce the risk of retaliation. Organizing empowers both individuals and the communities to which they belong.

More formally,

> Organizing is the process of helping people understand the shared problems they face while encouraging them to join together to fight back. Organizing builds on the social linkages and networks that bring people together to create firm bonds for collective action.

Organizing enables people and their communities to gain the capacity to take actions for change, a capacity that we label as development.

> Development is the ongoing creation of personal and collective resources that enable people to fight back and to take charge. Development includes building organizations that have the knowledge to help those in need, creating the bonds of trust between people that constitute community, sharing technical skills, and gaining ownership of material wealth in ways that improve the lives of those in need. Development is about building capacity for sustained change and empowerment.

Taken together, organizing and development are about

> creating local empowerment through groups of people with a shared mission acting collectively to control decisions, projects, programs and policies that affect them as a community.

> Organizing and development involve a struggle for power, often between the "haves" and "have-nots" (Alinsky 1969), between those who are in political office or who control wealth, and those who are not in office or lack material resources. In this battle,

> Power is the ability to affect decisions that shape social outcomes.

Fighting for Power

Power stems from many sources. For the haves, power comes from owning businesses and property, from occupying key political positions, from controlling public and private police forces, and from being accepted by the broader society as having a legitimate right to make decisions that influence social outcomes in ways that favor the powerful.

In community organizing, ordinary people come together to contest the tacit public agreement to allow financial, business, and political leaders to make all the major social policy decisions. Contestations occur over

- *How a problem is defined or framed.* Are people blamed for being poor because of their unwillingness to work or is there an understanding that poverty comes about because firms are allowed to maximize their profits no matter the consequences?
- *How decisions are made.* Should decisions be made by politicians beholden to big businesses, big businesses on their own, or should a more democratic system prevail?
- *Who carries out the decisions that are made.* Should government or businesses do things for or to people, or should people themselves carry out the policies that they have democratically determined?
- *Who benefits from a solution.* Are health plans set up to minimize the costs to employers or to assure that people receive the coverage they need?
- *How societal resources are allocated.* Should the rich continue to get richer while social programs that benefit the poor are eliminated, or can more just systems for allocating money be found?

When ordinary people begin a contest to obtain power, they lack wealth, rarely control force, and must contend with widespread beliefs that business or government are automatically right. Power, however, comes about as organizations bring people together and teach people needed skills. Businesses and the rich have more money with which to persuade politicians, but ordinary people can assemble in large numbers and persuade elected officials that if they do not help, they will be tossed out of office.

People obtain power step by step. Organizers work to increase awareness that many people face similar problems because of societal failings not individual faults. Next, people discover that they can join organizations that gain resources and focus collective energy on fighting back. Initial success leads to additional victories, as people master needed skills, enthusiasm and confidence increases, and others who initially stayed back become more willing to join in the struggle. Success at a shared task—organizing a neighborhood watch, reestablishing community businesses, pressuring a politician—empowers people. Participation in protest itself teaches people the need to fight and the possibility of winning, while creating broader political understanding:

> Through such protests . . . ordinary people construct a broader analysis of politics; they shift from a non-ideological stance to an ideological stance, from defining themselves as non-political to defining themselves as political, from having a deep faith in the established political system to developing a critical political analysis. This critical per-

spective . . . creates the potential for grass-root activists to play a more active and militant role. (Krauss, 1988, p. 259)

The more people participate in collective actions and gain a belief that change is possible, the greater their future capacity to solve community problems. Later, as people throughout the country join together in a shared cause, a social movement emerges. *Social movements* are

collective challenges by people with common purposes and solidarity in sustained interaction with elites, opponents, and authorities. (Tarrow, 1994, pp. 3–4)

Organizations need not win every campaign to bring about changes. A neighborhood organization might fight city hall on a redevelopment issue and lose but by its persistence convinces government to include affordable housing in future renewal efforts. During a sustained fight, power can slowly shift from business owners and government to representatives of ordinary people.

The purpose of such involvement is not to change one ruling group for another, but to gain power to solve problems. The goal of feminists is not dominating men but creating a society in which all people are judged on their accomplishments, not on their gender. When people form housing development organizations, their intent is to provide homes at affordable prices, not to drive for-profit firms out of business. *Power is not power over someone but rather the power to accomplish goals of social improvement.* But first, social-change groups need to be organized to be heard.

Power is Achieved by Expanding Democracy

Bringing about social change is a vital purpose of organizing, but social change must be accomplished in democratic ways. Democracy involves the informed participation of a large number of people in decisions that affect them. It requires that governmental bodies be accessible to all, and that policy issues be clearly stated and widely disseminated. Democracy allows for conflict as different interests are fought out through a fair and transparent decision-making process. Community organizing is about creating democratic involvement.

Every conceivable effort must be made to rekindle the fire of democracy. . . . A people can participate only if they have both the opportunity to formulate their program, which is the reason for participation, and a medium through which they can express and achieve their program. . . . The universal premise of any people's program is "We the people will work out our own destiny." . . . *Can there be a more fundamental democratic program than a democratically minded and participating people?* (Alinsky, 1969, pp. 196–197)

Social-change organizations must be run democratically, though there are a variety of ways of so doing. At the very least, decisions are made through votes in which all can participate. Alternatively, in organizations in which people know one another and have developed respect for each other, democratic decision making occurs when people talk together extensively, learn what each other wants, and build toward a consensus that respects the opinions of others (Mansbridge, 1980).

The ideals of democracy—a respect for the opinions of others and the full involvement of all in making core decisions—must be achieved in community or social-change organizations. Organizational leaders must strive to remain responsive to their members and make sure that procedures are in place that ensure all members, not simply self-selected leaders, are involved in setting the direction of the group.

Democracy is fragile. What destroys it most easily is lack of use. If people feel alienated and powerless—and thereby do not use the democratic rights they have—democracy dies. People who do not believe they can exercise power will not fight against infringements of their rights or the rights of others. Successful organizing gives the widest number of people possible a stake in preserving democracy and is part of creating a stable democratic society, open to all. By making real the democratic potential in society, community groups gain power to solve problems, and in the process, they rebuild democracy.

When Organizing and Development Efforts Succeed

Organizing efforts come about to solve shared problems. Neighbors argue for flood control and crime patrols; Native Americans press for compensation for the confiscation of their lands; housing advocates lobby for shelter for the homeless; environmentalists protest to stop the paving over of a wildlife refuge. Women employees in an industrial plant rebel against the sexist climate of their workplace. Gay people march for an end to job discrimination, while the wheelchair bound press for accessible buildings that can make the difference between a lifetime of dependence and a successful career. The energy for involvement in collective efforts comes from immediate and urgent problems faced by people in the same situation.

Recognition of a shared and urgent problem is the starting point, but to achieve a shared vision of what society can and should be requires building lasting democratically guided organizations. Visions for change can emerge as people work together and reflect on what they need to accomplish to solve problems they face. Such visions may stem from an underlying *ideology,* a lasting set of beliefs about what society should be like.

The means of achieving social change must be consistent with its goals. There cannot be racism or sexism in the process of organizing, if people hope to achieve a more just society. Solving complicated problems might require the help and support of experts, but experts should not be allowed to dominate the decision making; if they do, the goal of empowerment will not be achieved.

The goals of organizing may differ from person to person and from time to time. For us, the vision includes more fairly distributing wealth and power, encouraging those from different ethnic and cultural groups to work together, and eliminating the structural obstacles to a more just society, such as poverty and discrimination. Successful organizing implies a continuing capacity to address new problems as they emerge, as people develop confidence and skills and feel empowered to fight back. The ability to do so increases as people develop a sense of community in which individuals feel responsible for the collectivity.

People are Empowered

Organizing is about empowering people. Through involvement with community organizations, people develop confidence that they can succeed. People who control their work life, overcome personal problems, battle banks, or fight city hall and win are empowered. Empowerment increases as people work together to address societally caused problems, instead of judging success and failure in individual terms. Working collectively also empowers through the excitement that comes from being part of a larger cause.

People are empowered when they pull down the barriers of discrimination and get jobs based on their skills and experience, not their gender or ethnic background. They are empowered when they can solve financial problems, such as how to obtain a car loan or pay for child care. They are empowered by improving the appearance of their neighborhoods, when they can feel pride when they look around them and see that collectively they have improved their community.

Empowerment comes about as people learn skills to help themselves and others. As part of social change organizations, people learn to do things they never thought they could or even would have the opportunity to try: fund raising, public relations, negotiations, coalition building, public speaking, dealing with officials, designing public programs, repairing homes and neighborhoods, managing an office, or writing a press release. The confidence and skills people gained spill over into personal and work lives. People who participate in collective actions end up with a better image of themselves than people who are certain nothing can be done about problems.

Communities are Strengthened

Communities can be seen as physical places—people who live near one another; or, in terms of a shared social status—being a woman or a Native American; or, of people who confront a common problem—the parents of a disabled child. Successful organizing builds on communities already in place and helps to create new bonds among those who share difficulties. As people identify as members of a community, they learn that the problems they face and the solutions required are collective ones.

As part of the community building effort, people join groups with those in the same position as themselves, hear about each others' experiences, and gradually put together a picture of shared problems. Women learn that other women have been steered away from good jobs and that the inability to earn enough occurs because of unfair structures, not because of lack of ambition or knowledge or interpersonal skills. In chatting with those on the block, neighbors discover that Black, White, Hispanic, Asian, gay, and straight all suffer when the city fails to repair the streets or shut down a crack house.

As a sense of community is built and organizational successes become visible, power increases. In the economically disadvantaged Dudley Street neighborhood of

Boston, African American, White, Hispanic, and Cape Verdean people initially organized to stop illegal garbage dumping. This successful campaign showed people from the different ethnic groups the extent to which they all shared the neighborhood's problems. This initial success encouraged those in the neighborhood to continue working together and to tackle the more difficult problems of rebuilding homes and businesses that had been destroyed by arson and lack of investment (Medoff and Sklar, 1994).

As people discover that those in a community share a problem and that it must be combated collectively, they are able to discount the imposed myth of "rugged individualism," that discourages people from working together. This myth of rugged individualism suggests that an individual is free only if he or she is independent of others and fights adversity alone. Because individuals cannot fight big corporations or government by themselves, such a myth disempowers. The myth of rugged individualism is a framing imposed by those in power to prevent others from challenging social and political inequities. This myth

> leaves Americans with a stubborn fear of acknowledging structures of power and interdependence in a technologically complex society dominated by giant corporations and an increasingly powerful state. (Bellah, Madsen, Sullivan, Swidler, & Tipton, 1985, p. 25)

The belief in rugged individualism prevents people from joining together to fight back.

How the myth of rugged individualism disempowers is shown in the ways in which workers responded to their forced unemployment when plants shut down.

> Although they do not necessarily feel that their joblessness is their own fault, they retain other individualistic reactions. For example, they feel that going out to look for work for themselves is more effective than group political activity in their own behalf and that of their jobless colleagues. Being particularly vulnerable to feelings of worthlessness and depression, the unemployed feel an unusually strong need to be self-reliant and thus have a further reason to go out personally to seek work. (Gans, 1988, p. 78)

When people see themselves as members of a community that collectively face a problem, they discover they can fight back. Initially gays in Chicago, New York, and San Francisco fled discrimination, but eventually they came together and formed an activist community. By voting as a block, these organized communities were able to persuade city politicians and employees to listen to them, treat them with respect, and join them in the fight against homophobic prejudices.

Problems are Solved

Working together in community and social-change organizations people have solved a wide variety of problems. Neighborhood organizations have alleviated overcrowding in schools, forced drug peddlers to flee, have pushed for flood control measures to keep basements dry, and stopped highways from destroying intact communities. Community organizations have fought off government and businesses seeking to install toxic waste incinerators near residential areas. Other groups have brought back grocery stores to inner city neighborhoods. Some neighborhood associations have created neighborhood watches to improve physical safety; tenants' unions have successfully fought for heat and building repairs. Environmentalists have saved or restored wetlands where birds and animals can breed.

Victories multiply as one success enables others to occur. Starting with a single effort in Chicago, organizations nationally learned how to combat redlining, the unwillingness of banks to provide loans in poor neighborhoods. After a few well-publicized victories, community activists and labor unions now are able to join together throughout the country to expose and close down overcrowded, unsafe, and poorly lit sweat shops. An entire community development movement has grown up as activists in one community learn how to build affordable homes and then share this information with other less experienced organizations. Civil rights activists made it possible for African Americans to register and vote, creating a major tool for subsequent economic and political gains.

Problems Persist and More Efforts are Required

Community organizing has been successful in many ways, but problems persist that now cry out for immediate response. Even though in the last decade the economy has been healthy, inequality of income and wealth has increased. In addition, as the nation's population has become more diverse, tensions have grown between different cultural groups.

Economic inequality in the United States remains severe. The richest 1 percent of the population owns 39 percent of all wealth (Rossides, 1997, p. 134). The top 20 percent of the population earns 12.7 times the income of the bottom 20 percent, while in wealthier states such as New York the richest 20 percent of the population earns 19.5 times as much as the poorest 20 percent (Perez-Pena, 1997, p. A14). In fact, economic inequality has increased. In 1960, the top 5 percent of the population earned 15.5 percent of the national income while the bottom 40 percent earned 17.0 percent; 35 years later, in 1995, the earnings of the bottom 40 percent had dropped from 17 percent to 14.2 percent of the total; the top 5 percent increased their share from 15.5 percent to over 20 percent (Lauer, 1998, p. 219). The rich are getting richer while the poor are falling further behind.

Moreover, poverty is not evenly distributed across the population. The poor are disproportionately from minority groups. African American family income is only a little more than half that of White family income (Rossides, 1997, p. 397), the poverty rate of Hispanic families is more than twice that of non-Hispanic Whites (Rossides, 1997, p. 432), while the economic status of Native Americans is worse than that of Blacks or Hispanics. Further, within every minority group, the income of women, especially those raising children by themselves, is below that of comparable men.

To compound problems, economic inequality is associated with numerous social ills. The poor lack good medical care, are likely to face problems of crime, lack educational opportunities for their children, and do not have the economic resources to invest in their own homes or businesses. Since the Reagan presidency, and perhaps before, governmental social policies have helped those at the top of the economic hierarchy at the cost of those at the bottom (Gans, 1995). The people with the fewest resources to fight back confront the largest number of problems.

To us, economic inequality is the core problem our society faces, but a close second in importance is discrimination based on race, ethnicity, gender, and sexual orientation. Women and minorities get less respect and have fewer social and economic opportunities than do White males. Gays sometimes have difficulty renting apartments, may be forced out of jobs, and typically receive fewer benefits for their significant others. Further, divisions within discriminated groups make organizing difficult. Although all women are potentially subject to gender oppression they sometimes have trouble organizing to combat this problem because of differences in social class, race, occupation, or sexual orientation. The urban poor share many problems, but intergroup tensions, such as those between African Americans and Asians or between newer and older immigrant groups, can derail efforts to improve neighborhoods for everyone. Successful community organizing must help to build bridges between culturally diverse groups.

Economic inequality denies people resources to fight back, while tensions between different cultural groups make it harder to build communities among those who share similar problems. Current organizing work must address both issues.

Social Change is Accomplished Through a Variety of Democratic Organizations

Each woman who refuses to be treated in a demeaning way, each citizen who calls to complain about developers tearing down trees, and each young man who, during the Vietnam War era, burned his draft card, made a protest, joined a movement, contributed to social change. People rarely spontaneously rise up in protest, however, and when people protest one by one they often lack the power to bring about needed change. Instead people come together in *community and social-change organizations* that gain power by aggregating individual concerns and build the capacity to work toward needed solutions.

Over the years, there has been an incredible variety of social-change and community-based organizations. The lives of some have been brief, while others have lasted for generations. Some organizations focus on bringing people together who live in a particular geographic area; others deal with issues that confront people throughout the nation; still others focus on people from specific social groupings. Most people are familiar with those organizations that are noisy and conflict oriented. These gain the headlines, but the majority of community organizations work quietly to produce services or influence government.

The problems that community and social-change organizations combat vary from very specific matters of personal or economic interest to more abstract concerns of civil rights, civil liberties, or equality of opportunity. Demands made by a tenants' union for keeping rents within reason in one apartment building illustrate the concrete, economic end of this continuum. At the other extreme might be the actions taken by the Southern Poverty Law Center to protect minorities from racist actions or the work of the American Civil Liberties Union to defend the free speech of a flag burner.

Social change and community organizations can be classified according to their primary missions, to improve social equity, increase social justice, provide a good or service, enhance community identity, or strengthen community defense. In practice, most durable organizations combine several of these missions.

Social Equity.   *Social equity* organizations pressure government agencies to provide individualized benefits to their members and constituents. In the 1980s and 1990s social equity organizations supporting the homeless forced government to provide shelter for those in need. In previous decades, organizations of the aged, such as the Gray Panthers, worked to gain economic benefits for the elderly through improvements in social security and Medicare.

Social Justice.   *Social justice* organizations work on broad issues such as civil liberties, civil rights, and the protection of the environment. The benefits that these organizations seek are not separable, each group member doesn't get an allocation of clean air or one more civil liberty if the group's lobbying is successful. Rather, rights are secured for everyone. Organizations that have worked to reduce discrimination against gays and lesbians, civil rights organizations that a generation ago struggled to obtain the vote for minorities, and groups trying to assure procedural justice for immigrants are examples of social justice groups.

Social Production.   *Social production* organizations provide goods and services of economic or psychological value to their membership and the communities to which they belong. Support groups to help those with cancer or heart disease or to help victims of spouse or alcohol abuse are examples of such social production efforts, as are community-controlled health facilities such as women's health cooperatives. Other social production groups work to help neighborhoods restore needed businesses, teach the unemployed how to form businesses, or help lower-income people rent better apartments or buy homes.

Community Identity.   The goal of *community identity* organizations is to work with people to develop a sense of belonging and shared pride. Many gay rights organizations, as well as those that speak for particular ethnic groups, such as associations of Native Americans or Asian Americans, came about as assertions of community identity. Folk and food festivals sponsored by neighborhood associations, such as the Hill in St. Louis (Shoenberg, 1980) or ethnic art fairs at local cultural centers help people identify with others in their geographic community.

Gay pride organizations help gays recognize that being homosexual or lesbian is not a stigma that needs to be hidden. Gay pride organizations began by emphasizing the contributions and creativity of their members. Later, such organizations worked to secure the ability of gay couples to adopt and to receive health insurance benefits for long-time partners.

Community Defense.   Many organizations began as efforts to protect an identified social or geographic community from destructive outside pressures. Such *community defense* organizations emerge as neighbors join together to protest a highway that will destroy an intact community or to preserve affordable housing in a community in which wealthier people are displacing the poor. Other community defense organizations begin when those who share a social bond join together to protect themselves against collective threats. For example, community defense organizations among Spanish speakers work to protect immigrants' rights.

Organization Functions Blur and Evolve

In practice, the missions of the separate types of community and social change groups blur. An organization that defends a geographic community from outside economic forces may also provide a sense of pride and identity to those who live nearby. Many organizations that initially came into being to increase pride in a shared heritage end up demanding social services or economic improvement for their members. Some community organizations change from community defense to social production. For instance, in South Bend, Indiana, a neighborhood defense organization initially formed to combat redlining evolved into a social production organization that built the homes the neighborhood required.

Often the mission and actions of an organization are shaped through complicated and evolving relationships with government. *Pressure* organizations work within the conventional rules of the system—through lobbying, petitioning, or providing political support—to persuade politicians and bureaucrats to adopt policies the organization wants to see in place. In contrast, *protest* organizations work outside of the conventional rules, because those in the organization question the legitimacy of the rules. A sit-in for civil rights is a form of protest; working with elected officials to help rewrite laws to preserve open space from exploitation by oil companies is a form of pressure.

Social equity and social production organizations may work with government to produce a needed good or service, while some community organizations perform public services under government contracts (Smith and Lipsky, 1993). Other community groups partner with a government agency but do so in ways in which the organization's members define the problems and possible solutions and use public funds to carry out their plans. For instance, neighborhood housing organizations might decide which properties to rebuild and who should live there, while financial help for the projects might come from the government.

Social-change and community organizations come into being in many different ways. Part of the work of the *community organizer* is to encourage the formation of such organizations and provide focus to their missions. Organizers work with members of a community to help them identify a problem and motivate them to come together to solve the problem. Once such organizations are under way, community organizers help to keep them on their chosen course, encourage people to join up, and provide some of the technical knowledge needed to accomplish collective goals.

Contrasting Models of Organizing and Development

Models of organizing describe broader strategies for accomplishing a vision, the appropriate steps for getting there, and how to evaluate whether the means of getting there are consistent with the desired ends. Some models grow out of specific ideologies of change, but most emerge in response to concrete situations.

Organizers approach people to help them solve the immediate problems they face, not to carry out some abstract ideology. Unemployed community members aren't thinking abstractly about the world economy when their jobs disappear; they are worried about how they will pay their bills and whether they will ever be employed again. People organize to combat a specific, serious problem—their children contract leukemia and nearby chemical companies refuse to take responsibility; or White children are tracked into the college bound curriculum with the best teachers and the Black children are routinely assigned to the slower classes with less skilled teachers.

Organizers see much of their work in immediate and practical terms, not as a means to carry out some distant ideology. What motivates them is a sense of injustice that inflames them. Organizers respond to firsthand experiences and then share practical knowledge with one another: In leafletting, they learn to cover not only the immediate neighborhood but also adjacent areas as these people have similar problems and may join the fight. They learn to maintain an image of power: If the group looks like it is losing power, elected officials will not listen.

Over time, however, accumulated experiences can lead different groups to believe in distinct tactics. An organization might successfully pressure city officials to increase services to the neighborhood by massing people in the mayor's office. They may have failed in the past by simply requesting that the city provide a service. But a few blocks away, another community organization itself provides the service the city failed to provide. In the environmental movement, one social-change organization goes door to door to enlist members who then demonstrate against a chemical hazard, while another sends out mass mailings, raises funds, and hires professionals to lobby full time in Washington to make that chemical illegal.

Eventually such differences are almost codified in contrasting models of what organizing and development ought to be about. These emerging models develop passionate supporters and equally passionate detractors among practitioners and the academics who study organizing.

The models provide different answers to three related sets of questions. The first is how ideological should the community organizing effort be? The second is how important is it to solve problems in a particular way? If the problems are severe enough, is it ok to solve them even if the process isn't democratic or empowering? The third set of issues deals with how members should be recruited and what their roles should be after they are brought on board.

Can Social Change Be Brought about Nonideologically?

Any community organization that plans to be around for more than one campaign needs to address a very practical problem, how to decide what to work on first and what to work on next. One approach is to not answer the question abstractly but instead to determine to work on whatever seems urgent to members at the time. Some activists fear, however, that such an opportunistic approach won't add up to substantial gains and argue that it would be better if the efforts were sequenced in some way and progressed toward some goal.

At the other extreme, some community activists are ideological and want to move toward a society with less private ownership and far more collective responsibility for social welfare. Still others argue that organizing is not about fighting over the distribution of wealth but is more about rebuilding community and restoring collective responsibility. Such *value-based organizing* is largely influenced by progressive, socially responsible churches. Economic issues are not ignored, but economic improvement and equity are seen as a consequence of the restoration of core values, not as independent issues.

Saul Alinsky, one of the founders of modern neighborhood organizing, insisted that there ought to be no broad agenda, that community organizations should just focus on immediate problems. He believed that such pragmatism was the only way to motivate people to act, but, in part, he was trying to convince those in power that community groups were not ideological and would not turn into a communist movement, a very real fear during the 1940s and 1950s.

Alinsky's argument against taking an ideological approach has been influential, but following the model does not preclude building toward a broader goal. That goal might be greater participation of neighborhoods in budgetary decision making, or better relations between ethnic groups, or guaranteeing freedom of speech for everyone, or more independence for people with disabilities. While groups engage in smaller projects—arguing for a new community center or a wider door on a public building— the individual projects are chosen to cumulatively build toward the broader goal.

It is possible to work on organizing models that explicitly seek to ameliorate the harm that relatively unbridled capitalism creates without, at the same time, appearing to oppose entirely our current system in ways that invite massive opposition. For instance, many community organizations that focus on restoring neighborhood economies are avowedly capitalist, owning and managing property and encouraging the poor to become capitalist entrepreneurs on a small scale. Their goal is to share the wealth more evenly by making capitalism work for the poor.

In part, the battle between pragmatically guided and ideologically guided models reflects deeper concerns about how fundamental the changes are that should be sought. Should social-change and community organizations be primarily reformist or should they be more revolutionary? Reformist organizations tinker with the system, trying to make it work right, buying into current values but arguing that they have not yet been obtained. In contrast, revolutionary organizations question core assumptions and propose radically different alternatives. Few modern models for community work are avowedly revolutionary, but some have argued for basic changes in gender roles or the overthrow of racial and ethnic discrimination. Further, activists who argue that capitalism is not simply about bottom-line profits but should take into account human and community welfare, are proposing fairly radical changes.

Another ideological concern involves the decision on how confrontational a social change organization should be. Should such organizations directly assault the system through demonstrations, protests, or perhaps more radical tactics? Or should they negotiate with those in power, build consensus, and bring about change step by step?

Many community organizers view the tradeoff between direct action and negotiation as a pragmatic, tactical decision: is the immediate problem better resolved through a direct confrontation or will consensus building work better? Others see confrontation and negotiation as linked in stages: you try to negotiate, and that failing, escalate step by step until a direct confrontation is at hand, or confront first, having weakened the enemy and shown your own strength, then come to the bargaining table.

The choice between direct actions and consensus building, however, can have broader implications. Groups that routinely undertake direct actions do so because they believe the establishment is simply wrong; they feel that involvement in rallies, sit-ins, and other forms of protest, gives participants a sense that they can make the establishment quake. Direct actions are not simply about winning an issue, they can make people feel empowered, almost irrespective of what short-term changes are made or which problems are solved. In contrast, proponents of consensus building models argue that organizing succeeds when people learn to work together and that consensus means that community has been built.

Many of these strategic differences are subsumed as part of the differences between two contrasting thrusts to organizing. The first reflects a *social mobilization* tradition, the second a *social production* tradition.

In the *social mobilization, direct action* tradition, the core strategic goal is to get people to act together, to gain power through the numbers involved on the assumption that such pressures will make those in power comply with the demands these people make. In this tradition, the emphasis is on the mobilizing effort—contacting people and encouraging them to become socially and politically active. Social mobilization approaches encourage people to petition vigorously, protest, demonstrate, and not fear direct confrontations. Social mobilization efforts are labeled *campaigns,* efforts in which collective power is used to make others change. The changes brought about through campaigns are sometimes less important than the strength and unity that comes about through mobilization, because mobilization is empowering.

In the *social production* tradition, the strategic goal is to get services, material goods, or ownership of property for people in need. In this tradition, the core emphasis is on achieving the outcome—helping those in need with personal problems they face, providing jobs, better apartments, or ownership of homes. Under the social production model, people master the economic and managerial tools necessary to control newly found capital wealth or to administer needed social services.

In the social production model to obtain the needed goods, services, or redistribution, people are more likely to work with those in power than directly confront them. Social production approaches encourage people to learn how to participate in the political system and manage relationships with the agencies that provide social services. This model teaches people how to adapt the tools of a capitalist economy and those of social service agencies to their own ends. Social production efforts are usually labeled as *projects,* endeavors to create material goods or services that benefit those in need.

Tensions abound between those who support social mobilization models and advocates of the social production approach. Mobilizers claim that in the social production model, people are bought off by trivial changes, such as a slightly better job training program or one more community health center. As a result, people never gain the power required for needed fundamental change. In turn, supporters of the social production approach claim that mobilizers are so concerned with activating people and the glory of public demonstrations that little thought is given to assuring that the victories that occur through direct actions lead to lasting changes.

Choosing between Means and Ends

Even when there is agreement on what the overall goals of organizing are or should be, there may be disagreement on how to get there and especially on the balance between means and ends. These disputes are seen as organizers argue over strategies, that is, the statements about how goals should be achieved.

While most agree that community organizing is about solving problems collectively, what is less clear is whether solving the problems is more important than empowering people and community organizations. Is the transformation of people the goal itself or is it the means to alter the broader society (Hanna and Robertson, 1994)? Will an improved society make people feel more efficacious or must people first feel empowered before a society will change?

The balance between means and ends affects how organizers interpret the role of the community organization. Is the organization a tool to bring about change or is it an end to be achieved? There is no clear-cut answer here. Without a formal organization sustained action is impossible, the organization builds solidarity and community capacity that enable people to accomplish their shared goals. If the creation and maintenance of the organization becomes too important, however, raising funds and pleasing financial supporters may displace tackling important issues of interest to members. In this case, if the means, setting up an organization, becomes the end or goal, the real goal of community organizing can be thwarted.

Another tension between means and ends occurs as organizers worry about how to create solidarity among community members. In many situations, as organizing work begins, the basic sense of community, of trust, of knowledge of shared problems, is not there initially. The job of the organizer might be first to help build community, to create a base from which to take action. But building community solidarity can too easily become an end in itself, a goal to be worked for rather than a means to solve a problem. For example, in setting up an identity organization that encourages pride in being Black, or deaf, or being a member of the Beverly neighborhood, organizers might create other problems. For instance, to bring about neighborhood pride, the group might make improvements in housing that look great and symbolize renewal, but in doing so make the neighborhood unaffordable to the poor who live there, creating or exacerbating an economic problem.

Strategic Choices on Mobilization

Organizing models differ on how people should be recruited for social-change work and what roles those who have been recruited should play. Some of these decisions are tactical, based on what seems to work better in each situation. Whether to go door to door or to request a few supporters to hold meetings in their homes is a tactical decision: if people are shy about outsiders or much discussion is needed to learn what problems a neighborhood faces, home meetings work better; if the issues are clear and the neighbors generally trusting enough to open a door to strangers, door-to-door approaches work better.

In addition to these relatively unimportant issues of tactics, approaches to mobilizing also reflect strategic concerns. For instance, models differ on whether to mobilize people individually or work to mobilize existing organizations—churches, social clubs, ethnic pride groups, block watches. Such differences can affect the goals and strategies of the resulting community organization. Coalitions of existing organizations often are limited in what they can do to what all coalition members can accept. If any member of the coalition does not want to go along, the proposed campaign or action can fall apart. Direct membership organizations recruit people who agree with the initial ideas and will carry out a campaign or direct action like the one being proposed, but recruiting individuals is slower than recruiting existing organizations.

Another question of mobilization concerns what roles the members or recruits should play. At one extreme are fully democratic, participatory organizations in which only those who want to work join up, all decisions are made through (consensual) democracy, and the members themselves act as leaders, organizers, staff, and constituents. Some of the members become more active than others, pay attention to the decisions that have to be made, present issues to the others as well as the public, and generally act as leaders of the organization. With this approach, activists take on the role of organizer and staff member, helping to recruit new members, and trying to keep the organization focused and running smoothly, handling both the larger issues and day-to-day tasks. With this approach, organizational members are also the constituency, the people for whom the organization is trying to gain benefits.

At the opposite extreme are the national public interest groups or progressive advocacy organizations. People who agree with the positions these organizations take, such as favoring population control, saving the whales, or banning handguns, sign up and pay dues but have little say in the ordinary operation of the organization. Instead, a professional staff works full time to try to accomplish the organization's goals. Constituents need not be members: the American Civil Liberties Union protects free speech for everyone in the country, not just for organization members.

Between these extremes are a variety of options. Decisions can be made through democratic votes, through consensual discussions, or by elected representatives. A paid organizer can be spokesperson for the organization, or the group's elected leaders may play that role, or ordinary members may represent the group to the public. The organizers

TABLE 1.1   Ways in Which Models of Organizing Can Differ

Role of Ideology

Are projects selected on an ad hoc basis, or are they chosen with a fixed and broader goal in mind?

Does the organization accept capitalism, entrepreneurship, and individual ownership, or does it emphasize communal responsibilities and joint ownership?

To what extent are economic issues more central or are concerns with values and community building more important?

Is the group aiming for modest changes in the status quo, or are more radical changes sought?

Are social mobilization or social production approaches more important?

Means, Ends, and Goals

Problem solving may be more or less important than transformation of people

Creation and maintenance of formal organizations may be a means or an end of organizing

Mobilization Concerns

Organizations may recruit individual members or be built up of other organizations that form a coalition

Members may be more or less involved in decision making and day-to-day running of the organization

The role of the professional organizer can vary

---

may be hired staff members, with careers that take them from community group to community group, or they may be members of the community and permanently aligned with a single group and purpose. The actual options suggested depend on the model of organizing chosen.

No matter the model followed, when learning how to be organizers, most people focus first on the practical issues, as the technical details are important. A malfunctioning sound system or a locked restroom can turn a rally into chaos. An organizer has to know what to say to a potential recruit or contributor. In addition to mastering these details organizers also must think about the broader issues that underlie the different models, the tradeoffs between mobilization and production, between capacity building and problem solving. In Table 1.1, we summarize the differences in the various models of organizing.

Our Approach to Organizing and Development

The role of the organizer is to help create a sense that change is possible and show the way. The organizer's job is not an easy one. Building progressive community and social-change organizations requires dedication and energy, as well as knowledge and experience. Further, organizing work is often done in the face of larger economic and political forces that can sometimes overwhelm even the best community organizations. Regardless of skill levels, not every effort will succeed, but greater skill and knowledge such as that presented in this book improve the chances of success.

Our approach to organizing involves combining insights from a variety of models. Rather than promoting one approach or another, we argue that social mobilization (rallies, marches, and protests) and social production approaches (providing services, building homes, creating jobs) (Anner & Vogel, 1997) are complementary and compatible. Successful lobbying for laws that require buildings to be handicapped accessible are important; so are organizations that design and produce handicapped-accessible homes. If the goal is more independence for people whose mobility or dexterity is impaired, organizers must learn about both approaches.

We use numerous examples of social problems but recognize that the issues about which people get most upset change over time, as some problems are solved and others become more salient. The feminization of poverty continues while inequality in the distribution of wealth and opportunity gets worse. Problems with homelessness persist. Welfare programs have changed, pushing many to work in marginal jobs with marginal pay and highlighting the limited coverage of health insurance. Mergers of large companies and trends toward downsizing have threatened the jobs of the middle class and middle aged, those who felt most secure in society. At the same time, the number of babies born to unmarried young teens has gone down, and violent crime rates continue to drop as the society gets, on average, older. Past reckless consumption seems to be catching up with the world in the form of global warming, creating a mass of environmental problems, including more vicious storms that virtually wipe out more poorly constructed communities.

The problems and the programs designed to deal with them continue to change. Community organizers need to know the details of these programs, the problems they cause, and the opportunities they present and where to look for updated information. Organizers need to help frame the problems so that people can see that problems are shared and that collective solutions are possible and appropriate.

Successful organizers believe that community and social-change groups can create a more equal, democratic, and empowered society with a stronger sense of being part of a shared community. To achieve this vision organizers need to reflect on what has worked and what has not worked. As they reflect, organizers will develop their own theories of what tasks must be undertaken and how they are to be carried out. We hope that *Community Organizing and Development* will provide the tools that organizers need to start them on their work.

PART TWO

Resolving Social Problems through Organizing

Part Two of this book establishes the setting in which organizing occurs. Chapter 2 examines how shared framings of social problems affect community action, explores two illustrative problems, poverty and neighborhood decline, that have shaped community work, and indicates the overall ineffectiveness of government in handling many of these problems. Chapter 3 shows how community and social-change organizations wrestling with changing environments have brought together the weak, voiceless, and poor to successfully tackle tough problems.

2 Understanding and Combating Social Problems

Organizing is about people gaining power to undertake collective actions successfully. The purpose of these actions is to overcome shared problems that are systemic and structural and have been ignored or incorrectly handled by government, businesses, or charities.

Problems abound.

In the nation's poorest neighborhoods, unemployed men hang around street corners; others wake up early to take long bus rides to distant jobs for low wages. Public parks have become drug supermarkets. Downtowns flourish with new steel and glass office towers and rush-hour crowds, but the homeless still sleep on the streets. In inner-city neighborhoods, affordable housing is destroyed to make way for upscale condominiums for the middle class. People rush out to buy health foods and over-the-counter medical cures as health care becomes less accessible and more bureaucratic, especially for the poor. Children are beaten by their parents and aging parents abused by their children. Historic tensions between African Americans and Whites persist, while rivalries between other ethnic groups have worsened. Jail populations rise dramatically to accommodate the mass influx of those arrested for drug charges, while funding for job training and higher education declines as a proportion of state budgets.

Social problems have a profound personal impact. Middle-aged employees who have been thrown out of their decent-paying jobs because of corporate takeovers live in fear of losing their new, lower paying jobs. For those with prison records, a large and increasing proportion of the population, getting jobs is incredibly difficult, while in many inner-city neighborhoods, flipping hamburgers is seen as decent employment (Newman, 1999). Welfare laws have changed, requiring many who had received assistance to take on low-paid work, mostly without health insurance. Imagine the tension a single mother feels, now juggling work with child care, having to rely on an inadequate public transportation system to get to work, for a wage that fails to bring her out of poverty and doesn't pay for doctor bills for her children.

While problems abound, how people interpret and understand them differs dramatically. To some, a physical handicap is an individual problem, one to be handled through charity to the victim, with no broader implications. To others, this problem has an important social component because businesses, education, and government have failed to accommodate to the needs of those who have trouble walking, seeing, or hearing. The problems found in run-down neighborhoods can be understood as a result of the impersonal workings of the market in which people get what they can afford and can work harder if they want more. Or the presence of boarded up and broken-down apartment buildings can be alternatively understood as stemming from a lack of enforcement of local housing codes and tax policies that create profits for owners who do not maintain their properties.

An understanding of what constitutes a problem, what it means, and what actions are needed grows as people talk about their problems. Such *framings* are socially defined. How a problem is framed suggests why problems occur, who is responsible, what solutions people are willing to accept, and what actions are appropriate for combating the difficulties. Framings can be influenced by community organizations that want to solve problems and by their opponents who do not want change.

This chapter first describes how problems are socially constructed, arguing that those in social-change and community groups need to frame issues in ways that facilitate social change. The chapter then explores several major social problems that affect much of present day organizing, indicating the extent of the problem as well as the response or lack of response from the public sector.

What Constitutes a Problem is Socially Framed

A social problem is not something that exists as a natural thing on its own. Instead a problem is *socially constructed* as people share their understandings of what constitutes the matter, work out what its causes are, and then agree on what can and should be done about it. What is initially experienced personally is constructed as a social problem only after many people accept a shared understanding of the matter and agree that it has come about because of conditions created by society and is serious and widespread.

These socially constructed interpretations affect how the "facts of the matter," the *objective conditions,* are understood. To some, 12 percent unemployment means the economy is failing, 50 people working in a small factory creates unsafe overcrowding, and a highway with 12,000 cars a day means danger for school children. To others, however, 12 percent unemployment means people are too lazy to work, the crowded factory is a natural step on the path of business growth, and the busy highway is little more than a quick path to jobs and shopping.

These shared definitions of a social problem are put forth in *frames*—descriptive images—that indicate why something is problematic and how it is socially caused (Baylor, 1996; Goffman, 1974; Polletta, 1998; Snow & Benford, 1992, p. 137; Snow et al., 1986). The framings that are constructed influence what solutions people can accept. For example, those who oppose abortion frame the issue as protection of the unborn child. To them, abortion is murder. The solution is to ban abortions or terrorize abortionists so they won't kill infants. Those who support abortion rights frame the matter in terms of a woman's right to control her own reproductive system. For them, the issue is one of privacy and individual choice. Activists carefully frame issues to favor the outcomes they prefer and to win support from the public and from government.

As part of the battle over how to frame an issue, people argue over who is at fault. To what extent should individuals be blamed or does the problem stem from broader conditions? These interpretations affect what actions seem appropriate. For instance with spouse abuse

> [p]ast research shows that police did not arrest men who battered their wives, even when victims were in serious danger and directly asked officers to arrest. . . . Activists in the battered women's movement saw failure to arrest as tacit support for battering, contributing to the inability of women to escape violent relationships and in the escalation of abuse to domestic homicides. (Ferraro, 1989, p. 61)

Initially, battering was framed by those in positions of power as a private domestic problem with a biological and, hence, almost inevitable cause. Women activists eventually were able to reframe the issue so that battering was seen as a crime.

Framings are intentionally constructed by victims, by the media, and by those in positions of power. Conservative mayors explain housing deterioration as the result of irresponsible tenants and rampant crime and suggest tearing down slums. Progressive mayors frame the same issue in terms of the neglect of landlords and the lack of neighborhood-based policing. These various definitions of the situation are picked up by newspapers who agree with one side or the other and promoted by those who are affected by the different solutions suggested. Developers and perhaps their allies in government benefit if slums are torn down to make way for offices and high-rise residences for wealthier people. Community activists try to frame the same problem in terms of providing safe and healthy homes for current residents.

Framings are communicated through *typifications,* a kind of story, or set of examples, perhaps made up, that indicates what the problem is, why it occurs, and what should be done about it. President Reagan, for instance, offered such a typification by creating the image of a "welfare queen," a person stealing from the welfare system and driving a Cadillac. This framing suggested that the problem with welfare was the greed of lazy but clever people who rip off the system, and the solution was to end welfare. Typifications may vie with one another, for instance, the typification "the deserving poor" evokes an image of a disabled widow with young children, while the typification of "the undeserving poor" is that of an able-bodied young male who appears more willing to sell or use dope than find a job and, therefore, not worthy of any form of public support. Such negative typifications justified a "war against the poor" (Gans, 1995) by blaming poverty on moral defects of individuals.

Typifications have been misappropriated by those in power in ways that can harm the poor. For instance, the typification "underclass" was introduced by scholars (Wilson, 1987) as part of a sympathetic portrait of people who face numerous problems, many because of racism. The popular press and politicians, however, reframed the meaning of this typification in ways that disparaged the poor in attempts to end programs to help those in need. As Herbert Gans explains

> the term "underclass" has developed an attention-getting power. . . . The word has a technical aura that enables it to serve as a euphemism or code word to be used for labelling. Users of the label can thus hide their disapproval of the poor behind an impressive academic term.
>
> Because "underclass" is a code word that places some of the poor *under* society . . . users of the term can therefore favor excluding them from the rest of society without saying so. . . . Because "underclass" is also used as a racial and even ethnic code word, it is a convenient device for hiding anti-black or anti-Latino feelings. (Gans, 1995, p. 59)

To combat unfavorable typifications, activists must create alternative framings to communicate that those who suffer from problems are victims and not villains and are capable of helping themselves. For instance, to garner support for their work, developmental activists publicize success stories of poor people who build or repair their own homes after receiving small but desperately needed loans. The image here is of an "energetic self-starter" not of a person receiving "assistance."

Activists try to frame issues to enable others to recognize the social or structural causes of problems but in doing so must be careful not to suggest that the problems are inevitable. Instead, organizers need to demonstrate that there are ways of combating problems that are realistic and effective. For instance, activists might explain unemployment in terms of international competition that is causing many factory jobs to move abroad. Bringing back those industrial jobs might be impossible but setting up training programs in communities and schools to prepare people for new positions in the information age is a feasible, realistic option.

In establishing frames that motivate fighting back, organizers should avoid overly simplifying issues and instead recognize that social problems are complicated and often interdependent. Solutions that might appear to solve one problem can fail because another related problem interferes. Tenant-owned apartments are unlikely to solve housing shortages unless tenants also have steady sources of income and have some training in housing management.

Social Problems and Contemporary Organizing

Framings do reflect underlying social and economic conditions that affect the lives of the people with whom organizers work. To illustrate how such framings emerge from social and economic conditions and then are turned into policies to improve the situation, we discuss two broad issue areas; the first, individual and family poverty; and the second, the ongoing restructuring of urban space.

In the interest of space, we chose only two social problems, excluding literally hundreds of other issues of equal importance, including racial and ethnic prejudice, unequal treatment based on sexual orientation, and environmental degradation. Our discussion of these two areas is meant to illustrate a logic that organizers can use to assess social problems, no matter the issue area. First, obtain the facts of the matter, and learn to read these facts in light of how the problems have been framed by victims, by the broader public, and, in particular, by government. Then examine what programs or solutions have been proposed and figure out which ones have been more or less successful. Actions taken by social-change and community groups must be grounded in the facts of the matter but must also account for how people interpret the situation and what efforts, if any, government has made to solve the problems.

Poverty and Economic Inequality

Although the economy has fared well in the last decade, economic problems persist. Inequality between the rich and the poor has actually increased in recent years, and the poor are often barely able to survive. While income gaps between ethnic groups have declined, people of color still remain far poorer than others, and women as a group, particularly divorced or unmarried women with children, remain especially poor. Many people who work earn the minimum wage, often without health insurance, and have to work more than one job to pay the food and rent bills. Husbands and wives may both have to work, making child care problematic, and lack of health insurance makes every illness a financial catastrophe. Persistent poverty and its consequences have been and continue to be major stimuli for organizing.

To begin understanding a problem requires figuring out how it is measured. Government agencies assess employment, poverty, and wealth in different ways, each with its own twist for organizing. Government statistics consider that a person is working even if the job is temporary, irrespective of how much it pays, and whether or not it includes important fringe benefits such as health care. People are considered *unemployed* only if they are not in school and are actively seeking work and have failed to find it. People discouraged from trying and the ever burgeoning prison population (at present, nearly two million people disproportionately minority) do not count as unemployed. Real unemployment levels are thus considerably higher than official government statistics suggest.

The government measures the number of people who are poor by using an indicator called the *poverty level* that is supposed to be the amount of money required for minimal sustenance, for families of different sizes. Although the figure is very low, it is still much higher than what a person working full time at minimum wage would earn. The term *working poor* technically refers to those with full-time jobs whose income does not reach the poverty level but in practice describes anyone earning very low incomes. *Earned income* refers to money paid from jobs, while *total income* includes interest and dividends (virtually nil for the poor) as well as government assistance from programs such as Temporary Assistance to Needy Families (TANF) or the Earned Income Tax Credit (both explained ahead). Active debate exists on whether or not to count programs such as Medicaid, housing subsidies, or food stamps in tallying income. If these government benefits are counted as income, there are fewer people below the poverty level.

Income is vital for daily survival, but *economic assets*—a family's savings or equity in a home, car, or business—are also important. Assets (if they are sufficient) allow people to weather periods of unemployment or low income and medical emergencies. They also provide a pool that can be borrowed against (for instance, by increasing a mortgage) to provide investment funds for a business or to pay for a college education. Poor people typically have little or no economic assets in addition to limited incomes.

With these definitions in mind, the following is a quick sketch of the nature of present-day poverty. The numbers presented change from month to month, but historically the overall patterns of social and economic class, race, and gender-based inequality have remained fairly constant.

The overall distribution of income is highly skewed with those in the bottom fifth earning 15 percent of what those in the top fifth take home (Kornblum, Julian, and Smith, 1998, p. 232). Moreover, between 1977 and 1999 income inequality dramatically increased. The average after-tax income of the poorest one-fifth dropped 12 percent, while that of the richest one-fifth went up 38.2 percent. The richest 1 percent of the population (2.7 million people) have as much to spend as the bottom 100 million (Johnston, 1999, p. 14).

African Americans remain poorer than others, as do those from Spanish-speaking backgrounds, though incomes among those of Spanish descent differ widely, with Cubans being comparatively well-off and those from Puerto Rico being extremely poor. Geographically, poverty is least likely in the suburbs, most frequent in the central cities, and most extreme among the poor living in farm areas and on reservations. Female headed households with children constitute over half of the nation's poor—an illustration of the *feminization of poverty*. The family income of these households runs about 40 percent of the average. Families headed by minority females have even lower incomes on average. Overall poverty rates for people of color tend to run three times higher than the average.

With respect to wealth, as opposed to poverty rates, the top 1 percent own about a third of the nation's wealth. The wealth of the top 1 percent matches all the wealth owned by the entire bottom 95 percent. Black net worth is about 12 percent of white, while median Hispanic net worth is zero (United for a Fair Economy, 1999).

Poverty is associated with a wide variety of other problems. It can mean living in a house that is cold in winter, hot in summer, rat and roach infested, and located in dangerous neighborhoods; it often means a poor diet, few doctor visits (and those with underpaid Medicaid providers), and higher frequency of disease. Low-income women with children used to have the option to stay home and care for their kids, paying the bills with welfare payments, or working and relying on child care that may be unreliable or substandard. After welfare reform, many of these women no longer have the option of staying home to take care of their children. People from poor families on average have less formal education than others and may be prepared only for the industrial jobs that are rapidly disappearing. Children from poor families are more likely to drop out of school, have children out of marriage, and get entangled in crime. Those on welfare experience substantial hardships, with reports showing that during a year 15 percent of the families faced hunger, a like number had their utilities (light, heat, or telephone) shut off, and a fifth had to share housing with others (Edin & Lein, 1997). Poverty does not simply mean the lack of income but implies a myriad of associated and reinforcing problems.

For many people, the image of poverty is that of people on welfare, but this image is false. Most people who are poor remain poor even when they are working for a living. Over three-fourths of the poorest households have someone employed (Levitan, Gallo, & Shapiro, 1993). As another blow to the stereotype, most working poor families are intact, with a male in the household. The incomes and lifestyles of those on welfare and the working poor are remarkably similar (Edin & Lein, 1997). Literally millions of people are working full time and many others part time, striving to get by but not earning enough for a reasonable standard of living. While many of the working poor are eligible for Medicaid, food stamps, and housing assistance, they often don't use available governmental services. Many of the working poor are from recent immigrant groups, often Spanish speaking, using part of their meager salaries to support even poorer relatives back home. Further, the numbers of working poor are likely to increase because recent changes in welfare policy have forced many off welfare into marginal jobs. As Ira Cutler vividly describes

> Welfare reform has dramatically reduced the numbers of welfare recipients in our com-
> munities and just as dramatically increased the numbers of working poor families. It is
> as though, in a social policy version of the Invasion of the Body Snatchers, millions of
> families went to sleep one night as welfare recipients and woke the next morning as
> the working poor. (Cutler, 1999, p. 1)

Poverty has many consequences, each of which can motivate collective action. For example, activists might fight for higher minimum wages, universal health care, quality day care, or increased job security for workers in marginal jobs. Neighborhood organizing may occur around issues of jobs, homelessness, dilapidated housing, or crime in the nation's most economically depressed census tracts.

There is a shortage of housing available for those with low incomes. The numbers needing safe, affordable housing exceed the number of available units by 4.4 million. Three out of five poor renters pay more than half of their incomes for rent and utilities compared to a standard of 25 to 30 percent of income others spend for those purposes (Center on Budget and Policy Priorities, 1998). In recent years, the rent paid by the poorest 20 percent of Americans has increased twice as fast as their incomes, while the number of apartments with affordable rents (inflation corrected) declined in three years by almost a million units (Department of Housing and Urban Development, 1999). As the economy booms, housing prices increase, so that many of the poor, even those with federal subsidies, are unable to find dwellings they can afford. People are waiting longer for access to public housing; it can take years to obtain Section 8 vouchers (see ahead) that provide access to affordable housing in the private market (Department of Housing and Urban Development, 1999). With the homeless, problems of poverty are made worse by the breakdown in the delivery system for those with mental health problems (Jencks, 1994).

While poor people are found throughout the nation, poverty is most visible and devastating when concentrated in inner-city neighborhoods. These extremely poor areas of the city, often with poverty rates exceeding 40 percent, are described as hyperghettoes. These areas tend to be populated by minorities, have many dilapidated or abandoned buildings, lack jobs, and have high rates of violent crime. Most of the middle-class residents have fled these areas, as have the industries and the normal complement of commercial stores (Jargowsky, 1997). The concentration of poverty causes social problems to compound—the lack of jobs increases crime, the fear of crime discourages people from opening stores. The physical and social isolation of these areas enables middle-class society (and government officials, most of whom are middle class) to pretend that these hyperghettoes don't exist.

These intense concentrations of poor in inner-city neighborhoods reflect structural changes associated with a loss of higher paying industrial jobs. In the past, people with little education but with a willingness to work could find decent paying jobs in factories. Many of these jobs were located in inner-city areas because of the convenience of transportation and the presence of a pool of workers. Today, machinery has taken over some of these jobs, others have been exported to poor countries, and many of the remaining jobs are not unionized and pay poorly (Perrucci et al., 1988, p. 22). In the boom of the 1990s, these jobs have been replaced by service jobs, most of which are low-paid clerical and sales positions that lack security and fringes. Without a college degree, the economic prospects of even those willing and eager to work are seriously limited.

Urban Restructuring and Fights Over Space

Some structural problems that affect organizing result from (or at least are seen as) fights over geographic and social space. The movement to the suburbs, along with persistent social class and racial discrimination, have left geographic areas of concentrated poverty behind. In central cities, the homeless and the poor contend over space with gentrifiers and downtown developers. Ethnic groups vie over control of space, while environmentalists try to stop the conversion of farm land into suburban housing and malls. Fights over space reflect broader economic and social issues.

The Restructuring of Urban Areas

Recent decades have witnessed a massive restructuring of where people live and work, with employment and housing rapidly diffusing to the suburban ring. For decades, older inner cities have lost population and quality jobs to the suburbs. More recently, many central cities, especially those in the Sunbelt, have grown but not as quickly as the suburbs. Similarly, employment has grown faster in the suburbs than in the central cities. During the 1990s, the number of jobs increased 4.4 percent in the seventy-seven largest cities but 10.3 percent in the suburbs (Department of Housing and Urban Development, 1999, p. 11).

This slower job growth in the central cities has combined with a number of other factors to make life more difficult for the inner-city poor. Lacking reliable transportation, it is often near impossible for urban residents to commute to jobs in the suburbs. Inner-city schools often lack needed textbooks and computers and sometimes get the least qualified teachers, making it more difficult for residents in poor neighborhoods to compete for existing jobs. Many of the residents of these poor neighborhoods are minority members who face discrimination when they apply for jobs, further reducing their chances of being employed.

How is the Land to Be Used?

As people continue to move from central cities to suburbs and from inner suburbs to outer suburbs, battles occur over whether to convert more farmland into housing, shopping, and manufacturing areas. The result is often the degradation of the environment, destruction of wetlands, increase in traffic congestion and pollution, and further encouragement to empty out the existing older communities. In central cities with higher concentrations of the poor, the battles over land use are over whether to repair older structures or tear them down and replace them. What is taken down are single-room occupancy housing for the poor as well as older, dilapidated rental buildings and factories. It is seldom profitable to replace these structures with others that serve the same people, so the existing residents are ousted, to be replaced by upscale malls, middle-class condominiums, office buildings for middle-class jobs, and entertainment centers such as sports parks. These redevelopment projects are often subsidized by government.

In cities, the battle for renewal is also one that pits downtown against the neighborhoods. Big projects are funded for the downtowns, while neighborhoods may be relatively or even entirely neglected. Even routine expenses for road, sewer, water, and other infrastructure repairs are disproportionately spent in the downtown. One activist group discovered that in Chicago the two downtown wards received as much money for infrastructure as the other forty-eight wards combined.

In the recent past, government programs to build the highways that enable the suburban workers to commute from home to downtown jobs ended up displacing the urban poor, while other working-class communities have been destroyed to provide land for industrial or commercial use. On one occasion, General Motors threatened to abandon Detroit unless the city cleared hundreds of acres for a factory in Poletown. In response, "city officials had to acquire nearly seventeen hundred pieces of property, relocate more than thirty-five hundred residents, [and] demolish fifteen hundred residential and commercial structures" (Jones, Bachelor, & Wilson, 1986, p. 84). Similar destruction has occurred in other major cities, as housing is torn down to make room for museums, aquariums, and sports facilities.

In an effort to win back the middle and upper classes to city living, many city governments encourage *gentrification*. Older neighborhoods are recycled, either refurbished or knocked down and rebuilt, to provide elegant housing for wealthier people, often with quick access to downtown conveniences, such as upscale shopping, restaurants, theater, opera, and classy office buildings. Gentrification may force poor people from their homes, support networks, doctors, and ethnic stores and churches. The displaced may be forced to live among strangers in worse housing in more dangerous neighborhoods, move in with relatives or acquaintances, or pay more for equivalent housing.

A common pattern of gentrification occurs when speculators obtain property, often abandoned lofts, and lure in artists by charging very low rents. Attracted by the initial low prices, convenient location, and the cachet of living in an artistic area, young professionals arrive next, purchase older homes and begin to improve them. Landlords who house the poor then sell out for a profit, while people living in modest homes find that their taxes have gone up because taxes depend in part on the values of other homes in the area. The working poor are forced out.

Gentrifying areas often are adjacent to the few remaining inner-city manufacturing districts that employ those without college education. The professionals who live in gentrifying areas adjacent to manufacturing complain about truck traffic and odors, making life difficult for the small industrialists who quickly figure out that converting land to upscale housing is more profitable than using it for manufacturing. Gentrification exaggerates urban problems, by magnifying the loss of industrial jobs for those with low incomes and reducing the stock of affordable housing.

In some cities community groups have organized to convince the government to set up special *planned manufacturing districts* in which manufacturing firms that employ working-class citizens take priority over gentrified housing (Ducharme, 1991). Without such efforts, industries and lower income residents routinely lose out to gentrification.

Space and Ethnicity

Change in the ethnic mix of urban space shows the increasing importance of multicultural organizing. The composition of many of the poorest inner-city neighborhoods is often heavily minority, including new immigrant groups, who often contend with older groups for housing and jobs. The city of Los Angeles, for example, is home to 3.9 million immigrants; in the Los Angeles region, 27 percent of the population is foreign born (Waldinger & Bozorgmehr, 1996, p. 14). During the last generation, in Los Angeles County, "the Hispanic percentage has increased from 11 to 36 and the Asian percentage from 2 to 11" (Sabagh, Bozorgmeh, 1996, p. 87). Overall, "Latinos are rapidly becoming the nation's largest minority group" (Suro, 1998, p. 25). While Blacks, Native Americans, and some Hispanic groups have had trouble getting good enough jobs to leave the inner city, some immigrant groups have risen quickly economically and left their old neighborhoods behind. The constant influx of new immigrants, however, keeps the poverty level high in the old ethnic neighborhoods (Enchautegui, 1997).

Immigrants sometimes do not speak English, which accentuates cultural conflicts and makes intergroup communications and organizing quite difficult. In Los Angeles about 40 percent of the households do not speak English at home (Lopez, 1996, p. 142). While some immigrant groups have been able to earn enough to leave for the suburbs, many minorities and recent immigrants still remain in the inner cities having been kept out by suburbanites who reject their traditions and values. With so many minorities in so small a space, each fearing the other, yet wanting to assert their ethnic identity by establishing stores with familiar food and churches with remembered rituals, it is not surprising that many minorities end up battling each other for control of space.

Urban ethnic groups also vie with one another for jobs, especially entry-level positions for which newcomers, often with limited English language skills, are eligible. This competition may show up in an ethnic group's control of particular kinds of jobs. One family may establish a business and then hire only family members; when a member of the ethnic group becomes a manager in a company, he or she may hire only those from the same ethnic group.

When a given group dominates a particular business, academics call that kind of work an ethnic niche. The garment business in New York used to be Jewish dominated; in recent years, the dominant group has been Asian Americans. In parts of Texas, Spanish speakers from specific villages staff supermarkets, while South Asian Indians disproportionately are involved in the motel business. If the immigrant group is large and varied, it may create a kind of ethnic enclave in a geographic area in which those from the group patronize businesses owned by coethnics.

The existence of economic niches and enclaves can be beneficial to up and coming groups. Niches allow those with limited skills, knowledge, or contacts to enter the mainstream economy, because of family connections. The strength of an economic enclave is that wealth generated by some in the group provides jobs for others in the same group who then recirculate the money in stores owned by coethnics.

But the presence of ethnic niches and enclaves can create tension. In Miami, African Americans feel excluded from the Spanish economic enclave, and in New York City, African Americans and Puerto Ricans contend for government jobs (Torres, 1995). In some cities, tensions occur between Korean American owners of small stores (a niche they dominate) and the African American communities in which they are located. Such tensions sometimes spill over into violence, as occurred in South Central Los Angeles where Korean American liquor stores were burnt during urban uprisings (Sonnenshein, 1996). In New York City, a deal by an African American redevelopment group to partner with a supermarket chain to open a quality store that would employ community members was seen as a direct threat to the Spanish community whose members owned large numbers of small grocery stores.

Government Policies and Social Problems

Whether the decision of a city mayor to clear the streets of the homeless or the total revamping of welfare funding at the federal level, government actions dramatically affect the work of community and social-change organizations. Government funds a number of housing and redevelopment programs and sometimes enforces environmental or civil rights laws. At times, however, government fails to enforce laws or passes laws that directly harm the poor. To understand a problem, organizers must figure out what government has done and whether on a particular issue government is an ally or an opponent.

Through the speeches politicians give and the actions bureaucratic agencies take, government also helps construct the definitions of social problems and frames the solutions that broader public will accept. By building new jails and arguing for extreme penalties for narcotics offenses, government defines drugs as a problem, places the blame on immoral or criminal individuals, and decides imprisonment is the solution. Once government has framed a solution in this way, it is difficult to convince people that drug addiction is a medical problem or that drug dealing is a consequence of lack of legitimate employment opportunities.

Politicians describe and repeat examples that to them typify problems and from these typifications then justify their solutions. When conservatives talk about welfare cheats, they communicate that welfare has failed, an image that set the stage for a radical reduction in the social safety net. Labeling homes in need of repair as "blighted" justifies their destruction and replacement by upscale housing. Other typifications, such as the label "historic district," emphasize that a neighborhood is a community resource that needs to be fixed and preserved but not necessarily for the current residents. In framing what constitutes social problems and what are viable solutions, government has a disproportionate amount of influence.

In Chapter 12, we describe government structures and how to affect those in office. Here we provide an overview of how some government agencies define problems and how government policies affect the poor and influence battles over space. In doing so, we focus on policies about housing, community redevelopment, social welfare, and economic development. In the next chapter we briefly discuss government actions that have affected civil rights, feminism, and the environmental and disabilities movements. Organizing work is greatly affected by government policies, but because these policies change over time, those involved in any issue area should update themselves before launching a campaign.

Recent Overall Trends

From the late 1980s to the late 1990s (during the George Bush and William Clinton presidential administrations), there were some major broad changes in government policies that influenced virtually all issue areas. One trend has been called the *hollowing out* of government. Hollowing out refers to a decrease in government spending and personnel and an increase of contracting out to nongovernmental organizations for services. A second trend has been decentralization of functions from the federal government to the states, sometimes called *the devolution revolution.* A third trend has been a change in the willingness of the courts to require governments to carry out services and promises.

The hollowing of the federal government has resulted in budget and staffing cutbacks that have fallen more heavily on agencies working for the poor, especially the urban poor. For example, in the last few years, the Department of Housing and Urban Development has been dramatically cut back in staffing and has more programs to administer with the same or shrinking numbers of dollars.

In addition to cutting budgets, the hollowing out of government has included considerable contracting out for service delivery, often with little follow-up on how well the contractors are performing the service and little ability to accumulate experience from one contractor to another. For example, rather than pick up garbage with municipal employees, local governments often hire a private firm to collect the solid waste. State governments often contract out for social services.

Privatization (contracting out) provides both opportunities and problems for community groups. On the one hand, some community groups can get contracts to deliver services to their own constituents, supporting themselves and providing a needed service of high quality. On the other hand, sometimes private and nonprofit organizations get these contracts by charging low rates and then find they cannot afford to deliver quality services. As a result, they may harm institutionalized or dependent populations. One recent report noted that private providers of jails and reform schools for troubled teens sometimes kept their charges beyond their discharge dates, because the contractors were paid per inmate per day and wanted the revenue. Private firms may also be less amenable to public policies that urge fair wages and benefits or equal job opportunity for women and minorities.

Sometimes government agencies enter into *partnerships* or *coproduction* with private-sector organizations, not-for-profits, or citizen groups. In these partnerships, service delivery or costs may be shared. Parents might help coach softball games to help out a financially strapped park district that can't afford to staff the games (coproduction), or city hall might contribute funds to a local Chamber of Commerce to help finance a chamber initiative to bring in new businesses (partnership). Partnership programs do increase the impact of limited government money, but many partnership programs are disguised subsidies to businesses. Like contracting, they often weaken government's control over policy. In the economic development example, the Chamber of Commerce would be making the policy decisions that shape who benefits from new businesses.

Development occurs as programs and funding have been increasingly turned over from the federal government to the states. Often the funding has not matched the responsibilities that have been transferred. While the states have been empowered, relatively speaking, the cities have not because cities now have major responsibilities for handling social problems but are not being funded at former rates to pay for programs (Eisinger, 1998, p. 322). To worsen the situation, at the local level, tax limitation movements have reduced the money counties and cities can raise from their own sources, forcing them to choose between services such as police, fire, and public works on the one hand and social service efforts on the other.

As Eisinger ominously summarizes

the absence of a growing stream of federal dollars has meant that city political leaders cannot afford, fiscally or politically, to push an agenda of social and racial reform. . . . left to confront the great urban racial and economic polarities, few elected officials would be so foolhardy as to risk inevitable failure by initiating solutions based on the modest and limited resources that they themselves can raise. It is far easier—and the outcome more certain—to lower taxes, reduce public employment, and fill potholes. City limits have never been more in evidence. (Eisinger, 1998, pp. 322–323)

This retreat from social responsibility has occurred even though in recent years the federal budget has been healthy and seems now to be generating a surplus. Little of that expected surplus has been targeted for social programs; tax breaks for the wealthy have taken priority. Worse yet, the surpluses that will be used to fund these tax breaks will be created by cutting social programs much further in the next few years. As the surpluses are committed to future tax breaks, road projects, and debt repayment, the federal government seems to be cutting rather than adding to social programs to keep the budget balanced (Center on Budget and Policy Priorities, 1999).

The third broad trend of recent years, cutting across policy areas, has to do with the courts. In the recent past, when the government failed in its social responsibilities, lawsuits could be brought with a reasonable chance that the courts would mandate needed actions. In the last few years, courts have been less willing to listen to complaints about government neglect. Further, in 1999 the Supreme Court ruled that states cannot be sued by their citizens for enforcement of federal laws, weakening the ability of people to obtain redress if states violate federal laws, such as those against age discrimination. Other laws that have been imposed on the states might also fall into this category, possibly including open housing laws and those banning discrimination based on disabilities. Recent trends in court decisions mean that social change organizations might have to win battles in 50 states not just one battle at the federal level (Greenburg, 1999).

Federal Antipoverty and Social Service Programs

Much of current organizing against poverty is influenced by government actions. The federal government first became involved in antipoverty programs during the Great Depression of the 1930s to help unemployed and hungry people. Some programs paid for jobs for people who built or repaired roads, public buildings, and parks; others provided support for artists and writers to record the period. Most public employment programs faded away by the Second World War, but the income maintenance efforts in social security and welfare became institutionalized.

After World War II, from 1945 to the end of the 1950s, the country experienced an economic boom. Public attention to poverty faded. Instead, government sought to eliminate blight in cities and renew downtowns but did so by tearing down many neighborhoods that housed the poor. During the 1960s, poverty was rediscovered as a social problem, in part because of the interests of Presidents Kennedy and Johnson and, in part, from the pressures from civil rights campaigns that made it clear that many citizens had not benefited from the growth in the fifties.

In the 1960s, the federal government set up a wide array of programs to combat poverty and to improve deteriorated neighborhoods. Many were part of the *War on Poverty,* funded by the federal Office of Economic Opportunity and run by local Community Action Agencies. For a time, these agencies encouraged citizen participation and actually hired organizers to work in poor neighborhoods. Programs included Head Start, to help children of poor families learn enough to start school on equal footing with their peers, the Job Corp, a training and employment program, and the Food Stamp Program. In addition, the federal government helped fund Community Development Corporations (CDCs) to carry out community-based programs for economic and housing renewal. Another program set up at this time was Legal Services, which employed attorneys to help the poor in dealing with government bureaucracy or in handling relations with their landlords. Community organizations and welfare-advocacy groups worked with Legal Service attorneys to bring class-action suits to force changes in government and business policies toward the poor.

The elderly also benefited as social security payments were increased and health programs for the poor and the elderly were established. In addition, President Johnson supported the Older Americans Act (OAA), which paid public or nonprofit agencies for their efforts to help the elderly.

These government programs had a dual purpose: economic betterment and empowerment of the poor. The laws setting up these programs and the rules to implement them required citizen participation in the administration of social service, community development, and community mental health programs. In practice, many citizens did not take advantage of the chance to participate, in part discouraged by local government officials or business people who themselves actively sought leadership roles in these new social agencies. Though many of the War on Poverty programs failed to empower the program recipients, they did create a tradition of community participation and control that outlasted the federally funded Community Action Program (Fainstein et al., 1982, p. 18).

Policies adopted during the Republican Nixon and Ford administrations (1968–1976) weakened what remained of community control of federal social service programs, though the level of funding was only marginally reduced. The Office of Economic Opportunity was abolished, however, eliminating many bureaucrats who were willing to lobby for the poor.

To help the unemployed gain jobs, the Nixon administration funded the Comprehensive Employment Training Act (CETA). There is little evidence that the program actually created many new jobs for poorer people, although it did fund some temporary and entry-level positions in local government. Ironically, given the conservative nature of the Nixon administration, CETA helped sustain the community movement by allowing local governments to hire personnel for community-based social services.

The Nixon and Ford administrations were followed by Democratic President Jimmy Carter (1976–1980) who tried to reintroduce programs that benefited the poor and minorities and increase their funding. Localities were allowed to use money from the Community Development Block Grant (initially a physical redevelopment program) for social service activities. Social activists were appointed to federal positions and an Office of Neighborhoods was set up in the Department of Housing and Urban Development to coordinate federal antipoverty efforts.

The overriding goal of the Reagan administration (1980–1988) appeared to be to reduce the costs of social service programs. The president successfully framed societal concerns about antipoverty programs by talking about a (mythical) welfare queen who rode in a Cadillac and collected dozens of welfare checks. Playing on this image, and with support of conservative legislators, President Reagan cut back some social programs. For example, even ignoring the effects of inflation, early in the Reagan administration, Aid to Families with Dependent Children (AFDC, welfare) dropped 6 percent, food and nutrition assistance went up only 1.4 percent, and employment and training funds were halved (Weicher, 1984).

Efforts were made to obscure the size of these cuts (and to increase the power of state government in administering antipoverty efforts) by combining separate, earmarked federal grants into a single *block grant,* for such areas as community development or for social services. Before the block grants, the government used to make what was called *categorical grants,* that is, it would allocate money for specific narrowly defined programs, such as repairing blighted houses. A block grant combined several similar programs such as those for repairing blighted homes, sewer repair, and community redevelopment into one larger program with a locality determining how much should be spent for each of the formerly separate efforts. The total for the block grant was usually less than the sum of the individual categorical grants constituting it, but the locality could spend all of the grant on one effort and none on any of the others if it wanted.

The new flexibility in the block grants was not always beneficial to the poor. For instance, the Social Services Block Grant (SSBG) that included AFDC was redesigned so that the states did not need to target all of the money to the extremely poor. Moreover, the funding for the block grant was only 70 percent of the total of the categorical programs that it replaced. Fortunately, many states increased the share of money from state taxes going to help the extremely poor, though often at the cost of reducing funding for other programs, such as energy assistance (U.S. Conference of Mayors, 1986, pp. 177–178). When the Reagan administration cut the SSBG by another 50 percent, the states could not make up the gap, instead having to force the advocates of one worthwhile social program to compete against another vital service for the reduced funds.

President Clinton, a middle-of-the-road Democrat, followed the Republicans Reagan and Bush in 1992. For the poor, the most important policy change of this administration occurred in 1996 when the Democratic president and Republican Congress reached agreement on a total overhaul of federal antipoverty policy. The legislation ironically named the Personal Responsibility and Work Opportunity Reconciliation Act dramatically changed the support system for the very poor.

> The Personal Responsibility Act . . . limits the time (to 5 years) that a family head can receive cash assistance under the renamed program for Temporary Assistance to Needy Families (TANF). The law sets work requirements . . . half of all single parents must be working. For two-parent families, at least one parent will have to be working in 90 percent of the assisted families. Work activities are tightly defined in the law . . . The law requires unwed teen parents to live at home . . . and to be in school in order to receive benefits . . . there are even more detailed requirements for establishing the child-support responsibilities of noncustodial parents . . . for immigrants, the law is especially strict. (Nathan, 1998, p. 4)

States are allowed broad discretion in implementing the law, so long as their policies reduce welfare rolls consistent with federal goals. States determine who is eligible and define what is or is not a job-related activity. Recipients are no longer automatically Medicaid eligible, limits have been placed on the amount of Food Stamp money some recipients can receive, and funding for child nutrition has been cut (Sheets, 1997).

The increased discretion for the states is part of the rules for

> the TANF block grant . . . eliminates the entitlements . . . under . . . Aid to Families with Dependent Children (AFDC). Each state also receives a new child care block grant and can transfer up to 30% of the TANF block grant funds to the child care block grant and up to 10 percent of the pre-existing, broad gauged social services block grant. (Nathan, 1998, p. 4)

States readily accepted the new responsibilities because initially the funds provided exceeded the money they were then spending. The full impact of the changes will not become apparent while the economy remains robust and former welfare recipients can find jobs. With the economy booming, welfare rolls have contracted sharply, by 43 percent over four years. Of those, about two-thirds have found some kind of work, but the work is often low paid with wages hovering around the poverty level (Brauner & Lopest, 1999), and those last hired will be the first fired when the economy begins to contract.

Changes in welfare policy have spilled over into other policy areas. States quickly discovered that many welfare recipients require a variety of supporting programs to get off welfare, including assistance with transportation, medical care, day care, and family problems. Further, many on welfare who had been receiving federal housing subsidies found that when working they were no longer eligible to receive housing support, yet they did not earn enough money to pay for adequate housing on their own.

Optimists see an upside to the changes. For those who got jobs there is increased pride and empowerment that comes in joining the mainstream economy. Further, while wages for the formerly unemployed are often low, most of the working poor are eligible for the Earned Income Tax Credit, a cash return from the IRS for those who are working, but whose earnings are low. Pessimists consider the changes brought about by TANF as a shredding of the social safety net and anticipate real trouble the next time the economy enters a recession and the number of unemployed increases.

Federal Housing and Community Development Efforts

Federal urban renewal and housing policies have changed enormously over the last 45 years. The level of financial support has fluctuated, the definition of who is to be helped has shifted, and the respective powers and responsibilities of the federal government, localities, and community groups has varied. In recent years, states and localities have gained more power over housing and community development but have fewer resources to carry out such programs. In addition, nonprofit community development and community-based fair housing organizations have increased their role in delivering housing and renewal services.

In many ways, it appears that the middle class and businesses, rather than the poor and poor neighborhoods, have been the primary beneficiaries of federal redevelopment efforts. Urban redevelopment efforts begun after the Second World War cleared slums occupied by the poor, often removing African Americans, to make way for expanded central business districts. Some new housing was built including federally financed public housing projects and units funded under various categorical housing programs such as Section 221(d)3 or Section 202 that paid private developers to house the poor or the elderly. Displacement of the poor was high; for example, in New Haven 20 percent of the people in the city were moved, and overall "four dwelling units have been destroyed by renewal for everyone built" (Smith & Feagin, 1979, p. 241), while the poor who were housed often ended up in shoddily built places (M. Mayer, 1978). Further in the inner cities, people with multiple economic and social problems were forced to live in high-rise public housing buildings in neighborhoods without adequate schools, playgrounds, shopping, or security.

Meanwhile the federal government was aiding the middle-class flight to suburbia by providing tax breaks and subsidized mortgages, funding the construction of new highways from the cities to the suburbs, and paying for the building of new sewer and water systems. Subsidies to the middle and upper classes for housing far outstripped the costs of housing the poor. Overall, between 1949 and 1960 the total cost of public housing units constructed was matched by the average federal subsidy provided in a single year to the middle class (Struyk et al., 1988, p. 62).

In reaction to the failure of urban renewal to serve the poor and in response to increasing unrest in urban areas, President Lyndon Johnson initiated the Model Cities program. Model Cities joined efforts at physical redevelopment with the social service programs that were part of the War on Poverty. The impact of Model Cities, however, was greatly attenuated as Congress insisted that the small amount of money made available be shared by a large number of cities. The requirements for citizen participation in the Model Cities efforts encouraged the growth of community organizations; however, mayors resented the loss of their control and successfully demanded that the laws be changed so they, and not community groups, had effective say on how the money would be spent. Cities did gain more say when, in 1965, the Cabinet level Department of Housing and Urban Development was created, combining programs that support home mortgages with a variety of urban renewal efforts within one agency.

During the 1960s, government itself built about 27,000 public housing units each year; however, government sought to get out of doing construction and instead set up a variety of indirect subsidy programs to encourage the private sector to construct affordable apartments, repair older homes, and build less expensive houses, often by guaranteeing the mortgages on these buildings. These efforts often backfired. Many of the subsidized homes were shoddily built or not fully repaired, then aggressively marketed to people with incomes inadequate to pay the mortgages or maintain the properties; they often defaulted. Builders who made a profit on their sales and banks whose mortgage profits were guaranteed by the Federal Housing Authority cared little about the long-term consequences of these sales. Worse yet, unscrupulous real estate brokers played upon racial fears to encourage white families to sell their homes to speculators who in turn sold them to poor African American families who received federal mortgages but lacked the income to maintain the properties. Through such programs, government both facilitated "white flight" and funded neighborhoods that quickly became slums (Levine and Harmon, 1992).

Major changes in federal policy toward housing occurred in the Nixon-Ford years with the Housing and Community Development Act of 1974. Many separate redevelopment efforts were merged into the Community Development Block Grant (CDBG). CDBG brought together categorical programs for street repairs, sewer construction, housing construction and rehabilitation, urban planning, certain specified community services, the preservation of historic buildings, and economic development work. CDBG funds were allocated by a formula that provided more money to cities that were relatively poor and had an aging housing stock.

Local officials maintained substantial discretion in the expenditure of these funds so long as the projects were consistent with overall CDBG objectives. Cities receiving CDBGs were required to set up citizen advisory groups, but these citizen groups often had little say. How CDBG money was to be spent created numerous conflicts. Some local governments sought loopholes, for instance, by spending money in poor neighborhoods but on projects that benefited wealthier citizens, in effect using poverty funds to displace the poor. Over the decades, and because of the efforts of numerous community organizations, CDBG increasingly has been treated by city governments as money meant for the poor and poor communities. In many places, activist groups have gained effective say in how the money is spent, while many community groups receive part of their budget support from the block grant (Rich, 1993; Sanders, 1997).

During the Nixon administration, the Section 8 Housing Program dramatically changed how the federal government helped some of the poor pay for their housing. Section 8 provides vouchers to (a fraction of) those who need affordable housing. Voucher holders must locate HUD-approved housing on the free market and pay "fair market value rents." The voucher covers the rental costs that exceed a given percentage (initially 25%, now 30%) of the tenant's income. Another part of the Section 8 program provides subsidies for builders who construct apartment buildings in which a given percentage of the units are made available to Section 8 eligible individuals. In practice, not enough vouchers are made available and funding for the program has always been uncertain.

During the Ford administration the Home Mortgage Disclosure Act (HMDA) of 1975 was passed requiring banks to publicize by geographic area where mortgage loans were made. HMDA was the first step in providing data to combat redlining—discrimination by banks who refused to issue mortgages for homes in poor, primarily minority areas. In 1977, after pressure from activists, the government passed the Community Reinvestment Act (CRA) that allows federal agencies and banking supervisors to sanction banks that are not loaning money in or otherwise serving poor communities.

During the Carter years, HUD officials more aggressively fought efforts by White suburbs to exclude minorities. In part, these efforts were a response to the 1976 Supreme Court ruling in the Gautreaux case that mandated that because of discrimination on the part of the Chicago Housing Authority the poor had been precluded from suburban areas and that in response government must now provide Section 8 housing certificates to house the urban poor in suburban areas. Carter officials endorsed the decision and set about providing support services to those who were moved. Studies of Gautreaux and other similar programs have found that those relocated benefit by receiving both superior education and obtaining better jobs. Further, Carter appointed people sympathetic to the community movement to various HUD positions who, in turn, encouraged neighborhood organizations to monitor CDBG expenditures to assure that money was spent in programs that directly benefited poor individuals. In addition, HUD set up an Office of Neighborhoods that provided technical assistance for neighborhood organizations.

After the election of Ronald Reagan as president, the climate for housing and community development soured. Traditional grant programs were cut back and long-standing programs that funded affordable housing were stopped cold as funds for affordable housing dried up. At its peak in 1978, CDBG was funded at about $2.25 billion (in 1988 dollars). By 1988, at the end of the Reagan administration, funding had dropped to less than $1 billion, corrected for inflation. Further only 60 percent of CDBG money had to be targeted to the poor. Established businesses became eligible grant recipients. Under Reagan, those living in subsidized homes now had to spend 30 percent, up from 25 percent, of their income on rent, while few new homes were built. Combining all forms of housing assistance to the poor in 1977, the federal government aided about 500,000 households, a figure that had declined to 200,000 by 1985. Homelessness increased, in part, because there were fewer homes for the poor, while upper status people continued to benefit from the tax reduction for interest paid on their mortgages.

It appeared that few funds would be available for constructing affordable housing; this situation hurt not only the poor but also wealthier builders and banks that made profits from such projects. At the urging of a coalition of community groups, banks, and builders, Congress passed in 1986 what is known as the Low Income Housing Tax Credit (LIHTC). LIHTC allows wealthier corporations and banks who invest in affordable housing projects to receive a substantial tax reduction as long as they invest certain sums in housing construction for the poor. Although some activists complain that LIHTC is "feeding the sparrows by feeding the horses" (Hartman, 1992), overall LIHTC has provided billions for affordable housing and is now a mainstay of funding for affordable housing.

President Bush continued many of the Reagan policies but in more moderate ways. In 1990 Congress passed the National Affordable Housing Act that combined what was left of many federal housing programs into a lump sum payment to localities, while also reinstating the requirement that 70 percent of CDBG money go to low and moderate income communities. Other provisions encouraged local governments to improve public housing (the HOPE program) while offering subsidies to help the poor own their own homes (the HOME program). The Affordable Housing Act mandates that at least 15 percent of housing funds be set aside for projects developed by nonprofit, community-based organizations. The act authorized a large increase in federal money for housing but few new funds were forthcoming.

For those concerned about housing and community renewal programs, the Clinton years have been a terrifying roller coaster ride. Clinton appeared sympathetic to the causes of the urban poor, but has not been willing to fight hard for particular programs. His appointees at HUD were active supporters of community causes, worked closely with community groups, and tried to shape HUD in ways that would help the poor. Yet, at the same time HUD supported devolution, moving more responsibilities to the local governments without providing needed funds.

The Clinton administration's plans were on balance positive, but the Republican dominated Congress actively opposed programs for the poor. Pressures to balance the budget encouraged Congress to reduce social service, housing, and urban renewal programs. The Republican Congress threatened to abolish HUD, but the department hung on, coming up with one reform plan after another to improve financial management and cut staffing levels. Congress weakened fair-housing legislation and attacked the Community Reinvestment Act. To complicate matters, the welfare-to-work legislation required funds from the housing budget, to provide homes to those moving to obtain jobs, increasing demand on an already overwhelmed budget.

The Community Development Block Grant survived as a tool for urban renewal. For instance in the first three years of the Clinton administration CDBG paid for 641,000 affordable housing units and helped create 445,000 new jobs. The amounts budgeted for CDBG held steady, at around the $5 billion range, but the dollars had to go farther because many new earmarked programs were put into the CDBG program, spreading the same sum of money over many additional efforts. In addition, more cities are now eligible for money from the same pot, reducing the amount available for the most troubled big cities.

The major Clinton innovation to help urban areas was the Empowerment Zone Program, in which $100,000,000 grants (over ten years) are provided to a handful of cities that successfully competed for the money while some other cities designated as Enterprise Zones have received smaller grants. Firms in Empowerment Zones obtain special tax consideration and are encouraged to work with community groups, while community members (at least in theory) help plan local renewal. Many consider these two programs to be little more than a version of Model Cities and question their effectiveness and scope (Gittell & Vidal, 1998).

In late 1998, federal housing efforts dramatically changed with the passage of the Quality Housing and Work Responsibility Act. QHWR encouraged local Public Housing Agencies to tear down older, derelict projects and provide those displaced with Section 8 vouchers. In addition, funds from HOPE VI were to pay for comprehensive housing, planning, and social service efforts in areas surrounding public housing.

While, the destruction of crumbling units sounds like a good idea, these proposals are a mixed blessing. Some fear that destroying public housing projects located near the central business districts will simply allow gentrification. Further, there are not enough Section 8 vouchers (or landlords willing to accept Section 8 tenants) to house the individuals who once again are being displaced, and who could end up having no choice but to move in with friends or family or find inadequate housing in poor neighborhoods. Activist groups are torn on how to respond, hoping for an alternative to dilapidated public housing, appreciating the holistic HOPE VI programs, but fearing the changes will simply increase problems in poor and minority neighborhoods.

Matters are complicated by the uncertain fate of Section 8, especially what is known as the *expiring use permits*. In the past, Section 8 helped developers build apartments on the condition that the apartments be made affordable for a contractually determined number of years. Once those years have passed and the section 8 permits have expired, the owner can do as he or she wishes with the building. Further, getting Congress to appropriate HUD money for Section 8 has been a hassle and a cliffhanger every year.

At the federal level, then, many of the institutions and sources of housing and redevelopment for the poor remain under attack. The crucial Community Reinvestment Act has been threatened; HUD has dramatically shrunk its staffing; its existence as a cabinet level department has come into question; and the whole department is on a financial watch list for lax financial management. Program funding has been reduced or diverted. There have been practically no new public housing units, old units are being torn down, and the program that is intended to provide housing, the Section 8 subsidy program, has been underfunded while expansion of federal funding to handle new needs stemming from welfare reform has been inadequate.

Local Government and Economic Development Policies

As the federal government shrinks, local governments have an increasing responsibility to carry out welfare, housing, community redevelopment, and other social service programs. Some localities fund affordable housing programs out of recycled grant money or use their own taxes, while others only reluctantly spend the money provided by the federal government. In addition to the responsibilities that have devolved onto them, states and municipalities have many of their own policies and programs that affect community actions.

State and local governments often run their economic development programs in ways that affect community organizations. Some of these efforts offer incentives to businesses to relocate and by doing so take jobs away from other communities. Some localities sponsor economic development programs that help businesses if they promise a certain number of new jobs to local residents. In practice, few subsidy programs affect the decision of companies where to locate (Wolman & Spitzley, 1996) while the poorest cities that have the greatest social needs end up spending the most to help wealthier businesses (Rubin & Rubin, 1987). Too often, getting a business to move or concluding a deal becomes an end in itself instead of the means for alleviating poverty. As one observer noted,

> relatively few city officials recognize that economic development, as traditionally pursued, should have anything to do with poverty alleviation. The latter seems like just another social objective that obstructs entrepreneurial deal making and business attraction. (Giloth, 1995, p. 281)

When economic development activities go so badly awry, activist groups need to change the equation and ensure that local residents benefit from the deals being made.

Some cities have adopted programs that are more sensitive to neighborhood concerns. Such efforts include repairing streets and sidewalks, sanitary sewers, elevated train structures, lighting, or drainage, in poor communities so as to encourage businesses to expand or reopen (Imbroscio, 1997). Another approach to helping poorer neighborhoods is called *brownfield redevelopment* in which cities agitate to get federal money or use their own funds to help detoxify old industrial sites, which are almost always in the poorest neighborhoods. When the sites are usable again, new businesses can move in, generating jobs and helping to bring the whole neighborhood back. With another approach to protect existing jobs, cities establish zoning codes that prevent manufacturing districts from turning into gentrified housing or entertainment areas. By providing job training and funding transportation that enables people from poor communities to reach places that have jobs, local governments can bring some social equity to their economic development efforts.

With sufficient political pressure, cities can be persuaded to shift some of their resources from downtown–big business renewal to the needs of poor neighborhoods (Rast, 1999). Cities can also require that downtown businesses receiving government support help provide affordable housing or guarantee that certain numbers of the poor are employed. Most important, cities can work with and provide economic support to the numerous community-based organizations in poor neighborhoods that provide affordable housing, attract stores, and create new businesses (Rubin, 2000a).

To change the direction of local economic development policies requires that community activists work to reframe how issues are seen. At present, many public officials try to obscure what they are doing by calling the incentives offered to profit-making businesses *investments* but label the money spent by community redevelopment organizations *subsidies,* a term that carries a negative connotation of inefficiency. Elected officials sometimes use the phrase *economic development* to refer to programs that help businesses and restrict the term *community development* to those efforts involved in rebuilding poor neighborhoods. When used in this way, public officials are often trying to mislead by claiming that economic development benefits everyone while community development helps only the poor.

Implications for Organizers

To illustrate the background material organizers need, we have briefly sketched issues of poverty and urban decline and how government has responded to these problems. While we have only covered a small handful of the many problems communities face, the discussion suggests lessons that can help organizers, no matter what problems their groups are fighting.

Organizing is Guided by Analysis of What Causes Social Problems

To effectively design campaigns, activists must understand the source and background of different social programs. Without this understanding, efforts might be spent on the immediate symptoms of a problem while ignoring underlying issues. Fighting to keep a factory in a community is important, but working to persuade the city to provide job training for the poor and investments in firms set up by community members might be a better approach to handle the social causes of neighborhood job decline.

If the causes are not diagnosed with some degree of accuracy, then the organizing effort, even if successful, is not likely to have broader impacts. The solution may have the impact of a Band Aid when major surgery is called for. Today community groups work with labor organizations to try to improve conditions in inner-city factories, many of which are disguised sweatshops. Fixing the immediate problems of working conditions at a plant are important. Solutions will be more lasting, however, if organizers also work to bridge the gaps between males and females and between different ethnic groups that management exploits in its effort to distract attention from poor pay and working conditions.

Framing and Reframing Social Problems

Battles are often over how problems are framed. A first step in organizing is working with those who feel disempowered to develop a shared definition of why they face the problems they do and then convincing the broader society and those in government to accept this definition of the situation.

Organizers recognize that framing issues in ways that support their own interests is important. For example, conservatives often "blame the victim," that is, argue that the people suffering from a problem have created that problem themselves. Thus, people who are unemployed are out of work because they are lazy or cannot deal with authority, not because the jobs themselves are dirty, dangerous, back breaking, and monotonous, and not because there are not enough jobs to go around. To the extent that those in power manage to shift the blame to the victims, neither government nor business ends up with any responsibility to make changes. Polluting firms define their actions as creating jobs, denying any long-term social harm. Those in power create a story that omits major parts of reality, that makes them look good, and that makes it very difficult for others to question their actions. Organizers need to contest these disempowering framings and formulate and publicize counter stories. To fight the image of the undeserving poor, activists argue that many of the poor are elderly and frail or uneducated with responsibilities for children. Most of the poor are hard working and employed but end up in jobs that do not pay enough to survive.

The Unstable Policy Environment

Activists try to force changes in public policy or to monitor implementation of a law. The policies activists focus on may be highly visible, for example, when government forbids gays in the military or precludes gay marriages; or the policies may be less visible, as when subsidies on mortgages for the middle classes hasten suburbanization and leave central cities with a disproportionate number of poor people. Further, policy changes at one level of government may reverberate for years in different locations. When the federal government discontinued General Revenue Sharing (a type of grant), many cities reduced the social services that these funds supported.

Organizers need to pay attention to the constantly changing policy environment. Programs to encourage neighborhood empowerment under the Carter administration were reversed during the Reagan years. Vital laws such as the Community Reinvestment Act are constantly in danger of being eroded or terminated. Affirmative action has been weakened in recent years. Some states have curtailed abortion rights, some passing laws requiring minors to get their parent's permission before obtaining an abortion, others banning late-term abortions done with particular procedures. Even constitutional issues like the separation of church and state are continually changing.

Public policies are unstable because frequent elections provide the opportunity for those who oppose particular policies to try to undo them. Organizers and action groups need to dedicate time to assure that friends in office are not replaced by enemies. This is normally accomplished by working in coalitions with other progressive groups.

A Changing Social Environment

Some social problems endure over time. It seems that there will always be poor people while social and economic inequity persists. Ending the tensions between racial, ethnic, and religious groups is an ongoing task. But other problems have taken on new focuses as social attitudes evolve and as the legal and economic environment changes. Organizers should not assume that their prior understandings of problems and failed solutions are sufficient to guide present-day action.

For example, in the past, unions represented established ethnic groups and worked to prevent immigration, because they felt that immigrants and African Americans from the South would work for less money and take jobs from union members; unions also blocked membership in apprenticeship programs to minority group members. At that time, labor unions may not have made good allies. But in recent years, some unions have actively worked to organize minorities, others work with farm laborers or service workers of all colors and ethnic groups. Unions maintain the same anti–sweat shop orientation today that they had years ago, but now the goal is to protect newer immigrants. Also, unions have a major interest in trying to prevent jobs from moving abroad. Today unions and many community organizations have issues in common and union–community group alliances make sense.

Urban neighborhoods remain important as a focal point for organizing, but other types of organizing have gained prominence in recent years. Organizing around issues that go beyond a neighborhood and around personal identity, in terms of gender, ethnicity, or sexual orientation, have become more important and are carried out in many different places at once. Environmental concerns, for example, seldom limit themselves to a neighborhood; they may deal with watersheds, or regions of the country, or areas downwind of a nuclear power plant.

The old distinctions between cities, in which organizers work, and suburbs, that organizers ignore, have broken down as older suburbs begin to show signs of crumbling infrastructure and ethnically varied populations. Older suburbs have began tearing down older homes and factories to make way for newer structures. Social problems like gangs, drugs, and school violence have moved into the suburbs, attracting bored and unhappy youngsters. All these changes create new opportunities for organizing.

Changing demographics affect organizing work. The population at large is getting older, on average, increasing the importance of retirement funding and health care as issues about which to organize. At the same time, immigrant and minority groups have a younger population, one for which concerns about day care and schooling are much more important. Issues that resonate with one demographic group may be irrelevant to others.

The successes of past organizing efforts have changed the environment for present-day efforts. Thousands of community development groups now provide affordable homes for hundreds of thousands of poor families. In schools, in places of business, and in residential neighborhoods, more people of color are in positions of responsibility than ever before. Women have many more opportunities in sports, education, and jobs than a generation ago and are beginning to challenge the notion in medical research that women are just like men and that only men need to be studied. A generation ago, raw racism was (in certain social sectors) acceptable and the intentional and overt subordination of women was a common practice. Now racism and sexism, while still real, are no longer normative.

The improvements that have been made can distract from how much more progress is still needed. A woman who is now in medical school and would not have been a generation ago may still find herself relegated to relatively poorer paying and less prestigious specialities. Offsetting the increasing percent of Americans who own their own homes has been the increase in the number of homeless people sleeping on park benches, in cardboard boxes, under highway overpasses, and on grates over subways that let out a little warm air. The economy has been strong for a number of years, but almost all gains have been among the well-educated with those with little education having few opportunities. The people at the bottom still live from hand to mouth, without enough resources to cover emergencies. New jobs being created are still primarily of the low-paying variety, often without health-care benefits.

Social Problems Compound

Campaigns are often about a single issue—eliminating a drug house, changing the law about who can file a complaint in a spouse abuse case. Such efforts are important, especially because organizations that tackle too many issues at once may end up not accomplishing much. Yet organizers have to keep in mind that problems compound, appear in clusters, and, at times, have to be confronted all at once.

Neighborhoods with high unemployment have higher crime rates, fewer intact families, and tend to be those most neglected by government. Many homeless people need jobs, suffer from problems of substance abuse, have poor health, face psychological problems, and often lack the skills needed to help themselves. Jobs have moved to the suburbs, but because of the lack of affordable housing in the suburbs or mass transit from the inner cities to the jobs, the inner-city poor cannot follow the jobs. Battered women who end up in shelters often lack jobs skills and lack self-confidence as a result of prior beatings and the threat of future ones.

Because problems compound, sometimes solving one problem helps solve several others. Affordable housing adds stability to the lives of poor families, enabling their children to stay in one school, do better academically, and increase the chances for a decent job. Youngsters who are able to find part-time jobs, even McJobs, are more likely to graduate from high school and even go on to college. Job training for abused women may open up the possibility of moving away, may increase confidence, and provide the opportunity for health insurance, making physical problems more manageable.

When a single solution is likely to be drowned out by multiple problems, community groups can participate in a variety of local coalitions formed to coordinate fights against separate problems. Some community areas have begun Comprehensive Community Initiatives that coordinate multiprong attacks on a set of reinforcing social ills that hurt one geographic area.

Don't Act Alone

Organizing is about teaching community members the power of working together. Too often, though, community groups and action organizations basically work by themselves. In some urban neighborhoods, action and community groups end up rivaling one another, perhaps in competitive efforts to sign up the same members or in battles to obtain funds from the few local donors. Some groups philosophically disagree, as for instance when direct-action groups that picket those in office distrust community-based housing groups that take money from government.

When activist groups are trying to attack complex social problems, going it alone is likely to be ineffective. To persuade and pressure government, organizers must be part of coalitions that present a powerful voice to those in office. While nominal membership in a coalition—signing up, paying dues, and doing little else—is a start, effective coalitions come about only after individual groups develop trust by working together on a variety of issues. In urban communities, social service, neighborhood, and direct-action organizations need time to get to know one another. Ways to do so might include sharing festivities or victory celebrations with one another, holding workshops on changing government policies and funding, or just enjoying each others' company in social situations, such as going out to lunch or going to a baseball game together. By sharing stories informally, organizers learn how much all action groups have in common.

3 A Thumbnail Sketch of the History of Community Organizing

Community organizing is about solving present day problems. Why then should activists study the history of neighborhood organizing and social movements?

First, community organizers cannot do their jobs unless they have the confidence that success is possible. Organizers learn from history that a variety of social-change groups, faced with long odds and with slim beginnings, won out in the end. We know David can beat Goliath, because he has in the past.

Second, history lends us patience while teaching us persistence. Organizers discouraged by the slowness of progress learn that while past movements faced lean days in which few joined in the fight, there were frequent days of triumph and victory. When present community organizations encounter hard times—arsonists burn down affordable housing or a courageous organizer is knifed by opponents—organizers look back and see that other organizations overcame threats, had their members jailed, jobs taken away, their demonstrations broken up by violence, and survived. Bad times are turned to good purpose as activists create a shared history of solidarity and pride. History makes clear that slow times need not mean the death of hope.

Third, history provides concrete lessons on tactics and strategies allowing each generation to build on the knowledge of its predecessors. Activists learn that short-term victories are not enough unless an organization remains in place to assure that gains do not quickly evaporate. Reviewing the lessons of the past, organizers discover the importance of gaining public support, not just the quiet assent of government officials or a few business leaders. The now legendary antics of organizer Saul Alinksy teach us what can be accomplished by disruptive humor. The nonviolence of Dr. Martin Luther King, Jr. makes clear that unarmed people can face billy clubs and fire hoses and win not only symbolic but actual victories.

Past failures, too, teach present-day organizers. The women's movement lost the fight for the Equal Rights Amendment, in part, because of dissensus among activists. Community organizations have crashed and died when they overextended themselves financially.

Finally, history is about the problems people and their parents and grandparents have experienced and the solutions they achieved. History is a continuing story that can and should be shared. The narrating of history is empowering, to those who tell the tale and those who listen, as participants take pride in describing successes, while framing the issues in ways that encourage others to join in the fight.

In short, history sensitizes us to the problems and possibilities of change, provides concrete advice for present-day action, and sustains our action with the hope and pride that comes from learning of past successes.

A Brief History of Neighborhood Organizing

Neighborhood organizing is only one form of community organizing, but one whose history illustrates what has happened in other movements. Extending the work of Robert Fisher (1994), we divide the history of neighborhood organizing into seven periods. The first occurred during the Progressive Era, from approximately 1895 to 1920, during which progressives tried to document the social problems people were encountering— baby formula diluted with bacteria-laden water, overcrowded housing conditions—and during which wealthier people helped to socialize new immigrants into middle-class norms. During the second period, the severity of the Great Depression triggered broader concerns with social change leading to radical approaches to neighborhood work. During the years following the Second World War until the end of the Eisenhower Administration in 1960, much neighborhood work returned to a more conservative pattern, more concerned with protecting the status quo than in alleviating problems. In sharp contrast, in the 1960s, organizing was reinvigorated, as battles as against poverty, sexism, and racism took place as part of a broader social upheaval. The 1970s were a period in which past gains were solidified with issue organizing predominating over neighborhood action. During the Reagan-dominated 1980s, conservative forces fought back against many of the gains of the 1960s; by this time, though, both neighborhood and social-issue organizations were skilled enough to survive a social backlash. Most recently, during the Clinton period, a sophisticated, professional neighborhood and social change movement is able to go head-to-head against conservative forces.

Research Bureau and Social Welfare Neighborhood Organizing

Two distinct strands of community work marked the end of the nineteenth century and early part of the twentieth century: "bureau work" and social welfare organizing. Each represented a paternalistic effort of an upper class to help those in need.

Numerous concerned individuals, often those with a background in social work, worked in various research bureaus to document the extent and severity of problems. The underlying assumption was that once government and the community at large knew about problems, they would be forced by moral compulsion to solve them. Funding for this work came from prominent industrialists who were concerned about such issues as improving the education of their work force, but they did not allow researchers to investigate broader questions of social inequity. By the 20s and 30s, many of these research bureaus lost their concerns with the poor, often changing into antitax groups.

Social welfare organizers also worked to combat overcrowding and poor sanitation that new immigrants faced in urban communities while attempting to socialize these individuals into what these reformers felt was an American way of life. Middle- and upper-status individuals, working out of settlement houses like Hull House, taught immigrants English, instructed women in how to prepare American foods, and otherwise sought to help the new immigrants blend into middle-class life. Individuals were helped, but there were few efforts at empowerment or attempts to build pride and solidarity among the various ethnic groups. An exception was the International Institute, which set up a pluralistic approach to neighborhood organizing that celebrated separate ethnic traditions (Betten & Austin, 1990, p. 57).

By the end of the Progressive Era, a new, more radical model developed. The Cincinnati Social Unit Plan (1918–1920) showed the possibility of combining empowerment work with the amelioration of social problems. With this model, activists, mostly middle class, set up Social Units in poor areas, which were run democratically and were operated by block workers, who lived in the neighborhoods and regularly visited all the families in their Social Unit. Decisions were made by a policy council formed of the block workers and occupational councils made up mostly of professionals living in the neighborhood. With input from community members, these councils designed health programs among other efforts.

Even the small successes of this more participatory program roused opposition. Doctors feared that Social Unit actions would lower their income; the mayor opposed it, labeling the whole effort as Bolshevik; government agencies feared the councils would take away their responsibilities; and business people feared that cooperative buying by community members would cut into business profits. Not having anticipated such opposition and lacking deep community support, the movement faded away (Betten & Austin, 1990, pp. 35–53).

Organizing in the African American community took place separately from that in White neighborhoods. Activists such as Ida B. Wells-Barnett organized against lynchings, helped set up women's clubs for social services, and agitated against unfair treatment of African Americans, while other organizers such as Lugenia Burns Hope established various neighborhood service organizations in poor Black communities to improve health and education and to agitate (unsuccessfully) for better employment opportunities for African Americans. As a result of such efforts "in cities throughout the North and South, African Americans established hospitals, clinics, schools, kindergardens, Y's, homes for single working women, day nurseries, orphanages, mutual benefit societies . . . and old folks' homes . . . [often] supported and controlled by the African American community" (O'Donnell, 1995b, p. 15). Though several of the organizations had working class leaders, most of the leadership came from better off African Americans.

For neighborhood organizing, the Progressive Era displayed mixed themes. Concern was shown for the poor by some members of the middle and upper class, yet the fundamental thrust was to maintain the status quo. Though some efforts tried to preserve an ethnic heritage, the thrust of the early activists was to Americanize the foreigners and help the poor materially, but they did little to set up empowered community organizations.

Radical Neighborhood Organizing

The 1920s was a period of relative prosperity that ended abruptly with the Great Depression lasting over a decade. At its nadir, over a third of the working population was unemployed, casting serious doubts on the viability of American capitalism. For a time, no one assumed responsibility for the poor, but eventually, as part of the New Deal, the federal government initiated a series of social and economic services. During this period of national trauma, three forms of neighborhood organizing work occurred. The Communist Party organized unemployed workers, while a faction of radical social workers, a small portion of the larger numbers of people hired to carry out New Deal programs, tried to encourage militant actions in the neighborhoods. In a third thrust, Saul Alinsky established coalitions of neighborhood-based organizations in which community members agitated for needed social and economic reforms.

Capitalizing on depression-era fears, the Communist Party organized unemployed workers, directed sit-ins at relief offices, defended tenants evicted from apartments, and worked within Black communities to promote interracial cooperation. The party established neighborhood workers' councils, which demanded economic relief from government. Although the local councils were supposed to be run by community members, in general the movement remained centralized and under party control (Fisher, 1984, pp. 34–46). The party gradually deemphasized neighborhood action as it increasingly worked to organize against fascism during Hitler's rise to power.

In response to pressure from the left and in reaction to the suffering of the American public, the Roosevelt administration set up the New Deal, an evolving and overlapping assortment of federal programs that provided the origins of the modern welfare state. Relief programs for businesses, farmers, and ultimately the unemployed followed one another. Social Security, Aid to Families with Dependent Children, and capital projects to stimulate economic growth were initiated. As part of this broader effort, the number of social workers rose dramatically, though these early workers often lacked training (Ehrenreich, 1985, pp. 43–102).

A radical faction of social workers, the Rank and File Movement, moved from providing services to undertaking community organizing work (Wenocur & Reisch, 1989, pp. 182–207). Rank and File activists considered that they and their clients had to fight oppression together:

> Social workers fought to unionize and fought along with "clients" as tenants or as demonstrators themselves, not as a separate movement but as part of a growing movement organized along class lines. In this period, young caseworkers did not see a separation between themselves and their clients. (Wagner, 1989, p. 267)

The Rank and File lost much of its organizing momentum, however, as social workers were increasingly absorbed by the expansion of New Deal social welfare programs (Wenocur & Reisch, 1989, pp. 197–199).

Little influence on neighborhood organizing remains from the Communist Party or the efforts of the Rank and File Movement. In contrast, the work of Saul Alinsky has had a direct impact on present day community work (Reitzes & Reitzes, 1987;

Horwitt, 1989). Combining the belief that social problems have a community basis with the militant tactics used in labor organizing by John Lewis, Saul Alinsky set up problem-focused, nonideological community organizations.

Alinsky formed action organizations by gathering existing local groups into a coalition that then engaged in direct action campaigns meant to resolve immediate problems facing community members. These action organizations used dramatic and confrontational tactics; for instance, great numbers of poor people would enter upper-status department stores, or protesters would deposit on the lawns of politicians garbage from neighborhoods with infrequent pickup. These actions were meant to solve an immediate problem and to mobilize people for further efforts by showing the "have-nots" that through collective action they could gain power over the "haves."

The initial Alinsky group, The Back of the Yards Neighborhood Council, was set up in the densely populated, underserviced area surrounding the stockyards in Chicago (Slayton, 1986). The neighborhood was already in ferment from left-wing labor activists who were working to fight the awful working conditions at the meatpacking plants. Alinsky persuaded Catholic clergy, who feared the ideological left, that they should help form an indigenous, nonideological organization to solve economic and social problems. With church support, in 1939 Alinsky was able to persuade numerous church-based organizations and social and ethnic clubs in the Back of the Yards neighborhood to come together and form a neighborhood council.

Through participatory processes, the council decided to focus on immediate issues of concern to community members, such as improving employment opportunities or repairing deteriorated housing. The early work involved actions—mass efforts that usually included mocking humor—to gain small victories, such as the rerouting of garbage trucks, the installation of stop signs, and the provision of local health stations. The short-run goal was to win the issues, but the long-run purpose was to build a permanent organization that could keep up pressure on government and businesses. Day-to-day work of the organization was carried out by a professionally trained organizer who was an employee of the neighborhood coalition. In theory, the organizer was to work himself or herself out of a job and go on to other communities, as neighborhood people developed their own skills.

Post–Second World War Conservative Organizing

From 1945 to 1960 the United States experienced economic growth and rapid subur-banization but remained socially and politically conservative. National attention was focused on the Cold War, with problems of poverty and racism either ignored or bulldozed away. Urban renewal consisted of tearing down the homes of the poor (often the minority poor), while new highways allowed the middle and upper classes to quickly drive through these areas on their way to suburban homes.

Liberal, issue-oriented, social-movement organizations were alive, and Alinksy groups continued to protest, but far more efforts took place to preserve the status quo and to support businesses. For example, social welfare agencies set up the United Community Defense Services (UCDS), a centralized group that tried to organize business elites and welfare officials to fix local problems. The UCDS officials "fundamentally accepted the existing system and sought, within the limits of that system, to ameliorate social inequalities in support of the objectives of those in power" (Fisher, 1984, p. 71). Funding was slight and accomplishments minimal.

Within the new suburbs and within wealthier areas of older cities, conservative neighborhood improvement associations proliferated. As Fisher argues "the association serves to protect property values and community homogeneity by opposing commercial development and excluding members of lower classes and racial minorities" (Fisher, 1984, p. 73). To carry out their exclusionary work, these associations relied on restrictive covenants that forbad sales to specified minorities. After the Supreme Court ruled such covenants illegal, neighborhood associations switched tactics, pressuring suburban governments to adopt zoning and building codes that made houses too expensive for the poor (Danielson, 1976). In addition, real estate agents steered minorities away from such neighborhoods, while minority group members who persisted were subject to physical attacks and harassment.

The Drama of the 1960s

From 1960 to the early 1970s, the nation was in ferment, with hundreds of thousands involved in community organizing and social movement organizations. "Nothing was sacred, everything was challenged" and people had to consider "disturbing questions" such as whether America was racist, imperialist, or sexist (Anderson, 1995, p. i). Issues raised by the counterculture—drugs, freer sexual behavior, changes in dress—blurred into concerns with peace, environmentalism, racism, and sexism. Students, feminists, and civil rights workers all engaged in successful and overlapping battles. During this period the "old left" with its moribund, European, labor-oriented, socialist views was replaced by a "new left," vibrant with American ideals of promoting social justice, yet concerned with preserving individualism.

The federal government was both the devil and angel, the devil that waited too long to respond to problems and the angel that funded community work and passed laws that helped foster social change. Federal support, however, came about only after pressure was applied by community activists. The election of a more liberal president, John F. Kennedy, who was appalled by images of rural southern poverty, offered the possibility of improvement, but not much happened until after Kennedy's assassination when President Johnson supported changes in civil rights laws and persuaded Congress to increase funding for community action.

The courageous actions of civil rights workers in the south provided the most important impetus to change—in the Montgomery bus boycott, the sit-ins to desegregate public facilities, and later, in the voter-registration drives that succeeded only after both Black and White organizers had been murdered. Activists in the Southern Christian Leadership Conference (SCLC), the Congress of Racial Equality (CORE), the Student Non-Violent Coordinating Committee (SNCC), and hundreds of local people (Payne, 1995) confronted southern racism head-on. After much strife, Congress passed the civil rights and voting rights bills that provided the basis for subsequent social justice work.

As the civil rights movement moved north, minorities became active in protesting and rioting against horrible living conditions. A new round of actions was stimulated by the assassination of Dr. Martin Luther King, Jr. Partly in response to such protests and partially to carry out the unfulfilled promises of President Kennedy, the Johnson administration supported a series of community-based social welfare programs.

The federal government passed funding for a "War on Poverty," implemented a Model Cities program, and established the Office of Economic Opportunity (OEO) that became the institutional scaffolding for programs to aid the poor. Money was made available for affordable housing programs, Project Headstart helped poor preschoolers build skills, and food stamp programs helped feed the hungry. Federally funded Community Action Agencies (CAA) set up a permanent presence in localities to carry out social programs, while Community Development Corporations (CDCs) received government funds to build homes, create shopping areas, and provide jobs in areas of deep poverty. Concurrently, federal dollars supported community health-care and mental health agencies to work with community members. While large by historic standards, overall funding was still modest.

In many of these programs, federal dollars were to be spent only after "maximum feasible participation" by those affected by the programs (Brilliant, 1986, p. 574). Regulations required city officials to work with neighborhood organizations on setting priorities for spending funds. Community Action Agencies hired neighborhood organizers to organize the poor; the federal Volunteers in Service to America (VISTA) Program engaged volunteers, many of whom later became professional organizers; and the federal Legal Services Corporation employed attorneys funded to speak for the poor in court and to act as advocates in front of government agencies. For a while it seemed that community groups, supported by CAAs and Legal Services attorneys, would have an effective say in directing programs to alleviate poverty.

Concurrently, hundreds of smaller neighborhood organizations emerged as people got together to combat problems. Initially such community activism emerged from African American communities, but organizing quickly spread to other groups. Long-festering grievances among Hispanics turned into direct confrontations, as activists demanded community control (Chavez, 1998). Neighborhood groups opposed construction of federal highways that destroyed inner-city communities. In larger cities, such as New York, neighborhood organizations battled to gain a say in running the school system and demanded better employment and job training opportunities.

Protest groups carried out numerous direct actions. Through confrontations, Alinsky organizations such as Freedom Integration God Honor Today (FIGHT) in Rochester, New York, successfully demanded jobs for poor minorities, while former civil rights organizers formed the National Welfare Rights Organization (NWRO), which used sit-ins and marches to bolster their demands for more resources for the dependent poor. In the west, Cesar Chavez merged issues of ethnicity, civil rights, and labor in forming a farm workers' union. Through picketing, hunger strikes, and ultimately a nationwide boycott of grape products, the union improved the working conditions of farm laborers. Native Americans carried out numerous campaigns to publicize historic wrongs, reminding the country that their land had been taken from them by force and deceit, leaving them in poverty. An Asian American movement began to stir when working-class Asians fought displacement from transient hotels in big cities in California (Wei, 1993, pp. 22–23).

Organizations moved from protests to attempts to control the physical redevelopment of their neighborhoods. With the availability of federal social service and redevelopment funds, The Woodlawn Organization (TWO), an Alinsky direct action group, began providing services and undertaking physical renewal projects. In the west, Hispanic activist groups moved from direct action to setting up economic development corporations such as the East Los Angeles Community Union to provide jobs and stores for the poor (Chavez, 1998), and numerous CDCs, emulating the few dozen funded by the federal government, began building affordable homes in poor neighborhoods.

The agitation of the sixties began over issues of poverty and racial injustice, but other concerns emerged. On campuses, college students protested the rules and traditions that treated them as children and demanded educational reform. This reinvigoration of the student movement was most apparent among the activist left who formed organizations such as the Students for a Democratic Society (SDS). These student activists worked in the south as part of the civil rights movement and later organized in northern cities and in Appalachia, helping to build democratic self-help programs among the poor.

During the sixties, the women's rights movement, which had been relatively dormant for years, was resurrected. Women's groups demanded equal job opportunities, abortion rights, and a constitutional amendment guaranteeing women equal rights under the law; however, factions within the women's movement, between gay and straight women and between those of different social classes, weakened the effort and women did not get their amendment (Ryan, 1992).

Gay activists started to come out of the closet. The willingness shown by gays at the Stonewall Inn riots in New York City to physically fight back against state oppression symbolized the beginning of this fight for human rights. The environmentalist movement changed and became more radical and more broad based. Environmentalism had been characterized by upper-status people wanting to assure the purchase and preservation of national parks, but the 1960s saw the beginning of a mass movement concerned with preserving species and eliminating pesticides. Groups such as the Clamshell Alliance and the Abalone Alliance were willing to use direct actions (Gottlieb, 1993).

As the nation's involvement in Southeast Asia expanded, activists increasingly focused on the Vietnam War. First those from the peace movement, then the larger student population, and finally a cross section of the American public were in the streets asking why we were fighting half way across the world when numerous problems remained unsolved at home. The escalating costs of the war were pulling federal resources and attention away from antipoverty programs and efforts to enforce civil rights.

With this constant questioning of the status quo, a threatened establishment began to fight back. Protesters were portrayed as long-haired hippies in need of a bath, not messengers pointing out problems that needed to be addressed. In cities, mayors who resented citizen control of the CAAs complained to Congress and regained control of antipoverty funds. Local officials, who were often responsive to big business, ended up deciding what would be built and where. Although laws were put on the books guaranteeing voting and civil rights, enforcement was sporadic. Under the guise of helping localities, the federal Law Enforcement Assistance Administration provided local police with riot gear and armed vehicles to suppress social protests. State and federal officials spied on protesters, those engaged in antiwar efforts as well as those fighting for civil rights. Leaders such as Dr. Martin Luther King, Jr. were kept under constant FBI surveillance (Branch, 1998). With local officials trying to subvert antipoverty programs, the unwillingness of the federal government to end the Vietnam War, and federal agencies engaged in monitoring and suppression, activists began to distrust government and the electoral system.

By the end of the decade, many Alinsky-style organizations fell apart. After the initial organizer left, nothing held these coalitions together or gave them direction, with the consequence that "very few organizations survived when the organizers left town for a new venture" (Rogers, 1990, p. 88). To keep going after the initial organizer left, these Alinsky-style organizations needed a more permanent institutional framework and a continuing source of trained organizers. As a response, academies such as the Industrial Areas Foundations were set up to provide organizers with extensive training, better salaries, and more backup support, to enable organizing efforts to persist.

Other kinds of community groups also had troubles. White college students in the SDS never overcame the class and racial gaps between them and the minority communities they tried to help. Rather than work with the people they served as full-time organizers, they sometimes tried to manipulate the groups to reach decisions that the organizers preferred. While the movement preached equality, within many organizations women were exploited as second-class citizens, and racial tensions between Black, White, Brown, and Red weakened efforts to secure civil rights. Many activists became disillusioned and dropped out (Gitlin, 1989, p. 424).

Still, much was accomplished and the era of the 60s provided a lasting legacy for today. As Terry Anderson reflects:

> Since the sixties, all of the various movements have diminished. That is natural, for the activists succeeded in bringing about a sea change, a different America. . . . The first wave asked about the rights of black citizens, the rights of students, about their obligation to fight a distant and undeclared war. They provoked the nation to look in the mirror. The second wave expanded the issues to include all minorities and women. . . . Since, liberation and empowerment have become threads in the nation's multicultural social and political fabric. . . . By confronting the status quo, activists inspired a debate that since has taken place in Congress, courts, city halls, board room, streets, and even bedrooms. The debate involves the political and the personal, and it asks the central question of this democracy: What is the meaning of "America"? (Anderson, 1995, p. 423)

Nixon and Carter Eras

In spite of the more conservative environment during the Nixon and Carter years, many of the gains of the sixties were maintained. Both political and financial support, however, were reduced for community groups.

Much of the reduction occurred as President Nixon rolled many of the grants that had supported community action into a smaller number of block grants (described in the previous chapter). The block grants gave more discretion to local officials and forced the community groups to compete with each other for funding. When the size of block grants was reduced, the competition became fierce and funding for community groups uncertain. Such changes weakened neighborhood work, though during the later Carter years, neighborhood organizing again received a boost as the Department of Housing and Urban Development employed activists who ran some small programs that directly supported neighborhood groups.

Though the total amount of money available was reduced, money was still around for community-based housing and economic development, especially in minority neighborhoods. Activist groups that engaged in protest during the sixties refocused their efforts to build homes and create jobs in poor neighborhoods. In addition, numerous CDCs came about to create affordable housing and, as such, were eligible to receive federal money. Many CDCs expanded their mission to include creating jobs for the poor (Peirce & Steinbach, 1987).

Except for those engaged in housing, community groups had little chance of directing receiving federal funds. Realizing now how undependable that revenue source was, activists rebuilt the movement with backup support structures that helped maintain the community movement in these difficult times. Many of these support organizations carry out tasks that the federal government had formerly funded. The Center for Community Change, for instance, offers technical support to a wide array of activist organizations, while consulting firms and trade associations, such as the National Congress for Community Economic Development, provide networking and technical assistance for community-based economic development groups.

Broad-based neighborhood organizing continued, with notable successes among Hispanic populations in the Southwest, especially in Texas. These successes followed a revamping of the strategy of community work. Leaders such as Edward Chambers, Alinsky's successor, and Ernesto Cortes, among others, determined that neighborhood organizing could not succeed if it focused on only a single issue or if the core organization was dependent on an individual charismatic leader. The Industrial Areas Foundation argued that neighborhood groups should work to build an independent, local funding base and put aside sufficient money to survive occasional funding droughts. Such community organizations must be responsive to ordinary members and the leaders must be immediately accountable to the membership (Rogers, 1990, pp. 95–96).

Many organizations concerned about social, gender, and economic issues moved from organizing people to providing the needed services themselves. Women's groups, pressed for job and economic equality, sought federal support for the Equal Rights Amendment and worked to establish local organizations that helped victims of rape and spouse abuse. Some women's groups concentrated on maintaining access to safe abortions. Gay activists, mostly living in progressive communities, sought to end housing and job discrimination, while groups of seniors continued efforts to end age-based discrimination. A crucial victory for neighborhood activists came as a result of the work of the National Peoples' Action, a coalition set up by Gale Cincotta, that convinced Congress to pass the Community Reinvestment Act (CRA). The CRA gave neighborhood housing and redevelopment groups a new tool with which to battle bank-sponsored redlining.

Community organizations began to rethink what they were trying to achieve. Some women's groups changed their emphasis from achieving specific goals to the process of doing so, arguing that the way in which changes occurred could be as important as the change itself. Achieving goals was important but so was establishing the principles of nonhierarchical, democratic decision making (Deutschmann, 1988; Garland, 1988; Hooks, 1989; Iannello, 1988; Katzenstein, 1987; Nes & Iadicola, 1989; Rothschild, 1987).

Other community groups were swept up in a neopopulist revival that argued that democracy cannot occur in a society with a marked inequality in wealth. For instance, Dr. Martin Luther King, Jr. observed that it "made no sense to be able to sit down and order a hamburger if you could not afford one" (Delgado, 1986, p. 18). Issues of economic justice became part of broader agendas for social equality.

The Reagan-Bush Backlash

Throughout the 1980s and early 1990s, when Presidents Ronald Reagan and George Bush were in office, conservatives worked hard to undo the major accomplishments of the prior twenty years. The gains of women and minorities in the workplace were particularly galling to conservatives, who worked to rescind affirmative action and return women to their traditional subservient roles (Faludi, 1992). During this time, budgets for social programs were reduced, while increasingly conservative local governments used block-grant money in ways that did not help those most in need. Federal housing efforts virtually dried up and officials actively opposed to environmentalism were appointed to offices meant to monitor the environment.

In a hypocritical fashion, federal officials spoke about the importance of self-help, but to them self-help implied a voluntarism of benevolent charities, rather than a movement to empower local social-change organizations. Neighborhood organizing took on a perverse face as wealthier individuals increasingly moved into physically and socially controlled gated communities, set up primarily to exclude the poor and those of color (Blakely & Snyder, 1997).

In spite of the lack of national support for social change causes, community activism remained very much alive, taking on new and sophisticated forms. Activist groups learned to combine direct action street campaigns with sustained lobbying efforts. Campaigns run by Associations of Community Organizations for Reform Now (ACORN) for instance, put together militant actions such as squatting to take over abandoned homes for the poor, with a legislative push for more affordable housing. Later, ACORN began doing housing development work on its own. Advocates for the disabled successfully lobbied Congress for passage of the Americans with Disabilities Act. That legislation became a wedge for pressuring public and private authorities to accommodate the needs of those with disabilities. Community-based development groups, no longer routinely receiving money for housing, expanded their missions to include efforts at economic development and learned how to play the capitalist system to leverage needed funds. Building on the successes of Black studies programs, students from Hispanic and Asian groups pressed for university programs that would educate themselves and others about their national heritage and recent history.

In many cities, activist organizations and their coalitions were sufficiently accepted to be routinely consulted by those in office. Many groups routinely received Community Development Block Grant funds, perhaps softening somewhat their militance but assuring that they would remain alive. Progressive cities devolved decision-making functions to elected neighborhood groups, at times allowing full veto on neighborhood projects to these groups (Berry, Portney, & Thomson, 1993; Goetz & Sidney, 1994a; Medoff & Sklar, 1994). In Texas neo-Alinsky groups were able to influence the public agenda at both city, such as San Antonio, and state levels (Wilson, 1997). In Chicago, a coalition of neighborhood groups successfully campaigned for Harold Washington as the city's first African American and community-focused mayor. In many areas, ethnic assertion was converted to political clout with neighborhood groups sponsoring African American, Hispanic, and Asian people in their often successful bids for public office.

In part, success was attributable to an increasing sophistication among social change and community groups. Many funded permanent lobbying organizations in Washington and in some state capitals. To provide training and support, networks of organizations expanded their activities. The Industrial Areas Foundation set up by Alinsky a generation ago, ACORN, Pacific Institute for Community Organization (PICO), Direct Action and Research Training (DART), Neighborhood People's Action (NPA), Gamaliel, and other networks of neighborhood groups now provided technical assistance and offered training to an emerging coterie of professional organizers.

These networking and technical assistance groups helped community organizations adapt and think through the appropriateness of their strategies. At annual meetings, activists talked with one another about what adaptations were needed, while networks such as the Industrial Areas Foundation changed their approaches, moving from colorful campaigns to faith-based organizing and increasingly emphasizing the importance of building a permanent organization. Technical assistance organizations did background research to inform campaigns, for instance, pinpointing banks engaged in redlining or highlighting neighborhoods most affected by deindustrialization. As they adapted, many in community work recognized that they were dependent on the public sector. As Robert Fisher summarizes, organizers learned that

> a primary target for contemporary grassroots efforts must be a responsible public sector. . . . effective community organizing requires a legitimate and accountable public sector and a zeitgeist, a spirit of the time, that encourages its citizens to be active in public life. (Fisher, 1994, p. 175)

The Clinton Era

With the election of William Clinton, a moderate Democrat who respected the community movement, activists anticipated that the regime would support housing, be proenvironment, and supportive of feminist causes. Conservative forces in Congress and in many localities, however, were able to continue the backlash of the previous decade. During this era, community action increasingly concentrated on pressuring states and localities because major federal social welfare programs had devolved to the states, and local governments became involved in the issues of abortion and gay rights.

New welfare programs passed by Congress emphasized getting people off welfare into jobs. Housing programs deemphasized public housing projects and favored a decentralized market-based approach that gave needy families subsidies to pay rent in privately owned buildings. Some organizers shifted their focus to helping people cope with these welfare-to-work programs, while the physical destruction of high-rise public housing forced other organizers to change their efforts to ensure that the displaced poor were still housed in safe locations accessible to transportation.

New activist groups started up to deal with some of these emerging issues. For example, the Kensington Welfare Rights Organization lobbied and used direct actions to gain services for its membership in poor neighborhoods in Philadelphia. A little later, the group organized a coalition of poor peoples' organizations to campaign nationally to protest the decline in programs to help the poor.

Even with a Democrat as president, the times remained conservative, keeping social change and community organizations on the defensive. Grass roots environmentalists continued efforts to preserve open space and fight pollution but were opposed by conservative elements that persuaded the courts to weaken proenvironment legislation. Federal support for affirmative action declined, while in the face of some negative court cases, states and cities found it increasingly difficult to maintain their own affirmative action programs. Housing and neighborhood groups spent much effort to preserve the Community Reinvestment Act that was under attack by conservatives and bankers. During this period, major foundations pushed for consensus organizing, an explicit repudiation of Alinsky activism. Although, the community-based housing and development movement rapidly expanded, some feared that such organizations were so focused on building homes and creating jobs that they neglected their broader mission of empowerment (Stoecker, 1997).

Historic activist agendas remained but took on new twists. Neighborhood groups tried to protect the poor from displacement as gentrification accelerated around the cores of many major cities. In inner cities, neighborhood organizations focused on the concerns of legal and illegal immigrants and found to their dismay that groups of the poor from different ethnic backgrounds were contending with each other for the same limited resources.

In prior eras, activist groups tended to specialize in one issue area or another, though some neighborhood organizations saw linkages between different concerns. By the nineties, social-change organizations, government, and funders increasingly recognized that solving inner-city problems requires simultaneously thinking about housing, jobs, transportation, education, and crime. In response, action organizations began to expand their missions and to work out ways of coordinating with each other to bring about more comprehensive programs of renewal.

Lessons from History

An examination of the history of community organizing offers much for organizers to use immediately. Past organizing efforts reveal a variety of strategies and tactics and demonstrate which approaches are chosen depends on the spirit of the times. A second theme in this brief history is that community organizations do not work alone but instead depend on other social-change organizations, socially concerned churches, foundations, and organizations that provide technical support and advice. A third theme is that long-term success is hard to sustain and requires framing issues and choosing symbols in ways that gain lasting public support.

A study of history also underscores that some of the problems and obstacles to successful organizing emerge from within the movement. For example, some community organizations representing different ethnic groups have become competitors for limited funds and publicity, while advocacy groups have been unable to bridge social gaps between racial or income groupings inside the organization. In some groups, the organizer has become so prominent that it is difficult to build the skills of and empower members. Organizations have lost recruits as a result of contradictions between the organization's espoused values and the way it operated. For instance, feminists left some social-change organizations once they discovered that to fight against male dominance and bullying, they needed to work in democratic, consensual organizations, not in patriarchically structured groups.

Two Steps Forward and One Step Back

History demonstrates that considerable progress has been made in empowering neighborhoods and in bringing about social reforms. Unions are legal. Laws require reasonable accommodation to people with various disabilities. Minority group members register and vote, have access to better jobs than in the past, and are subject to fewer racist encounters. Community members run neighborhood focused social service programs, CDCs build affordable homes, and abortion is still legal, despite a determined opposition. Tenant organizations are common. Community groups and neighborhoods oppose industry when it poisons streams and drinking water and pollutes the air. Discrimination against women and minorities in business organizations is now illegal, and antigay discrimination is declining. While public resources for economic renewal still favor the rich and downtown property owners, poor neighborhoods are not entirely excluded from public largess. History shows, however, that we still have a long way to go to build a society that no longer discriminates on race, gender, or sexual orientation and has a more egalitarian distribution of wealth.

How quickly progress can be made depends on whether conservatives or liberals are dominant in politics. Conservatives tend to blame individuals for the problems people face and recommend that people solve problems by themselves. Those unable to help themselves can rely on private and religiously based charities. Liberals are more likely to argue that many of the problems people face are caused by factors over which individuals have limited control, such as industries moving abroad, the elimination of good paying low-skilled jobs, gentrification that pushes up the costs of housing, and persistent structural racism or sexism. Such problems and their consequences are best fought through collective, organized social action.

Society sometimes loses its ability to see social injustice. For generations, many White people looked at segregated facilities, toilets for Whites and toilets for Blacks, drinking fountains for Blacks and drinking fountains for Whites, and did not cringe.

More recently, many Whites look at schools with mainly Black students and do not see sagging roofs, broken windows, sporadic heat in winter, and old text books. Wealthier people often ignore the inner city with its dilapidated housing, vacant lots, lack of stores, and day labor. At other times, however, society can see what it is shown. The sight of poverty in Appalachia pricked the conscience of a president and through him the conscience of the country. The image of Black children being marched off to jail during the civil rights era mobilized a nation and gave impetus to a social revolution.

Problems do not necessarily stay solved but reappear under new guise. Recent waves of immigrants have stimulated fear and prejudice, resulting in denying public benefits not only to illegal aliens but also to legal immigrants. Political pressure has increased to eliminate bilingualism and promote English as the only language of instruction in public schools.

What can be accomplished by community organizations depends on the social climate and the political culture at the time the organizing takes place. A campaign that would be inconceivable at one time may be successful at another time. One cannot easily imagine gay pride parades in the 1920s or 1950s, but today gay actions are common and cities have adopted ordinances that forbid discrimination on sexual orientation. Chicago's government under former mayor Richard J. Daley attacked civil rights activists and helped destroy neighborhoods through so-called renewal programs; a generation later, under Mayor Washington, leaders and staff from neighborhood groups were appointed to public office and the city funded activist community groups. After Mayor Washington's death, the city returned to a more conservative business–oriented model, but the rampant racism of the past has been reduced, and poor neighborhoods receive an increased, albeit not yet a proportionate, share of redevelopment money.

Part of the reason for the swing between more and less favorable periods for organizing is that the successes themselves have the effect of lowering enthusiasm and involvement. When the problems have eased, the motivation to participate is less and the ability to catch public attention is reduced. Some people who have benefited from social change see the gains as solid and permanent, so no further effort is required. Others feel that they won their positions based on their own achievement and assume others can and should too. They resent sharing the credit with the community groups who made their successes possible. Conservative groups use these beneficiaries of past gains to argue against the need for further collective action.

Matching Tactics to Climate and Philosophy

History teaches us how tactics have changed over time and political circumstances. Community actions have varied from broad humor, such as a sit-in in public restrooms, to the deadly serious confrontations of civil rights workers with racists in the South. Some involved the massing of tens of thousands or even hundreds of thousands of people, such as for antiwar and civil rights protests, while others involved quiet consultations at city hall. What worked at one time and place, might well have failed somewhere else or at another time.

One element of choosing tactics is the appropriateness of the tactic to the organization's goal. A hunger strike to support the unionization drive of Hispanic agricultural workers made sense, given the poor working and living conditions, the horrible pay, and the intense opposition the farm workers encountered. A hunger strike would seem inappropriate, however, in a campaign to add art and drama to the school curriculum. Polite lobbying may be sufficient and appropriate to persuade public officials to support a partnership to build affordable housing or to convince public officials that new buildings should be handicapped accessible. More aggressive action would be appropriate in a situation in which the legitimate demands of the community group were repeatedly ignored or where opposition was substantial and vocal. When the government ignored the plight of the homeless while warehousing unoccupied homes, ACORN members felt that they had to be more obtrusive. They squatted on the premises and forced the issue.

The choice of tactics also depends on the conservativeness of the time or place. A gay pride parade might work in New York City but might increase opposition to gays in small rural towns. A rally to support the right to bear arms would have more positive effect in states where original settlers and later farmers routinely shot "varmints" that threatened their homestead or livestock than it would in neighborhoods where gang warfare often catches school children in the crossfire.

History allows us to figure out what works and when and teaches us the necessity of choosing tactics that will match an evolving political and social climate. Despite this pragmatism, however, activists do not simply make it up as they go along. Having examined history and become familiar with its traditions, activists distill this learning into the models of organizing discussed in Chapter 1.

Linkages Within Social Change and Community Movements

When neighbors get together to combat a local problem, they often face a sense of isolation, of being the only ones that seem to care about the deteriorated schools or the drugs on the streets. An examination of the history of the neighborhood movement and social-change efforts, however, shows the tight interconnections of activists over time and between movements.

Approaches taken by one organizer or group are learned by others, who then go on to add to the body of knowledge and the shared lore of successful strategies. Success inspires others to emulate the same techniques, while the frequent moves of professional organizers from one community to another help to disseminate ideas. Alinsky who was himself influenced by the labor organizer John Lewis, taught Fred Ross and Ernesto Cortes, who in turn inspired Cesar Chavez (Reitzes & Reitzes, 1987). Both working with and emulating civil rights activists, SDSers Tom Hayden and Steve Max became leading advocates of neopopulism.

Not only have some organizers taught others, but some organizations and movements have emulated others or been stimulated by them. Organizations such as ACORN grew out of experiences in welfare organizing and the civil rights campaigns. While women activists have had a proud history of their own, the revitalization of their movement emerged out of the activism of the sixties. Historic movements of Hispanic activism were reinvigorated in part in emulation of African American activism, while collectively these different movements of ethnic assertion inspired Native Americans and later Asian Americans. Activist Alinsky groups such as the early Woodlawn Organization were intimately linked with civil rights groups such as CORE. In general, the sixties became a cauldron of activity in which counter culturalists met with civil rights activists, joined with environmentalists, encountered the peace movement, and all merged with various movements of ethnic assertion and empowerment (Anderson, 1995).

The flow of ideas and sharing of successful tactics was facilitated by extensive networks. Successful local organizations created networks such as the Industrial Areas Foundation (IAF), PICO, DART, Gamaliel, and ACORN to train others. Another way of sharing ideas occurred at a retreat for organizers. For instance, the Highlander Center in the rural south, set up by Myles Horton, provided a safe place for activists to talk and plan social-change efforts and, not so incidentally, allowed Blacks and Whites in the segregated south to socialize together and share ideas. Foundations too helped disseminate successful accomplishments of one group to other organizations that they also funded.

Organizations symbolize their victories by making icons out of core events or documents that then become models that other groups can emulate. The Seneca Falls women's rights conference in 1848, which presented a declaration of rights including that all men and women are created equal, was the trigger for much of the women's activism that followed. It became a symbolic event, that could be referred to briefly and be widely understood by organizers. Particular confrontations—Greensboro, Birmingham, Montgomery or Selma for the African American civil rights movements, Wounded Knee for the Native American, Stonewall Inn for gay activism, or Sproul Hall in the student protests—became symbols as well. For example, when police came to break up a gay gathering at the Stonewall Inn, for the first time, gays fought back. Stonewall was the beginning of what has been a very successful movement, it represented a turning point. Martin Luther King's jailing and Cesar Chavez's fast still resonate among a wide variety of activists far beyond the civil rights movements. For many, the phrase "that summer" (Dittmer, 1994) evokes the Freedom Summer of 1964 in which Black and White, male and female converged on Mississippi in a collective and public outcry for social justice. A single term or phrase carries whole stories and is packed with emotion. The danger, the courage, and success of the civil rights movement became such an important touchstone for all organizers that many other protest groups continue to sing the songs of the civil rights movement.

The history of different groups has sometimes been recorded in documentary form and is generally available to all actual and would-be organizers. Activists reflect upon SDS's Port Huron Statement, Dr. King's Letters from a Birmingham Jail, and the various manifestos put out by ACORN, and now readily accessible on the Internet. Alinsky's two books *Reveille for Radicals* and *Rules for Radicals,* though somewhat dated, still represent a common lore shared by those involved in social-change organizations.

Finally, social movement information passes from one group to another through individuals who are involved in several organizations at once or who move from group to group. People who are willing to fight one issue are often more willing to fight another one, as we detail in Chapter 7, so there is always substantial overlap between those involved in separate issues, for example, between the peace movement and environmentalism (Zisk, 1992, p. 182).

Endemic Tensions in Social Change Movements

Activists are constantly assessing the effectiveness of the strategies they use to accomplish campaign goals. Those strategies that help the organization win are vigorously pursued while others are dropped. Sometimes, however, it is not clear from the organization's own experiences what the best way to go is. In these circumstances, examining some historic patterns can provide some guidance.

For example, history points out the need to balance the role of heroes and the need to recognize the ordinary people who do the daily work, and, in many cases, take on large risks. Heroes are important. A hero symbolizes the cause, focuses media attention, and motivates others to join in. It is hard to think about the Women's Movement without recognizing Susan B. Anthony or to talk about the civil rights movement without also talking about Dr. Martin Luther King, Jr. Cesar Chavez came to represent the farm workers in their effort to unionize; to many Lois Gibbs came to represent the battle against toxic wastes; Maggie Kuhn came to represent the empowerment movement for the elderly. Within particular neighborhoods a handful of individuals become identified with the cause; activists refer to Dennis West's organization or to Pete Garcia's projects, rather than Eastside Community Investment or Chicanos por la Causa, two community development corporations.

Yet, successful organizations are far more than an extension of their leaders. Hundreds, if not thousands, of ordinary people, "local people" (Dittmer, 1994) are what make movements and organizations work. It took more than a Dr. King to fill up the Birmingham jails, and though Russell Means and Dennis Banks were central to the American Indian Movement, the seizure of Alcatraz or the standoffs at Wounded Knee were collective efforts (Nagel, 1996).

History can also be a pretty good guide on the question of how radical an organization should be. Incremental change is easier and more comfortable for members but may never reach the goal; more radical challenges not only have the possibility of achieving more dramatic outcomes but also invite more opposition and suppression and sometimes scare away potential members.

For much of its history, the National Association for the Advancement of Colored People (NAACP) tried to bring about incremental improvement by working through the courts and with those in government. In contrast, the Southern Christian Leadership Conference in its attempts to desegregate bus systems and the Congress of Racial Equality and the Southern Nonviolent Coordinating Committee in their direct attacks on Jim Crow laws felt that anything short of bringing about new rules of the game would be insufficient.

Confrontational tactics resulted in violence and bitter repression but were effective in calling attention to the problems and helped create the symbolic leaders who caught and channeled media attention. Community organizers cannot routinely expect large numbers of people to put their lives and homes on the line. When it happens, though, say when many people volunteer for direct actions that will result in arrest and imprisonment, the result can be morally powerful. The apparent contradiction between the potential for success in more militant movements and the possibility that the public will turn against the movement because it is fomenting violence have made more aggressive tactics a difficult choice.

History suggests that the most successful approach is to have different groups pursue strategies with varying degrees of militance. Members who feel comfortable with the level of aggressiveness sort themselves among the groups. Popular anger and fear of the more radical groups may actually enhance the bargaining power of the more moderate groups, creating breakthroughs that would not otherwise occur. If one group can call attention to the problems with dramatic confrontations while another shepherds court cases through the legal system, the total impact may be more powerful than either approach alone.

Community groups can find some guidance from history on another troublesome strategic choice. If the community groups focus on issues that are too narrow, they can't get many members or make much impact on larger problems; however, if they focus on larger groups and build broader membership bases, the cleavages among their members may become destabilizing. For example, feminist groups that aim to improve the status of women attract women of different ethnic and social class backgrounds who might have trouble understanding that they share problems. Separate groups with smaller constituencies may find it difficult to form alliances when they need to. Distinct Cuban, Puerto Rican, Mexican American, and Salvadorian groups each push for civil rights but have difficulty working with one another as Latinos, while organizations representing inner-city poor Latinos and those representing inner-city poor African Americans are often at loggerheads (Suro, 1998).

With careful framing of the issues, many community groups have been able to unite those from separate backgrounds, creating a pattern that is available to other groups. Issues of rape and abortion cross class lines among women and can form the basis of a broader membership base. Groups representing the disabled were able to come together with housing organizations to provide shelter for the disabled. Skillful coalition builders can bring community groups together, at least temporarily, to design new programs, press for funding, or argue for needed legislation.

Besides the specific lessons for present-day organizers, history offers three important themes that form a set of assumptions underlying organizing. One is that over the years there has been progress, sometimes faster and sometimes slower, but real and cumulative. A second theme is that community organizations have to deal not only with threats from outside the organization, from people who oppose its goals or methods, but also with threats from inside, especially the antagonisms that keep one disempowered group separated from another. The third theme is that activists learn how to crystallize their victories in symbols that are easily communicated and that together they create a shared model of what ought to be and what can be.

Community Organizing and Social Work Education

The relationship between community organizing and social work has been close over the years, but it has been a complicated and changing relationship. Early community organizing at the turn of the century was often spearheaded by social workers who wanted to create better lives for the poor and improve living conditions in the over-crowded cities. Initially, social workers came from middle- and upper-class backgrounds and saw their mission as one of teaching immigrants how to talk, cook, and act like middle-class Americans. These social activists generally did not work to empower the poor or encourage cultural differences.

During a brief period during the Great Depression of the 1930s, social workers were more radical, but they soon were absorbed into the Roosevelt-era social programs. Social workers staffed many of the agencies set up during the War on Poverty in the late 1960s and early 1970s and from those positions, a small number vigorously promoted community organizing and direct actions. For example, during that period social work activists and educators Frances Fox Piven and Richard Cloward (Piven & Cloward, 1977, 1978) called for street activism. Parts of the social work profession blended into the community organizing world.

If the relationship between social work and community organizing has sometimes been cooperative, more often social work has taken a different and even contradictory approach to social problems. Alinsky left social work in rebellion against its support of the status quo. Outstanding historic figures in social work education such as Mary Richmond or Bertha Reynolds were exemplars of the activist approach, but they are seen as exceptions. Even during the activist 1960s, social work education moved only slightly toward a community organizing orientation, with the Piven and Cloward wing of the field being in the minority.

Even in the War on Poverty, the bulk of social work agencies "contrary to expectations failed to promote social change and used the federal poverty funds to expand their traditional casework approach" (Ehrenreich, 1985, p. 179). In part, social workers ended up responding to government pressures to calm problems not bring about social restructuring. Social workers were becoming increasingly professionalized and skilled in psychological models, pulling them further away from concerns with community empowerment.

Wenocur and Reisch argue that social work was shaken by the social turmoil of the 1960s but had returned to its individual-oriented case work approach by the 1970s.

> Although the social work enterprise remained preoccupied with issues pertinent to professionalization . . . the political turmoil of the 1960s—the social movement for peace, civil rights, women's liberation, an end to poverty, welfare reform and the government's expansion of the welfare state—did shake it from absorption with matters of "function" for a short time. . . . The social ferment in and around social work pushed the enterprise as in the 1930s, to reexamine its commitment to helping the disadvantaged and correct social injustices through institutional reform. With the return to social equilibrium and conservatism in the mid-1970s and 1980s, social workers again turned to their preoccupation with "function," [and] initiated a new cycle of emphasis on individually oriented clinical social work. (Wenocour & Reisch, 1989, p. 268)

Harry Specht and Mark Courtney lament this return to a microapproach. They point out that the personal preference among social workers for case work has been reinforced by the education provided by schools of social work whose course work mandates studies of individuals and their problems, paying far less attention to institutional and structural causes (Specht and Courtney, 1994). According to these activist educators, social workers have become "fallen angels," in part because the Council on Social Work Education (CSWE) does not have any "requirement that students complete courses on . . . publicly supported social services, community work, work with groups or the law" (Specht and Courtney, 1994, p. 149).

Despite the difference in approaches between case-oriented social work and community organizing, the prognosis for closer integration between social work and community action is reasonably good. Specht and Courtney (1994, pp. 152–175) detail the possibilities of recreating a community-focused emphasis within social work education, while many teachers and students of social work are actively engaged in Comprehensive Community Initiatives (R. Stone, 1996), community renewal programs that tie together social services, organizing, and community-based development. Feminist social workers, such as Cheryl Hyde or Marie Weil, show how providing social services can complement social change efforts, with the services reaching out to people who then join activist movements to combat the causes of the problems (Fisher, 1994, p. 204). Association for Community Organization & Social Administration (ACOSA), an active professional association, links together teachers of community organizing and social services administration, encouraging more active involvement of students in social action. Increasingly, electronic lists such as COMM-ORG provide a medium in which social workers, community organizers, and others involved in social action communicate and debate values and goals.

Conclusion

In Chapter 2 we described social problems that communities and the disempowered face and some of the major government programs meant to combat these problems. That chapter explored how social issues are framed and interpreted in ways that create the current environment for community action. That environment has also been shaped by a history of prior social policies and community response. This chapter sketched out the historic part of the action environment.

History shows that while success has sometimes been slow, and prior efforts have sometimes been undone, progress has been real and hope for the future is legitimate. Heroes of the past, both the ones we know by name and the anonymous heroes who marched and rallied and filled the jails in protest, provide inspiration to today's activists. Today's organizers can find some solutions to their present problems by examining the tactics and choices of past organizations. They can also learn what to expect when times do not favor community organizing. Patience, persistence, and understanding are all vital to achieving long-term success.

History also shows that those engaged in community organizing and social activism do not always agree with each other and can compete with each other. Many of the barriers between organizations, however, can be brought down by skillful framing of issues to emphasize what groups have in common. What seems to work best is a variety of groups, each with their own constituencies and goals, that come together in coalitions when needed and that can rely on support organizations for research, ideas, and sometimes financial support.

PART THREE

Empowerment and Community Building

Organizing and development means creating local empowerment through groups of people with a shared mission acting collectively to control decisions, projects, programs, and policies that affect them as a community. Part Three of this book examines what is meant by empowerment and how organizers work to build communities.

Chapter 4 portrays how the rich and powerful attempt to deprive others of a sense of control over their own lives and details the ways in which people recognize such oppression, and then develop the capacity to fight back. Chapter 5 explores the meaning of the term *community,* both as physical place and as the psychological sense of belonging to a group. The chapter examines how community comes about by creating and building on the social capital that links individuals.

4 Creating Empowerment for Collective Action

The victories described in the previous chapters demonstrate what can occur when ordinary people work together in ways that empower themselves and their communities. *Empowerment* is a core goal of organizing, but what is meant by the term is not always clear, especially because many in government or business who oppose change falsely use an empowerment rhetoric. In this chapter, we explore the different meanings of the term, examine why people are not already empowered, and examine ways that organizers help people begin to become so.

The Multiple Meanings of Empowerment

Empowerment is a psychological feeling that individuals have when they believe they can accomplish chosen goals; it is also political or organizational strength that enables people to collectively carry out their will. Empowerment occurs when ordinary people discover that they have the capacity to solve the problems they face, control the means to do so, and have final, authoritative say in decision making (Perkins, 1995). Empowered individuals are willing and able to assert their collective wills, even when faced with opposition from the established political or economic structure. To activists, political empowerment is achieved when previously oppressed individuals take over the formal reins of elected office and are actually in charge (Jennings, 1990).

Empowerment is the tool through which ordinary people collectively combat the *mobilization of bias*. This bias stems from the

> set of structures including norms, beliefs, rituals, institutions, organizations and proce-
> dures ("rules of the game") that operate systematically to benefit certain groups and
> persons at the expense of others . . . . (Bachrach & Botwinick, 1992, p. 14)

As part of growing up in a culture in which the rich and the business classes dominate, ordinary people accept these biased rules. Such a willingness to capitulate can occur because people feel they are alone with their problems (Seitz, 1995, p. 7). When people feel devalued and looked down on and do not know that others share these feelings, they often withdraw, ceasing to participate in collective activities and failing to understand the sources of their problems. When that happens, "a society . . . is robbed of the will to understand its own pain, sickness, suffering and dying" (Rappaport, 1985, p. 15). People accept whatever decisions are made, even when those decisions are harmful to them, without fighting back. Disempowerment occurs because people, often without thinking of their own interests, accept the rules of the game that put others in charge.

Instead, as Jacqueline Mondros and Scott Wilson have argued

> People want not only power, but to feel empowered. . . . From welfare mothers, women, gays and lesbians, farm workers, homeless people, blue-collar workers we have heard time and time again how they feel ignored, belittled and diminished in our society. Social action organizations are places where they feel competent, capable, in charge, and they can act on those feelings. (Mondros & Wilson, 1994, p. 244)

Empowerment occurs as those in community and social-change organizations confront the tacit rules that favor the rich, the owners of large businesses, and government agencies. *Organizers work to help people empower themselves by combating the cultural rules that result in their subordination.* But battling cultural rules is far from easy, because the rules are set up to convince people they cannot succeed. To begin this battle, organizers help people gain a sense of their own power step by step, with small collective victories showing the potential for larger and more lasting results.

This feeling of empowerment, along with the organizational capacity to bring it about, enables people to develop a "sense of competence, control and entitlement" that lets them legitimately pursue activities that will make them powerful (Mondros & Wilson, 1994, p. 5). Empowerment occurs collectively, through organizations (Speer & Hughey, 1995, 1996). People

> are empowered to the extent they understand that their own access to social power exists through organization, through the strength of relationships among individual members in that organization, and through active participation in their organization and subsequent reflection on their involvement. (Speer & Hughey, 1995, p. 737)

People feel empowered when they recognize that their contribution helps the group succeed (Speer & Hughey, 1996, p. 185). Power comes from solidarity, from membership in a group, where the efforts of individuals are channeled, focused, and effective.

People learn they can use collective power to shape outcomes that benefit them, to control their own world, and to escape subordination from others. The belief that empowerment is possible gives people the confidence to build the organizations that once in place work to change the cultural rules that have kept people subordinate.

A feeling of empowerment grows when people who understand that there are collective solutions to their problems begin to fight back and take some control. Rather than living passively as a tenant in public housing, residents empower themselves by setting up elected tenants' councils to improve the conditions in which they live. People who successfully pressure elected officials to enforce zoning ordinances and prohibit obnoxious uses of property become empowered. Residents who patrol their own neighborhoods to drive out drug hustlers feel empowered. Learning how to fight back and pressure government and business to respond is empowering.

Empowerment, however, can also occur in other ways. By gaining a material and social stake in society people gain a self-confidence that empowers. This can come about by mastering the skills needed for a better job or by moving into and perhaps owning a new home. As Herbert Rubin was told by a community developer, empowerment comes about:

> When people have a decent place to live, to go home to everyday, their ability to deal with every other issue that's out there is greatly increased. I don't have to worry about where I am going to live, what I am going to pay for rent, I can move onto that next step and worry about a whole lot of other things. . . . It is a self-actualization thing. You take care of your most basic needs and then you can move on to the secondary level, up the ladder. . . . **Poor people need to own things.** (Rubin, 1994, p. 413)

The pride of ownership, the learning that goes into maintaining property, and the sense that a variety of basic problems have been solved are all empowering. People who own homes for the first time also have more stake in the community and are more willing to fight to protect the neighborhood. They contribute to the solidarity of the neighborhood, provide a resource for others, and, as part of becoming empowered, accept a *responsibility* to continue to work to solve problems.

Empowerment links the personal and the political by enabling people to escape from the humiliation they feel when they are put down by others. As bell hooks describes, when a White man puts down a woman or ignores the input from a member of a minority group, the humiliation is intensely personal, but the cause is embedded in institutional structures of domination, and the remedy has to be collective. Those who have suffered from sexism or racism need to see that what has happened to them is not personal, that it happens to many others, and that they can do something about it collectively. People feel empowered when they fight back politically to overcome personal oppression.

Finally, people are empowered when they control the environment in which they live. That means that cars do not speed through residential streets endangering children; it means that toxic waste does not drift down on the neighborhood from a nearby incinerator; it means that the neighborhood is not a market place for drugs or prostitution. Such empowerment comes about when neighbors working with neighbors and local police and planning agencies and newspaper reporters create a safe community and keep it safe. It also means that the residents of the neighborhood control its resources, own its businesses and homes, and that the money spent by the community does not leave the community, stripping it of resources.

How People are Kept Disempowered

To help people become empowered, organizers first have to understand and battle the feeling of powerlessness that stops people from joining collective actions. Many people are afraid, while others blame themselves for the problems they face, not recognizing they are victims of broader structural forces. People fear retaliation and are terrified of attacking the organizations on which they are economically dependent. People hesitate to fight back because they are often isolated from each other and think that they are alone. People are disempowered when they accept the beliefs that wealthy and powerful people deserve to be in charge and that to protest their decisions is wrong.

Further, society and culture have a range of mechanisms to convince people that they lack the capacity to take charge and should remain subordinate. When people are blamed for their problems, *humiliation* often renders them powerless. *Learned inefficacy* convinces people they lack the capacity to succeed. The *organization of consent* tricks people into competing against each other rather than against those in power. Further when people buy into the legitimacy of *stratification* by class, race, or gender they implicitly accept inequality and make it hard to fight back.

In direct confrontations with those in power, other mechanisms come into play to keep people subordinate. Through *personalization* people are tricked into taking blame for their own problems; by defining situations as *zero-sum,* people in power turn one oppressed group against another; and finally, even when people want to fight back, *system bias* prevents the poor, minorities, and the oppressed from offering effective input into decisions.

These mechanisms of disempowerment are what organizers must learn to fight, but the very mechanisms of control can create the resentments that provide the motivation for fighting back. When people are humiliated, they are disempowered but also angry. They can see from their experiences in the unemployment lines and the kind of treatment they get in clinics when they present their benefits cards, they understand when public officials reply to them snidely when they testify at public meetings, that they are being intentionally humiliated. When people who are in wheelchairs know they are bright and able and can work but everywhere they turn there are unnecessary obstacles in their path, they recognize prejudice. People know what is happening to them but accept the situation because they feel powerless to change it. *Organizing is about building on these sparks of resistance to overcome the many mechanisms of disempowerment.*

Humiliation and Self-Blame

People often blame themselves for the bad things that happen to them. When a woman is beaten by her husband, she wonders what she has done wrong to deserve this treatment; relatives who see her swollen face may ask her what she did to provoke him. People who are out of work, looking for jobs unsuccessfully, come to accept their lack of value on the market as a reflection on their lack of skills or personality. As long as people look inward for the causes of their problems, they fail to discover the social forces that have created their difficulties.

Worse yet, people often interpret their problems as humiliations to be hidden and this sense of shame keeps people from joining together. Not all that long ago, a handicapped person would stay at home, embarrassed by his or her handicap; people would go without adequate food rather than to admit to others that they could not earn enough to feed themselves. Their humiliation kept them isolated and powerless.

Sometimes people blame themselves because they feel other people blame them. *Blaming the victim* is a form of social control that disempowers by denying people a legitimate focus for complaint. Police and the courts have often blamed women who have been raped for "asking for it" by dressing sexily or going to a man's apartment. Marchers who are beaten by onlookers or police are often criticized for the violence. If they hadn't protested, violence would not have occurred. Poor people with no medical insurance are blamed for not saving money to pay for medical bills. The poor who feel they are at fault for earning so little do not ask who is benefiting from their low salary and long hours. Instead they bear the guilt along with their problems.

Another variation of this form of disempowering is *blame shifting* in which people are told that their solutions should not be accepted because they will create even worse difficulties. For instance, instead of the owners of polluting factories accepting responsibility for poisoning people, owners blame shift by claiming that if the community group's demands for clean air were met, the cost of installing scrubbers would make the firm declare bankruptcy, throwing large numbers of people out of work. People may be convinced by such arguments to accept the pollution to keep their jobs. Business organizations may blame environmentalists for the costs of cleaning the air or water claiming that those extra costs forced the company to eliminate jobs to restore profitability.

Learned Inefficacy

Disempowerment also occurs because people *learn inefficacy*, that is, they accept the false belief that they are not competent to even try to fix a problem. Learned inefficacy is reinforced as people accept the argument that only experts or those with money or degrees have the skills to succeed. People are led to believe that to contact government requires expensive lawyers or arcane knowledge of bureaucratic and legislative procedures. They assume that starting a small business is an impossible task. They fear freedom and independence because they think they will fail. So they remain in minimum wage jobs. By believing they will fail, people fail.

A sense of inefficacy is taught intentionally by those in power to put down any opposition. Officials might tell citizens that they should not comment on the issue at hand because they have been in the community only a few years and don't know the history of it. Bankers justify denying loans to small businesses in poor neighborhoods by arguing that such businesses are bound to fail. How can they succeed when they lack the money to get started? People learn from newspapers and classrooms that business lobbyists control decision making. They conclude the system is not open to influence, and there is no point in participating.

Learned inefficacy is also taught through the ordinary occurrences in life. Public schools impress upon students that if they have no natural talent for something they should not try to do it. Art, math, and athletics are treated as gifts that you either have or do not have, not things that can be learned. Rather than a place where people learn confidence in their ability, school becomes a series of narrowed possibilities. Expectations of students are low, especially in inner-city schools. Fearing failure and embarrassment, young people learn not to try.

Television reinforces the elimination of possibilities by showing the poor and stigmatized in a negative way. Programs show African Americans as drug dealers not successful business people. Pictures of inner-city neighborhoods emphasize empty lots, dilapidated housing, and unemployed young men hanging out on the streets. Television rarely presents stories about poor people starting their own firms or community groups building new homes to revitalize their neighborhoods or single mothers getting college degrees, one course at a time. People who live in poor communities see these biased televised portraits of their neighborhoods and conclude there is not much possibility for change.

Underlying learned inefficacy is the notion that whatever one wishes to do is limited by biology—one must be White or male or of a certain age, size, strength, intelligence, or have some natural skill or ability. Women have been told that they would not be good politicians because they lack the biological aggressiveness of males or that they would fail as lobbyists, because they would not be accepted by hard drinking, male politicians.

An acceptance of learned inefficacy precludes the learning, change, or growth and the possibility of mastering the skills or talents required to succeed. Learned inefficacy forces people to accept their lower status as inevitable. *Organizing is about learning skills and capacities that help reverse learned inefficacy.*

The Organization of Consent

The *organization of consent* is another way in which those in charge convince dominated groups to accept the values that keep them subordinated. What occurs is that people are convinced to compete with one another to please those in positions of authority rather than join together in collective efforts. This social control mechanism is most easily seen in the workplace in which competition among workers is used as a way of benefiting the company. In this situation

> . . . consent is generated and sustained [by] . . . the seductive practice of fulfilling quotas and getting assigned work done with the least amount of effort . . . even the most antagonistic workers [participate] in the interest of achievement, piece-rates, and promotion. . . . This form of pragmatic acceptance of capitalist domination on the part of workers disperses conflict laterally (between workers) instead of vertically (between workers and capitalists) muting class antagonisms. (Isaac, 1987, pp. 131–132)

The organization of consent causes workers (or any of those who are dominated) to focus on competition with one another rather on the structures by which they are dominated.

In multicultural cities, politicians use a similar logic to play off one ethnic group against another. Elected officials from different ethnic communities each want to bring home projects to their neighborhoods. They compete with each other for a few more homes for the needy or extended hours on some bus routes. By accepting this competitive model and the belief that politics is about dividing up a limited pool of resources, neighborhood politicians ignore the broader question of why the poor communities receive only the table scraps and the larger projects remain downtown.

Competition between downtrodden groups occurs because many of those who are disempowered adopt the ideology and values of the few who are in charge. On a personal level, people of modest means sometimes seek to imitate the rich and powerful and compete with one another for symbols of success. People who can barely make the rent payment imagine being the landlord. Instead of joining a rent strike, individuals try to get a job collecting rents from others, while fantasizing about owning the building. If you identify with the boss, you are unlikely to organize a protest against him or her.

One reason the organization of consent and other similar forms of disempowerment are effective is that people accept the broader cultural values that attribute success to personal hard work and that blame failure on the individual. This framing is reinforced when elites call attention to the exceptional individuals among the disempowered who do succeed. A brilliant child of a migrant farm laborer might become the chief of staff of a major research hospital, but this prestigious position is far more likely to be held by the son (sexism intentional) of a person already well-off and socially successful. Rather than point out the obstacles the poor face, those in power argue "so and so made it, so why can't you?"

The culturally imposed belief that success is possible through competitive achievement ends up as a way of preserving present structures. As long as people think that the path to success is through personal effort, they are unwilling to join together and fight back against the system and are unlikely to be sympathetic to those who do.

Disguising Stratification

Cultural values put forth by dominant groups, and unfortunately accepted by many others, rank people by gender, race, ethnicity, class, and wealth, with men favored over women, light-skinned over dark, northern European ethnic groups over others, and rich over poor. Many in positions of power have found being of the right race, gender, or class has helped them succeed. They prefer to claim, however, that they have succeeded because of merit, and tend to deny the importance of their sex, skin color, or inheritance.

Another form of disempowerment comes about when the oppressed do not acknowledge the extent to which these culturally imposed status rankings limit their career choices and opportunities. People growing up secure in an ethnic neighborhood or in a religious tradition, or young women who have always been cherished at home, may find it impossible to imagine that they were passed over for a job or a raise because of their ethnic background, their religion, or their gender. They do not want to see themselves in a despised or ignored social category; it is too different from the self-image they grew up with.

Because so many people are uncomfortable acknowledging the importance of social rankings, people who argue that stratification disempowers have difficulty persuading others. Even when people recognize that they are being looked down on because of their lower status, it can be difficult to raise the issue and break down the pretense. Bringing concerns with race or gender or economic status into the open is awkward, because they are supposed to be irrelevant.

Sometimes, though, relative status is clearly invoked as a way of choking off argument. The use of status may be so blatant that those so dismissed acknowledge that they have been put down. One example occurred in a battle between poor minority women and hospital administrators over the closing of women's health clinics. During the battle, a spokesperson for the hospital attacked the demands of the protesters, telling them, "You don't 'demand' of doctors. You wouldn't make demands of your husbands" (Morgen, 1988, p. 105). This reply made it clear that the protesters were viewed as patients and as wives, two subservient roles whose arguments were treated as illegitimate, regardless of their content.

> What had begun as a feeling of being denied access to the decision to close the clinics was transformed through direct contact with the doctors and the hospital into a recognition . . . that "they think we are stupid and unworthy of having our views taken seriously." (Morgen, 1988, p. 104)

In the case of the battle for the clinics, the put-down was so obviously based on status ranking that people could easily understand how they were being disempowered. Often, though, such forms of psychological disempowerment take more effort to bring to light. Suppose staff members of a housing agency have preconceptions that poor minority groups lack the ability to manage a housing complex. The housing staff are unlikely to air such views in public. Instead, they argue that the tenants do not know how to monitor boilers or maintain equipment or handle rent. If the residents of the housing complex try to answer these technical charges, they get nowhere, and some other reason is given, because the real issue is a disdain for the poor. Not only is such a situation confusing, because the housing staff are saying one thing but meaning something else, but the residents may accept the argument that they lack the ability to manage the complex.

In short, people in power often treat people badly because they consider them of lower status, while pretending that the substance of the matter is really what is of concern. Such disempowerment will last until activists develop "conceptual frameworks that capture the complex ways that gender, race, ethnicity, and class become politically meaningful" (Morgen, 1988, p. 113). Empowerment comes about when people are willing to fully confront, both with themselves and others, how their status—race, gender, ethnicity, age, size—is influencing the discussion.

Recognizing Social Psychological Disempowerment

Learned inefficacy, fear of humiliation and self-blame, the organization of consent, and discrimination against less favored groups weaken the ability of people to take charge. To begin to convince people to fight back, organizers work to combat the mechanisms that disempower people.

In working to help people become empowered, organizers must recognize and combat the shame and fear of humiliation that keep people from publicly expressing their needs. To do that, organizers emphasize the social rather than individual causes of problems so people understand that they should not feel inadequate because they are experiencing a problem. Similarly, organizers teach that having a problem should not be a source of embarrassment, it is not shameful. Women who have been beaten by a spouse may hide the bruises and deny the problem. They do not want anyone to know what has befallen them, that their lives are not perfect. (They may also fear that embarrassing their husbands will provoke a new round of violence.) As long as they cannot talk about what has happened to them they cannot agitate for collective solutions. Providing social support in a shelter where other abused women are living can be helpful in getting women to talk about what happened without feeling shame.

Organizers try to prevent people from blaming themselves. An objective of the battered women's movement is to show the women that they are not to blame for provoking abuse (Schillinger, 1988, p. 469). Organizing among the unemployed begins with research showing how the profit margins of the company increased after the firm was bought out and the new owners sold off needed assets. People understand that if they are unemployed because shareholders are benefiting from the destruction of the factory, they should feel angry, not guilty.

The first step in combating status put-downs based on the hidden dimensions of stratification is to recognize what is going on; the second step is to make it explicit and public. In the case of the housing agency staff, the residents needed to listen to the staff's arguments and respond to the underlying issue. If after several rounds of charges and answers, more excuses are made, the housing development residents might say, "Are you saying we are incompetent and cannot learn?" Or, "the housing project in Glenview is run by the tenants, are you saying we are less competent or knowledgeable than they are?" Another approach might be, "How about doing this on a trial basis. If at the end of 6 months we have not demonstrated that we can run this place, we can return to the status quo." In the case of the women and the health clinic, the women can raise the issue of gender in the press. A newspaper headline might read, "Doctors Call Women Subservient." Presumably the authorities would be embarrassed, and other women in the neighborhood might begin to see a link between the low esteem in which the women are held and the closing of the clinics. Raising the issue of the status put-down can be a terrific organizing issue: "We will show them what women can do."

In battling disempowerment caused by the organization of consent, organizers must grapple with accepted cultural beliefs that maintain the present structures of control, such as that hard work alone leads to career success. Organizers should help people understand that the game is fixed, that opportunities are structured according to status, and that there are institutional barriers that must be removed. As a renter, you can't become the landlord while working on a minimum wage job with no possibility of savings, especially if banks redline, that is, do not lend money because they define the neighborhood as a poor investment. Organizers may need to demonstrate to potential activists that only a few of those who are structurally disadvantaged can make it, for most, unless the path is widened the obstacles remain overwhelming. Between the fantasy and the reality action is needed to bring about better schools and access to better paying jobs, and bank loans.

Once community organizers have dismantled whatever disempowering mechanisms prevent people from becoming active, and the group's new members begin to demand better schools or better employment opportunities or health services in poor neighborhoods, group members are likely to confront further efforts to disempower them. These, too, must be fought.

When confronted with the demands of a community organization, people in positions of power often raise two types of manipulative arguments, the first, disparaging people who protest through *personalization* and, the second, creating psychological and organizational disunity by claiming that resources are limited and one group's gains are another group's losses, the *zero-sum* argument. At a more fundamental level, people are disempowered because of *system bias,* the political structures that restrict access to decision making and obscure the permitted patterns of influence.

Personalization

Personalization is a manipulation those in power use to play on the insecurities of people who are just beginning to have the courage to become involved. When confronted by requests from the disempowered, business leaders or those in high position argue that *they*—elected officials or heads of businesses—represent the general interest and that members of a community or social change organization, by contrast, are worried only about their personal concerns.

For example, a request for a company-sponsored day-care facility might be put down by management as a selfish attempt on the part of women (not men) to have someone take over their responsibilities. This argument denies women's legitimate need to ensure the health and safety of their children while they work and tries to humiliate the requester. In a slightly different example, environmentalists might argue with a city council to preserve open space for the flora and fauna. Prodevelopment council members attack the group, arguing that the environmentalists want the luxury of the park for their own recreational purposes. They further charge that satisfying the request for open space will stop the economic development, taking jobs away from those in need. Those on the city council claim they are protecting the broader public, when in fact the ones who will benefit most from despoiling the land are the housing and mall developers who contribute to the political campaign expenses of council members. In this case, the argument simultaneously shifts blame and attributes personal motives.

Zero-Sum Arguments

Another manipulation that those in power use to limit demands for change is to play upon a shared belief that power and resources are *zero-sum,* that is, gains by one group can only occur if they are compensated by losses from another group. Elected officials sometimes promote the idea that there is only a limited amount of money for community groups and to fund one would be to deny another, instead of, for example, looking for other sources of money to fund them all. These arguments create competition between community groups, reducing the chance of people working together in ways that might benefit everyone.

Zero-sum arguments are frequently used by those who oppose any kind of affirmative action. We only have a limited number of positions, they argue, and if we hire women or minorities, well-qualified White men will not be hired. In the past, in the U.S. South, the zero-sum logic was used to convince poor Whites who were only slightly better-off than poor Blacks, that if Black people were to gain the Whites would lose out. This belief encouraged virulent racism and distracted from the overall unfairness of an economic system that made so many Whites and Blacks poor.

In general, by convincing others that the zero-sum model really describes politics and economics, those in power encourage each group to get its own piece, rather than to build toward a collective effort to expand the pie. Doing so creates contention rather than cooperation between different ethnic and racial groups and between providers of different kinds of social services. These manipulations disempower the dispossessed by making it difficult for them to work together as a powerful moral force.

System Bias

Many of the mechanisms of disempowerment work because they are built on cultural beliefs that the poor and vulnerable accept: Those in power deserve to be in power, they work hard, and I should give them respect. I am responsible for my own problems, my best strategy is to try to keep my problems to myself. I cannot fight back, I would not even know where to begin, and if I tried I would probably fail. These beliefs are reinforced by popular novels, movies, and news stories, by schools, and by the forms and letters sent out to the public that are so complicated and cumbersome, people feel they need help from experts to read and respond to them.

Further, people have been convinced not to fight back through the use of force and violence, especially to repress unions and minority group members; however, the use of force by government is costly; a regime that depends on force can be overthrown by force, and excessive use of violence can discredit the people who use it, especially because people are taught to believe that real power does not require the use of force. Governments prefer to control potential threats to the status quo in much quieter ways. One way this is done is through a *system bias* that both structurally and psychologically biases government toward the rich and powerful.

System bias comes about as those from business classes, through campaign contributions, influence people who run for office and then reinforce this influence through maintaining lobbyists. Further, many government decision makers often come from the same social strata as do business leaders. They share many of the same values and goals because of their common background, education, and socialization. Neither business leaders nor former lawyers now in elected office need to be convinced that managers should run companies and workers should obey or that capitalism is essentially a fair system.

When those in office need advice, or even when they are relaxing but talking about more serious issues, they are more likely to be with those from the business community and other upper status people. During these contacts, values, goals, and ideas are informally communicated and in the absence of other knowledge these are the ideas that shape political outcomes. How does a politician learn about the long-term costs of pollution, when his or her friends are from the business community and always talk about the new jobs they will bring?

The result is a general tilt of government toward business and wealthy citizens. Those with demands that might threaten the status quo are kept out of the decisional loop in such a way that they often cannot see their exclusion and so cannot publicize or protest it. The resulting pattern of behavior is called *system bias* or the more encompassing term of *ecological power* (Stone, 1976, 1989) through which "the power-wielder is effective without having to engage in direct action to prevail over opposition or to prevent opposition from developing" (Stone, 1976, p. 105).

System bias is often built into the structures of government, where it becomes accepted as the way things are done and, hence, becomes invisible. The origin of this biased structure is so buried in the distant past that its consequences are hard to see now. For example, the council-manager form of municipal government is touted as good government, professional government, led by a professional, trained staff responsive to an elected city council. This form of government is supposed to take the politics out of cities and provide well-managed programs at reasonable cost.

In reality, city managers usually are trained to think in ways that support the business community. Historically, the council-manager form of government was put in place to disempower the poor.

> the new reform [was not] a revitalization of popular government. . . . What they sought was the replacement of the ward system . . . with a centralized administration that would organize municipal services according to the business view of what was good for the community. City manager government promised to accomplish all of this. Businessmen could then reduce the influence of lower-class groups in city government and advance their own notions of public policy. (Scheisl, 1977, p. 176)

The actions undertaken by the city manager in accordance with his or her training would tilt toward those preferred by the business community and, in doing so, disempower the poor, in ways that were far from obvious.

A subtle aspect of system bias is that many of the decisions that are made that favor business are done quietly, without any public airing. Government transactions with the business community are kept secret, not because of corruption, but because of the shared belief that business won't deal with the city if its negotiations are made public. Deals are locked in stone before they are announced, with the claim that if the discussions had been made public businesses would not have participated in negotiations.

The language used in political discourse reflects system bias. Many public officials talk about "incentives" to encourage businesses to expand or move to the city and argue that when cities provide such incentives they are working "for the common good" and the money spent is an "investment." In contrast, help to the poor is labeled as "subsidies" or "welfare" and considered to be money targeted for benefit of individuals, with no benefit to the collectivity. Advocates for children and those who oppose public subsidies to business make the opposite case, that subsidies to businesses take from everyone and give to a limited number of corporations without any collective benefit; they call these subsidies "corporate welfare," and they describe money spent on children's education and health as "investments." The vocabulary used indicates that a number of public officials (though not all) are biased advocates of the business community.

A related, but even more subtle form of disempowerment involves what is called *nondecisions* (Bachrach & Baratz, 1963). A nondecision means that important questions about the allocation of resources or actions of government are never asked, there is no forum for their discussion, so that contention over these issues cannot possibly take place. When budgets are being discussed, people focus on details, not on general policies. Most of the budget is exactly as it was the previous year, and the small part of the budget that is up for discussion is often framed in terms of very narrow choices, such as shall we put $20,000 more into the annual fund balance or shall we hire a part-time secretary. The broader questions, such as what services should the city provide and should the city subsidize upscale housing, are often not discussed in public. The answers to these unasked questions are assumed in ways that favor the status quo. Because the nondecisions are not visible, people do not realize they have been left out of the decision making.

Building toward Empowerment

What can organizers learn from this discussion of empowerment? First, empowerment is about both improving individuals' confidence in their ability to challenge the status quo and about increasing community groups' capacity to accomplish collective goals. Empowerment requires organizers to combat the cultural beliefs that keep people isolated and make them feel inadequate. Further, empowerment can come about by establishing a positive cycle in which personal and collective successes reinforce one another. People who feel they can make a difference join community organizations aimed at change; when these organizations succeed, their members feel an increased sense of personal efficacy.

Organizers, however, must not forget that the empowerment of individuals and community organizations is threatening to the establishment that wants to discourage community action. Sometimes those in leading political or business positions try to humiliate and derail protesters through direct put-downs, but more often disempowerment occurs in subtler ways, such as not providing a setting in which fundamental policy choices can be discussed. Organizers may have to help create a forum for the discussion of such issues, through direct actions, through framing of issues and dramatic revelations of conditions, and by using the repressive responses of campaign targets to create sympathy for the cause.

In the remainder of this chapter, we discuss how community organizers can take advantage of the positive cycle that links personal and collective empowerment, first helping people to overcome their isolation and feelings of incompetence, and then building the capacity of community organizations.

Consciousness Raising

The initial step in building personal empowerment takes place as people recognize that they are victims of problems that are shared by many others. This recognition occurs when people get together, talk about what bothers them, and share experiences of oppression. In these discussions—*consciousness raising* sessions—people discover that their personal problems are caused by the broader social structure and occur because they redound to the advantages of others. Initially these reflective group conversations were popularized by feminists who encouraged women to talk and discover shared problems, but today consciousness raising is an appropriate tactic whenever it is important to create awareness of the social basis of a problem.

Consciousness raising helps people learn that they are not alone in experiencing a problem and that the problem is not their fault. Women talking together may find that regardless of their income or education, men stereotype them as emotional, incomprehensible, and spending machines. They may share episodes of humiliation or may discuss how men discouraged them from getting more education, or trying a new career, or even making their opinions known. People who have tried to buy homes and failed may share incidents in which banks refused them mortgages and provided little information on how to go about getting needed funds. They may learn that their problems are not simply the result of a slight blemish on their credit records, that the problem is not their fault, that banks always find something wrong with the applications from anyone in their neighborhood. Through narratives shared with one another people learn that the problem is socially caused (Rappaport, 1995).

Through sharing their stories, people gradually learn to think more critically about the economic and social structures that oppress them. As they take action on their new understanding, they develop what Freire calls a *critical consciousness*. For example, as part of the action campaigns within the civil rights movement, people came together to learn how to successfully register to vote. As they talked to each other in this specific campaign, they also talked about other problems they shared and increased their willingness to battle a broader oppression (Payne, 1995). Once a critical consciousness has developed, people are better able to analyze and combat cultural beliefs that have kept them disempowered.

Consciousness raising sessions need to be followed up by action challenging the cause of the problem. In her study of how Appalachian women fought back against gender and economic subordination, Virginia Rinaldo Seitz argues:

> . . . their own consciousness may have been raised: they may have *questioned* the right of men to batter, of an employer to take advantage of them, and of a social worker to demean them. . . . But they did not necessarily actively *challenge* the right of men to batter, of capitalists to exploit, or of the market to define culture. They did not have the critical consciousness (Freire, 1972) that is grounded in the political or collective *practice* of opposition. . . . personal experience is politicized, but politics is more than individual action. (Seitz, 1995, p. 225)

Consciousness raising helps break down individual disempowerment but is only a first step toward collective actions.

Self-Assertion

After people recognize that problems are shared and structurally caused, the next step is self-assertion. People vent their anger in public declarations and by individually and collectively acting against those who cause the problem. Individual resistance and self-assertion can be empowering. An individual may learn to talk back to a landlord, demanding and getting heating and plumbing repairs for one apartment, but it is even more empowering if tenants of a whole building can pressure the landlord to provide improved housing conditions or charge fairer rents to everyone. These acts of self-assertion combat the cultural belief that owners have a right to charge what they want or allow a property to get run down. Such "stories of resistance are . . . assertions of self-respect" (Dill, 1988, p. 43).

Resistance can involve not backing down when confronted with an evasive answer or not being intimidated by an authority figure. An employee may publicly insist that the boss clearly set forth job responsibilities or express a preference for being called Mrs. Jones rather than Betty. Individuals may demand information from banks about where housing loans are being made. Organizers work hard to encourage people to speak out in public, to find their voice, and to talk back (hooks, 1989). Learning to resist demeaning behavior is empowering. Talking back teaches those who have been dominated that they can make their arguments even when those in power would prefer not to hear them. It also demonstrates to others that people can gain the courage to resist.

Framing the Agenda

The next step is for the community or social change organization to frame the issues to get them on the public agenda. The goal is to present these issues in such a way that the public recognizes the wrongs that have been done and those in power are no longer able to hide from these concerns.

A public demonstration or a media campaign can make people aware of issues. Through such agenda-setting tactics, the community organization can turn what those in power have treated as nondecisions into issues that are now to be contested. Few politicians or bureaucrats advocate poor housing, loss of jobs, neglect of AIDS patients, leaving the homeless on the streets, isolating the elderly, polluting the environment, or poorly educating the young. These are problems that once raised people agree should be solved, but because the costs of solving these problems is often perceived as too high, those in power may see to it that there is no forum in which to discuss the issues. Community and social-change organizations focus public attention on these issues, putting them back on the public agenda.

In many cities, residents treat the homeless as invisible, they have learned not to see the problem. They step across the bodies of sleeping homeless people in doorways to get into their buildings in the morning, but have no idea who the homeless are or why they are there or what it would take to move them into a better situation. Community organizations fighting homelessness not only have to make the invisible real and human, they have to frame the issue in ways that gained public support. One way to do this is to introduce the homeless, many of whom are children, to the neighbors; rather than faceless vagabonds, the homeless become children who have had a bad break and deserve some help. Another approach is to present a program in which the homeless are working to improve their lives but need some help. Maybe they can learn to build a temporary residence if they get donated materials and some guidance on how to do it. Or maybe they can demand community facilities where the homeless can get medical treatment and supervision. In each case, the homeless are presented in favorable terms that match the culture—as children needing help from adults, as people trying to get skills and work, as patients needing medical care.

Setting a public agenda is empowering in two ways. The success of getting the broader community to see the issues in a favorable light is a milestone; combating the system bias that kept the issues off the public agenda gives group members a new sense of possibilities.

Building Power

Through efforts to assert themselves and frame the agenda individuals work to

> create political space for the underclasses to acquire voice and a more empowered sense of community involvement, thereby enabling them to compete more effectively with the upper classes in all arenas of politics. (Bachrach & Botwinick, 1992, p. 12)

Participatory community and social change organizations control political space. Such organizations *gain power through committed members.* The number of members alone is impressive, their dedication is even more impressive. Business groups may have more money, but when the goal is to influence government, it is the people with votes, who commit time not money, who count.

Numbers and enthusiasm are two sources of power; other sources include *legal actions, expertise,* and *the threat of force.* Bringing suit to stop the dumping of toxic material is an example of using legal authority; learning how to interpret budgets of government agencies to find out who is getting what is an instance of using expertise. Actual disruption of traffic or the threat of disruption of water supplies represents force and the threat of force. These are not easy tools to use: The law is complex, it may be difficult to get a clear decision, and courts are very slow. Mastering expertise, say, in learning how to read mortality tables to figure out whether your neighborhood is suffering a higher than expected rate of childhood cancers, can be a slow task. The use of force is risky—it invites counterforce—and often puts public opinion against the group and the campaign. Each of these strategies, however, involves the use of power and, when carefully implemented, may bring about victories. Of equal import, using these strategies shows people that they can fight back, that they do have power. It also shows them that they can learn what they need to know; they don't have to be born knowing the law or how to use health statistics.

Capacity Building

An organizer works to help community members build the *capacity* to fight back. Capacity has two components. One component is knowledge, a set of skills, useful for building organizations and carrying out campaigns and useful in other areas of life. Mastering new skills is personally and psychologically empowering. The second component of capacity is the belief, often based on experience, that effort will be rewarded, that the organization has power, its framing of the issues is astute and choice of tactic effective. Members have to believe that if they take action to solve problems collectively, they can win. *Capacity building is the antidote to learned inefficacy.*

Individual capacity can be bolstered in a variety of ways. Through running training programs and through encouraging schools to improve their curriculum, community organizations help people learn new skills. Some skills such as bookkeeping or marketing enable people to get better jobs; others such as running meetings or preparing flyers assist the organization in running successful campaigns. Those who learn new skills can get an additional boost in confidence from sharing their new skills with others.

Some community organizations help people to own or manage property. Land or property ownership or management builds skills and confidence and helps make people more willing to organize and participate in politics (Rohe, 1994). Studies of tenant management in low-income housing shows that "involving residents in the management and ownership of low-income housing leads to an increased sense of control and ownership, two key aspects of the notion of empowerment (Van Ryzin, 1994, p. 250)." *Capacity building involves acquiring the skills to succeed and the confidence to try.* Ownership and management of property seem to contribute to both skills and confidence at the same time.

The belief that efforts will be rewarded, that public actions can bring about victories, not punishments and humiliation, is usually based on experience. Past accomplishments of a community organization testify to the possibility of future successes. Small successes can help create confidence that bigger victories are within reach. Campaigns or projects in which a community member has participated and which reached a satisfactory outcome are the most powerful reasons to believe that a community group can be successful. New moderate-priced housing in a dilapidated neighborhood or a new business that has hired five local residents constitute incontrovertible evidence that community organizations can win.

Successful actions are incredibly empowering, as explained by a member of an organization for the disabled:

> Before the project I felt helpless about the decisions that were affecting my life. But then we visited our legislators at the Capitol and learned that letters and phone calls are taken seriously and can be effective in decisions. (Checkoway & Norsman, 1986, p. 270)

The campaign helped change their view of themselves, helped them to see themselves as a political unit, and enabled them to represent their interests in public (Checkoway & Norsman, 1986, pp. 274–275).

It is possible to increase capacity, that is increase individual learning and instill a belief that community groups can succeed, without achieving the last step, which is to go beyond individual benefits and problems to responsibility for the community. If the cause of a problem is diagnosed as sexism of physicians, and sexism of physicians is reduced, then the whole community benefits. During the consciousness raising stage, the group leaders have to be careful to focus on societal causes of problems. If that does not happen, and members want to use the collective power of the organization to solve their individual problems, the result may be that one individual gets more schooling or one individual gets a job, but the community's capacity to solve collective problems is not enhanced. hooks calls this focus on the individual *narcissism* (hooks, 1989, p. 105).

Bootstrapping toward Empowerment

Victories reinforce capacity. Empowerment comes about step by step as community and social change organizations "take advantage of the cracks in the system to win victories and demonstrate that authority can be challenged and that people can generate power" (Perlman, 1979, p. 423).

In San Antonio, Communities Organized for Public Service (COPS) first worked to change the voting system from one that discouraged Hispanics from voting to one that gave them a real say. With this victory under their belt, they then worked to elect their own representatives from the predominantly Spanish-speaking district in which they lived. A highly visible success showed the possibility for continued action. Following a similar logic, community development groups often work to repair the worst buildings in the neighborhood just to show others that it can be done (Rubin, 2000).

Such actions are a form of *bootstrapping* in which the confidence and the skills that come from one victory or completed project enable the organization to attempt the next. Organizers encourage groups to undertake small projects that when successful provide the sense of achievement that further collective action is possible and worthwhile. Fair Share, in Massachusetts, illustrates the bootstrapping process:

> Fair Share concentrated on small victories at the local level. Tax abatements in Dorchester, bridge repairs in East Boston, a dump relocation in Worcester. These issues . . . engage people in work that teaches them something about power. . . . The actions were picked to be winnable. (Zald & McCarthy, 1979, p. 30)

Bootstrapping has two stages. The first is to carry out an activity that has low costs to community members, that teaches them something of import, and that yields a victory. For example, the organization gets a politician who has avoided constituents to show up at a meeting, perhaps convinces city hall to put in a needed stop sign, or gets people interested in working on a crime-watch detail. Next, the group moves to larger issues, such as working to make the neighborhood safe and attractive for the children. To bootstrap successfully, community groups must choose issues carefully: They must be important enough to engage people and must teach lessons on which people can build, yet at the same time the issues must be winnable.

In doing a small project it is easy to lose sight of larger goals. Even small actions like agitating for a stop sign must be framed as collective undertakings, maybe accomplished by holding a mass meeting at city hall. Another way of creating a sense of community through small projects is to design work in which many people can pitch in, such as repairing a deteriorating home. In some neighborhoods, organizations run "caulk of the town" days in which people come out together to do minor home repairs for the elderly or disabled. In other neighborhoods, prayer vigils around crack houses enable residents to fight together a shared problem. Each action is small, doable, yet brings people together to see the potential for future collective actions.

Collective Empowerment

The idea of creating collective empowerment is slightly different from that of individual empowerment. Individuals who feel they can succeed are empowered; collective empowerment comes about as people learn that they share a responsibility for one another and by doing so help create *social capital,* a resource for future community actions.

For example, people who initially came together to combat poor housing conditions might later form a development corporation that helps others acquire ownership in affordable housing. As a means toward collective empowerment, the development corporation improves the physical neighborhood through new homes and provides people with a sense that together the community can improve.

By acting together, people strengthen community bonds, the sense of belonging that gives security and at the same time imposes obligations. These strengthened ties are part of a community's *social capital.* Social capital consists of "the resources embedded in social relations among persons and organizations that facilitate cooperation and collaboration in communities" (Committee for Economic Development, 1995, p. 12). Putnam (1993) and many others have argued that social capital, the networks of people with complementary skills and the trust and belief in one another that bind community members to one another, enables individuals to work together effectively, and, through this work, to strengthen the community.

As people feel empowered, their communities gain in social capital as neighbors feel confident to help one another. In turn, in neighborhoods in which there is a rich supply of social capital and help for problems can be found, people on a personal level feel empowered. For instance, people might work together to create a safe block, learning how to set up a block watch or make contact with the police. Such efforts makes others believe that the neighborhood will remain viable and that they should contribute to community actions. This feeling of shared responsibility is a vital form of social capital.

With increased confidence and belief in the community, people become willing to join in common efforts, for instance, participating in a neighborhood paint-up, fix-up campaign. The success of these neighborhood improvement programs (perhaps when supplemented with some direct pressure tactics) encourages banks to loan money enabling improvements to be financed. With the support of the bank, others can now make needed repairs to their homes, increasing the overall quality of life in the neighborhood.

The key step in creating collective empowerment is to help people learn that through their collective actions they become responsible for each other and the community as a whole. Collective empowerment comes about when people gain the confidence and experience that by helping others they also help themselves. To work, however, participation in community organizations must be seen as effective and people must be able to see the connection between their individual effort and the community outcome. Just showing up a meeting is not enough; people have to understand that their actions bring about desired results.

For instance, in the Dudley Street section of Boston, community members formed the Dudley Street Neighborhood Initiative (DSNI) in which people were individually and collectively involved in planning and voting on how to rejuvenate their neighborhood. They convinced the city of Boston to give DSNI the eminent domain power necessary to clear slum property to build homes for community members. The initiative obtained funding from foundations and got advice from technical experts but insisted that individual community members be trained in new skills. Each action taken was discussed and approved by a large, ethnically representative, elected board of community members. Community participation was real and understood as such by those in the neighborhood. Projects were accomplished by the members of the organization, and, as a result, collective empowerment occurred (Medoff & Sklar, 1994).

When organizations are in place that involve people in the decisions and accomplish needed tasks, people no longer feel disempowered or sense that they lack control. Collectively individuals are able to achieve goals that they could not achieve alone, develop new skills while doing so, and gain an empowering confidence in themselves and their communities. When people form and control community groups that determine public agendas and thereby become effective political actors, they can counteract system bias.

Through acting collectively, people learn about the political nature of dominance, that they are not alone as victims of social and systemic problems. Organization members learn respect and tolerance and how to cooperate with one another. Ultimately, people learn to see that battling back against disempowerment is not simply for themselves or their families but is part of their responsibility to a shared and evolving community. As people work for each other, they expand the social capital that makes future community projects and improvements easier. By making their opinions count they give reality to democracy.

CHAPTER

5

Understanding Community

Empowerment is about people gaining confidence to fight back, not only for themselves but for the community of which they are part. But what is meant by *community?* Organizers use the term in different but related ways, each implying strategies for getting people to work together.

- Community describes a *geographic place,* a neighborhood, perhaps a large housing complex, or a park in which the homeless congregate. People live in this place and interact with each other, at least occasionally.
- Community refers to the *bonds* that people share because of *ascriptive ties,* that is, ties based on place of birth (such as people from the same village in the old country), common cultural beliefs, religious heritage, or racial background. Groups based on these ties are often called *solidarity communities.*
- Community applies to a group of people who *share concerns about specific issues,* such as the environment, affordable housing, or facilities for the disabled. A *community of interest* emerges when individuals who share these interests develop a common *framing* or interpretation of what is wrong and what can be done.
- More generally, community is the set of *obligations and responsibilities that people assume when they are willing to help one another.* Such bonds might preexist as they do within solidarity group or they can be the *product* that emerges as people work together to achieve a common goal.

Building community means creating or increasing peoples' feelings of *social solidarity,* that is, the sense of belonging to and feeling responsible for a group or territory. Community is built on *social capital,* "the stocks of social trust, norms, and networks that people can draw upon in order to solve common problems" (Lang & Hornburg, 1998, p. 4). If there is inadequate social capital, it is difficult to build a sense of community.

One form of social capital—*social glue*—describes the bonds and obligations that link individuals. Social glue refers to "the degree to which people take part in group life [and also] the amount of trust or the comfort level that people feel when participating in these groups" (Lang & Hornburg, 1998, p. 4).

Social glue can be strong or weak. When strong, people are linked through many different ties. Individuals may do business together, go to the same churches, participate in the same service clubs, and share the same ethnic traditions. Social glue is typically strong in established *solidarity communities,* communities formed of people who share a common ethnic, cultural, or religious heritage. People in solidarity communities tend to trust each other because of their shared backgrounds, common histories, and long memories. Even relative strangers can be held accountable, because their family is known even when they are not.

In some places, social glue is weak, for example, when neighborhoods are occupied primarily by renters, who come into the community for a short time and then move elsewhere, or by commuters, who live in the community but work elsewhere, patronize businesses where they work, and have little identification with or concern for the place in which they live. Sometimes the bonds within specific groups in a geographic area are strong, but the linkages between the separate groups remain weak. One neighborhood we studied had a half dozen rival Korean clubs. Within the clubs the social ties were strong, but rivalries between the clubs precluded them from working together even though individuals shared a common ethnic culture.

Social glue is often weak within *communities of interest,* composed of people who share concern about an issue, may be willing to take action on this issue, but may have little else in common. They may live almost any place and be linked to each other by a newsletter. The intensity of feelings on the issue, however, can make up for the lack of social glue.

Social capital also comes about by building *social bridges,* links that join people within a group to the broader, outside world. Such links "are vital because they not only connect groups to one another but also give members in any one group access to the larger world outside their social circle through a chain of affiliations" (Lang & Hornburg, 1998, p. 4). Middle-class people who meet each other in college and then live in different cities but maintain contact with one another form a social bridge, that, for instance, enables a city official to easily contact an executive in a business; however, there tend to be fewer social bridges in poor communities. People in poor neighborhoods might want to help one another find jobs but lack the contacts—the social bridges—to employers outside of the neighborhood that hire people at better wages. Part of organizing is in helping people strengthen their communities by building social bridges.

No matter whether working with geographic, solidarity, or interest group communities, organizers first ascertain whether a sufficient sense of community can be found on which to build an activist group. When it appears that social capital is lacking, that is, a sense of trust and mutual obligation are low, then early efforts should be focused on building solidarity.

Fortunately, such community-building efforts *bootstrap,* that is, an initial success in bringing about an increase in a sense of mutual obligation sets up a base on which to build toward a shared sense of community. People might join a block association without having much sense of group obligation, to protect their own homes or children. If the actions of the block association are seen to help, perhaps by cleaning up a park in which the children play, families that benefit feel more obligated to help others in the group on future issues. This sense of obligation creates social capital for continued involvement (Hirsch, 1986).

People who are drawn into a social action for individualistic reasons end up through the experience of working together creating loyalty and trust with one another. The very act of struggling together and displaying a shared resistance creates a common identity among the poor, the dispossessed, or the disempowered. This *emergent solidarity* increases the social capital by turning personal concerns into a collective responsibility. Rick Fantasia illustrated how this process works among community members who joined together, initially quite reluctantly, in a strike against the town's major employer. During the strike

> the workers had defied company authority at its highest levels, and a strong sense of solidarity had emerged, growing strong at each phase of the action. Solidarity among the workers was not an a prior "fact," but grew out of this interactive process of negotiation between workers in their confrontations with authorities. (Fantasia, 1988, p. 88)

Less dramatic involvement also builds social bonds. In some cities, for instance, people participate in community councils that have some say in local matters. Observers of these councils have noted that "there is a strong and positive relationship between level of participation and sense of community" (Berry, Portney, & Thomson, 1993, p. 290). Just having some say over a neighborhood expands peoples' sense of belongness and creates a solidarity with others in the community.

The effort of working or fighting side by side brings about a mutual trust, a form of social glue, that becomes available for subsequent efforts. In addition, those who are involved in a battle use their own social bridges to find support that can be linked to the current battle. These efforts join people involved in local efforts to larger networks of concerned people and in doing so "facilitate(s) the emergence of new networks, which in turn allow advocacy groups, citizens' organizations, action committees, and alternative intellectuals and artists to be more influential in processes of political and cultural change" (Diani, 1997, p. 35).

An initial involvement, even at a minimal level, can start the process of creating the shared bonds of community that support collective actions; however, beginning this bootstrapping toward community can be difficult. In this chapter we examine how differences between geographic, solidarity, and issue communities might create problems in stimulating the creation of the social capital on which organizations depend. What should be done in neighborhoods that appear to lack social capital? In neighborhoods built up of people from many separate cultural groups can the necessary social bridges be found to create multicultural organizations?

Building Community Within Neighborhoods

In the Alinsky tradition, street-level organizing is about bringing people together to combat neighborhood problems. What constitutes a neighborhood, physically, legally, or socially? Determining neighborhood boundaries can be important, as people identify with this territory and can be mobilized in its defense.

Geographic neighborhoods are separated from one another by major highways, large parks, or busy shopping strips. Others are defined as the service areas for a grammar school, a parish, or a community center. In older cities, neighborhoods might be remnants of areas set up to house workers for major industrial activities, such as the animal slaughtering that occurred in the Back of the Yards neighborhood or the rail car construction in Pullman areas in Chicago. In larger cities, many neighborhoods were originally small villages that later were incorporated into a growing metropolis. In suburban areas and growing cities, the boundaries of neighborhoods are often the subdivisions that were built at one time by housing developers.

Over time, people can contest how neighborhood boundaries are labeled. To those involved, belonging to a particular neighborhood may either confer or deny social status. For instance, in Chicago's Uptown area, residents argued about whether to include particular blocks in the neighborhood because of concerns about their social and economic composition (Bennett, 1997).

City governments often designate a geographic area as a neighborhood and then use this territory for planning purposes or as a service area, regardless of whether people in that locale initially identify with one another. Organizing is then required to respond to officialdom. Chicago, for instance, has seventy some named neighborhood areas, as does the much smaller Minneapolis. Dayton, San Antonio, Birmingham, and numerous other cities have divided themselves into neighborhood planning areas (Berry, Portnoy, & Thomson, 1993).

Sometimes local governments decentralize decision making to the neighborhood level. Under Mayor Flynn in Boston and Mayor Washington in Chicago, City Hall gave neighborhood organizations some power over public decisions, while police and public safety functions are often administered in districts that overlap with city neighborhoods. In other cities, zoning, land use, and large infrastructure projects, and in some cases, parts of the city budget, must be approved by a recognized community organization, usually elected by neighborhood residents (Berry, Portnoy, & Thomson, 1993). When neighborhoods and neighborhood organizations have real decisions to make, residents may interact more often as they choose representatives, create committees, think about neighborhood problems and priorities, and come up with plans. As such, the government labeling of a locale as a neighborhood encourages people to feel more bound to one another. Recent research has shown that

> city government sponsored neighborhood associations, **if given genuine power over local affairs** [emphasis Rubin], appear to be more effective in involving and empowering disadvantaged minorities and generating a deeper sense of community than the voluntary organizations usually stressed in the civil society argument. (Foley & Edwards, 1997, p. 559)

A sense of neighborhood may be mandated from above and take on reality as citizens implement new powers and responsibilities, or it may emerge on its own. Because of their geographic proximity, those in a neighborhood confront common problems, varying from concentrated poverty and heavy traffic to poor schools, street crime, and flooding. Neighborhoods are easiest to organize when those who live there see that they face a common problem and will sustain a loss if the community does not take action. Decisions by government that threaten neighborhoods can also bring neighbors together to resist the onslaught even if they had few prior connections. Bonds quickly form among residents whose homes will be destroyed if the city and state construct a planned highway or neighbors may join in an effort to prevent a local school from closing (Crenshaw & St. John, 1989). A sense of community develops as people respond to such threats.

Community organizing is easier in some neighborhoods than others, but the mere presence of social glue does not necessarily mean that people are willing to be involved. In fact, individuals who are relatively alienated from the community may be more likely to organize than people who are more integrated. As Crenson describes:

> the residents who make these contributions [toward organizing] are often people who exhibit some of the symptoms of the loss of community . . . deliberations about matters of community concern occur in an atmosphere of neighborly tension, not neighborly solidarity. (Crenson, 1983, p. 154)

Probably the easiest neighborhoods to organize are those that already have a reputation for activism and so attract residents who find the sense of community appealing and want a lifestyle of community involvement. The Cedar-Riverside neighborhood in Minneapolis lured in individuals interested in establishing alternative economic and social systems (Stoecker, 1994); the Castro community in San Francisco has been open to people associated with the gay lifestyle. Areas such as the Five Oaks neighborhood in Dayton, Ohio form

> an "ideological community." . . . That is, residents choose the neighborhood in part because of its urbaness and diversity and because they consciously seek a neighborhood that will serve as a community. (Majka & Donnelly, 1988, p. 158)

Such places permit and encourage innovative experiments in organizing.

In contrast to those people who relish the variety of urban life and want to create community that crosses ordinary boundaries, other people move to "gated communities," neighborhoods that are homogeneous (middle or upper class) and intentionally cut off from people who live differently (Blakely & Snyder, 1997). While people in these neighborhoods might have to contribute money to pay for crime patrols and ground crews, this type of mandated participation usually does not bring about the sense of responsibility for the collectivity that constitutes true community.

Neighborhoods as Contested Space

Social and economic interests often vie for control over physical space in neighborhoods (Wright, 1997). The homeless and the extremely poor might occupy territory that is fought over when banking, real estate, or the government want to convert the space into more profitable uses for wealthier people. Ethnic groups contend over the symbolic and material ownership of neighborhood space, sometimes rejecting each other's claims, and battling over whose stores, churches, or social mores should dominate.

In battles to control contested space, banks, developers, and wealthy property owners denigrate the value of inner-city neighborhoods, claiming that such areas are run-down and crime-ridden, worthy only of being demolished and replaced with more expensive and more elegant homes. Organizers have found that people in these targeted neighborhoods are willing to fight back to preserve their communities. As David Hummon describes

> although national culture often stigmatizes such inner-city neighborhoods as not only environmentally but morally deficient, community activists may provide counterclaims that stress the vitality of their local areas. (Hummon, 1990, p. 28)

Neighborhoods are also arenas of social conflict when groups define themselves in terms of the territory they control. Such conflicts may show up as battles between street gangs over turf conflict, or over the use of playgrounds and hanging places such as taverns, or ethnic claims to particular churches, stores and restaurants. Those conflicts may be unusually bitter because they involve identity. Stephen Nathan Haymes describes the vehemence with which African American communities defend their neighborhoods:

> black urban communities resist white supremacists' urban meanings and urban forms by constructing alternative images and representations of place. By doing so, urban blacks construct self-definitions, their making of place is tied to the construction of their identity as blacks. (Haymes, 1995, p. 9)

It is within these (social psychologically constructed) spaces that groups work to define who they are and of what their culture consists. As Haymes continues to explain

> black settlement space is the location from which urban blacks construct alternative experiences of time, space, and interpersonal relationships or community, an alternative culture to that of white supremacist Capitalist patriarchy. (Haymes, 1995, pp. 13–14)

Control of space permits a definition and expression of culture, especially a culture that stands in opposition to dominant groups.

This concern with controlling space is reflected in the ways in which African Americans participate in collective actions. In comparison to other groups, African Americans are less likely to be involved in broader issue–based organizing but are more likely to be active members of neighborhood associations that fight to protect their settlement space (Portney & Berry, 1997, pp. 637, 643).

Neighborhoods, Ethnicity, and Multiculturalism

Though less than in the past, neighborhoods remain the home of *solidarity communities.* Solidarity communities are composed of people in the same racial or ethnic group, who share history, culture, language, or religion. Solidarity ties are usually based on birth. They are a given, not something to be created; however, definitions of who is in and who is out can evolve and may be the subject of controversy. Certain orthodox Hasidic Jews who live together in urban neighborhoods define less religious Jews as not truly of the same faith and, hence, not part of their solidarity community. Slavic groups who were antagonistic to one another in Europe accepted a common cultural identity in the United States as part of their effort to unite to gain political clout (Kornblum, 1974).

Understanding linkages within solidarity communities is important if members of that group are to be mobilized. Cultural pride and ethnic identity provide the social glue that enables people to come together on issues that affect the whole group, whether or not specific individuals in the group are immediately affected. People are likely to give to charities sponsored by their solidarity group, even if the contributors don't foresee that they themselves are likely to need support. Or people of a given ethnic neighborhood may rally when a hurricane devastates their ancestral homeland, collecting food and clothes in local churches. Or those within a solidarity community may band together to support new immigrants from the old country, sponsoring them for jobs and giving them temporary shelter.

Solidarity communities reinforce their connectedness through shared rituals, holidays, festivals, and evocations of a common history. To build organizations within solidarity communities, organizers promote the art, social events, and stories that relate shared historic sufferings of the group to its current members. These stories replay past traumas and humiliations, forced migrations for Native Americans, incarceration in concentration camps for Japanese Americans during World War II, slavery for American Blacks. By sharing these experiences and vulnerabilities, members of the solidarity community rediscover what membership entails and why future collective actions might be required. These historic, mutual experiences can be a cause for pride—we went through all this and survived—as well as a cause for rebellion. Native American organizers build solidarity within the group both by narrating how the mainstream society stole Native American land and then by demanding that government restore traditional hunting, fishing, and land rights, which it had taken away.

By reframing how the past is understood, solidarity groups can turn prior humiliation into a source of pride. One way of doing this is to point out that the group's beliefs contradict those of the oppressing society. Padilla describes the development of an activist Puerto Rican ideology that emphasizes the differences in values from the dominant Caucasian groups:

> An essential feature of this ideology is the rejection of "white definitions" and myths of subordination and their replacement by Puerto Rican definitions. . . . This ideology defines Puerto Ricans as possessing precisely those human qualities in which dominant white America is so morally deficient, and some of the very qualities by which white America defines this subordinate group are transformed from denigration to approbation. (Padilla, 1987, p. 65)

Organizers working in solidarity communities rely on these two ideas, using history of the group to reinforce the solidarity that legitimizes social action and redefining humiliating elements of the history into sources of pride. Such strategies may be sufficient to build an action community if the issue affects primarily the members of one ethnic group, such as demands for compensatory payment for lands or property seized from them. If the neighborhood consists of multiple ethnic groups, however, building a neighborhood organization by emphasizing cultural values of the separate groups can prove problematic.

With the major exceptions of African American neighborhoods and a handful of Hispanic areas (Massey & Denton, 1993), few neighborhoods are racially, ethnically, or culturally homogeneous, at least, much beyond the block level. Miami neighborhoods are often an uneasy mix of different Spanish speaking groups and African Americans. Los Angeles neighborhoods are famous for their variety of residents, including a selection of people from separate Spanish speaking countries, a number of distinct Asian groups, Caucasians, and African Americans (Waldinger & Bozorgmehr, 1996). Older and newer ethnic groups contend for dominance in suburban areas (Horton, 1995), while city neighborhoods must deal with multiple ethnic/cultural groups sharing a common space (Goode & Schneider, 1994).

Both suburban and central city neighborhoods are ports of intake for new immigrant groups from abroad and internal migrants from Puerto Rico. To some extent people from different cultural communities clash with one another. When many languages are spoken in one neighborhood, communications can be difficult; there may be contention about what language should be spoken in stores, government offices, social service agencies, or even by the organizers themselves. Multicultural organizing presents problems that go well beyond the techniques needed for organizing solidarity communities. These issues are discussed later in this chapter.

Economically Deprived Neighborhoods

Of particular interest to progressive organizers are older minority neighborhoods, especially those that have lost many middle- and upper-status individuals who moved to more upscale places. As a result of these migrations, African American (and to a lesser extent Hispanic) neighborhoods have split into three types of residential communities. An increasing number of upper-status African Americans live in racially mixed suburbs. A second group live within primarily poor but not destitute neighborhoods in the central cities. These communities are often stable with rich traditions and developed helping networks. Then there is a third category, neighborhoods of desperate need, *hyperghettos*. A hyperghetto is an African American neighborhood that

> has lost much of its organizational strength—the "pulpit and the press," for instance have virtually collapsed as collective agencies—as it has become increasingly marginal economically; its activities are no longer structured around an internal and relatively autonomous social space that duplicates the institutional structure of the larger society and provides basic minimal resources for social mobility. (Warcquant & Wilson, 1989, p. 15)

Scholars argue about how many neighborhoods actually fit the economic extremes of the hyperghetto model, though all accept that poverty is geographically concentrated.

Organizers working in poor neighborhoods (neighborhoods in which from 20% to over 40% of the inhabitants have incomes at the poverty level or below) must be aware of the overlapping problems that confront people and make organizing difficult. These neighborhoods are characterized by many female-headed households, by deteriorated physical structures, by low levels of education, lack of jobs, and high crime rates (Jargowsky, 1997, pp. 29–110). In addition, individuals living in poor communities are less likely than others to be socially connected to those who have contacts for jobs or services (Tigges, Browne, & Green, 1998). Both social glue and social bridges are missing.

From the perspective of an organizer, areas of extreme poverty present a challenge, as many appear to lack the social infrastructure on which to start to build. Organizers may have to begin their work by emphasizing projects that show the possibilities for bootstrapping by helping to solve immediate problems in a visible way. For instance, community groups that help people own their own homes or start their own businesses increase neighborhood bonds and produce visible signs that change is possible. Where Community Development Corporations (CDCs) have built affordable homes or encouraged residents to be involved in management of apartment buildings and co-ops, poor people develop increased attachment to one another and to the wider neighborhood (Briggs, Mueller, & Sullivan, 1997).

In general, as people see that collective action works to reduce social problems, they increase involvement in local organizations. Success encourages participation that creates social capital which in turn helps solve community problems. For instance, even in the poorest and most crime ridden neighborhoods "collective efficacy, defined as social cohesion among neighbors . . . is linked to reduced violence" (Sampson, Raudenbusch, & Earls, 1997) that comes about through community crime patrols. In addition, social bonds and the power to fight back are strengthened as the organizations that do exist, such as churches, recreational clubs, and business groups, form networks among themselves (Mesch & Schwirian, 1996). By building on whatever social capital is found, organizers help community members identify with and take responsibility for the geographic area and provide a base for involvement later on.

Neighborhoods and Social Capital

The presence of social capital, the stock of social trust, norms, and networks that bind people together, enables individuals to cope with personal emergencies while strengthening the overall community. Social capital includes the obligations people feel toward one another; the informational channels they share; and the way they sanction each other when they fail to respond. When people feel obligated to help one another, a parent can leave a child with a neighbor, if he or she has to rush to the doctors, while people within the neighborhood share information about jobs located elsewhere. Apartment buildings within neighborhoods whose people are linked together by the norms of trust and mutual obligation are seen as more secure (Saegert & Winkel, 1998, p. 47). In general, studies show that neighborhoods with more social capital are less likely to decline economically and socially and "more likely to remain stable over time" (Temkin and Rohe, 1998, pp. 81, 84).

In neighborhoods in which social capital seems inadequate, an early, major goal for the organizing effort is to build bonds between people by creating situations in which people can help one another. In these efforts, skillful organizers don't assume that social capital is absent but instead consider that it remains to be discovered. Organizers work with community activists to find out who associates with whom, and who helps whom. Is there an association of church leaders? Do the pastors, preachers, rabbis, or imams meet on a regular basis to discuss common problems? Do they respond together when something bad happens in the neighborhood, such as a highly visible hate crime? Are the churches, mosques, and synagogues connected to social service agencies? Do they provide social services themselves, such as day care, after school programs, or housing for the homeless? Is there an association of small business people? Do most of the small business owners belong to it? Is there a linkage between the business owners and the schools, so that children can expect employment on graduation? Is there an active parent-teacher organization? Does it meet formally or informally with other governmental agencies that are related to schooling, such as the library board or the parks department? Are there block clubs? Do most blocks have them? Are they active? Do they ever interact with each other, for a big party or for planning or lobbying? Are there political clubs, such as Democratic or Reform party clubs?

What about newspapers or newsletters or local television programs; is there any way that neighbors can find out what is going on in the neighborhood, what block parties are coming up or what street festivals or art shows, what school board meetings?

How do people handle situations in which neighbors in multifamily units create fire hazards? Or how do they handle loud parties or drug transactions that take place out in the open?

Once organizers have a good handle on the level of social capital and where it is strong or weak, they can try any of several strategies to bootstrap from what is present. If there are no block associations, a block party can help neighbors get to know each other and pave the way for more organized activities. If there is no way for residents to discover events or follow news in the neighborhood, a few community members can write and distribute a newsletter. If the clergy never seem to get behind a single project or event, an organizer can suggest that the religious leaders form a plan for how to respond to hate crimes.

With even relatively small amounts of social capital in place, it is easier to organize for some collective problem solving, which in turn facilitates the creation of more social capital. Three specific examples of ways to start organizing in neighborhoods with little social capital are using economic development programs, undertaking faith-based organizing and supporting community building initiatives.

Creating Social Capital through Community-Based Economic Development

Programs.   Community-based economic development programs can be as much about the process of creating social capital as they are about increasing wealth. For example, microenterprise programs are set up to help poor women establish income producing firms, but in doing so they increase the amount of community social capital. As Lisa Servon describes

> microenterprise programs are typically thought of as economic development strategies . . . the community development element—which involves connecting people to each other and to critical organizations—is often over-looked. . . . Microenterprise . . . programs (have) emphasis on relationship building. . . . (Servon, 1998)

Microenterprises contribute directly to the creation of social capital by connecting people to each other and with community institutions. For example, such programs may link poor women with banks or foundations to get startup capital and with community colleges to get training for bookkeeping and other basic business skills. In doing so, these economic development programs help create needed social bridges.

Faith-Base Organizing.   Within many neighborhoods, churches are the repository of place-based social capital, uniting people who share core values. Church members often take on obligations of supporting and helping congregation members (Nash, 1993). Churches from different neighborhoods can be more readily linked to one another than can individuals, creating the social bridges that provide resources to communities in need.

The Industrial Areas Foundation's faith-based model of organizing builds on these ties to create powerful community groups. People who are united by a common faith and set of values, especially values that include helping neighbors, can more easily work together to solve collective problems. Linkages between churches provide economic and political resources that enable those from one neighborhood to help those in another neighborhood achieve social and political goals (Cortes, 1996; Warren, 1998; Wood, 1998).

Community Building Initiatives.   Advocates of Comprehensive Community Building Initiatives (CBI) (Kubisch, 1996; Smock, 1997; Stone, 1996) work to create a sense of community in the poorest neighborhoods. The goal is to create a healthy community that is able to coordinate neighborhood assets to begin a multipronged attack on what ails the area, while recognizing that a single effort is unlikely to solve a complicated set of interdependent problems. Helping teenagers requires better schools, systems of mentoring, linkages to the job market, and recreational opportunities. Poor people need jobs, but they also need affordable housing and are more likely than others to be deprived of adequate medical care.

CBI is built upon eight premises, each of which seeks to strengthen local networks and feelings of mutual obligation. CBI is intended to:

Integrate community development and human service strategies
Forge partnerships through collaboration
Build on community strengths
Start from local conditions
Foster broad community participation
Require racial equity

Value cultural strengths

Support families and children (*www.ncbn.org/about/principle.htm*)

In the CBI model, the social bonds that constitute community are activated by establishing linkages between neighborhood groups, churches, governmental organizations, and a myriad of neighborhood-based social service, housing, and economic development organizations.

Social capital is increased as the different organizations begin to work together, for instance when a housing group assists a job training service to find employment for tenants. Further, each separate organization creates social bridges to economic and knowledge resources outside the neighborhood, by networking to similar organizations throughout the nation. A neighborhood group may be affiliated with the Gamaliel Network, or a CDC may be hooked up to a national organization of housing developers and funders, bringing new knowledge and resources into the community.

An increase in community social capital emerges as social networks link individuals to each other and to organizations and from networks that link organizations to one another. Comprehensive Community Building is about coordinating this process of expanding social capital in ways that change "thinking and practice among all of the actors involved in addressing poverty . . . creating new, more resilient relationships among them" (p. 13, *www.ncbn.org/directry/profile/Boston.html*).

Constructing Community Memberships

At first, it would seem that the structures and membership of a community are visible and obvious to all. City maps or planning documents specify boundaries for labeled neighborhoods; community groups designate in their charters the blocks on which they work. Most solidarity groups have their own criteria for determining who belongs and who doesn't, in terms of descent, surname, membership in a given church, mosque, or synagogue, or a shared history. Just because people live near one another or have a shared history or surname, however, does not mean they consider themselves part of that community. People might live in a legally defined neighborhood and even know one another, but for community to exist, individuals must recognize that they share issues and obligations. Water in the basement is an individual homeowners' problem, until neighbors get together and frame the issue as the unwillingness of the city to reduce flooding.

Constructing Community among Solidarity Groups

By definition people are members of an ascriptive community, regardless of what choices they make. Even in this situation, however, what constitutes a racial, religious, cultural, or ethnic group can differ from time to time and from place to place. Does skin color matter? Is surname important? Is it religious belief or cultural practice that establishes an ethnic community?

Further, even when ascriptive characteristics seem apparent to outsiders—color of skin, gender, surnames—individuals still determine on their own whether to consider themselves as part of a solidarity community. To what extent do people of African descent who came to the United States from Haiti or the Dominican Republic see themselves as part of the same solidarity community as other African Americans? Does someone from Japan identify as an Asian American or as a Japanese American or neither or both? When and in what place? A person is born as a female but chooses whether to be a feminist, and, if so, what feminist beliefs to hold. Why have dozens of Native American groups have come together in the American Indian Movement, while creating unity among Spanish speakers from Mexico, Central America, Puerto Rico, and other Caribbean Islands has proved problematic?

Organizers are usually safe in assuming that people who live near one another are more likely to share problems than those far apart. Similarly, those who label themselves as belonging to a solidarity community—through membership in ethnic or religious organizations, participation in shared holidays, or perhaps even in terms of matters of dress or speech—are more likely to share linkages than are strangers. *Still each generation constructs anew what parts of a shared past to emphasize.* Do African Americans emphasize the experience of slavery or the unrecognized triumphs of the past or both? Is Black culture seen as complementary to, a predecessor of, or separate from White culture? Do American-born Japanese build their identities around a shared culture that emphasizes courtesy, calmness, and loyalty to the group over the individual, values that go back to the old country? Or do they emphasize the abuses of the imprisonment during the Second World War, events that underscore their common history in the United States? Is language something to be fought over as core to the cultural identity, which occurs among some Spanish speaking groups, or is religious practice the defining characteristic of group membership and identity?

Social constructionists argue that the criteria for membership within a solidarity community emerges over time. As individuals prepare for collective actions, they emphasize certain bonds, discount others, and actually invent some new ones. Further, a constructionist view of ethnicity

> stresses the fluid, situational, volitional, and dynamic character of ethnic identification, organization, and action. . . . The construction of ethnicity is an ongoing process that combines the past and the present into building material for new or revitalized identities and groups. (Nagel, 1996, p. 19)

As ethnic groups construct or reconstruct definitions of who they are, certain symbols (either older historic one or those newly invented) become the resources around which organizing takes place. Some of these symbols speak to individuals directly, as does the pride of a past victory, while others play a more instrumental role in the organizing. Places take on symbolic value and as such are used as part of the mobilization process. Ethnic churches, associations, restaurants, and other locales associated with the cultural group serve as meeting places, spots in which information is shared, or places to raise funds to support the organizing effort. A building identified with a group can serve as a symbol of the community, indicating that this is where people who share a common background can come together (Nagel, 1996, p. 26).

By forging new symbols and accentuating the bonds that foster solidarity, the organizing campaign contributes to the creation of community. The African American civil rights movement built on preexisting solidarity bonds, but the terrors of working together in a hostile environment strengthened cultural linkages and by doing so facilitated further organizing (McAdam, 1994). Individuals of Asian descent in the United States worked to create solidarity in their own separate groups—Chinese Americans, Japanese Americans, or Filipino Americans—while at the same time developing an overarching sense of an Asian American identity (Wei, 1993). As the American Indian Movement began to chalk up impressive successes, more people of Native American descent began to identify themselves as Native American when asked by the United States census. This willingness to label oneself as a Native American was partly the result of increased material benefits Native Americans received, but it was also the result of the skillful use by organizers of Native American symbols and ceremonies that created pride among those in the solidarity community. In general, solidarity communities provide a basis for organizing work, but conversely the strengthening of a solidarity community is often what the initial organizing effort is about.

Constructing Communities of Interest

Communities of interest come about when people join together to battle a problem that is shared. Communities of interest can grow into social movements as people join to work for a better environment, accessibility for the disabled, civil rights for minorities, speech rights, gun control, affordable housing, or just about any issue that motivates collective action for change. Communities of interest come about through an intentional process in which issues are constructed in ways that create the bonds that unite people.

Organizers recognize that abstract problems do not provide a base for organizing, if people do not agree about how the issue is to be framed. Issue communities emerge only after people discuss, negotiate, and define for one another the meaning of a problem and then recognize that when defined this way the problem is one that is shared. Those in an issue community need to agree on the causes and solutions of the problem. It is difficult to organize a group to combat poor wages if some people feel that the problem comes about because capitalists exploit laborers, while others feel that workers would earn more if they had better education. Does a solution involve improvement of inner-city schools or working to set up industrial cooperatives in which the workers own the places where they work?

Issue communities emerge as large numbers of people agree on the causes of a problem and collectively accept certain steps toward its solution. This construction of an issue community requires both overt and tacit negotiations among potential activists. Issue communities come about as a product of a *discursive politics* that

> seeks to reinterpret, reformulate, rethink, and rewrite the norms and practices of society and the state. . . . Discursive politics relies heavily, but not exclusively on language.

> Its vehicle is both speech and print—conversations, debate, conferences, essays, stories, newsletters, books. (Katzenstein, 1995, p. 35)

Any particular problem can be viewed in a number of different ways and at different levels of specificity. If an industrial plant is polluting a particular river, killing the fish and threatening water supplies, the problem can be viewed as one of controlling a particular effluent from this plant, or cleaning up this river, or it can be defined in terms of the lack of enforcement of existing laws because of public officials' fears of putting an economic burden on a major industry. Advocates for the wheelchair bound can focus on a number of different aspects of the issue, from discrimination in hiring, to accessible buildings, to changing public attitudes toward people with disabilities. How the problem is defined affects which and how many people might be interested in getting involved and suggests particular solutions.

Communities of interest come about as people develop common *framings*—interpretations and understandings—that enable them to work together in ways that redefine problems not only for themselves but also for the society. These framings within a social movement community create common values that in many ways constitute a shared culture. For instance, those people who came together to demand rights for the hearing disabled

> equat(e) disability with civil rights: to them deafness is not a disability but a culture—like being Jewish, Irish, or Navajo. (Shapiro, 1993, p. 85)

These efforts not only created a framing that drew supporters to the cause and turned what had been viewed as a disability into a source of pride but also suggested strategies and helped change the public's view.

The issues that turn a community of interest into a social movement emerge from debate and discussion that occurs among individuals who identify themselves as being disempowered by the problem. The precise nature of the problem, its causes, consequences on the individual, and the appropriateness of different solutions emerges as a result of ongoing negotiations. These discussions define what the movement is about for its members and for the broader public.

In general, whether mobilizing people within geographic areas, building on solidarity relationships, or forming an issue-based movement, organizers must remember that community is built rather than preexisting. Sometimes the community has to be created from scratch, as when people develop an issue-based community to solve an emerging problem. At other times, social bonds may exist before organizing begins but may need to be redefined or energized to facilitate organizing.

Network Linkages

One way organizers help build community is by reinforcing the interpersonal linkages between people, strengthening the form of social capital called a network. Networks join people in solidarity groups, represent the links between neighbors, and emerge in issue communities, as people discover others who share similar problems.

Social networks are the paths of contact, the connections, between individuals. People may be connected to each other through church groups, parent-teacher organizations, health clubs, or political groups, through friendship, blood, relationships, by being neighbors or coworkers. Networks that support community work come about as a consequence of organizing, especially from linkages formed during previous collective actions during which people forged shared values and learned to trust and help one another. For instance, historically, people decided to be fully committed to the civil rights struggle only after getting support from their immediate social networks (McAdam & Paulsen, 1993). Once engaged in the civil rights' movement, activists met one another and during campaigns often lived together in safe-houses. Through such joint action people set up lasting networks that reinforced their own images as activists and deepened their commitment to the ideology of the cause, in this case bringing about change in a nonviolent fashion (Morris, 1984).

Even loose networks can provide a basis for organizing. In what is termed *liberated networks* (Wellman & Leighton, 1979), indirect connections are made between people that in turn set a basis for collective action on a shared cause. A person may need counseling for a child in trouble and have no knowledge of how to find such assistance. By talking to people at church or in a bowling league, he or she learns about a support group and eventually works with others to improve services for children. Such liberated networks constitute the *social bridges* that enable people to reach out for resources and information not available in their immediate environment.

Liberated networks—those with loose social ties—(Granovetter, 1973) open up a wide world of knowledge beyond peoples' immediate contacts and by linking individuals to others with quite different experiences. Tightly knit groups might lack the knowledge or resources needed to solve problems that are new to all those in the group but can gain such knowledge through these looser connections. For example, MacLeod (1995) compared the success of members of two gangs within a poor community, one that was more tightly linked to neighbors and the other with more social bridges to the outside world. He found that individuals in the gang with better networks to the outside were more likely to succeed at getting jobs or going to college because people outside the gang's immediate world could provide them with needed information that was lacking among their neighbors.

An important step in organizing is in finding preexisting social networks and building on them to create communities of mutual support. Doing so helps people discover that they are not alone and there are others who will help. The knowledge that support can be found gives people courage to become involved in community and social change efforts.

How Social Bonds Can Divide

By building on bonds within existing communities, organizers encourage the social solidarity that facilitates collective actions. This initial effort to get people together bootstraps as people who have joined together on one issue frequently remain part of a continuing network (Mueller, 1994), ready for collective action to solve other problems.

Creating groups that share cultural symbols, however, might inadvertently divide one segment of the population from another. People who come together because of an array of cultural, religious, and historic linkages often become hostile to outsiders. Pride in shared culture may result in denigrating those who are not part of the culture or who do not accept the intense feeling that defines a solidarity community.

Efforts to unite based only on ethnic pride can be antagonistic to a broader goal of creating a multiethnic, multiracial group to combat shared problems. In Chicago, for instance, organizers of White ethnic groups played on shared religious and cultural history to build coalitions to fight crime, end real estate abuses, and demand that government funds be spent in the neighborhoods not just downtown. Yet, the very basis for solidarity, shared ethnic history, also emphasized and accentuated historic Black-White antagonisms (Green, 1988). Similarly, observers have noted that in multicultural communities of different minority groups, the efforts to create ethnic solidarity within each group plays on negative stereotypes one group has of the other and as such divides neighbors from one another (Goode & Schneider, 1994, pp. 209–241).

The very cultural values that define solidarity communities can make it difficult to unite people in broader, issue-based communities. For example, building on shared religious and cultural values, African American churches have united congregants in efforts to renew neighborhoods, support housing development, and, most importantly, provide a home for the civil rights movement. Yet, the values that bind the congregants make it difficult to join with others as part of progressive social change networks. For example, a number of Black churches have taken stands against gay rights (hooks, 1989, p. 123). In a similar matter, the Catholic church–based Campaign for Human Development that has united many people who share religious values to work on causes of economic justice "will not consider projects or organizations which promote or support abortion, euthanasia, the death penalty, or any other affront to human life or dignity" as defined by Catholic church doctrine (Fellner, 1998, p. 21).

In Hispanic communities, the traditional solidarity values that unite coethnics vie with feminist concerns. Cultural values in the Hispanic community emphasize hierarchical control, while feminists emphasize collective decision making. For Hispanic men, politics is separate from the personal, while for the women the political and personal blend together (Hardy-Fanta, 1993, p. 34). Even the understanding of what constitutes political action differs. For the women "politics appears to mean the power to effect change rather than the power over others" (Hardy-Fanta, 1993, p. 30) as it does for the men.

Careful balance is required when building organizations based on solidarity values to assure that doing so does not preclude working with others on broader issues.

Building Community in Multicultural Settings

The multicultural and multiethnic composition of many major cities complicates the problems of building community solidarity. Typically larger cities, and even smaller cities, are now populated with crosscutting arrays of different ethnic and language groups. Further, people labeled by outsiders as belonging to one cultural group may in fact consist of numerous contending subgroups—Asians divide into Chinese, Japanese, Koreans, Filipinos, Vietnamese, Thai, and a few mountain tribes from Southeast Asia (Horton, 1995). Spanish speakers are divided by country of origin, by social class, and by political history. In some cities particular neighborhoods are known for their concentration of gays. Sometimes one group dominates a neighborhood, but groups may mix, sharing neighborhoods or even blocks.

In this setting, tensions are no longer simply those of Black and White, but of African American and Korean, Hispanic and Black, Chinese and Japanese. People of different religious background may struggle to define holiday celebrations in schools. Gays may fight for increased rights while their religiously based opponents with a firm base in a solidarity community try to block their efforts.

Regardless of the ethnicity, language, or traditions of its residents, people who live near each other face problems in common—inadequate transportation, infrequent garbage pick up, a dearth of jobs, or dilapidated school buildings. Building community within "bubbling cauldrons" (Smith & Feagin, 1995) of overlapping ethnic groups is complicated.

One approach to organizing in multicultural, multiethnic neighborhoods is to examine each cultural group carefully for common concerns and efforts that could unite their work (Rivera & Erlich, 1995). Maybe two groups that at first appear antagonistic are concerned that their children gain upward mobility through education and would be willing to work on improvement of the schools. Perhaps two minority groups with very different religions can agree that government should not support any religious symbols at all. Groups that can work with each other on particular projects of common interest may learn to trust each other and later work on broader neighborhood issues.

Another approach is to examine the traditions of each group to find the cultural support for community organizing. For example, Islam has a very strong moral value on helping the poor; that value can be the basis of multicultural work. Some ethnic groups have a strong emphasis on hospitality and helping strangers, even when those strangers are from a different ethnic group. Some groups emphasize mutual aid. Such norms and values can be extended across groups with a little reinterpretation.

While gaps between groups are real and persistent, by paying attention to the mechanics of cultural translation, organizers can help overcome them. Many first generation and newly immigrant people do not speak the same language so multilingual organizers might succeed where those speaking only one language may fail. To help bridge language gaps, interpreters should be available at key organizing meetings in which different language groups are present, not only to assure that the meaning is understood but also as a mark of respect. Similarly, at such meetings, to show respect, organizers should not give priority to one language, such as English.

Language translation is more than a mechanical process because words must not only communicate literal meanings but also must resonate culturally. An English language religious metaphor might be offensive when translated. In addition,

> translation demands more than simply literally transcribing what is being said. In order to transmit the real meaning and invite participation, says Peter Cervantes-Cautschi,

director of the Portland Oregon Workers Organizing Committee, "the critical thing is that the [translator] has to be into the movement. Because if [that person] doesn't really understand what we're trying to accomplish, then they are not going to get it right." (Anner, 1996, p. 162)

Having the words translated is but one part of a broader process of cultural communication. Multicultural groups can work to improve their members' understanding about each others' heritage. One technique is to introduce individuals of different ethnic groups in settings where they can comfortably get to know each other. Another is to challenge bigoted statements. A third approach is to provide educational sessions on each others' background. For example, a Protestant church in Little Rock, Arkansas invited a rabbi to explain to some of the congregation a new statement of faith that was roiling reformed Jews. Another avenue is to organize antiracism campaigns.

Stereotypes that make multicultural organizing difficult can be broken down through direct contact and firsthand information. Mutual respect between groups is increased as people watch those different ethnicities function well in leadership positions. Accordingly, in forming a community group that cuts across ethnic, religious, racial, or other groupings, it is vital to assure that all key groups have members in leadership positions. Not only does each group feel more represented, but other groups get a chance to see that people in other groups are competent and concerned (Anner, 1996, p. 167).

Breaking down stereotypes is useful, but typically few people get involved in such extended cultural education activities (Goode & Schneider, 1994, p. 255). Another approach to organizing across solidarity communities is to shape an issue in a way that simultaneously appeals to different groups (Delgado, 1993; Lee, H., 1996; Lee, N., 1996). Campaigns for multicultural education or improving the schools, advocacy of public support for neighborhood (ethnic) businesses, or efforts to protect new immigrants from sweatshop working conditions of long hours, low pay, and poor light and ventilation are all issues that attract participation from a variety of ethnic and religious groups. Safer neighborhoods, better city services, access to job training and employment are also issues likely to bring people together. As people from different groups work on the same campaigns, multicultural communities gradually emerge.

Visualizing Community

The term *community* refers to a geographic place or an identifiable social group, but most importantly it describes the sense of belonging that people have when they share obligations, support each other, and feel concern for one another. In efforts to mobilize people, organizers rely on knowledge about how community bonds come about and what they accomplish.

Organizers unite people by building upon preexisting community bonds, recognizing that individuals who share a history of collective persecutions or a similarity in religious beliefs, are easier to bring together because of these linkages. In these efforts, though, care is taken to make sure the solidarity bonds that unite some people do not divide one group from another.

Organizers recognize that community bonds are strengthened after people have individually benefited from a group's activities, as people then feel a sense of responsibility to reciprocate and help others in the community. Social solidarity increases after people have worked together to solve a common problem and now feel part of a group. This sense of belonging empowers because it makes people feel they are not alone, that others care and are available to help. Much of the work of organizers that we shall discuss in the next section of this book involves starting this process of creating community solidarity by setting up neighborhood associations, building coalitions of churches, putting out newsletters, and generally enabling people to meet one another and become aware of shared problems.

PART FOUR

Mobilizing and Sustaining Community Activism

Part Four examines why people decide to join community and social-change organizations, how organizers work, and the ways in which collective actions are sustained by building lasting organizations.

Chapter 6 explores the role of the professional organizer in catalyzing social change, while Chapter 7 examines reasons why people join in collective actions and the techniques for encouraging them to do so. People join to fight back after they understand problems they face and discover that the problems can be solved. How to obtain knowledge about community and social problems is described in Chapter 8.

To sustain collective action requires an ongoing organization. Chapter 9 describes how to structure organizations in ways that accomplish ends efficiently and democratically. The goals of democratic organizations are determined at public meetings, while individuals gain the skills and confidence needed to be part of an empowering movement through shared training sessions. Chapter 10 describes a variety of meetings that reinforce peoples' decisions to join in collective action and provide them with the tools to succeed.

6 Organizers

What They Do and How
They Learn To Do It

Help Wanted: An Organizer
Willing to work long and inconvenient hours at less pay than could be earned elsewhere. Must have the patience of Job and a hide thick enough to withstand constant criticism and slow progress. Must be willing to accept the blame for failures. Must not try to claim personal credit for successes. Must be willing to learn new skills while helping others discover how to work together in organizations that bring about social change. Good communication and analytical skills desirable. Being able to articulate a vision of the future and having an empathetic personality a plus.

Organizing involves mobilizing others into action in ways that empower both the individuals involved and their broader community. What part does a professional organizer play in these efforts? What skills and training do organizers require? How are these skills obtained, from whom and where? To what extent is organizing an avocation motivated by a desire to help others and to what extent is it a job requiring material rewards? What sort of person becomes an organizer and why?

Jacqueline Mondros and Scott Wilson define organizers as "the salaried staff of social action organizations . . . the fact that they are employed and remunerated gives them special status within the organization and holds them accountable in special ways" (Mondros & Wilson, 1994, p. 7). In contrast to this workday description, Alinsky portrayed the work of organizers with a rhetorical flourish:

> It is the job of building broad, deep Peoples' Organizations which are all-inclusive of both the people and their many organizations. It is the job of uniting through a common interest which far transcends individual differences, all the institutions and agencies representative of the people. It is the job of building a People's Organization so that people will have faith in themselves and in their fellow men [sic]. It is the job of educating our people so they will be informed to the point of being able to exercise an intelligent critical choice as to what is true and what is false. (Alinsky, 1969, p. 202)

To Ernesto Cortes, a community activist in Texas, organizers are those whose job it is to help build the linkages between people required for collective actions:

> organizing is a fancy word for relationship building. No organizer ever organizes a community. What an organizer does is identify, test out, and develop leadership. And the leadership builds the relationships and the networks and following that does the organizing. (Rogers, 1990, p. 17)

What motivates both the organizer and the group's leadership is an abiding anger at social injustice that the organizer helps turn into a honed political tool (Rogers, 1990, p. 17).

Individual organizers have a spirit, a sense of soul, that motivates the oppressed to fight back. In his work, Cesar Chavez, a successful organizer of migrant farm workers, communicated a spirit of the possible. He preached, *"Si se Puede"* [Yes, it can be done] (del Castillo & Garcia, 1995, p. xiv). Organizers are catalysts, rousing others, and facilitating their collective actions. Organizers empower community members themselves to plan and run campaigns.

People become organizers in a variety of ways. Some begin their work as angry neighborhood residents who knock on doors and call friends and neighbors to come together to rid their neighborhood of prostitutes or fight the city's decision to locate an incinerator nearby or demand that leaky school roofs be repaired. Others become involved because of personal experiences, perhaps as victims of crime or as sufferers from a particular disease that the medical establishment ignores. These individuals educate themselves about the problems they face and then work to motivate others with similar difficulties to take the actions needed to improve their situation.

After reflecting on their own experiences or observing a world of injustice, other individuals are sufficiently angered to want to bring about change and start the effort of learning how to become an organizer. They read books such as this one or study in the community track in social work programs in colleges and universities. Others enroll in training academies for organizers sponsored by Associations of Community Organizations for Reform Now (ACORN), the Organizer Training Center, the Industrial Areas Foundations, or the Midwest Academy. Some learn on the job while being mentored by more experienced organizers from the Center for Community Change or the Gamaliel Institute, national organizations that help teach people the skills required to work in poor neighborhoods.

Many *street level organizers,* those who build organizations controlled by a local membership and that tackle issues that affect a specific geographic or social community, begin their work, often as interns, by responding to advertisements such as the following:

> Community Organizers—Summer Apprenticeship and Permanent Positions Available
>
> General description: Apprenticeships available . . . working at one of three grassroots community organizations—New York ACORN, Mothers on the Move, or the Northwest Bronx Community and Clergy Coalition. These grassroots organizations work to build an organized base of low- and moderate-income residents to fight for social and economic justice on issues such as affordable housing, workfare rights,

parent-led school reform, police accountability, and better neighbor-hood services.

Responsibilities include: Organizing tenant, block, worker, and parent groups on local issues; researching issues and developing strategies for organizing drives; recruiting new members and identifying community leaders; conducting grassroots fundraising drives; participating in weekly classroom discussions and training on skills and policy issues.

Qualifications: Commitment to social and economic justice. Some cam-pus, labor and/or community organizing experience desirable. Good writing skills and computer knowledge helpful. Spanish-speaking help-ful. Salary/benefits: $920/month stipend.

Expect more than 50 hours per week including evenings and some weekends.

Full-time, permanent positions are available at the end of program for successful organizers. Permanent positions range from $17–23,000 plus health benefits.

Such apprenticeships often turn into more permanent jobs paid by churches, neighbor-hood groups, or by social-change organizations. These internships, though, provide exposure to the harsh realities of organizing work in which much hard effort may produce few gains.

Some organizers are employed by *issue networks* that battle for specific causes such as fighting to improve the lot of women, the disabled, minorities, the homeless, displaced workers, or the elderly to bring about civil rights or to pressure for affordable housing. Others work to preserve the environment, reduce armaments, encourage world peace, or advocate for safer foods.

Historically, *union organizing* was considered as a separate path from street level or issue-based organizing. Today, organizers hired by progressive unions work within poor neighborhoods to stem the loss of working class jobs (Simmons, 1994). Organizers who work for unions of service workers, many from poor immigrant communities, join with street-level organizers to battle the neglect that confronts the neighborhoods in which immigrants are forced to live (Needleman, 1998).

Other organizers—*institutional organizers*—work for social service or develop-ment agencies that receive their budgets from mainstream charities or even from the public sector. These agencies help abused women, the mentally handicapped, and the homeless, promote neighborhood economic development, and provide job training. Much of the work of institutional organizers is similar to conventional social service employees; however, in addition to serving their clients, institutional organizers try to encourage those they serve to join together to battle the problems they face. Those employed by women's shelters might work to build an activist group among battered women and rape victims (Ecklein, 1984).

Developmental activists are organizers whose work is in building affordable homes, creating community jobs, and providing needed shopping within poor neighborhoods. Some developmental activists do little more than build homes and stores, an important service but not one that might empower community members. Other developmental activists encourage those who receive better homes or new jobs to get together and work to further improve their community, for instance by setting up an anticrime patrol. Some developmental activists work with women, many recently removed from welfare, to help them become certified day-care providers who provide needed services to neighborhoods that lack affordable day care.

The work of street-level, issue, institutional, and developmental organizers is helped by activists who work as employees in a wide variety of *support organizations.* Individuals employed by support organizations such as the Woodstock Institute in Chicago or the Center for Community Change in Washington, D.C., the Pratt Institute, or the Center for Urban Economic Development in Chicago garner technical information needed by social-change groups. Many who are employed in these support organizations began their own careers as street level or developmental organizers. For example, John Taylor whose career began as a developmental activist in Somerville, MA now runs the National Community Reinvestment Coalition (NCRC), which battles efforts of banks to weaken the Community Reinvestment Act. Similarly, Cushing Dolbeare, a former organizer, founded the National Low Income Housing Coalition that advocates for affordable housing and to protect the homeless.

Individuals who work for support organizations might analyze financial records to learn which banks are redlining poor communities, document the extent of neighborhood poverty and neglect, or examine the changing quality of housing. With the help of support organizations, issue-organizers in San Jose and Chicago successfully battled for the rights of the homeless (Wright, 1997). Some support organizations, such as the National Low Income Housing Coalition, also employ activists who lobby government for the changes that street-level organizers need in their work.

During their careers, organizers often take on a wide variety of jobs. Heather Booth started her career

> in the civil rights and early women's movements. She founded and still serves as president of Midwest Academy, one of the country's leading organizer training centers . . . founded the Citizen Labor Energy Coalition, and was a founder, . . . former president of Citizen Action . . . she served as director of National Mobilization for Choice. (Booth, 1994, p. 8)

A street-level organizer working to improve schools might recognize that problems stem from racial injustice and switch the focus to such concerns; feminists who begin organizing in support of women's reproductive rights might became institutional organizers working to ensure women equal job opportunities.

Many developmental activists began their careers as street organizers and changed their approach after concluding that the poor would gain more power by owning property than simply asking government for help. Support organizations are staffed by former neighborhood activists who want to share their knowledge and experiences beyond the communities in which they began their work. For instance, the National Low Income Housing Coalition hired a person who

> will be working at the coalition as Research Manager. He comes to us from the AFL-CIO, where he worked on corporate shareholder initiatives. . . . The bulk of his work experience has been at ACORN, where he worked for seven years, first as a local organizer . . . and then as Research Director. . . . He has also worked . . . for the

National Congress for Community Economic Development and the Center for Community Change. (e-newsletter NHLIC 2/6/1998)

The variety of career opportunities in organizing is clear from a brief glance at the membership of the National Organizers Alliance (NOA) a professional association of organizers. NOA's steering committee has on it people who have worked as labor organizers and as neighborhood activists, those who fight for gender and sexual preference equality, organizers in Latina causes, several who are employed by training centers, people concerned with tenants' rights, organizers who work to improve the environment, and those concerned about welfare reform and rural poverty.

Tensions do occur among different types of organizers, particularly between those who have become development activists (the social production model) and others engaged in street-level or issue organizing (the social mobilization approach). Very few individuals have personalities that allow them in the morning to yell at a politician and then work on a project spread sheet with the politician's staff later in the same day. The perspectives do seem mutually exclusive.

> The point of organizing is to force the . . . power structure to respond to community demands . . . development is a business that involves carefully collecting the necessary financing, permits, permission, grants and other requirements for building units of housing, businesses, etc. Developers have lunch with bankers and try to show them why the bank should get involved in affordable housing. Organizers storm into bank offices with angry protesters demanding that bank officers take immediate action. It's hard to imagine doing both at the same time. (Anner & Vogel, 1997, p. 3)

Yet, in practice both approaches are important, each empowering people in separate ways. Street-level and issue organizers force those in power to pay attention, while developmental activists enable ordinary people to take more permanent control of the changes that have been made.

Sketches of Organizing Work

The daily work of organizers differs greatly, but all contribute to the broader task of social change. In the early civil rights era in the South, Septima Clark, a person who grew up in the deep south, worked behind the scenes to organize citizenship schools that gave people the confidence to try to battle Jim Crow. Though her work was vital for the civil rights movement, she received little public acclaim. By contrast, Martin Luther King, Jr. became an international figure.

A generation ago everyone knew of Saul Alinsky who wrote two major books on organizing, founded the Industrial Areas Foundation (IAF) to train many others, organized the Back of the Yards in Chicago, and helped set up the Woodlawn Organization in Chicago and worked with Ed Chambers to set up Freedom, Integration, God, Honor, Today (FIGHT) to combat racial discrimination in Rochester. Today the Alinsky approach to organizing is carried out on a daily basis by people such as Hugo Rojas who work in virtual anonymity to organize people in Chicago's poorer areas to demand fair services. Mr. Rojas tries to do his work so that others obtain the credit, while in the past when Saul Alinsky arrived in a community the newspapers bannered his stay.

Organizers differ in how they relate to government and business. A number of years ago, Stokely Charmichael rallied many young Black people and created fear among the power structure with his cries for "Black Power" that were heard as a direct threat to government and businesses. Today, another organizer, Mike Eichler, works behind the scenes to encourage community members to build community groups that work hand in glove with businesses, foundations, and government to restore neighborhoods. Some organizers in ACORN picket financial institutions and have been cited for contempt of Congress; other individuals also working for ACORN rely on federal housing programs and banks to obtain the funds to provide shelter for the poor.

Though many organizers receive formal training, others teach themselves through their work in confronting the problems their communities face. Lois Gibbs had been working as a housewife when she became aware of the illness caused by the pollution in Loves Canal from the dumping by Hooker Chemical Company. She organized her neighbors by going door to door to form Loves Canal Homeowners Association, got technical help from sympathetic academics, and eventually pressured both government and industry to obtain compensation for the community for the harm done by the polluting firms. Larry Kramer moved from being a social service activist working with victims of autoimmune deficiency syndrome (AIDS), to teaching himself and others the militant and confrontational tactics required to make an issue salient to those in power. The result of his work was the formation of AIDS Coalition to Unleash Power (ACTUP), a social change organization that has dramatically pressured government to help AIDS victims (Foreman, 1995).

Much of organizing is undertaken by *ordinary people* who no longer are willing to put up with problems they face. The historian Charles M. Payne described how many African Americans living in the most racist areas of the South quietly and carefully went from neighbor to neighbor to set up the networks that supported the civil rights fights of the 1960s (Payne, 1995). These local people—merchants in the African American community, household workers in White homes, some rural farmers, African Americans working in the post office—joined with Black college students to overturn century-old injustices (Dittmer, 1994; Payne, 1995). Ordinary people successfully organized and changed the nation.

In *A Life in the Struggle: Ivory Perry and the Culture of Oppression,* George Lipsitz (1995) described how by fighting back against adverse circumstances he and other minorities faced, Ivory Perry, a poor African American, empowered himself and those with whom he worked. As an activist, Perry took actions that were courageous and often dangerous—facing brutality in the civil rights' drive in the South or blocking traffic with his body in St. Louis. He went door to door to increase Black power in the South, to fight poverty in St. Louis, to combat unjust landlords and to agitate against lead-based paint, which was poisoning children. Often, he worked on his own, at other times with Black social-change organizations, and for a while, during the War-on-Poverty era, was an employee of a poverty agency. His actions, though, were usually behind the scenes, as a friend described:

The interesting thing about Ivory Perry was that he didn't shoot for the limelight. You'd always see him in a secondary role getting the job done. Ivory was always there, and I always understood that, well, this guy's legitimate. He's there because there's a mission to be accomplished and he's not hogging the headlines. (Lipsitz, 1988, p. 74)

Social change comes about through the work of ordinary people and thousands of unheralded organizers, who spend years to bring about needed improvements. For example, the Dudley Street Neighborhood Initiative (DSNI) rebuilt a neighborhood the city had abandoned. Through direct actions the group stopped arsonists from burning apartments and eliminated illegal garbage dumping. The DSNI has received much publicity, including a movie, *Holding Ground* (New Day Films). These accomplishments required thousands of hours of work by ordinary community members. Individuals such as Adalberto Teixera first canvassed the Dudley Street community, that is, went door to door, to discover what problems people shared. Then he helped to arrange community meetings, encouraging people to attend by distributing flyers and continuing to knock on doors (Medoff & Sklar, 1994).

Most of the organizers' time is spent on routine activity, with much failure and fatigue and little public glory. Organizing involves knocking on dozens of doors, handing out flyers, chatting with people, only to discover that few are willing to show up at a meeting. At times organizers find that they spend so much time raising money that there is little left over for doing community work.

For instance, a typical day for a street-level organizer, Gabriel Gonzales, began late in the morning (because he had been at a meeting the previous night). Gonzales first scanned the newspapers for stories about his neighborhood and about actions of local government that would affect his community. While checking with his office to assure that thousands of flyers announcing a meeting had been distributed, he received a call from a city council member. He told the council member to call an elected board member of the organization, since he, Gonzales, was simply an employee of the community group.

Gonzales spent the afternoon with the board members planning what to schedule at a major community meeting and then phoned several allies in other community groups to work out a strategy to pressure a recalcitrant public agency to provide a needed service. He took some time to teach interns how to strategize for a direct action against a public office. Gonzales then spent a frustrating hour locating a key for a public hall that had been loaned to the group for a meeting. The day ended with a community workshop discussing what to do about overcrowded public schools.

A developmental activist, Bob Brehm, described the kinds of things he routinely does. Much of his work is in making sure funds are on hand to pay for needed projects. He sometimes works with the board of a cooperative apartment set up by the community group, to plan how to battle encroaching gentrifiers. He spends a lot of his time negotiating with bankers about loans needed for community work. He has to check every day to see that physical construction of the group's projects is on schedule and deal with any delays or emergencies.

Direct action organizers who challenge the system with demonstrations or civil disobedience experience excitement or even terror in their work. They often risk being beaten or even killed; however, even these individuals are mostly involved with routine activities. During the civil rights campaigns, for example, organizers from the Student Nonviolent Coordinating Committee (SNCC) spent much of their time canvassing house to house, encouraging people to register to vote. They set up schools to teach people how to register, established a speaker's bureau, spent meetings planning how to deal with arrest and what to do once they were in jail. They chatted with people informally in coffee shops and barber shops to learn their fears and gain their confidence (Payne, 1995, pp. 244 ff). Bob Zellner, one of the early SNCC organizers,

> once compared organizing to a juggling act—how many plates can you keep spinning at once? Organizers had to be morale boosters, teachers, welfare agents, transportation coordinators, canvassers, public speakers, negotiators, lawyers, all the while communicating with people ranging from illiterate sharecroppers to well-off professionals and while enduring harassment from the agents of the law and listening with one ear for the threats of violence. Exciting days and major victories are rare. Progress is a few dollars raised, a few more people coming to pay poll tax. (Payne, 1995, p. 246)

Much of the organizing occurs behind the scenes, and most organizers remain unknown. Still, a few organizers earn recognition as public heroes. Through the publicity they receive such well-known activists as Martin Luther King, Jr., Ernesto Cortez, or Saul Alinksy call attention to an issue and by doing so rally thousands of supporters to the cause. These *symbolic organizers* help give shape to what people understand are the issues at stake, especially through dramatic and visible events, such as Martin Luther King, Jr. being carted off to jail in Birmingham, Alabama in the fight for civil rights or Cesar Chavez fasting during the effort to unionize farm workers.

The Skills and Roles of the Organizer

An organizer is partly an agitator, administrator, propagandist, bookkeeper, solicitor of funds, assuager of hurt feelings, public speaker, backroom negotiator, and, in many cases, general handy person. In the morning, an organizer listens to the problems community members face, in the afternoon desperately tries to reconcile the increasing expenses of the organization with an uncertain funding base, and at night canvasses to increase the organization's membership. Organizers need technical skills to raise funds, run meetings and conferences, bring law suits, do action research, and deal with the press, among many other items. Through their ability to frame action issues, organizers give voice and image to what social change efforts are about.

In addition, organizers must know how to build unity in communities, to calm hurt egos when tensions are high, to bridge differences between committed volunteers, and to reassure members when failures occur. As Mondros and Wilson argue "perhaps the most difficult task of an organizer is to orchestrate relationships among leaders and members when there is internal conflict" (Mondros and Wilson, 1994, p. 92). Organizations divided by endless interpersonal tensions self-destruct.

Interpersonal skills involve more than the ability to assuage hurt egos. Organizers must be able to listen to and understand what others have to say and then figure out which issues are really important and how willing people are to join and work together. To learn what people think, organizers canvass the neighborhood, going door to door and listen to complaints and suggestions. Organizers set up meetings during which community members share their ideas, concerns, and sometimes their anger.

An organizer must be empathetic enough to encourage people to talk openly and honestly and skilled enough to be able to hear not only what is said but also what is meant. Are people really concerned about that stop sign or is the complaint about the sign just another way of saying that nobody cares about the neighborhood? When people disagree on what issue to tackle first, how much is that disagreement on the substance of the matter, how much is a battle of egos on whose ideas will prevail? Are people speaking openly and plainly, or is courtesy covering up racial, gender, or ethnic animosities that are the real issues?

Such empathetic listening skills are especially vital in working in multicultural environments and in those in which gendered issues are central (Bradshaw et al., 1994; Gutierrez et al., 1996; Rivera & Erlich, 1995). Organizers must learn that people with different cultural backgrounds, and males and females convey information in different ways. People from some groups tend to speak indirectly, taking awhile before coming to the main concern; others may be very direct and approach the subject quickly. Women often communicate information more indirectly than do men. An organizer may have to become a *cultural broker* who not only understands what people from what different backgrounds are trying to get across but who can also communicate these insights to others.

In general, organizers play four complementary roles. As catalysts, they stimulate others to take action on problems; as teachers, organizers work with people to help them develop capacity to solve their own problems; as facilitators, they provide information and handle many of the important routine tasks of the organization; and, as linking people, organizers seek out information, allies, and technical knowledge from outsider supporters while working to create linkages within the community.

Organizers as Catalysts.   Organizers *catalyze* others into action by canvassing and arranging meetings that allow people to share problems and concerns. At such meetings, organizers help participants understand how to battle a sense of disempowerment through collective political action. As catalysts organizers show the possibility of change by communicating how others have succeeded (Fisher & Kling, 1994) and build confidence by suggesting ways the present group can proceed.

Organizers work with *local leaders* but play a different role. Local leaders are long-time community members, who know many people in the neighborhood, are familiar with community problems, but lack hours in the day or the technical skills needed to do the myriad of tasks that organizers undertake. Over time, organizers do communicate these skills to the local leaders, hoping to work themselves out of a job, keeping in mind as they do so the advice provided by Ernesto Cortez of the IAF:

> You see, there's an Iron Rule in organizing. It is a little different from the Golden Rule. The Iron Rule says: *Never, ever, do for people* what they can do for themselves. And, it is a very difficult rule to follow. (Rogers, 1990, p. 15)

As a catalyst, the professional organizer releases the power that is already there among the local leaders. As civil rights organizers explained "in many cases, SNCC did not so much develop leadership as remove barriers, so that leadership that was already there might emerge" (Payne, 1995, p. 194).

Organizers as Teachers.   Organizers are teachers who help others learn how to do a wide variety of tasks—how to contact politicians, to lobby with them, deal with the press, or prepare and implement a budget. As mentoring teachers, organizers guide others in a gentle and nonauthoritarian manner that encourages people to reflect about relevant issues, "What do you think might happen if we did that?" "How many people do you think it would take to do that task?" The goal of the organizer as teacher is to help organizational members develop the abilities to ask themselves needed questions.

Organizers are not the teachers who stand in front of a classroom spouting facts or theories assuming that the students are ignorant. Instead, the role of this type of teacher is to make people feel comfortable sharing their experiences by asking the questions to which members can relate. Organizers listen and summarize the answers in ways that others can understand. Organizers structure discussions in ways that allow each person a chance to air his or her opinions and do not allow the meetings to run on endlessly, wasting everyone's times. Organizers teach through example and share their own experiences to show possibilities for success and to lay out a variety of options that other groups have tried.

Part of this type of teaching is to put tools into easy reach and show people how to use them; this is what capacity building is about. Rather than the organizer scouting a site for a protest, he or she should teach others what to look for and have them accomplish the task. Organizers teach community members what a valuable tool the Internet is for action research but have organizational members do the work to find the addresses of corporate leaders whose companies are polluting the area or look for statistics on illness, to see if the rate of disease in the neighborhood is higher than typical.

Like the best teachers, organizers encourage people to follow up their own ideas even if these are not the ideas the organizers would have chosen. If success occurs, people feel empowered, while if failures happen, the organizer helps them learn from their mistakes. An organizer is there to make sure the thrown rider gets back on the horse and tries again.

Organizers as Facilitators.   Organization members often have good ideas for action campaigns or for social production projects, but nothing happens because of lack of time, money, or knowledge. As a facilitator, an organizer provides follow through, helping to raise funds and carry out routine tasks.

As staff members, organizers often do the less glamorous tasks involved in running an organization, carrying out an action, or building a project. Facilitators make sure that the halls are rented for the mass meetings, or double check the schedules of the politicians to assure that when the membership arrives the politicians are present. They take the time to figure out how to fill out loan applications for home repairs and mortgages and then teach others how to do it. Facilitators keep abreast of news stories, read technical publications about community projects, and follow the vagaries of local politics.

Some of facilitator's tasks are mundane; anyone can do them, but people rarely have the time. Someone has to arrive at a meeting early to set up chairs in their proper place. Other tasks require some technical knowledge and concern for detail: making sure an audit is done and appropriate reports are sent to foundations or government organizations that might provide funding for the group. While part of the teaching role of the organizer is to help people learn to do these tasks, many fall on the shoulders of the facilitator who is paid to handle such daily details. Without the concern for administrative detail that a facilitator can provide many collective efforts might end in failure.

Organizers in a Linking Role.   Part of the role of organizers is to link their organizations to the wider world. When organizers attend conferences sponsored by foundations or support groups, they bring back new program ideas, knowledge on how to pay for activities, and information on how to accomplish tasks. The initial contacts for coalition building typically come about as organizers undertake their linking roles. Organizers from different groups often meet together, share ideas, or plan joint strategies that are then discussed with the organizational membership.

Organizers also link their organizations to the outside world through contacts with the press, though the official spokesperson for the organization should be a local leader. The organizer discovers which reporters are most likely to be sympathetic to the cause. While organizers might answer background questions posed by the media, simply because he or she is around the office more than elected leaders, major questions should be referred to the elected board to emphasize to the media that the organization is owned by its members not by its staff.

Framing What Should Be and Can Be Done

The roles of catalyst, teacher, facilitator, and linking person describe what organizers do on a daily basis and point out what is to be avoided—taking charge, bossing others, or acting as a know-it-all. In addition, organizers carry out another set of activities that help frame for the members and the public what the group is about. In their guise as *organic intellectuals* and as *symbolic leaders,* organizers help interpret past experience, articulating what is possible and why it is necessary to fight back.

Organic Intellectuals

Successful organizers have taught themselves how to learn from experiences and then share with others what they have discovered. Many organizers have worked out an *organic theory,* based on reflection on their experiences and that of their organizations, that explains to themselves and others what should be done, what has worked, and why. These activists have become what the Marxist intellectual Antonio Gramsci termed *organic intellectuals.* An

organic intellectual [is] a manipulator of signs and symbols, an educator and an agitator rationally translating the needs and aspirations of [the] community into effective action. . . . In order to succeed, organic intellectuals rely on collective memory—shared experiences and perceptions about the past that legitimate action in the present—and on social learning—experiences with contestation in the present that transform values and goals for the future. (Lipsitz, 1988, p. 228)

As organic intellectuals, organizers build on experiential knowledge to shape future action.

Rather than rely on book learning, organic intellectuals have taught themselves to analyze the situations they face and from such reflection work out what actions should be taken. Their understanding grows from contact with the oppressed, not from academic theories. Dr. King's organizing skills grew as he learned how people responded during the rapidly changing events of the Montgomery bus boycott, building from the real world events a model for collective action.

Some of what organic theorists learn is about ordinary matters that motivate people to join together. From hearing about the experiences poor people face when applying for social welfare benefits, organizers learn of the power of humiliation to motivate collective response. A developmental activist explained to Herbert Rubin how he learned about problems people faced when they were refused mortgages or denied loans for housing repair.

> I didn't get [this knowledge] out of no book, I got it out of the streets.
> I got [what] was a real problem, I listened to the people, I was there
> holding their hands. I know what the problems are.

From their daily encounters organic intellectuals learn what will motivate people to join in the fight and discover the tools needed to succeed. For example, Cathy Hinds was upset when doctors and public authorities could not answer questions about her children's bad reactions to local water. She discovered that such problems were shared by her neighbors, and she then taught herself how to get water analyzed. With this knowledge in hand, Ms. Hinds was able to organize her neighbors and pressure government to act until the homes of victims of the poisoning were purchased and the site was designated for clean up (Garland, 1988).

Organizers as Symbolic Leaders

Organizers can become symbolic leaders for the broader cause, helping people frame the issue so that it can be communicated to others. Symbolic leaders speak in ways that shape and frame how people understand the issues at hand. Their voices carry to those who are fighting back and to those in positions of power.

Martin Luther King, Jr., for instance, gave voice to the sufferings of African Americans in moving and eloquent language; the "I Have a Dream Speech" has become part of American cultural lore. Local organizers carry out this important role of symbolizing the need for change. Mrs. Fannie Lou Hamer was a symbolic organizer who gave voice to collective suffering:

> Immediately, an electric atmosphere suffused the entire church. Men and women alike
> began to stand up, to call out her name, and to urge her on. . . . She went on to speak
> about the moral evil of racism itself and the grievous harm it was doing to the souls of

white people in Mississippi. . . . She did not do so in accusation, but with a kind of redemptive reconciliation, articulating a vision of justice that embraced everyone. She ended up leading the assembly in chorus after chorus of a rousing old Negro spiritual. . . . When she finished, the entire assembly was deeply shaken emotionally. People crowded around her to promise they would join the struggle. (Conversation with Robert Jackall reported in Payne, 1995, p. 242)

Through their actions, symbolic leaders can shape the definition of problems and solutions, as understood by those within the organization and outsiders. Cesar Chavez became a symbolic leader in his acceptance of arrest and in his hunger strikes. Dr. Martin Luther King, Jr., by accepting jailing in a dignified matter, redefined jailing from a situation of humiliation to one of pride (Branch, 1988) and provided a model that others emulated. For instance, civil rights activist Ivory Perry argued:

If he could be picked up and jailed for a crime he did not commit, he might as well go to jail for a cause. In that way he could turn an indignity into a badge of honor, transforming incarceration from a random blow of fate into a conscious strategy to undermine the power of those seeking to intimidate him. (Lipsky, 1988, p. 80)

When organizers act as symbolic leaders, they draw on their own experiences and what they have learned from others to shape a political language that communicates the need for change. Symbolic leaders collect the humiliations and disempowerments of the oppressed and transform these stories into motivation for collective action. They express the problems and solutions in a way that explains to the broader society why change is necessary. In general,

Symbolic leaders give voice and image where there was noise; they define humiliation as a collective experience and transform that experience into political energy for change.

Because symbolic leaders and organizers can be seen as embodiments of the values of the organization, they must reflect on their own behavior and values, to assure that the image they communicate is appropriate. As such organizers have to live their values in a visible way, which means that those values have to be deeply and sincerely felt. Organizers must not forget they are always on display, which means even in their leisure time, they have to avoid playing status games, acting as if they were bosses, showing favoritism, or ignoring important cultural values. Charles Payne, for instance, points out, how the courageous civil rights workers from the North lost support because their sexual behaviors were not compatible with those in the conservative South (Payne, 1995).

Values, Theories, Ideologies, and Models

An organizer should not try to impose his or her beliefs on community members. Doing so belies the very philosophy of empowerment. As a consequence, in the past, some schools of thought about organizing argued that the professional organizer should be a neutral professional, accomplishing a variety of assigned tasks without advocating a specific set of values or theories. Nowadays few agree with this.

Instead of pretending ideology does not exist, organizers must be aware of their values and implicit ideologies and those among the members of the organization. Even Saul Alinsky, who argued that community organizations should concentrate on the immediate obstacles that face people, still claimed that successful organizing required an understanding of the broader socioeconomic forces that created local problems (Horwitt, 1989, p. 108). Mondros and Wilson (1994, p. 14) point out that people become organizers to achieve the values they cherish, while Fisher has more boldly stated that "organizing must create a more consciously ideological practice" (Fisher, 1994, p. 228).

As teachers, organizers work with those in community and social change groups to reflect on (a) why problems occur; (b) whether the proposed solutions accomplish broader ends; and (c) whether the means of achieving these ends are consistent with the values to be achieved. Such reflections point out why certain actions are needed and how best to carry them out.

For instance, the organization might picket city hall to pressure for the resources needed to build a new school to alleviate crowding. But in taking time to reflect on why the organization had to rely on direct action, community members collectively discover that the system is biased against the poor. Through such reflections, organization members may then move from the specific problems of the school overcrowding to other problems that affect them as poor people, or even further, begin to better understand the importance of undoing broad inequalities in political power.

Once a group has begun to think about the broader goals of organizing, organizers can help direct attention to how well the organization's means and methods of operation match with these broader goals. For example, are women's ideas given less respectful attention in planning for community actions, indicating an underlying sexism? To what extent does the ethnic or racial origin of activists affect the positions they take in the action organization? Is the organization reproducing the same disempowering mechanisms as the broader society, requiring members to agree or get out? What steps has the organization taken to assure that decisions are made by the whole group, rather than a narrow group of activists?

Organizers should not impose a set of values on the organizations with which they work. Still, part of their responsibility is to help people discover from their own experiences the values and implicit ideologies that guide the actions that are taken. Organizers need to not only assure that they themselves exemplify these broader values but also assure that members are conscious of their overall goals and do not adopt means that contradict their own values.

Learning to Be an Organizer

Real world experience, with its successes and failures, is the primary teaching tool through which reflective organizers build their skills. To go beyond their own experiences, however, organizers sometimes attend training centers or take courses in the community tracks of social work programs, either to get a broad base in the field or to obtain knowledge on how to handle specific problems.

The programs at organizer training centers tend to be narrowly focused, to cover specific skills or opportunities in a short period of time, often a week or less. Topics covered might include fund raising or relationship with board members or implications of a new tax law for housing projects. Programs in social work schools often last several years, allowing time to reflect more on issues of history, urban affairs, government, and technical aspects of organizational administration. Organizer training centers and schools of social work often are structured to carry out different models of practice, ranging from those that teach militant approaches to those that advocate consensual, social production activities.

Organizer Training Centers

Some organizer training centers are associated with the separate networks of community organizations that, in turn, carry out different approaches to community work. For example, the Center for Community Change provides training that focuses on the work organizers do in very low income communities. The Center for Third World Organizing runs programs to help people of color and to promote multicultural organizing, while the Consensus Organizing Institute teaches how community groups can work with government and businesses.

Many training centers are associated with activist organizations that later employ those trained. Pacific Institute for Community Organizing (PICO), for example, helps organizers gain experience and then helps them obtain work in a wide variety of community action efforts (O'Brien, 1994). The National Training and Information Center (NTIC), teaches people direct action techniques that are most appropriate for the work done by organizations affiliated with Neighborhood Peoples' Action (NPA). The IAF trains a professional cadre of skilled organizers who while employed by the IAF are indirectly paid by funds raised in the communities in which they work (Delgado, 1994, pp. 87–93).

Training programs differ widely, from short, focused courses that teach one or two technical procedures, to more philosophical approaches that explore what community work is all about; some programs provide both. The Center for Third World Organizing's Saturday School for leaders "offers a wide variety of Bay Area organizations the opportunity to interact in a five-week training session that offers both skills and opportunities to examine issues through a lens of race, class, and gender" (Delgado, 1994, p. 72), while the IAF program for leaders has "training sessions [that] offer local leaders an introduction to community development, organizational structure, and community power, as well as some of the techniques of skills for effective leadership" (Reitzes & Reitzes, 1987, p. 101). Much of the IAF training is on how to build relationships between community members and between different groups in the community. Thousands of organizers have taken the five-day courses offered by the Midwest Academy that include technical issues such as recruitment of members, issue selection, investigative research, and grassroots fund-raising, as well as general background on the purpose of community organizing, the dynamics of power, and coalition building (Reitzes & Reitzes, 1987, p. 154).

Training academies teach different philosophies of organizing. Some concentrate on training local leaders rather than professional staff, fearing that highly trained organizers will find it difficult to act in a democratic, consensual way. Programs differ in their emphasis on confrontation or consensus, though the emphasis has evolved over time. Initially, IAF encouraged organizers to carry out the Alinsky model of direct confrontation tempered by humor. Today, IAF's approach has been toned down to emphasize the importance of building on shared values and compromising with those in power (Fisher, 1994, pp. 192–196). By contrast ACORN is still committed to a "radical ideology and confrontational tactics" (Fisher, 1994, p. 197). Similarly, the training provided by the Midwest Academy assumes that organizers will be involved in direct action campaigns (Bobo et al., 1991).

Recently Michael Eichler, a developmental activist, set up a training institute in consensual organizing, in which organizers are taught how to bring community groups, businesses, and government officials together to participate in programs to physically renew poor communities.

As one interviewee reported to Herbert Rubin,

> What Mike Eichler is doing, is he's figured out how to organize around consensus as opposed, I would suggest, to Alinsky's adversarial organizing. . . . What Mike does is he goes into a situation and he says, "We need to have some very, very clear incentives here that people can understand will be available to reward their hard work." . . . he really begins to take people through understanding of how everyone within a community can really be part of the development of the transformation of that community.

Schools of Social Work

The training received at each organizing center is of excellent quality, but it is of necessity brief and often concentrates on the immediate and practical. In addition, each center usually teaches only one of the many possible models of organizing work. For those who want a broader perspective examining a variety of orientations to community organizing, studies in the community track of social work schools may be more effective.

Models taught in schools of social work vary from social planning, in which community members collectively suggest what should be done to improve their neighborhoods, to professionally trained city employees, to political and social action models in which people take charge themselves (Weil, 1996). Programs range from those that emphasize ways of raising peoples' awareness of common problems and willingness to fight back to those that emphasize the mechanics of social administration (Weil, 1996, pp. 42–44). All these different points of view are reflected in the *Journal of Community Practice,* a publication put out by the Association for Community Organization and Social Administration (ACOSA) whose members are teachers of the community approach in schools of social work.

The extended curriculum in schools of social work allows time to reflect on core goals of organizing and to master complicated technical skills. Course work often includes studying social and economic problems that affect community work, the mechanics of keeping a social change organization alive, and the history of organizing. Such programs introduce future organizers to the heroes of the field and lead them to understand that they are going to be part of a proud and successful tradition.

Schools of social work can help future organizers develop the cultural awareness necessary for successful community work. Internships and class projects expose students, many of whom come from the more economically fortunate groups, to those who suffer disempowerment from poverty, discrimination, age, or disabilities. Skillful teaching helps students reflect on their experiences and develop the ability to form their own theories of community work that will improve subsequent practice.

In recent years, two important concerns have entered into the community organizing curricula in schools of social work. The first, a feminist perspective, emphasizes the importance of not simply bringing about change but paying attention to how the change is to be accomplished (Hyde, 1996). Feminist practice

> includes humanistic qualities such as caring and nurturance, coupled with the use of democratic processes and structures. . . . the feminist organizing perspective is concerned with fundamental cultural and political change—the elimination of patriarchy. (Hyde, 1996, p. 130)

The second recent emphasis has been on teaching organizers how to work in multicultural environments. The goal is for students to learn how to work with people from different cultures while at the same time encouraging those from different cultures to work together on shared problems (Bradshaw, 1994; Rivera & Erlich, 1995).

Organizer training centers and schools of social work, as well as the school of hard knocks, all contribute to the ongoing education of organizers. Whether or not an organizer gets formal training, however, learning is a lifelong effort. The problems that people face keep changing, government programs and funding sources evolve, and philosophies of organizing differ over time. Organizers need to keep listening and reflecting about what can and should be done.

Organizing is Both a Calling and a Career

Many people begin their organizing work because of an impassioned response to fight a social injustice, a "cold anger" in Cesar Chavez's terms. Others become organizers because they are moved by deeply held religious or social convictions, a vision of what can be and should be. For such people, organizing is an avocation, work done out of dedication and concern. The rewards for these individuals come from the intrinsic value of what they are doing.

With the hours long, the pay moderate, and success never sure, people don't simply choose to be organizers by sitting down in a career counselor's office and discussing the possibilities. Still for those who are planning a career in the organizing world, there are many practical questions.

First among them is, where are the jobs? How do you get them? Many begin their organizing career as volunteers or interns working for a specific cause about which they care deeply and by finding funding from the community, foundations, or even government, eventually turning their efforts into a full-time career. People who attend training centers or schools of social work are often placed in internships that can lead to a full job as an organizer. Once involved in a community or action organization, as a volunteer or intern, new organizers find future employment through networking among activists working in sister organizations who discover the need for more full-time organizers.

With experience or training in hand, organizers looking for work respond to job ads. The National Organizing Alliance gathers information about potential jobs and circulates it in news bulletins and electronically. Magazines, journals, and newsletters that support social-change efforts often carry job advertisements. For neighborhood and urban issue organizing, community-oriented magazines such as *City Limits* are places to look, while for development activists the advertisements in the publications put out by the National Congress for Community Economic Development provide a start. Job information can be found on sites on the world wide web. By pointing a web browser at *www.nonprofjobs.org,* an organizer can find a data bank of work in the nonprofit world categorized by skills and types of positions. Still, the most likely route for gaining a job is through volunteer work or an internship in one organization that opens the networks to the broader world of community action.

An examination of the advertisements for the field shows a wide variety of skills and backgrounds that are needed and acceptable, as well as starting salaries in the $20,000 to $30,000 range. Many positions include health benefits. For those with a college education, backgrounds in sociology, social work, planning, and political science are appropriate. Law and business are also appropriate training for some kinds of organizing work.

Job descriptions emphasize the variety of skills and experiences required. As an instance, one advertisement for a street-level organizer described:

> newly formed organization of homeless families and advocates seeks Lead Community Organizer. The Lead Organizer will be the primary staff person responsible for organizing families in Trenton who are homeless, formerly homeless, or at-risk of homelessness. The organizer will play a key role working to empower families living in poverty to: identify issues of concern, develop realistic strategies for addressing identified issues, and take effective action to realize change. Qualifications include: 3–5 years successful community organizing experience, preferably with people who have been homeless or who are at risk of homelessness; leadership development skills, and good written and verbal communication skills. . . . Some evening and weekend work required.

Other advertisements mention skills such as "good at working with and motivating people"; "competent with word processing software"; "fluent in Spanish and English";

"able to prepare an operating budget"; "successful fund raiser"; "knowledgeable about public/private sector funding programs"; and "experienced in nonprofit management."

Such advertisements cover many types of positions. A set of advertisements in a NOA publication were for union organizers, those who can teach popular education, tenants' organizers, and one or two positions for activists to promote cultural pride among different ethnic groups. Many NOA advertisements were for grassroots, neighborhood work.

> Californians for Justice, a grassroots organization working to build power in communities of color and among young and poor people of all colors. . . . Responsibilities include developing, coordinating, and implementing grassroots organizing efforts . . . training and supervising . . . organizing staff, building relationships with allied organizations, recruiting members and volunteers, grassroots funding-raising . . .

Developmental activists find positions by examining a different set of magazines or trade association bulletins that focus on jobs in redevelopment work. Often these positions are termed "executive directors" rather than "organizers" and require skills in fund-raising, project administration, and financial management. The following ad in a National Congress for Community Economic Development (NCCED) publication emphasizes these managerial skills.

> NHS of Camden is recruiting an Executive Director with at least 3–5 years of experience in the field of Housing and Community Revitalization who is able to lead the organization in building a strong niche in homeownership and lending services. We are seeking a candidate who possesses the skills and expertise to form partnerships and leverage community resources to expand homeownership opportunities city wide. Specific skills sought include fund-raising, hands-on housing/lending, finance, staff management and planning. Starting salary is $40,000.

Many of the positions available are in support organizations. The Center for Community Change and numerous other Washington–based organizations hire people who combine policy advocacy and policy analysis skills to examine social data and determine what actions should be taken. Advocacy organizations hire lawyers, coalitions require coordinators, and established social production organizations need people with specific technical skills—grants writing, apartment management and upkeep, or job training and placement.

The rewards of an organizing career are marvelous; people can earn a modest living doing such incredible work; however, organizing is difficult, the skills required are extensive, the funding base is uncertain, and the hours are long. Burnout is a problem, as discouragement sets in. Burnout may show up as emotional withdrawal, or as physical symptoms, including backaches, stomach aches, and headaches.

Organizers learn from one another the importance of anticipating burnout and work to prevent it from occurring or at least moderate its impact. One approach is to build in time for reflection so that activists caught up in the tensions of daily life can remind themselves of what they are trying to accomplish and the overall importance of social-change work. On a daily basis, to keep up motivation, organizers build some fun into their projects, put some humor in a protest, perform satirical skits at a meeting, or sing and dance at an ethnic festival or block party. Training sessions and retreats provide a chance for organizers to regain their energies, as they sit back and reflect on what has been accomplished and the potential for further gains.

The best antidote to burnout is a successful campaign or project that empowers members and the community. While attempting larger, more complicated work is important, organizers make sure some smaller projects are ongoing that have a good chance of succeeding. Winning a battle energizes, boosting the morale not only of organizational members but of the organizer him- or herself. Seeing a homeless person housed or a downtrodden person speak with confidence admonishing those in power or watching people from a wide variety of cultural and ethnic backgrounds come together to overcome shared problems are the successes that conquer burnout.

Victories are so important, they need to be marked and celebrated and become part of the lore, the memories that can sustain organizer and members through leaner times. As one activist told us

> After every project you must celebrate because you've built yourself up and up and up and all of a sudden when it's done you think, "Hey, but it's not [done]. It just isn't." And that's why you have to celebrate it. You have to force yourself into celebrating and saying, "We did a good job." I mean, you just fight so many people and you fight so many different funders to finally get it there that it's like, Whew, I'm just glad this is done and I think that's why people get burned out of this field very quickly and leave it. You've got to celebrate. You gotta celebrate every little victory. It's mandatory.

When organizers are overwhelmed in their work or fear that no one understands or need a boost after a defeat or require technical knowledge that they lack, they seek support from one another. Within every major city, organizers are networked and call each other frequently. The rapid expansion of organizations such as the NOA suggests that organizers need a forum in which to share frustrations and need colleagues to support them when they are feeling low. In addition, associations like NOA help improve the conditions under which organizers work, for instance, by establishing retirement funds that follow the organizers as they move from job to job. Organizers also meet each other in action coalitions set up in different cities to coordinate battles against big business or government. Meeting in coalitions organizers learn techniques from one another, share the burdens of their jobs, and learn that they are not alone.

Studies show that organizers enjoy their work. One individual, who at different times has been a street-level organizer and a developmental activist, described how he feels when negotiating with bankers for projects that benefit the poor.

> There's a side of me that loves that shit, cause I could mess with these guys. And I can understand them. I have a mind that works on the math and the notion of lawsuits and stuff and that's a hard thing. . . . I can sit with Fannie Mae and negotiate with them and stuff and I can understand the legal documents in a reasonable amount of time so that you don't get lost with just lawyers controlling it.

Another person described himself as loving the excitement of building a community project when funding is scarce and risk is high. A similar enthusiasm for their work was found among neighborhood-based community organizers in Chicago. Career satisfaction is high.

> Organizers are sustained in their jobs by their commitment to the ideals of organizing and by a sense of efficacy in pursuing these ideals. In addition, Chicago organizers are sustained by the more mundane advantages of the job—the joy of "wins," the variety of tasks and skills the job demands, and autonomy and flexibility of determining how to get the job done. (O'Donnell, 1995a, p. 8)

Other studies have also shown that pride in bringing about social change remains an important motivator for those in social action organizations (Sherkat & Block, 1997).

Conclusion

Some of what organizers do might appear to be contradictory. Organizers become experts by learning numerous skills, from books, from classes and training sessions, and from experience. Mastering these skills allows professional organizers to become central players in community efforts to change social and political policies.

Yet, at the same time that organizers are gaining skills as professional activists they must keep in mind that the purpose of organizing is to empower others. An organizer has failed when those outside the community, or worse yet, the community members themselves, identify the cause and the campaign as belonging to the organizer rather than the neighborhood or the organization's members. An organizer facilitates, motivates, and teaches but must not take away ownership of the result from the newly empowered, activist community.

An organizer reflecting on the tension between what he and his organization can accomplish and the need for broader empowerment offered this insight, comparing organizing work to that of a catalyst in chemistry:

> We think of ourselves as catalysts and in the true sense of the word, a catalyst doesn't get used up in the reaction. . . . [if our effort] doesn't ignite activism and ignite a sense among people about what can be done when people work collectively and struggle for what is needed, then we've done little.

CHAPTER

7 Mobilizing for
Collective Action

Acting as catalysts, organizers mobilize people to join together to combat shared problems. In general, *political mobilization is the process of moving personal grievances to the realm of collective, organized, social action.*

Mobilization begins when an individual overcomes psychological barriers to fighting back. Personal mobilization might begin with a "click" event (*click* as when a light turns on) that forces an individual to link personal oppression to broader political or social problems. A male attorney insists that the female attorneys fetch the coffee, citizens whose children are diseased discover that companies have lied about toxic wastes, or homes are destroyed by local government to make way for a mall that residents oppose. Click events that mobilize individuals

> spring from "practical" matters which cause fear and anger in peoples' lives, such as parents' horror when they find out that their children have been drinking water polluted by toxic chemicals. (Krauss, 1988, p. 260)

Organizers build on these events and work to reframe personal experiences and individual grievances so those involved can see that their problems are socially caused. Then to bring about collective action, organizers work to "eliminat[e] barriers to participation through setting agendas and defining issues" and "shap[e] belief systems, ideologies or shared consciousness" in ways that enable people to understand how their actions may succeed in bringing about change (Speer & Hughey, 1996, p. 178). Without such reframing some victims of a problem may try to persuade others not to fight back because they are fearful,

> neighbors and fellow citizens resent dissenters, and tell them that their mobilization will harm property values, chase away employers, and make matters worse. Dissenters are also vulnerable to ostracism and the "blaming the messenger" phenomenon. (Woliver, 1996, p. 141)

Successful mobilization is about overcoming systemic forms of disempowerment—fear, learned inefficacy, the organization of consent, and the system bias—that allow those in power to stymie collective action.

Mobilization Bootstraps

Bootstrapping means to start small and then build on successes to create the resources that allow an organization to take the next step. Successful mobilization requires such bootstrapping during which the victories achieved by a handful of concerned individuals slowly motivate others to join in the fight.

A neighborhood organization formed by a few long-term residents might at first appear quiescent. The meetings and festivities sponsored by such an organization, however, provide a locale in which new residents can meet with one another and share their concerns about the community (Frankfort-Nachmias, 1993, p. 8). A few volunteers from a church might repair a handful of homes and, by doing so, motivate others to form a Community Development Corporation. A successful effort by a neighborhood association to chase drug pushers from one park encourages other community members to join in future efforts to take back the streets. Activists on the board of a low-income housing cooperative might initially find it difficult to encourage others to become involved in bettering the living environment, but once some visible changes are made, even small ones such as the improved appearance of the entrance, people feel empowered and are increasingly willing to participate in the work of self-management (Saegert & Winkel, 1996).

Just fighting along with others who believe in the same issues strengthens social bonds and makes further mobilization efforts easier, even when the initial efforts appeared to have failed. For example, civil rights organizing in the Woodlawn Community in Chicago had been going nowhere until the Woodlawn Organization hosted a rally for returning Freedom Riders (people who courageously fought for voting rights in the South). The possibilities for success that were shown by the Freedom Riders who spoke at the rally triggered mobilization in the south side of Chicago as "Woodlawn had turned out en masse for the Freedom Riders" (Horwitt, 1989, p. 400). Nicholas von Hoffman, the Alinsky organizer who was working in the Woodlawn community, described the explosion:

> I think we should toss out everything we are doing organizationally and work on the premise that this is the moment of the whirlwind, that we are no longer organizing but guiding a social movement. (Horwitt, 1989, p. 401)

Participation in a battle strengthens peoples, commitment to the cause, making sustained mobilization easier (Speer et al., 1995). For instance, in a labor strike, management called in police and strike breakers, whose brutality against the activists increased their commitment to the cause and their willingness to stay the course, while encouraging others from the broader community to provide assistance (Fantasia, 1988, p. 174).

By knocking on doors and holding meetings, an organizer provides the initial spark that brings a few people together and that creates the possibility that further mobilization will continue in a self-sustaining way. Meetings held in individuals' homes or in churches, libraries, or restaurants encourage people to share their feelings, increasing community solidarity, a form of the social capital, which, in turn, reinforces the enthusiasm to work together. As people find out more information about the problems they face, their shared anger encourages them to join together to bring about change, while the information they communicate gives them confidence that they can succeed.

Theories and Research Findings about Mobilization

For the organizer, mobilization involves day-in, day-out contact with potential organization members to learn what grievances they have. Who is most likely to become involved and what triggers such involvement?

Research suggests several complementary answers. Material on *political participation* points out personal characteristics that distinguish people who become involved from those who remain indifferent. The literature on *resource mobilization* indicates what broader conditions in the society influence when mobilization is likely to occur. *New social movements theory* and, in particular, what is known as *identity theory*, examine how specific framings of issues encourage mobilization. Understanding these three theories helps organizers figure out which tactics to try and when.

Political Participation

Studies about political participation provide information about who gets involved and under what circumstances. Initially, political participation researchers grouped people into four categories of lesser to greater degrees of involvement—political apathetics, spectators, foot soldiers, and gladiators (Milbrath, 1977).

Apathetics are politically and socially inactive. Organizers focus very little effort on these people because they have made a decision to drop out of the political process. Unfortunately, in many communities apathetics are the largest group. Political *spectators* are more active, do pay attention to some public events and can be recruited. Spectators are unlikely to perform the detailed work of running an organization, but they can be convinced to appear at a public rally, vote for a candidate who supports an organization's cause, and perhaps contribute nominal amounts of money.

More active still are the *foot soldiers,* people who routinely show up at meetings, hand out fliers, lick stamps, and campaign in support of community issues. Organizers work to assure that foot soldiers gain sufficient positive feedback from their work to continue their participation. Finally, *gladiators* are highly involved individuals, who lead organizations, place their bodies on the line in confrontations, spend many hours working to keep the organization alive, and, if necessary, subject themselves to arrest in support of organizational goals.

Political participation research shows that mobilization campaigns rarely change people's values and beliefs; instead mobilization involves encouraging those who already support a cause to increase their degree of commitment. Organizers do not try to recruit a White racist to a Black activist group or an avid capitalist to a workers' cooperative, especially because these efforts may backfire, by encouraging an opponent to work against the cause. Instead, time is better spent in turning passive supporters into active participants and in helping local leaders gain the skills to become gladiators.

Studies of political participation suggest ways of increasing people's involvement. To begin, the less demanding the task, the more likely that people will join in. Overall, almost a third of people claim to have been active in some political activity (Milbrath, 1977, p. 22). About 8 percent of the population is involved in some community organization (defined broadly), about 14 percent have made contact with government officials, 30 percent work with others on local problems, while only a handful, 3 percent, claim that they would participate in public demonstrations (Milbrath, 1977, pp. 18–19).

Data on who participates indicate that the well-educated are politically more involved than the poorly educated; majority-group members are more active than are minority-group members; the wealthy participate more than the poor; and people in professional occupations participate more than blue-collar workers (Smith, Reddy, & Baldwin, 1980; Steggert, 1975, pp. 13–15). Furthermore, people who feel alienated and inefficacious do not undertake political action (Milbrath, 1977, pp. 7, 66).

At first, such findings appear disheartening for working with the poor or minorities; but other research offers more hope by explaining that participation rates among the poor and the disempowered may have been underestimated by the initial statistics. For instance,

> social background loses much or most of its explanatory power in predicting participation in voluntary associations when intervening attitudes, personality, and situational variables are controlled statistically. It is possible, for instance that those groups who avoid participation in the larger social fabric because of their perceived inefficacy, will respond to an arena of concrete, visible concerns such as their own block. (Wandersman, 1981, p. 37)

If people are interested in a particular local problem, they may participate regardless of their educational or economic background. An unwillingness to try to change national policy need not imply a reluctance to work toward improving local police protection.

Other predictors of participation may provide helpful guidance to organizers. People who have lived in a community longer are more likely to be active (Smith, Reddy, & Baldwin, 1972, p. 219). People with stronger organizational linkages are more likely to become active, as models of social capital would suggest. For example, studies of Latino/Latina communities in which participation overall is quite low, show that women, who are far more "embedded in (and more aware of their embeddedness in) social relations than are men," are more likely to form participatory and politically active social networks than are the men (Hardy-Fanta, 1993, p. 24). Similarly, overall participation in neighborhood anticrime activities is quite low; only about 10 percent of the people are involved. But of people who are already members of any neighborhood group, over 50 percent participate in anticrime activities (Podolefsky & DuBow, 1981, p. 111). Even being a client of a neighborhood service organization, one form of community integration, increases involvement in other local organizations (Thomas, 1986).

Identifying with almost any local group increases the willingness of individuals to become involved while those who feel that a collectivity to which they belong is politically efficacious are more likely to join in with others in political actions (Yeich

& Levine, 1994). Those who live in cooperative apartment buildings and feel that other coowners are active are more ready to join collective activities (Saegert & Winkel, 1996). Similarly, studies of unions show that the workers who are most likely to be active are those with the strongest identification with the group (Kelly & Kelly, 1994). Strong cultural or ethnic identification also increases political involvement. For instance, even though African Americans are less politically active than Caucasians, for those African Americans who strongly identify with their blackness, participation is as high as for Whites (Milbrath, 1977, p. 57). People who have strong interpersonal linkages within their neighborhoods but are highly dissatisfied with city services are very likely to join in collective activities (Ahlbrandt & Cunninghman, 1979; Crenson, 1983). These apparently alienated individuals are dissatisfied enough to want to undertake action, and their strong linkages to the community motivate them to work to improve the locale in which they live.

Caution is necessary, however, in assuming that a willingness to participate, or even mild participation such as voting, extends to more intense social action. Far more people express support for an issue than are willing to demonstrate or even sign a petition for that issue. For instance, a suggestive study of participation in peace demonstrations in Europe shows that concern about an issue, even one as important as having nuclear missiles nearby, might not necessarily translate into political action. In a survey, 74 percent of the people who were affected by the deployment of nuclear missiles opposed their placement. Eighty percent of those expressing opposition were contacted by activists who were setting up a demonstration. Even so, only 1 of 6 promised to show up and worse yet, only 1 out of 25 actually did (Klandermans & Oegema, 1987).

A continuation of this study sought out why people were unwilling to be involved even when they supported the issue. *The most important reason was that they had not been personally contacted by an organizer to encourage them to stay involved.* In addition, many people who said they opposed the missiles were only marginally opposed, did not want to disagree with the government officials who supported the deployment of the missiles, and were involved in peer and friendship groups that did not agree with the protest (Oegema & Klandermans, 1994). Personal persuasion can increase involvement, but the effectiveness of contact can be diminished if the social networks in which people are involved offer a message opposite to that given by organizers.

The research on political participation can be boiled down to four lessons for organizers. First, don't expect everyone to join, even those that agree with the issues. Second, those who do sign up to be members of an action organization need continual reinforcement, because the opposition will be trying to discourage them from participating. Third, participation in social-change and community organizations is most likely among those already involved in similar activities and among those who have strong linkages to the community. Effort to build community integration, by increasing social capital, is well worth the time because the presence of strong community bonds increases mobilization.

Fourth, gladiators are most likely to share two characteristics. They feel strongly about the issue or take pride in the community to which they belong, yet at the same time feel that those in power neglect their neighborhood or group. Those who run block parties and complain to city hall about poor street repairs, or people who actively speak with pride about being gay, or those with disabilities who vociferously demand equal access and equal opportunity, are potential leaders. Organizers do not have to persuade such people about the need to participate or the justice of the issue. Instead, organizers work to strengthen the networks local leaders share, while helping them structure an organization to carry out the collective work.

Resource Mobilization

Political participation models identify which individuals are most likely to get involved. Resource mobilization theories provide complementary insights, emphasizing how the political and social climate affects participation (McCarthy & Zald, 1987).

The central premise of resource mobilization theory is that at any time there is sufficient discontent in society to generate collective political action but that an external *trigger event,* a dramatic and public event, is required to mobilize those who are discontent. Organizers await for a trigger event that dramatically highlights the problem and then work to jell the preexisting, free-floating discontent that people feel into an organized and focused social-change effort.

For many social issues—civil rights, affordable homes, abortion, antigay discrimination, drunk driving, women's rights, neighborhood concerns—organizations started by people dedicated to a cause are already in place because of past events. Though initially lacking a mass base, these organizations can survive for a time by subsisting on funds obtained from "conscience constituencies," that is, wealthier individuals and foundations who feel strongly (or guilty) about a problem. These existing social-movement organizations employ professional organizers who, once the trigger event occurs, step in and bring about mobilization by showing people activated by the trigger event how, by joining the organization, they can fight back.

The trigger may be a dramatic and visible failure of government that points out underlying problems, such as rape in which police stand by and watch, or a community mental health movement that closed mental hospitals and left the mentally ill on the streets. Deaths from a toxic waste spill may trigger thinking about the causes such as lack of enforcement of the antipollution laws or corporate dominance of regulatory agencies. Slow response to an earthquake or hurricane highlights governmental incompetence or underfunding or indifference to suffering of the poor and homeless. Reduction in the number of bus routes or hours of service can be a trigger for action by neighborhoods of transit-dependent residents. The tearing down of affordable housing to make room for a mall owned by outsiders or the city's unwillingness to repair potholes big enough to swallow a van may be the trigger that mobilizes the poor to fight back.

Activists and organizers sometimes stage trigger events. In the civil rights era, when young Blacks sat at lunch counters reserved for Whites, they knew they were likely to be met with violence; the massive voter registration drives defied local Whites who had long denied Blacks the right to vote and stimulated oppressive actions. Sufferers from black lung disease in the coal industry and brown lung in the textile industry were made aware of how they were neglected when outside physicians funded by the United Church of Christ and the (Catholic) Campaign for Human Development came to town and showed that company doctors had been lying about the health of the workers. In each case, organizers knew that the drama of the situation would publicize the problems and help mobilize people into action.

People understand the problems before the trigger events—African Americans in the South knew they could not vote; coal miners were aware that they had trouble breathing; and those who suffer from a disability each day confront the obstacles society places in their path. What a trigger event does is highlight the problem so dramatically that both victims and the broader population can no longer deny its existence or importance.

Organizers build upon the trigger events to bring about political action. Professional organizers interpret or *frame* the trigger events to show possible participants that the immediate, personal problems they face are part of a broader problem that the trigger event now makes visible (Snow et al., 1986; Snow & Benford, 1992). For instance, an incident in the Chicago area in which drunk police officers chased and shot at a Black couple driving their car may resonate with many Blacks who have been harassed by police in lesser but still frightening and humiliating ways. A shooting of a woman by an estranged husband may legitimize the fears of other women who have been abused while bringing the problem to public attention. Organizers frame issues to link personal grievances to the broader social concerns for which their organizations provide an answer and, in doing so, encourage newly mobilized people to join an existing social-movement organization.

To summarize, the resource mobilization approach teaches organizers that a core part of their work is in crystallizing preexisting feelings among the disempowered, rather than initially searching for what bothers people. The key step in mobilization is framing or defining the broader issue, the one made apparent through the dramatic trigger event, in ways that mesh with the concerns and fears that people already have. The next step is to publicize how the social-movement organization can fight the problem and, by doing so, encourage people to join an action organization already in place.

New Social Movements

In recent years, organizing has taken place among people, even those of higher economic status, who because of personal characteristics or social identities, share a common oppression. These *identity issues* of gender, sexual orientation, racial/ethnic identity, or biologically based physical conditions provide the basis for what scholars term "the new social movements" (NSM) (Buechler, 1995; Johnston, Larana, and Gusfeld, 1994; Larana, 1994).

The literature on NSM describes that mobilization occurs when people reach agreement that they share a common characteristic that has led to their oppression. NSM theory emphasizes that these shared characteristics are constructed over time through an ongoing process of negotiation and framing. Mobilization occurs as people buy into a shared definition, almost an ideology, of what constitutes the problem and then identify as part of the victim group.

People negotiate over the definition of the problems they face, and in doing so define those who should be mobilized in an action organization. For example, if those involved in an activist women's organization define the core problem as one of job opportunity, then women who stay at home and raise children are not part of the group. Conversely, the self-definition of activists limit what problems the organization confronts. Gays and lesbians might organize separately, if gender is of primary concern, but might join together if sexual orientation is core to the constructed identity. For instance, the organization Queer Nation has successfully communicated that the oppression that both gays and lesbians face is part of the broader problem of homophobia and that consequently, gays and lesbians can fight together.

Identities may be reframed to increase the number of people who can work together. Organizing among Asian groups in the United States was more successful after people of Chinese, Japanese, and Filipino descent reframed the problems they faced as stemming from their common Asian heritage to work together (Wei, 1993). Similarly, after long-term negotiations and argumentation, the separate but politically weak cultural groups that were in North America before European settlement determined they would be more effective in fighting oppression if they accepted a shared definition as "Native Americans" or "Indians" (Nagel, 1996). In a like manner, the idea of what constitutes women's liberation did not emerge full blown. Instead, over many years, separate groups—women who were concerned about being underpaid, others who resented the subordination of lesbians, and those who focused on the oppression of minority women—noted that members of each group were victims of a pervasive subordination of females and that change would more likely come about if this broader issue were faced collectively (Mueller, 1994).

Identity issues can be reframed so that people no longer avoid joining in action. For example, not so many years ago, being disabled meant being perceived as helpless and incompetent. Many individuals with physical impairments sought to disassociate themselves from disabilities (Scotch, 1988, p. 161). As those with physical problems came to know and talk to each other, however, they reframed the problems in ways that encouraged collective action:

> a redefinition of disability was required—one that treated disability as a label for a group of people who had the potential for political action and who were unfairly excluded from mainstream social institutions on the basis of their physical or mental impairments. (Scotch, 1988, p. 163)

To summarize, the new social movements' literature should make organizers aware that problems are not necessarily objective, hard-nosed matters of fact about which people simply need be made aware. Rather, mobilization comes about after either tacit or explicit negotiation among those affected. Building a shared identity sometimes helps create a common definition of the problem that enables those who originally saw issues in a different way to work together. Still, the ongoing negotiation of what constitutes the problems and who is involved might preclude some and include others from working on one cause.

Implications for Organizing

Taken together, the three traditions of research on political and social participation suggest several lessons.

First, organizers should have realistic expectations about how many people will be involved in any event or campaign. Not everyone is going to join, no matter what the organizer does. If the expectation is too high about how many people will undertake actions, the organizer is likely to get discouraged and burn out. Moreover, estimates that are too high lead to unrealistic goals for what the organization can accomplish; an agenda that is too ambitious may lead to defeats, discouraging future mobilization.

Second, existing action organizations already in place can take advantage of trigger events or even stimulate them to bolster membership. When trigger events do occur, activists need to think about how to frame the events so that as large a number of people as possible see that they are affected by the problem and become willing to join the group.

Third, those involved in complex problem areas, such as people facing racial oppression, homelessness, or sexual harassment on the job, need to work on defining their issues in ways that enable people with initially different perspectives to join together. A stronger organization is built when issues are framed in ways that enable large numbers to accept that they face a common problem.

Mobilization Models

Knowing theories of how and why mobilization works is important, but these theories are not carried out in the abstract. Organizers don't talk about theories of participation or resource mobilization. Instead, in their efforts to convince people to join an organization and carry out needed actions, organizers guide their actions by following one of six different models. Each model suggests ways to approach individuals to encourage them to become involved.

The Direct Membership or Boston Model

With the direct membership, or as it is sometimes called the Boston model, organizers talk to individuals one-on-one to bring them together in a single-issue, membership organization. The organizer

> first talks with key "gatekeepers" in the community who, once convinced of the merits of the organizing effort, provide a "contact list" of potential members for the organizer to visit. The organizer then meets with those contacts (adding new ones in snowball fashion as s/he goes along) and pulls together an organizing committee that provides the initial core group for the organizing drive. (Staples, 1984, p. 20)

This logic was prominent in the early welfare rights movement and was followed by civil rights workers organizing in the South (Payne, 1995). Most neighborhood associations formed to combat an immediate threat—too much traffic, an increase in crime, gentrification, and displacement—are usually set up using the direct membership approach.

The Alinsky Model

The Boston model builds an organization one person at a time. In sharp contrast, the Alinsky model brings together existing organizations in a community to fight for a wide variety of neighborhood issues.

Organizers who follow this approach, come into the community only after some local groups invite them and show their sincerity by raising the funds necessary for the initial work. With a funding base in place, Alinsky organizers, part of the Industrial Areas Foundation (IAF) network, go into the community and learn about its physical, ethnic, and cultural structures using the research techniques described in the next chapter. Working with the leaders of established organizations, and especially with clergy of concerned churches, the organizers locate other community groups and organizations that might want to join a neighborhood federation. With this temporary alliance in place, the organizers form a transitional steering committee for a new community organization (for which the organizer acts as an adviser). This committee convenes a community convention during which people describe the problems they face and work out ideas for their solution. Under the Alinsky approach, the core goal is to establish a permanent democratic organization that can speak for the neighborhood as a whole on a wide variety of issues.

The ACORN Model

Associations of Community Organizations for Reform Now (ACORN) has set up a nationwide network of neighborhood organizations that, not unlike the Alinsky model, work to overcome a wide array of issues that affect poor communities. Within each neighborhood, professional ACORN organizers recruit organization members one by one, usually through a door knocking or house meeting approach, at which a supporter of the group invites in friends and neighbors to meet with the organizer and discuss problems. Organizers encourage people to join ACORN to solve the immediate neighborhood problems, but in doing so slant the mobilizing appeal to the issues that are of concern to the ACORN network as a whole. Today, much of ACORN organizing is about improving the conditions of housing in poor communities.

ACORN organizers assume that many existing local organizations are controlled by the established power structure that has intentionally excluded the poor. By forming its own network of community groups built up of the mobilized poor, ACORN gains the power to oppose the establishment. To maintain its independence and to form a political structure independent of those already in power, ACORN tries to obtain most of its funding from membership fees rather than from foundation or church contributions.

Consensus Organizing

The Alinsky, Boston, and ACORN models are oppositional and mobilize people by encouraging them to take on the power structure. The consensus organizing model works on dramatically different assumptions. With this model, the goal is

> building consensus and unity among all segments of the community: neighborhood residents, bankers, business people, religious leaders, politicians, and government offi-

> cials. No one is to be embarrassed, no resentments rubbed raw . . . consensual . . .
> organizing strategy tends to see the fundamental goal as rebuilding community, forging
> a sense of unity among fragmented elements, and gathering resources to perform specific
> community tasks. (Fisher, 1994, p. 188)

The goal is to link poor neighborhoods to the established political structures so that
collaborative work can be accomplished. This work is often led by community development corporations that try to physically repair the neighborhoods.

To build consensus organizations, several outreach efforts are made simultaneously. Professional organizers, trained at the Consensus Organizing Institute meet
with community groups, and then encourage leaders of those groups to mobilize ordinary
community members to join in with the redevelopment work. At the same, those from
the organizing group work with government, banks, and business people to convince
those in the power structure why they should help renew poor communities. Organizers
emphasize the need for cooperation and the hopes for the future rather than concentrate
on complaints or problems.

Planning and Governance Models

A different approach to mobilizing comes about as part of a top-down, community
planning model. In this case, government, foundations, or business coalitions mobilize
community members by asking them to set up organizations to provide input to government about neighborhood priorities, needs, and hopes (Brown, 1996; M.M. Stone,
1996). Often the community group submits a report and little occurs.

On occasion, neighborhood planning groups take on an important role when
neighbors carry out their own ideas and empower their communities. In an exemplary
case, the Dudley Street Neighborhood Initiative created a neighborhood plan, got city
approval for the plan, and obtained the resources needed to carry out many of its own
ideas (Gittell et al., 1998; Medoff & Sklar, 1994).

Getting people involved in community planning efforts occurs in two steps. First,
either government officials or community activists carry out a door knocking campaign,
set up public meetings, and hold press conferences for local papers to convince people
to come to a meeting to talk over problems, goals, and priorities. For instance, in the
Dudley Street neighborhood, organizers knocked on every door, explained what the
organizing was about, and encouraged people to show up to discuss community issues.

Next, organizers hold planning meetings during which community members discuss their hopes as well as what they want government to accomplish for the neighborhood. A development activist illustrated how his organization set up such a planning
session to figure out what the community and the city could do about a derelict strip
of stores. A neighborhood organizer, Gladys

> essentially organized people to get them out to meetings. . . . we had
> as many as 200 people at these meetings and people were excited, peo-
> ple were pessimistic, said it would never happen. Gladys helps us orga-
> nize . . . meaning get out the flyers, telephone the folks, lend credibility.

The city and the development group had initially intended to build new and updated stores. But community members feared that outsiders would own those stores and insisted on and got affordable housing for the neighborhood.

Progressive Advocacy Models

A large number of national organizations work full time on social equity and social justice causes. These groups protect civil liberties, preserve the separation of church and state, or promote environmental legislation. They speak for the ill-housed, the homeless, the elderly, children, immigrants, or crime victims. Many of these progressive advocacy organizations are run by a full-time professional staff who advocate for needed legislation or changes in government rules. While the staff members of these organizations work for the membership, individual members rarely get involved in daily activity.

For progressive advocacy organizations, mobilization means increasing the dues-paying membership, both to obtain funds and to provide evidence to politicians that the group speaks for a large constituency. To recruit people, appeals are made usually by mail or phone. The goal is to locate individuals who already support the issues at hand and persuade them to send in membership fees; rarely do such groups try to persuade the uncommitted. That is what is to be accomplished later in the social action campaigns.

Some of these progressive advocacy organizations are actually national coalitions that represent dozens, sometimes hundreds, of local organizations. For instance the National Low Income Housing Coalition (NLIHC) speaks for hundreds of smaller community groups that represent the ill-housed. The coalition holds an annual meeting with its membership groups to determine overall policies, but the daily work of lobbying at the federal level is done by the NLIHC's staff.

Members of progressive advocacy organizations are encouraged by the national leadership to make contact with their local legislators on issues that affect the group. To help this occur, the national groups keep the membership informed on what is going on through frequent newsletters, web-based and/or hard copy. In addition, phone banks and e-mail lists are used to call out the troops. The details of these tactics will be discussed in the chapters on social action campaigns.

Mobilization Tactics

Various mobilization tactics are followed including:

- activating established organizations
- encouraging individuals to join through one-on-one encounters
- evoking social and political networks of individuals.

Historically, adherents of different organizing models have followed distinct tactics, but increasingly organizers tend to use whatever tools seem to work, no matter the model that initially suggested the approach. Organizers make their appeals at churches, social clubs, or neighborhood watch groups simply because large numbers of people can be addressed at once. An advocacy group may knock on doors, rather than sending out mailings. Few of the members recruited through door-knocking campaigns are asked to do much more than pay dues or send an occasional letter; still door knocking is an effective technique for raising funds, and enables organizers to hear firsthand what community members feel and think.

What happens during the one-on-one conversations varies depending on the purpose of the visit. For instance, in door-knocking campaigns set up to build a neighborhood organization, organizers ask people they meet questions about general problems they face and then listen carefully to the responses. The specific issue discussed is often less important than convincing people that the organization is concerned about what they think and will address matters community members suggest. By contrast, with issue-based organizing, during one-on-one recruitment efforts, the organizer tries to persuade individuals to join with others who want to combat a specific problem. In this case, the organizer tries to keep the conversation focused on the problem at hand, encouraging people to talk about how the problem affects them.

In mobilization efforts, face-to-face communications work best, whether door-to-door or at community meetings. Whether recruiting individuals or groups, there is no substitute for being there, listening, linking perceived problems to broader issues, and explaining how the group works and how successful it has been. Organizers need to be careful about how they express their own opinions during these conversations. They must show that they are concerned about the issues yet not be so assertive that they fail to show respect to the opinions of those they are seeking to mobilize.

Mobilizing with Organizations

One of the quickest ways to mobilize people is to bring together established community groups, thus uniting their existing membership. Respected heads of established organizations lend credibility to new organizing efforts. An organizer might ask a clergy person to encourage congregants to join in the community group or to show up as part of a demonstration. As one organizer noted,

> Organizing individuals . . . is "the slowest road to hell." It was by recruiting groups, not individuals, that the coalition was able to build as quickly and strongly as it did. (Henig, 1982, p. 88)

To mobilize in this way, activists first take an inventory of community assets and identify the organizations that might participate, such as church groups, social organizations, block associations, tenants' groups, youth groups, and unions. Then the organizer talks to leaders of these groups to encourage them to join the community effort that will be run as a confederation organization with its own independent governing board.

Building a new community group based on existing organizations has its difficulties. In communities with competing ethnic or religious groups, it is difficult to choose which to use as an organizational home. For instance in his work in Chicago, Alinsky made sure that the support organizations included not only White ethnic Catholic churches but also some Black Protestant groups. In Rochester, New York, the Alinsky organization Freedom, Integration, God, Honor, Today (FIGHT) was sponsored by Black Protestant churches. To provide balance, without hurting ethnic sensitivities, another separate group, Friends of FIGHT, was formed, with a White membership.

Other groups have cleverly bypassed these problems by making sure that each community constituency has representation in the federated organization, as shown, for example, in the Dudley Street Neighborhood Initiative (DSNI). To mobilize different constituencies and to assure none feel left out, the DSNI board is elected by citizens who vote for seats controlled by their ethnic groups. In addition, the board, while dominated by community members, maintains representatives from a wide array of other, established community organizations:

> **Board of Directors of the Dudley Street Neighborhood Initiative**
> 12 Community Members elected separately from Black, Cape Verdean, Latino, and White constituencies
> 5 members of nonprofit agencies from Health and Human Services
> 2 members of community development corporations
> 2 small-business persons
> 2 broader business community members
> 2 religious community members
> 2 members of nonprofits from an adjacent area
> 1 city official
> 1 state official
> 2 others chosen by the board to assure racial/ethnic/age/sex representation. (Mcdoff & Sklar, 1994, p. 58)

Another problem that can occur is that leaders of the separate organizations vie with each other to direct the confederation. The organizer must use tact and skill to prevent this from happening, because each of the separate constituencies that the local leaders reach is necessary for overall success. If building a permanent confederation proves too difficult, it may be better to set up a temporary coalition in which the individual organizations work together on a case-by-case basis.

Mobilizing through Individual Encounters

A wide variety of ways are used to contact individuals to convince them to join a community or social-change organization. These recruitment efforts can be done by sending written material, holding meetings in private houses, chatting with people at barbershops, laundermats, and coffee shops, and going door-to-door to canvass the neighborhood.

Mobilizing individuals is not about persuading those who oppose the group to change their minds but instead should focus on locating people who are in general agreement about needed changes. The organizer *reinforces* these shared beliefs, *per-*

suades people that it is possible to fight back, and *encourages* them to join and participate in the organization. The key to mobilization is convincing individuals that they should work together to bring about necessary changes, rather than teaching them about problems that they already recognize.

Canvassing.   For neighborhood organizing, canvassing, that is going door-to-door and talking with people, is vital. New organizers are often assigned to canvassing work, in part to test their mettle and, in part, so they can learn firsthand about the problems people face. Canvassing is important because

> Person-to-person contacts build organizations where people feel equally valued. When someone takes the trouble to visit you and talk with you about his or her organization, it means something, especially when you know that the person is not being paid to hustle you. (Kahn, 1982, p. 110)

While canvassing is generally door-to-door, sometimes this form of recruitment proceeds along social networks. With this approach, organizers first talk to local leaders, and if they seem sympathetic, ask for their help in identifying others to approach. Initially the Gay Alliances in San Francisco were built up along networks (Castells, 1983), while in the civil rights era in the South, organizers had to travel along social networks lest they talk with the wrong people and maybe get shot at, beat up, or killed (Payne, 1995).

Canvassing, whether along networks or door-to-door, is mostly about listening. The organizer asks people what they feel is wrong. This is courteous, shows interest and respect, and when people raise an issue, they are more likely to commit themselves to act on that issue.

> Long experience with organizing has shown that people tend to support decisions they feel involved in making. When they feel they were not consulted, that they did not have a part in the decision-making process, they tend to vote with their feet and walk in the other direction. (Kahn, 1982, p. 69)

The problems organizers hear about come from the everyday experiences of people they canvass. Individuals don't talk about income distributions; they worry whether they earn enough. People don't think about urban planning, but they care if the traffic is increasing on streets that their kids have to cross. "As one activist put it, 'At the local level, you organize around dog shit, stop signs, whatever people are talking about'" (Cassidy, 1980, p. 72).

Though the organizer wants people to join an organization, it is best during canvassing efforts to focus on the problems mentioned and the possible solutions rather than talk about the organization itself, other than letting people know it's there. Sometimes people are just waiting for an opportunity to complain, and the organizer provides that opportunity. At other times, organizers may have to start off the conversation by asking some questions in ways that don't put words in people's mouths. If a canvasser begins the conversation by asking, "Is dirty drinking water a problem for you?" and the resident answers, "Yes, but . . ." and the canvasser says to him or herself, "Aha, dirty water is a problem," a wrong conclusion might be drawn. The person could be bothered by the water, but won't take action on this issue, because there was something more important he or she wanted to say but didn't get a chance to express.

During a conversation held while canvassing, several things are accomplished, sometimes simultaneously:

- An organizer introduces himself or herself and suggests general concerns that might affect the overall community.
- The organizer encourages the people being canvassed to talk about the problems they feel strongly about.
- The organizer briefly describes the community organization, suggesting how that organization can help overcome the problems mentioned.
- The organizer encourages the person to join the organization and to show up for its meetings.

The organizer must balance listening to what bothers people and letting people know what the organization can accomplish. For instance,

> **ORGANIZER:** Hello, I'm Herb Rubin a neighbor who is working for SDA, the Southside DeKalb Association. You've probably heard of the work we've done in pressuring city hall to pay more attention to the neighborhoods, especially the flood and sewer problems, as the city rapidly grows.
>
> **SPECTATOR:** Yes
>
> **ORGANIZER:** Well, we're trying to get some people together who are worried about how all the new housing might cause more flood problems. Are you concerned about problems of rapid growth?
>
> **SPECTATOR:** Yes, but my house doesn't flood. I'm affected by the increased traffic with all the new stores and traffic signals. I also worry about whether the growth will increase our taxes.
>
> **ORGANIZER:** That's interesting. In particular, what about the traffic or taxes bothers you? . . .

The organizer then listens to the problems that the person expresses and indicates that others are also concerned about similar problems. The organizer would then indicate that the SDA is working on these problems and suggest that the person might want to sign up and attend a meeting.

In this case, the SDA is about preserving a neighborhood. Handling flood problems is important, but so are the concerns about traffic; the point is to get people together. The organizer must listen carefully to the needs of the people because ultimately people only participate for problems that they feel are real and affect them individually.

Once conversations are begun, however, it is sometimes difficult to get people to stop; they have found a sympathetic ear and want to pour out their frustrations. Skillful canvassers learn to listen and then draw the conversation to a close by showing how by working together neighbors can solve the problems they share.

When canvassing is being done by organizations that focus on specific issues—tenants' rights, for example, in a neighborhood owned by absentee slumlords—during the initial comments, the organizer should emphasize the immediate problem. He or she specifies that the group has been set up to help tenants get better services for their rent dollars. The organizer encourages the potential recruit to talk about problems with housing, about services received, dealings with the landlord, and other similar matters. When the person wants to discuss other issues—lack of jobs, poor neighborhood schools—the canvasser has to perform a juggling act—empathizing with expressed concerns, while at the same time steering the conversation back to the problems of housing and tenant-landlord relationships.

Difficulties do occur with canvassing. In many neighborhoods it is hard to get people to open the door and talk, those who feel disempowered sometimes are just too discouraged to be involved. Others are too tired or busy, and some are simply afraid to open doors to strangers. Canvassers though show up night after night in the same community, and over time even nervous people begin to recognize them and will open the doors and chat.

Another difficulty in getting people to participate is that they fear sticking out, being different from others, or being first. To handle such concerns, it can be useful to sign up local leaders before beginning the canvass and include their names in brochures and conversations.

Canvassers hear excuses for noninvolvement that they recognize might not be real. For instance, a person might say "I am too busy to spend an evening a month at organization meetings" when in fact the real reason is he or she is afraid of being criticized by people in authority. People may say they don't think a crime patrol will work, but they may mean that they don't want to get involved with the police under any circumstances. To handle such situations, "learn to search out the rationalizations, treat them as rationalizations, and break through" (Alinsky, 1971, p. 112). Organizers listen to the reasons people give for not being involved in collective activities and try to hear which ones ring true. Unexpressed fears must be overcome. For instance, people in the Edgewater neighborhood in Chicago hesitated to participate in an anticrime organization lest they stand out in court. In response to these fears, the organization set up a system in which community members went together when one was to testify in court (Marciniak, 1981).

House Meetings.   Many community and social change organizations mobilize members by holding house meetings. A house meeting is little more than people getting together at someone's home to informally discuss problems. When neighbors are concerned about community decay, or people from an oppressed group need to talk about common problems, they often begin by sharing coffee, wine, or beer at someone's home and talking. House meetings might end up as consciousness raising sessions in which people first learn they share a problem, discover that the problem is socially caused, and then search for ways to collectively fight back.

Meetings are scheduled at the homes of volunteers, who are asked to invite friends. Only a few are invited each time to prevent people from being embarrassed about saying what is on their minds in front of a large group. At the meetings, organizers try to encourage people to express their concerns and think about the reasons why they all face the same problems. As people recognize that they share the same problems and have been put down in a like manner, organizers describe how these problems can be overcome by working together in a community or social-change organization.

Cesar Chavez, the farm-worker activist, organized primarily through house meetings:

> Cesar opened with a few introductory remarks and then, suddenly leaning forward as though about to confide some marvelous secret, asked softly if they had heard of the new organization he was building in the valley—the Farm Workers Association. None of them had, of course, nor was he all that familiar with it himself, having just that day decided on the name. But the words held magic, because heads came straining forward.
>
> He sat in silence, letting the suspense mount before he went on. It is a movement, he said, in which farm workers could struggle to free themselves from the injustice of the job, the government, and life in general. There was no ready-made plan, he assured them. This was one of the reasons he was meeting with them and other workers—to gradually put together ideas based upon what they wanted, along with some of his own. He then passed around some self-addressed three-by-five cards with the lines on the back for the name and address of the worker, and for what the worker considered a just hourly wage.
>
> The idea was an instant hit. Always before, one worker said, others had decided what he deserved. Now he, himself, was being consulted. "It's like letting us vote," he said, "on what we think." . . .
>
> Cesar called for more questions and other issues were raised—the use of Mexican braceros who took the jobs away from local people, the many times they had been cheated by labor contractors, the lack of toilets and clean, cold water in the fields.
>
> They could have gone on all night, but Cesar cut in, explaining that when the workers had their own Association, many of these things would be changed. They would be able to stand up to the growers, he told them, and demand an end to the injustices they had been suffering for so many years. (Levy, 1975, pp. xxi–xxii)

During civil rights campaigns in the South, African Americans who were more financially secure than others, particularly those who held federal jobs, hosted house meetings. At these meetings, people voiced complaints about the many injustices Black people faced. Organizers listened, explained how campaigning for voting rights would be an important way of overcoming these problems, and then encouraged people to join in voter registration drives (Payne, 1995).

A house meeting provides some protection for individuals so disempowered that they are afraid of openly defying their oppressors. People who have good reason to be afraid of threatening bosses—farm workers who hold transient jobs, or African Americans whose livelihoods depended on the people who oppressed them—do not meet alone with an organizer. A house meeting provides some protection, because individuals don't stand out as defiant, and the meeting with the organizer is less visible than it would be on the street or in a shop or restaurant.

This logic was used in efforts to organize ill-paid, immigrant workers in the garment industry, though meetings were not held in their homes. Because of the resistance of management, union organizers were unable to meet with potential members at places of work, while workers were afraid to be seen talking with the organizers even in their homes. Instead, labor unions, working with community agencies, helped set up social service agencies to assist workers and their families. As workers and their families visited these agencies, organizers talked with them and encouraged them to join the labor union. The social service agency created a setting similar to that found in a house meeting (Needleman, 1998).

Mobilizing Along Networks.   Networks are the bonds between people who know each other socially, as kin, or through work. People are most likely to be mobilized into action when they already belong to a network of those who care about the issue, as studies of feminist activism have shown (Cable, 1992). Further, even when people believe in a cause they do not become active unless they are closely connected to others in their social networks who also support the cause (McAdam and Paulsen, 1993). If my friends and relatives say it is okay to join in, it is okay.

Organizers recognize that mobilization occurs as people within a network encourage one another to become active, rather than through direct communications with the organizer. With this in mind, organizers seek out and talk with opinion leaders who are central to a network and hope the message influences others. In doing so, however, organizers must keep in mind that opinion leaders are effective because they reflect the sentiments of others to whom they are linked, not because people simply follow them. Further, depending on the issue, opinion leaders differ. A person who can mobilize support for a social justice campaign might not be the same individual whose help is needed to activate people in a housing project.

Networks are mobilized by convincing people who already have opinions on the topic that they can do something about the issue by working together. For instance, people already linked together in a helping network—to provide assistance in times of financial trouble or death, to aid the elderly, or to assist those with disabilities—have already defined themselves as potential activists on the issues for which the network initially came into being.

National level progressive advocacy organizations work this way. A handful of activists who work for the organization pay close attention to governmental actions that might affect the organization's membership. When broad support is needed, a national issue network is mobilized by sending out letters or e-mail or using phone trees to encourage people to contact elected officials. For example after a Supreme Court ruling that weakened abortion rights, advocacy organizations like Planned Parenthood, the National Abortion Rights Action League, People for the American Way, and the American Civil Liberties Union sent out mailings to their membership throughout the country to call and write legislators to support freedom of choice. Activists in support of affordable housing and fair housing legislation now rely upon electronic communications to activate their networks of supporters when threats to the Community Reinvestment Act appear or when conservatives try to gut the federal budgets that support housing programs for the poor.

Incentives that Encourage Individual Participation

Gladiators are so irritated at a problem that when an organizer appears and describes an organization that can fight back, they jump at the opportunity to join in. Many spectators, though, need an extra boost to move them from quiet anger to a willingness to be active. For some, articulating their anger in the company of other angry people provides a sufficient boost, while others won't join in unless they feel they will get something individually out of the effort, such as the chance to improve their income or housing circumstances. Others are less motivated by material rewards the pleasure that comes about from belonging to a community or being part of a winning team.

Individualized, Material Incentives.   One motivation for people to work in a community organization is to get something of economic value for themselves. Such *material incentives* might include free or subsidized day care, job counseling, group insurance, or a low-cost mortgage. Organizations do not last, however, if the only reason people join is for an immediate material good, as shown by what happened to the Massachusetts Welfare Rights Organization (MWRO).

> MWRO organizers were able to promise welfare recipients that if they participated in welfare rights activities, they would soon be rewarded by supplementary welfare grants. . . . With the passage of time . . . many of the general membership gained enough confidence to make demands of the welfare office personnel without belonging to a group. Others soon found that after a few major supplementary welfare checks had been won, there was little more that the group could continue to offer them.
>   Thus all components in the welfare rights movement—members, organizers, and leaders—began to lose interest in maintaining the local affiliates and the groups began to fade away. (Bailis, 1974, p. 3)

It is possible, though, to provide individual services or goods in ways that encourage people to stick with the broader social action program. For example, some community-based development organizations make available affordable housing for community members, but those who are housed are strongly encouraged to join tenants' associations or cooperative boards and committees that run the new complexes. Once involved in these activities, people soon discover the advantages of providing a community service such as summer programs for their children or neighborhood watches (Briggs, Mueller, & Sullivan, 1997).

Solidarity and Expressive Incentives.   Another way an organizer can move a spectator to become a gladiator is by evoking a sense of communal solidarity in which people assume a responsibility toward the groups with which they identify.

Solidarity incentives "derive in the main from acts of associating and include such rewards as socializing, congeniality, the sense of group membership and identification, the status resulting from membership, fun, conviviality, and so on." (Clark & Wilson quoted in Sharp, 1981, p. 419)

Solidarity appeals mobilize people in several ways. First people become active to protect a group with which they psychologically identify. Initially people join to reinforce their own sense of belonging. In doing so they recognize that they now have an obligation to take actions to defend and support the broader (solidarity) community. "If the highway goes through here, the Armenian [Greek, Turkish . . .] Church will be unable to keep its social program. Kids will find it harder to keep up the traditions. Perhaps I should join the Stop the Highway Organization?" To construct such appeals, organizers must understand the many factors—shared traditions, common ancestral language, beliefs in common heroes—that give meaning to a solidarity community.

Second, people are willing to work in support of identity groups to which they belong—being gay, disabled, an environmentalist, feminist, or any other collectively framed image of self. Although individuals in such identity groups do gain personal benefits—for the wheelchair-bound obtaining ramp access to buildings—often the benefits are diffuse and only slowly trickle down to individuals. For example, as the society becomes less homophobic, gays find daily life less stressful, though the impact of any one particular action of the group on bringing about such improvement is not always obvious. Environmentalists take pleasure in breathing clean air but gain psychological satisfaction from realizing that some species in some faroff place has a better chance to survive. Older women might march to support abortion rights, even though they are unlikely to need abortions themselves. Instead they are acting on a connection to all women, to their daughters, nieces, friends, and acquaintances, becoming active because they see themselves as a part of an identity group.

People are mobilized through solidarity appeals when organizers show how collective actions promote deeply held core cultural values. Such values can include the importance of education or a belief in charity toward neighbors. This approach to mobilizing is now part of the Industrial Areas Foundation (IAF) strategy.

IAF training began to combine the two earlier Alinsky themes of listening to community culture and individual self-interest to gain a different view of what motivates individuals. It began to distinguish between "self-interest" and "selfishness," arguing that people's basic concerns are not only for themselves in an immediate short-term sense . . . people . . . evidence a strong interest in the intangibles of their lives—their families' well-being, their own sense of contribution and dignity, their core beliefs, their friends and closest associates, and their sense of efficacy in the world. (Boyte, 1989, p. 89)

People are mobilized, in part, because they feel good about themselves when they work to preserve shared values and beliefs.

Organizational Participation and Success as a Sustaining Incentive.   Organizations that are run democratically are more likely to get people involved, while organizations that enable people to work on tasks they feel confident to perform increase peoples' willingness to join in a broader effort. People stick with the group because of the satisfaction of shaping the direction that the organization takes (Jenkins & Perrow, 1977; Knoke & Wood, 1981; Kweit & Kweit, 1981). The initial mobilization is reinforced by being in a leadership position in a community group, being active in a tenants' association, or gaining public recognition by holding an office in an organization that others recognize and respect.

Further, as the bootstrapping model implies, people want to be with a winner, so organizations encourage people to join by talking about the successes already obtained and how future victories will come about. Social action organizations that follow the Boston, ACORN, or Alinsky models quickly seek out a visible victory even if on a small issue, while development groups build a new home in a conspicuous location to show people what can be done. People want a major change, but after getting nothing for many years, even a small victory is empowering.

Participation that achieves even small victories can build loyalty to the organization, increase bonds with other members of the group, and, by doing so, reinforce the decision to be involved. What Hirsch describes for activists in block associations holds true in general:

> Those who come to block clubs and tenant unions to attempt to find a solution for a narrow economic problem often quickly stop participating once that issue has been resolved one way or the other. Very active block club members may be motivated primarily by social, i.e., solidary incentives. Reciprocity may be the crucial motivator for those who make the jump to community-wide work. And the most active leaders may be motivated primarily . . . by commitment to the collective goals of the group. (Hirsch, 1986, p. 384)

The trick in creating sustained mobilization is to provide the early victories so that people stick around until they develop a sense of reciprocal obligation and group loyalty.

In protest organizations, each time the enemy is discomforted can be defined as a victory. Alinsky advised organizers to "personalize the issue," that is, identify the problems with a politician, banker, an interfering judge, or bureaucrat. That way, the organization can work on a series of easily accomplished actions, such as picketing the person's home or distributing fliers that show the errors of the target's ways. Each such action provides a short-term victory that keeps people engaged.

Similar ends can be achieved by undertaking actions that are amusing, mock those in power, are exciting, and create the camaraderie that comes from doing something fun together. These visible efforts involve many people, show quick results, and yet are not very threatening to those participating:

> Here's an example of how to put fun in your fight. When we started the antiredlining battle the bank president told us that the bank didn't make loans in our area because it was a slum, recalled Shel Trapp. Needless to say, people got mad about that. But what could they do? We had only $36,000 in deposits in that bank. . . . We tried picketing. Nothing. We kept picketing. No results. They just ignored us and went on with business.
>   Then one of our ladies said, "Let's have a bank-in!" We said, "Great idea!" Then asked, "What the hell's a bank-in?"

The next day, we had our bank-in. We put five of our people at each of the windows. They would each withdraw a dollar. Then they'd deposit a dollar. Then they'd ask for change. We even tied up the drive-in windows. And we sent in a racially mixed couple to get a loan.

Then Josephine . . . dropped two dollars in pennies on the floor. All the guards came rushing over to pick the money up. She thanked them, and dropped the coins again. Finally, the bank president came running out to the office asking what we wanted. We told him we wanted a meeting with the bank's board of directors that afternoon at two o'clock. "But all the directors live in the suburbs!" he bellowed. "Right," we said, "that's the problem—they live in the suburbs and won't make loans in the city."

Well, we got our meeting, and we got a $4 million loan commitment, a review of all previously turned-down loans *and* a $1,000 contribution to the community organization. (Cassidy, 1980, pp. 80–81)

Victories such as this one are stimulating and encourage people to stay involved. Still, organizations need not succeed on every issue once people have developed commitment to the group. Any loyalist to a losing baseball team that *sometimes* beats the league leader demonstrates this principle. *Intermittent reinforcement*—that is, an occasional success—is sufficient to keep many members active.

Even the act of building and maintaining a community or social-change organization reinforces the mobilization cycle. Having a large number of people show up at a meeting is a victory, an increase in paid membership is a victory, getting the newsletter out is a victory, having a politician come to the group's meetings is a victory. Peoples' commitments are strengthened when they are involved in performing even routine tasks, so long as the tasks do not become tedious. Making a reasonable number of phone calls to mobilize others can reinforce the commitment of those who do the calling.

Part of the reason why community and social action groups have so many committees is that much work must be done. But another reason is that the committee work encourages people to be involved, doing necessary tasks to accomplish the organization's goals, and, by so doing, reinforces their initial decision to join.

Committees that deal with publicity are particularly important. People feel useful when they write and circulate a newsletter or put items on a web page. Just getting the newspaper out or keeping the electronic medium up to date is a victory. Moreover, such communication publicizes the successes of the group, encouraging others to join in and strengthening the willingness of older members to stay the course.

In fact, it is primarily through such mass media and Internet communications that national progressive organizations reinforce members' commitment. The newsletters describe the accomplishment and victories, while action alerts, e-mailed notices about problems, encourage people to phone or write legislators, giving members something important to do and reminding them why they joined in the first place.

Tailoring Mobilizing Tactics

To mobilize members, different organizations build on tactics particular to their group, though there is no reason why others cannot copy these ideas. Feminists, for example, recruit using consciousness raising sessions of the sort that often occurs in house meetings. In addition, organizing among women is holistic rather than based on narrow issues. It is clear to many women, for example, that day care is a personal problem, but that it stems from sexism in the society that leaves the major burden of child rearing to women and gives them few financial resources with which to procure day-care services. The connection between the separate problems has the effect of helping to draw together women of different social classes, ethnicity, and marital status into a single organization, because each group is affected by the broader problem.

Mobilization strategies that work for one group may not work for others. Appeals to solidarity across tribal lines has enabled Native Americans to join together, at least politically, but the same kind of appeal of a newly framed and created ethnicity has worked less well for Asians. In some neighborhoods, door-to-door canvassing may be impossible, buildings may be locked, or residents might not let anyone into the building out of fear of crime so one-on-one meetings are problematic. Churches in some communities may be very helpful in mobilizing congregants but in other communities may fear offending the richer people who fund them.

No one approach works all the time. The basic idea, however, of reaching out to people, listening to their needs, and then reinforcing their hopes that change can come about through involvement in organizational activity still provides a guiding model.

Sustaining Mobilization

Getting people initially involved is only the beginning of the mobilization process, as the commitments to the organization must persist over time and through numerous activities. Members might be drawn to an organization initially because they think it will improve their property values or increase access to low-cost day care, but later, they may stay in the organization because they have made friends and enjoy the sociability. People may join an organization because other people they know are active and only later discover the excitement of participating in a winning campaign.

Organizers need to pay attention to ways of holding on to existing members. Techniques for doing so include celebrating victories and replaying together the humor built into some pressure tactics but can also involve setting up tasks that keep people interested, involved, and motivated. Organizers don't just put out a newsletter, instead they encourage those working on the task to learn desktop publishing and use their creativity to produce a product of which they are proud and incidentally learn skills that will be marketable.

If the organizer knows that members enjoy the sociability of the group, he or she designs tasks, even simple ones such as folding flyers so several people can work together. The organizer should be cautious about assigning too much work to any one individual because those who feel overburdened may drop out of the organization. The organizer must also be flexible. Community organizations are built on volunteers who cannot always be active. To handle the unreliability that may result, work should be done by teams so that tasks get accomplished whether or not any one individual is involved. Keeping people involved can be hard work, but successes can be joyous, campaigns can be fun, and even routine efforts can be absorbing and rewarding learning experiences.

8 Gaining Power through Community Research

Research can improve community action. Research empowers group members as they discover the causes of problems and how to bring about solutions. Research documents that the private and individual sufferings of community members are widespread and social. Studies that document a problem are a first step toward the collective action that provides an avenue out of shared helplessness.

What Topics Do Community and Social-Change Organizations Research?

Research takes place at nearly every stage of organizing. Initially community activists want to find out how people see the problems they face and then document the extent of those problems. Some problems are quite visible to all, such as "wall people," the unemployed who hang around corners or appear to spend their days leaning against walls. Other problems are discovered through interviewing people about the difficulties they face in finding homes, getting services, shopping, or obtaining and keeping jobs. Observations about the number and types of businesses there are in the community, or the number of drug pushers in the parks, document community problems.

Organizers want to know how people understand the problems they face and how issues are framed. They learn this information by talking with people, perhaps as part of the canvassing effort. Later on, activists hold focus groups—collective interviews—in which people spark off one another to explore their feelings about problems they face and the possibilities of finding solutions.

Organizers also need to learn what resources are available upon which the organization may build. Do people have a strong sense of belonging to a community? How much effort is required to create the social capital upon which community is built? As part of such inquiries, activists might find out how many groups are in the neighborhood, who belongs, whether these groups cooperate with one another, and the extent of social networks that join people together. Community researchers may examine the neighborhood for segregated playgrounds, the ethnicity of churches and of the owners of the stores, and the presence of needed facilities such as gyms, swimming pools, or day-care centers. Researchers try to see if there are institutions that bring people together from different social classes or ethnic backgrounds, such as unions or religious organizations or schools.

Research is also done to learn about the economic, political, and social environments in which action will be undertaken. Organizations need to know who might support them financially, what grants are available, and which banks might loan them money for which kinds of projects. What types of projects and organizations do foundations now support?

Researchers examine governmental agencies to learn which policies affect the social change organization and to find out what help might be available. Does new or pending legislation speak to the problems at hand? Which officials are in favor of the organization's goals? Who seems to be opposed, and how important or powerful is the opposition? What are the weaknesses or vulnerabilities of opponents?

Organizers need to keep generally informed about changing social conditions, government programs, and the responses of other groups to emerging problems. To keep informed, community organizers often start the day with a careful reading of the local newspaper, looking for stories on local politics. What does it mean when a local alderperson is reassigned to an important committee? Will it help or hurt the neighborhood movement when a senior bureaucrat who has been open with community people is technically promoted to be in charge of the airport but no longer works downtown?

Activists routinely peruse magazines such as *City Limits* for the New York area, the *Third Force* on the west coast, and *Social Policy* for national issues that detail action campaigns and provide background on local social issues. In Chicago, a typical issue of *The Neighborhood Works* has a piece describing how housing activists pressured the city to commit millions to affordable housing, providing examples that other groups might emulate (Ervin, 1994). The National Neighborhood Coalition circulates newsletters that provide background information and the names of contact people on a wide variety of approaches to neighborhood activism. Every few months San Francisco's Organizer Training Center circulates (for a small fee) reprints of a wide array of journal and newspaper stories that describe action campaigns and discuss more philosophical issues of organizing. The typical package of *The Organizer Mailing* contains 150 to 200 pages of such clippings, ranging from stories about the changing political environment to detailed narrations of actual action campaigns. Community researchers would rarely read a whole package, but any one issue has half a dozen stories that probably speak to the concerns of the group.

Numerous activist organizations maintain web pages that describe their groups and present step-by-step narratives of how to conduct a campaign. One of the most exciting sites is put up by the Kensington Welfare Rights Union (KWRU) (*www.liberty-net.org/kwru/kwru/kwru.html*) of Philadelphia. This web page describes how KWRU bootstrapped itself to obtain power by detailing several local campaigns and then describes its national efforts to build a movement for economic justice. The Handsnet web page describes a wide variety of campaigns, while the Community Information Exchange (CIE) maintains a data base on funding opportunities. CIE also circulates reports that detail new approaches toward community renewal. For instance, one described how to use health-care services to help stimulate neighborhood economic development.

One of the best sites for activists is Comm-Org, maintained by Randy Stoecker at the University of Toledo. This web page links to numerous activist groups and archives material on a wide variety of organizing techniques. In addition, Comm-Org electronically distributes a series of papers in which both organizers and academics discuss important issues in organizing philosophy and techniques, ranging from examination of important victories to contentious debates about whether social production drives out direct action.

For those involved in housing and economic development, membership in National Congress for Community Economic Development (NCCED) guarantees receiving a supply of relevant information. NCCED circulates special pamphlets on projects that community groups might want to do, such as those linking social services to housing redevelopment. The National Low Income Housing Coalition (NLIHC) provides crucial information on government support for housing and monitors changes in social welfare policy that might affect housing. The monthly journal *Shelterforce* summarizes the world of affordable housing, detailing activist campaigns and physical redevelopment programs.

For those engaged in either direct action work among the poor or community renewal efforts, contact with the Center for Community Change (CCC) is a must. This organization monitors a range of issues that affect the poor, provides detailed reports on campaigns community groups have undertaken, and sends out action alerts to mobilize people to contact public officials especially on federal policies that could adversely affect the poor. In its journal *Community Change,* the CCC provides detailed how-to-do-it advice, such as ways to influence the mass media. Periodically, the journal provides thoughtful summaries of the extent of poverty and changing public policies toward the poor. The CCC also circulates backup information on long-term projects it runs. For example, those interested in housing trust funds (ways of subsidizing affordable housing) can obtain from the CCC continual updates of action campaigns for setting up such funds.

No one can possibly keep up with all these sources of information on social activism. Because it is important to create a sense of the possible and to make people feel empowered, care must be taken to make sure that people are not flooded with data, much of which is not that useful. The idea is to pick a few sources, subscribe, skim the table of contents (or web pages), and then look in more depth when the information seems relevant. Community researchers need not discover everything about a problem but instead should focus on obtaining the information that speaks immediately to the issues at hand.

Doing the Research

Research must be accurate but done in ways that teach and empower organizational members. Balancing the expertise needed to accomplish research in a technically appropriate way while encouraging participation can take some thought and requires balancing a variety of tasks. Depending on the types of research, activists can play a variety of roles from passive consumers of data to aggressively integrating the research into an action campaign.

As *research consumers,* activists build upon information that others have collected. Universities, support groups, think tanks, and government agencies all collect data on communities and their problems that social change groups rely upon to document the issues. Government agencies routinely collect information on the extent of problems, the distribution of wealth, the conditions of housing, and employment in different locales that would be too expensive for individual groups to obtain on their own.

Activists build on such available data but then need to supplement it to focus on the group's immediate concerns. If organization members need to know the rate of illness at a particular factory or in a specific neighborhood, they may need to collect the data themselves. In following a *participatory action research* (PAR) model community researchers choose the topic, design the way in which data are gathered, collect the information, and do their own analysis (summarized from Stoecker, 1998).

Participatory action research (PAR) helps people document the problems they face while giving voice to the oppressed. For instance, in Appalachia, the Highlander Center using the PAR approach undertook a multistate, multiyear study of land ownership to find out which businesses had exploited the poor and harmed the environment. In a big city neighborhood, community PAR researchers staked out a drug house and tailed the person who collected the rent to locate the owner of the property and eventually pressured him to evict the dope pushers. PAR researchers have documented problems caused by toxic waste, for instance, by noting how many days children in an impacted neighborhood have missed school or had to visit a doctor or nurse with complaints of difficulty in breathing, nausea, or skin rashes. PAR researchers followed up such findings by surveying community members about health problems they have faced and, while doing the survey, introduced their organization to others in the neighborhood.

Some research, though, requires technical skills beyond what members of the action organization can learn in the time they have available. In such circumstances, social-change and community groups can enter into *collaborative research partnerships* with progressive universities or policy research action groups (Nyden et al., 1997). In such partnerships

> academics and nonacademics work together in identifying the research issue, developing the research design, collecting the data, analyzing the data, writing up the results, and even working with policy makers and practitioners in designing programs and policies. (Nyden et al., 1997, p. 4)

Professors can provide technical expertise to design a study and do the more complicated statistical analyses, while the organization members determine what is to be researched, provide much of the labor in gathering the data, and help process the data.

The community response to the environmental disaster at Love Canal shows how collaborative research can come about (A. Levine, 1982). After the Hooker Chemical Company had filled up Love Canal with noxious chemicals and covered it over, people unwittingly purchased homes nearby. Eventually residents noticed a high rate of health problems and began to suspect that poisonous chemicals were leaking into their basements. To combat the problem residents set up the Love Canal Homeowners' Association led by Lois Gibbs, a local housewife turned organizer.

The organization initially appealed to government to explain to them what was happening. After first denying there was a problem, public agencies prepared technical reports, but these reports minimized the health problems. Because community members had talked with one another and knew about the effects of the chemicals on their families, members of the Homeowners' Association were not willing to accept a report that minimized the health problems. Instead, these homeowners worked with university scientists to reexamine the official data. This collaborative effort documented the extremely high rates of illness and provided the information for the subsequent campaign in which the community group was able to pressure the government to declare an emergency and compensate homeowners and allow them to afford to move away.

Data Gathering Techniques

While community activists rarely have the time to become full-fledged researchers, they should be aware of the wide variety of techniques for obtaining needed information. To begin, activists can build on information that others have obtained, much of which is now available on the Internet. As participating members of a neighborhood or social-issue community, activists can observe what is happening and then later interview people about the problems they face and solutions they propose. Sometimes such interviews are conducted at great length and depth, seeking out both detail and individual experiences, while at other times large numbers of people are surveyed to obtain numeric data on specific issues. With focus groups, researchers listen as several people discuss problems at once; with techniques such as network analysis, activist researchers try to discover the linkages between individuals that provide a basis for collective action.

Using Available Data

Community researchers use available data to help document problems, such as unemployment or pollution, environment-related illnesses, or overcrowding in poor neighborhoods. Vast amounts of data on social problems can be found in public sources such as the U.S. Census, local traffic records, or congressional hearings.

It helps to know who collects what kind of information so organization members don't have to sort through too much. For example, the Center for Disease Control (CDC) in Atlanta monitors death rates by cause and can be useful for groups interested in diseases, such as breast cancer or AIDS. CDC data provides insights into environmental problems, as the Center investigates hot spots, areas of the country with unexpectedly high death rates. Besides counting people by location, the U.S. Census collects information on income and education by race and age; data can also be found on employment and housing. If an organization needs to understand the relationship between education and income, in general, over time, and by location (roughly) the Census is the place to look. For information on welfare reform programs, research institutes like the Urban Institute in Washington, D.C., should be the first stop.

Today community researchers can utilize the Internet to find much available data (Schwartz, 1996), including census data, information from the CDC, some of the reports of the Urban Institute, and literally tens of thousands of other items. The Internet refers to five connected tools:

E-mail	Through electronic mail researchers inquire about programs, policies, and problems from other organizations that have faced similar situations.
Lists	Activists become members of lists—mass electronic mailings—in which people each receive and can reply to information about shared interests.
Chat rooms	People with similar interests are on-line at the same time and can discuss and respond to each others concerns, almost as if a face-to-face conversation were occurring.
Web pages	Web pages are the heart of the Internet. On a web page an individual, group, or organization puts up information that others can then access. Such information can vary from official government documents to census material to sets of undigested opinions.
	Quality web pages include indexes or search engines that allow users to search the site using topics or key words.
	Some web pages allow users to pose questions of a database. For instance, a neighborhood group can query the web page maintained by the Census Bureau to learn the average income within a zip code.
	Web pages are linked to other sites of interest. A page describing renewal projects in a neighborhood might be linked to one providing facts and figures on Community Development Corporations, local organizations that build projects in poor communities. These links make research much easier.
Search engines	The amount of information on the Internet is escalating rapidly. People use search engines to locate relevant web pages. A search engine is a program that looks through web sites to find needed information. The user enters key words; the search engine produces a list of web pages in which these words are found.

Available Data on the Federal Government.   Community researchers need to pay close attention to federal programs and funding sources. How much money is available, for what purposes, and from what agencies? What changes have taken place in laws and regulations, and who is affected by these changes? How did particular politicians vote on social issues? Which legislators are on the side of the community or social action organization, and which ones are wavering but could possibly be persuaded to support a particular campaign? What legislation has Congress posed and passed, and what comments did legislators make about the bills?

Studying the federal level is an ongoing activity, because policies and funding are almost always in flux. Decisions can be made by different agencies that contradict one another, and several different departments may have programs on one issue. Community groups concerned with employment and training programs for the poor must monitor the Department of Housing and Urban Development (HUD), the Department of Health and Human Services, and the Department of Labor.

Proposals made in the House of Representatives on an issue might be quite dissimilar from those made by the Senate. Initial decisions might not be followed through and require continual research. For instance, one year, HUD received nearly sufficient funds to maintain the Section 8 housing program, but later on that year Congress took this money to pay for disaster relief, promising to restore it later. Careful monitoring is required to see if promised funds are there when the time comes to spend them.

With the major exception of material on espionage and some parts of the defense budget, most information on the federal government needed by community and social action organizations is public and available, much of it on the Internet. Some of the information is directly provided by government agencies; other material is gathered by support organizations specializing in a given policy area, such as housing or economic redevelopment or income inequality.

Information on funding sources is readily available on the web pages of individual bureaucratic agencies. HUD's web pages are a good place to start, because they are well organized and user friendly, having information about HUD programs and funding and providing links to the Federal Register and the Catalogue of Domestic Assistance, both of which describe sources of money. HUD's web page has buttons connecting to information sources about federal policies and actions on the elderly, the homeless, Native Americans, and the handicapped. HUD also posts NOFAs or notices of funding availability, that is, what grants are available.

The budget as proposed by the president is posted on the website of the Office of Management and Budget. To see what is happening to budget proposals, researchers must examine the legislation as it is passing through both houses of Congress. Budget bills don't become law until they have passed both houses and usually been through a conference of the House and Senate and have been signed by the president. These public laws are posted on the Internet by the Library of Congress (the site is called Thomas after Thomas Jefferson) and are searchable by keywords, such as *housing* or *handicapped* or *environment*. The researcher gets summaries and text, if desired, for all laws passed in a specified term of Congress that contain the researcher's key words somewhere in the legislation.

Thomas (*http://www.Thomas.loc.gov*) is a good place to start for information on a whole array of legislative matters besides the text of laws. This site allows keyword searches of the Congressional Record, so a researcher can see what was said on the House or Senate floor about particular legislation. Thomas has links to the House and Senate websites, which maintain information on committee and subcommittee structures and upcoming hearings and suggest whom to contact and about what. Some committees provide transcripts of selected hearings. Majority and minority parties often maintain separate websites with political interpretations of recent legislation. Thomas also offers links to federal agencies and state and local sites.

Thomas enables researchers to do a quick search initiated by almost any appropriate set of keywords that describe policies or legislation of concern. A researcher might start out looking up major legislation by topic, such as housing or homelessness, AIDS, or veterans hospitals. The more specific the words the better—House Bill 2876 works fine—but almost any set of key words can start the process, such as toxic waste (and) community development. "Housing" and "appropriation" bring up the legislation to fund the Department of Housing and Urban Development.

Thomas lists all roll-call votes for the current session, including how senators and representatives voted on the initial proposal, the amendments, and the final version. If a particular congressperson introduced an amendment to completely gut a piece of legislation advocated by a community group or coalition and then voted for the final version and claimed that he or she supported the legislation, the researchers can see through the claims. Advocacy organizations that want to know what a representative or senator said on the floor about the topic can look up the Congressional Record—just click on the box in the Thomas site—and enter into the search both the topic of concern and the legislator's name. What appears is a list of the speeches made by that person on that topic.

Another search strategy is to go directly to the committees in each house that have jurisdiction over areas that interest the action organization and look up hearings, documents, or press releases. Keep in mind, however, that sometimes a single program is overseen by several different congressional committees. By examining the hearings, an action organization can figure out where controversies are likely to occur; by noting who testified and what they said, group members can determine potential allies and enemies on this issue. Powerful computer search engines allow researchers to find information quickly on specific topics of their concern pulling out the relevant parts from hearing transcripts that may be six-hundred pages long.

While such work is relatively easy, organization members may not have the time for it, in which case, the organization may want to use material that has already been summarized for them by many Washington-based advocacy and information gathering organizations that maintain the information on their web-sites. Recognizing that web addresses change sometimes, we offer some of our favorite sites: *http://www.rtk.net, http://www.ombwatch.org/ombwatch.html, http://www.cbpp.org, http://www.policy.com,* and *http://epn.org.*

Almost all these sites provide news or in-depth reports on policy issues, such as federal funding for housing or whether people leaving welfare are getting jobs and keeping them. Right To Know (RTK) is a public information access group that organizes electronic information on a variety of action issues. Besides keeping track of federal legislation, RTK provides free databases, announces activist conferences, and often posts the speeches and workshops from relevant conferences. Policy.com and epn (electronic policy network) bring together the work of a variety of think tanks, foundations, university programs, and businesses to provide news on current policy issues and make available the publications of the member organizations. OMBWATCH and the Center for Budget and Policy Priorities (CBPP) monitor governmental budgeting; CBPP is well known for trenchant, technically accurate reports on the impacts of legislative or administrative proposals on children and the poor. Some of these sites allow the reader to pick a topic that the site monitors and have e-mail on that topic sent to the individual.

In addition to monitoring the five sites just described, we subscribe to two e-services, HANDSNET and NLIHC. HANDSNET provides a weekly news summary that compiles reports prepared by other organizations that pay close attention to issues such as housing, welfare, children's services, community development, and AIDS-HIV research. Its approximately five-thousand subscribers gain access to a user-friendly interface that has an e-mail facility and discussion forums in different areas of interest to social activists. The service encourages participants to post news, services, and ideas for social action organizations. HANDSNET also provides a custom electronic news clipping service, which locates materials from a profile provided by the subscriber.

The National Low Income Housing Coalition (NLIHC) is an activist coalition that works in support of affordable housing. Besides its lobbying work, NLIHC maintains an active home page that links to information sources on state, federal, and, at times, local housing concerns. Each week, NLIHC electronically circulates to its members synopses of changes that have taken place that affect housing policy. Its electronic newsletters provide details on congressional committee actions, program changes, funding levels, and policy shifts. The weekly bulletin also monitors pressures to change key legislation such as the Community Reinvestment Act.

Researchers who subscribe to any of these services also receive ACTION ALERTS, sent to the news services by other organizations. ACTION ALERTS points out pending legislation of vital importance to social action organizations and then specify which public officials should be contacted on the issue, often providing telephone or e-mail addresses. On a weekly basis, HANDSNET summarizes a wide variety of ACTION ALERTS. On one occasion all subscribers to OMBWATCH received an ACTION ALERT at 10 o'clock at night, when a conservative congressperson tried sneakily to add provisions to a bill that would have stopped nonprofits from lobbying.

Available Data on Neighborhoods.   Community researchers can locate a vast amount of data on their neighborhoods. Information collected by government is particularly valuable, not because it is better than data activists collect, but because government agencies are more likely to believe data they collect themselves.

Local government offices keep records that are descriptive of communities, such as crime rates by location and type, traffic accidents by intersection, housing complaints against particular buildings, the location of road repair projects, and the emergency response time for police, fire, and ambulance. Other data maintained by city or county departments includes land use by residential, commercial, and industrial categories, requests for zoning changes, and building permits. City and county community development agencies submit grant proposals to other public organizations that require back up data on such matters as poverty levels, the quality of housing, and social welfare needs. Annual financial reports often list the largest property tax payers in the city or county. Such information can be useful in planning campaigns and in providing background data on the community.

The Department of Housing and Urban Development maintains data bases, many accessible through the Internet, that provide information on local problems. Such information is most likely to be available on the country's most distressed neighborhoods. HUD provides software (called *Community 2020*) that enables users to access demographic data and housing information for small geographic areas.

HUD maintains on its website the backup documents that cities, and within selected cities, Empowerment Zones, provide, describing the economic, housing, and social problems they face. This data may or may not be broken down by neighborhoods. Statistical information can be obtained from HUD on public housing projects in specified geographic areas and on an indirect subsidy (called the Low Income Housing Tax Credit) that can help community groups that are planning to build affordable housing. Such data are probably best accessed as part of a collaborative research project because more complicated statistical tools are necessary to make sense of them.

An increasing number of neighborhoods maintain their own home pages describing social conditions in the communities and actions community members have taken to regain control. Many of these web pages that are descriptive of neighborhoods can be found through *http://www.libertynet.org/*. While the data speak to different communities than the one in which the researchers are working, the available material suggests the types of information that can be collected for almost any neighborhood.

The Department of Labor releases material on unemployment rates, while state employment offices prepare material on both new hires and unemployment for many locales. Such data must be examined with care because unemployment figures only include those who are currently unemployed and are looking for work. The numbers do not include those who have taken lesser jobs or people who have given up looking for work. They usually only go down to the county level, not to the level of cities or neighborhoods.

Private commercial surveys can be of use in measuring economic conditions within communities. Dun & Bradstreet provides information on turnover in local businesses, vacancies in office buildings, capitalization of business, and other figures that suggest where economic problems might occur. Commercial vacancy rates can be estimated by looking out of a car window or by asking commercial real estate firms for such data.

The U.S. Census.   A major source of social, economic, and demographic data about local communities are the various surveys and censuses carried out or contracted for by the federal Bureau of the Census. Every ten years, the Bureau counts each individual in the country, obtains some background data from all, and more detailed information from a sample of the total population. This more detailed information includes age, family status, family and personal income, race and ethnic background, gender, education, employment status, commute to work, and the type, quality, and expense of housing in which people live. Major pressure from members of Congress to reduce the cost of the census and its intrusiveness in people's lives and business may reduce this source of information in the future. In addition to the population census, the Bureau of the

Census conducts a survey of housing conditions in major metropolitan areas every few years. For wealthier communities, census material is considered quite accurate, but unfortunately, in poorer and minority communities, many individuals are missed, distorting the overall information.

Population and housing data are released by census tracts, geographic areas that usually contain about four-thousand people. The Census Bureau tries to maintain the same geographic boundaries for census tracts from one census to the another to observe changes; as a consequence census tracts that house the poorest part of the population tend to be smaller, as people have moved out of these areas, though the number of such tracts containing very poor people has increased.

In larger cities, the Census Bureau tries to match the boundaries of the tracts to neighborhoods, at least as the city officials define neighborhoods. In practice, community researchers have to combine data from separate tracts to match the actual neighborhoods their organizations represent. Data are not released on individuals, only on groups within areas, and if too few individuals of a given social background are found in any tract, that category is excluded from the published data. Some data is also compiled by ZIP code, and all data are aggregated by cities (or their equivalent) as well as by counties.

In any one community, researchers can examine census data to learn about the poverty level, quality of housing, the amount of education people have, and other quality–of–life indicators. Comparisons of census data over time point out trends that can guide community work, such as the expanding number of female-headed households or the increasing likelihood that children will live in poor households. Census data also permit comparisons of wealth, unemployment, or living conditions by racial and ethnic groups.

Raw census data is released in printed form, on computer tapes, and in many cases can be accessed through the Internet. In recent years, the federal government has cut back the budget of the Census Bureau so that the Bureau is less willing to produce reports that focus on specific, narrowly defined geographic areas or do the more sophisticated multivariate analyses. It is still easy to find out how many poor there are in a community, but researchers either have to work with raw census data tapes or hire a commercial service to determine, for instance, the relationships among education, family status, ethnicity, and the economic well-being of children. Handling census tapes can be tricky so collaborative research is advised.

For quick statistical descriptions on communities, researchers can electronically query the web page of the census bureau. By clicking on a map or by specifying census tracts, ZIP codes, or the names of places, the researcher is presented with a list of census variables. He or she checks off the ones for which information is required. Almost instantly, the information appears.

To obtain more detailed information community researchers can acquire census tapes or CD-ROMs with census data and do the data analysis themselves. For aggregate analysis at the tract level, such research is possible, but the Census Bureau does not release raw data on individuals, so certain forms of analysis are difficult. A researcher can figure out that areas in which people lack adequate education and are predominately minority have low incomes. The data do not permit examining if it is the individual minority people themselves who are poor and lack the education or if other people who live in the same area are the ones in economic trouble.

Participant Observation

Researchers can find out from data from the Census Bureau and other government agencies about basic problems such as the number of people on welfare, the amount of overcrowding, or the ratio of dependents, old and young, to working people. There are many things about a community, however, that are relevant for organizing that do not show up in available data. Some of that information can be gleaned from being in the community, watching, writing down what the researcher sees, and analyzing it afterward. That kind of research is called participant observation.

Participant observation can be useful in documenting problems when there is little available data, when getting it proves difficult, or when vivid types of description are required to supplement cold statistics. For example, to measure the intensity of police patrol, an observer can stand at a corner and count the number of squad cars that pass by. To find out about garbage services, organization members can walk through the streets the day after garbage has been picked up and note the thoroughness of the job. To document the under serving of the medically poor, researchers can go to the emergency room of the local hospital, which often is the primary source of medical care for the poor, and measure how long people with various problems have to wait for service.

Community researchers can walk around a neighborhood and note what is located in each lot—a house, apartment building, store, park, service station, dump—then observe whether each structure is dilapidated or if windows are broken. A visual survey of the neighborhood reveals such problems as broken sidewalks, unpaved or chip-and-seal roads, and gaping potholes. Poor drainage shows up in flooded underpasses; sewer backups are apparent through their stench, especially after a heavy rain. Environmentalists can count dead animals in polluted watersheds or walk along waterways and note illegal dumping of industrial waste.

If the community has many homeless people, they are visible on the streets. Are parks controlled by hoodlums? How old are the school buildings, and what shape are they in? If the schools have playgrounds, are they black-topped (dangerous if children fall) or do they have rubber or sand flooring? Are public buildings accessible to the disabled?

Through an observational tour, community researchers may see teenagers hanging around street corners or game rooms or observe the spray-painted names of street gangs on the walls. They may watch people catching the bus after a long wait in rain or snow. Or, they may see people hurrying home at dusk, trying not to be caught out alone after dark.

Observations can also help document economic problems in the community that are hard or impossible to see in available data. Researchers can compare food prices in the markets and find that they are higher than elsewhere in the city, maybe because the neighborhood is served only by small and overpriced minimarts. Bulletin boards in markets or laundermats may show a number of people looking for odd jobs, suggesting underemployment or an inability to get by on low-salaried jobs. Frequent advertisements to sell household goods might indicate lots of people moving in and out. If there are many day-labor employment offices in the community, there are probably a number of people with low skill levels, while a lot of empty storefronts suggests a shrinking economy. The researcher might also note whether the community is served by branch banks with reasonable fee structures or whether the financial needs of the residents are being met only by money exchanges, with their high costs for routine services.

If there are only a few local stores, money rapidly leaks out of the community as people have to buy goods elsewhere. The businesses that do exist may require little capital investment, such as barbers or beauty salons. There may be many shops that sell pornographic materials or drug paraphernalia. An observational study may show, as one did in the burned down areas of Los Angeles, the presence of more liquor stores than in any other part of the city. All these are indicators of an unhealthy economy.

Skilled observers cannot only see the amount of change in a neighborhood but also, to some extent, its direction. For example, in larger cities, the presence of artists in loft apartments can be a sign that real estate people plan to gentrify the community, renting first to artists who want large inexpensive space, then slowly increasing rents, improving apartments, and then eventually displacing the poor.

Community organizers need to know not only what problems exist but also how community members feel about these problems. The organizer in his or her role as researcher can chat with neighbors, talk to people about their problems at supermarkets, or discuss community matters while waiting for a bus. To supplement what is heard at these encounters, activist researchers attend community meetings or go to neighborhood social clubs and listen to peoples' complaints and try to hear how community members interpret their world. Is it a world of hope and potential or one in which the people have given up? Do people blame themselves for their problems, the system, or other ethnic groups?

As organizers listen, they might hear men talking among themselves, complaining about the difficulty of finding jobs because of affirmative action. The problem is jobs, or the lack of them, but these people have been distracted into a useless and generally unfounded anger. They need more information about where their jobs really went. The task of a community organization might be to document the loss of jobs and try to figure out where they went, why they went, and whom to target to stop the outward flow.

In addition to pointing out problems, participant observation can help document resources. The physical location of a neighborhood itself can be an asset. For example, if the neighborhood is located within easy distance of a vibrant downtown, the community organization might be able to develop some local businesses, employing local residents, to supply the needs of the downtown. Another asset might be small manufacturing plants that hire people at living wages. These plants can employ the young from the neighborhood or provide the customers for luncheonettes. In poor neighborhoods buildings have been torn down. As long as this vacant space has adequate sewer and water, as almost always is the case in urban areas, these apparently desolate spaces provide the sites to construct affordable homes and needed community businesses.

Communities are more easily rebuilt by working with facilities already in place. What facilities are available, and what additional businesses might service them? For example, is there a busy community medical or mental health facility? Are there hospices for the terminally ill? Is there a van that transports the elderly to clinics or shopping, and are there special housing facilities for the old? Are such facilities located within easy walking distance of stores or recreation? Are there youth centers and places for day care for children and the dependent elderly?

Social organizations are also a community asset. For instance, "researchers in one low income Chicago neighborhood found over 150 associations" varying from political clubs, to square dancers, to religious groups, to women's organizations, to Alcoholics Anonymous (Kretzman and McKnight, 1993, p. 111). Researchers can explore whether the churches provide needed social services or if the clergy are willing to take a lead role in combating social problems. Colleges are often located near poor neighborhoods—real estate is less expensive—and might provide a wealth of resources that the community could use, as do the public libraries. Banks might sponsor social services, and in some neighborhoods, community organizations have encouraged even currency exchanges to fund neighborhood renewal programs.

Sometimes walking around the community while observing and recording information can suggest possible organizing issues or strategies. For example, if the parks seem to be used by some ethnic groups but not by others who also live nearby, community activists might be cautious about proposing organizing issues that require cooperation between ethnic groups in a given neighborhood. Organizing along solidarity lines might be more successful, at least initially.

Participant observers in community organizations may try to figure out the amount of social glue that links people together. Do people know their neighbors? What holidays bring people together? Are there local festivals that celebrate the traditions and contributions of different ethnic or cultural groups? Have neighbors faced a common problem, such as flooded basements, tracking of economically deprived children to slower classes in school, or the closing of a major store? If so, they have already joined together in a common effort and are more likely to work together again.

Focused In-Depth Interviews

In-depth interviews allow the researcher to ask questions and listen to the answers and then follow up with further questions to really understand what people feel and think. One key function of in-depth interviews is to elicit detailed and sensitive stories about people's experiences with problems that are amenable to collective solution. People may describe embarrassing encounters with police, frustration at the inability to use a restroom in a wheelchair, or humiliation at a public meeting when asking a question. These stories may highlight problems that organizers already know about, or they may bring to light situations that the organizers never thought about. Interviewees might describe being falsely accused and arrested and being unable to prove their innocence; or, they might talk about coming home from work to find the baby-sitter gone and the baby all alone. People might talk about their fear of walking from public transportation to their apartments after dark or their difficulty paying doctor bills. Each of these, should they prove to be common problems, could provide the subject for a campaign or collective activity.

In-depth interviews can also help design or redesign programs. An interviewer working with a community employment agency might be curious why teenagers fail to get jobs, even when they have the requisite skills. Rather than guessing, he or she asks individual teenagers to describe the day of the interview in detail. From their descriptions, the interviewer learns that these young people did not know how to dress. The researcher also discovers that when those hiring asked pointed, personal questions, the teenagers acted hurt or defensive. Based on this knowledge, the community agency can redesign its program, to include advice on dressing and how to respond to pointed or even personal questions.

In-depth interviews are a little like ordinary conversation but concentrate on only one or two matters that are discussed in greater detail than in a normal conversation. To get the kind of detail that is necessary, the researcher has to let interviewees know that their experiences are worth sharing. When people begin a story, interviewers encourage people to provide details through body language (leaning forward slightly, maintaining eye contact) and brief statements, such as "that's interesting" or "please continue." Interviewers solicit details with gentle probes or follow-up questions such as "then what happened?" or "you've described a bad incident with the landlord, have you had other such experiences?" (Rubin & Rubin, 1995).

If the interviewer is trying to find out what might motivate people to organize to fight back, the general opinions of those being interviewed are less important than information on actual incidents. If an organizer asks a community member his or her opinion of city hall, and the answer is "they are a bunch of s.o.b.'s," the organizer still does not know what the issues are or what a solution might consist of. A more pointed set of questions, such as, "have you had experience with city hall? if so, what was it like? what happened? can you describe it to me?" is more likely to reveal a potential organizing issue and the emotion surrounding it.

Researchers try to keep people focused on the general topic of concern. An activist researcher for a consumer group steers conversations to problems in dealing with stores and firms rather than the failure of the Department of Defense. The trick is to keep people on the major topic without the activists imposing their own views on community members.

If the goal is to learn general information about a community, researchers should talk to a wide array of people. Once a problem has been specified, in-depth interviews are most meaningful especially when carried out with those most concerned with the issue. Leaders of tenants' groups are best attuned to problems with landlords, while clergy or those running social service agencies often keep on top of family difficulties. Still a variety of perspectives is required to best understand the situation and to learn what can be done. If people in the neighborhood are thinking about setting up a crime watch, researchers might interview victims of crimes, the police, and business owners and residents in the areas with the most crimes. In addition, interviews in similar neighborhoods that already have a crime watch probably will provide insights about what to do and what to avoid in setting up a similar program.

In figuring out whom to interview, care is required to assure that researchers get the information needed and that they gain a variety of perspectives. After interviewing an informed person, researchers ask for suggestions on others who are in the know. A person on the board of a housing development organization might recommend talking with those from a social agency that helps people prepare their finances so that banks will approve a mortgage loan. Activists involved in one issue almost always know others who are also so engaged.

Especially if the organization is planning action on an issue, make sure a wide variety of perspectives are covered. If a person being interviewed strongly advocates one side, the researcher might want to ask the names of people with whom this person disagrees and then follow up by interviewing them. Common sense often suggests who might have different perspectives. In one neighborhood, interviewers talked with tenant activists who wanted to reduce automobile traffic to protect their children and then followed up by talking with the local merchants who wanted more parking to lure in customers. These interviews provided information that enabled the action organization to prepare a plan that included off-street parking that protected most residential streets. The proposal satisfied (at least in part) both neighborhood factions and enabled the community group to succeed.

Focus Group Interviewing

People talk together informally at social occasions and at any place where friends or neighbors gather. Community researchers listen carefully to such sessions to gather ideas on community needs, especially from people who might be too shy to share what they feel in a one-on-one interview. Similarly, at consciousness-raising sessions and at house-meetings potential activists share their understandings of the problems they face. A focus group tries to recreate the exchanges that occur in such informal conversations, though in ways that focus on a topic chosen by the researcher (Greenbaum, 1998; Morgan, 1988).

In setting up focus groups, activist researchers first determine the types of information needed and then choose participants accordingly. If the goal is to learn about typical problems in the community, researchers might invite an array of individuals from the neighborhood to match roughly the various demographic categories. For example, there could be one focus group of the elderly, one group of males and one of females, and different groups representing major ethnic or racial groups in the neighborhood. If the information needed is ways of improving a day-care center, one focus group might be made up of parents whose children are attending one and another might consist of parents who have decided not to use the service. If the problem is that participation in meetings at a housing cooperative has declined, researchers might invite board members to one focus group, regular attendees to another, and people who don't attend the meetings to a third.

To encourage people to talk, focus groups are kept small. Once a focus group has been assembled and participants have had some time to socialize over coffee, the moderator, often the community organizer himself or herself, introduces the topic and, if needed, makes a few comments to get the conversation going. Sometimes he or she calls on people to assure that everyone has a chance to talk but otherwise does not participate in the conversation. While people talk about the subject matter at hand, they are videotaped or tape recorded for later analysis. Usually an hour or so is set aside for the discussion.

The moderator introduces the topic in general terms. What needs improvement in the neighborhood? What can we do about the interethnic tensions in the neighborhood? Early in the session, participants may be asked to jot down a few ideas and then speak briefly on them without others responding. This is done to assure that everyone's ideas are on the table rather than letting the more aggressive attendees set the agenda. Once this initial round has taken place, people are encouraged to talk about their feelings, experiences, and ideas for improvement on the matter at hand, each taking turns speaking but following no particular order. People can respond to each other's ideas and present the things they thought of themselves.

When a topic seems to have been exhausted, the moderator might suggest moving on. He or she can summarize the conversation to that point and ask if that is a good description of how people feel or if it leaves some important theme out. If necessary, a moderator might toss out a different slant to stimulate further conversation. "Seems like everyone wants new affordable housing in the neighborhood. Does that mean that you are less interested in luring some stores back in?" If the conversation seems to be getting too raucous, the moderator tries to calm it down.

The tapes of the focus group session contain a lot of information. Focus groups are like a dozen in-depth interviews occurring at the same time, with many people sharing their experiences on a single topic. The stories and experiences told by one person often jog the memories of others who are then able to narrate occurrences that they probably would not have thought of otherwise. Researchers who observe the group dynamics can sometimes find patterns that might affect the success of the organizing effort. For example, as the discussion continues, do people work out a shared understanding of a problem or do they grow contentious? Are there tensions and disagreements on substance between people from different ethnic groups? Are these disagreements in narrowly focused areas that can be avoided in later meetings, or are tensions so high that people from different ethnic groups disagree no matter what the issue?

Focus groups can reveal important cleavages. For instance, a focus group was held among community activists who were preparing applications for federal housing assistance. All agreed on the need for more housing and the reluctance of government to provide it, but the activists strongly disagreed about how to define the eligibility level for those receiving housing assistance. Some community activists wanted the funds to go only to help individuals in extreme distress while others wanted money to help poorer working-class people buy small homes to help stabilize economically declining communities. The focus group discussions brought these divisions to light, and the participants worked out the issues in later meetings.

Survey Interviewing

In a survey, a set of uniform questions, usually with standardized categories for answers, is asked of a large number of respondents. From surveys, community researchers can learn such things as the satisfaction of people with their housing, public transportation, or community services. Survey respondents state whether they have been victims of crime or till the rent they pay, among hundreds of other topics. For state and national organizations, a survey might be the only practical way of learning what the widely scattered membership wants the organization to do.

Sometimes organizations are surveyed, for instance, to find out which funding sources housing organizations use or to tally the accomplishments of community development groups (National Congress for Community Economic Development, 1995). Recently, organizers in Ohio surveyed an array of neighborhood and community groups to learn what types of technical assistance these newer organizations would need and whether they would be willing to join a state-wide coalition (West, 1998).

Unlike in-depth interviewing in which details from a few are found, the purpose of a survey is to determine overall sentiment. When survey respondents are chosen through a *scientific sampling procedure,* answers from a modest number of people can be generalized to a larger number with a specified degree of accuracy. Survey answers, however, lack the depth and detail of focused interviews and require people to react to questions posed by the researcher rather than articulate their own perspectives. Surveys are used better to determine how many face a problem or how much people spend and other straightforward factual matters, rather than how people frame and understand issues.

Still surveys can provide needed background information. In *needs assessments surveys,* respondents are asked about the problems they face and their willingness to join in collective action to solve them. *Satisfaction* or *evaluation surveys* determine the extent to which people are content with something such as a service they've received, while in *outcome surveys* organizations are queried to learn how much they have produced, for example, the number and cost of housing units they have built.

Some surveys attempt to tap *general information* about a community and provide data to help focus organizational action. Community members are asked whether they are likely to volunteer and for how long or their respective interests in a variety of tasks the community group could undertake. Community members are asked about skills they have and groups to which they belong, as part of an effort to measure the amount of social capital. Though the topics for surveys are nearly endless, the goal is to make sure that the information collected is focused on community needs and can lead to subsequent action and is not simply collected to keep people busy.

Surveys are probably best done as part of a collaborative research project as writing questions, choosing a sample, and carrying out the statistical analysis require experience and formal training. In preparing surveys or working with those who do, keep in mind the following hints about writing questions and selecting a sample.

Preparing Questions.   Several rules guide the writing of more meaningful survey questions:

1. *Questions must make sense and seem important to the respondent.* Questions should be relevant to the immediate situation people face and not be on some distant concern. A researcher would ask housing cooperative members about housing conditions but probably shouldn't pose questions about issues of war and peace.

2. *Don't collect more information than is needed.* Keep survey instruments as short as possible by making sure that any question asked provides information necessary to the action organization. If working on setting up a day-care facility for the elderly, questions on the number of elderly in each household or the medical coverage they now have would be relevant, while general opinions about Social Security or Medicare would probably be of little use.

3. *Word questions carefully.* The language should be simple, direct, and familiar to the respondents. Avoid using technical terms or government jargon, unless surveying people who use such terms in their daily work. Do not ask about "a unit" when you want to know about an apartment or a home. To assure that survey wording is understandable, items on the survey should be tested with people similar to those being studied before the questionnaire is used.

Avoid questions that are loaded or double barreled. A loaded question virtually forces a given answer, for example, how can someone say no to "Do you oppose dumping of toxic chemicals?" A double-barrelled question asks two items in one question, such as "Do you want to tear down existing housing and build a home for the elderly?" People who want to keep the old housing in place but still support housing for the elderly cannot answer such questions in a meaningful way.

4. *Keep the answer categories fairly simple, and make sure each category is distinct.* The answer categories must be short and easily understood. With opinion questions, standard categories such as "strongly agree," "agree," "neutral," "disagree," and "strongly disagree" or "very satisfied" . . . "very dissatisfied" are easily understood. Make sure all possible answer categories are covered, including, if necessary, a category called "other" or "no opinion."

Sometimes a needs assessment survey asks people to order the importance of problems such as lack of shopping, crime, or the inconvenience of mass transportation. If using a ranking, don't try to compare more than three or four items in one question and make sure that the comparisons are between similar items. People might have concerns about Social Security cost-of-living increases and be worried about whether they will get enough heat in their apartment building, but comparing actions at the federal level with problems with landlords really makes little sense.

5. *Be cautious about using open-ended questions on a survey.* Fixed format means that the answer categories are already given, while open-ended means that the respondent can say whatever he or she feels is correct. For the most part, open-ended answers on surveys confuse more than they illuminate, as people vary in the clarity, scope, and depth of what they say. If researchers want to explore issues to obtain what people think in detail, they are advised to use an in-depth interview, not a survey. Still, if part of the initial canvassing to mobilize people involves asking survey questions, organizers might want to include some open-ended questions that then become the topic for an immediate in-depth conversation.

Choosing a Sample.   The goal of surveys is to find out how common an attitude or experience is and among which groups: What percent of people are angry enough at city hall to work against the mayor? How long does it take the average person to get to work, and what percent of people use public transportation? Are African Americans more likely to be denied a loan than members of other groups?

To find out these answers might seem to require talking to far more people than the organization has time or money to survey. If people are chosen for the survey using *scientific sampling procedures,* however, answers from a smaller number of people can be generalized to the entire community with a known degree of confidence.

Scientific sampling requires following exact procedures in choosing survey respondents. Talking with the first few people contacted, or surveying only friends and neighbors simply doesn't work as these people are more likely to have similar opinions. While the technicalities of scientific sampling can be complicated and probably should be done as part of collaborative research, as long as three basic principles are followed, the results tend to be accurate (Rubin, 1983, pp. 131–162).

First, researchers specify the broader group whose opinions, concerns, or factual descriptions are of interest, the *overall population.* If the researchers want to know what problems adults in the neighborhood feel are important, the population might be all people over eighteen who live in the neighborhood. In this case, a couple living with two college-aged children would count as four people. If on the other hand, the organization is interested in measuring the extent of housing blight, each dwelling place is treated as one member of the population (of housing units) no matter whether it is empty or three families are sharing it.

In a national survey of organizations that build affordable homes, the researchers have to decide whether to include in the population all organizations that build homes, even if that is not their main goal, or only those that specialize in community-based housing development. In the former case, churches that build one or two homes a year would be part of the population, in the latter case they would not be considered so.

Once the population is specified, the researcher prepares a system for uniquely identifying each member of the population. For voters, lists can be obtained from boards of elections and broken down by precincts. If the population consists of housing units, a listing of addresses can be prepared by walking around a number of blocks and writing down the addresses or by using a current city directory. For a national organization, each member normally has an identifying number; those numbers can be used to list the population.

Sometimes, appropriate lists are not available. In this case, researchers must avoid just grabbing anything that looks like a list, lest doing so distort the results. For example, using a sign-up sheet for those who attended a city-sponsored neighborhood planning session would be useful only for choosing the most active, not for community members more generally.

Often substitutes are available that function like a list. Most people live in houses, apartments, or prefab homes so the addresses of homes substitutes for the list of people, as long as a rule is set up for determining whom to interview in each home. Even the homeless have been "listed" by clever researchers working for advocacy groups. One team mapped out a city to locate alleys, doorways, and other places the homeless might sleep and conducted a survey of those locations in the early hours of the morning (Rossi and Wright, 1989).

If a researcher *randomly* chooses people (or organizations) from the lists, the answers that these people provide can be mathematically extended to the whole population described by the list. *Random* does not mean hopping and skipping down the list any old way, rather it does mean using a statistical procedure so that each person on the list has an equal chance of being chosen, but no one knows in advance who will be picked. Usually a table of random numbers, sometimes one generated by a computer, is used to choose the numbers.

There are a few catches. People must be willing to answer the questions in a truthful manner. Further, if large numbers of listed people cannot be found, or many simply refuse to answer, the sample might not really be random. If only the most angry or most active people answer the survey, while the others refuse, a totally distorted view of the community could result. Activists might falsely assume many people would show up at a demonstration because these are the ones who replied to the form, when in fact, most people were unwilling.

Network Analysis

Communities are places in which both people and organizations are linked to one another in ways that allow exchanges of information, social support, and material resources. To discover these linkages, community researchers undertake *social network analyses,* that is asking who knows whom, what people share with one another, and what organizations are linked to one another and how.

Community researchers undertake network analysis by asking individuals whom they know, whom they would go to for support, whom they have helped, and who has helped them. Researchers ask people how many friends they have living nearby and to whom they talk about problems. From whom do they learn about job opportunities? Whose advice is sought on how to vote? Are the networks tightly enough linked so that mobilizing one person encourages many others to join the organization? In ascertaining the amount of social capital, researchers look for support networks. Can people who are unemployed find help in putting food on the table, or do they know someone who will introduce them to a potential employer? Are people networked within a solidarity community that enables them to borrow funds from kin or coethnics, perhaps to start a small business?

Network analysis provides information on how easily a message or request for support will spread. Do the social networks of those who know each other from work, politics, and recreation overlap so that a wide variety of people are connected to one another? Are there cliques of people connected among themselves but isolated from other groups? Do issue networks overlap, that is, do people who are fighting for day care also work to preserve the environment or defend civil liberties?

Organization Sets.   Part of network analysis involves discovering the organization set to which the community group belongs. An *organization set* is made up of those organizations whose actions influence another specified organization. In mapping out an organization set, a researcher tries to find the allies, government agencies, rival organizations, and protest targets that influence the focal community group.

This is done in two ways. First, the researcher examines the actual dealings the community organization has with other organizations and notes the transactions involved: When the community organization seeks out financial support, it talks with officials at the Steelcase Foundation; when it seeks help on managing affordable housing, it calls up the Enterprise Foundation. In this part of the analysis, community researchers locate relevant organizations in the community and national advocacy groups that might help local groups.

Another approach to learning about organization sets is compiling a list of organizations and institutions in the neighborhood, perhaps by taking a walking tour, by inspecting neighborhood directories, or even by thumbing through phone books. The researcher then picks core issues—a protest to preserve affordable housing from demolition when a sports stadium is proposed or an effort to encourage a supermarket to move in—and examines which organizations were involved in the issue and what they attempted to achieve. The researcher then notes the relationships of these organizations to the core community group and to each other. For instance, a community-based redevelopment group may receive indirect help from the city's community development department because it pressured county officials to provide more services in poor neighborhoods.

Organization sets differ depending on the particular issues, but linked groups can usually be classified in terms of a few categories, as we illustrate for a community redevelopment organization. First, there are the *potential partisans,* organizations that might help the redevelopment group in action campaigns. Next, there are *local allies* such as sympathetic church groups and merchants' associations that might help in the physical redevelopment projects. *External allies,* organizations outside of the neighborhood, such as the Local Initiatives Support Corporation (LISC), provide grants, loans, and technical advice on housing and commercial development. *Bureaucratic linkages* are those maintained with public offices, such as the community development office at city hall or the regional office of the Department of Housing and Urban Development. *Rival organizations* are important parts of the organization set because they might oppose some of the efforts made by the core group. Finally, organizations confront *targets*—businesses such as banks or real estate companies—whose efforts have to be thwarted to bring about community-controlled redevelopment.

Planning and Combining Different Data Gathering Procedures

To obtain the data needed for most campaigns and projects, community researchers usually combine several different data-gathering procedures. Suppose that community members are interested in documenting the fairness and efficiency of the services provided by government, because activists believe that some neighborhoods get better service than others and some neighborhood residents are harassed more than others. To measure the number of police officers, the organization simply looks in the available budgets and annual reports. Information on how police are assigned to different parts of the town might require doing in-depth interviews of police department officials or, if cooperation is not forthcoming, extensive observations of actual patrol strategies. Background surveys of community members can determine whether or not people from different ethnic groups are more or less likely to have contact with the police.

If the problem the group is researching is the deterioration of the rental property in the community, the problem can be broken into smaller research questions, each investigated with separate data-gathering techniques. For example, commercial financial services such as Moody's or Standard and Poor's provide information on the percentage of property taxes levied that are actually collected. A figure under 95 percent indicates a serious problem, such as landlords running their properties into the ground and refusing to pay property taxes. Some cities have housing courts where tenants can bring complaints about the lack of heat in winter or broken toilets that are never fixed. Participant observation in such courts may give a good view of the problem with particular landlords and give a feeling as to how widespread the discontent. Many communities have community relations offices, which mediate landlord-tenant disputes. These offices have records that community groups may use to identify particularly troublesome property owners, or they may provide sites for participant observation. Interviewing the community relations officers may also prove helpful. Information on how to retrofit apartments for people with various physical limitations can be found from Internet sites, while the newsletters of other organizations mention sources of funding for housing projects.

Sometimes a target of a campaign might be a large company that appears to be leaving the neighborhood or is seen as discriminatory in its hiring policy. To pressure such a company, information is required that in many cases can be found on the Internet (summarized from Mattera post to comm-org Saturday Oct. 23, 1999). Several different sites, such as *www.hoovers.com* or *www.companiesonline.com,* provide brief descriptions of firms, while for larger companies the Federal Securities and Exchange Commission requires electronic filings that describe the owners of the company, major stockholders, and others who could be pressured. Increasingly, Secretary of States' offices post background on companies. By examining sites such as the one maintained by the Center for Responsive Politics (*www.crp.org*) activists can find which corporate political action companies have contributed to what politicians.

Using the Research Data

Once collected and analyzed, activists use research data in a wide variety of ways. Background information stimulates community discussions on what problems should be tackled first and why. The community is becoming multiethnic; how do we take into account different cultural traditions?; rents are rising faster than incomes; people are afraid they won't be able to pay their rent; and certain buildings are being gentrified. How should we respond? There is a large unmet need for day care for the elderly parents of working families; can community groups do something about this problems?

Research can show how to solve problems, for example, a social production organization might want to imitate the New Communities Corporation (a community development group in Newark, NJ) that figured out how to tie together day care and job training. Data obtained becomes part of a proposal for funding from foundations and government agencies. In a request to fund a neighborhood watch program, the community group would want to show (a) that crime is a problem, perhaps using police records supplemented by a community survey, and then (b) provide evidence, perhaps from an Internet search, that in similar communities neighborhood watch programs do work.

Research data is publicized to persuade government, pressure businesses, and motivate community members into action. Multiple sources of data are more convincing than are single sources, while official sources have more credibility with government.

Politicians have a hard time ignoring the data that their planners or the Census Bureau have collected.

Information collected for action organizations has to be communicated dramatically and credibly to frame the issue in a way that creates support. Numbers are important but often seem dry so that statistical reports should be complemented with stories and descriptions that make problems real and vivid, perhaps by putting a photo of the victims of problems on a web page. When presenting numeric data, assume that people (especially elected officials) won't read tables; instead prepare graphs or pictures that make the findings come alive. Today with computers and programs such as PowerPoint, visually exciting displays of data can be prepared and the community researchers can quickly try out different types of graphs to see which look best. Maps are good for showing the extent and location of problems. Maps take on special importance when dealing with elected public officials who think in terms of voting districts. With modern computer technology, researchers can present a map and then sequentially overlay measures of different community problems.

Whether talking to the organization's own membership or making presentations to public officials, research presenters should include descriptions of the goals to be accomplished and demands for future action. For example:

Conclusion of Report on Health Care in Southside

[*Goal*] To improve the health conditions in Southside [*Information on the problem*] in which 15% of the children show below normal growth patterns resulting from protein deficiency [*Action*]. Southside Community Organization strongly advocates that the city finance a combination day-care and food cooperative that [*Information on resources for action*] can be paid for using money from the Social Services Block Grant.

Conclusion of a Report on Housing Conditions in Northside

[*Information on the problem*] Our community survey showed that 60% of the housing in Northside is owner occupied by working people with modest incomes. Two-thirds of this property needs repair. [*Action*] Northside Community Redevelopment organization will establish a revolving loan program for home repair. [*Information on resources*] Start up funds have been promised by Conglomerate Bank that has also promised to double the home repair money lent in Northside. [*Further action*] Northside Community Redevelopment will join with Neighborhoods for An Improved Northside in pressuring other banks to live up to their CRA responsibilities and provide more money for repairs. [*Long run goal*] The home repair program will help improve housing for people now resident in the community.

Community research is part of the broader organizing process for social action and social production organizations. Doing the research can involve many organization members; coming up with useful findings is empowering to those involved. Such research helps guide action campaigns, pointing out what issues will mobilize people, the vulnerabilities of the targets, and what changes can be made. The information helps community groups formulate their own projects and obtain grants. Community groups can search for information about how problems have been solved by others.

No matter whether the research is used to design a development campaign, as ammunition to knock an opponent or as a red flag to mobilize community members, people must understand the findings. The data must appear sound and the results presented in a convincing and understandable way. Most important, the research must lead to action that brings about needed social change.

CHAPTER

9 Building Capacity in an Empowered Organization

Through mobilization efforts, activists build democratic organizations that create power, maintain expertise, provide continuity, and permit quick reactions to problems. Ongoing, empowered organizations help guide social change efforts, while enabling people to obtain the self-confidence and technical skills they need to accomplish shared goals. Maintaining an effective organization, however, requires mastery of an array of technical and financial tools such as those for budgeting, housing finance, law, fund-raising, personnel management, and similar matters. To master these skills some individuals need to develop expertise, but by becoming expert they may fail to empower others.

In this chapter, we describe what social change organizations can accomplish, argue for the importance of learning technical skills in ways that empower the membership, and examine the vulnerability of community and social change organizations because of their small size and financial dependence. We then introduce some of the core technical skills needed to make organizations run well.

What Organizations Accomplish

A single person can complain to city hall about a problem and may get results, but he or she is unlikely to bring about lasting change in the city laws or an interpretation that sets a precedent for others. A complaint to a company about a faulty product might result in the individual receiving a free case of the product, but he or she is less likely to bring about changes in the way the product is made or the working conditions faced by the laborers. To stop a protest, government or businesses might promise to make policy changes, but unless there is an organization in place to follow up, activists have no way of making sure that promises are kept. A permanent community or social change organization can coordinate the concerns of numerous individuals, monitor the target to make sure promises are kept, or, even provide lasting solutions by running programs itself. Community and social change organizations focus power, provide continuity, gather and use expertise, and react quickly to changing events.

Organizations Focus Power

Social-change organizations focus resources, in terms of people, expertise, energy, motivation, money, and time, and turn those resources into power to affect decisions.

The very existence of a community or social change organization shows those in positions of power that ordinary people are willing to fight collectively and stay the course.

Organizations coordinate the actions of large numbers of people to oppose existing structures. Politicians pay attention because community organizations can get out the vote and turn unresponsive officials out of office. Chief executive officers (CEOs) worry that organizations will buy stock and orchestrate the membership to attend meetings and argue for important social changes. The ability to focus people power is a core source of organizational power.

Organizations Provide Continuity

Confronted with worker or citizen demands, those in power delay responding, hoping that activists lose interest and go away. Having an organization in place, especially one with a paid staff, communicates that those making demands have staying power and that some response is necessary.

Organizations have the capacity to take the time necessary to obtain evidence that a problem exists. Community groups can investigate housing discrimination by sending couples of various ethnic, racial, and religious backgrounds to respond to advertisements and see how often the test couples are referred elsewhere. To document the effects of polluted water, action organizations can meticulously go over medical data to determine the frequency of illnesses. Gathering backup data takes the time and persistence that many individuals lack but that organizations provide.

When those in power make promises, organizations can monitor whether these promises are kept. They can check whether grant funds were spent to house the poor, as the new policy provides, or find out how well an antipollution law is enforced. Organizations are around to publicize failures on the part of public authority, mobilize people if promises are broken, or perhaps sue.

In addition, established community organizations can undertake tasks themselves, using funds provided by others. Community organizations provide direct services, whether providing medicines to AIDS patients, assistance to new parents, day care to people struggling to get off welfare, or job training for new immigrants. Social production organizations can borrow money and build houses and stores, because they employ the staff with the necessary knowledge and have established the track records that let banks know that they will be around to pay off the debts.

Organizations Garner Expertise

Though volunteers in community organizations acquire many skills, numerous tasks that are needed for social-change work require specialized knowledge that might take years to acquire. Organizations can hire people, responsive to community members, who know how to prepare budgets, read legal documents, or find the best price for a service or product. The professional organizer is such an expert, as is the president of a community development corporation (CDC) or the executive director of a community-controlled social service agency.

Setting up a facility to care for young children with AIDS requires more than compassion; service providers must know day-care regulations and have a wealth of medical knowledge. Advocates for the poor must master the complicated information on how the regulations for one social program affects how others can be administered. For instance, recent changes in welfare laws would have made many people ineligible for affordable housing programs until experts working for community and social change organizations convinced government officials to change these contradictory rules.

Expertise is not simply measured in terms of the technical knowledge of a few employees but instead resides in the organization as a whole. Organizations learn from the experiences they have, maintain records, and enable people to share memories with one another. Such records and shared memories are passed from one generation of members and staff to the next, as they talk to each other and tell each other stories of past events. Promises made in response to community actions are recorded, vulnerabilities of targets are noted, and successful strategies are remembered.

Organizations Can React Quickly

Political and social situations rapidly change. Drug dealers might move into a neighborhood or conservative legislators introduce amendments to gut existing social legislation. If each time such changes occurred, activists had to begin mobilizing people, the game would be over before progressive groups could get their point of view across.

Established organizations constantly scan the action environment, noting what has changed and responding quickly to prevent problems from getting out of hand. Activists closely monitor city hall to make sure that council decisions don't negatively affect the neighborhoods. A permanent neighborhood organization has a police liaison who can immediately inform authorities of drug traders in the tot lot, while a social production organization has a full-time grants person who learns where money can be found for community projects. In general, communities with extant organizations are better able than communities that lack organizations they control to react quickly to neighborhood problems (Briggs, 1997; Henig, 1982; Sullivan, 1993), simply because people know to whom to report when emergencies arise.

Support organizations such as the Center for Community Change (CCC) or the National Low Income Housing Coalition (NLIHC) maintain a permanent presence in Washington, DC and in state capitols. When national legislation is proposed that can affect members' interests, messages quickly go out mobilizing people to phone their elected officials. For example, when conservatives tried to weaken the provisions of the Community Reinvestment Act, progressive lobbyists buttonholed supporters and put out electronic messages to groups throughout the nation to speak up to preserve this legislation.

Organizational Tensions

In working hard to gain needed technical skills, progressive organizations chance losing sight of the goal of empowering the membership. Organizations need dynamic leaders, experts with knowledge about government and big business, and money from government and foundations to accomplish collective tasks. But organizational leaders may dominate decisions, experts may do the work themselves rather than teaching the members how to do it, and those who provide the funds may set the goals for the group. Care is required to make sure that social change organizations are both effective at their tasks and empower their membership.

Resolving Leadership Tensions

An organization without a visible leader has difficulty in gaining public attention; however, when an organization is led by dominant individuals, the broader public may attribute successes solely to the personality of this individual. Martin Luther King, Jr. was crucial to the success of the Southern Christian Leadership Conference; Cesar Chavez to the Farm Workers Union; and Monsigneur William Lindner catalyzed the New Communities Corporation (NCC) to rebuild central Newark. People are less aware that civil rights efforts involved thousands of ordinary people (Payne, 1995), while NCC success requires a dedicated board and the actions of dozens of community members.

The publicity that charismatic leaders receive makes the broader public aware of problems by personalizing the issues. Yet organizations led by such dynamic leaders can fail to encourage other members to make decisions and might neglect to set up a permanent structure that will be in place when the leader is gone. Leaders of organizations should work hard to become symbols to the broader public of what the organization is about. Yet, the organizational members must stay alert lest charismatic leaders, through the attention their pronouncements receive, arrogate to themselves the policy decisions that should be made by the broader membership.

Organizations should not be so afraid of powerful leadership that they drift leaderless and fail to develop the concentrated focus necessary for success. As Zisk argues, creative leadership can empower the group:

> The near-paranoid way some Greens view their leaders, is best solved by changing that attitude i.e. for Greens to learn to distinguish between creative leadership that is empowering for all vs. the sort of power-grabbing style they fear. (Zisk, 1989b, p. 14)

Bad leaders seek their own glory. In contrast, creative leadership is about showing members and the public that change is possible and success is likely. Further, creative leaders make sure that the mechanical and administrative tasks needed to sustain an organization are in place. They chair meetings and work with organizational staff to handle many of the housekeeping activities of a group—preparing budgets, assuring bills get paid, planning and circulating meeting agendas, and getting out newsletters and press releases.

Leaders coordinate complicated social action campaigns and take responsibility for sequencing what is done and making the adjustments needed to quickly respond to changing events. Someone must decide on the spot what to do if the police start arresting the demonstrators. In social production organizations, leaders try to convince funders to pay for a project that the membership wants rather than simply carry out the funders' agenda. While the overall goals of a community organization and its guiding philosophy of action (e.g., the choice of whether to use civil disobedience or not) must be decided through the democratic involvement of the membership, having a leader coordinate the details involves minimal loss of member control.

Through the force of their personalities and their courage, creative leaders frame social and political issues so that change can occur. Such leaders *transform* the membership by impressing on them the importance of assuming a collective responsibility. This comes about as

> followers feel trust, admiration, loyalty, and respect toward the leader, and they are motivated to do more than originally expected to do. A leader can transform followers by: (1) making them more aware of the importance of the task outcomes. (2) inducing them to transcend their own self interest for the sake of the organization. . . . Transformation leaders influence followers by arousing strong emotions and identification with the leader, but they may also transform followers by serving as a coach, teacher, and mentor. (Yukl, 1989, p. 211)

The actions and words of the leaders can reinforce a democratic organizational culture by encouraging involvement and by teaching people to respect each others' opinions (modified from Schein, 1985). Leaders encourage others to participate by fully recognizing and respecting opinions not their own. Leaders help people build on their own strengths by moving people along the paths the membership has chosen to achieve collectively determined goals.

To make sure that leaders do not overstep their bounds and threaten the democratic nature of the organization, progressive organizations make sure that overall policy is set at membership meetings that involve either all members or democratically elected representatives, depending on the size of the group. In addition, boards of directors must be democratically elected and should have frequent enough meetings to insure that the leaders' actions are consistent with the general direction given by the membership.

Maintaining Democracy in Formal Organizations

Most effective organizations set up a formal structure, with officers, lines of authority, and designated work assignments. Structure includes relatively permanent patterns of organizational behavior such as ways in which people are recruited, who does the hiring and training, or rules on when meetings are held. In addition, structure describes how different parts of the organization coordinate their work. Written rules, such as details of how to solicit funds or hire and fire staff, are part of the broader organizational structure as are the understandings on whether the rules always need to be followed.

Having a carefully delineated structure can increase organizational efficiency. Rather than spending time inventing a new way to do the work every time a new recruit is brought on board, step-by-step procedures are in place to teach the newcomer what to do. When many tasks are routinized, organizational members can concentrate their time on the more difficult problems.

If there is too much emphasis on formal structure, however, the organization may alienate its members. Efficient, hierarchical, bureaucratic structure might make democratic participation difficult, if not impossible. In response to this problem, in the sixties and early seventies, some organizations such as the Students for a Democratic Society (SDS) avoided hierarchy and tried to carry out a full participatory democracy in which members deliberated about each issue as a group. As a result, SDS did a lot of talking and took very little action (Gitlin, 1989; Miller, 1987). Rather than promote pure democracy, such loosely structured organizations end up with a *"tyranny of structurelessness"* in which there is the

> development of informal leaders—individuals who gained power due to media attention or personal characteristics. Such leaders were not chosen by the group and thus could not be removed by the group. (Iannello, 1988, pp. 4–5)

A lack of structure doesn't promote either democracy or efficiency.

Much thought has to go into finding the right balance between achieving bureaucratic efficiency and democratic involvement. Several approaches appear to work. In one, organizations start out with minimal structure, imposing rules only after they are shown to be absolutely needed. In another approach, the founding leaders of the organization work hard to create a democratic organizational culture in which people recognize that their opinions count, democratic involvement is encouraged, yet, when needed, bureaucratic rules can be put in place.

Let Structures Emerge to Mesh with Strategies.   To help insure that progressive organizations are effective and democratic, rules should be kept to a minimum. Without any structure, work might not get done at all; but too much structure and organizational members lack the freedom to accomplish their tasks. An organization that routinely undertakes complicated renewal projects that require many interdependent technical steps, or one that needs tight coordination between legal and direct action tactics might have to set up a moderately strict hierarchy. By contrast, a counselor in a community-run antisuicide hot line can't check out each emergency with a boss and doesn't have to coordinate his or her decisions with those of many other people. Bureaucratic procedures should be added only when absolutely necessary.

Beginning in a period of great ferment, an organization starts with a flexible structure and a handful of guiding procedures, with the expectation that rules will emerge that speak to the specific tasks to be accomplished. There are few routines and everything is discovery. But as the organization learns that certain solutions work, it builds routines to insure that these solutions are in place. A day-care center need not reformulate its mission every month, as long as community members monitor the center to make sure that it is helping children grow emotionally, socially, and intellectually.

As strategies and goals change, however, so should structure to prevent the organization from becoming rigid. A protest organization using the tactics of the 1960s in the political environment of the 2000s is likely to be ignored or laughed at. When community development groups that depended on government grants were unwilling to develop new funding sources, they died for lack of money when government cut back what it was willing to supply. Organizations can wither if they fail to ask if the prior routines are suitable for the current problems.

Fighting Formalization by Creating a Democratic Organizational Culture.   Initially, small organizations may be able to make decisions consensually, but as organizations age, some degree of bureaucratization is likely to set in. Either specialists are hired or some staff and volunteers develop expertise that separates them from others. Organizations need this expertise but must use it in a way that carries out the goals democratically set by the membership.

In a housing organization, someone must know the technical details of how to fund apartments with tax credits, but that individual must remain responsive to community members who democratically decide where the housing is to be, for whom, and how it should be managed. An advocacy organization requires a professional lobbyist who stays informed on which elected officials are wavering on key issues, but the lobbyist should not be the one who determines which issue the organization pursues. Those decisions should be made by the membership as a whole.

The best protection against over bureaucratization is an *organizational culture* (Schein, 1985, p. 6) that values dissent and participation and that expects the membership to direct the organization. Democratic organizational cultures just don't happen but rather grow out of the actions taken by the founders. When organizational leaders listen to others with respect, convene group discussions, search for answers from any and all within the organization, not from just those at the top of the hierarchy, they communicate to staff and members that all opinions count and that the organization is owned by its members and not by a handful of leaders.

In an organization with a democratic culture, staff and volunteers habitually question rules and oppose the tendency to set up a rigid hierarchy. Those who work in an organization with a democratic culture are not frightened of their bosses and do not act in a bossy way to their subordinates. People understand that responsibility is shared, and even those higher up in the chain of authority must solicit others' opinions about proposals. Members of democratic organizations assume that criticism of procedures is good, as long as it is not couched roughly or hurtfully (Rothschild & Whitt, 1986, p. 84).

Today, many activist feminist organizations are set up to reinforce a democratic organizational culture (Ferree & Martin, 1995). These organizations build on what was learned in the sixties during which activists, following feminist philosophies, set up a variety of *democratic-collectivist* organizations. This model of organizing reconciles membership participation with effectiveness (Rothschild & Whitt, 1986), though it seems to work best in small organizations that provide social services, especially to the membership itself or in small community businesses (Iannello, 1988; Milofsky, 1988).

Democratic-collectivist organizations minimize formal rules and reduce the hierarchy of positions by concentrating authority in the whole group, rather than just the administrators or officers. To avoid the need for top-down decision making, these organizations emphasize a consensual structure in which "control rests ultimately and overwhelmingly with member-employees-owners, regardless of the particular legal framework through which this is achieved" (Rothschild & Whitt, 1986, p. 2). Such organizations recognize that technical knowledge is required, but rather than hire expertise, the ethos of the democratic-collectivist organization is to recognize "ability or expertise within the membership" (Iannello, 1988, p. 21). In organizations that emphasize consensus decision making, workers are often friends with one another and may join the organization because they like the atmosphere and feel empowered by it.

Gaining Funding without Losing Empowerment Goals

To pay for office and project expenses, community groups need money. They may seek funding from government, foundations, or the private sector. In taking funds from others, however, organizations chance being coopted, that is adopting another's agenda as their own. To avoid this problem, activist organizations such as Associations of Community Organizations for Reform Now (ACORN) try to pay their expenses almost entirely through membership dues, while Industrial Areas Foundation (IAF) affiliates try to get as much money as possible from local churches that share their community empowerment agenda. Groups doing capital intensive projects, however, such as building affordable homes or those that provide a subsidized social service, need a stream of external funds beyond what the membership or local churches can provide. Activists must make sure that the organization is attempting a project because it is what the membership wants, not just because it is for what funders will pay.

A more subtle problem that reduces democracy and organizational empowerment can occur when accepting money from supportive funders. As a condition of receiving the funds, the organization is asked to make what appear to be reasonable structural changes. For instance, to obtain low-income housing tax-credit money, federal agencies require that community-based development organizations establish independent, non-profit subsidiaries. To manage these subsidiaries necessitates setting up a business-like structure and hiring people with expertise in financial matters. The subsidiary can end up being the tail that wags the larger organizational dog.

Further, funders often decide which organizations to support on the basis of whether these groups receiving the money are structured in ways that make the granters feel comfortable (DiMaggio & Powell, 1991, p. 73; Meyer & Rowan, 1991). A funder might require that a community group hire an accountant, rather than relying on volunteers to manage large grants. Accountants usually believe in a set of values, such as efficiency and extreme caution about spending money, that are antagonistic to the community groups' goals. An accountant may be reluctant to put money into risky ventures run by less experienced community members, while the community group may feel that is precisely what they are supposed to be doing. An accountant may feel that his or her expertise should be listened to, while the community group may feel that technical staff should listen to the membership. Those responsible for paying the bills might want to treat those being housed as merely rent-paying tenants, not participants in a community project set up to teach people empowering skills. As a result of complying with funder requirements for safeguarding money, community groups might follow a business model.

Further, organizations staffed by professionals have better opportunities for obtaining funding but the more the organization is run by professionals, the less it is run by community members. Women's shelters have experienced this problem.

> Shelters had to lay their claim to expertise in order to ward off competition from more traditional agencies and obtain funding. . . . Adding more difficulties, funding agencies, boards and some staff advocated or demanded the hiring of professional directors or counseling staff in order to acquire the expertise needed to survive and help battered women. (Schecter, 1982, pp. 107–108)

Organizational structures, especially those set up to please outsiders, carry with them values and directions that can change the organization's mission and make it less participatory and empowering to the membership.

Organizational Transformations

Organizations are live, dynamic, evolving entities. Most begin as an informal gathering of a handful of people affected by a problem. The first set of changes occurs as this informal group incorporates, sets up officers, and hires staff. Other changes occur as the mission evolves to handle changing community needs. For instance, many community social production and social service organizations begin as activist, neighborhood groups. The activist group was democratically administered by a board and a few officers; however, once the organization begins complicated social service or physical development projects, it has to hire people with technical skills.

How can groups sustain a democratic culture while accomplishing complicated projects? One effective approach is to maintain the core neighborhood organization, in which decisions are made democratically, and set up the social service or physical development group as a separate but related organization. People from the neighborhood organization can serve as board members for the new offspring, providing direction and information. For example, to fight neighborhood deterioration, people in Sherman Park in Milwaukee formed the Sherman Park Neighborhood Association. To handle the technical tasks of building and repairing homes, the neighborhood group spun off of the Sherman Park Redevelopment Corporation. Both organizations share a building and the boards are closely connected.

Social change and social production organizations sometimes die. Some organizations are set up to accomplish a single task, and when that task is done, the organization goes out of business. Other organizations disintegrate when members disagree strongly on what their purposes ought to be. The Whittier Alliance in Minneapolis, a successful community organization for many years, died when staff and board disagreed about whether the group should fight for poor minorities or work to preserve the middle-class character of the neighborhood (Rubin, 2000).

Sometimes organizational death occurs when the task exceeds the technical or administrative capacity of the organization. In the last few years, for instance, a number of prominent community housing and economic development organizations have folded including Eastside Community Investment in Indianapolis, ESHAC (East Side Housing Action Committee) in Milwaukee, and Peoples' Housing in Chicago. The organizations were trying to accomplish a vital community task but were not economically viable.

Striving to accomplish what others think impossible is what community organizations ought to be about. Because what they try to do is often so difficult or so new, some failures are inevitable. While for the group's members and staff the demise of the organization is sad, other community organizations learn from its problems and work more effectively on similar problems. More unfortunate are those cases in which the death is unnecessary because the organization lacked routine financial or managerial skills.

A Prelude to Organizational Administration

Enthusiasm and dedication among activists and staff of social-change organizations are vital, but without understanding how to manage the organization democratically, yet efficiently, even the best ideas fail. If the organization is underfunded, projects languish. If administration is heavy handed, employees and volunteers might lose the fervor necessary to succeed. The organization cannot borrow money and build affordable homes if it lacks financial controls. In contrast, good administration enables work to get done, builds capacity, and empowers the organization and the community it serves.

In the remainder of this chapter we provide a brief introduction to the details of administration. Those who intend to go into social activism as a career or work in social production organizations may wish to take courses in social service administration or enroll in programs that teach managerial skills to organizers.

Establishing the Overall Structure

Organizational structure should emerge slowly to accommodate the action environment. Still, certain decisions on structure have to be made early in the organization's history. To begin, organizations should incorporate as nonprofits and carefully select a board of directors. Then members must determine how the organization is to be led, through collective leadership, an executive director, a president, or in other ways.

Incorporate as a Not-for-Profit Corporation.   If the organization plans to be around for a while, it makes sense to incorporate as a *not-for-profit corporation.* Incorporation turns the organization into a legal "person" that can own, buy, and sell property, contract debt, sign contracts, sue and be sued, and receive and spend money. After incorporation, Mary Jane is no longer personally responsible for the phone bill, the East Side Neighborhood Redevelopment Corporation is the entity that has to pay the bills.

Incorporation is a relatively simple and inexpensive matter, handled by the state government, usually by the office of the Secretary of State. In the application, the group, sometimes with the help of an attorney, describes its purposes, provides an address, notes the names of the board of directors and officers, and chooses a unique name. Sometimes incorporation papers also specify bylaws, that is the rules to be followed in running the organization. As long as a charitable, educational, or public purpose is being served, as interpreted by the tax code, nonprofits can own property, sell services, and otherwise act like a business, with the important exception that no individuals working for the nonprofit share in the money made (beyond a reasonable and fair salary).

Once incorporated, most community and social production groups are eligible to apply for a tax-exempt status under Section 501(c)(3) of the Internal Revenue Code.

Nonprofits that are primarily involved in advocacy and undertake substantial amounts of lobbying are not eligible for 501(c)(3) designation. Usually it takes awhile for the Internal Revenue Service (IRS) to approve the 501(c)(3) status, but start-up groups can find a temporary home as part of another nonprofit that has received the designation. A neighborhood social service organization might be run as a project of a local church, until the community organization receives its nonprofit, tax-exempt status.

The IRS considers public or charitable services to be tax exempt. A tax-exempt organization does not have to pay federal taxes on income collected for specified tax-exempt purposes. The organization can also apply to the state government for an exemption from sales taxes. Most important, donors receive a tax break when they contribute. Private foundations, such as the Ford Foundation, are largely restricted to giving their money to other tax-exempt organizations. Many federal agencies give grants only to not-for-profits. In addition to the tax deduction for donations, tax laws provide advantages to businesses that partner with not-for-profits in housing and renewal efforts. Finally, professionals such as lawyers and accountants are ethically obligated to do some *pro bono* (free) services and prefer to provide them to not-for-profit organizations.

There is an important catch: a 501(c)(3) organization is not allowed to spend a substantial amount of its time in direct efforts to influence legislation. In Chapter 12, on political action, we discuss these constraints in more detail. Overall, these rules should not handicap actions because setting up another organization that focuses on political work is easy.

Choosing a Board of Directors.   The board of directors is legally responsible for the organization. Depending on state laws and the wording of the incorporation papers, boards adopt the goals of the organization, hire and fire the chief officers, and sometimes have a say in other personnel matters. The board approves the organization's budget and is the legal signatory for most contracts, though, at times, this authority can be delegated. The board can help link the organization to the rest of the community; sometimes it provides know-how or fund-raising contacts; and it can help keep the organization focused on community goals.

Selecting board members requires some thought and involves some tradeoffs. Having upper-status professionals on the board can be advantageous, because they bring expertise and experience and they give foundations and other contributors confidence that the group will be managed well. On the down side, high-status people rarely are representative of the communities being served and might attempt to impose a paternalistic and charitable model rather than promote community empowerment. Boards of democratic organizations should have at least some people on them who come from the communities being served or who have personally faced the problems that the organization is set up to resolve. Boards work best when they mix some upper-status professionals with community members. Such mixed boards encourage their members to talk and learn from one another. We have observed boards in which street activists and CEOs of Fortune 500 and billion-dollar foundations talk on a first-name basis and vigorously debate ideas with one another.

Efforts are required to assure the board represents people from different social, economic, political, and ethnic constituency groups. In one approach, the board of the Dudley Street Neighborhood Initiative mandated representation from each ethnic group in the community and assigned seats to representatives from other community organizations, foundation people, and one for a government official.

The organization must assure that the board members chosen agree with the purpose of the group and have had time at workshops and retreats to reach consensus on these goals. A strongly divided board can spend so much time fighting that the organization loses sight of its overall mission. Board members must be prepared to ask staff difficult questions that keep the organization on target, effective, and open.

In choosing board members, the following questions should be kept in mind:

1. Is the person really interested in the organization and willing to spend time to help? Politicians might appear to provide good contacts, but if they never show up to a meeting they are useless.
2. Does the person have some skill or resource that is badly needed by the organization? Skills might be technical ones such as accounting or the law, but they also might involve the ability to network with community members.
3. Might there be a possible conflict of interest? Housing development organizations might think twice before inviting the head of a construction firm on the board, if that firm will be seeking work from the group.
4. Will the proposed board member help lend legitimacy and visibility to the organization? Political notables and successful business people often provide outsiders with a comfort level with the organization. Care is needed lest such individuals try to take over the group. Established clergy from neighborhood churches can provide legitimacy with less fear of cooptation.
5. Are some board members personally familiar with the tasks to be accomplished? Tenants' organizations often choose tenants as members of their boards, assuring that the boards have access to first-hand familiarity with the building's problems, but service providers sometimes choose funders and outside experts forgetting to put former clients on their boards.
6. Are there members on the board to represent gender, racial, ethnic, geographic, or interest groups in the community? Some organizations reserve a few seats for constituency groups.

Nonprofit boards are rarely paid, even though the members have great responsibilities. A description of the problems of being a board member in a housing cooperative applies to board work more generally in the not-for-profit world.

> with the exception of psychic rewards of prestige, status, and a sense of involvement, membership on the board of a cooperative does not present an attractive package of rewards and perquisites . . . members receive no compensation . . . for the long hours . . . which probably helps explain why more people do not run for the board and why turnover is so high. (Greenberg, 1986, p. 54)

It is one thing to think about the criteria for choosing individual board members and another to think how these people might work together. In less successful boards, the diversity of membership increases conflict and misunderstanding (Daley & Angulo,

1994, p. 175), but if everyone thinks the same way, major problems may be missed, and new solutions may be overlooked. Good boards develop a dynamic in which people play off each other's strengths and complement one another's knowledge.

Staff, particularly the president or executive director, might prefer a captured board, that is a group of people who go along with their recommendations. While having curmudgeons on the board is no fun, having sheep does not serve the organization well. An active board should ask hard-nosed questions about why people are hired and the way money is being spent. Even more important, the board should ask staff members questions that force the staff to look beyond day-to-day problems and keep the organization focused.

In the best circumstances, the board

> . . . provides an opportunity for shared wisdom. Ideally, it places at the disposal of an institution, the knowledge, insights, and personal contacts of a group of unusually able people who have wide-spread spheres of influence. . . . *Most of the time the members devote to a board is spent in aiding and supporting the institution not in controlling it.* [emphasis added] (Houle, 1989, pp. 7–8)

In addition, a good board can help the organization manage its environment without being coopted. For example, nonprofit boards facilitate cooperation with government while guarding essential organizational values (Stone, 1996, p. 64). As government has assigned more social service and development tasks to nonprofits, this intermediating task has become more important.

The Chief Executive Officer.   Another important administrative decision is how to govern the organization on a daily basis. Here, too, form should fit function.

Some smaller groups are run through a collective leadership, where the board, or less formally, a leadership committee, makes the routine decisions. More often, especially for direct action and neighborhood organizations, the board hires a professional organizer who runs the organization on a daily basis while the board or the membership as a whole elects a president from the membership as chief officer. In this structure, the board sets overall policy, the president and the organizer confer frequently, the president does the public speaking for the group, and the organizer, as chief staff member, handles routine administrative matters and coordinates mobilization efforts.

Social production organizations may be more formal and like businesses. The board is in charge, but the chair of the board (sometimes confusingly labeled as the president) concentrates on issues affecting overall policy. A professional is hired to run the organization on a daily basis. He or she handles budget and staffing issues and plays a crucial role in suggesting projects to the board. In social service organizations, this professional is often called the executive director, while in CDCs, the title president is taken to show to the financial and governmental community that a CDC is a business, albeit a community-controlled one.

Conglomerate Structures.   Most neighborhood organizations have simple formal structures with a board, perhaps a CEO and/or an organizer and a few staff members.

For many groups such a structure is sufficient. As organizations grow and take on a multitude of tasks, new sections might be added, perhaps with one concentrating on organizing community members, another on building homes, a third on managing rental property, and a fourth on running a job training program. Such sections are often set up to carry out grants for specific projects. To ensure that the expanding organization continues to function well, people in the different sections need to interact frequently with one another—staff meetings are a must and contact can be facilitated by having a single coffee pot in a common lounge.

At times, more complicated structures are required either by funders or by the law. For instance, a 501(c)(3) organization that wants to actively lobby might want to spin off an affiliated group to do the lobbying. Coordination between the organization and its lobbying wing can be achieved through overlapping membership of the two boards. Social production organizations often partner with for-profits to build homes or set up community enterprises that are managed in part by those from the business community (see Chapter 16). By law, some of these partnerships must be for-profit businesses while the nonprofit becomes a stockholder in a joint enterprise.

Establishing such complicated, conglomerate forms can be advantageous for community groups. For instance, a neighborhood group might attempt risky projects, renting to the very poor or helping establish a microenterprise that can lose money. Establishing a conglomerate structure legally separates the risky enterprises from the core neighborhood organization so that if the business goes under the community group still survives.

Managing Staff

Once an organization increases beyond a minimal size, leaders have to pay close attention to how to work with staff members. The objective is to develop a management style that empowers the organizational staff while creating a consensus on what the organization is to accomplish (Latting & Blanchard, 1997). Hierarchical decision making should be minimized; ways of amiably settling conflicts should be devised, and work should be structured so that the staff develops confidence in their own abilities.

Light-Handed Supervision Empowers.   With care in hiring to make sure that people share the ideological goals of the organization, supervision can be reduced to a minimum. For instance, organizations, such as cooperatives, in which staff feel they are the owners, require fewer supervisors than other organizations (Jackall, 1984, p. 7).

In general, those higher up in the hierarchy should try to avoid managing through threats. Good management requires skillful interpersonal negotiation, reconciling individual goals with the broader needs of the organization. Supervisors need to be cautious to make sure when they provide advice they do so in ways that avoid demeaning people. To the extent possible, evaluation of work should recognize and encourage good performance rather than criticize tasks that have been poorly done. Evaluation should entail public praise, especially the sort that lets people know they are contributing toward organizational goals.

The role of the supervisor is to figure out solutions rather than blame employees. For example, volunteers who are constantly late in the morning might better be assigned to afternoon and evening work. Perhaps these individuals cannot count on their day-care providers, suggesting a service the organization might provide.

Training Empowers.   Quality training programs help empower both permanent staff and volunteers while improving organizational output. Training is about building capacity and enabling people to master a variety of skills that help them develop a sense of their own competence (Speer & Hughey, 1995).

To begin, people empower each other by training one another. Volunteers who have experience answering a suicide hotline can teach others how to do it. Volunteers, interns, and new staff can observe as developmental activists negotiate with cities for funding for affordable homes. As group members each learn a wide variety of tasks, backup personnel for crucial work become available. In addition, such training enables people to learn how the whole organization functions, not just one little corner of it. When individuals are sent off to receive specialized training from others, make sure on their return they share what they have learned with the group.

Assigning and Scheduling Work.   In a new organization, members may be required to try their hands at a variety of tasks, learning as they go. As the organization grows, however, organizational leaders may have to assign tasks to those with greater expertise, while making sure someone accomplishes the daily work that must be done. The goal is to make sure the assignment of work is motivating and not discouraging, disparaging, or excessively boring.

Volunteers must see how their task contributes to the achievement of the long-run goal of the organization and that progress is being made. Knocking on doors and leafletting can be boring (or scary), but people become more motivated for such tasks when they see an increase in turnout at the next rally.

Boring assignments should be rotated with more interesting ones, and, when possible, boring work should be done in groups, so people can chat and create a stimulating or fun atmosphere. Licking stamps is just plain tedious, but it is more enjoyable in a group. More glamorous tasks might involve speech making, dealing with the press, and coming up with strategies for protest activities. Rather than limit these tasks to a few, most organization members should have an opportunity to be involved in these exciting efforts.

Conflict Management.   When highly motivated people work together on controversial tasks, conflict is almost inevitable. People quarrel about who will get limited resources, disagree about priorities, and may resent others who they think are not doing their share of work. In neighborhood organizations, conflicts can be exacerbated by underlying racial, ethnic, or religious tensions. Of course, people sometimes fight with each other because they can't get along as individuals.

One approach to reducing conflicts is to keep basic information about resources, goals, and progress widely accessible. If members know how limited the budget is, they might not squabble over funds they know are not there. If everyone understands the strings attached to grants, members are less likely to argue about how the money will be spent. Another way of reducing fights over grant money is to think of ways of informally sharing the funds. For instance, grant money that is earmarked for refurbishing a park cannot legally be spent on staffing a food pantry, but if the grant comes with some overhead money, the overhead could be used to purchase a computer that others in the group could use.

When quarrels do occur over substance, someone with good mediation skills can help, talking to both sides and trying to find a position that will be acceptable to everyone. The individuals involved can be requested to come up with a new approach that would satisfy them both. In general, the goal is for organizational leaders to channel conflict toward productive ends.

Larger organizations with a more divisional structure sometimes experience tension between the divisions. The parts of the organization that do physical renewal or building projects employ people with very different world views than those who do advocacy organizing. Each unit may feel its needs are most urgent and resent resources being spent elsewhere. Each cent that is spent on setting up a day-care center, for instance, means that much less money for helping restore neighborhood shopping. Try to avoid such problems so that one part of the organization does not see another section's gain as their loss. Perhaps the day-care center can be built in a place that helps those who work in the neighborhood stores.

In smaller organizations, work groups can form loyalties and rivalries with other work groups. To prevent such work groups from becoming factions with their own agendas, rotate the membership of the work groups and change work assignments from time to time.

Getting Money

Organizations often start up with volunteer labor and donated resources. One organizer described to us how his group began.

> We had been a cause, we had been totally unorganized, I like to talk about it as a kitchen table organization. Where the work was done around somebody's kitchen table. Where the financial records were kept? In a shoe box. You know. Totally informal.

Another group that ended up as a sophisticated CDC began as "six people in my living room saying 'boy am I sick of looking at this stuff. Let's build a factory.' . . . No one had the faintest idea what we were talking about, including us."

Other organizations begin as projects of churches or civic groups, where the parent group absorbs the costs of providing office space, telephone, and photocopy machine and might pay for an organizer or two. Eventually, to sustain itself and gain the resources to undertake projects, however, a systematic way of funding is needed.

Fund-raising is difficult and takes time away from action campaigns and social production work. Obtaining large sums means applying for grants from government agencies and foundations, chancing that the organization will have to carry out the agenda of the funding agency. In the most extreme case, the organization becomes so concerned with maintaining its funding that it forgets its social and activist mission. Still, without funding, little is accomplished over the long run.

Fund-raising does take time, but it need not distract from the principal mission of the group. By obtaining small sums of money from multiple sources, the organization can protect itself from being captured by any one funder. Fund-raising itself can be part of spreading the mission of the group; each time a potential contributor is solicited, the fund-raiser can talk about the overall goals and purposes of the organization.

Organizations categorize money into different pots that are used for separate purposes. *Operating funds* pay for ordinary daily expenses—salaries of organizers, office rents, light, heat, postage, and insurance. *Project funds* pay for the costs of a specific service or activity. *Capital funds* are those spent for one-time outlays or for items that will last a long time, like furniture, automobiles or vans, or buildings. In Chapter 16 we describe how community organizations can obtain money for capital expenses and for sustained social production projects, like offering day care. In this chapter we focus on obtaining operating expenses.

Operating expenses are the hardest to obtain. A foundation that provides project or capital funds for refurbishing an old building can show a product to its board, but money spent for operating expenses such as telephones and toilet tissue leaves no visible trace to brag about. One way of getting needed operating funds is to specify in a project grant that a certain amount of money will go for overall organizational expenses, for instance, by attributing part of the organizer's time to a grant-funded project.

Another way social-change organizations obtain operating funds is by soliciting members, community residents, local businesses, and community institutions, especially local churches, for modest contributions. Smaller organizations can earn money for operating costs through a variety of special events—fairs, bingo, fund-raising meals— as well as from fees obtained from services and projects.

Where a community organization gets its money can be important, because some money comes with restrictions on how it can be spent. Donations from individuals are usually seen as flexible, while money from the United Way has more strings. Contributions from foundations and corporations are considered worth pursuing because of their size and relative flexibility (Groenjberg, 1993, p. 149).

Membership and Community Contributions.   Funds are sought from community members, churches, and local businesses through face-to-face canvassing or through mail or telephone solicitations. In organizations that work in a geographic neighborhood, all three approaches can be tried, while national social-action groups are more or less restricted to fund-raising by mail or telephone.

Successful fund-raisers offer the following advice:

1. People give to people. Ask in person.
2. The best people you can ask for money are those who already have given money. Keep complete records of your donors.
3. People cannot respond unless you tell them what you want. Always ask for a specific amount or item. Be enthusiastic, optimistic, and bold. You get what you ask for.
4. People who ask for money become better givers. People who give money become better askers.

5. People want to back a winner. Be proud of your organization, what you do, and how you do it. Success breeds success!
6. More people mean more money and more funds. Find a job for every volunteer. Make it more fun to be on the inside participating than on the outside looking in.
7. People want recognition. Send thank-you notes! (Flanagan, 1982, pp. 170–171)

Standard books such as Kim Klein's *Fundraising for Social Change,* third edition (1996), and updates in periodicals such as the *Grassroots Funding Journal,* provide a wealth of additional tips on philosophies and techniques of obtaining funds.

Many progressive organizations favor door-to-door fund raising because such canvassing enables organizers to talk to people, find out what they feel, and dramatically increase the likelihood that people will join the group and contribute. Organizations such as ACORN that try to fund themselves entirely from membership dues rely heavily on the canvassing model. A canvasser is a member of the organization, often on its staff, who goes door to door describing the organization, soliciting funds, and signing up people for the group.

Canvassers should wear something identifying their organization. After being greeted at the door, the canvasser should present his or her name, the organization's name, its purpose, its accomplishments, the nature of the problem the group is now confronting and how the person being canvassed can help. The initial message has to be presented briefly:

> [Name and identification] My name is Deanne Sassafras and my family and I live around the corner on Elm Street. [Organization's identification] I'm a member of the Working Mother's Association [accomplishments] the group that stopped the closing of the Medical Clinic. [Current problem] This time we are fighting to keep the Community Day-Care Center open near the south-side office complex. [What the person can do] To help us put out flyers and pay for the legal fees to fight the city's decision [amount of contribution] we're asking each family to contribute $10. Will you help us?

The message describes the group, the issues faced, and links the actions that can be taken to specific outcomes, all in a short presentation. Follow-up discussions can be held requesting that the person join the group and pay membership dues. Note that the canvasser is focusing on specific issues and the overall value of the group and not on such mundane things as paying the heat and light bills.

When talking to community businesses and social and religious organizations, canvassers must show how the interests of the other groups coincide with those of the action organization. When asking for money, the action organization can explicitly mention overhead needs because businesses and social and religious organizations recognize the legitimacy of such needs and can provide *in-kind* contributions. The owner of a partially empty business block might be willing to contribute a store front to a community renewal group. Churches might allow the use of a community room and let the action organization use their phones or photocopying machines. Food stores might provide the refreshments that encourage community members to show up at meetings.

Most organizations that focus on social issues—the environment, women's rights, speech rights, antidiscrimination—seek out a city-wide, state, or even a national membership, thus making face-to-face canvassing quite difficult. Fund-raising from members and small contributors must be done by telephone or through mailings.

Mail or phone appeals made to current members and contributors should begin with thanks for past support as well as some indication of what the group has accomplished with the money. Then the messages explain on what the group intends to continue to work, often focusing on an immediate issue that has received media attention. In mailings, the organization should be clearly identified, perhaps by including a brief annual report or a glossy flier describing what the group is about. For people already members of the organization, the mail or telephone solicitation often contains a request to take some political action, such as contacting a congressperson or sending an enclosed card demanding that a company stop polluting. The message repeats what has been achieved and should be explicit in asking for a given amount of money and providing a way of transmitting the funds. Many people do not give out credit card numbers, so phone solicitors coordinate their work with mailers who quickly send out a clearly labeled pledge card and postage-paid return envelope.

Community organizations sometimes make special appeals when there is an urgent issue coming up in Congress, for example, or when a foundation or business has offered funding on a matching basis. In the latter case, the more money the organization can raise on its own, the more it can get from the original donor. Some organizations have also tried to solicit bequests, asking members or the public more broadly to write the organization into their wills.

Board members can be asked for substantial contributions. Such money need not come from the board member's own pocket; each board member can be made responsible for raising a fixed amount of money for the organization.

Special Events.   The purpose of special events is to obtain unrestricted money by charging fees for a service, product, or activity. Many organizations that need only small budgets keep afloat by periodically having bake sales, fish fries, or bingo nights.

Keep in mind that the work of preparing special events can distract from the organization's ongoing mission, so they are best used for funding one-time expenses. For example, a group can hold a combined bake sale and yard sale to get the money to rent buses to take activists to a march in Washington. Sales of this sort rarely produce enough money to sustain an organization over the long run.

Special events are likely to be less distracting if the same type of event is offered each year, so that it becomes routine enough to reduce the time involved. A historical preservation society might hold an open house in a restored building, charging a small fee for the tour and selling food on the lawn. A wildlife preservation organization can collect fees for leading canoe tours down a lonely river, both making money and showing others the wonders that are being protected. For neighborhood organizations special events can both raise funds and help build a stronger sense of community integration. For example, a street fair with ethnic foods; booths with art, jewelry, or clothes made by community members; and ethnic music can symbolize the cultural richness and integration of community life.

Obtaining Core Funds from Foundations and Government.   Some groups can survive on dues, contributions from small businesses, and the revenue generated from special events. Larger chunks of money, however, are required to sustain an ongoing organization, especially one that wants to maintain a permanent office and keep qualified people employed.

For start-up organizations the problem of finding funding for operating expenses is difficult but not impossible. For broad issues of social justice, benevolent millionaires such as George Soros have made contributions and established liberal foundations such as the Ford Foundation have provided start-up grants. The Catholic Campaign for Human Development and similar church-related foundations in other denominations occasionally fund core operating expenses, especially for organizations concerned with fighting poverty among minority groups. Periodically, foundations seek to fund start-up neighborhood groups that are planning to work on issues of concern to the foundation. In recent years, for instance, the MacArthur Foundation has funded groups interested in holistic programs of neighborhood renewal, designating most of the money for established organizations, but setting aside a small pool for start-up groups.

For the most part, though, the large national foundations pay little attention to start-up organizations. Still, it is worthwhile to examine the web pages of the foundations from time to time, because what foundations think is worth funding changes quite rapidly. For newer organizations, local foundations are a better bet, however. Many cities, including quite small ones, have community foundations whose mission is to focus on local needs. These foundations can be persuaded to pay a few thousand dollars for overhead office expenses. One of our students persuaded her hometown foundation to pay for printing, photocopying, and the travel necessary to train people in the anticrime tenants' association she founded. Neighborhood business owners, especially those who can see that the community group will serve their interests, for example, in cleaning up eyesores or chasing away the dope trade, might help fund some overhead costs. To meet their Community Reinvestment Act requirements, banks sometimes pay the core expenses of community housing and tenants' associations.

Surprisingly, even government can be a source of funds for core expenses. For the most part, the Community Development Block Grant (CDBG) funds material projects, but regulations permit the money to be spent for operating expenses of community groups that have a neighborhood focus. For example, Minneapolis has used CDBG funds in each of its separate neighborhoods to set up community-based planning organizations that act as general neighborhood advocates. In Chicago, starting with the progressive Mayor Washington, numerous groups were designated as delegate organizations, receiving money for undertaking city services in the neighborhoods. They were allowed to use the money for general overhead expenses.

Personal contacts count in fund-raising. Organizations should contact people in banks who have the responsibility for giving small grants and becoming acquainted with program officers in foundations. Organizers must find out in what projects these funders are interested. Having some kind of track record of successful projects and good management is helpful. With patience, things might just click, as illustrated by the story told by a community activist who worked hard to obtain start-up money for a neighborhood improvement group:

The next problem here is that we couldn't get funded. We were operating voluntary, had a free office over there. I was living on love. And, we couldn't get funded. I would go to all kinds of funding sources, . . . I wrote proposal after proposal, no one would touch us. We didn't fit in social service. We didn't fit in housing. We wanted to do a shopping center on Franklin Avenue, it was unheard of. . . . Got turned down by all of them. . . . Finally, I don't even know how. I remember it was December. I was extremely pregnant, I was trudging around taking buses, I looked just pitiful. . . . I mean being pitifully pregnant is the best fund-raising technique but I can't do that every year. . . . I remember I went to the [major community foundation] and they are known to be innovative and they take risks. . . . And, I told him my story and he asked me all kinds of questions. And, I said, "I don't know." We were so dumb. And, I was honest, I don't know but we will figure it out. And, they agreed to give me a $10,000 start-up grant.

The moral of the story is not to be "dumb" but to be persistent. If the organization keeps trying and balances what it wants to do with what the funders are willing to support, it should eventually get funded.

Using Profits to Pay for Core Expenses.   Increasingly, nonprofit community organizations are providing a social service or doing housing or economic development, often under contract to government (Smith & Lipsky, 1993). Organizations engaged in housing development obtain a fee when the project is completed. Service organizations are allowed overhead expenses. When community groups partner with commercial firms, for instance, to maintain an office building or factory space in the neighborhood, they get to keep their share of the profits, if any.

At times, such efforts pay off and help provide core operating expenses. The New Communities Corporation, a CDC in Newark, NJ, earns thousands of dollars in profits from its partnership with PathMark Supermarkets from a jointly owned store. In many cities, CDCs are expected to support themselves from the profits made when a housing project is complete.

Most of the time, however, such projects do not earn a profit. If the activity were profitable, private sector firms would probably have undertaken it and the community group would not have had to fill the niche. Well-known neighborhood groups such as ESCHAC in Milwaukee and CDCs such as Eastside Community Investment (ECI) in Indianapolis lost so much money in commercial endeavors that they had to fold. One community housing organization started a factory (to repair industrial pallets) to make money for the organization. The organization wanted to "develop that rascal into a full fledged, well-bred, nicely cared for cash cow" only to discover they lost money on the factory, because the organization did not have the capacity to do its core tasks and on the side manage an ongoing business (Rubin, 2000a). More generally, managing affordable housing is economically marginal, at best (Bratt et al., 1994), and the effort to make a profit can distract organization members from what should be more central tasks. Commercial endeavors can be great projects for a community group, but they are not reliable sources of funding for operating expenses.

Our advice is as follows. If the mission of the organization is to provide a service, help start stores in the neighborhood, build homes, or the like, focus on that mission and hope to run in the black but make sure the service is provided by a subsidiary so that if financial troubles occur it doesn't destroy the core group. Services are legitimate activities for community groups; however, for groups primarily involved in other activities—neighborhood advocacy, for instance—trying to run a business to make a profit for the core mission is more likely to distract from the mission than to make any money.

Managing Money through Good Fiscal Practices

No matter how money is obtained, it must be wisely managed by following sound fiscal practices. While the business management techniques described here may not sound like the heart of social-change work, they are very important for keeping an organization alive.

> No matter how dedicated the membership and how worthy the cause, without proper fiscal management, community organizations will collapse.

Good financial management has immediate payoffs. Organizations that have cash in hand don't have to borrow, thereby saving interest charges. Money in the bank earns interest and organizations that can pay cash for needed goods and services often receive a discount. Steady streams of money are necessary to pay staff; good staff who do not get paid regularly quickly start looking for other jobs. In a financially well-managed organization, replacement of equipment or repair of storm damage does not threaten the entire project, because money has been set aside for emergencies, while key elements of the operation are insured. Community and social-change organizations that demonstrate good fiscal practices appear efficient and honest to potential donors, lenders, and to their own membership.

Members want to know that their money is being spent effectively and as promised. It is horribly discouraging to discover that no one can account for the money set aside for a project. What may appear to be corruption may be adaptation to an uncertain revenue flow or result from lack of planning, but it looks bad just the same. Money being saved to open the community center next year may have been used to pay this month's rent and light bill.

Donors want to know that the organization will spend the money in accordance with their specifications. Donors often require that a recipient organization has proven capacity to track funds and has the bookkeeping systems that assure that money earmarked for one purpose is not spent for another. Most government and foundation grants require full audits—legal verification by accountants on how money has been spent. Agencies such as the United Way refuse to provide money to groups that lack financial management systems.

Through budgeting and accounting, organizations keep track of where and how much money is being spent. Groups keep afloat by carefully balancing revenues and expenditures. Staff and board members should set aside some time to work out measures of cost control and to assure that money is being spent efficiently. Finally, to protect the organization from financial disaster, systems of risk management need be in place.

Budgeting and Accounting.   The heart of good financial management is a two-step process of budgeting and accounting. Together, budgeting links revenues to plans for projects and accounting demonstrates that money was spent appropriately and wisely. In addition, budgeting and accounting ensure that enough money is on hand at the time it is needed to avoid borrowing.

A budget is a statement that balances estimates of future revenues and expenditures, while allocating money to accomplish the tasks the membership wants to accomplish. To receive grants or loans for major buildings and social service activities the organization must prepare a budget in advance, that estimates costs and likely revenues. When other groups have done similar projects, estimates can be obtained from them. Those estimates then have to be adjusted to local circumstances, including salaries, rents, and projected revenues. Another group may have done a day-care center that is twice the size that the local group can afford, so drawing up the budget may mean figuring out how to scale back plans and still have a functioning project.

Because budgets depend on local conditions, they have to be built up from details. How many staff members will it take, at what salaries? How much will rent be? How many toys, at what cost, will be needed the first year of the day-care center? What will be the capital costs of running the office—for furniture, computers, printers, photocopy machines, or postage meters? All the costs to run the office plus the costs of the project must be figured out realistically and added up and then whittled back to fit within realistic estimates of revenue.

Budgeting for personnel takes real skill and sensitivity. Even a group that has little money to spend should not expect people to work for free. Professional organizers and staff members of nonprofits deserve medical coverage and should receive some contribution to their retirement. How many people should be hired? Too many and funds run out; too few and work doesn't get done. To complicate matters, laying off people is emotionally difficult, especially for a group that is about empowering people, so there is a tendency to hire too few to prevent the need for layoffs.

In general, budgets are built up in *service levels* or cost packages: that is, the organization plans a given amount of service or activities at a fixed cost. Some activities can be increased in small units. Leaflets cost so much a thousand, so if there is more money than planned, one thousand more leaflets can be printed and distributed. Other activities are lumpier. It is hard to rehabilitate half a building and leave the rest to the rats. Until the capacity of a kitchen to feed the homeless is reached, providing extra hot meals depends only on whether a little more money is available, but after space limits are reached, the organization would need a whole new kitchen to serve any additional meals, with all the costs implied in such an endeavor.

All organizations need to budget for *contingencies,* emergencies that are hard to predict such as broken equipment or unexpected lapses in funding. Congressional funding for a program may not be renewed, or money from an earmarked fund may be spent for other purposes, sending community groups scrambling until the funds can be restored.

Community organizations should also budget some *seed money.* It takes time to find outside funding for major projects, and most funders would like to see evidence that the idea is working before they agree to fund a project. As a result, the organization may need to pay for the start-up period itself. Or the organization may have to demonstrate the feasibility of an idea by doing a market survey, for example, or demonstrating the extent of the underserved population. Suppose a local funder indicates that it is

willing to help support community super markets, and a neighborhood has some abandoned retail space that appears to be ideal. The organization would be well advised to
spend some money to hire a consultant to determine if the project makes financial sense.

One of the basic tasks of budgeting is estimating the day-to-day costs of operations.
Operating costs should be framed by operating revenues, that is, recurring funds that
the organization can more or less plan on that are not earmarked for other purposes. A
key component of these revenues is dues. Budgeters need to look up the number of
members and the cost of dues, double checking to see that there has not been dramatic
fluctuation in membership or a recent decline that might affect the revenue predictions.
Another component of operating revenue may be grants that are likely to continue from
year to year, from the government or from foundations. Some checking is in order to
find out if the amounts are likely to drop during the budget year. Revenue from special
events can go toward operating expenses. These revenues should be based on prior
years' revenues from the same events, but estimating a little low, in case weather is
bad or the turnout is otherwise below predictions. The figure included in the budget
should be *net revenues,* that is, the income from an event minus the costs of putting it
on. For example, a hall must be rented for bingo, a street fair may require rental of
Port-A-Potties, and a fish fry involves the costs of the fish, even if the cooks are
volunteers.

Some revenues are hard to count on, they may occur or they may not. If the group
is engaging in a door-to-door campaign to raise funds, the outcome in dollars is hard
to predict, but it probably won't fall below historic levels for similar kinds of solicitations.
A reasonable, but low, estimate can be included in the budget, without encouraging
spending more than actual revenues permit. The payoff from an application for a new
grant is so unsure that the organization is better off not budgeting the revenue for
ongoing expenses that cannot be easily terminated if the grant does not show up.

Balancing Revenues and Expenditures.   To the extent possible, organizations should
try to balance revenues and expenditures. If deficits begin to appear, staff members
have to spend more time raising funds. The core mission of the organization may be
relegated to second place. If these emergency fund-raising tactics are unsuccessful, the
organization goes belly-up.

Even the most progressive social and community groups need to be *fiscally conservative,* that is very careful with money. (Fiscal conservatism has nothing to do with
being politically or socially conservative.) The most fiscally conservative approach is
to not allow fixed and recurring expenditures to exceed income that the organization
is virtually certain to obtain. Only after paying rent, salaries, heat, light, and the like
should the organization think about nonrecurring expenses, such as the purchase of
special equipment.

Fiscal conservatism prevents deficits but can prevent taking needed action when
problems are urgent. If the homeless should rapidly increase, or if a major employer
goes out of business, the neighborhood group has a moral obligation to try to alleviate
misery, even if the funds are not immediately at hand. Sometimes a local foundation
will come through with money to help handle the emergency. Another approach for
handling such emergencies might be to get permission from funders to reprogram money

from ongoing projects. A city might allow a change in the use of CDBG money if a business were suddenly to leave the neighborhood. If these options do not work, the organization may have to try some door-to-door or phone solicitations and cut back operating expenses in the interim.

Accounting and Cost Control.   Some kind of bookkeeping system should be started as soon as the organization is set up to record money received and money spent. For a small, informal community group, recording and keeping checking stubs might be sufficient. For groups running several programs at once, a more complicated system must be set up by an accountant.

A good accounting system tracks dollars, reporting on when they came in and where they went. Such information is necessary to reassure funders that money is being spent as intended. *Cash flow* statements let those in the organization know how much money is at hand at any time, allowing expenditures to be planned. Knowing that a large grant will be received in the third quarter suggests postponing expenses until then. Some organizations do, for a time, run a surplus; such funds should be kept in interest-bearing accounts, especially in the banks that have a policy of investing in community-based projects.

Good accounting data enables people to monitor how much things cost and to figure out where money can be saved. A community group can compare its expenses to those of other community groups or compare the costs of running a particular project to those of other similar projects. If heating costs in a home for the elderly seem too high, perhaps the group might consider investing in better insulation.

Periodically government or foundations fund national studies that audit community projects. One such financial audit found out that groups that were providing affordable housing were charging such low rents (because tenants could not afford more money) that almost no money was being set aside for capital repairs, such as replacing furnaces when needed (Hebert et al., 1993).

Risk Management.   Community organizations, especially those working with volunteers on controversial issues, must be prepared for financial risks that can occur because of accidents, malevolence, or lawsuits. Anticipating such costs is termed *risk management.* Risk is often handled by purchasing insurance.

What type of insurance to get depends on the mission of the group, though in most cases a general umbrella policy should be obtained to handle unforeseen circumstances. Almost all organizations need routine fire, theft, and liability insurance, in case an accident occurs on the premises. Special insurance is required for vehicles used in providing a service such as taking the elderly shopping. For groups providing support for the abused, health services, or child care, professional malpractice insurance is a must.

If some members of the organization handle large amounts of money, they should be bonded. Bonding is a guarantee that if someone runs off with the organization's money, the insurance company will make up the loss. Of course, before such protection is issued, the insurance company will check out the background of people handling the funds.

Insurance can be expensive, especially for small organizations. Fortunately, professional associations of community organizations now offer group rates, somewhat lowering the costs.

Building Empowered Organizations

In this chapter we first described a philosophy for administering community and social-change organizations and then talked about the technical skills needed to accomplish collective goals. Activists must balance the efficiency of an organization with its empowerment goals. To do so, activist groups are set up to empower employees, volunteers, and those who are served and are structured to avoid excessive bureaucracy yet maintain accountability and efficiency. Finally, activists must master the budgeting skills that reassure funders and that enable the organization to accomplish as much as possible with the limited money available.

CHAPTER

10 Developing Capacity through Participatory Meetings

Democratically run meetings help change personal indignation into collective action by increasing peoples' motivation to fight back, while giving them the tools to do so effectively. Meetings can be part of campaigns to share information or report on progress or to provide a forum to question those whom the organization has targeted. Meetings provide an opportunity to learn, through instruction provided by trainers or through peer instruction as activists teach one another and share their experiences. Meetings are about building capacity and increasing the confidence that success will be obtained.

Membership meetings and annual conferences create a forum at which major policies of an organization are determined and overall priorities are hashed out. More specific decisions are argued at standing committees, in task forces set up to handle pressing issues, or at the meetings of an elected steering committee or board. At *decision-making meetings* people work in a democratic way to determine what should be done, when, and by whom. At action meetings and rallies, activists present rousing speeches, sharing a collective narrative of triumph over oppression in ways that encourage people to continue the fight.

What is accomplished at meetings is important, but so are the procedures followed. Meetings must be run in ways that balance democratic participation with effective decision making. Skillful leaders and facilitators ensure that broad-scale participation occurs and that tasks are accomplished.

Characteristics of Good Meetings

No matter what the format or purpose of the meeting, certain skills are required to carry it off successfully. A badly run meeting can negate all the work that has been done in mobilizing people. A good meeting moves toward accomplishing goals, whether setting up a community day-care center or leading a protest against a Fortune 500 company. Holding a good meeting increases peoples' confidence that their organization can succeed and that it is worth their time to stay involved.

How do good and bad meetings differ? Bad meetings are long and boring. Nothing is accomplished. They are often chaotic and decisions are made even when necessary information is not at hand. Bad meetings alienate people; they sit there but don't really feel part of what is going on and become angry at one another. Perhaps most important, bad meetings create a sense of the impossible: How can we defeat them, if we can't even run a simple meeting?

Good meetings are exhilarating. They flow from issue to issue in a fast-paced, logical progression. A skilled chairperson ensures democratic participation by following a meaningful agenda set up in advance and enforcing rules that encourage participation and turn taking. Information is available in time to make decisions. People who attend these meetings feel that they own the outcomes and have a responsibility for carrying them out. Members interact and learn that their opinions really count. Such meetings create an increased sense of unity and possibility: How can anyone stand in our way when we are so strong together?

Regardless of the type of meeting, preparation is required to make them go smoothly. Someone must decide where they are to be held, obtain a room of the appropriate size, and arrange furniture to encourage dialogue. Those setting up the meetings must see that flip charts or blackboards are available, that speaker systems work, that coffee and refreshments are served, and that restrooms are accessible.

Participants must learn when the meeting will take place. Meetings of the boards or tasks forces should be held at announced and regularly scheduled times. In case people forget, written or phone notices should be sent as reminders. To remind people about community meetings, activists go door to door; doing so also provides another opportunity for recruiting. Leafletting the neighborhood is appropriate, as is placing posters that describe the when, where, and what of the meetings on bulletin boards of housing complexes, in store windows, and in other public places. In addition, the organization should draw up a press release for radio stations or local newspapers, making it clear that everyone is invited to attend.

What at first appear to be technical details in arranging a meeting can affect attendance. Is the location for the meeting one that will attract individuals from different groups in the neighborhood without turning off others? Some people might be uncomfortable meeting at the Catholic church, while others might feel out of place at the Hispanic center. Organizational headquarters are usually fine for smaller workshops and decision meetings among activists, but headquarters are usually too small for membership meetings. Sometimes, it's worth renting a room so the meeting place is not identified with any particular faction or ideology.

The physical layout for a meeting affects outcomes. If the room is too small, people feel uncomfortable, perhaps can't see what is going on and want to go home as soon as possible. If the room is too large and looks empty, it appears that no one cared enough to come. Light furniture is useful. More chairs may be set up if additional people come to a membership meeting, and in training sessions movable furniture allows people to break into smaller groups to practice what is being taught.

Make sure people can clearly hear the speakers. A room with too many corners creates an echo that makes speech sound noisy and indistinct; look for a room with acoustical tiles or carpeting, but not so much that the sounds are swallowed. When using a public address system make sure it works.

Everyone can easily see and hear if the room is set up with wider but fewer rows of chairs rather than a narrow deep layout. Members are more likely to feel close to the speakers and to the action if they are in the first few rows. While it is easier to see and hear the speakers if they are on a raised platform, such an arrangement suggests hierarchy. Instead, if the meeting room has a raised platform, organizers might want to put the podium to one side, and seat part of the audience on the platform. If the speakers are on the platform, they should address the members, not others on the platform. At the initial community meeting of the Dudley Street Neighborhood Initiative, the funders sat above the membership. The whole flavor of the meeting changed when a community activist grabbed a microphone and turned her back to those on the platform to address the membership (Medoff & Sklar, 1994).

For small meetings, having a single table around which everyone can sit adds to the feeling of solidarity. If possible, choose a round table without an obvious head position. People who sit opposite one another may act antagonistic, so encourage those who might disagree to sit next to one another. Meetings held around a coffee table encourage people to chat and share impressions, allowing them to gradually work out shared framings of problems.

In bilingual or multilingual communities, those organizing the meeting should try to have comments translated into each of the languages involved. It is best if the speakers present their ideas in several languages, alternating which language is presented first. It doesn't matter if the speaker is not terribly skilled in one of the languages, effort counts, and the effort is a mark of respect. Sometimes, however, translators are needed. People from a single language group should sit near one another and have an interpreter in their midst or, better yet, have earphones that broadcast a concurrent translation.

If the meeting is going to last for a while, the schedule should include time for sociability. Start off with coffee and a little bit of pleasant chatter. Have frequent breaks, and make sure coffee is available. If possible, try to arrange that people have the opportunity to eat together at some time during the meeting; don't let everyone go off on his or her own for lunch; and try not to let people go off together in cliques. Informal mealtime conversations can defuse potential antagonisms.

National meetings almost always balance formal workshops with sociability. People who have not yet met are encouraged to share a meal. Workshops are interspersed with informal tours to see what other organizations have accomplished. Receptions are set up for late in the day so that people have a chance to socialize. Developmental activists often meet informally in buildings that host organizations have rebuilt, creating an opportunity to meet casually while learning about successful projects.

Membership Meetings

General membership meetings (sometimes known as annual meetings or community conferences) enable the overall membership to set policy. In culturally mixed neighborhoods, such meetings can help people from different parts of the neighborhood and different ethnic backgrounds discover their common interests and frustrations.

At the initial membership meetings, people work out the goals of the new organization and choose (temporary) officers and members of a steering committee. Leaders from the community, often those who called the initial meeting, and professional organizers introduce themselves and discuss the problems of the neighborhood. In new organizations, recruitment committees and committees to organize the next meeting must be quickly established, but the membership might not yet be familiar with those who want to serve. One approach is to elect temporary representatives, who serve for a short time, until people get to know each other better.

At membership meetings, organizers need to be sure to get the names, addresses, and phone numbers of people who attend. Recruitment literature should be made available. Collection of dues is important because the organization needs the money, and paying dues reinforces peoples' identification with the organization.

In full membership meetings, the role of the chair is important. Initially, the chair might be the professional organizer, but as soon as possible an elected leader should take over. This person must have good speaking skills, a touch of humor, and an ability to play on emotions. In multicultural and multilingual neighborhoods, language skills are plus. The chair must show vision and portray goals that members understand, while at the same time instilling a sense that the goals can be accomplished. Speeches should be dramatic, vividly recounting recent battles and earlier victories of the organization, so that those who are new to the group begin to share past experiences. Such speeches build confidence by describing clever tactics that were successful and frame the possibilities of accomplishing the broader mission of the organization.

In an ongoing organization, membership meetings are held regularly to discuss progress and difficulties, choose new officers and consider the effectiveness of the steering committee. At membership meetings, members can express general concerns, comment on what has already occurred, and discuss new efforts. Meeting organizers should encourage debate and discussion, allowing a certain amount of anger to be expressed, as long as basic information is communicated and the meeting proceeds in a more or less orderly fashion.

Membership meetings are opportunities to show members and the invited press what the community has accomplished by working together. For example, Communities Organized for Public Services (COPS), a strong neighborhood federation in San Antonio, Texas, at its tenth annual meeting described to its membership that the organization was now part of a broader state-wide alliance that had national influence. The enthusiasm generated during membership meetings is intended to keep campaigns going and to encourage participation in organizational efforts. If difficulties are occurring, the members may have to decide whether to terminate a particular project.

After the meeting has been concluded, leaders and organizers should hold an evaluation session to examine the issues raised, think about whether the organization has gotten off track, and figure out which of the members' suggestions can be implemented. In addition, leaders should review the meeting to see if it was conducted in ways that encouraged participation and followed democratic procedures.

Agendas, Bylaws, and Rules of Procedure

Meetings, especially those of the full membership, can be complicated affairs, so while it is important to maintain a tone of informality to encourage people to participate, it is also necessary to maintain order and direction. The proper use of agendas, bylaws, and rules of procedure can encourage reasonably focused discussion in which those who wish to speak have the opportunity to do so, speakers can be heard, and decisions are recorded for future action.

Agendas enable people to plan in advance what topics will be covered and in what order they will be discussed. They keep the meeting on target. Bylaws and rules of procedure allow meetings to be conducted in an orderly and democratic fashion by regulating who can talk and when. The goal is to prevent a few determined souls from dominating the discussion. Bylaws promote democratic governance and help avoid conflicts by specifying how often membership meetings take place, the eligibility requirements for voting and standing for office, and the minimum number of people who must be in attendance for decisions to be made. These rules help prevent a minority faction from taking over and assure that the membership as a whole will be consulted on major issues. Rules are meant to facilitate discussions and actions rather than limit them and need not be followed rigidly unless order appears to be breaking down.

How many and what rules are needed vary from organization to organization. Bylaws might say that committee membership is determined by lottery from among the entire membership or specify very detailed voting procedures. Sometimes key constituency groups, representing different ethnicities or a variety of neighborhood and service organizations in the community, are automatically assigned a seat on key committees. Almost any procedure is appropriate if it assures fair representation and the inclusion of less dominant members, but some procedures should be worked out in advance.

Similarly, decisions should be made in advance to determine who can vote. The most common arrangement is for dues paying members to vote and for staff not to. If this rule is adopted, it must be widely advertised, or all those who attend a meeting may think they have a vote and be frustrated or irritated when they discover they do not. In organizations that provide social services, staff would more likely have a vote, but distinctions may have to be made between part timers and full timers or temporary and permanent staff. The group may need to decide how to handle volunteers, whether they should have the same vote as staff and client representatives.

In democratic organizations, issues must be fully discussed, different sides aired, and some accommodation reached. If a very small group, however, feels strongly that its opinions must prevail and disrupts discussion, making every meeting tense, such factionalism eventually will destroy the organization. To reduce the tyranny of a small minority, bylaws might specify a minimum number of members that must be present before business can take place—a quorum—and set that number larger than the size of small factional groups. Another bylaw that can reduce unnecessary conflict is one that requires all final decisions to be made only at meetings that are announced well in advance and then only on issues that have been included on the agenda that is circulated before the meeting. That way, new issues cannot be introduced and voted on at the last minute.

For most meetings, the agenda should be widely publicized. It should have on it only a limited number of items, because many people will want to talk, and slogging through a long list is demoralizing. Agenda items should be linked to actions and not just declarations of intent. Having an agenda item to condemn the lack of bilingual education is not enough; instead, the items should demand that the school district give special help to students who don't speak English at home. Assuming the item is passed, the organization then sets up a committee to contact and pressure the school board. In addition, agenda items should include brief reports on work in progress and accomplishments to date.

Putting new items on the agenda during the meeting for discussion at that same meeting is problematic because group members don't have a chance to think about the issues in advance. It is better to have committee meetings before the membership meeting in which people suggest and debate items to go on the agenda. Only in real emergencies should organizational leaders add items to the agenda at the last moment, and then they must include a full explanation of why the rush. An agenda committee can work out which issues must be handled at the full membership meeting, what problems can be solved immediately without going to the meeting, and what situations require further deliberation before being presented to the entire assembly.

Bylaws, formal meeting rules, and carefully worked out agendas reduce the chance of meetings being so contentious that members don't get a chance to discuss things or fully listen to each other's arguments. Often bylaws are adopted from standard publications such as *Robert's Rules of Order* (Robert and Evans, 1991), though most organizations simplify these detailed rules. For instance, *Robert's Rules of Order* specifies that unless recognized by the chair, people should not speak, except to clarify procedures. Rather than hold haphazard discussion, issues are only discussed after *motions* are made that suggest the necessary actions. *Discussion* is then limited to the content of the motions, with the chair working to assure that what is said is germane to the topic at hand. A skillful chair makes sure that all sides have had a say, before a decision is made, usually through a vote.

Such formal procedures are too intimidating for some people and might limit the discussion. To ensure that other matters can be raised, many meetings leave time for expressing general grievances; usually after the formal items on the agenda have been discussed. During these gripe sessions, few limits are placed and the conversation can move from topic to topic. When an issue raised this way seems important enough, the chair should assign it to a committee for further thought, encourage people to meet informally on the topic, and then bring it back to the next meeting as an item on the agenda.

Another crucial set of rules speaks to how final decisions are made, whether through formal voting or consensus discussions. In formal voting, a certain percent, usually a majority, must agree on an issue. For major issues, a two-thirds majority might be required for passage.

In an alternative system, consensus decision making, everyone has to agree, more or less, to the proposition on the table before it can pass. Consensus decision making is democratic and empowers everyone because anyone can veto a decision. In the full participatory democracy models of consensus decision making, minimal structure is imposed. Rather than taking votes, individuals try to persuade each other by explaining their reasoning; they listen to each other and decide based on what they hear, reformulating the proposition until everyone can agree with it.

The goal of everyone having a say with minimal controlling hierarchical structure, though appearing to be a good one, in practice excludes the less aggressive and can be quite undemocratic. With consensus systems, a very small minority can disrupt a group, leading to no decision being taken at all.

> "Consensus" voting, where people discuss an issue until a formulation is reached with which everyone agrees is . . . both elitist and undemocratic. It is elitist because consensus meetings can go on for hours—hours that working people and parents do not have. It is undemocratic because it assumes that disagreement is a sign of group weakness rather than actual strength. (Burghardt, 1982a, p. 54)

The history of the Students for Democratic Society (SDS) (that made all decisions through participatory democracy approach) shows that meetings at which full consensus is required collapse under their own weight (Gitlin, 1989; Miller, 1987). Even more damning, feminist literature shows that with the lack of structure involved in consensus meetings, women had far less opportunity to speak than men. Further, when a consensus is required, it is often hard to delegate work to a committee, because the proposal a committee might achieve by consensus could easily end up being unacceptable to the larger group (Zisk, 1989b).

Fortunately, consensus decision making can be modified in ways that reduce many of its drawbacks. One approach is not to require 100 percent of the members to concur. Discussion continues until almost everyone agrees. Then those who still are not satisfied are asked if "they can live with the decision that the others want." If they say "yes," the discussion is then ended. The principle respects the opinions of the minority, while letting those in the majority know that they should try to accommodate actions to those not yet in full agreement (Avery et al., 1981). Another way is to put a time limit on the discussion with the discussion arranged in ways that everyone gets a chance to speak and to react to the opinions being expressed. If the group cannot achieve consensus within the time limit, some other procedure may be invoked, such as turning the decision over to a steering committee. Presumably the threat of loss of control over the outcome encourages people to come to consensus more quickly.

Focused Decision-Making Meetings

When many technical details must be considered before reaching a conclusion, a mass meeting is an inappropriate setting. A large group is unlikely to read background material. The open give and take needed to explore a variety of options is impossible when dozens or hundreds of people are involved.

Broad policy directions may be decided in the membership meetings, but the smaller decisions intended to implement those overall goals are often made in committee. The membership meeting might discuss which community problems are most important and should be tackled first; committees might then weigh strategies to deal with those problems and decide on specific tactics, targets, and timing. Committees also typically deal with issues of hiring and firing staff and with internal stress between factions with different points of view or between competing ethnic or language groups or neighborhoods.

In examining specific options, committees often have to deal with financial or political risk. Can a social production organization afford to risk all its capital in sponsoring a needed neighborhood supermarket? If a protest group attacks the mayor on one issue, will it lose his support on other issues on which the mayor has been helpful? Committees may decide not only how a project or program will be done but also with whom, which bank or foundation will be approached for funding, or which other community groups would make effective allies.

Effective decision-making groups are structured to encourage creative problem solving, maintain democratic involvement, and prevent people from being too intimidated to express their real opinions. If a committee works out solutions that incorporate the key ideas that have been discussed, participants will feel that they have been heard, and will feel responsible for the decision (Kaner et al., 1996). Success is more likely when meetings are guided by structure and rules, but are carried out in settings that are warm, fun, and informal. In such a setting, people feel comfortable and secure and enjoy what can be a difficult task. Table 10.1 illustrates what happens if there is too little or too much structure.

Structuring Good Decision-Making Meetings

To enable give and take to occur, decision-making meetings are usually fairly small, usually no larger than a dozen people. Successful groups meld together in several stages, creating a shared culture that facilitates effective discussions (Kowitz & Knutson, 1960, p. 344).

In the first few meetings, an *orientation* takes place as those in the group discover each other's personalities, strengths, and weaknesses. Next, in the *formation* stage, the roles of individuals are resolved. Some group members may maintain the harmony of the group, while others provide technical information. Still others reinforce the culture by sharing the history of the decisions already made and reminding the participants of the processes the group has been using. In the third stage, *coordination,* negotiations occur between group members over the meaning of information and the priorities of the different goals. Finally, in the *formalization* stage, the group determines a course of action. If the decision has been made by consensus, there should be lots of support for the chosen strategy; if a majority voted for one strategy, some time may be used to persuade those who didn't agree to support it.

Decisions made with broad input are not only more empowering to the members, they are often better because they are more thoroughly examined. To prevent a chair from dominating the discussion and ensure this broad participation, some groups set up what is known as a *traveling chair.* With a traveling chair

> the person who is talking is responsible for calling on the next participant. She or he speaks and then calls on someone else who has indicated a desire to contribute. The process shares the responsibility and power of recognizing speakers . . . and generally increases participation, commitment, and involvement. (Avery et al., 1981)

TABLE 10.1   Decision-Making Groups Require Balance in How They Discuss Issues

More	Less
Structure	
With too much structure, talking is inhibited because people are afraid of making a procedural error	With too little structure, people defer to either the more aggressive or the high-status people and fear to talk
Leadership	
Too strong a leadership makes group members fear to contribute	With too weak a leadership, the discussion wanders and loses focus
Cohesion	
With too much emphasis on cohesion, people defer to the majority opinion, irrespective of what they individually think	With too little cohesion, people are afraid to present their ideas
Conflict	
Constant conflict disrupts meetings, leads to leadership fights, and makes reaching a decision that people will actually follow harder	Without conflict, weaker ideas go untested

Another approach is to have decision-making groups work with a professional *facilitator*, whose job is to run meetings smoothly and democratically while encouraging group members to explore a variety of ideas. A facilitator is not a voting member of the decision-making group and might be hired from outside of the organization.

Facilitators keep a meeting flowing and encourage participation in several different ways:

- They emphasize what people have said by repeating the key ideas that have been raised to make sure everyone has heard and registered them.
- They encourage people to take turns in talking rather than allow a few to dominate the conversation.
- They show respect for all ideas, even those that at first appear to be silly. A good idea may be presented in jest to deflect criticism or ridicule.
- When people don't complete their thoughts, the facilitator probes for further details but otherwise does not contribute his or her own thoughts.
- The facilitator works to gently keep the discussion on target, often by repeating the core questions at intervals or when the discussion seems to be wandering.
- The facilitator keeps people on their own schedules by reminding them when they agreed to stop.

- After a while people seem to run out of ideas. Facilitators know that decision-making groups get a second wind and encourage people to stick at the task a while longer. (adapted from Kaner, 1996)

Facilitators do not contribute to the substance of the discussion. In contrast, the professional organizers and staff members who attend decision-making meetings provide backup information and answer questions.

To make people feel comfortable and encourage them to participate, group leaders

1. Keep groups small. It is better to form several subcommittees than have one large one in which some are too intimidated to talk.
2. Arrange the physical setting in ways that symbolize equality. Sitting at a circular table is less formal than sitting at a conference table with a head.
3. Follow a prearranged agenda. Everyone's time is valued, there is little meandering over the different topics.
4. Don't try to accomplish everything in one meeting. Time should be allowed for people to get to know each other and take on specific roles before the group feels comfortable enough to make difficult decisions.
5. Share history through narratives and stories. Shared history creates trust among members and gives them common examples to draw on.
6. Leave time for informal conversations. Such exchanges enable people to get to know each other and increase their willingness to listen to each other.
7. Assign responsibility for carrying out the group's decisions. It is frustrating to call another meeting to continue working on a problem and find out that the previous decisions have not yet been carried out. (adapted from Jones, Barlund, & Haion, 1980; Kowitz & Knutson, 1980)

Agendas help regulate the flow of the meeting. Here are several recommendations for arranging an agenda:

- Place some routine business or announcements first. Read brief reports, if there are any.
- Place the most important decisions (or most controversial topics) about 15 to 20 minutes after the start. People tend to be most alert at this point.
- Limit the number of difficult or controversial items to be handled at any one meeting. Estimate the time to be spent on each item. When people see that a discussion is supposed to last no more than half an hour, they try to reach a decision in that time. Of course, if the item proves more difficult, extra time can be allowed, or the unfinished items could be placed on the agenda of the next meeting.
- Wrap up a meeting with noncontroversial items such as authorizing the payment of routine bills.

If the agenda seems too long, routine items that need little or no discussion can be grouped together within a *consent agenda*. Items on the consent agenda are made available but not read aloud unless someone asks a question.

Agendas are intended to guide meetings so that progress can be made and time is not wasted on minor matters. Agendas should not become so rigid, however, that they restrict the number and variety of clever ideas that are brought forth. If some topics are too complex to deal with all at once, the group can hold separate meetings to discuss various options and then bring back their decisions to the next board or steering committee meeting for ratification.

Creating and Stimulating a Variety of Ideas

Some of the problems confronting community organizations and social-change groups are truly perplexing. How does one reduce pervasive, lingering pockets of poverty? How can one successfully oppose irresponsible landlords or companies that put their profit margins before health and safety? Community organizations have to come up with answers that not only work but also appeal to the membership.

Decision-making meetings must be conducted in such a way that people feel comfortable generating possible solutions to these complicated problems, even if some of the ideas might not work. Whoever is playing the role of chair can make some suggestions, but should be careful not to force his or her perspective on the group. A leader helps people build on the ideas they suggest.

One task of the group leader is to help frame the issues so they appear solvable. If committee members express concern that the problem is overwhelming, the chair can try to reframe the issue so there are several viable ways to approach it. If committee members are skeptical about having the time to do one more thing, the chair might suggest breaking up the tasks into smaller parts and prioritizing them. If the fear expressed is that the project will take more money than the group has, the leader can steer the conversation to fund-raising strategies (adapted from Kaner, 1996, p. 196).

The discussion leader sets the tone for the committee. Leaders don't yell at those who get excited or out of hand, but rather gently ask them to tone down the discussion. Continued courtesy in the face of rudeness shows people the need to respect each other's ideas while discouraging disruptive personality conflicts. Determined calmness and unfailing courtesy creates an environment in which people are willing to speak. Wherever possible, avoid criticizing or blaming people, because blame and criticism inhibit people from offering their ideas.

> When defining an issue or problem always define it as shared. Responsibility for a conflict never lies with just one person or faction. Say, "We do not agree about the distribution of office space," *not* "Jack refuses to share his desk." Say, "Mary and Tom have a problem coordinating their work schedules," *not* "Tom is never around when Mary needs to consult with him." (Avery et al., 1981)

Discussion leaders call on individuals who have not spoken much to help explore all sides of an issue. He or she might ask the speaker to elaborate a bit. "I understand the first part of what you said, but I'm not sure what you think we ought to do after the meeting with the alderperson." Next, the leader encourages others to explore the idea at hand so that many people have ownership of what has been suggested. If only one side of an argument is being presented, the discussion leader can ask for opposing views or shortcomings of the proposal.

The leader can summarize his or her understanding of the emerging consensus and see if others agree on this summary. Sometimes merging existing themes can take a bit of cleverness. One person may have argued for a demonstration against drug dealers, while another may have talked about the frustration of being ignored by city hall. The leader can combine the ideas to suggest a well-publicized sit-in at the city plaza with oversized pictures of brazen drug transactions.

Getting agreement can take some skill. The goal is to find a solution that incorporates the feelings of virtually all those involved. The first step might be to find out where people stand and to see if peoples' views overlap. The group may then want to explore some of the overlapping responses in more detail, because those have a substantial amount of support to begin with. Those who support particular ideas may then try to convince the others. There is no need to try to converge at a consensus all at once (Kaner, 1996, pp. 148–149).

Even in the most effective, harmonious groups, ideas evolve over time. A good idea may have to simmer for a while until it has been refined and gradually becomes group property and not simply an individual's pet scheme. The first time the idea comes up, it may meet with criticism and be tabled or even die. If it has considerable appeal, it will come back again later, in somewhat modified form, to handle prior criticism. "The same basic solution may go through a number of such transformations before it is accepted" (Jones et al., 1980, p. 166). Social psychologists term this process of letting an idea simmer *decision modification*. Effective discussion leaders encourage this recycling of ideas until they become group property.

Generating a Wide Variety of Ideas.   Decision-making groups can use a number of techniques to encourage wide participation and lots of suggestions.

One way to come up with ideas is through *brainstorming,*

> . . . a procedure wherein members are encouraged to suggest any idea about the problem that comes to mind. The ideas are written on a blackboard or flip chart, and no positive or negative evaluation of the ideas is permitted, included scowls, groans, signs or gestures. (Yukl, 1989, p. 250)

The presentation of one idea may stimulate others, and the excitement generated should encourage people to jump in with additional thoughts. The leader of brainstorming sessions must make it clear that no idea will be immediately evaluated, that what might appear to be way out might turn out to be worthwhile (Kaner, 1996, p. 100).

A variant of brainstorming is called *round robin* (Moore, 1987). In this case, somebody suggests an idea and writes it down on a pad. The pad is circulated, and everyone is required to add or cross out a statement that somehow builds on the original ideas. The obligation to write something forces people to contribute, and because no emendations are signed, anonymity is preserved. A more lively variant of this process is a *structured go around* (Kaner, 1996, p. 80) in which, depending on the variation chosen (a) people sit in a circle and the person clockwise to the speaker speaks next; (b) the speaker tosses a bean bag (or some such thing) and the person who catches it must contribute an idea. The goal is to free people from the embarrassment of choosing to talk because the way the game is set up, they have no choice.

With *nominal group techniques* (from Delbecq, van de Ven, & Gustafson, 1975, revised by Moore, 1987) or *individual writing* (Kaner, 1996, p. 80), people jot down their ideas on slips of paper that are shuffled before the ideas are placed on the board, without any names being attached. Once the initial set of ideas has been collected, the leader or facilitator tries to get each member of the group to discuss the strengths and weaknesses of the individual ideas. Better yet, the group as a whole might suggest how separate ideas can be combined into a stronger approach.

Sometimes people get excited and jump in, not letting others speak, intimidating those with less confidence or lower social status. A skillful facilitator can normally restore order with a few polite words. Another approach that encourages critical discussion while preserving order is to use a *talking stick*. An object, such as a stick, is placed in the middle of the room. People agree to talk only when they are holding the talking stick. When they finish talking, they place the stick back in the middle where the next person then picks it up. People who want to shout out usually curtail themselves because they know they will get a turn.

Group members can come up with some terrific ideas using these techniques, but the process should not stop when the first good idea surfaces. It needs to be evaluated, to see if it would work, or what its shortcomings might be. To assure that the idea is tested, each group should select one or more *devil's advocates*. The role of the devil's advocate is to look for weaknesses and report back to the group later before any action is taken (Yukl, 1989, p. 225). This approach allows people to put forth clever ideas in a spontaneous manner but gives the group a chance to reflect before going off half-cocked.

Problems of Cohesion, Satisfaction, and Groupthink

Enthusiasm and spirit permeates decision-making groups for community and social-change organizations: We're finally together; we're going to rebuild the neighborhood or teach those chauvinist pigs that women are not decorations. When people work together in groups that are highly motivated and get along well, they are more willing to present ideas and accept ownership of group decisions. Because the group, rather than individuals, makes the decisions, even fearful group members can help make risky decisions. Groups, however, can become too cohesive. Members can become too concerned about their acceptance in the group to challenge ideas that really have problems in them. Janis called this phenomenon *groupthink* (Janis, 1982, p. 9).

The way action organizations are formed can encourage groupthink. People join because they care deeply about some issues and feel that by working together they can prevail. They are likely to demonize their opposition and feel that right is on their side. Members of an action organization may feel invincible and, therefore, have no need to check out the feasibility of their plans. Or they may be so fearful of falling out among themselves that they apply strong pressure on anyone who dissents, resulting in an inability to evaluate their own proposals (Janis, 1982, pp. 174–175).

The result of groupthink may be unwise decisions, failed campaigns, and loss of membership. If decision makers feel invulnerable, they may underestimate the strength of opponents. Or they may be so convinced of the rightness of what they are doing that they forget to build support for the project and are blindsided by opposition or lack of funding. To prevent groupthink, decision-making groups should be forced to gain the concurrence of others before acting. The need to convince those not immediately in the group forces people to examine the strengths and weaknesses of their own arguments. Another approach to preventing groupthink is to set up workshops to examine past actions. Knowing that past policies did not always work encourages people to reflect on what might be wrong with their current ideas.

Handling Conflict

A community group has to be prepared to deal with conflict among members, but conflict can get out of hand and become all consuming. Some of these conflicts emerge because people are frustrated by long and difficult meetings that don't lead to acceptable solutions. Others result from personality clashes or because people feel that they are being ignored.

Sometimes all that is needed is to call a break so that people can calm down. When two people radically disagree, the leader can call on others to move the discussion along. When someone is getting strident in an effort to be heard, the facilitator summarizes the arguments being made, including those of the person who thinks he or she is being ignored (adapted from Kaner, 1996, pp. 114–119).

As long as conflicts are not based on personalities or on core values that guide the group, fully articulated disagreements can get people actively involved and act as a safety valve for frustrations (Jones et al., 1980, pp. 153–154). Groups that know how to handle conflicts usually produce better decisions, generate more alternative solutions, create more interesting meetings, and force members to be specific about the information needed to resolve problems (Kowitz & Knutson, 1980, pp. 171–175).

Discussion leaders handle conflict differently depending on the matter under dispute (Jones et al., pp. 146–147). A conflict based on prejudice needs to be handled differently from one based on disagreements about focus or logic.

Individuals might disagree on assertions, that is, untested statements of personal preference or belief. These assertions may reflect unresolved feelings about race, ethnicity, gender, or people in certain occupational positions. Such statements can derail a discussion or an effort to make a decision. One approach to handling conflict of this sort is for the discussion leader to particularize. For example, if Mr. Jones asserts, "It is impossible to work with bankers," the discussion leader might ask, "Do you think you can work with Ms. Smith?" (Ms. Smith is a community banker that has helped fund the group before). "Of course, I can. Ms. Smith is an exception, not like those folk from downtown." Such an agreement can resolve the immediate conflict, without speaking to the broader question of whether or not bankers can be trusted.

Individuals might disagree on the logic of an argument. Sometimes further explication of the facts or spelling out the logic in more detail resolves the difficulty. For instance, a leader of a community-run social service agency might take a position against financing a shelter for abused women. Spelled out, the reasoning is that in this middle-class community few women would need or ask for these services and the shelter might attract people from elsewhere. When others point out the number of police calls made by abused women in their community, the person who objected to the proposal is likely to back off.

Sometimes it is the evidence itself that people disagree on. For example, a group member might argue, "We can't target Exxon to clean up the river, it will cost too much, and one industry will never pay that amount." In this case the conflict can be bridged by finding out the actual cleanup expenses involved and learning the history of cases in which environmental groups pressured industries to pay for problems businesses created. When disagreements occur on evidence, a committee can be set up with people on both sides to look up the facts.

The most difficult conflicts to resolve are those on values, that is, fundamental beliefs. These beliefs may be about the goals, what equality means, for example, or about the means, such as whether violence is ever justified. Such values often stem from deeply felt religious or ideological beliefs and can be intense. People may come together initially because they are disempowered in a similar way—because of the color of their skins, their gender, or the coincidence of living together in a neglected neighborhood. Once together, however, they discover they differ in values. In such circumstance, as has occurred in the civil rights era, among feminists, and environmentalists, different groups spin off, agreeing on the need to solve core problems of racism, gender inequality, or environmental deterioration but having to work separately because they disagree about what actions are appropriate.

Training Meetings

To bring about changes, organizations need the capacity—the technical and social skills—to fight back. In training meetings, community members, volunteers working with the staff, learn the technical tools of direct action, of managing social production projects, and of maintaining the organization itself. People learn how to run meetings, raise funds, prepare press releases, make budgets, direct projects, apply for grants, and virtually any other action needed to build organizational and community capacity.

Training may be focused on how to carry out specific actions. During the civil rights era, citizenship schools were set up as training academies to teach people how to register to vote and what to do once the vote was obtained. Some of the schools taught the literacy skills and civic knowledge needed to register. If an organization is planning an action involving civil disobedience, members have to learn first what to do and why they need to do it that way. Even organizing people to testify at city hall requires rehearsing.

Bringing about community-based economic and social production necessitates that people master new skills. Activists in the Dudley Street Initiative worked with professional planners and architects and taught themselves the techniques for physically restoring their neighborhood. Tenant management groups, as well as boards of housing and worker-owned cooperatives, must learn the details of property and fiscal management. People who join lending circles—ways of acquiring small amounts of capital for microenterprises—have to learn how to draw up business plans and how to manage debt. Those involved in community development learn to borrow for housing or commercial projects, then learn how to manage the property they buy or build.

Sometimes the basic work of the community group is to train members for jobs. Feminist organizations have helped teach their members how to work in banks (Tom, 1995), and community-based development organizations have sponsored training programs that teach women on welfare to become owners of their own day-care businesses (Rubin, 1994).

As members and staff master skills, the organization becomes more successful and community capacity increases. Learning new things enhances individuals' willingness to work with the group while the confidence that develops is empowering. People are more likely to learn when the training avoids a formal top-down approach that equates the teacher with knowledge and authority and the student with ignorance and submission. Training models that follow the philosophy of the pedagogy of the oppressed (Freire, 1970) break down the border between student and teacher, as they teach each other about their experiences and what actions will work.

The details of training programs differ depending on the subject matter. Learning how to eliminate hazardous material (a common problem in redeveloping inner-city properties) is done in a hands-on manner on site. Learning how to plan a budget takes place in a small room, where people sit with computer-generated spreadsheets and collectively watch how the numbers change, as different assumptions are entered into the calculations. In spite of these substantive differences, there are many commonalities in how empowering training sessions should and can be run.

Training sessions should be involving for the individuals, rather than being a passive exercise. Formal lectures, in which people just sit in the audience and listen, should be kept to a minimum. General principles can be discussed at a brief general session, which then breaks up into smaller workshops. Samples should be handed around, of budgets, or news releases, or loan agreements, or whatever it is the members are learning how to do. Trainees should get a chance to watch someone do the task and get a chance to do it themselves.

Training sessions must balance the need to communicate specific skills with the requirement to create an environment that makes people comfortable in learning together. If trainees have a list of criteria by which to judge a good budget or a good grant application, they can critique each others' products or proposals without being embarrassed that a teacher is judging or criticizing them.

The trainer is supposed to know more on the subject of the training than those who come to learn; however, if an outside expert lectures to the group, he or she might inadvertently reinforce peoples' sense of ignorance and incompetence. To avoid such disempowering action, trainers should be group members who have participated as learners in other sessions. When the trainer in protest tactics sits down and learns from others how to do a budget, the message is given that we are all students who can learn from one another. Learning and teaching styles that bring the learners into the process in an active way can also be helpful. Simulations, in which the attendees work out solutions in groups and then discuss them, can be useful tools that avoid formal teacher and student roles.

The personality and speaking skills of the trainer are important. The speaker should use a bit of humor and indicate that he or she has been there before—led a demonstration, been audited, arrested, or applied for a grant—and was successful. The trainer must indicate that there is nothing he or she has done that others in the group cannot also do. The trainer should have similar background to those in the group and be able to say, "Five years ago I was sitting where you are now." "Here's how it works, I did it, you can do it, try it now." If the trainer looks and sounds like those who are taught, this message is more likely to get across.

For instance, a developmental activist described a successful training program for young people run in a community-based auto-repair shop located in a Hispanic neighborhood. The training

> gave the [youth] an exposure that is not the summer job where you push a broom, pick up paper, cut grass. We put them to work with the computers and in the departments. You put them with a role model, a person looks like them, eats like them, lives where they live, didn't have a lot of education. . . . You take a kid and have him go to a lawyer downtown [a program the city sponsored], he is an alien to them. They don't think they can be ever like that guy. They don't ever want to be like that guy. But if we assign a student to Jose who has a 4th grade education and who is now the general manager here. They know, they say, "hey, I could be a general manager of a place because Jose did it." . . . That makes a whole different world. Those are people you need to put those kids with, people they can identify with who have made it.

Effective training builds on references and examples familiar to those who are learning. A person teaching about budgets should use the organization's own budget or one from a similar group. If the training session is about property management, the trainer can work with the tenants' organizations on an actual problem they face. The closer the training is to what people recognize they need to know, the more eager they will be to learn what is offered.

To get some of the technical material across without being intimidating, a lot of trainers prepare folders that link backup material with the speakers' presentations. If the first speaker is talking about legal constraints on door-to-door solicitations, the first tab might contain a copy of the state laws on solicitation of funds. The information included should make the speaker's comments clearer and provide reference material for later use. Backup material also helps people pay attention to the speaker, because they don't have to take notes.

In general, trainers have four responsibilities: they should build skills, integrate values with the skills taught, help set realistic goals for those learning new material, and generate enthusiasm for the topic at hand.

Build Skills.   At the training session, have people practice. Don't let people leave until they have shown that they can use the knowledge they gained. People learning to do a community analysis, for instance, can practice using demographic data on the neighborhood or can take a walking tour to demonstrate their new skill at documenting community problems.

Another way to build skills is to have people play roles that grow out of the training. For instance, let some members take the role of the neighbor being asked for money, while others practice making an appeal. Role playing teaches, but it also can be very funny or very dramatic. One community member can represent advocates for clean air and back a polluting business owner into a legal jam; or one of the trainees can make a plea for funding that represents graphically what drug rehab means to addicts with kids. The silence when other members of the group pause to listen, fascinated by the story, reflects respect and absorption.

Integrate Values with Skills.   The success of training sessions reinforces the belief that people can learn and succeed, a core value of organizing and development. Technical skills should be integrated with the underlying values or philosophies that make them valuable. For instance, in training for civil disobedience, people learn how to accept arrest passively or how to act as a dead weight when the police cart them out of a building. These skills are meaningful only when the philosophy of nonviolence is understood.

Effective training teaches people not only how to piece together resources to restore a strip of stores in a poor neighborhood but also why it is important to keep money in a community and recirculate wealth. Particular techniques might change over time—funding sources evolve—but the core reasons for action stay the same and should be explained.

Be Realistic.   Trainers should be realistic in teaching people what to expect. Trainers should provide information on how many grants are submitted and how many receive money. They should let trainees know how often people will slam doors in their faces or make false promises to attend neighborhood meetings. The group as a whole should encourage love of the neighborhood, but the trainer also has to warn the future canvassers that door-knocking in some neighborhoods can be dangerous and that it is better if people do it in pairs. If group members expect too much, they will get discouraged the first time they have a grant application rejected or the first time a neighbor won't talk to them.

Build Enthusiasm.   It is possible to be realistic and build enthusiasm at the same time. For example, the trainer can explain that while members won't succeed in every instance, even a small number of victories can be very important. Any new member a canvasser can bring helps keep the organization alive and activities funded. Some of the instances of pollution that members document will result in Environmental Protection Agency (EPA) action and an eventual cleanup of the site. People become more enthusiastic when they can see how their efforts can be effective.

Excitement is catching. If the trainer is enthused about the subject, he or she can rouse the group. That excitement comes across in examples that are well chosen of fun campaigns or successful projects with good outcomes. A well-told story makes the trainees feel like they are there, for instance, engaged in a successful fund-raiser or pressure campaign. A dramatic story builds excitement and a successful outcome reinforces the feeling that "Yes, we can do this, and now we know how."

The Role of Democratic Leadership

Meetings highlight the role of organizational leaders who appear on the podium or take the responsibility for guiding decision-making meetings or leading training sessions. As we discussed in Chapter 6, symbolic leaders are important as they provide the voice that others hear and the personal examples of courage that are emulated. At meetings, leaders stimulate others. People such as Ernesto Cortez can turn a quiet meeting into an enthused rally by making people understand that they share problems and can fight back. Leaders frame the possibilities for change and provide overall guidance to the group.

While their role is important, organizational leaders or even technical experts must not use their position to dominate decisions, even if problems seem to require quick action. Doing so belies the empowerment ideals of organizing. Sometimes experts may feel entitled to push decision-making groups in their direction because they feel they know best, while those who found organizations feel a proprietary sense of ownership and want others to go along with their ideas. Even right decisions taken at the behest of a few or short-term victories brought about by following the ideas of leaders might hurt the broader organizing effort. If people feel they have little part in making decisions, they won't feel empowered and will drop out. A victory that comes about simply by following the actions of a leader, rather than enhance mobilization, might discourage people who feel their opinions don't matter.

At meetings and through their overall actions, leaders should work to build organizational capacity and help to empower organizational members. Building capacity is about teaching others how to do something and then enabling others to do the work themselves. Winning an immediate battle against oppressors is important, but it must be done in ways that help the membership gain capacity.

In general, leaders and organizers should function as catalysts and teachers, as facilitators, not owners or managers of the organization. The founders should try to see themselves as trustees who have taken on a collective burden until others can assume the role. This is the lesson taught through democratic, participatory meetings.

The Social Action Model

Social change can be accomplished through several complementary approaches. Through *social-action campaigns,* pressure and protest organizations call attention to problems to compel government or businesses to make changes. With the *social-production approach,* community organizations provide services or material goods, or orchestrate neighborhood reconstruction. In Part Five we examine the social-action model, while in Part Six we discuss the social-production approach.

Chapter 11 presents a philosophy of social-action campaigns, showing the importance of acting in ways that are dignified and empowering and framing issues in ways that support social-change efforts. In Chapter 12, we discuss two styles of political action that can influence government. The first is pressuring those in office to comply with community needs, and the second is community members themselves trying directly to bring about legislative change.

When lobbying and low-key pressure fails, confrontations are required. Chapter 13 describes litigation as a way of increasing pressure and then explores a variety of direct actions such as civil disobedience and rallies that confront those in power. Chapter 14 examines how social-change organizations gain effectiveness through working in coalitions, by skillfully using the mass media, and by mastering the bargaining skills required to assure that what is gained through direct action is not lost at the negotiating table.

CHAPTER

11   An Overview of Action Campaigns

Through action campaigns, members of social mobilization organizations contend with authorities to challenge the inequalities that limit life opportunities. The scope of action campaigns varies greatly. Community groups might conduct one-shot efforts to force a city council to put in a needed stop sign at a dangerous intersection, or neighborhood housing organizations might rally in support of increased investments in poor communities. National organizations have carried out campaigns for gender or racial equality that lasted decades, bringing about fundamental changes in political and social values.

Action campaigns involve people coming together to pressure racist or sexist individuals and institutions—unscrupulous landlords, irresponsible businesses, banks, hospitals, and even government—to compel these powerful entities to change. In such campaigns, people

> **Define** or **frame** a problem, **document** its extent, **target** those who can effect a solution, use **direct pressures** on the target, and work to ensure the **implementation** of promised changes.

A *campaign* is a planned and coordinated effort to cause an opponent to concede to the demands of the social action organization. Campaigns follow long-term *strategies* that describe what goals to work toward, which targets to pressure, what actions are acceptable, and how success is to be measured. Campaigns build in pauses so activists can evaluate progress and change tactics if necessary: Perhaps picketing would be more effective than a sit-in or maybe the organization should target the corporate headquarters instead of the local branch. Is the concession made by the target truly a victory, or is it an intentional distraction?

Tactics are the specific activities undertaken to bring about change—lobbying, phone calls, sit-ins, on up to sabotage. An *action* occurs when members of a social mobilization organization carry out a specific tactic, for instance, by showing up en masse at city hall and demanding that the code enforcement officer explain why no fines have been levied against landlords whose buildings are firetraps. In a single campaign, the actions chosen depend upon the perceived vulnerabilities of the target and the willingness of organization members to participate. Activists might decide that a hunger strike could shame religious leaders into spending more to help the poor. To stop an unneeded highway, members of militant organizations might destroy construction equipment; others who believe in nonviolence might decide to lie down in front of the bulldozers. Some might be willing to accept arrest for trespassing by refusing to move from an old and cherished neighborhood building that is about to be torn down.

Tactics cluster in several groupings. With *pressure tactics*— lobbying, petitioning, working with bureaucrats—organization members accept the legitimacy of the system and play by its rules, for instance, by showing up at government hearings and respectfully requesting officials to make needed changes. The implication is that the system itself is working, but that it needs prodding. *Legal tactics*—law suits, court appearances, and restraining orders—indicate that the action organization feels that the targets have failed to abide by the rules of the game and need to be forced to do so. In contrast, with *confrontations* or *direct actions*—sit-ins, pickets, breaking unjust laws, aggression at targets—the action organization indicates that existing political, economic, or social structures are so biased that ordinary people cannot prevail. Old rules must be violated, and new ones promulgated and enforced.

Confrontations get public attention and show authorities that the action organization has the power to extract a cost if change is not made. Suppose stores sell products made by exploiting child labor and refuse to stop when requested by social-justice organizations. In response, the members of the organization might march around the store or tie up its counters by sending in (fake) customers who demand services. Confrontations are social explosions that yell, "Pay attention! There is a problem here! And, if you don't find a solution, we will make our own."

Confrontations are intended to force targets to promise to change. To assure lasting victories, however, social action organizations have to think about ways to permanently alter laws, regulations, and policies. Tenants can't conduct a rent strike each time a landlord turns off the heat. What the striking tenants are after is enforcement of city codes that require landlords to provide adequate heat. New laws lock in the gains made through confrontations.

In practice, organizations combine several tactics in their campaigns. For instance, Communities Organized for Public Services (COPS) in San Antonio began using direct actions and confrontations but is now powerful enough to exercise direct political influence (Sanders, 1997; Sekul, 1983). COPS was formed in the early 1970s in San Antonio by mobilizing Mexican-Americans whose neighborhoods were devastated by floods to demand a fair share of the federal money for infrastructure improvement.

Initially, confrontional tactics were used. For instance, when the city manager refused to release needed funds to poor neighborhoods, "a delegation of COPS people, led by president Carmen Badillo, paid [the city manager] a visit in his office. They demanded with TV cameras present that the [city manager] meet with them" (Sekul, 1983, pp. 181–182). COPS is still willing to bring out the people but today is more likely to use political lobbying as it is a recognized power in the city. By mobilizing individuals, churches, and neighborhood groups within a coalition, COPS offers support to its candidates for office who will keep promises to the poor neighborhoods. For instance, because of COPS, a very large portion of federal development money that San Antonio receives is now spent in poor neighborhoods on projects community members have chosen (Sanders, 1997, p. 56).

Action campaigns can be effective, but community groups must be clear about their aims and be able to recognize how long it takes to win difficult battles. Further, while success is important, it must be obtained in ways that emphasize the overall goals and values of the members of the organization. For instance, in the fervor of an *accountability session*—when elected officials are challenged to answer questions in a public forum sponsored by the community group—it is easy to forget that the goal is to solve a problem not discomfort a politician.

The Overall Purposes of Social Action Campaigns

Though less press attention is now paid, social action efforts are almost as popular now as they were during the 1960s, when protests were held on a wide variety of issues (Beckwith, 1998). Today, students demonstrate to force Nike to stop exploiting workers overseas; gays, lesbians, and their supporters campaign to end discrimination based on sexual orientation; public housing tenants picket the Department of Housing and Urban Development (HUD) to assure that affordable housing is made available when older units are torn down. The Kensington Welfare Rights Union, along with numerous local antipoverty organizations, struggles to ensure that welfare reform does not make life worse for the nation's poorest citizens. Associations of Community Organizations for Reform Now (ACORN) join with progressive unions to assure that people coming off welfare do not displace the working poor. Numerous groups have convinced cities to award contracts only to firms that pay their employees a living wage substantially above the poverty level.

What questions should activists ask themselves when choosing issues? Ideally, a successful campaign should address and help solve societal problems; it should help strengthen the community organization and empower its members; and it should raise the level of public discussion on matters of concern to the action organization.

First, *are the issues framed in ways that speak to broad social problems, such as those of social justice and economic inequality?* Campaigns to pull down institutional structures that discriminate against minorities, women, older citizens, or gays make real the possibility of individual mobility and success and energize the society. Actions to eliminate severe economic inequalities reinforce the ideals of our society. A system that allows people to work full time and yet not reach the poverty line or one in which government allows wealthy people special tax protections while the poor lack medical care is unjust and inspires people to join in. What makes these social justice issues especially suitable for action campaigns is that the public basically agrees with the values that guide the efforts, though people have to be shown how far they have strayed from their beliefs.

If actions are going to resonate with the public and achieve more fundamental changes, they need to be framed in terms of the larger issues. Thus a campaign to stop one company from dumping hazardous waste illegally ought to be framed as part of a broader concern about safe water and breathable air. The public at large understands the importance of cleaning up toxic waste, whether or not they live near the polluting plant or the dump site. A campaign to free one death row inmate from prison because of a faulty trial can be framed as a case against police and judicial procedures that assign incompetent lawyers to poor people and use confessions that were extracted under duress. If the campaign cannot evoke any broader principles, perhaps it should not be undertaken.

A second question in evaluating a campaign issue is whether or not *the issue helps mobilize people and by doing so strengthens the social action organization.* Regardless of the broader social value of an issue, if the concern does not appeal to community members or frightens them, organizations should think twice about taking it on. Campaigns build on what people know and feel. Community members might not recognize how federal immigration policy keeps wages low and be unwilling to join a campaign to change the policy. They do know, however, they are poorly paid and that their bosses are often abusive. They may be more willing to join a campaign that is aimed directly at those problems. Trying to end housing discrimination in a community might seem overwhelming, but fighting for better enforcement of the building code to prevent blight might seem more manageable. Small successes reinforce people's willingness to stay in the group and can jump start the building of an empowered organization.

A third criteria for evaluating a campaign issue is *the extent to which working on the issue helps educate community members and the public.* If the issue is framed properly, even relatively narrow concerns can help raise people's awareness of broader matters. A battle to stop development of one farm property into large-lot suburban homes becomes a way of teaching people the costs and consequences of suburban sprawl. A community action to protest city subsidies to a firm that has abandoned a poor neighborhood might educate participants about how tax subsidies unjustly support the well-to-do. A campaign to clean up a particular river can teach participants about pollutants, illegal dumping, and the lax enforcement that lets businesses get away with poisoning fish and fouling public waters.

Successful campaigns teach people that they do have power over those who appear to be in superior positions. If the group represents a large number of constituents, politicians will show up to accountability sessions at which organization leaders and members ask prepared questions, usually about community needs, promises made, and services not provided. Participants at such sessions do not accept vague answers or smokescreens; they demand straightforward answers and enforceable solutions. Organization members learn that they can make elected officials quake and need not be dependent on the good will or favors of those in office.

Before and during action campaigns, activists share with one another *narratives* that elucidate in personal terms how they have been harmed by the problem at hand. People teach each other what they have learned. In the civil rights era, for instance, individuals who learned from each other's experiences while attending the Highlander Citizenship School later established citizenship schools in poor communities that taught people sufficient literacy skills to become registered voters. While learning these skills, people talked together and shared their stories of oppression, and collectively worked out ways of fighting back.

In meetings during campaigns, women narrate stories of abuse, people of color describe incidents of racial oppression, environmentalists share reports of vanishing species and land turned into arid scrub by overgrazing. The disabled talk about their frustration and humiliations when they could not gain access to buildings or restrooms.

Through such stories people teach each other that they are not alone with their problem and that their problems have structural, not personal, causes.

Sharing narratives strengthens bonds between people and helps create *affinity groups* of individuals who develop trust and respect for each other because of shared beliefs and experiences. When targets of campaigns pressure individuals to withdraw from action campaigns, the bonds within the affinity group give people the courage to stay the course. If group members are evicted or fired, they know that they will help each other. When those in power try to divide and conquer those in activist organizations, perhaps by giving leaders a promotion or fixing up their apartments, the solidarity of the group prevents people from deserting the cause.

Understanding Perceptions and Realities of Power

Campaigns are about gaining the power to affect decisions that shape social outcomes. Power can be gained through the manipulations of symbols that portray how an issue is framed, through the use of numbers of those mobilized, and by the threat of disruption or embarrassment.

Creating Power through Issue Framing

Framing refers to the way in which an issue is understood, or, for that matter, whether or not an issue is seen as a problem. Frames are ideological and conceptual lenses that "interpret, define and give meaning to social and cultural phenomenon" (Baylor, 1996, p. 242 from Goffman, 1974).

Frames help determine what issues will be discussed and how people understand their meanings.

Are people who receive welfare lazy cheats or are they primarily seen as mothers with hungry children?

Is the factory a place that provides jobs or a source of environmental pollution?

Are stock-piled nuclear weapons a defense against tyranny or means of mass destruction?

Action groups seek to define issues in ways that build unity within the organization, battle false images spread by the opponents, and convince the public of the justice of the cause. For example, people with disabilities used to be portrayed as helpless charity cases. Activists in the disabilities movement worked to convince government, the public, and many with disabilities to reframe the issue as one of bringing about justice, equal access, and opportunity (Shapiro, 1993).

Effective framings convince others that the difficulties people face are problems worth battling, not minor complaints (Best, 1995; Rochefort & Cobb, 1994). Sexual harassment (or even stalking) was initially portrayed as boys being boys, not as an outward sign of structural sexism; not until women were able to reframe the argument so their complaints were seen as legitimate could any action be taken to stop the harassment. When religious leaders and protesters against U.S. policies in Latin America banded together to offer sanctuary to refugees, the U.S. government tried to frame the issue as aiding illegal immigrants. In response, protesters worked to frame the issue as one of defending religious and political freedom.

Action organizations work to *construct* interpretive frames that provide support for their demands that challenge the arguments that protect the status quo. Society often accepts the argument that the rich deserve to be rich and get tax breaks because wealthy people risk their money and create jobs for others. This framing ignores the fact that workers take risks with their health—more precious than money—when they handle pesticides or chemicals or work on scaffolding or in tunnels. Or as another example of false construction, business people sometimes argue that they are being fair and legal when they offer only a minimum wage rather than the living wage needed for people to survive. That framing ignores the social consequences of large numbers of working poor, without health insurance or pensions and with no one home to watch the children. Justifications of inequality and injustice must be examined and challenged.

The framing of the issues enables members of a social action group themselves to see the legitimacy of fighting back.

> Excluded groups are always objectively deprived but this does not mean that they will uniformly perceive these conditions as socially unjust and alterable. . . . Objective social inequalities have to be collectively redefined as the source of social injustices that can be remedied by collective action. (Jenkins, 1985, p. 5)

Before people get involved they have to believe they have a right to do so. For instance, in battling business interests, action organizations must persuade even their own members that the free market is not always right (or even free) and that social needs are as valuable as economic profit. Keeping a neighborhood socially intact is more valuable than allowing a few to profit from gentrifying property.

Organizational members must see that there is a possibility of change, that is, there is an *agency* that causes the problem and another that can bring about a solution. The voice of the status quo argues that things just happen to be the way they are because of economic or social laws that are naturally occurring, so that battling them is futile. In contrast, activists frame issues to show that problems are caused by someone who benefits (slumlords get rich while people live in hovels) and argue that there are ways of changing the situation (having government enforce laws on housing standards) (Gamson, 1997a).

In individual campaigns, issues are framed to mesh with the particular targets being fought. For instance, Schneider (1997) describes two framings evoked in campaigns held by Puerto Rican activists in different parts of New York City.

> In Williamsburg . . . the political power of the Hasidim encouraged Puerto Rican activists to use an anticolonial frame. This frame linked local struggles around housing, AIDS, and drug abuse to the independence and anticolonial struggles of Puerto Rico. . . .

Activists were able to mobilize the Puerto Rican community by stressing cultural pride and independence and by targeting the Hasidim as colonialists. . . . In the South Bronx, where Puerto Rican activists challenged a machine controlled by a Puerto Rican boss, activists used an antisystem frame; attacking the political system itself, and political parties, and politicians associated with the system. (Schneider, 1997, p. 241)

Each group has to frame the issues in a way that motivates its members to participate, leading to the same issue being framed in multiple ways. For example, activists in the gay-lesbian movement disagree on whether the goal is to gain cultural acceptance or increased legal and political rights. A comparative study showed

New York City activists consistently privileged strategies that challenged dominant cultural values over those that would maximize the likelihood of policy success. By refusing to hold private hearings with the Human Rights Commission, activists increased the scope of conflict. Rather than allaying the fears of legislators and the public by reassuring them of the incremental nature of the policy reform activists exacerbated those fears by having transvestites testify at public hearings. In Oregon, activists were content to hold secret meetings with lawmakers in order to gain legal change. (Bernstein, 1997, p. 546)

In New York, it was more important for those in the movement to emphasize their culture than to win the immediate issues. In Oregon, activists were willing to accept a small gain in their political rights, even if it meant hiding issues of their personal identity. To sustain mobilization, distinct framings might have to be chosen to appeal to those in separate social change organizations.

Another function of framing is for activists to combat the images that the opposition uses to make the action organization look bad. In a battle over affirmative action involving sit-ins and protests, an organization might frame the issue in terms of undoing past injustice, while the opponents counter that activists are demanding special privileges. In addition, opponents may try to argue that the organization's tactics are inappropriate, arguing that responsible citizens quietly petition for changes or hire lawyers rather than carry out mass demonstrations. Opponents try to frame the lack of decorum shown in a sit-in as an indication that the action organization is too antisystem to deserve support. Of course, this framing neglects to mention that the rules of the system favor the status quo. For instance, in the 1960s, welfare rights organizations used militant tactics as part of their fight to humanize bureaucratic procedures and to end hunger and cold among the poor; their opponents tried to frame the issue as street bullies using force to cheat the honest taxpayer (Bailis, 1974; West, 1981).

Media coverage often supports the establishment's perspective. To frame their concerns as a search for historic justice, Native American activists physically took over symbolically important sites (places at which treaties had been negotiated that were later violated by the U.S. government). Unfortunately, the media concentrated on the militant tactics, ignoring the underlying issues of stealing land from Native Americans (Baylor, 1996). A protest organization must be aware that the public, informed only by an established press, sees the world through frames that disparage direct actions and that reinforce the images preferred by the establishment.

Activists in the housing movement studied how the public interpreted their actions and concluded that proponents of social change needed to change their strategies. Initially housing activists thought that people would be upset that the rich received large subsidies through the mortgage interest deduction and would be sympathetic toward the poor who were forced to live in horrible housing. The studies showed that neither image was the case and efforts to garner support by appealing to concerns with economic injustice would fail. Fortunately, "there was a sense of injustice in people having to make a choice between housing and other necessities," and people respected the poor when the poor themselves worked to rebuild their own homes. As a result, activist coalitions reframed their campaigns to show the willingness of the poor to care for homes they own and apartments that they managed. By reframing issues to show that the poor are willing to put energy into solving their housing problems, housing groups gained increased public support (NLIHC web page).

Successful framings not only generate support within a community group and among the public, but they also help action organizations build coalitions (Snow, Rochford, Worden, & Benford, 1986; Snow & Benford, 1992). One approach to coalition building is to find a common *bridging theme* among groups working for the same cause, such as when separate organizations share a belief that poverty results from economic exploitation, even if initially one group had focused on poverty among women and another within an ethnic group (Carroll & Ratner, 1996, p. 609). Sometimes by *amplifying the frame,* coalitions are built as separate groups see how their concerns come together. For instance, peace activists trying to stop a foreign war might argue that the reasons for the war are to enrich the arms manufacturers who have disproportionate influence on Congress, thereby uniting the peace movement with those who worry about excessive business influence on Congress.

Sometimes an issue has to be reframed in ways that enable potential allies to reframe how they see the issues. For instance, business owners of polluting industrial plants have long framed the issue as pollution versus jobs; if you want jobs; you have to accept pollution. Environmentalists discovered that many of these industries were moving to poor, rural, primarily black areas because more prosperous areas would not accept the pollution. The environmentalists then redefined the frame away from the divisive issues of jobs versus pollution to that of environmental racism, showing how pollution was targeted at minority groups. Under the new framing, environmentalists and groups working for racial equality could join forces.

Symbols and Agenda Setting

Action organizations and their opponents fight to define the issues in terms of symbols that support their cause. A *symbol* is a word, phrase, image, icon, or person that stands for deeper, more complicated ideas. Symbols frame issues by providing people with simplified explanations of the problem as well as the possibility of solutions.

Some symbols have positive connotations, others have negative ones. For example, public officials may argue that inner-city problems are caused by "drug pushers." "Drug pusher" is a symbol, suggesting an individual with no morals, an object of legitimate hate, and best taken care of by putting the scum in jail. The cause of urban poverty is symbolically attributed to the moral values of individuals; the implied solution is supporting "law and order."

By contrast, a neighborhood action organization may attribute urban poverty to a lack of job opportunities, symbolized by footloose firms that have abandoned communities. When people cannot see a legitimate way to earn a living they search for profitable, albeit illegal, economic niches. The drug trade is hence a consequence not a cause of urban problems. The symbol of this campaign could be the rich suburban industrialist who worked laborers hard, took financial help from taxpayers, and then abandoned the city to find less expensive workers. The solution would be an economic one, helping those in the inner city start up their own firms or providing job-training programs so people can find jobs outside the drug trade.

Action campaigns work to associate positive cultural symbols with their efforts and create new and compelling symbols that support the cause of social change, while preventing those in power from identifying the organization with negative symbols. A group might portray its efforts as *redressing grievances,* a term that echoes the demands of the colonists in the Declaration of Independence (a positive symbol); at the same time the targets of the protest may label the demonstrators as *disorderly, lawless,* and *outside of proper channels.* Those who opposed feminists called them *bra burners,* which became a symbol of people without respect for social proprieties. Feminists labeled their movement *women's liberation* suggesting a positive linkage to the civil rights movement and freedom from enslavement.

In choosing symbols for a campaign, there are a number of strategies to keep in mind.

Create a Sense of Organizational Unity. Action organizations must symbolize the *we-ness* in the group. Keep in mind, though, what works well within the group may sound threatening to the outsider, as do symbols of ethnic pride such as *Black Power.* At times, the threat can be intentional, for instance

> . . . the term *Chicano* increasingly became the symbol of self-identification for many activities. . . . For many people Chicano connoted a militant stance, confrontation actions and intense pride associated with the movement for brown identity and power. (Hammerback et al., 1984, p. 5)

A sense of we-ness can be symbolized in ways that give pride to the group and that also appeal to a broader public. For instance, activist groups that press for neighborhood improvement might want to symbolize their cause with a picture of an attractive streetscape, while solidarity organizations might portray a unifying festivity.

Come up with Catchy Typifications. When possible, campaign symbols should typify the problem in an easily communicable fashion. The pro-choice and pro-life movements both have such powerful symbols with the coathanger and the partially formed fetus. Pictures of the cooling towers of nuclear reactors communicate the dangers of present-day nuclear technology.

Songs and their titles (e.g., "We Shall Overcome") create powerful symbols of an issue. Songs can provide unity to a movement while highlighting the issues under dispute. Protest song lyrics often provide "diagnoses of what is wrong with the present order of things . . ." (Lewis, 1987, pp. 169–170).

The actions taken by groups, when suitably publicized, can end up symbolizing the problem and suggesting possible solutions. For example, in the past, to protest apartheid in South Africa and, more recently, to protest homelessness, students have constructed and briefly live in shantytowns on the lawns of universities. The shantytowns are easy to portray in the media, represent the problem, and personalize the issues (Fordham, 1986).

Symbols are most effective when they evoke broader societal values. The image of civil rights workers facing police dogs shows the nature of oppression; no one in our society should be treated that way. The image becomes a symbol of what is wrong. When Greenpeace surrounds nuclear Navy vessels with its small dinghies, the image is of David taking on Goliath. The public may subconsciously begin to root for David.

Personalize.   To weaken the argument for policy changes, those in power blame social problems on unworthy individuals. President Reagan, for instance, created a vivid symbol of a welfare queen bleeding the system dry, rather than confronting the core question of why people did not have jobs. Opponents of affirmative action promote the symbol of an incompetent minority doctor or a woman promoted to boss with no experience. People involuntarily cringe at either idea. Such symbolizations are hard to counter because they are more easily understood than explanations of structural unemployment or institutional racism.

In response, those in action organizations create counter symbols that create appealing human scale images of the problems faced. For instance, one such powerful symbol is that of the *victim,* the blameless individual whose difficulties are so clearly caused by a problem that he or she did not create. A sick child becomes the symbol of toxic waste; a surgically mutilated house pet symbolizes the victims of medical experimentation run wild. During the Vietnam War era, peace activists were handed a dramatic symbol of the victim when television cameras recorded the agony of a young Vietnamese girl covered with burning napalm, running screaming down the street.

A symbol that is somewhat trickier to use is that of the *enemy,* "identifiable persons or stereotypes of persons to whom evil traits, intentions or attentions can be attributed" (Edelman, 1988, p. 87). Alinsky's classic advice was to "pick the target, freeze it, *personalize* it, and polarize it" (Alinsky, 1971, p. 128, emphasis added). Doing so can focus attention on a problem in terms that people can grasp. The Vietnam War became President Johnson's war, Sheriff Bull Connor, who turned the dogs loose on civil rights protesters, symbolized the racist south.

On the other hand, symbolizing a problem in terms of an individual enemy or even a victim can distract attention from the social causes that created the difficulty. Finding a suitable individual to demonize can be problematic. For instance, the chief executive officers of major companies are often colorless individuals; they are rarely good symbols for corporate malfeasance. In campaigns targeted at political officials, the same person who could be used as the symbol of the problem (the enemy) might be the person whose support is needed to bring about a solution. Demonizing him or her would not be an effective strategy.

Create Symbols of Success No Matter What Actually Happened.   In many campaigns,victory and defeat are hard to define. Beliefs

> . . . about success and failure are among the most arbitrary of political constructions and perhaps the least likely to be recognized as arbitrary. . . . The issue turns on which actions and which consequences are to be highlighted and which ignored. (Edelman, 1988, p. 43)

Even the jailing or death of organizational activists can be interpreted as a victory by creating the symbol of a martyr for the cause, which occurred when leading civil rights activists were murdered.

When immediate objectives of a campaign have not been accomplished, symbolize the victory in terms of the striving that occurred, the ongoing battle against the odds, and the ability to motivate participation. When specific aims of a campaign are not achieved, talk about the positive changes that did occur. For instance, Mansbridge concludes after describing the defeat of the Equal Rights Amendment (ERA): "Because the ratification campaign raised consciousness, helped women organize politically, and stimulated legislative and judicial action, that campaign was worth the effort put into it" (Mansbridge, 1986, p. 188).

To summarize, one way in which action organizations get their issues on the public agenda is through the thoughtful use of symbols that are the primary language of public discourse. At the beginning of a campaign, one must use symbols to justify taking public actions and to legitimate the tactics to be used. During the campaign, the organization must develop symbols that focus attention on core parts of the problem that also create sympathy for the organization and its cause, for example, the undernourished child sewing clothes in a sweat shop. Toward the end of the campaign, the organization has to symbolize the progress made and the victories achieved, to keep up morale among its members and to demonstrate to the public that change is possible.

Tactical Power

The power that an action organization has can expand and contract and can be created and enhanced in a variety of ways. To begin, social action organizations gain power by documenting and publicizing the extent of a problem. Information campaigns create power by trying to make authorities live up to the values they espouse. City council members are less likely to tolerate apartments with rodents and vermin once the problem has been shown on television; if they don't take action it looks like they don't favor clean and safe housing.

Sometimes campaigns embarrass companies or individuals by pointing out contradictions in their values. Showing that a company that profits from sales to minorities has few executives from minority groups might create pressure for change. Why buy from someone who won't hire you? Large international corporations such as Nike or manufacturers of designer clothes have been embarrassed by showing that their expensive, prestige goods are manufactured by exploiting child labor.

Sometimes action organizations can increase their power by threatening to delay decisions, which can cost their opponents money. For instance, banks feel they have to merge with one another or lose out in the competitive market; however, mergers require approval of public authorities and by law such approval cannot be given if the banks are not reinvesting money in the communities they serve. Community groups can threaten to hold up the merger by protesting to the public authorities that the banks have not increased their community investment portfolios. The delay can cost the banks more money than they would have to spend if they agreed to fair reinvestment policies.

Power can come about from a threat, perhaps of disrupting business as usual for those who are targeted by the campaign. When possible, however, actual disruption should be avoided, because those not involved might be inconvenienced and feel anger against the organization. If an organization ties up traffic on freeways in Los Angeles to protest inadequate public transit, the group demonstrates power but infuriates hundreds of thousands of people. The awareness that the organization is willing to create traffic chaos, though, might be sufficient to pressure a city council to add new bus routes or change schedules.

The prime source of power for action organizations is their ability to mobilize people in large numbers. If one family pays the rent late, the slumlord may be irritated but unconcerned, because that family can be evicted; however, if many families band together and intentionally withhold rent until the landlord fixes the plumbing and provides heat, that same slumlord is financially threatened. Politicians respond when organizations mobilize a bloc of voters to protest a development or to demand jobs, especially if they think that these organized people will vote. Large numbers can bring real power to bear if they boycott a particular product or picket stores that discriminate.

The effective use of power requires understanding the strengths and weaknesses of the opponents. As part of planning campaign strategy, think about the following questions:

1. *Can the target grant the demands made by the action organization?* Has the organization picked the right target—the state level government, rather than the national level, or the corporate offices of a company rather than those of a branch? Does the target have the legal right or the resources to respond? Targets of campaigns must be able to effect a solution.

2. *What is the power base of the opponent, and which parts of that base are most vulnerable to attack?* Is the strength of the opponent based on corporate wealth, a strong client-base, or only on a razor-thin electoral victory? Does a company need a favorable decision by a regulator that the community organization can influence or delay? Is a company particularly vulnerable to bad publicity at the time of stockholders' meetings?

3. *How willing and able are the opponents to strike back?* Have opponents hired professionals to advise them on how to break up a union or how to combat consumer boycotts? Has the city arrested people during demonstrations, or have they kept the police away for fear of provoking a violent confrontation? Can the targets disempower individual activists by pressuring their employers to fire them?

4. *What sort of support do your opponents have from others and can this support be weakened?* When elected officials depend upon support from the business community, pressuring business might be the way to persuade government. During the civil rights actions in the sixties, business people lost trade because of boycotts; to preserve their income, these businesses pressured government to concede on social issues.

It is also useful to know when your targets are so trapped by their supporters that it is nearly impossible for them to concede. For instance, activists in support of gay rights might try to pressure politicians, only to discover that even moderate Republicans can do little because they fear opposition in the primaries from the antigay, religious right.

5. *How much knowledge do your opponents have of your group?* In campaigns, an organization that is known for hanging tough is more likely to prevail. If a group has won previous battles, make sure new opponents are aware of past successes.

Keep in mind, however, that opponents also can learn about an organization's weaknesses. Rent strikes fail if landlords figure out which tenants can be bought off, while bosses are often aware of the economic needs of those on strike. When action organizations are labeled by the larger public as being extreme or "un-American," opponents can get away with calling in the police or using physical force.

6. *For what tactics are the opponents prepared and for which are they most vulnerable?* A heavily bankrolled company can withstand an economic boycott, while landlords with vast holdings might be impervious to rent strikes. Government agencies or schools that have large open and unsecure buildings might be vulnerable to sit-ins, especially if the targets are concerned with the bad public opinion that would occur if arrests were made.

Today most larger companies, schools, and businesses have standard procedures for handling picketing, demonstrations, and other common tactics, weakening the effectiveness of this approach. If that is the case, cleverness is appropriate, perhaps by adding a mocking humor to what people expect to be an acrimonious confrontation.

7. *Can arguments be reframed in ways that build upon accepted moral values?* If the opponent preaches moral values—as churches do—point out that its actions are keeping people cold and hungry. If government argues that it is responsive to the will of the people, but means to the will of big business, accept these pronouncements at face value and demand a public hearing.

8. *Can your organization increase its power through political jiu-jitsu?* Action organizations are usually economically weaker than their opponents and control far less force. In such a situation, think how to flip the actions of the opposition around, so they hurt the target more than the action organization. When passively resisted, an intimidating use of police force can be made to appear as a brutal attempt to suppress political freedom. Withholding of information can be made to look like stonewalling or temporizing.

In answering these questions, one must keep in mind that action organizations have no permanent friends, but, equally, they have no permanent enemies. A city that has allowed slumlords to flourish can be pressured to provide grant money for community groups to do housing inspections. Chambers of Commerce who may oppose community groups on many grounds, can become allies in efforts to renew neighborhoods.

Action Campaigns are Part of a Long Process Built Up of Intermittent Successes and Failures

Action campaigns are part of a stream of linked events. Long-term successes are based as much on learning from prior failures as they are from building on prior victories, while much learning takes place as separate social action organizations help one another.

People active in one cause directly assist those working on another by joining or providing advice to other groups (Carroll & Ratner, 1996; Meyer & Whittier, 1994). Approaches developed in one context, for one cause, get applied to different causes. For example, the feminist revolution changed how later peace organizations went about their work:

> . . . the feminist movement led the 1980s peace movement to differ in several important ways from earlier waves of peace activism. Ideological frames linked militarism to patriarchy. . . . Organizational structures reflect the concerns with process, consensus, and avoidance of hierarchy. . . . Finally, the emergence of visible women leaders in both wings of the movement reflects the influence of feminism. . . . (Meyer & Whittier, 1994, pp. 292–293)

Success often occurs in bursts with long intervals of quiescence in between. After years of isolated attempts to combat racial injustice, a flowering of actions occurred during the sixties, standing Jim Crow on his head, and changing both law and custom. These changes took place because of the courage of thousands of individuals and numerous local campaigns, but victory was made easier because of a gradually improving climate of support at the federal level, a climate of support that, in turn, was a result of prior efforts by activists.

Success can depend on the *political opportunity structure,* that is, the political factors that can affect outcomes but over which the action organizations have little immediate control. Tarrow explains

> . . . the concept of political opportunity emphasizes resources *external* to the group—unlike money or power—that can be taken advantage of even by weak or disorganized challengers. Social movements form when ordinary citizens, sometimes encouraged by leaders, respond to changes in opportunities that lower the costs of collective action, reveal potential allies, and show where elites and authorities are vulnerable.
>
> The most salient changes in opportunity structure result from the opening up of access to power, from shifts in ruling alignments, from the availability of influential allies and from cleavages within and among elites. (Tarrow, 1994, p. 18)

Actions that might fail at one time might succeed at another; in the short term, victory and failure may not be within the immediate control of those engaged in social action campaigns. The result is that community groups may put themselves on the line, work extremely hard, and still seem to fail. Morale can be a serious problem; maintaining membership when groups seem to fail requires a long-term view.

Keeping Up Morale over the Long Run

Given the opposition faced and the difficulties of the tasks involved, campaigns sometimes collapse. When an effort does not succeed, step back and figure out what should be done differently next time. Were the tactics inappropriate? Was timing wrong? Did the opponents capture the symbols that garner public support? Were activists so split that a coherent effort was not possible?

Sometimes community efforts seem to take so long that activists get discouraged and participants drop out. This loss of morale is most apparent in fights that persist over several generations, such as those for civil rights, gender equality, increased worker control, and a more equitable distribution of income. Victories occur, but so do numerous discouraging defeats. Group members may feel more downhearted than warranted by the actual situation.

> Within a few years after achieving the goals of "take-off," every major social movement of the past twenty years has undergone a significant collapse, in which activists believed that their movement had failed, the power institutions were too powerful, and their own efforts were futile. This has happened even when movements were actually progressing reasonably well along the normal path taken by past successful movements! (Moyer, 1987, p. 1)

The effort of continually campaigning can leave people depleted. For example, after years of fighting for civil rights and battling to end the Vietnam War, many activists were burned out (Gitlin, 1989, p. 424).

What does an organization do to cope with the loss of morale during long-run campaigns? One response is to concentrate on smaller efforts for which a quick and reinforcing victory is possible. Working toward a neighborhood park can be the first step in reclaiming an entire community. Celebrate this victory as a step toward the larger goal. If a frontal assault on the target exceeds the capacity of the group, think of smaller efforts that will contribute to better outcomes. If legislation can't be changed at the federal level, work in the more progressive states to start the ball rolling.

When people get discouraged, spend some time together reviewing the history of other successful movements. Examine how long they took to bring about important changes. Remind those who seem discouraged that the basic rights that they now assume came about only after a long struggle in which defeats were frequent. For instance, federal recognition of the right to unionize only dates back half a century and took two generations to bring about. The United States is only one generation removed from legalized racial discrimination. The young women of today are the second generation who have legal access to birth control. A generation ago most gays were still in the closet, while people with disabilities were often treated as charity cases. Some of these campaigns still have a ways to go, but improvement has come.

Activists should understand that there will be times in which action seems to stop (Taylor, 1997). During these interludes, organizations have time to figure out how to accommodate their actions to the changing political climate and recruit new members less fatigued by the battles of the past (Staggenborg, 1998; Whittier, 1997).

Keep in mind that if success were easy, the struggle would not be necessary. As Gitlin describes in his reflections on the partial successes of the sixties: "'It was not granted you to complete the task,' said Rabbi Tarfon nineteen hundred years ago, 'and yet you may not give it up'" (Gitlin, 1989, p. 438).

The Target Strikes Back

Campaigns are sometimes defeated because the opposition fights back successfully. People in power stall, deny the legitimacy of demands, demean the protesters, or refuse to take up the issue.

Opponents may employ severe countermeasures. They may try to discredit the action organization, claiming it represents the opinions of only a handful of discontents. The enemy may investigate the organization, seizing its books, records, and mailing lists, looking for financial irregularities, and trying to taint the protest group with scandal. Individual activists may be pressured to withdraw their protests or face losing their jobs, eviction from their apartments, or blackballing—refusal by almost any company to hire them anywhere.

Protesters have to be prepared for the possibility of physical repression. "Goon squads" were used against labor organizers and tactical police against war protesters. Southern law enforcement personnel assisted local hooligans in beating up civil rights workers. During the sixties, police raided homes of African American militants and killed them. Repression against African American and Native American militants included "eavesdropping, bogus mail, 'black propaganda operations,' disinformation, harassment arrests, infiltration, snitch-jacketing—creating suspicion—through the spreading of rumors, manufacturing of evidence—that bona fide organization members . . . are FBI/police informers—, fabrication of evidence and even assassination" (Churchill & Wall, 1988). From documents now made available, we know that in the 1960s public authorities, including the FBI and state level police, spied on protesters, planted stories to discredit leaders such as Martin Luther King, Jr., and delayed enforcing laws that would have protected civil rights protesters (Branch, 1998).

Less extreme than violence, but in the long run probably of greater importance, progressive movements are opposed by countermovements that come about to undo changes that have been made. The right-to-life movement came into being to fight the gains of the pro-choice movement; after affirmative action enabled women and minorities to have fairer access to jobs, construction contracts, and educational opportunities, a strong countermovement grew up that has made affirmative action illegal in many areas.

Backlash movements can use a variety of tactics. For example, renters in a poorer neighborhood of Minneapolis working through a community association had organized committees to pressure for tenants' rights and had set up a community development corporation (CDC) to produce affordable housing. Landlords who had been threatened by the poor organized and encouraged their supporters to show up at the election meeting of the community group. The tenants no longer felt a need to attend this meeting and so the landlord group was able to take over the organization, destroying its affordable housing programs and the tenants' associations (Goetz & Sidney, 1994b; Rubin, 2000a).

Those in the countermovement have tried to change laws that allow activists a public voice. For instance, business and conservative groups resent the accomplishments of nonprofits who have persuaded public officials to help their causes. To limit the constitutional rights of activists groups to provide information to elected officials, conservative groups working through Representative Daniel Istook (R, Oklahoma) introduced legislation to forbid any organization receiving federal support from using federal money or other money that it raises to lobby public officials. So far this legislation has failed to pass (in part, because it would hurt such mainstream groups as the American Red Cross), but it represents an attempt to change the rules of the game to silence those who oppose the status quo.

Values that Guide Social Action Campaigns

Action organizations need to choose tactics in proportion to the problem at hand and that reflect the values of those in the group. Few neighborhood associations would conduct a violent demonstration to convince the city council to provide an additional stop sign; on the other hand, peaceful petitions to racist voting registrars in the South, at best, got a scornful dismissal, so more vigorous and confrontional efforts were required.

Tactics used must reflect the fundamental moral and political beliefs of those in the organization or else the campaigns will fail. Activists differ in their beliefs about the value and sanctity of private property and construct campaigns consistent with these beliefs. For instance, for radical organizations, such as some environmental groups, animal advocates, and antiabortion groups, the destruction of physical property, even when people are threatened, might be acceptable; for ideological supporters of non-violence, no cause is worth harming others physically. Some who accept the religiously based premises of liberation theology (Smith, 1991) question private ownership of property, if the owners are using that property to oppress the poor. Though the ACORN model is nominally nonideological, ACORN puts forth strong populists beliefs that question capitalist ideas about private ownership:

> ACORN expresses the idea that "the land and commodities of America belong not to some but to all the American people" in both word and deed. (Russell, 1990, p. 36)

ACORN is willing to attack property. For instance, one ACORN tactic is to mobilize illhoused or homeless people to squat in abandoned buildings that are still owned by government or private individuals, demanding that the property be turned over to those in need. In contrast, proponents of consensus organizing believe that business can be persuaded to form partnerships to help the poor so that direct actions that threaten private property would not be inappropriate.

The major purpose of action campaigns is to solve problems, but, in addition, campaigns are about mobilizing people to build a lasting community organization. Sometimes, organizers must consider whether a tactic that appears to be effective to quickly solve a problem hurts mobilization efforts. Legal tactics may paralyze an opponent but involve only a handful of skilled participants. Picketing or leafletting may be less effective but allows everyone to join in. ACORN is as much concerned about teaching previously disempowered people that their opinions count as it is about winning immediate issues. ACORN tries to choose tactics—rallies, sit-ins, or voter registration drives—that can involve all community members, even if other approaches might more quickly result in a victory.

The Legitimacy of Protest Tactics

For tactics to work, at least over the long run, organization members and the public have to accept the legitimacy of what is done. To use a shockingly inappropriate action may cost the group support. Kidnapping a business executive to protest the dumping of toxic waste might appeal to some but would rarely be seen as legitimate. Less harmful but still deviant acts, such as protesters throwing pies at executives or men undressing in public to protest the exploitation of women, might work. Some "socially unacceptable forms of protest will gain attention precisely because they are socially unacceptable" (Crozat, 1998, p. 59).

Unfortunately, the legitimacy of tactics is often defined by the establishment. Appeals, petitions, and other types of suppliant actions are almost always considered legitimate. More militant actions, consistent with the form and style of American protest, such as picketing, boycotts, or sit-ins, are considered appropriate if the issues being fought are seen as extremely important. When famous people concur with a tactic, it may become more acceptable to the public. When Senator Robert Kennedy flew to the west coast to be with Cesar Chavez during a protest fast, the senator helped legitimate the efforts of the farm workers to unionize and the use of a hunger strike as a tactic.

What tactics are considered appropriate changes over time and can differ by locale. Studies in Europe show rapidly changing fashions in what forms of unconventional politics are acceptable. For example, large-scale demonstrations are no longer seen as a revolutionary threat (Rucht, 1998). In American politics, a wide variety of direct actions are now part of a conventional repertoire of political action, but their public acceptance still remains in doubt.

> Protest methods may well have been employed more often and by a wider panoply of groups than twenty years ago, in spite of the fact that popular acceptance of the forms has not changed considerably. What this would mean is that the increase in frequency of protest has not desensitized the observing public to the actions themselves. (Crozat, 1998, p. 81)

In choosing tactics, a rule of thumb is that the more extreme the problem, the more accepting the public is of a militant tactic. To picket city hall over a speeding ticket is illegitimate; no broader issue is being raised. But if the organization pickets city hall, claiming that a disproportionate number of traffic stops are made on people of color, then a more fundamental issue is at stake, and the organization is seen as justified in its use of militant tactics.

Means and Ends.   Whether a tactic is viewed as legitimate, depends in part on whether the means and the ends can be reconciled. For some, the ends may justify the means, and a wide variety of choices would be considered ethical. Thus radical environmentalists put spikes in trees, ruining them for lumber, and creating a risk of injury of lumberjacks. For others, the ends never justifies the means. If something is wrong, it is always wrong, regardless of the circumstances or who is getting hurt. Such groups might believe that power obtained through intimidation is incompatible with deeper, democratic beliefs that respect the rights of all individuals. Or they might avoid deceiving the opponent into thinking they have more power than they do, because deception is wrong.

As Alinsky described, what might not be ethical in one situation might be appropriate and moral in another. For him, whether a tactic was right or wrong depended on the circumstances. He was particularly concerned that the opponents would demand that a community group meet unrealistic ethical standards and thereby render it impotent. To avoid such situations, Alinsky offered the following advice:

1. One's concerns with the ethics of means and ends varies inversely with one's personal interest in the issue.
2. The judgment of the ethics of means is dependent upon the political position of those sitting in judgment.
3. In war the end justifies almost any means.
4. Judgment must be made in the context of the times in which the action occurred and not from any other chronological vantage point.
5. Concern with ethics increases with the number of means available and vice versa.
6. The less important the end to be desired, the more one can afford to engage in ethical evaluation of means.
7. Generally, success or failure is a mighty determinant of ethics.
8. The morality of means depends upon whether the means is being employed at a time of imminent defeat or imminent victory.
9. Any effective means is automatically judged by the opposition as being unethical.
10. You do what you can with what you have and clothe it with moral garments.
11. Goals must be phrased in general terms like "Liberty, Equality, Fraternity," "Of the Common Welfare," "Pursuit of Happiness," or "Bread and Peace." (Alinsky, 1971, pp. 24–27)

It is possible to be ethical and still win issues, but, as Alinsky points out, not if the group follows the moral standards set for it by its opponents.

Balancing means and ends is very difficult when contemplating illegal actions. It is wrong for leaders of a protest organization to deceive their members about planned illegal actions, but if the members know and agree, should the group engage in illegal actions? Is a break-in to obtain documents that seriously compromise a target (a planning report that shows that a company knew that the pollutant would cause cancer) worth the violation of law and the chance of being caught? It may be appropriate to violate a law when the intent is to publicly demonstrate the injustice of that law. So when Black and White civil rights workers entered restaurants together, shared drinking fountains, and shared seats on public transportation, they violated southern Jim Crow laws intentionally to show how wrong the laws were.

When violating unjust laws, people must be willing to accept arrests. Being arrested demonstrates their commitment to bring about change and their willingness to accept the consequences. Activists who face arrest often risk their lives for the cause by blocking factory entrances to protest the production of weapons or chaining themselves to bulldozers. It is precisely because they accept known risks that their actions resonate with the public.

The way in which the group violates the law should call attention to the absurdity or unfairness of the law. Sitting in and being arrested in a bank lobby to symbolize the bank's unwillingness to provide loans in the community is clearly a political protest and may gain public sympathy. Robbing the bank, even if the money is given to the poor, is likely to gain widespread opposition, confusing the group with robbers and threatening private property more generally.

Violence and Ideological Nonviolence.   When is violence appropriate in action campaigns? This is far from a theoretical question. The history of labor organizing involves picketers fighting scabs and public or private police attacking union members. During antiwar protests, street demonstrations became massive brawls as taunts turned into fisticuffs. Antiabortion militants have bombed abortion clinics, and environmentalists have destroyed equipment for building roads. Civil rights workers were beaten and shot, and many died.

Social change organizations are philosophically divided on the question of violence. ACT-UP, the gay organization set up to battle the public sector's indifference toward the AIDS epidemic, is made up of people willing to use disruptive, potentially violent tactics. Even here, however, the willingness to use disruptive tactics depends on the "perceived stakes, of how much impact governmental decisions are expected to have on individuals and their solidary groups" (Jennings & Andersen, 1996). Violence, to ACT-UP, is a calibrated means to achieve a calculated end. The Students for a Democratic Society (SDS) grew out of pacifistic movements, yet the Weather Faction of SDS advocated sabotage because of the failure of nonviolent means to stop the war in Vietnam. In the civil rights movement, the nonviolent leadership of Martin Luther King, Jr. stands in sharp contrast to the advocacy of militancy and violent self-defense philosophies of Malcolm X or H. "Rap" Brown. Even among the militant, however, violence was more about posturing to scare those in power than about hurting people.

Still, the potential for violence is endemic in almost any community action in which opponents directly confront one another. Angry words easily can turn into pushing. Protesters may goad police, trying to elicit an overreaction that will make the police look bad, or police may provoke protesters by walking too closely or physically directing marchers one way or another. They may be looking for an excuse to beat up the protesters or to charge them with resisting arrest.

With *active nonviolence* people refuse to fight back when provoked, passively accepting abuse and going limp when being arrested. Active nonviolence reflects a philosophy in which participants publicly take the moral highroad. As expressed by Martin Luther King, Jr.:

1. Nonviolence is a way of life for courageous people
2. Nonviolence seeks to win friendship and understanding
3. Nonviolence seeks to defeat injustice, not people
4. Nonviolence holds that suffering can educate and transform
5. Nonviolence chooses love instead of hate
6. The believer in nonviolence has a deep faith in the future

We do not advocate intentionally seeking violent encounters. There is a contradiction between trying to defeat someone with violence and the respect for human dignity and autonomy that underlies a sense of community. As Cesar Chavez argued:

> If we had used violence we would have won contracts a long time ago but they wouldn't have been lasting because we wouldn't have won respect. Wages are not the main issue in the strike. . . . No what is at stake is human dignity. If a man [sic] is not accorded respect, he cannot respect himself and if he does not respect himself, he cannot demand it. (Chavez quoted in Ecklein, 1984, p. 15)

Nonviolence does not mean that the organization should capitulate to power. Rather, nonviolence is a way of turning brute power against itself, a form of political *jiu-jitsu*. When opponents use repressive force, it redounds against them (Sharp 1973, p. 110). Society has fairly strong norms against anyone hitting or shooting an unarmed person. Nonviolence is a public demonstration of being unarmed; anyone who would attack a nonviolent group looks like a bully. In addition, nonviolent tactics can persuade the broader public by creating a moral image of those in the action organization and making it clear how much the power the opponents depends on repressive force.

Ultimately, as Martin Luther King, Jr., argued, the ends are present in the means (Branch, 1988, p. 871). Arguing that the means justifies the ends assumes a limited definition of the outcome, such as a good contract or an agreement to provide protective equipment to workers spraying toxic chemicals in the field. Other outcomes are involved, however, when the values of organization members corrode as they come to see violence as acceptable. Activists have to be concerned about whether, to achieve a limited victory, they adopt the morality of the enemy.

Values and Philosophies Evolve

Within most organizations core values and philosophies are unlikely to change dramatically over the short run. Instead, when some members of an organization seriously disagree on the appropriateness of particular tactics, they break off and create a new group. Over time, however, representatives of different groups and approaches meet and argue about what works best, and individual groups may gradually modify their view of what tactics are acceptable or appropriate.

ACORN, for instance, has moved from directly pressuring government through demonstrations to trying to win office and to working on affordable housing but in ways that guarantee that poor communities benefit. While its tactics have changed, ACORN still insists on widespread participation in its campaigns. While ACORN activists are now willing to work with bankers, they recognize that bankers may need to be persuaded through confrontational tactics. The core values of the organization remain, though the tactics followed have changed.

In its campaigns, IAF still carries out its historic pattern of uniting different church congregations that in turn pressure government on an array of topics (Rogers, 1990; Rooney, 1995; Wilson, 1997). Yet, today, like many other alliances, the IAF now partners with government to help rebuild homes and neighborhoods. Still, IAF activists and theorists such as Ernesto Cortes claim that their historic mission remains constant.

> The work of IAF is to establish a public space in which ordinary people can learn and develop the skills of public life, and create the institutions of a new democratic politics. With organized citizens and strong mediating institutions, our communities can address structural inequalities of the economy for themselves, restore health and integrity to our political process, mitigate the distortions created by organized concentrations of wealth, and—in the end—reclaim the vision and promise of American life. (Cortes, 1996)

Creating a Campaign Using a Variety of Tactics

Campaigns are planned and coordinated efforts to cause an opponent to accede to the demands of the social action organization. Action organizations need to get issues on the public agenda, demonstrate the power to disrupt and the power to reformulate agendas, and indicate to others that they have the staying power to assure that promises will be kept. An action organization creates power as it combines pressure and legal and confrontation tactics in ongoing campaigns that are oriented to winning issues and building the organization.

At intervals, action organizations evaluate and reformulate their overall strategies. Members ask, for example, in what ways the choice of issues and actions has affected the image of the organization. Is the organization seen as part of the broader community it serves, or are the members perceived as wild-eyed quasi-terrorists? Is the organization now a player in the political game, one to be consulted and respected, or is it an intermittent participant mostly to be ignored? Does the organization have the staying power to contest a complicated agenda, or must it focus mainly on narrow issues that lead to quick resolution? Are those who were involved in the campaign now feeling successful and empowered? Have people learned new skills that can be continually used? Have the campaigns enabled community leaders to emerge, and if so, what role do they now play? What tactics are now mastered that will stand in good stead in the next campaign? Have alliances of peoples' organizations been formed and strengthened in ways that allow separate organizations to help and learn from one another?

The next three chapters assume that broad issues of strategy have been worked out and concentrate on how to implement particular tactics to achieve the agreed on goals. We outline ways of influencing the political system in a peaceful fashion and describe the confrontations that make the system pay attention to community group issues. We also talk about ways to extend the organization's power by building coalitions of like-minded groups or by mastering publicity that persuades the public. Then we discuss how to solidify a victory at the bargaining table.

CHAPTER

12 Influencing the Political System

In this chapter, we examine the conventional political tactics meant to influence elected officials and the bureaucrats who run public agencies. Through lobbying, petitioning, having its members serve on civic boards, and by political campaigning, social action organizations get laws passed and enforced and assure that regulations are implemented. In these efforts, government can be a target, an ally, a neutral arbitrator, or a prize to be captured. Government must be viewed as changing and complex, as part of a world in which activists rarely have permanent allies or permanent enemies. The same agencies that provide resources for affordable housing or that enforce civil rights laws may be working to support tax legislation that helps big business. Strategies to work within the political system need to be flexible, and actions chosen must not alienate those who might later be in a position to help.

Government cannot be ignored. Elected officials and bureaucrats design social and economic programs, collect taxes and allocate funds, provide direct services for citizens, build projects, award and supervise contracts, enforce laws, set up and maintain regulations, plan for the future, help negotiate between community and private interests, and mediate some disputes. Those in the public sector make choices on spending that affect community groups and poor people. Will money be used for armaments or for job retraining, or for health care and if so, for whom? Will funds be spent to expand airports to facilitate business travel or to clean up toxic wastes in old industrial neighborhoods?

Government determines the scope and intensity of regulation. Is food quality monitored in restaurants and grocery stores and if so, how carefully? Is meat inspected for safety? Are building standards maintained so that homes don't burn down and foundations don't crack, or are standards so unreasonably strict that only the rich can afford housing? What kind of restrictions are there on radium in the water or on the use of pesticides or insecticides? Does government require business owners to make equipment safe for workers?

As we described in Chapters 2 and 3, success in gaining civil rights, in housing programs, school reform, gender equality, environmental justice, in social welfare, and many other areas required national political support. In localities, when progressive administrations (Clavel, 1986; Clavel & Wiewel, 1991) have taken over city hall, attention is paid to neighborhood needs and needs of the poor rather than to downtown developers.

Working with government, however, requires constant vigilance. Even after gains have been made, opponents try to reverse public actions. At the federal level, conservatives continue to try to undo the Community Reinvestment Act (CRA) and to shrink programs of income support for the poor and elderly. A backlash against affirmative action and abortion rights has been prominent at the state level. At the local level, neighborhood gains seem inevitably to be followed by a resurgence of influence by business groups, and each small victory by environmentalists is followed by an onslaught from developers.

This chapter describes government structure, how policies get made, and two different approaches to influence those policies. With the first, *lobbying,* social activists try to persuade public officials that there is a problem needing fixing and that government should accept the solutions proposed by the activists. With the second approach, *direct involvement,* social action organizations try to pass referenda, have members run for office, or seek out appointments to commissions or planning bodies.

Understanding Governmental Structures and Policy Making

The word *government* is a misleading term as it implies a single, large entity with one set of rules to enforce. Instead, in the United States, government is an aggregate, a mixture of many different agencies and elected bodies at the federal, state, and local levels. Each unit of government may have administrative, legislative, and, at times, judicial responsibilities, while separate federal, state, and local agencies carry out the will of their chief executives and legislative bodies. To complicate matters, federal, state, and local governments have separate but overlapping responsibilities. Successful community and action organizations work to understand this structure and learn case by case where it is best to try to intervene.

There are over 80,000 distinct units of government in the United States, including the federal government, states, counties, municipalities, towns and townships, and special districts that can be responsible for anything from schools to eradicating mosquitoes. Most, but not all, levels of government divide activities into executive and administrative functions of running and coordinating programs and administering bureaucratic agencies; legislative functions, such as determining what programs to adopt and how to fund them; and judicial actions, such as determining if laws have been broken and if decisions made are consistent with fundamental constitutional provisions.

Which agency or which institutional actor is responsible for what decisions can be difficult to track down. Policy proposals at the federal level can originate in Congress or in the executive branch. They can be modified by the Office of Management and Budget acting for the president, or by Congress acting in committee or as a whole. Once approved by Congress and signed by the president into law, decisions can be modified by bureaucratic agencies who carry out the policies, or by Congress pressuring the agencies on which rules to follow. At any time after passage, the Supreme Court could declare a law unconstitutional, forcing it to be dropped or modified. In the states, power is diffused between governors, legislators, the courts, and administrators. In most states, the governor is the most powerful actor, but agency bureaucrats can make end runs around the governor, and legislators may have the power to bargain for pieces of legislation. At the state level, too, courts can overturn legislative or executive decisions.

Most levels of government are technically run by elected officials—politicians—who are subject to electoral will, serve fixed terms, but need not have any special technical competence for the position other than obtaining the votes. At the federal and state level, the heads of most bureaucratic agencies are appointees who serve at the pleasure of either the executive or legislative body. Local governments often appoint professional managers who are chosen for their technical competence and serve only at the will of the executive or council (depending on the locale).

The heads of public sector agencies are career, bureaucratic administrators chosen for their technical competence and training; services are provided by well over ten million public sector employees—technically bureaucrats—ranging from police, social workers, and individuals who allocate government grants to community groups and nuclear scientists working in government labs. Bureaucrats can be removed for cause, though many have civil service protection, which allows them to make a career within government serving under many different politicians.

At the federal level, most agencies are located in one or another cabinet level department, while some agencies, such as the Environmental Protection Agency (EPA), are independent, not located in any department. Each of the cabinet departments has an overall focus, although many programs end up in one department or another because of political reasons rather than because of the similarity in their purposes. The Department of Housing and Urban Development (HUD) carries out housing and urban renewal programs; the Department of Labor is concerned with unemployment and training programs; the Agriculture Department is concerned with forestry, farms, and food production and inspection; and most social service programs are run out of the Department of Health and Human Services (DHHS). The separate departments are often supervised by different congressional committees that differ in terms of how accessible they are to community and social change organizations.

The independent agencies, bureaucracies that are not part of the cabinet departments, perform a variety of functions that affect community and social-change organizations. Among many independent agencies are the EPA, the Equal Employment Opportunity Commission (EEOC), as well as agencies that supervise banks in ways that buffer the banking system from politicians. Independent agencies are generally more difficult for community groups to influence directly, while neither Congress nor the president have as much control over them as they do over the cabinet departments.

Independent agencies have analogues at the state level. Most states have utility commissions that set and monitor utility rates and the performance of utility companies and building authorities that borrow money for public construction. These independent agencies have their own boards and the degree of supervision by elected officials is usually far less than for regular administrative agencies, but the situation varies case by case.

In recent years, the national government has assigned responsibilities (and often provided funding) to the fifty states to carry out tasks that had previously been the responsibility of the federal government. For instance, welfare and job training programs are now state responsibilities (with certain federal controls). Battles over civil rights, affirmative action, abortion, and privacy are increasingly fought out at the state level. As a result of such decentralization, fifty state level policies may replace one national guideline.

Most of the state governments are structured like the federal government, with an executive branch that supervises numerous administrative agencies, two legislative houses (with Nebraska as an exception), and a judiciary. Most governors have more control over the state budget than does the president over the federal budget, and most governors can more easily control the actions of administrative agencies than would be possible at the federal level.

Only rarely do small social action or community groups directly pressure the federal government. Usually, such action is done as part of a broader coalition, often one that has the necessary expertise and knows whom to pressure, when, and what to say. As we shall describe in Chapter 17, social-change organizations have established national groups with professional staffs to pressure the federal government.

Community organizations now increasingly target the states as they take on more program responsibilities. Agency directors and reporting structures change fairly often, making it difficult to figure out who has the governor's ear, or more generally, who has the power to grant the community organization's demands. In the last two decades, state–wide coalitions of action organizations have been formed to coordinate political efforts at the state capitals, but in contrast to coalitions at the federal level, state action coalitions lack staff and long-term experience.

Most neighborhood and community organizations work with local government. Each individual group must learn how their own city functions, who has power and resources, and who will listen to their requests. An overview is possible, however, because differences between local governments fall along a limited number of dimensions, that vary in terms of the scope of responsibility, how much independence localities have from the state, and the balance of power between the executive and legislature.

The scope of powers and responsibilities of *general-purpose local governments*—municipalities, counties and townships—differ depending on the state, and within states, by the size of the localities, with larger entities likely to have more autonomy. A broad-scope local government might be responsible for an array of local services, including police, fire, sanitation, zoning, social services, community development, job training, education, and parks and recreation, while a narrow-scope government might control only the police and zoning, contracting with other agencies for some other services, relying on other units of government, such as fire protection districts, for the rest. In most places counties have narrow powers, so cities are a more important target for community action. In rapidly growing areas, however, counties do vie with municipalities on who should provide what services, with welfare, social services, and overall planning being crucial areas of contention (Teaford, 1997).

Generally, local governments have only those responsibilities specifically delegated to them by the states, but such responsibilities vary. Some states grant cities, usually larger ones, a greater autonomy by delegating to them *home-rule* powers. What is included in home-rule powers varies, but it generally includes the ability to set up administrative structures to provide a wide variety of services without gaining state approval, greater freedom in levying taxes, and an ability to borrow money for capital projects without undertaking a referendum, which is required in many non–home-rule communities.

Constraints exist, however, on raising taxes. In several states and localities, referenda have been passed, ordinances adopted, or even constitutional changes made that limit tax increases. These *tax caps* restrict the amount of money local government can collect and thereby limit the services that can be provided. Many tax caps, however, have provisions that allow communities to increase taxes if the citizens approve at a referendum.

General-purpose local governments are usually run by an elected council that decides on overall policies and an elected executive (mayor or county board chairperson) who makes recommendations and supervises implementation. In the council–manager form of government, the council and mayor appoint a professional administrator to manage the local government and supervise the departments, most of which also have their own directors. In the mayor–council form, the elected mayor takes on the responsibilities of chief administrator, though he or she often has support staff to help. In a strong-mayor form of government, mayors have primary power over the budget, appoint the heads of city departments and the members of citizen advisory boards, and often have a veto over legislation the council passes. In weak-mayor cities, the mayor is just one member of the council who sometimes only has some additional ceremonial responsibilities. The commission form of government is a less common structure in which individuals are elected as a council (called a commission) with each commissioner also heading a department such as police or fire.

Most people are aware of general purpose local governments, because mayors often appear on television and are blamed or praised for what happens in their cities. Residents are less aware of special purpose governments, often termed *districts,* that are set up to serve just one function rather than a number of them. The best known special purpose government is a school district, but there may also be a variety of others such as fire protection districts, sanitary districts, drainage districts, mosquito abatement districts, park districts, and special recreation districts. In some locales, bridges and highways are the responsibility of special districts, while other locales have set up redevelopment authorities, a type of special district, with powers to borrow money, buy real estate, and help fund renewal projects. In some states, neighborhoods are allowed to set up their own special service districts in which neighbors can tax themselves more heavily to provide services that others in the city don't get such as more policing, lighting, more frequent sweeping or snow plowing, or additional maintenance of neighborhood parks.

Most special-purpose governments are run by an elected board, though some are headed by people appointed by other elected officials. Few voters are familiar with all the special districts in their areas or with the candidates running for these offices and turnouts for elections for special district boards are sparse. Because many districts have independent taxing powers and are responsible for a wide range of tasks, community groups may want to try to swing an election and create a board sympathetic to community issues.

For many action campaigns, knowledge of a handful of specific agencies is sufficient. If neighborhoods want more community policing, talking with the police department, the mayor, and the council is certainly the way to begin. Matters are often more complicated, however, as many programs of interest to action organizations are simultaneously the responsibility of several levels of government. The target for the action organization is not an individual government office but all the agencies working on the issue at different levels of government.

As an example, in dealing with wetlands, someone from the national Army Corp of Engineers might work with a state level EPA and a city planner. Or, for a community group wanting affordable housing, having the mayor's support is of value, but the city is just one player in a complicated network of agencies. In this case, a city housing official typically works with state counterparts who allocate tax credits (a technical way of funding affordable homes), while support from federal HUD officials comes into play to provide subsidies for the poor. Success for action groups requires simultaneously persuading bureaucrats and politicians who work for different levels of government to accept the action organization's agenda.

Further, action organizations have to monitor changes in government personnel and programs. Those holding elected office change frequently, at times creating dramatic differences in what will be supported. For years, the housing committees in Congress were chaired by representatives who supported affordable housing and were advocates for the CRA; in 1999 the chair was an opponent of CRA and not all that friendly toward housing subsidies. Similarly, new laws can affect established ones, sometimes by inadvertence. For instance, the changes in welfare legislation were worded in such a way as to deny housing subsidies to a third of those in Cleveland receiving them, all quite by accident. In this case, activists successfully convinced both local and federal officials to change the regulations to reconcile the requirements for housing subsidies with those for the new welfare programs.

Cultures of Support

In addition to understanding the formal structure of government, activists must also learn about differences in how people in office behave and their expectations about community groups. These differences reflect historic patterns that reflect a culture, a set of shared beliefs, on the role of the public sector and its participants.

One such cultural distinction is the difference between *reformed* or *unreformed* city governments. Historically, unreformed cities were those dominated by political machines that bought support from new immigrants with jobs and food. Most such political machines have disappeared, but in some cities, organized groups are still able to elect and reelect the same mayor, who then acts in an unreformed manner, dominating the city council. In such cities, action organizations need access to the mayor, but must keep in mind that individual council members may control sufficient resources to handle neighborhood issues on their own. In these cities, action organizations gain power by demonstrating their ability to reward allies with votes.

In reformed cities, the political culture discourages the use of government resources to sustain people in office. In such places, individual council members have less control of resources and the mayor may lack independent power. Daily administration is carried out by a professionally trained city manager who is responsible for running the city in a fiscally prudent way, assuring the routines of government are conducted efficiently. The manager maintains control over the departments by appointing and, if necessary, firing department heads. The watchwords of reformed governments are efficiency and fairness, at least in carrying out the rules on the books. Action organizations gain influence through knowledge of these rules and by working to assure that the written rules favor the communities they represent.

In recent years, political scientists and urbanists have introduced another, broader way of viewing city governments, called the *urban regime* approach. An urban regime "refers to (a) the public officials and private interests that function together as allies in the city's *governing coalition* and (b) the nature of the policy agenda pursued by this coalition" (Imbroscio, 1997, p. 6). In this approach, the culture of government emerges through the interaction that takes place between public officials and selected constituency groups. What characterizes a regime is an ongoing discussion through citizen advisory groups and informal, social contacts between favored constituents and elected officials. Because public officials tend to appoint to boards only those with whom they agree and then interact with these individuals socially, the advice received tends to be limited and slanted in ways that benefit those within the regime.

In most cities, business interests dominate the urban regime. In such corporate regimes "private interests (large downtown businesses) play a major role in guiding development policy with the effect that public authority and resources are used to subsidize private investment" (Whelan, Young, & Lauria, 1994, p. 2). Still, with persistent participation in the electoral process, coalitions of community organizations have established progressive regimes in which

> . . . middle and lower class neighborhood groups play a major role in policy making. When dominant, a progressive regime will expand services, pursue redistributive policies, and perhaps, limit growth and place controls on land developers. (Whelan, Young, & Lauria, 1994, p. 2)

In contrast to the downtown focus of corporate regimes, progressive regimes target programs to neighborhoods in need, often by working with community-based organizations (Imbroscio, 1997, pp. 97–138). In addition, progressive regimes open up access to a different set of constituencies. For example, in cities with progressive regimes, groups of gays and lesbians who had become politically active gained the ear of those in office (Rosenthal, 1996, p. 45).

The best known progressive regime came about when, with the support of numerous community and social change organizations, Harold Washington was elected mayor of Chicago. With Washington in office, important government positions were staffed by community activists, previously hidden city records were made open to community groups, funding dramatically increased for both economic development and social services in neighborhoods of need, and community groups received funding to provide public services. Of equal import, with the progressive culture in place, neighborhood and social change activists were able to interact with bureaucrats and elected officials, and help reframe their understanding about the purposes and goals of local government (Clavel & Wiewell, 1991).

Even when progressives are not in office, community groups can play a significant role in policy formulation. For example, the Texas Industrial Areas Foundation (TIAF) had conducted protests and had been involved in electoral politics in ways that convinced local officials to recognize the group as a significant player whose concerns mattered. Having gained such access, TIAF is now able to focus attention on issues that the power structure had tried to ignore. For instance, based on its support in many localities, TIAF was able to create a multicity coalition that pressured the state government to help the many cities that had underfunded schools. This action helped TIAF consolidate its position as part of the local governing regime and enhanced its ability to speak up on other issues (Wilson & Hadden, 1997, pp. 275–288).

The Policy Process

One goal of social action campaigns is to shape the policy agenda followed by elected and bureaucratic officials. For instance, the National Congress for Community Economic Development (NCCED), an organization that supports affordable housing, at one time was active in trying to influence twelve policy areas ranging from protecting CRA to establishing social programs to enable the poor to save money for education. To influence policy making, activists have to understand the policy process that can involve

- making issues salient to those in office by carefully framing them consistent with the goals of the social-change organization
- working out a variety of acceptable options
- communicating to those in office what options are desired
- pressuring those individuals to adopt the ideas proposed by the social change organization
- and, then making sure that the new policies are actually carried out.

Framing Issues and Establishing Policy Alternatives.   The first step in the policy process is to make those in office aware of the concerns. Sometimes this has already happened because action organizations have carried out demonstrations making the issues salient, or because newspaper accounts have made the general public aware of the concerns. On occasion, even government bureaucrats become allies, using pressure from action organizations to convince politicians to adopt policies that the bureaucrats themselves know are right.

Care is required in how problems are framed. Portraying a drug problem as one of inadequate police protection could result in crackdowns against minorities, which is not what the action organizations want. A better framing would carefully link the sale of drugs to the lack of jobs in the legitimate economy and then argue for improved programs in job training, creation, and placement.

An issue might be framed differently depending on whether it is the attention of politicians or bureaucrats that is being sought. Politicians are more likely to accept policies that provide visible resources to constituency groups for which the politician gains electoral credit; bureaucrats are more amenable to framings that emphasize fairness or equal treatment or that show their political bosses that the bureaucrats are doing a good job.

Points of Discretion, Points of Power.   Action organizations need to find the people who have power, funds, or discretion to make the decisions the action organization seeks. Sometimes the responsibilities of particular positions are clear. For example, you would probably contact a public works department about fixing potholes. However, for major changes in laws or policy, legislative action is required. To make this happen, social-change organizations must know the cumbersome process of passing laws and the different points at which pressure can be exerted.

The passage of a federal law requires action by the entire membership of both the Senate and the House of Representatives and presidential approval. Most of the time, proposals are drafted, and compromises are made at the legislative committee or subcommittee level. Action organizations first find out which committees handle issues of concern to the group, recognizing that some legislation falls into the jurisdiction of several different committees. The titles of committees might not be good clues to what they do. For example, the House Banking Committee is the one that has jurisdiction over housing. One way to track which committees are likely to have jurisdiction is to look at previous legislative efforts on the same subject and see which committees held hearings on the topic. While several different committees could deal with the issue of concern to the group, try to get the matter discussed by the one that has historically shown support for community issues; check out its voting record in committee minutes.

If committee members, especially from the majority party, support the policy proposal, they then assign committee staff, experts in writing laws, to help draft the requested legislation, and if the issue appears to be one in which politicians could gain credit, the committee might schedule public hearings. Part of the purpose of hearings is to solicit the opinions of supporters and others who may be affected by legislation. Few hearings, however, are actually for the purpose of gathering new information, but instead they are about providing a public framing of the issue at hand. If the legislation is still alive after hearings, the committee may hold a markup session during which the proposed law is rewritten in ways that will gain the support of enough legislators to pass the bill.

In complex legislation in which more than one committee has jurisdiction, a bill may go from one committee to another and from one set of hearings to another. Once approved by the committee(s), the bill is forwarded to the floor of the legislative chamber. Sometimes four or five versions of the same bill may be circulating at the same time. Action groups need to monitor all the versions because parts of some may be incorporated into the others. The other house may be considering a similar bill at the same time, or it may wait until one house has passed its bill and then respond to the proposed legislation. If both houses pass different versions, the separate bills go to a conference where individuals from each house work out a single version. In the past, the conference usually decided between one of the two bills, perhaps making slight modifications in each. Recently, conference committees have begun to change the bills considerably, a cause for concern for community groups especially when opponents of the social change matter appear at the conference. After both the House and the Senate have passed identical bills, the proposal then goes to the White House for the president to sign or veto.

Even if the legislation passes, the work of the action organization is not through. For a new program to be effective it must be funded, and obtaining funding at the federal level requires an entirely separate legislative procedure. In each house, there is a budget committee that establishes overall ceilings on spending for a series of related programs, such as for housing or the environment, and then within this limit subcommittees appropriate money for the separate program. Because each subcommittee is working within an assigned spending ceiling, if committee members raise the appropriation of one agency, they have to lower something else in their jurisdiction. Money spent on housing the elderly might mean less for housing poor families. Some programs, however, called entitlements, don't go through the appropriation process, as their costs are determined automatically, often by a formula. Under current law, however, increasing benefits of entitlements requires either new taxes or a cut in another entitlement program.

At the state level, the legislative and funding process can differ from place to place. For instance, the two houses may have joint committees and hold only one hearing. Financing may occur at the same time as program design. Community groups and their coalitions have to delineate the process in each state in which they plan to campaign for legislation or budget. At the local level, the process is likely to be simpler. Community organizations can ask the mayor or manager to introduce their proposal to the council, or a friendly council member can introduce the measure.

Regardless of the level of government, significant bills normally run into opposition. Opponents may introduce amendments that will weaken the proposal or render it inoperable or vote the whole bill down. To strengthen their case, progressive organizations must agree in advance on one proposal that they can defend against opponents. For example, before Congress passed legislation that funded affordable housing, a wide variety of community housing organizations—varying from those who work comfortably with bankers to those who have protested the same banks—negotiated and agreed among themselves what they would present to Congress. Congress heard a united voice and that voice prevailed over opposition.

As legislation goes through committees and between houses or branches of government, changes can be made, now improving the situation, now making it worse. Devastating amendments may be proposed, and defeated, or passed, only to be dropped again in conference. Sometimes legislation is dropped one year only to be picked up again the next. Community organizations have to follow the progress of the bill intently, be ready to react, mobilize support, lobby, or make a new proposal at a moment's notice.

To accomplish this requires patience and staying power. A group that presents an idea and then fades away is unlikely to succeed. A principal strength of conservative business and social interests is their ability to follow up their issues over time. Through a variety of coalitions, trade associations, and support groups (see Chapter 17) social-change organizations are beginning to match the presence during the legislative process of business groups.

Rule Making and Implementation.   The passage of legislation is not the end of the policy process. Once bills become laws, bureaucratic agencies are responsible for carrying out what has been legislated. This *implementation* stage requires the agency to interpret the law and to make up rules to accomplish legislative intent. Sometimes it is easy to figure out how the law is being implemented. If the city council has passed a bill authorizing a new traffic light, group members can go out and see if the light has been installed. If an increase in minority or female hiring was mandated, organization members can look at new hires to see if the target figure was achieved. Sometimes, however, measuring the degree to which a law is being implemented or tracking how well it is carried out is more difficult.

Many legislative bills specify general principles without spelling out how the policy should be carried out, for instance, not detailing formulas for allocating money or indicating how to measure the success of the program. Instead, bureaucratic agencies are required to set up rules that are consistent with legislative intent. How an agency designs and interprets these rules can dramatically influence the impact of the program or policy. For example, for programs designed to benefit poor people, agencies have to specify how poverty is to be measured. Agencies may also have to determine whether a new program can be contracted for in the private sector, or whether legislators really intended the contracts to be carried out by not-for-profit organizations.

Federal bureaucratic agencies and some state agencies must announce in advance the rules that they are considering. At the federal level, these announcements are made in the *Federal Register,* which also includes where to send comments and alternative ideas before the final set of rules appear. To assure proper implementation of policies, action organizations must make sure their ideas become part of the way in which agencies implement policies. In addition, action organizations must make sure that the rules are actually followed. During the Reagan administration people who held offices at HUD opposed affordable housing and were so negligent in following the program rules that nonprofit housing developers were unable to get funds that Congress had intended.

Regulatory agencies may require especially close supervision. Such agencies are often understaffed and respond by working closely with the very businesses they are supposedly regulating. Regulatory agencies tend to be flexible in how they implement rules; they may be so amenable to businesses' objections to particular rules that they lose sight of the needs of the broader public. Social change organizations must keep close watch on such agencies to make sure that the agencies do not forget that their purpose is to ensure pure food, effective medicines, clean air and water, and safe workplaces and not simply to save businesses money.

Two Styles of Political Action

Community and social change organizations can choose between two broad sets of conventional tactics to influence government. With *lobbying,* organizations persuade officials to pass laws and implement regulations the community organizations want. *Direct involvement tactics* turn community members from petitioners to decision makers, who run for office or sponsor initiatives or referenda through which voters directly decide policies. Both lobbying and direct involvement are more likely to be effective when backed by mass mobilization of community members.

There are no fixed rules on when which approach is appropriate. In a progressive city, effective lobbying might be accomplished by a simple phone call because supporters are already in office. By contrast, when conservatives dominate government, getting the message across in a nonconfrontational manner may be very difficult. The group may have to work through other lobbying organizations or coalitions that are more acceptable to those in power. If a group cannot make any headway in this manner, it may be better to work on direct involvement or rely on the confrontations described in Chapter 13.

In choosing tactics, organizations have to consider the impact on the members of the organization. For instance, policy advocacy involves near full-time work by specialists who have at their fingertips numerous details—how many are homeless, where they are located, how many have tuberculosis or AIDS. These specialists have to know the legislative process inside and out, minute by minute, and understand how the programs they support relate to other policy areas. Policy advocacy can be quite effective, but maintaining advocates in Washington and in the state capitals is expensive and rarely empowers most organization members who are not involved on a daily basis. Organizations have to decide if winning on particular issues is worthwhile if group members are not part of the process.

Effective political tactics necessitate that organizational leaders work closely with those in power, risking cooptation, that is, agreeing with those in office simply because of the frequent contact made and losing sight of members' goals. Through extended contact with government officials, advocates discover that to get changes they want, some compromise might be needed. Vigilance by other members not involved in the daily encounters with those in office is required to assure that representatives of action organizations are not slowly coopted but instead are making only the minimal compromises needed to get action.

Lobbying Tactics and Procedures

Lobbying involves communicating with those in office about the background of an issue, possible solutions, and the sentiments of those in the organization on how the public sector should act. Lobbying entails a presentation of information and opinions that takes place through long conversations with those in office, and when group members call or write elected officials. Lobbying is usually done in a quiet voice that gains power because politicians know it represents the opinions of thousands of voters.

Lobbying is an ongoing process, not an episodic one. Effective neighborhood organizations make sure some of its members attend all city council meetings and major committee meetings, even if no immediate issues of concern to the group are being discussed. Doing so shows politicians that the group is aware of upcoming issues, knows how councilmembers stand on various matters, and reminds elected officials of the presence of the organization. In this manner, activists define themselves as players who need to be consulted when their issues come up.

Complicated issues—the needs of the disabled, improving the environment, and controlling growth—are rarely decided once and for all, but rather are visited and revisited by politicians on numerous occasions. To make sure their voice is heard over the long run on complicated matters, social action organizations band together to form *advocacy coalitions* (Sabatier & Jenkins-Smith, 1993) that work out a common (or at least overlapping) policy agenda between the separate groups and employ lobbyists to speak for the broader coalition. For instance, in Spring 1999, eleven different organizations that support affordable housing, varying from the development activists in the NCCED to the street level organizers within the National Low Income Housing Coalition, met in Washington to coordinate their agendas that were then presented to the House and Senate (NCCED, 1999).

Effective lobbying requires perseverance. A lobbyist who has been following an issue for a long time knows what has been tried before, what was rejected and why, and what suggestions are likely to garner support now. Any lobbyist who has been around awhile has a track record and has already shown the politicians that the information he or she provides is reliable. Further, the continued presence of a lobbyist makes it clear to the elected officials that this group will not go away. In contrast, an organization that comes in at the last moment with its ideas will probably have little impact, no matter the quality of the ideas. One of the reasons given for the failure of the Equal Rights Amendment (ERA) to gain the needed thirty-eight states for constitutional ratification was that many feminist organizations that were lobbying showed little staying power.

> In spite of the ERA activists' mottoes, "We won't go away," that was exactly what the state legislators expected them to do. The legislators expected, and often got, sporadic initiatives, intense one-time activity, and little follow-through. (Mansbridge, 1986, p. 158)

When action organizations maintain a permanent lobbying presence, they are ready to suggest new policies when opportunities appear. After a disaster like the Exxon Valdez oil spill, environmental lobbyists, already an established force in Washington, pressed for stricter enforcement of environmental laws.

Further, an ongoing lobbying presence is required to prevent the opposition from sneaking through legislation that will hurt progressive causes, especially by reducing the funding available. For instance, conservatives have argued for a tax cut in ways that take money away from social programs, while supporting bills that would make it difficult or impossible for progressive groups to lobby.

With conservative forces now dominant at the federal level, progressive organizations have changed their approaches to lobbying. As suggested by the Center for Community Change, progressive organizations should:

> *Carefully pick your issues.* Prioritize issues and make sure those chosen are vital to the group and are those with which group members are familiar.

> *Make a commitment to it and assign responsibility.* Make sure someone is in charge to follow up on the issue.

> *Recognize that there's been a sea change in who has power.* When conservative Republicans chair important committees, activist groups need to build new relationships.

> *Don't assume that an ideological difference is insurmountable.* Even conservatives are willing to work with groups that show a strong reliance on self-help.

Examine your language. With conservatives in office, militant language does not work as well as framing issues in ways that appeal to the right. Label the poor as workers not sponges and talk about everyone's desire to own property.

Expand your horizons. Lobbying coalitions can bring together street activists and social service providers.

Don't let one "no" stop you. When ignored, you can make some noise through direct action, but in any case, don't give up.

Never stop having your members educate the people in power. Encourage calls from community members, and, on local issues, have people make frequent visits to those in office.

Use the media both to educate and pressure legislators. While talking with legislators make sure to provide stories to the press to bring public attention to the issues.

Be willing to confront and express outrage. Lobbying does tone down confrontations, but when necessary express anger, perhaps in a dramatic way.

Be prepared for a long struggle. Few issues are resolved in one-time approaches to politicians; decades of education and pressure may be required (adapted from Center for Community Change, 1996, pp. 17–20).

Lobbying is Mostly about Being There and Providing Information

Lobbying is about providing the information that government officials lack, in ways that will make them see the issue in your way. Lobbying is less about direct persuasion than it is about giving politicians who already lean your way the background material they need. Sometimes lobbying involves little more than just telling elected officials that their constituents face a problem such as when environmental lobbyists show officials that toxic waste sites are located within electoral districts that they represent.

As representatives of organizations that can bring out the vote or that can create disturbances, lobbyists gain attention because of the potential threats they represent. Effective lobbyists, however, don't evoke these threats; they understand that public officials do not want to be seen as losing face by capitulating to raw force. Instead, lobbyists provide the information and recommendations that enable politicians to support the social-change organization but appear to be doing so because of the facts of the matter.

In dealing with friendly legislators, lobbyists provide the specific information legislative supporters need to defend their positions. For instance, advocates for the CRA provide sympathetic officials with figures on how many banks are obeying the law, what improvements in housing have come about because of the law, the low default rate on CRA loans, and the fact that banks make money from CRA loans.

Elected officials want the facts that back up a case before they go public with a position. So in arguing against an ill-thought-out land clearance and redevelopment project, a lobbyist for low- and moderate-income housing should not just oppose the project, but find previous studies that show how many people will be displaced from their homes, how many small businesses will be destroyed, and, using engineering research, how many accidents will be caused by the new traffic patterns. It helps if the lobbyist puts a human face on the problems and the causes, maybe quoting stories of people who had been displaced and had to share small apartments with their relatives.

In lobbying, the facts presented must be correct, even if they slightly weaken the case being made. To be sure the information is accurate, lobbyists should collect the information themselves, paying careful attention to the rules of research detailed in Chapter 8. Community members, however, should not expect those in office to believe everything; they will be hearing the opposite side at the same time, and arguments of the opponents will also sound credible.

Sometimes lobbyists can use official government data to make a case. At the national level, the General Accounting Office, the Office of Management and Budget, the Bureau of Labor Statistics, and the Bureau of the Census, among many other agencies, produce reams of material that may speak to the issues. These data may be used to document the need for income supplements, the lack of funding for affordable housing, the discriminatory consequences of new tax changes, or the number of industrial sites that are polluted and in need of cleanup. At the local level, data collected by county or city departments can turn into lobbying ammunition in support of neighborhood improvement programs. Engineering departments do traffic counts that document the need for traffic signals and stop signs. Community development departments keep records on the number of households below the poverty line and the number of dilapidated buildings. The county clerk has evidence on the number of houses being rapidly sold in one area (which can be an indication of block busting). Police departments typically keep data on the amount, type, and location of crime. It is easier for a politician to support additional money for street repair if data gathered by the city's development department demonstrates the need. Community group members should not assume that because local government departments produced it that elected officials are aware of it.

The facts and figures lobbyists gather provide politicians with an acceptable *rationale* for supporting a cause, so they do not appear simply to be capitulating to pressure. A good rationale, that is, an acceptable framing of an issue, provides facts that politicians then can use to defend a controversial decision: yes, the refusal of the rezoning cost a few jobs, but approval of the rezoning would have increased truck traffic by 40 percent in a neighborhood filled with children.

Often opponents distort information, however, so that part of a lobbying effort involves providing data that inoculates politicians against such misleading arguments. Banks had argued for years that they did not discriminate against African Americans, simply that African Americans were poorer than others and poorer people received fewer loans. Affordable housing advocates located official data collected by banking supervisors and showed that what the banks were saying was wrong: even when income and other background factors were the same, African Americans still were less likely to receive loans. Similarly, companies that received contracts from cities vociferously argued that living-wage ordinances would bankrupt them. These arguments were weakened once a few cities had adopted such ordinances and evidence was at hand to demonstrate that the policies helped workers and caused no harm to their employers.

In working with politicians, effective lobbyists recognize the cross-pressures from different constituency groups that politicians face. Clever lobbying suggests ways to the politicians of satisfying what at first might appear to be contradictory demands. For instance, housing lobbyists pressured Congress for money to fund affordable housing at the same time that corporate interests were pressing for lower taxes. Lobbyists for housing groups came up with the idea of introducing special tax credits that would allow rich companies that invested in affordable housing projects to substantially reduce their tax bills. This idea enabled legislators to satisfy what at first appeared to be irreconcilable differences between business and the poor.

Another constraint politicians face is the lack of money to fund every worthwhile idea. Effective lobbyists work to find out where funds can be found. To do so, activists might have to study budgets and themselves become expert in public finance. After examining a city's finances, a neighborhood organization might argue that the city can refund an expiring bond at a lower rate of interest and use the difference to repair neighborhood schools. Officials, especially in smaller and middle-sized cities, don't always understand how federal grant money can be used. For instance, with *categorical grants,* money can be used only in the exact manner specified by federal law—money for road repairs cannot be used to build a new school house. But much of the grant money that cities receive is in the form of *block grants* that allow funds to be spent in a wide variety of related areas. There are block grants for community renewal and for social services that cities have traditionally used to fund a handful of specific types of projects. Lobbyists for community groups have taught city officials how to use block grants for innovative projects that benefit the neighborhoods in ways that don't increase any local expenses.

Persuading Staff

Lobbying is about personal persuasion, albeit persuasion that can be backed up by the force of numbers of people that action organizations can mobilize. It is best to lobby directly with the elected officials, but high-ranking federal officials or mayors of large cities might lack the time to deal with each organization. In such cases, community groups can approach politicians indirectly through their staff, who then boil down an argument and communicate it to the decision maker. Staff members have more time to talk with those in action organizations and might feel insulted if they are bypassed. Staff members are often knowledgeable about issues and can warn activists when they are approaching politically sensitive areas.

Federal, and at times state legislators, hire staff who specialize in hearing constituency requests, and they employ individuals who are expert in the particular programs of concern. Effective lobbyists find these people and work with them, not simply to persuade the politicians, but to seek out help from the staff in drafting the legislation. In cities, the heads of the separate departments act as staff for the city councils and as such should be approached with new ideas, as these are the individuals who make recommendations to the council.

In addition, some local governments employ advocacy or social equity planners. The job of these individuals is to determine the impact of public projects on community members. Progressive planners call attention to needs, such as for affordable housing, employment training, and adequate and affordable health care. Equity planners might find the data to show how proposed highway projects would break up intact (usually poor) neighborhoods. As part of the lobbying effort, action organizations are well advised to seek alliances with advocacy and social equity planners.

Learn the Decorum for Public Meetings, Hearings, and Markup Sessions

Lobbying can involve private discussions with officials or staff, but it also occurs at public meetings, hearings, and at markup sessions in which legislative committees work out the details of bills. Most such meetings are public, but that does not necessarily mean a community group will have an opportunity to speak. Fortunately, many cities schedule times at council meetings for citizen commentary; all an organization has to do is to sign up. Also, when cities determine how to spend money received from the federal government—*pass-through grants*—they are required to hold public hearings, often run by advisory councils. By law, any citizen has a right to speak at such meetings.

At the federal and state levels, witnesses are invited to testify at hearings by committee staff. The trick is to get on the witness list. In Congress, both majority and minority staff get to choose those who testify; however, the hearing itself is orchestrated by the majority party. Organizations that have their representatives in Washington are more likely to be called to hearings, in part because people are available quickly and there are no travel costs. Even if an organization is not invited to testify, it can submit written testimony that will appear in the printed form of the hearing and be included in the records.

Public hearings, markup sessions, and council meetings are formal occasions, during which visitors are expected to show respect for the process. Having many people from an organization attend a meeting makes sense, but these people (usually) should behave in a respectful and quiet manner. While community and social change organizations might want to carry out demonstrations, rallies, and other direct actions while hearings are occurring, the events should be separated, as elected officials resent having meetings disrupted and are likely to turn against a group that creates such tumult.

Because the norms of how to behave at public meetings do differ from place to place, attend a few meetings and observe what is expected. Does the speaker address the council or legislators, or does he or she address the audience? Do those making presentations to the elected officials use formal titles or personal names? How do witnesses dress? Pay attention to the mannerisms of lawyers and highly paid business lobbyists. In their speeches, they are calm, polite, and factual. They recognize that while the immediate issue is important, so is maintaining long-term access to the legislative body.

The amount of time allowed for a presentation will differ. At the state and federal level, speakers negotiate in advance for how long they will speak, with the legislative body trying to provide some balance between opposing sides. Experienced activists know their time will be limited so they work out carefully what they will say beforehand, often summarizing the material orally and presenting a fuller version in writing for the record. Advocacy coalitions usually try to have their best speakers present a summary and then, if time permits, have people from individual groups add details. If an organization has two-hundred people willing to show up to a meeting, one of them should present a carefully prepared statement. The speaker should ask the people in the audience who support what he or she is saying to stand up.

Sometimes city council members want to hear from anyone who wants to speak, but only for a few minutes each. In this case, an action organization should plan out a sequence of linked speeches that together present the overall argument. The first speaker should present the gist of the argument. Then members of the group can elaborate on individual points, for example, by taking one topic and showing the impact on that person. The lead speaker might talk about how many children have to be bussed because of the lack of neighborhood schools. Then a parent might describe what time his child has to leave home and when the child returns home. Another parent might describe what happened when her child, who was at school some distance from home, got sick during the day. The wrap up speaker might summarize the group's proposal, underscoring its feasibility.

In general, statements made at hearings, council meetings, and legislative discussions should be brief, focused, and logical. When the arguments require statistical data (or, when pictures speak louder than words) attractive charts or graphs should be posted or handed to the councilmembers. Statistical material should not be read out loud, it is boring and hard to follow.

When appropriate, individual presentations should balance facts with personal narratives: "I oppose the rezoning because, as the engineering department figures show, it will increase traffic by 40 percent near the Jefferson school. I have two children attending that school and the existing level of traffic makes me nervous." After several such presentations, a speaker should then summarize the arguments in terms of a broader public interest so as to frame the issues in ways that elected officials can endorse. "Development ought not be accomplished in such a way as to endanger school children."

Dramatic presentations can be effective as long as they make a clear point. For example, a legislator who worked with community groups that helped the disabled described a presentation he planned:

> We brought out a fellow who has cerebral palsy. . . . I mean he could talk but you couldn't understand him. He had an interpreter who could understand him and then she would tell you what he was saying. You saw somebody who definitely was unemployable.
>
> Instead he owns a business now that employs 11 people. . . . It's a small newspaper, community newspaper. . . . And he is an entrepreneur. . . . We brought him in to testify and once people saw that. I mean their mouths dropped. No one said a word against him in both houses.

The legislation passed, in part, because people learned that those with disabilities can work and be productive. The presentation was really attention grabbing.

At public sessions, opponents may fight vigorously for their side of the issue. The trick is to avoid direct confrontations but at the same time not allow opponents or legislators that favor the opponents' side to twist your words. Tact is required.

If a legislator, while questioning you, asserts facts you know aren't correct, simply cite the source of your correct facts. You don't want to make an opponent lose face in a hearing, but you do want to show that his facts are wrong. Present the correction, calmly and forthrightly, setting aside your emotions. (Alderson & Sentman, 1979, p. 282)

When someone asks a hostile question, try to treat it with respect, showing that you understand the premises but want to correct misunderstandings. Suppose an alderperson harshly questions a representative of a spouse-abuse center. "Those women in the shelter can't be from our community, they must be coming from neighborhood towns. Spouse abuse is what happens to poor people, when the men are out of work." A respectful and informative response could be, "Economic stress is certainly a cause of violence, as the alderperson indicates, but there are other causes. Spousal abuse happens at all economic levels and more than 70 percent of those in the center have local addresses."

Refuting arguments that opponents might make is difficult because hearings are not debates but presentations that are prepared in advance. To some extent, the opponents' arguments have to be anticipated. Spend time and look up arguments they have made at similar hearings or read their literature. If possible, prepare a set of questions that your opponent might have difficulty answering and, well in advance, hand these questions to a legislator or city council person who supports your side. Members of elected bodies are usually allowed to question speakers, creating some give and take at the meetings.

If your group knows enough about the arguments of opponents it can include refutations in its presentation. Suppose a community group is trying to stop a developer who wants city permission to build a large housing complex that would destroy a grove of trees. Spokespeople for the environmental group can

1. *Disagree w ith the evidence presented.* The developer will describe the amount of green space to be left when the project is completed. Environmentalists point out most of that space will be in small front yards, not in parks and open areas that everyone can use.

2. *Point out inconsistencies in the arguments.* The developer describes how easily the city can accommodate the small increase in population, while describing how much more money the city will get in taxes. You argue that either growth is moderate or the gain in taxes is moderate. The developer can't have it both ways.

3. *Challenge the assumptions in the arguments.* The developer argues that traffic congestion will not be a problem. After examining his back-up information you learn that he assumes only one car per family, while modern developments average 1.8 cars.

4. *Challenge the priorities within the arguments.* The developer argues that housing is needed because people want to move to the suburbs. Environmentalists argue that the reason people moved to the suburbs was to get open space and if the proposed development goes in, congestion will replace that open space.

5. *Challenge the track record of the opponent.* The spokespeople for the environmental organization present pictures of other projects built by the developer,

showing that they result in high density and crowding. (modified from Alderson & Sentman, 1979, pp. 236–239)

Demonstrating Mass Support in Lobbying Campaigns

Through extended conversations with those in office and through appearances at committee meetings, city council sessions, and markup sessions, activists communicate their organization's goals for policy changes. Face-to-face lobbying is strengthened when large numbers of people make it known to those in office that they too support the proposed policy.

Letter-writing campaigns are one way of enabling large numbers of people to lobby public officials. Leaders of a social action group can encourage its members to write, perhaps by sharing sample letters at meetings or in printed or electronic newsletters. Established national organizations maintain lists of members who have volunteered to write or call public officials and use electronic mail or telephone trees to activate these individuals to contact legislators quickly.

Other organizations arrange for their members to have brief face-to-face lobbying encounters with their elected representatives. For instance, on a yearly basis, coalitions of CDCs, and in separate efforts, coalitions of housing advocates meet in Washington. As part of their conference, they send conference attendees to visit their legislators on Capitol Hill to let them know what issues deserve support. Similarly, "some groups, such as the Sierra Club, have a membership lobbying corps, which comes to Washington when key bills are under consideration to lobby members and their staffs" (Wilcox, 1997, p. 97). Other national groups ask volunteers in communities across the country to make themselves known to their local legislators. When lobbying is required these individuals phone or appear in person in the district offices of their national legislators to make the organization's case.

In mass lobbying efforts, people should be polite and to the point, describing the problem and how it affects them as individuals. Letters should be brief and focus on only one problem. Effective letters indicate that the writer is aware of what the official has already done on the issue, while providing suggestions about what future actions are needed. These contacts should not contain even veiled threats. After an issue has been decided, it's a good practice to write to thank politicians for their support.

Organizations work to make letter writing easy to encourage their supporters to join in; however, "congressional offices are routinely barraged by postcards and form letters, and most of them by now merely count these mass-produced communications, but do not reply to them. More effective are handwritten, individual letters" (Wilcox, 1998, p. 96). Personal letters that provide anecdotes that make a problem real to a politician are probably the most effective form of mail communication.

Electronic communications, such as faxes and e-mail, have become major tools for mass lobbying. Homepages and mailing lists allow for rapid mobilization of national organizations (Schwartz, 1996). Websites can be designed to allow any one to click on, compose a letter, and send it to specified members of Congress (Lyman, 1998). Increasingly, electronically circulated *sign-on letters* have become a tool for lobbying.

With a sign-on letter, organizations send copies of policy statements to potential sup-porters, asking people to sign their names and organizational affiliation and pass on the letter to other similar groups. At the end, the letter returns to the initiating organization that then can hand it to the appropriate officials. Especially when time horizons are short (such as when opponents have convinced someone to change a bill during a markup session), electronic media are an important way to get supporters to lobby legislators.

With increasing frequency, city governments are setting up web pages, many of which allow for constituent comments. A decade back, Santa Monica set up a Public Electronic Network that enabled citizens to participate in electronic discussions of policies about homelessness. City policies changed as a result of these discussions, but the network was shut down after some of the communications became too vitriolic (Schmitz et al., 1995). Recently, the city restarted the network after the League of Women Voters volunteered to assure that conversations would stay civil (Santa Monica, 1998).

No one knows for sure how effective electronic communications are in persuading legislators. Some legislators are not electronically sophisticated, while others consider electronic lobbying as just a sophisticated form letter. A study of how those in Congress respond to electronic communications concluded that personal contact is still far more effective than conventional or electronic mail, but that personalized e-mail is becoming more effective. Overall, those in Congress were not yet geared up to capitalize on the electronic revolution, but it seemed likely that would change soon (OMB Watch, 1998).

Constraints on Lobbying

Both individuals and small groups of citizen activists can lobby to their hearts' content, but different rules apply to organizations. For instance, to obtain legal, administrative, and financial benefits, social change and neighborhood organizations incorporate as 501(c)(3) charitable nonprofits. Such organizations are limited by law in the amount of lobbying they can undertake, as spelled out in the Lobbying Disclosure Act of 1995.

Nonprofits that employ at least one person who spends at least 20 percent of his or her time in lobbying or that spend $20,000 semiannually on lobbying must register as lobbying groups. Once registered, such organizations can lose their tax-exempt status if they exceed certain limits on their lobbying. Fortunately, the provisions are fairly liberal and apply only to the federal level. Many activities do not count against the limits, for instance, teaching about an issue, broadly defined, or doing technical analysis or studies. Distributing nonpartisan back-up material on issues, providing testimony at the request of the legislature, or defending the organization from attacks by opponents are *not* considered as lobbying. As the legislation stands, it allows for as much effort as most groups are able to undertake, with the main problem the need for detailed record keeping (paraphrased from Trister, 1995; Center for Community Change, 1996).

Some conservative interests are trying to reduce the amount of lobbying in which nonprofits can engage. Representatives have introduced legislation that would preclude any organization that receives federal money from direct lobbying. So far such bills have failed, in part, because a vast number of nonprofits have mobilized to fight the changes and have kept on top of the issue through electronic communications. To be on the safe side, some organizations have set up affiliates that do all the lobbying, allowing the main group to do the projects that require grants.

Direct-Involvement Politics

Through lobbying, community and social-change organizations work to influence government officials who in turn are the ones who bring about changes. Direct-involvement politics carries the process of political involvement one step further, as activists run for office, serve on boards, or sponsor referenda or initiatives that make a direct appeal to the electorate to change a law.

Direct-involvement politics would seem to be the height of empowerment; however, caution is required because serving in public office creates responsibilities that go well beyond pushing for a social-change agenda. Elected officials must deal openly with people with whom they disagree, find that they have to make compromises, and chance accepting establishment values. Further, activists in office tend to become separated from ordinary members of the organization, might absorb a go-along-to-get-along mentality, and may be increasingly reluctant to press for the more radical alternatives preferred by the organization's membership.

Still, direct-involvement politics has its pluses. Members of neighborhood boards can have authoritative say over changes that affect community members, referenda can put laws in place that accomplish community goals, and having sympathetic candidates in office certainly beats continually fighting politicians who oppose the goals of community groups.

Community Boards and Neighborhood Governance

Citizens serve on a wide array of community and neighborhood boards that vary in power and effectiveness. Such boards range from citizen advisory groups mandated by the federal government, such as those set up to recommend spending priorities for community development block grants, to local commissions that have a say on zoning and land use matters. Many cities set up neighborhood-based planning boards to advise on projects and problems within an area. Sometimes these boards have a role in planning budgets.

Just labeling a board "participatory" or "community-based" does not make it so, however. Most community boards are run by a self-perpetuating local elite and allow for very little effective involvement by ordinary citizens (Cnaan, 1991). A study of federally mandated citizen boards showed that in most cases

1. [There is] a lack of representativeness of participants
2. The most successful citizen inputs are found in programs which seem to require the least expertise
3. Overall, the impact of citizens groups has been limited

4. Most participatory programs are geared to intervention at the local administrative or service delivery level, leaving the vast reaches of agenda-setting and policy prescription relatively untouched. (Crosby, Kelly, & Schaefer, 1986, p. 170)

Other scholars worry that rather than empower, community boards pit neighborhood against neighborhood. As described in New York City:

. . . with a shrinking pie, a division of the city into separate community boards tended to place neighborhood interests in competition with each other. Neighborhoods were divided from each other, not united, by the arrangement. (Marcuse, 1988, p. 281)

While older studies showed a certain skepticism about citizen boards, more recent research has shown the potential for such boards to be effective. One national study examined cities in which there was high participation in community boards and asked why such empowerment came about. The study discovered that in effective boards citizens demanded the right to be involved while local officials supported their demands. Next, effective boards were found in communities in which face-to-face communications were already under way and, in which cities encouraged a two-way flow of information, rather than a top-down model. Real efforts were made to assure that the boards were free of partisan politics. Finally, sufficient money was made available for boards to accomplish their tasks (Berry, Portney, & Thomson, 1993, pp. 48–51). As a consequence, people in neighborhoods with effective boards were more likely to become politically involved than were people from other communities.

Experience confirms the potential for community boards to empower people. For instance, prodded by action organizations, community members have joined local school boards that brought about progressive educational and social reform (Lee, 1996). In Boston, the Dudley Street Neighborhood Initiative prepared the redevelopment plan for its community that the city adopted, had real input into zoning decisions, and was given the right of "eminent domain," that is, it could exercise the city's power to forceably purchase land needed to improve the community (Medoff & Sklar, 1994; Tulloss, 1998). In Minneapolis, a series of Neighborhood Revitalization Boards have an effective say in allocating redevelopment funds and strong powers on zoning cases (Nickel, 1995). Cities that have set up Housing Trust Funds, ways of funding affordable housing, often ask neighborhood activists to be on the boards that allocate the money.

Active citizens can empower boards, but cooperation is still required from officials. For instance, in Dayton, Ohio, citizens from separate neighborhoods are members of priority boards that have effective say in shaping the city's budget. The boards are elected from distinct parts of the city with neighborhood associations guaranteed a seat. The priority boards are treated seriously because they are knowledgeable, while city officials are instructed to accept a board's recommendations unless there are powerful reasons to disagree. Much effort is required to make the boards work well. City officials spend a lot of time teaching citizens about the technicalities of budget making. Before making recommendations, the members of priority boards consult with one another and with people who work with CDCs.

Before advising members to get involved in neighborhood boards, an action organization might want to assure that participation is not a waste of time. Are the decisions made by the board binding, rather than being merely recommendations? Are the stakes high enough to be worth the time? Having a say on a city budget or zoning is probably worth the effort, but being on the advisory board of a planning effort can often turn out to be a waste of everyone's time if the plan is not taken seriously. Are democratic procedures followed in choosing who is going to be on the board? Appointed boards are easier to coopt as part of a political machine, while elected boards might stimulate community involvement.

Referenda and Initiatives: Forms of Direct Democracy

In about two dozen states and in many localities, citizens can propose legislation, called *initiatives*, can vote on legislation through *referenda*, or advise legislators on what people feel about an issue with a nonbinding vote, or even expel a sitting official from office through a *recall* election.

Every year dozens of major referenda take place. In 1998, referenda and initiatives were held on affirmative action, the legalization of marijuana for medical use, animal rights, gender equality, legalization of gambling, and cigarette taxes (Verhovek, 1998). Another issue that has come up recently is the legality of physician-assisted suicide. Tax limits are a perennial favorite. Community groups have sponsored local referenda to stop block busting in racially changing neighborhoods (Scheiber, 1987), and social movement organizations have set up votes to oppose nuclear weapons (Zisk, 1989b).

Direct democracy can be used by conservative groups to undo legislative gains that action organizations have obtained. Referenda sponsored by conservatives groups to cap local taxes pull money away from public schools and needed social services, while direct-action politics in California have harmed immigrant groups and weakened affirmative action. Such backlash movements garner huge support and, unfortunately, in many cases "campaign spending is the single most powerful predictor of who wins and who loses" (Cronin, 1989, p. 112). Still, the power of money does not always prevail over the power of numbers. For instance,

> Out of 72 city or county ballot measure campaigns that pitted poorly funded local residents and environmentalists against the overwhelming spending of developers, the developers *lost* two-thirds! (Schmidt, 1989, p. 36)

Social-change organizations must be ready to fight against backlash referenda. For instance, in 1998 in California, legislation was proposed through a referendum that would forbid any money deducted from employees' checks to be used for any political purpose, unless the employees explicitly approved of each case. Because some of the money that charities receive are used for lobbying, and payroll deductions are used to pay union dues, this bill would have harmed both nonprofits and unions, making it more difficult for either of them to lobby. Progressive organizations fought this referendum and prevailed (Bass, 1998).

Trying to pass a statewide referendum can be so time consuming that an organization can do little else. To get onto the ballot requires a large number of signatures, so the organization has to have people working throughout the state, and working quickly, because usually there are strict time limits on signature gathering (Dresang & Gosling, 1989, p. 180). Sometimes professionals are hired to collect signatures. It is questionable how often an issue merits the huge efforts that referenda entail.

The structure of a mass ballot forces issues to be phrased so that they can be answered with a yes or no. Such wording oversimplifies complicated issues and by doing so chances trampling on minority rights (Cronin, 1989, p. 98). For instance, referenda posed as yes or no questions on health matters have sought to isolate AIDS victims, while others phrased in terms of bureaucratic efficiency have tried to mandate that only English be spoken by state bureaucrats. People do not have simple feelings about abortion, but referenda do not allow for tapping complicated opinions. With only two choices allowed, moderates might be forced to the extreme and an extreme opinion might be adopted as policy when in fact, few prefer it. What appears democratic may not be democratic at all.

Holding Office and Working in Electoral Campaigns

The extent to which action organizations should be directly involved in political campaigns, especially in having organizational leaders running for office, is very contentious. Having supporters in office is almost always a plus, but getting them elected and spending time governing can distract from the broader concerns of social change organizations.

Studies show that when progressive officials are in office, community and social-change organizations benefit, especially when those in office came from the neighborhood movement. Pierre Clavel argues that

> . . . progressive governments did make a difference. [They provided] support for neighborhood organizations and pressured local administrations to depart from the traditional hierarchical models of government. (Clavel, 1986, pp. 215, 233)

Further, with activists in office, governments are more likely to fund advocacy and equity planners who work with neighborhood groups and speak for the poor.

Mayors Flynn of Boston, Goldschmidt of Portland, and Washington of Chicago all emerged from the neighborhood movement and once in positions of power were open to community concerns, supported programs that helped neighborhood causes, and appointed people to office who were active in the community movement. In smaller cities, such as Santa Monica, California or the multicultural Monterey, California (Horton et al., 1995) neighborhoods worked to get their slates in office to bring about specific changes, in the former, rent control and in the latter, increased sensitivity to the needs of the different cultural groups (such as having multilingual signs). In general, minorities seem better able to protect social and economic gains when representatives from their groups serve as the elected officials (Browning et al., 1997).

Historically, as part of civil rights organizing, action organizations created alternative political parties. The Freedom Democratic Party in Mississippi slated many of the local activists in the voting rights movement for office. In Chicago, Jesse Jackson's tries for the presidency built up his Rainbow Coalition that in turn mobilized large numbers of voters who then worked for other community causes. The involvement of the Industrial Areas Foundation in electoral politics, in supporting candidates and in getting voters to register and vote, has increased the clout of neighborhood coalitions (Ross, 1996).

There are real advantages of having community supporters in office, but working full time in campaigns can be a losing proposition. Backing the opponent of an incumbent can permanently alienate the incumbent, and if the rival has no chance of winning the organization might never get to speak to the incumbent again. Elections often pit people from different ethnic or cultural groups against each other, creating friction instead of the unity necessary to work to improve schools or jobs. The time required to run an electoral campaign is so great that little else gets accomplished by the group, and "even committed activists eventually grow weary of putting their energies into progressive races that are clearly doomed from the start" (Ashkenaz, 1986, p. 17).

Even winning does not necessarily mean that desired changes will come about. Other officials remain in office and might dominate decision making. Further, once in office, activists have legal and moral responsibilities for more people than those that backed them during the election. Worse yet, once in office, people tend to want to stay there and may compromise the platforms on which they were elected to gain wider support.

Seeking the middle ground may be the best strategy. Community groups can endorse particular candidates for office and encourage group members to vote for them but should probably avoid the cumbersome effort of running campaigns to get organizational leaders into elected positions. The work is onerous and can distract from efforts to get policies passed. Activists should pay close attention to how elected officials vote and work to get the organization's concerns on the policy agenda. Further, through accountability sessions, activists can maintain pressure on elected officials to keep their promises to the group and seriously embarrass those who fail to do so.

Conventional political activity is a necessary part of community and social-change work. Only the public sector can pass needed laws, provide funding, and assure that policies are implemented. Conventional political activity, however, is seldom sufficient to bring about major changes. Instead, community and social-change organizations have to create their own sources of power by forcing their way onto the political agenda through the direct (and sometimes disruptive) actions that we discuss in the next chapter.

13 Confrontational Approaches

Direct Actions and Litigation

When lobbying is insufficient, social change organizations rely on pressureful, confrontational strategies. With litigation, organizations evoke and use the power of the courts to compel government and business to live up to their own rules or stop harmful policies. With direct actions—demonstrations, sit-ins, picketing, boycotts, and other forms of confrontations—activists vigorously demand that changes be made now. With direct actions "the squeaky wheel gets the oil. . . . So we squeak." (Medoff & Sklar, 1994, pp. 84–85)

Confrontations force responses from targets by making them fear continual disruption, a fear that gains credibility as activists literally put their bodies on the line. Massive demonstrations helped end the war in Vietnam; daring sit-ins, boycotts, and civil disobedience helped bring down state sanctioned discrimination and segregation.

Confrontational tactics make problems visible. A few people might pass the homeless sleeping in parks and doorways, but millions see pictures on the six o'clock news of the shantytowns set up on the capital lawn to illustrate the plight of the extremely poor. Disruptions led by the AIDS Coalition to Unleash Power (ACT-UP) focused attention on public neglect of the AIDS epidemic; confrontations inspired by the Justices for Janitors Campaign (McCarthy & McPhail, 1998) made clear to the broader public persistant economic discrimination against those working in less desirable jobs. Direct-action campaigns led by battered women taught the public about the structural forces that made it hard for women to escape abusive relationships (Kendrick, 1998, p. 160).

Direct actions catch the public eye, scaring the targets while rallying others to the cause. The drama of the tactics used—flamboyant demonstrations, rallies with thousands participating, daring sit-ins, and at times, human chains to block streets and even construction equipment—serve to mobilize people beyond the initial activists. The daring visibility of the few suggests that now is the time to join the battle (Woliver, 1996). Activism bootstraps as people who become involved feel empowered and become even more willing to continue the fight. Large numbers of Native Americans joined a battle for their civil rights after seeing the bravery of a few at the sit-ins at Alcatraz; in the civil rights era the broader public was moved to join in by those who were willing to put their bodies on the line.

Direct action organizations blend visible assaults on the establishment with longer term efforts to build a strong core organization. Over two years of effort, the Kensington

Welfare Rights Union (KWRU) set up a tent city to protest the failure of the housing shelter system, took over a church to house homeless families, and led two long marches (of over a 100 miles) to protest new welfare laws, all while coordinating other groups in a national campaign to call attention to persistent poverty. Concurrently, KWRU expanded its institutional capacity by setting up a Poor People's Center to lobby in the state capital and building a Human Rights House, which became the organization's office, a place to hold membership meetings, and a distribution point for commodities for poor people (*http://www.libernet.org./kwru/kwru*).

Litigation

Litigation targets officials and businesses that fail to uphold the law, ignore existing regulations, or violate constitutional rights. Court actions can stop landlords from evicting tenants, mandate compensation for toxic wastes, halt highway construction, force businesses to comply with antidiscrimination legislation, or require schools to make facilities handicapped accessible. Action organizations can go to court to demand police records to end profiling by race—the practice of stopping minorities who are doing nothing wrong, because police think they might be guilty of something. National coalitions work through the courts to assure that states do not violate the rights of those coming off welfare by imposing onerous workfare requirements. Social change organizations use the courts to protect people who suffer discrimination because of their religion, ethnicity, and increasingly, sexual orientation.

Legal actions help legitimate a social change organization in the eyes of the public. The opposition tries to portray activists as a bunch of rabble rousers, but in court the public face of the group is a neatly dressed lawyer whose presence suggests respectability and legitimacy. Further the act of bringing a legal case helps frame an issue by providing it with an official label.

Legal actions are usually just one part of a broader action campaign. Court actions stall the opponents until the action organization builds broader political support for its cause. For instance, if a government redevelopment authority issues dispossession notices to residents, a group can sue to get the time to organize a response. Legal tactics can halt the destruction of public housing until new apartments have been found for those being displaced. Suits to enforce the endangered species act have stopped lumbering or development on land harboring protected plants and animals.

One important legal tactic involves *discovery motions* that require documents germane to a case to be made available. Using discovery, environmental organizations located internal reports of the Department of Interior that showed that public water was being sold at far below market costs to large-scale commercial farmers, making transparent one way the government subsidizes the rich. In environmental suits, discovery enables activists to find out where toxic wastes are being dumped, while similar legal tactics have yielded internal personnel records of companies that show patterns of gender or race-based discrimination.

The fear of being engaged in an expensive legal fight can force opponents to negotiate, as the public sector has shown with the tobacco industry and increasingly with gun manufacturers. For banks and builders, time is money. If a community organization can obtain an injunction against a builder to stop construction, the builder cannot sell homes to pay back borrowed money. It is often cheaper for the developer to build some affordable homes than to resist the pressures from the action organization.

Litigation becomes part of a direct action within campaigns of *legal mobilization.* For example, in efforts to assure pay equity at work, lawsuits create publicity and help mobilize people who then participate in demonstrations and conventional politics (McCann, 1994, p. 48).

Forms of Legal Action

Most legal actions involve either injunctions or lawsuits. *Injunctions* are court orders to stop possibly harmful actions until additional facts are gathered. A city might be enjoined not to distribute block grant money until it can show that federal rules for fair allocation of the funds have been followed. *Suits* are filed to right a wrong, to claim compensation for harm done, or to make a party live up to an agreement. *Performance suits* are meant to force a party to carry out a contract already signed or a law already on the books. *Substantive suits* are intended to gain compensation for harm done, such as when people get hurt from working in unsafe conditions.

Often the harm caused to an individual is so small that bringing suit would be prohibitively expensive. In such cases, *class-action suits* are filed in which many small complaints are lumped together. Such efforts are of particular import when consumer or environmental issues are involved; however, companies have responded to the threat of class actions by trying to convince government to make them illegal. For example, businesses lobbied for laws to mandate that before lawyers can bring a class-action suit, they have to get all their clients' permission in writing, a difficult task if people are scattered throughout the country. In response, rather than bringing a class-action suit, social change organizations try to pressure government regulatory agencies, which have legal authority, to bring the suits instead.

A *procedural suit* can force a government agency, regulatory body, or, in some certain circumstances, a business, to follow its own rules. Activists have sued the Food and Drug Administration when it appeared to be excessively slow in approving necessary medicines such as those that combat AIDS. Activist organizations that focus on issues of gender discrimination can bring a procedural suit when hiring, firing, or promotion practices follow different paths for men than they do for women.

Problems with Legal Tactics

While they may produce major victories, community organizations have to be alert to the difficulties inherent in legal approaches. Some of these problems are technical; others deal more with organizational capacity building.

One of the technical problems is that deciding where to sue can be difficult. Is this a criminal or civil case? Should it be brought before a petty claims or a housing court? Should it be a local case, a state case, or a federal case? Have civil rights been violated? Is the group seeking compensation for damages? The standards of evidence are easier in some kinds of cases, which may make them easier to win, but in these cases the ability to establish a precedent is lower.

Another difficulty with legal strategies is that countersuits are increasingly frequent, putting action organizations on the defensive. When action organizations attempt to run boycotts, companies sue asking for damages from lost business. Protesters can be ordered by the courts to stay away from sites they want to picket; violations of these orders put action organizations in contempt of court. In many locales, action organizations have lost suits to be allowed to picket, demonstrate, or even hand out information at private shopping centers and in malls. During the civil rights era, segregationists mastered a series of legal tactics that seriously handicapped those trying to change the status quo (Barkan, 1997).

A third problem is that laws differ place by place, so what has been learned in one case might not work elsewhere. For example, the legal rights of tenants vary from Indiana, with weak protenant laws, to Massachusetts, where tenants are protected by implied warranties that housing is habitable, have a right to deduct repair costs from rents, and cannot be evicted for taking action to promote their rights (Joseph, 1983, p. 133). Laws allow rent strikes in New Jersey, while elsewhere those conducting such a strike could find themselves under court sanction.

An additional drawback to legal strategies is that they are expensive because they require hiring professionals who, in turn, need backup support. Affordable legal information can be obtained from activist law centers such as the Welfare Law Center (*http://www.welfare.law.org*), which litigates for and provides information about abuses of welfare law. Support organizations and national coalitions, the American Civil Liberties Union (ACLU), Mexican American Legal Defense Fund, and other groups, have full-time attorneys on hand that work for progressive causes, but the number of cases they can take is limited.

But even when the organization can afford the expenses, it is questionable whether using hired professionals is a way of building organizational capacity and empowering the membership, especially because legal processes are often so slow that people lose interest. As activists warn

> . . . trials are held during the day, which often precludes attendance by workers. The litigation time line is not controlled by members and can be lengthy. The role that members can play is extremely limited, so a litigation project does not facilitate leadership development. It is difficult to recruit members around legal cases for these reasons, which means it is difficult to build the power of the organization. (Gaventa et al., 1990, p. 115)

One response is to try to bring more members into the legal fight. For instance, the Association for Community Organizations for Reform Now (ACORN) worked out a way for members of tenants' organizations to participate in legal campaigns by serving papers on their opponents.

> [This] offers exciting opportunities: "I went right up to the door of that mansion. You should have seen the look on his face when he took the paper. I thought I was nothing

compared to him, but he had to take the paper from me and see the medicine we had planned for him." (McCreight, 1984, p. 183)

Other organizations ask their members to help with the information gathering and detective work in preparation for court hearings. Housing activists track down ownership of derelict properties so their attorneys know whom to sue.

A second way to involve people in legal campaigns is to make sure group members are directing the strategies followed by the attorneys. In Chicago, as the Department of Housing and Urban Development (HUD) sought to tear down derelict, affordable apartments, activists followed an array of strategies including seeking ownership of the buildings. Legal help was needed to draw up incorporation papers and to sue HUD to force it to follow its own regulations. Attorneys were hired but were given detailed direction by community members (Nyden & Adams, 1996).

To summarize, legal tactics are varied and often effective, though slow and expensive. Despite major outlays, some legal tactics fail in court and many tactics seem to exclude organization members. The need to win the case may give attorneys disproportionate say over how the case is brought, threatening the sense of empowerment of members. Legal tactics should be used sparingly, only when needed, and, almost always, as only one part of a broader campaign.

Overview of Direct Actions

Direct action tactics range from noisy demonstrations to silent prayer vigils; they may be as active as marches or as immobile as sit-ins; they may work by threatening finances, as do boycotts and rent strikes, or by creating delays, as in traffic or construction stoppages. Direct actions can be utterly serious or humorously mocking. They can be blatantly illegal or well within the law. Direct actions should be attention getting and communicate a clear message, but they should *not* be undertaken simply because they gain the limelight or make group members feel important. Direct actions require the time and moral commitment of people to the issue and often involve some risk.

Choosing Actions

In determining whether to rely on direct actions and then which ones to choose, activists should reflect on three issues:

First, determine if the tactic will work and at what cost? If a boycott or picketing brings opponents to the bargaining table, the tactic may be worthwhile, even if the store, its employees, or an industry is hurt in the short run. Sabotaging equipment may slow down or stop the construction of a highway, but it also risks hurting construction workers and turning the public against the group. In this case, the costs may outstrip the benefits. How effective will the tactic be in motivating and empowering supporters? If there is much publicity but little follow-up, organization members will be demoralized.

Second, does the direct action frame issues in ways that make a good argument for the cause? The action needs to gain attention and to symbolize the issue. Throwing money into the trading pits on Wall Street attracted attention and symbolized greed; blocking a public health facility caught the public's eye and called attention to lack of care for AIDS victims.

With *sociodrama* members of the organization act out the harm people face unless changes are made, for instance, by setting up shanty housing in public squares or by having people lie down as if dead next to a nuclear reactor site. To symbolize the unfair way in which the federal budget is allocated, activists publicized how little money goes to poor people by making an eleven-foot budget pie (out of ice cream) and then cut out the tiny slice that went to those in need. The KWRU set up mock tribunals to provide evidence that the U.S. government was guilty of human rights violations because of the way the poor are treated. Large groups of antiwar people have held silent vigils around Army bases as if to mourn the (future) dead.

A dramatic turning point occurred in the civil rights campaign in Birmingham, Alabama when the children began to march. The children were in danger, symbolizing the depth of their and their parents' commitment and the meanness of the segregationists who arrested nonviolent children.

> Reporters saw things they had never seen before. George Wall, a tough-looking police captain, confronted a group of thirty-eight elementary-school children and did his best to cajole or intimidate them into leaving the lines, but they all said they knew what they were doing. Asked her age as she climbed into a paddy wagon, a tiny girl called out that she was six. (Branch, 1988, p. 757)

The knowledge that the nonviolent protester is putting his or her life in danger becomes a powerful symbol of a movement. Environmentalists who sail into nuclear test zones are risking their lives to make apparent the danger of nuclear weapons to wildlife and people. Preservationists have chained themselves to trees to block development; if the trees were to be cut down the activists would be torn apart. These protest actions are dramatic, attention focusing, and make a relevant political point.

The third set of issues activists need to consider is whether the direct actions they are considering are consistent with their values and the moral premises of the public. For groups that endorse nonviolence, are the actions they plan fully nonviolent? Do members understand the risks involved? Do the actions educate the press and the public? If participants are seen as precipitating violence, they may lose public support, even if the arguments are popular. If the direct action inconveniences large numbers of people, without a good symbolic link to the issue, it may also alienate the public. Blocking traffic may make sense in a campaign for more public transportation, but it may not make much sense in a campaign for more jobs for the unemployed.

The Acceptability of Direct Actions

Direct actions are most effective when the broader public is willing to accept them as right and just. Action organizations are caught in an interesting bind: tactics chosen must be strong enough to be compelling and outrageous enough to attract attention, yet be sufficiently acceptable to the mainstream to avoid alienating the public.

Violent and disruptive tactics are considered acceptable only in very serious situations. Over a long period of time, "unruly groups, those that use violence, strikes, and other constraints, have better than average success" (Gamson, 1997b, p. 364), but these groups were successful because the situations they faced were deemed serious enough to warrant confrontations. Rather than being punished,

> . . . those who use more unruly tactics escape misfortune because they are clever enough to use these tactics primarily in situations where public sentiment neutralizes the normal deviance of the action, thus reducing the likelihood and effectiveness of counterattack. (Gamson, 1997b, p. 364)

Another approach that allows a certain amount of disruption without retaliation occurs as activists negotiate what is planned with authorities, sometimes called the "institutionalization of protest." Activists and authorities discuss and tacitly or explicitly agree about what will occur and how (McCarthy & McPhail, 1998). As result of the institutionalization of protest, activists have won fights to carry out some disruptive activities in public forums (McCarthy & McPhail, 1998, pp. 87–91). Today, public authorities, especially the police, expect protesters to negotiate their plans in advance, to prevent the harm that occurs when people fail to understand what others intend.

Action organizations do flamboyant things:

> . . . initiating traffic blockades . . . ; chaining themselves to buildings of targets . . . and to the White House fence, disrupting network television broadcasts . . . occupying legislators' offices . . . and the U.S. Capitol (where thousands of blood-stained pennies were scattered); setting off stink bombs in the U.S. Congress . . . illegally distributing hypodermic needles to drug addicts . . . and even covering Senator Jesse Helm's house with a giant replica of a condom. (McCarthy & McPhail, 1998, pp. 102–103)

Arrests often follow such tactics, but who is arrested and when may be negotiated with public authorities, who promise not to use force in return for the tacit cooperation of the action organization (McCarthy & McPhail, 1998, p. 103). Scholars argue about whether negotiations with authorities reduce the effectiveness of protests by making their occurrence predictable. Such negotiations, though, enable activists to gain access to forums—malls, for instance, or coverage on television—that they previously lacked and reduce the chance of violence (McCarthy & McPhail, 1998, p. 109).

Guiding Direct-Action Campaigns

Community and social-action organizations plan, guide, and evaluate their direct-action campaigns. Campaigns are more likely to be successful if they are viewed as part of a broader bargaining process and tactics are chosen and implemented with this larger picture in mind.

Alinsky Tactics for Direct-Action Campaigns

Saul Alinsky focused his advice for direct action on the implicit bargaining strategies involved. For example, he argued that the organization's tactics must always keep the members involved and interested. If the members are not active and engaged, the direct action won't have any punch. He emphasized different ways that an organization with relatively less power than the opponents could win, including building an image of power, going outside the experience of the opponents, keeping the public on your side, and using ju jitsu, that is capitalizing on the mistakes of opponents.

Tactics Must Receive Support from within the Organization.   To encourage people to join in, tactics must be those enjoyed by the members of the action organization. Campaigns must be focused and when possible brief because activists want to see immediate progress (Alinsky, 1971, pp. 127–130).

Effective tactics might gently threaten those in power, only hinting at greater power. Alinsky once got the city of Chicago to concede a point, by threatening to have organization members occupy each bathroom stall at the airport. Mock press conferences can satirize people in power and have the additional advantage of being fun. Humorous tactics must be steadily applied to wear down the opposition in ways they do not expect.

Whether tactics are humorous or not, the issues have to be understandable to members. Alinsky argued that people deal better with concrete issues and clear causes than abstractions. Fighting a corporation like the telephone company can seem futile, but putting pressure on an individual with a name, a house, and a reputation in the community seems more doable. As Alinsky argued, "Pick the target, freeze it, personalize it, and polarize it" (Alinsky, 1971, pp. 127–130).

Direct Actions Should Enhance the Image of Power of Your Organization. Opponents are often stronger than community groups, so tactics may involve bluffs and threats. As Alinsky argued, "Power is not only what you have but what the enemy thinks you have" (1971, pp. 127–130). The potential for disruption may be more effective than disruption itself. Elected officials might work with an organization to prevent a mob scene in the council chambers, but if an actual demonstration occurs, they may use the police to quell the uprising and show who is in charge. The actual disruption inconveniences many and may turn potential supporters against the group, minimizing the chance of successful negotiations.

Mock the Rules of the Game.   Because opponents often control the use of force, an indirect and legal approach may be better than a head-on attack. Rather than directly challenging an unjust rule or procedure, following it to the letter can often underscore its absurdity. For example, during the Vietnam War era, protesters obeyed the law and flooded Selective Service offices (draft boards) with mail describing each change in their status. As one of the organizers explained

> We want everyone to take this law so seriously that they inform their board of every single change, even if they're over age or have already completed their service. This means wives, mothers, and friends as well. They should submit documents attesting to any change in the status of the registrant. The Selective Service just cannot stand up administratively to absolute obedience to the draft laws. (Sharp, 1973, p. 417)

Be Patient until Your Opponents Make a Mistake.   A goal of keeping the pressure up is to cause the opponents to make a mistake. Perhaps they will call the police to break up a meeting and create sympathy for those unjustly carted off. Perhaps they will deny members of the action organization the right to free speech, leading to law suits or highly publicized reversals of prior decisions.

Recently, on a college campus, an action organization was gaining little attention in its effort to protest Nike's use of sweatshops. Fortunately, a foolish campus administrator stopped the group from putting up posters. The fight over the posters and free speech gave the action organization far more publicity than did the initial cause.

Sometimes the desire of public officials to prevent a scene is so strong that they overreact. Protests in Seattle in 1999 against the World Trade Organization (WTO) provoked massive police action, including beating and arrest of a reporter trying to show his press credentials. While the media in general opposed the demonstrations, portraying them as antitrade, protest groups did succeed for the first time in drawing national attention to some key issues, showing that the WTO was overruling individual country's antipollution laws. The public learned about the underlying issues.

Anticipate the Opponent's Reaction.   Action organizations can expect opponents to arrest demonstrators or try to fire activists from their jobs. Organizations have to be prepared to support these victims. What is often harder to handle is when the opponent pretends to be conceding the issues but in fact is simply stalling. Opponents might set up a committee to investigate the problem, while planning to do nothing.

Another diversionary tactic might be for the opponent to concede that the problems are real, then demand that the action organization take responsibility for the solution. If the target is willing to provide the organization with the technical and economic resources to do so and accepts the organization's proposals with minimal change, the group members have won. Often, though, the target concedes the issue but does not provide the wherewithal to bring about an effective solution. Don't fall for this trap.

Contemporary organizers do not necessarily accept all parts of the Alinsky model but do agree that activists need to make sure that tactics are acceptable to organization members and must realistically reflect the power of the group. Further, organizers have to keep inventing new tactics to keep opponents off balance (McAdam, 1997, p. 355).

Organizational Coordination of Direct-Action Tactics

Effective campaigns require planning and monitoring. Matters that need to be addressed in advance range from deciding how disruptive or passive to be down to the details of getting parade permits or securing permission for rally sites. When civil disobedience is planned or when large groups are to assemble, organizations often negotiate with the police to establish *public order management systems* (McCarthy & McPhail, 1998, p. 104), agreeing on what rules are to be followed in carrying out their actions.

If actions are part of a broader campaign, the timing of the separate tactics has to be worked out. Picketing, for example, might precede sit-ins, and publicity may accompany both phases. Carrying out a series of linked events requires budgeting of an organization's financial and personnel resources. If the campaign is supposed to build to a crescendo, but, as time passes, the organization can get fewer and fewer people to picket or rally, the campaign will fail.

Individual actions also require detailed planning. If a group is planning to take over a floor of a building for a sit-in, leaders of the event must be sure they can get demonstrators into the building, have access to rest rooms and water, can feed the participants, and can communicate with the press, police, and emergency services. In one case, activists from a national coalition planned to occupy a federal educational agency to demand a meeting with the director to complain about the neglect of schools in poor communities. The activists rushed the building expecting to find token opposition (and even sympathy) among the targets, only to be met with strong police opposition. In its planning, the organization did not notice that a government intelligence agency shared the premises with the educational bureaucracy.

There may be many steps to be taken before the action starts. When the Dudley Street Neighborhood Initiative picketed to shut down illegal garbage sites within the community, they did a lot of preparation first:

> . . . leaflets had been dropped at hundreds of homes; follow-up home calls had been made during the previous two nights; several city officials had been invited to attend and had confirmed; hundreds of "Don't Dump on Us" buttons had been produced in three languages; rides, child care, refreshments, and translations had all been arranged. (Medoff & Sklar, 1994, p. 71)

As part of the initial planning for confrontations, event organizers should sit in a room together and predict what could possibly happen and plan how to react. What should the organization do if the police start hitting protesters? Should more militant tactics be used if the media are ignoring the events? What should the group do if the target offers to negotiate? Or if a target refuses to meet with them? What if opponents try to separate professional organizers from the group and treat them differently? Plan for every situation.

During action campaigns, organization staff should be on alert. During civil rights' protests, people from headquarters had to rush to different cities to bail people out of jail or to locate activists who had disappeared and might have been hurt or killed. Staff may maintain phone trees in case they need to call out others. If arrests are anticipated, bail money is kept in an accessible place, and activists who have checking accounts may leave signed blank checks at headquarters to pay for unseen contingencies, such as ambulance rides. Competent and supportive lawyers must be on call. Activists must have communication gear and batteries or electricity with which to power equipment if coordination is needed within a large group.

All this readiness is necessary because in the middle of a campaign a group may need to act quickly. When government officials feared that poor Haitians might be bringing AIDS to the United States, these Haitians were often detained. Campus activists found they needed to take quick action to prevent unjust deportations.

> So, instead of asking for representatives from different groups to come to meetings to "discuss what to do," the organizers publicized "emergency meetings" with an action agenda and immediate things that needed to be done. Announcements were made in classrooms and cafeterias; teach-ins were held that turned into work sessions for painting banners; everything possible was done to fill large numbers of students with an urgent sense of mission. (Jones, 1996, p. 75)

Part of readiness is training for those who will participate in any direct action. In a rally, march, or demonstration, participants must learn how to respond quickly to signals from marshals, to advance, retreat, sit down where they are, or quiet down. Targets are impressed when a large unruly crowd suddenly becomes silent at the mere suggestion of the leaders; making sure that happens requires practice.

Training can include instruction on how to breath (for a little while) when under tear gas assault, or how to deal with arrest. Everyone should have change to call the organization's lawyer, access to bail money, and have nothing in their pockets that can be construed as a weapon, not even a nail file. Participants must be sure they are not carrying any drugs or anything that could be mistaken for illegal drugs. Such items can turn an arrest for trespassing or failure to disperse into a more serious charge.

Nonviolent civil disobedience works if participants believe that violence is harmful and have undergone substantial training. Unfortunately, few people can stand a beating without wanting to fight back, so screening is required to make sure these people avoid nonviolent demonstrations. During the Montgomery bus boycotts, action organizations conducted training schools in nonviolence, and only people trained and experienced in nonviolence were allowed to become Freedom Riders (Branch, 1988, p. 438). Even after selecting the people most likely to resist provocation, organizers would be wise to make sure that those with the greatest experience are scattered throughout the group, ready to intervene if, in the heat of the moment, tempers flare.

Nonviolence training involves anywhere from a few hours to several months. Some of the training is aimed at showing the harm done by violence, while other sessions explain safety issues, such as how to protect the head when being kicked or how to fall limp, avoiding harm while inconveniencing the arresting officer. Training has to be done carefully, to avoid pushing people beyond their commitment (Branch, 1988, pp. 471–472).

Remember, even if a group has trained members to be nonviolent, the police do not always cooperate. They may take one provocation from a few people as an excuse to beat up on a large number of peaceful protesters, or they may decide to clear the streets by arresting everyone in sight. When possible, action organizations should encourage neutral parties to observe what is going on. When arrests occur, these observers can testify to what happened, identify witnesses, and otherwise assure that if the case comes to court, the protesters' side of the issue will get a fair hearing.

Forms of Direct Action

The techniques used in direct-action campaigns run from petition campaigns to sabotage. Regardless of the militancy of the tactics, however, all direct-action tactics are geared to accomplishing three ends:

- Widely publicize an issue and by so doing frame the cause and the solution in ways consonant with the goals of the action organization
- Increase the commitment of activists while mobilizing others to join in the collective efforts
- Force those in power a step closer to accepting the solution wanted by those in the action organization

Direct-action tactics fall (loosely) into three broad categories—education, mass mobilization and confrontation, and economic campaigns. With education tactics, power stems from the action organization's ability to frame the issues and shame officials and business leaders; in mass mobilization, activists create a fear of what will happen if large numbers of supporters are roused; in economic campaigns, targets are forced to comply because of financial losses they incur.

Education Tactics

Information campaigns spotlight problems and suggest solutions. Social-change organizations publicize their issues dramatically, so that officials and the public cannot ignore the problem.

Documenting Issues. Community and social policy groups document problems and publicize the results. Public interest research groups may discover stores that are misgrading meat, corporations that are selling faulty and dangerous products, or the source of polluted streams. For example,

> Equipped with hipboots, maps of streams, data sheets and a list of industries and their discharge permits, students would hike or canoe along stream beds and make systematic assessments of sources of pollution. Their findings . . . were used by local community and environmental groups as well as understaffed county, state, and federal agencies charged with monitoring industrial discharges. (Griffin, 1987, pp. 19–20)

Community groups can do their own digging for information. In Chicago, a coalition of neighborhood groups gathered figures about how much money the city spent on capital projects such as roads, sewers, and transit facilities in different parts of the city. To do this work, community members learned how to examine a capital budget, discovered that most neighborhoods (other than downtown) were short-changed, and, with the evidence in hand, demanded that the mayor set up a fairer allocation of the capital budget (Rubin, 2000b).

Sometimes the information helps shape the demands made, while other times it is used to encourage people to join the campaign, such as during a *teach-in,* which mobilizes people who might not yet be willing to join in a march or demonstration but want to learn more about what is going on. During a teach-in, people with experience and first-hand knowledge share their information, especially material that contradicts the official versions. Mass mobilizations against the war in Vietnam were inspired by dozens of such teach-ins (Gitlin, 1989, pp. 187–188), as were direct actions on environmental and health issues.

Speakers at teach-ins take apart the misleading information put out by those in power and offer alternative framings. The Vietnam teach-ins were led by academics who had been doing research on southeast Asia and had solid information to report. Employees of the State Department were invited to speak but mainly provided the official line in a constrained fashion. The energetic and direct speaking style of the war opponents combined with their scholarly mastery made the representatives of the government look duplicitous and unconvincing. Audiences composed of those soon to be drafted were eager for real news and were personally concerned with separating propaganda from fact.

Skillfully orchestrated teach-ins and community education programs are a form of ju jitsu in which opponents can be trapped into discrediting themselves. For instance,

> . . . antinuclear activists have sometimes sponsored debates with representatives of the nuclear power industry. By inviting sympathetic scientists . . . the group can directly challenge corporate or government arguments. Many groups report that industry or government representatives are often so ill-informed or deceptive that they discredit themselves. An official of Dow Chemical, for example, testified at a California public hearing on [a pesticide] that despite animal research showing testicular damage from the pesticide, it had not occurred to Dow that it might also harm human male reproductive ability. (Freudenberg, 1984, p. 139)

Complaint Tactics.   Once a group has uncovered the background of a problem, it must call attention to the issue and ask for redress. Petitions and complaints are conventional responses that can blend into direct action. A petition is a written document addressed to elected officials that contains a statement of the problems faced and a demand or request (depending upon how confrontational the group wants to be) that the problem be fixed. The documents are signed by those who agree with the statement, giving names and addresses, and often indicating voting districts, so the forms can be targeted to appropriate officials. A more modern version involves signing and circulating an electronic petition that is then routed to an elected official.

A complaint is a description of a problem that needs redressing. Complaints might be about violations of building or safety codes, speeding on residential streets, or police who ignore illegal drug supermarkets in public parks. A complaint is addressed to the responsible bureaucrat asking that the problem be repaired. Complaints become a form of direct action when an organization coordinates many people who submit their concerns at one time. Petition drives can be widely publicized through the mass media, and group members can collect signatures at malls and in public facilities. The petitions are presented to elected officials, often with many complainants and the press present. The petition or complaint can be reproduced as a large poster or attached to a roll of paper that is unrolled in public revealing thousands of signatures at once, further publicizing the cause.

More aggressive variants of petition and complaint drives have been used, for example, a fax-in. In one state, the legislature and governor had been cutting back funding for affordable housing. Rather than simply request that the money be restored, action organizations held the

> . . . first annual neighborhood fax-in . . . community organizing for the 90's. We found out that there were two fax machines in the house, two in the Senate, and one in the governor's office. And we inundated those SOB's. We set out so many faxes . . . We get a phone call . . . "the governor just called, the governor's office just called and they're listening . . . knock it off!!" and . . . it had only been two hours and we said "well gee you know, we're really not capable of doing that. We've turned them all loose." (Rubin 2000b, p. 241–242)

Fax-ins can tie up a bureaucratic office or business sponsoring a project the social action group opposes.

Cool Media Events.   Cool media events are intended to gain attention for the cause and, at the same time, indicate a solution is needed now. The events must be flamboyant enough to catch media attention but must not distract from the core message. Some efforts can backfire. For instance, gay activists have held massive marches, only to find that the press focused not on the message about discrimination but on showy cross dressers. The intended message was lost. An "outing," in which gay activists reveal that key establishment figures are homosexuals, catches media attention, portrays the hypocrisy of those in power, but can cause a backlash because the tactic violates personal privacy.

Media events should symbolize the problem in a way that is either poignant or humorous. If people are crying along with the group, as they might with a sociodrama portraying AIDS' deaths, or laughing, as they did with Alinsky's bathroom takeovers, the message can be communicated with little backlash. Symbolism must be clear:

1. Protesting the lack of rat-control measures in poor neighborhoods in Washington, DC, activist Julius Hobson threatened to trap large numbers of rats and release them in Georgetown, a posh residential area. He then drove through Georgetown with cages of rats atop his car to make the threat more dramatic.
2. To bring home the importance of water pollution, one community organization collected a bucketful of foul-smelling effluent from a factory outflow pipe at the river's edge and poured the effluent over the plush carpeting at corporate headquarters.

3. To demonstrate the hazards of radiation escaping from nuclear power plants, Californians released 2,000 helium-filled balloons at a power plant site, with the attached message: as easily as this balloon reached you, so could the radiation from Diable Canyon Nuclear Power Plant if the plant goes into operation. (1–3 from Alderson & Sentman, 1979, pp. 214–215)

4. In reaction to the firing of a secretary for not making coffee for her boss, Women Employed arrived en masse (followed by a TV camera) to a Chicago law firm. While the camera whirled, they taught the lawyers how to make coffee. (Boyte, 1980, p. 111)

5. When a representative of *Playboy* was speaking on the campus of Grinnel College, both male and female students publicly took off their clothes to protest the portrayal of women in the magazine. (Deckard, 1983, p. 339)

6. "In Yellowstone National Park . . . [environmental activists] dressed in bear suits to protest a new hotel smack in the middle of traditional grizzly bear feeding ground. When asked to leave, several members checked into the hotel and ordered berries from room service." (Savage, 1986, p. 36)

7. After being ignored by Housing Secretary Jack Kemp who had made promises to help them, the activist housing group ONE "sent a singing telegraph to one of Kemp's representative (sic) who was addressing a public meeting in Boston. Just as the representative [was] about to speak, the telegraph was delivered by a person dressed up as a chicken who sang "Jack the Giant Windbag" to the tune of "Puff the Magic Dragon." The event was reported in the *New York Times* and encouraged Congress to question Secretary Kemp. (Nyden, 1996, p. 19)

The national organization United for a Fair Economy (UFE) specializes in producing cool media events that catch public attention on issues of economic injustice. An UFE activist described a sociodrama held in Boston harbor. As explained on the Internet site Comm-Org

> Rep. Dick Armey was in Boston to promote regressive flat tax and sales tax proposals. But we're ready for him. As he was about to dump the tax code in the harbor a plastic dingy boat suddenly appeared with two protesters from UFE dressed as a working family complete with a baby doll and a sign that read "Working Family Lifeboat." At the same time members of the "Rich People's Liberation Front" started shouting for him to "Sink 'em with the Sales Tax" etc. When Armey dropped the tax code, he overturned the dingy, forcing the working family to swim to shore. We stole the show. (reported on Comm-Org 4/16/98)

In *The Activist Cookbook: Creative Actions for a Fair Economy* (United for a Fair Economy, 1997), UFE builds on insights from protest and performance art to detail a wide variety of creative, cool media events. Some of these actions involve clever design of posters—a Sun Maid Raisins' poster with a skeleton rather than the healthy woman on it, to symbolize death from herbicides—to street or guerrilla theater in which activists take over a public forum and perform skits that symbolize the problems at hand:

1. When conservatives were to end a dinner by carving up a 17-foot pie (that symbolized that everyone gets a share), activists dressed as rich business people jumped into the pie shouting out "it's all for me."
2. Activist groups will label money for instance by putting gay or lesbian stamps on dollar bills and then circulate the bills to show the importance of the gay community to the economy.
3. Public housing tenants who were receiving no help from the housing authority to set up a day-care facility, marched into the authority's office along with children and toys to set up such a center in the office.
4. Activists dressed as government and business people got into bed with each other and rolled the bed into the halls of a legislature to symbolize the tight connections between government and business (UFE, 1997, pp. 1, 10, 12, 32).

As direct actions, cool media events catch attention but rarely trigger the needed changes. Instead, they become part of a broader campaign in which other tactics more directly pressure public officials or business owners to make the needed changes.

Moral Demonstrations. In contrast to the humorous tone of the cool media events, moral demonstrations—voluntary jailing, fasts, and vigils—are totally somber events. Moral demonstrations are intended to gain attention, help mobilize additional participants, and publicly frame the issues to potential allies.

In a moral crusade, especially one that studiously follows the tenets of nonviolence, participants put themselves in danger while indicating they will not fight back. People can die during hunger strikes, they can be beat up in jail, and they can be harassed during vigils. To block construction, environmentalists fasten themselves to trees, risking their lives if bulldozers knock down the trees. The danger to the participants is what creates the power of moral demonstrations. Organizers hope that the targets of a moral campaign will concede the issue rather than face the blame if protesters are hurt or killed.

A *vigil* is a type of moral demonstration that occurs when large numbers of people appear at a location that represents the problem—a drug "shooting gallery" or the headquarters of a company that exploits child labor—and by their quiet presence call attention to the problem. During vigils people may march quietly or pray. Vigils have been held outside of jails where civil rights' workers were incarcerated. The Dudley Street Neighborhood Initiative held a vigil outside of a park that dope pushers had taken over, while in Chicago, Bethel New Life, led a prayer vigil at a hospital site to prevent its closing. Public authorities often respond positively to vigils, but even when they do not, the problem has been publicized and members mobilized.

While rare in the United States, a *hunger strike* can be an effective moral demonstration that discomforts the enemy, calls attention to the cause, and rallies supporters for further efforts. For instance, during rougher moments in the effort to unionize farm workers, Cesar Chavez, a community and labor organizer, fasted.

(Chavez) set up a monastic cell, with a small cot and a few religious articles. Soon hundreds of farm-worker families began appearing . . . to show their support for Chavez and to attend the daily mass with him. A huge tent-city, with thousands of farm workers, sprang up. . . . There was a tremendous outpouring of emotion during the masses . . . the fast became an important means of unifying farm workers and educating them about the importance of the strike and boycott. (del Castillo & Garcia, 1995, pp. 85–86)

Chavez's fast communicated to the outside world the seriousness of the workers' plight and created fear among those in power lest Chavez were to die. In addition, the fast helped unify some quarrelsome factions among movement members by evoking "part of the Mexican culture—the penance, the whole idea of suffering for something, of self-inflicted punishment" (Levy, 1975, p. 277).

Being *jailed* can be part of a moral protest. Civil rights leaders decided if arrested whether to remain in jail. For instance, as part of the Birmingham campaign, Dr. Martin Luther King, Jr., was arrested and jailed. Numerous individuals (including opponents) offered to pay his bail, but as a moral demonstration he refused to accept. The enemy was discomforted while allies in government were motivated to take action lest King be harmed. While in jail, Dr. King wrote and smuggled out his eloquent *Letter from a Birmingham Jail* that explained the moral basis of the civil rights movement.

Physical Confrontations and Mass Mobilization Tactics

Rallies, marches, sit-ins, as well as slow-downs of services, traffic blockages, and demonstrations are confrontations involving masses of individuals. These tactics are intended to interrupt the normal flow of activity and intimidate those in power. At the extreme, confrontations involve sabotage and destruction, but more often they entail a large group of people articulating complaints and demanding solutions by waving banners and making speeches. The drama of confrontations invites news coverage, while the large numbers involved suggest the possibility of disruption or, at the very least, that a block of voters will be mobilized during the next election.

Forcing Accountability on Officials.   Public officials often fail to carry out campaign promises. To help prevent politicians from reneging on promises to poor communities, the IAF uses *accountability sessions.* The organization invites politicians to attend mass meetings and the politicians accept because of the known ability of IAF to get out the vote. The politician is then seated by himself or herself on a stage and members of the group ask questions about core issues. Waffling and evasion are not allowed. Unless a clear-cut *yes* or *no* is given, the audience heckles the official. Observers describe

> Whether politicians are intimidated by the organization's ability to inform large numbers of potential voters of any failure to make or carry out a commitment or are merely impressed by the confrontation with large numbers of well-informed, low-income constituents, it is clear that the accountability sessions are the primary image of the TIAF Network carried in the minds of many politicians. (Lavine, 1997, pp. 144–145)

TIAF also used direct actions to demand accountability. For instance, Texas state representatives had promised to support a reform in a health package, but opponents used a threat of a filibuster. Members from the Texas IAF were in Austin pressuring for the bill and noted the stalling and backsliding. Then

> [r]ight at the moment that the legislative session was gaveled to end, several things happened. Members of the TIAF organizations flooded the capitol dome, yelling, charging, and effectively blocking the major exits. A group of Hispanic legislators went to the Governor's Office, accompanied by Ernie Cortes [the staff organizer] and leaders of the TIAF organization, to demand an immediate special session. . . . under all these pressures, the governor had no choice but to call a special session to begin the following day. (Wong, 1997, p. 112)

Gaining the initial access to politicians, especially for poor people's organizations, can be difficult. When one organizer was asked how his neighborhood group managed to meet privately with federal Education Secretary Riley to talk about desperately needed school construction, he responded, "when we were in Washington, I paid a visit to Riley's office, *along with six hundred of my close friends.*" He elaborated, explaining that as part of a Neighborhood Peoples' Action conference in DC, ten bus loads of people were driven to the Department of Education's office building to pressure Riley to meet with community groups. The ensemble stormed the building and demanded of a guard that Riley be informed that a meeting was wanted. Riley was out of town, but the number two in the department quickly set up a session.

Successfully carrying off such an encounter requires discipline, lest the assembled activists turn into an unruly mob, legitimating arrest. When the number two person in the education department appeared to talk with the group, there was too much noise for him or the leaders to be heard. A signal was given by one of the organizers, monitors in the group quickly passed on the sign, and complete silence instantly descended, reportedly impressing the officials with how well the protesters were organized.

Sometimes, the purpose of direct actions is more about publicizing the issue than reaching a politician. ACORN set up its national convention in Milwaukee to call attention to problems with welfare reform that appeared to be most acute in Wisconsin. As part of the convention, group members engaged in direct actions.

> The target was Wisconsin Governor Tommy Thompson, the architect of W-2 [the state's welfare to work program] who was attending a $250-a-plate dinner celebrating the opening of Milwaukee's new $200 million convention center. As guests in tuxedos and evening gowns made their way down the red carpet to the entrance, picketers marched alongside them chanting "Hey, hey, ho, ho, W-2 has got to go." Circling the entire block-long building, ACORN members made sure that Thomson couldn't escape the message even though he snuck in the back door. (*http://www.igc.apc.prog/community/reports/acornrep908.1998.contemt.html*)

Successful direct action empowers members of the organization. After one such escapade, the homeless in Illinois found that the governor of the state was willing to meet with them. And,

Alan, a Homeless on the Move for Equality (H.O.M.E) activist commented, the least powerful person[s] in this state have met the most powerful person in the state. That's what shocked a lot of people, that homeless people can go in there and speak to the governor. A lot of people spent fifty or sixty thousand dollars in his campaign and can't go in there and see him any time they want to. All we got to do is sit out there and protest and the next day we seen the governor. (Wright, 1997, p. 189)

Rallies and Public Demonstrations.   In rallies and public demonstrations, the organization (or, coalitions of like-minded groups) arrange that large numbers of people appear at one time and at one spot. Rallies and public demonstrations

- Provide supporters and potential allies with information about the issue, indicate that they are not alone, and mobilize people for further electoral and confrontational actions.
- Present information in ways that provide to the public the organization's framing of the issue. The large numbers involved in a rally are the lure meant to attract the mass media, that, in turn, communicate the campaign's message to the public.
- Show the opposition that the action organization is capable of mobilizing large numbers of people. Much of the impact of a rally comes from showing that the group can successfully carry it off.

Care is needed so that the different objectives of a rally or demonstration remain compatible. Speakers should make strong, enthusiastic statements that inspire the troops and prepare for further action, but these statements have to be constructed to communicate well in the mass media. The goal is to explain the problem and the need for a solution, not to turn the demonstration itself into the object of media attention. The news should lead off with "people displaced by the new highway demand safe housing" not "police curtail unruly mob."

The history of social activism provides many examples of effective public demonstrations. The 1963 March on Washington for Civil Rights is legendary for Dr. King's "I Have a Dream" speech and for the size and excitement of the huge crowd. The whole nation (including the president and vice president) were exposed to the power of King's oratory. Hundreds of thousands participated in that rally. Another huge rally took place to support maintaining abortion rights when the Supreme Court seemed to be weakening those rights.

Small rallies and demonstrations can also be effective, especially if used as part of a larger campaign. In recent years, campus groups in the United States have demonstrated against Nike and other clothing manufacturers who exploit child labor in manufacturing their products. These efforts are part of campaigns to pressure stores not to purchase the products and to insist that universities not allow their logos to be used on goods made by sweatshop labor. Activists have also mounted direct actions to support living wage ordinances at city halls all over the country. These ordinances prevent cities from lowering costs by contracting out services to companies that pay very low wages. Protesters have rallied outside city hall to make their case and to indicate the breadth of community support for such ordinances.

Core to any rally are the speakers; sometimes who speaks is as important as what is said. As part of a campaign to stop illegal dumping in their neighborhood, the Dudley Street Neighborhood Initiative (DSNI) held a rally next to the dump site. Mayor Flynn got word of what was happening, and with staff and media in tow, showed up, spoke to the group, and promised his support. His presence helped to solve the immediate problem and, equally important, gave the DSNI visibility and legitimacy.

At rallies, speakers engage those in the audience, asking for a show of hands and inviting boisterous responses such as cheers, applause, amens, or shouted encouragements. Speeches portray the problem of concern and outline the solutions the group is demanding. Effective speeches combine motivating rhetoric and background information that teaches those attending the rally and the public about the issue.

One observer described a series of rallies, with crowds from 70 to 8,000 people, sponsored by the South Bronx Churches, an IAF affiliate, who were campaigning to gain control over land and obtain the financing to build affordable housing. Speakers emphasized the need for the improved housing and, then "dripping with contempt" and "pound[ing] home a class-driven analysis" (Rooney, 1995, p. 142) speakers contrasted the more affordable, better quality single-family homes that the IAF wanted to build with smaller condos that the city was willing to provide. People were then asked to join in the ongoing political battle (Rooney, 1995, pp. 141–149).

While few organizers plan huge national rallies, the chances are good that a more modest rally will end up part of a local campaign. Such events require considerable attention to detail. The following are some guidelines (modified from Burghardt, 1982a; Cassidy, 1980; Midwest Academy, 1976/1981):

1. Look over the rally site. If it's a wide plaza, make sure the camera will be located in places that make the group appear larger. Place loudspeakers so everyone can hear. If the rally is taking place inside a building, make sure people can get in. If the rally is being held in a public forum or on the turf controlled by the opposition, plant somebody inside just in case the opposition tries to lock the door.

2. Publicize the event, but in doing so slightly underestimate the size of the turnout. If activists estimate that 100 people will be there, announce that 75 will show up and try to get a space that will hold 70 to 100. Don't underestimate by too much, though, lest supporters be discouraged and not show.

3. Do the leg work to ensure that people will turn out. Don't rely on mass advertising alone. If it is a neighborhood rally, leaflet each home, a day or two in advance. Maintain a telephone network of supporters and call them; have supportive clergy announce the event in church.

Make sure that the events are held at convenient times. For larger rallies that are often held away from peoples' homes, arrange for transportation. If a rally is to be held at a distant site, buses must be chartered (and paid for) in advance, and adequate time provided for the trip. Use the time in driving to let people get to know each other better, share stories about the problems they face, and talk about how to behave during the speeches.

4. Both activists and speakers should work out in advance what will happen at the rally. The time to come up with creative ideas is in the working sessions held while planning the event, not in front of the mass media. A call for a frontal rush on the guarded office of the target at a nonviolent rally or an unplanned request that large numbers of people sit-in in business offices can leave a group in disarray.

5. Arrange for crowd control. Avoid chaos by making sure enough bathrooms and drinking water are available. Encourage people to listen respectfully to speakers, to feel free to show enthusiasm but to do so in ways that reflect positively on the group. For large rallies, marshals should be placed strategically throughout the group, to watch for excessively boisterous participants, or plants from the enemy, and to coordinate action, such as a safe retreat.

6. Music can be an important part of a rally. Protest songs give off the core message of the group, while singing together helps unify people. An active band on the podium quickly gets the attention of large numbers of people and can help maintain focus if the crowd becomes restless.

7. Try to make sure that speeches, messages on signs, and other communications are easily available to the mass media. If speeches are written out in advance make sure the media receive a copy. If the highlight of the rally is a flag burning and that is the image the group wants to communicate make sure the media know where to point their cameras. If the goal is to communicate factual details—mortgage discrimination, for instance—make sure that the media receive a fact sheet, and make sure the rally hears comments by a young couple talking about their inability to find housing. Assign an articulate spokesperson to work with the media.

8. Try to arrange speeches in ways that balance those meant to intimidate opponents with those that stir up supporters. Because people who are undecided about issues might be paying attention to rallies, in dress and mannerisms try to present a "cooler"—less disruptive—image than the content of the messages might indicate. A neatly dressed speaker can get away with a militant speech without appearing so threatening on the six o'clock news that the message is ignored. Clergy, especially those from churches that encourage oratorical skill, make especially fine speakers. Their cloth gives off an image of social morality, and most people listen courteously to religious folk, especially when their message is phrased in religious parables.

Paint slogans or complaints neatly to encourage them to be photographed, but if even mild threats are part of the rally, try not to put them in easily photographable formats. Targets will hear the threats anyway, so why chance alienating others.

Rallies are a good time to stage imaginative media events. A musical chairs game in which each chair represents a missing job, and someone gets left out at the end, might symbolize a shrinking economy. A mock funeral, for example, burying an effigy of "affirmative action" after the state stops enforcing it, makes the point clearly, yet maintains the culturally accepted solemnity of a funeral.

9. Plan the end of the rally. Organizers should not leave large numbers of inflamed people milling around. Police raids can occur after the speeches are over. Trouble makers may prey on chatting groups of demonstrators, trying to start a violent episode. One way to end the rally is to march together singing solidarity songs, which keep up the spirit and which make sure people are leaving together in an orderly fashion.

10. Make sure that information is available at the rally site for those who want to join the organization.

Marches.   A march is a demonstration on the move. The themes of marches are presented on banners and signs and in accompanying press releases. Marches are meant to widely publicize a problem, by literally bringing it in front of many people.

Recently the KWRU organized a series of national marches and caravans— marches by car—pointing out the plight of the welfare and working poor. Signs communicated the campaign messages, "Housing is a Human Right"; "Poverty is not a Crime"; "End Poverty Not Welfare." The demonstrators also ask for support: "Honk for Justice." The signs indicated the variety of groups that supported the action (Orland, 1998). The KWRU-inspired marches originated in separate cities, gained participants from a variety of neighborhood action organizations, and converged on important symbolic sites, such as Washington, DC or Wall Street. Antiwar marches have targeted the Pentagon or military bases; after arriving at the site, organizations hold a rally.

For the most part, marches are intended to publicize an issue and show that many people care about the issue. At times, however, marches can be disruptive. Bicyclists, for example, might take over roads through a bike-in march, to demand more bike lanes and saner transportation policies.

The form of marches (sometimes done in vehicles rather than on foot) can symbolize issues. To preserve abortion rights, three generations of women marched together, symbolizing the issues that unified them. During the civil rights era, Freedom Riders rode in integrated buses through the segregated South, symbolizing the brutality of the opposition (as some buses were destroyed) and the courageous dedication of the protesters (Payne, 1995, p. 107 ff). To show that segregation was not simply a Southern problem, Dr. Martin Luther King, Jr. led marches in Chicago and nearby Cicero where participants were taunted and stoned.

A number of steps have to be taken in advance to assure a successful march. In most cities permits are required. Routes must be carefully chosen. When marches are held at distant places, transportation has to be planned. No matter what the focus of the march, signs are needed to convey the group's message. March monitors have to be chosen and trained to guide the assembled group and to calm down the fracas if one occurs.

Picketing.   Picketing is more aggressive than marching. Its purpose is less to publicize a problem than to embarrass and inconvenience opponents, while loudly proclaiming the misdeeds of the target.

With picketing, activists choose a site of symbolic importance or of value to the opponents, such as a nuclear plant or a sweat shop. Activists march around the site, expressing their grievance on signs or with chanted slogans. In *informational picketing* activists march at a site but do not block entrances or exits, allowing customers and workers to come and go. With more aggressive picketing that might violate laws against trespassing activists surround a site, march around its entrances and exits, and while not physically stopping someone from entering or leaving, try to make it socially awkward for people to cross the picket line.

To oppose redlining, protesters have picketed banks in ways that inconvenience customers and embarrass the managers. People from the Dudley Street neighborhood picketed illegal dump sites, blocking vehicles and forcing the city to shut down these health hazards. Daring individuals from neighborhoods beset with drug problems have picketed the open-air "drug supermarkets" in their communities, sometimes also picketing the homes of suburban customers of the dope dealers. Protesters have surrounded nuclear reactor sites to point out the dangers of nuclear energy, while members of the Love Canal Homeowners Association in their fight against toxic wastes picketed the governor of New York and later President Carter. In the Vietnam War era, activists picketed military draft boards and recruitment offices, while today, the home offices of manufacturers that exploit labor are the subjects of informational picketing.

Social change organizations use picketing to achieve immediate solutions; they promise to stop picketing when their problems are addressed. Through a combination of picketing and cool media events, ACT-UP has gained publicity for AIDS victims and changed government policies. ACT-UP picketed a cardinal (whose pronouncements seemed unsympathetic to AIDS victims), pharmaceutical companies, and the offices of government bureaucrats. Their aggressive actions have had an impact:

> "There's no doubt that they've had an enormous effect," said Dr. Stephen C. Joseph, the New York City Health Commissioner who himself has been a target of ACT-UP's ire. "We've basically changed the way we make drugs available in the last year." (DeParle, 1990, p. 11)

Today help for AIDS victims can be obtained through conventional politics, but it took the aggressive direct actions of groups such as ACT-UP to put the issue on the policy agenda.

In planning picketing, community and social-action organizations need to consider several issues. Where should the group do its picketing? Try to choose a place that best communicates the group's concerns. Seriously inconveniencing a bank that won't make loans in the neighborhood sends a more effective message than picketing a minor retail outlet that sells clothing made with ill-paid foreign labor. Is there sufficient support from the broader public to make the picketing effective? If people simply cross the picket lines, shouting angrily at the picketers, perhaps informational picketing should be done first. Picketing that inconveniences a broad, uninformed public might create sympathy for the target. People who want to buy milk at the super market on their way home from work, might not be sympathetic to picketers' demands that the store buy fruits only from farms that reduce the use of pesticides. Will counterpicketing occur, leading to distracting confrontations between two groups? If so, the group should plan to get its message across in press releases or in interviews away from the immediate scene of the picketing.

Volunteers need to be trained, especially not to respond to taunts or provocations. Some cities restrict the types of materials that can be used for picket signs to prevent them from turning into weapons. Activists must find out the laws and use the appropriate materials for pickets. Finally, the organization needs to take the usual preparations to handle arrests.

Sit-Ins. In sit-ins, activists take over space by occupying an area and refusing to move. When target organizations are more or less sympathetic to activists, sit-ins can blur into a form of cool media event. For instance, students concerned about exploited labor in the clothing industry have taken over university offices and held knit-ins to pressure universities not to allow their logos to be used on products made by exploited laborers (Van der Werf, 1999, p. A38).

Sit-ins inconvenience the opponent by taking over offices or shutting down highways, lunch counters, lobbies, or other public places. Advocates for the homeless have encamped in public parks and outside government buildings, demanding that the public sector pay attention to their plight (Wright, 1997). Typically, they have been forceably removed by the police. Native Americans have seized small military facilities, demanding that the land be converted to Indian cultural centers (Nagel, 1996, p. 165). Sit-ins can be confrontational and lead to arrest because the activists are trespassing.

To succeed, sit-ins must visibly symbolize the problem and focus the disruption on those opponents who can resolve the issue. African Americans who refused to move from lunch counters until they were served symbolized the injustice and humiliation of segregation. When state laws abrogated the fishing rights of Native Americans (rights guaranteed by treaties), activists staged a fish-in, an active form of a sit-in, catching fish (illegally, according to state law) in full sight of the game warden (Sharp, 1973, p. 318).

Leaders of sit-ins often press for immediate gains. Activists in the welfare rights movement in Massachusetts sat in the offices of the welfare agencies demanding services to which the law entitled them (Bailis, 1974, pp. 47–54). The directors of the offices had the authority to grant their demands and often did. More recently, student activists have used sit-ins in university presidents' offices to demand better racial balances on campuses or the start of study programs that emphasize multicultural concerns.

Sit-ins work by disrupting a flow of people or of work and can be accomplished in ways that do not physically involve trespass. For example, when employees want to change rules of their organization, they are already in place, so a sit-in makes little sense. Instead, protesters might employ a tactic called *working to the rule*. Rather than staying home from work or directly fighting absurd organizational procedures, employees so precisely follow each procedure that the whole flow of work slows down. In a campaign to improve salaries and facilities, doctors at Boston City Hospital held a heal-in. They admitted every patient who could possibly benefit from hospital care and then provided the best medical service possible. The facility was soon overcrowded, and serious negotiation with the hospital administration began (Sharp, 1973, p. 394).

Sit-ins require careful preparation. First, some knowledge of how the target is likely to respond is important. Will the police be called in to arrest the participants or will the target try to maintain a good public image by supplying food and water? Second, check out the site carefully. Who controls the water and from what location? If water and electricity are shut off to the building being occupied, what other buildings will be affected? Where are the bathrooms? Can the police sneak in through a back door? Will those arrested be carried out through a door that the media cannot see? Are participants prepared to tolerate long periods of boredom? Do people have sleeping bags if a long action is planned? Make sure people who need medicines have them with them, and, if arrest is possible, make sure that participants have bail arranged and don't have anything incriminating on their persons. If arrest is not wanted, check out if there are escape routes. Plan to use the time in sitting-in to share information or experiences about the problem at hand, especially if the media are present.

Because the goal of a sit-in is to force some immediate concessions, members of the action organization must be available to negotiate with the target. Details on how to plan for such negotiations will be presented in the next chapter. Just make sure that there is careful coordination between the timing of sit-ins and that of the negotiations. Giving up the sit-in too early weakens the leverage of the action organization; too late, and the organization appears unwilling to negotiate and gets labeled as more interested in the glory of the action than in resolving problems.

Destructive Violence and Monkey Wrenching. In many campaigns, progress can appear particularly slow and victories scarce. In response, some organizations resort to violence. During the Vietnam War era, the Weather Faction broke off from the Students for a Democratic Society and its members engaged in sabotage and bombings. Road Rage in England publicizes ways of physically destroying road construction equipment to stop highways, carefully details how to mob the police to help people avoid arrest, and describes ways of responding to tear gas attacks. Militant animal rights groups invade medical and scientific laboratories, destroying equipment and releasing the animals. While most of the emphasis during the civil rights era was on nonviolent actions, groups such as the Deacons for Defense armed themselves, and members of militant ethnic power movements are often pictured with their weapons.

Monkey wrenching involves sabotaging the work of the opponent. It lies on the border between symbolic and violent protest. For instance, to protest overfishing, a flotilla of small fishing boats in Canada surrounded larger ships, literally stopping commerce. Other organizations intentionally deface signs and billboards to present their case—antismoking slogans written over pictures of the Marlboro man, for instance. Opponents of lumbering that denudes mountains sometimes put spikes in trees, which destroys the trees' economic value as lumber. If lumberjacks hit the spikes, they can get seriously injured. Even though activist groups warn that trees have been spiked, we oppose such tactics because of their potential for harm.

Monkey wrenching has proved popular. Primers on the subject sell well (Russell, 1987, p. 31) and numerous Internet sites exist that focus on more destructive tactics. Why? In part, people get frustrated by the slow speed of change and the indifference of government to some problems. In the short run, sabotage and monkey wrenching seem effective: Trees with spikes are not cut down. But activists should question whether such short-run successes contribute to the longer-term economic and political changes needed to resolve the problems.

Economic Tactics

Economic campaigns are intended to bring about change by causing financial hardships for the opponents. Given the severe imbalance in financial strength between most activist organizations and their targets, economic tactics usually require that the broader public or the government be brought into the fray.

Effective *coercive* sanctions occur when activists pressure government to use its economic power against the opponent. To combat mortgage discrimination, housing activists rely upon economic sanctions that the government can impose on financial institutions. By law, banks require permission from government regulators to merge or open new branches but cannot be given such permission if they are shown not to be in compliance with the Community Reinvestment Act (CRA). If banks seem to be discriminating against poor communities, activists try to force regulatory agencies to hold time-consuming hearings before the regulators grant the permission. The delays that could occur would be sufficiently costly that banks find that it is smarter to enter into community reinvestment agreements than to battle the community groups.

In a *boycott,* people refuse to purchase from a company or buy particular products unless and until certain changes are made. Consumer groups sometimes sponsor boycotts to protest price increases, ethnic groups organize tourism and convention boycotts of cities that discriminate, and feminist organizations tried to set up boycotts of states that refused to pass the Equal Rights Amendment. Environmentalists have organized boycotts of tuna that was caught in ways that endanger dolphins, and Greenpeace tried to organize a boycott of all products from nations that refused to stop whaling.

On occasion, if the membership and immediate supporters of an action organization are numerous enough, their boycott can have an impact on the targets. When the African American community boycotted stores in smaller and middle-sized southern cities, the economic loss was sufficient to convince the small merchants to hire Black sales staff and be more courteous in selling to African Americans. Usually, however, the number of people actively involved in the direct action organization is too small to have much of an impact, so allies are needed. The most famous boycott in recent times was part of the campaign led by Cesar Chavez to organize farm labor. Workers' strikes were not enough, but owners eventually gave in when a nationwide boycott of scab grapes was organized and supported by organized labor.

In addition, a company that has a reputation for social responsibility to uphold or one that has had recent economic difficulties may be vulnerable to a boycott (Friedman, 1996, pp. 161–162). For example, an action organization set up an international boycott against Nestles for marketing baby formula in poor countries. The formula was less healthy than breast feeding. The direct economic impact was minor compared to the negative publicity that implied a company that sells baby food was not concerned about the health of babies. Recently, groups organized boycotts against designer labels made in plants that exploit child labor. These boycotts are part of a broader campaign that also involves picketing sweat shops and a series of cool media events that bring negative publicity on the celebrities who endorse the product (Salomon, 1996). In this case, it is the publicity more than the economic loss that is effective.

Laws against secondary boycott, in which a merchant who sells a targeted product is avoided, make it difficult to carry out some actions. While it is legal to encourage people not to buy a particular product such as Nikes, it is illegal to tell them not to shop in a store that sells Nikes. It is possible to get around such limitations. For instance, during the era of the grape boycott with a

> "shop-in" . . . a respectable-looking housewife entered the store, filled her basket and then suddenly discovered that these were scab grapes. She demanded to see the manager. How could he put scab grapes on the shelves when some farm worker's children were starving? The drama became the center of attention. With the eyes of the checkers and customers riveted on the front of the store, the housewife lectured the grocer and then triumphantly marched from the store with children in tow. (Jenkins, 1985, pp. 168–169)

Other approaches are used to create indirect economic pressure. Activists can buy stock in large companies and show up at the annual meetings to ask questions about dubious policies. Increasingly companies have set up rules for conducting annual meetings that make it harder for small stock owners to voice their concerns.

A *strike* is an economic sanction in which workers deprive companies of labor to improve their salaries or work conditions. Historically, community organizers have had little to do with labor battles. In recent years, though, people have learned that management decisions to reduce salaries, cut back the labor force, or shut down a plant, warehouse, or office affect far more than the firm's employees. Today, while laborers are carrying out a strike, community members organize to provide backup support, through food donations, help on the picket line, or by convincing businesses not to demand cash from those on strike.

In a *tenants' strike,* renters living in a building or complex who confront a problem, such as poor maintenance or lack of heat, band together and refuse to pay rent until the landlord has solved the problem. On occasion, a sympathetic city government might help the tenants by stepping up code enforcement, but for the most part tenants are on their own. Tenants' strikes usually focus on unscrupulous landlords, but public housing authorities can also be targeted, as much of public housing is poorly maintained. In recent years, as HUD has started to tear down public housing, activists have organized people to withhold rent until adequate replacement housing is guaranteed.

Tenants' strikes are difficult to pull off. Unlike picketing or public demonstrations that can be seen as protected speech rights or labor actions that are guaranteed by the National Labor Relations Board, in many states tenants are not allowed to withhold rent, no matter what the landlord is doing. Fortunately, in other states, tenants experiencing inadequate services can legally withhold rent, but the rent money must be set aside in an escrow account that is held by a third party until the dispute is resolved. In some places, the tenants' organization can withdraw money from the escrow account to make repairs in the building if the landlord does not make them.

Convincing people to participate in a tenants' strike can prove difficult, because renters are afraid they will be evicted. During rent strikes, landlords often try to destroy tenant solidarity by pressuring or bribing a few to break ranks with costrikers. Several counter-strategies are used. In one

> . . . organizers promoted what they called the "rent slowdown" . . . a strategy in which all tenants held back their rents until the middle of the month, when the tenant leader handed them all to the landlord at the same time. It was an eloquent demonstration of tenant solidarity, and therefore, also a warning to the landlord, who often responded to tenant grievances at this point. For the tenants, it was in fact an organizational and emotional preparation for a strike should the landlord ignore the warning. (Lawson, 1986, pp. 227–238)

Organizers of tenants' strikes try to meet frequently with participants, usually in group sessions, to bolster resolve. Another way of creating group solidarity is for tenants' groups from different housing complexes to schedule rolling rent strikes. With this approach, only selected landlords are struck, but tenants in the allied groups support and encourage the strikers. Doing so can divide landlord against landlord rather than tenant against tenant.

Problems with Confrontation Tactics

Because confrontation tactics can be risky, their benefits and costs must be carefully thought out. Will the proposed actions get attention, properly frame the issue, and pressure the target to change? Or will they be more a form of showmanship that might feel good but accomplishes little? Will confrontations help build solidarity among different social-change groups or will they exacerbate tensions? For example, are the participants primarily males of a certain color, leaving out females and people of other colors? Will mainstream, feminist activists get upset when more militant, lesbian groups gain attention through a march, but in doing so frame the issue as one of gender orientation rather than sexual discrimination?

Do the direct actions truly cause the opposition to capitulate, or are they more likely to backfire and become an excuse for the opponents to fight back with increased force? Are demonstrators getting beat up and arrested? Are legislators passing restrictive laws making protests more difficult and repression easier? Are targets fighting back by spreading rumors about the sexual morality of those leading direct actions or raising questions of financial propriety? Do confrontations motivate opponents to work with those in office to undo progressive changes?

Confrontations often motivate opponents to fight back. For instance, in response to direct actions by feminist groups, conservatives led by Phyllis Schlafly "established a national movement STOP ERA . . . within months Schlafly had constructed a minutely organized campaign which could respond immediately where action was necessary" (Hartman, 1989, p. 136).

Direct-action tactics can lead to vindictive behavior against innocent bystanders. In one case, as part of a direct-action campaign parents conducted to improve schools,

> [t]he teachers raised the stakes with retribution on the activists' children and even in some cases on whole classes of children. Some of our children soon went for days without being called on. . . . Retribution on the children was one of the teachers' most effective ways of fragmenting parental opposition, deterring parents from "making waves." (Stern, 1998, p. 121)

When demonstrations, marches, picketing, or boycotts are over, organizers must ask what has been accomplished. A successful teach-in or march gives glory to all who are involved, but has preparing for the event taken away time from more fundamental work? Cesar Chavez, who gained fame from moral demonstrations, picketing, and protest marches, still emphasized that

> . . . a movement with some lasting organization is a lot less dramatic than a movement with a lot of demonstrations and a lot of marches and so forth. The more dramatic organization does catch attention quicker. Over the long haul, however, it's a lot more difficult to keep together because you're not building solid. (Chavez, 1984, p. 28)

Environmentalists in mainstream groups such as the Sierra Club, often consider direct-action organizations such as Earth First! as showboaters. During the civil rights era, members of the Student Non-Violent Coordinating Committee (SNCC) who worked day-in-day-out to help African Americans organize, learn how to run their own organizations, and gain voting rights, resented the publicity and acclaim from the large demonstrations led by Dr. Martin Luther King, Jr. (Payne, 1995). Activists in Appalachia managed to shut down strip mines and enforce reclamation laws using direct actions, but strip-mining persisted, because the opposition had better staying power. As an organizer explained:

> . . . it is clear that we did not give enough thought to how direct action would translate into a movement capable of mobilizing a lot of people. . . . Some of us were influenced by romantic slogans and the notions of armed struggle which were part of the antiwar movement of the late 1960s. We did not appreciate the long, slow work that fundamental social change requires. (Bingham, 1993, pp. 28–29)

"Building solid" should always be a goal, even when engaged in direct action. People are empowered only when they control an organization that has staying power. By encouraging new participants to join the organization, confrontation tactics can help build community capacity.

The final and most important concern about confrontation tactics is whether they lead to long-term solutions. Faced with the threat of a sit-in or ongoing demonstrations, an opponent might concede for the moment, only to renege later on. To stop the direct actions, those in power might propose a variety of *pseudosolutions* that do little to solve the underlying problem. Is establishing a human relations committee sufficient to solve fundamental problems of racism or sexism, or is it merely a ploy to quiet things down?

Successful direct-action campaigns should lead to long-lasting institutional solutions. Ideally, tenants should aim not only to convince landlords to provide the needed services but also to change the laws so that courts support tenants in housing disputes. Housing advocates should not only achieve the promise of some additional affordable houses or apartments but also work for legislation that will fund affordable housing over the long haul and will give community groups influence over how that money will be spent.

Long-term vigilance is required or the benefits from direct action will turn out not to be real. Through action campaigns, citizens in Chicago were able to convince the police to set up community policing programs. But doubts persisted on how well the program was being implemented. To find out, the Chicago Alliance for Neighborhood Safety had to sue the police department using the Illinois Freedom of Information Act (Anonymous, 1998, pp. 1–2). In response to both legal and direct action campaigns, banks in many cities have agreed to set up community reinvestment efforts. These programs have dramatically increased the amount of money for affordable housing but have done little to assure that business and commercial loans that are also needed are made available in poorer communities. Further, banks continue to pressure federal authorities to weaken CRA requirements, and increasingly loans are made by new financial entities that are not covered by CRA requirements (Schwartz, 1998).

To summarize, direct actions can be stimulating, intimidate the opposition, entice organizational members and supporters to join together, while dramatically calling attention to problems. Yet, the possibility of violence and the threat that the enemy will vigorously strike back should create caution among those contemplating confrontational tactics. The drama of the actions should not distract from their fundamental purpose of forcing changes upon recalcitrant opponents. Equally important, community and social action organizations must look beyond the immediate tactics, to assure that laws are changed and that agreements are implemented.

14 Extending Power through Coalitions, Publicity, and Skillful Negotiations

Through political tactics and direct actions, social-change organizations pressure opponents to make needed changes. Succeeding can be difficult as the opponents are usually wealthier than the social-change group, while the mass media tends to favor those already in power. To increase the chances that campaigns against powerful opponents will bring about change, organizers set up *coalitions* of community and social-change organizations that add numbers and expertise to their side. In addition, activists learn how to garner the *publicity* that reframes issues in support of social change, while working to master the *bargaining and negotiations* skills that assure what is won in the streets or through political work is not lost at the bargaining table.

Working with Other Organizations

A *coalition* involves two or more organizations working together to accomplish a common purpose (Roberts-DeGennnaro, 1997). Some coalitions involve separate groups from one neighborhood acting together to preserve the community against a common threat, such as a highway that destroys the neighborhood or overcrowding in schools, while others such as the National Low Income Housing Coalition coordinate tactics of its widely scattered national membership in campaigns to bring about affordable housing.

Coalitions enable organizations to work together even when their aims and approaches are not entirely the same. Neighborhood groups that fear the breakdown of community can work with labor unions concerned about the loss of jobs in joint efforts to pressure manufacturers not to abandon working class neighborhoods (Nissen, 1995; Simmons, 1994). Inner-city organizations have formed coalitions with suburban groups concerned with finding jobs for the underemployed (Orfield, 1998). During the campaign for the Equal Rights Amendment:

> One organization within the [coalition] movement would attract a more conservative membership, another a more radical one. Internally, this decentralization let members of each group feel more comfortable with one another. Externally, the division of labor made possible a "Mutt and Jeff" (or "good cop"/"bad cop") act, in which the more conservative organization could tell relevant power holders that if certain concessions

> were not forthcoming it could not hold back the radicals much longer. (Mansbridge, 1986, p. 194)

During the civil rights movement in the 1960s, groups that differed in the respective importance of fighting for jobs, the end of Jim Crow, or voting rights joined umbrella coalitions such as Council of Federated Organizations (COFO) and collectively fought against racist local governments (Payne, 1995). In Chicago, a housing alliance brought together activists who used militant tactics to demand funds for affordable housing with the development organizations that built the homes. The Environmental Justice Movement unites those who oppose new industrial plants that destroy the environment with African American activists who want more jobs for the poor. Working together in coalitions, these separate groups fight together to bring about jobs that respect the environment and the health of the workers.

Once people work together in coalitions they discover common problems and framings that encourage future joint actions. After joining together in some common battles, women's groups that had formed separately to work on a wide array of causes—low pay, sexual exploitation, day care—discovered the underlying gendered nature of many of the problems they shared (Naples, 1998). In Milwaukee, after an arrested African American man died under suspicious circumstances, over five dozen groups came together, ranging from neighborhood associations to revolutionary African American organizations (Woliver, 1993, p. 81). The coalition, initially set up to obtain justice in this one case, enabled people to address the structural racism that permitted the abuse of police power.

Organizations that fear retribution from those in power are more likely to fight back as part of a coalition. For instance, housing organizations find they have to conduct direct action campaigns against the agencies who allocate needed funds. They appear to be biting the hand that feeds them, but without the pressure money will not be forthcoming. So instead of individually confronting the funders, coalitions do the pressuring, as an activist described:

> . . . there is a strategy you're finding more, especially with this [more conservative city] administration in office. People are creating [pause], I tend to call them shell coalitions. And, a shell coalition stands up and say [shouts] "Mayor so and so." And, so you [the mayor] get mad at that coalition and mad at that staff person executive director of the coalition. (Rubin, 2000b)

In Chicago, the Neighborhood Capital Budget Group (NCBG) formed a shell coalition of housing advocates, economic developers, community developers, and neighborhood groups. This coalition conducted direct actions to redirect the city's capital budget, an approach that threatened Chicago's politics as usual. During the campaign, people employed by the shell coalition led the aggressive actions, allowing the housing organizations to avoid offending the people who would fund them (Rubin, 2000b). Shell coalitions protect their members from retaliation by creating a buffer between those who need the money and those who are pressuring government for the funds.

Coalitional Structures

Coalitions come in many forms, some short lived, others lasting for generations. Among the short-lived coalitions are *coordinating committees* that organize a particular event, such as a march, and then disband once the event is over. A variety of neighborhood associations might come together this way, for instance, to protest an interstate highway, and then once the actions are over resume their separate activities.

Response networks provide another form of short-lived and intermittent cooperation in which separate organizations keep in contact with each other, monitor problems and when the issues overlap work together for a time. For instance, when abortion rights are attacked, feminist and civil libertarian organizations unite and then go their own way once the immediate crisis has passed. In battles to stop the construction of dangerous rubbish incinerators, environmental organizations join with neighborhood groups in such response networks (Walsh et al., 1997, p. 89). Such cooperative efforts ebb and flow over time.

Action organizations from different neighborhoods or cities that share a philosophy about how to battle problems join together in more permanent *networks* or *alliances*. Well-known national networks include Associations of Community Organizations for Reform Now (ACORN), Citizens Action, National People's Action, the Industrial Areas Foundation, Pacific Institute for Community Organizations (PICO), Direct Action for Research Training (DART), and Gamaliel. Most networks maintain a central staff to provide technical assistance to member groups, sponsor training programs, and share information on national political and social trends. The network highlights the national problem, while the affiliates carry out actions locally.

Many issues require more time to monitor than individual community or social change organizations can afford. To stay on top of these matters, smaller organizations form *support coalitions* whose staff spends full time monitoring and lobbying on shared issues. Neighborhood housing organizations establish city-wide housing coalitions to keep watch over city hall; these supportive coalitions call for help from members only when pressure is required (Goetz, 1993). In Washington, DC, the National Community Reinvestment Coalition spends full time making sure that Congress does not gut the Community Reinvestment Act (CRA). When aggressive action is needed the coalition phones and e-mails its members, urging them to lobby their legislators or join in direct actions to preserve CRA.

Building Coalitions

The advantages gained from coalition work seem obvious—larger numbers of people confront the opponent, retaliation is harder, and each organization can share what it learned with the others, reducing future mistakes. Yet, in practice, coalition work is difficult. Potential allies may resent the loss of autonomy or may disagree about the legitimacy of specific tactics. Organizations can be more or less militant, more or less revolutionary, and differ in their willingness to engage in civil disobedience. In the antinuclear campaigns, for instance, coalitions were hard to form because

> [m]any of the people who might have pushed strongly for a low keyed grassroots strategy were not only worried about opposition strength, but profoundly concerned about re-

maining respectable and disassociated with those who did civil disobedience. (Zisk, 1989b, pp. 18–19)

Coalitions break apart over philosophical differences. Though helping each other in the vicious civil rights battles in the South, the members of the COFO coalition could not see eye-to-eye on electoral politics, and, as a result, the coalition fell apart (Dittmer, 1994, pp. 338–362). Individual organizations might quarrel over money, membership, or credit claiming, while racial rivalries that divide neighborhoods can disrupt community coalitions. Organizations compete with each other to obtain the increasingly limited number of grants available. Societal stratification can make coalition work difficult, for example, when the homeless felt they were treated as second class citizens by their financially better-off allies within the same coalition (Wright, 1997, p. 223).

To build coalitions with any sticking power, activists need to learn how to develop unity between different organizations. Coalitions are more likely to work if member organizations agree on ideology or share similar understandings of why problems occur. The chances of coordination increase between organizations if they are equally skilled in administrative matters. Groups with similar organizational cultures work together more easily. For instance, organizations that make decisions by consensus are unlikely to work easily with groups that deferently follow a charismatic leader, no matter how similar the organizations are in their goals. The more frequent the contact between members of different organizations, the greater the likelihood of successful coordination (Rogers & Whetten, 1982, pp. 54–94). Coordination is more effective when either the leaders of the group or the professional organizers staffing the group know one another and have shared experiences (Galaskiewicz & Stein, 1981). One purpose of the conferences held by the National Organizers Alliance is to facilitate this sharing and make it easier for groups to coordinate future efforts.

Sometimes the actions of the enemy virtually force organizations to come together, almost irrespective of their ideologies. Because of the ideological competition within the different sectors of the women's movement, long-term coalitions have been hard to maintain (Ryan, 1992), but when core issues are at stake—the right to abortion, for instance—numerous groups form a coalition.

Even when conditions are favorable, much effort may be required to bring about joint action (Alexander, 1995, pp. 117–198). Fortunately, looser forms of coordination or cooperation are easier to achieve. People in different organizations who know each other may share information. Sometimes there are organizations that help bring different groups together simply by making available a time or place at which activists can chat. For instance, in the homeless movement, soup kitchens become the meeting place for people from an array of groups who formed the personal linkages that later facilitated more formal cooperation (Wright, 1997, p. 234).

Cutting the Issue.   To sustain formal coordination, issues have to be framed so that each participating organization can see the benefits of working with others. Fortunately, if issues are framed properly, even organizations that have seemingly contradictory goals can discover a common purpose. For example, those trying to create new blue-collar jobs have often been at loggerheads with environmentalists, whose push for a cleaner environment seems to reduce industries' ability to compete in an international market. Recently, environmentalists have reframed the issues, as one of battling for the health of workers, especially those in minority communities. As an example, in Los Angeles, labor unions with large minority membership formed a coalition with environmental organizations and together combated the recycling of toxic wastes that hurt the environment and threatened the health of laborers (Bacon, 1996, p. 109).

In general, organizers work to *cut the issue* to show different groups why they should cooperate.

> Take the issue of public transportation. Senior citizen groups could support it because most seniors either don't drive or don't have the income to own cars. . . . Unions might support it because it would mean additional jobs in construction and in operating an improved mass transit system. Women's organizations might support it if there were particular guarantees written into the program to assure safety at night. . . . Minority organizations might support a plan which assured service between their neighborhoods and places where jobs were available. (Kahn, 1982, p. 279)

Careful framing is a must in organizing coalitions among multicultural constituencies. As a case in point, until they recut the issue in terms of shared oppression of women, organizers had real difficulty in bridging the cultural gaps that made it difficult to build a coalition among minority immigrant groups from Southeast Asia. This framing in terms of the oppression of women worked because "the needs and constraints of most refugee women . . . were so similar that the bonds of commonality were firmly established and cultural distinctions seemed slight" (Bays, 1998, p. 313). Similarly, the economic problems that divided Black from Hispanic neighborhoods in Oakland initially prevented the formation of a multicultural coalition. Then activists discovered reports showing that children in all the neighborhoods were being poisoned through lead-based paint and that health officials were ignoring the problem. Organizers were able to build a coalition on this shared threat to the children.

Sometimes coalition organizers have to cut an issue to battle the efforts of opponents to turn one coalition member against another. In planning urban redevelopment, government often sets aside a small amount of money for which individual neighborhoods compete, while reserving the bulk of the funds for downtown. Neighborhood groups end up fighting one another for crumbs rather than working together. To combat this manipulation, the Neighborhood Capital Budget Group in Chicago prepared and circulated a report to all the neighborhoods showing how little money each received. The information in this report motivated formerly competitive community organizations to join together in a city-wide campaign to reallocate funds for infrastructure redevelopment to the neighborhoods and away from the downtown (Rubin, 2000b).

Tactics of Coalition Campaigns

Coalitions can undertake actions that are not possible for a single organization. For instance, in many states, legislators from the big cities, suburbs, and rural areas rarely agree but can be persuaded to support a common program after being individually lobbied by a coalition of groups from the separate parts of the state. Coalitions allow finer gradation of pressure tactics than an individual group itself can usually accomplish. In Boston, as an example, developmental activists joined with street-level activists in a coalition to conduct a campaign to convince banks to fund affordable homes. The more cooperative banks were approached by the developmental activists who in face-to-face negotiations worked out financing agreements, while the homes of presidents of banks that refused to participate were picketed by more militant, often minority, organizations. Eventually most banks signed up.

If staying power is an issue, but some members of a coalition do not have the needed time, one group may become the lead organization, handling all the administrative work and calling on its allies only for shows of support (Hula, 1995). Another approach is to set up a staffed coalition organization that keeps on top of the problem and summons its members to action when the need arises (Rubin, 2000b). Lobbying by advocacy coalitions in Washington is done by only a handful of organizations, with other participants providing moral support and perhaps a few phone calls. Legislators assume that the less visible participants will become more active if the coalition does not get what it is pressing for.

Coalitions are handy because some organizations are better at pressuring government—the so-called "tree shakers"—while others are better at implementing projects with the new funds—the "jam makers" (Peirce & Steinbach, 1990). The jam makers have staying power to assure that promises made by the targets are kept. For example, activist coalitions of neighborhood groups, housing advocates, and development corporations pressure banks (and cities) to set up agreements to fund affordable housing. The temporary action coalition then forms a steering group to ensure that the banks' promises are kept, while neighborhood controlled development groups actually build the homes (Squires, 1992).

While there are obvious advantages to combining organizations that are good at pressure tactics with those skilled at carrying out programs, the focus of the two kinds of groups is so different that difficulties can occur. One coalition director described:

> I hear this everywhere I go around the country: God Damn developers. You don't come out when we picket. You don't come out when we have these press conferences. You don't come out and call the mayor a SOB. But when we go out and do it and shake the apple tree and some apples come down. You are the son of the bitches who get 80% of the apples and you didn't do any of the work. Damn it. Which is true. (Rubin, 2000b)

Despite these resentments, however, both groups are better able to achieve their goals of increased affordable housing by working together than by working apart.

Publicity

Through publicity, action organizations reach out to their membership, reframe issues, and embarrass uncooperative targets. They can publicize successes, demonstrating that problems can be solved, and attract new members. Success increases mobilization by creating an image of power.

For neighborhood groups and national organizations with up-to-date membership lists, reaching out to constituents is straightforward. In newsletters, a neighborhood organization tells residents about a new community center that it pressed the city to build or a neighborhood watch program it got up and running. The image of success is reinforced by the insignias worn by watch volunteers or through prominently displayed signs indicating this is a neighborhood watch community. National groups send out electronic and conventional mailings that brag about their accomplishments. An environmental group might boast about a bird coming off the endangered species list, having made a widely acclaimed comeback from near extinction; a civil liberties group might describe a case in which it protected unpopular speech rights.

Reaching out to targets, future members, and the public requires working with the mass media. Getting the media's attention and getting accurate stories broadcast and printed can be problematic. Even though many journalists are concerned with social issues, newspapers and television are businesses that depend on business advertisers and often reflect more politically conservative values.

To attract media attention, action organizations need to create their own form of political ju jitsu. The media world is very competitive. Making a story attractive enough for one outlet to cover virtually forces others to pay attention. A central purpose of the *cool media events,* the *moral demonstrations,* and the large-scale marches, is to create events of such interest that the media has no choice but to cover them. While it is fairly easy to get the media to cover the conflict involved in a direct action, it is far harder to persuade the media to focus on the message that the organization wants to communicate—end poverty, eliminate racism and sexism, or repair the environment.

With skill, even a routine event can gain media appeal. In one instance, an environmental organization wanted to disseminate a technical report on how strip mining in the Cumberland Mountains destroyed the land near a beautiful water fall that could become a tourist attraction. The group created a media event by designing a huge banner—100 feet long and weighing 200 pounds—and hanging it over the waterfall, a dramatic and difficult task. The waterfall and banner provided an eye-catching backdrop for a scheduled press conference and did lure in the media (Center for Community Change, 1997a, p. 36).

In general, publicity efforts are "frame contests" (Ryan, 1991, pp. 75–90) over whose images of what is important should prevail. Success occurs when framings build on widely shared symbols and values and peoples' personal experiences rather than on vague abstractions (Center for Community Change, 1997b). In a unionization effort, activists communicate that the battles are about workers' rights, the end of exploitation, and how everyone benefits when workers are justly compensated.

Action organizations cannot fully control the framings imposed by the media. News stories may attempt to portray unions as selfish, trying to maximize the salaries of union members, or as a special interest working against the free market (Ryan, 1991, p. 59). The media also tend to cover the violence that occurs rather than the purpose of the campaign, as one observer of a direct-action campaign led by Native Americans noted.

. . . violent tactics will not elicit media support . . . the decision to stage confrontational events to gain media attention is a risky choice. This is especially true for movements who wish to convey a frame that does not already conform to some widespread and beneficial cultural frame. . . . The belief that . . . [an organization's] message will receive a fair hearing . . . is somewhat naive. (Baylor, 1996, p. 251)

Preparing for Media Campaigns

To assure that the media gets the message, a successful publicity campaign should include several steps.

Determine Which Audience Should Be the Target.   Is it worth the extensive effort to gain the attention of the national audience or is access to a community cable station or a neighborhood paper sufficient? Must the public be reached or is the campaign actually focused on a narrow target? Thom Clark of the Community Media Workshop convinced activists in Chicago to design an entire media campaign to get the attention of one person, Chicago's mayor, who read newspaper columns and editorials but was thought to ignore placards that protesters might carry (Center for Community Change, 1997b, p. 31).

Test the Message to See How Others Understand It.   Sophisticated social change organizations try out their messages on *focus groups*. Either volunteers or paid individuals similar to those at whom the message is targeted are exposed to the message and then asked to discuss how they react and why. A message intended to show the power of the action organization—portraying a successful sit-in—might be coded by the public as indicating that the organization is just a disorderly mob. By using focus-group research, housing activists learned that people responded well to messages that describe self-help efforts by poor people but cared little about messages concerning social inequality.

Examine Practical Constraints.   Campaigns must respond to the financial and practical constraints that limit what the mass media covers. Mass media need to make a profit. An attractive story that can be covered at less expense—a demonstration held next to city hall—is more likely to get space than a more expensive story taking place in a distant neighborhood. One low-cost approach is to tag the community organization's events onto activities that the media are covering anyway. Before the 1992 Democratic Convention in Chicago, the Community News Project prepared a list of hundreds of personal contacts, events, and visually interesting settings that supported progressive urban causes and sent the list to the media to encourage them while in Chicago and waiting for convention stories to make contact with activist community groups (Center for Community Change, 1997a, p. 58). Making life easier for the press helps gain coverage.

Learn to time stories to fit into media rhythms. An anti–drunk driving campaign is more likely to get attention on New Year's Eve or on prom nights when the press is concerned about drunk driving. Stories released on a Friday are more likely to be covered in the paper but less likely to be read. An action done midmorning can make the afternoon papers and evening news, but an evening event, at best, will not get reported until the next day. An event scheduled too close to a media deadline will get ignored; why should reporters kill themselves to make a deadline when other stories are available?

Media hunger for stories varies over time. A war, disaster, or political scandal might absorb all reporters and dominate headlines, but during a lull, community groups can more easily gain access. When a lot is going on, talk shows might not want to interview people from an action organization but when other stories are scarce might want to do so. Persistence and willingness to appear at the drop of a hat can gain the organization greater visibility.

Work with Reporters.   Press relations are ongoing, not one shot, one-time activities. Invite reporters to visit your office, provide them with background on your group, and always answer their questions, even if doing so might reveal some weaknesses. Reporters respect such frankness and are more ready to listen when their support is really needed during action campaigns. Have information well organized, making sure file material and photographs or videos are available.

In the crunch of a campaign, reporters need reliable information quickly. Assign personnel to a media team who can meet with reporters and locate material reporters need to complete their stories. Designate a press information officer (PIO) who is on call 24 hours a day to meet with reporters (Kleyman, 1974). Make sure that the PIO has made contact with reporters long before the action begins, perhaps by inviting them out for coffee or lunch to describe what the organization is about.

Be honest. If a reporter catches a deception, the group loses credibility. If an organization routinely gives reporters good stories that they can run with, the reporters will be back whenever they need a story. Stories should be balanced and easy to check out. Reporters want to be seen as unbiased professionals, not flacks for a community organization.

Gaining Attention with the Newsworthy Story

The bottom line in gaining media attention is having a newsworthy story. Publishers want their newspapers to sell, and television stations need an audience. The Center for Community Change offers thirteen rules used by the media to judge whether a story is newsworthy:

Is it timely?
Is it new?
Is there conflict?
Does it involve a scandal?
Is it visual?
Does it involve prominent players or famous faces?
Is there broad and passionate support?
Is it possible?
Is it credible?
Is there human interest? A good story?
Is there paradox, irony, hypocrisy, or the unexpected?
Is it meaningful to readers or viewers? (Center for Community Change, 1997b, pp. 45–48)

Such rules suggest how to structure media events to increase the chance that they will be covered. The media are more likely to pick up on a story if a celebrity participates. The demonstrations that occurred after the shooting of an unarmed Black immigrant by four New York police officers gained media attention; to sustain interest, activists arranged for famous entertainers and politicians to appear, make speeches, and help blockade public buildings. Stories are also more likely to be picked up if they highlight an irony, such as cigarette companies, who spend a lot of money marketing to young people, supporting a campaign to discourage children from smoking. Human interest can be provided by focus on individuals who have been victimized by chemicals or particles in the air at work, by a medical establishment that used them as guinea pigs without their consent or knowledge, or by companies that made faulty products. Victims of government policies may also have dramatic stories to tell.

The need to make a story interesting makes it hard to communicate facts or figures, unless the numbers are put in human terms. An estimate that a community needs $48 million in mortgage money doesn't explain what a housing shortage entails as well as a tour showing four families sharing an overcrowded apartment. Human interest stories are most successful if they can create visually dramatic symbols of the cause.

> . . . the redlining issue is hooked to an attractive young couple with five kids who can't get a mortgage. The expressway issue is hooked to a particularly handsome church which would be torn down. The zoning violation is hooked to a rich absentee landlord who lives in the suburbs. (Cunningham & Kotler, 1983, p. 175)

Abstract issues don't communicate well through the media. For a story to fly, an exciting concrete event is needed as a peg or a hook. A rally with large numbers of people creates such a hook, as would evidence of corruption, such as contracts granted to developers who are friends of the mayor. The peg, however, can distract from the more fundamental issues.

> Pegs are not neutral packaging devices; they imply frames, and usually favor the dominant frame. They reinforce the legitimacy of official voices. . . . For instance, what could be more innocent than pegging a story on the homeless to a drop in temperature? . . . The peg moves coverage away from the fundamental issue of poor shelter . . . [and] leads audiences to ask whether the homeless have temporary shelters, not who is homeless and why. (Ryan, 1991, p. 98)

A story pegged this way could create sympathy for individuals with a problem but do little to encourage broader solutions.

More Controlled Messages

Once organizational members have developed working relationships with the press, they need to think out the content of the message and make sure that message is disseminated. Several tactics allow for good control of the message.

First, activists can use existing channels that take a message or announcement just as it is written. For example, community organizations can use public service messages on radio to announce meetings or major events. Members can write letters to the editor of newspapers. Such letters may be shortened, but if they are accepted for publication, are usually printed as submitted. Larger papers often run "op eds," thoughtful commentaries written by advocates of particular views. Organization members who are good writers can explain some current event framed by the organization. For example, gay rights groups can write about a recent case of harassment or murder of a gay soldier as an illustration of the failure of the government's "don't ask, don't tell" policy; or a gun control group can write about the mass shootings in public schools as a reason to curtail the availability of automatic weapons, rifles, and handguns.

Most of the time, community organizations are not publicizing something by placing it, unedited, in a local newspaper or on a radio station. Rather they create a story, which is covered by reporters, who may ask questions of group members, bystanders, opponents, and even people who were not there, and then write their own story. By the time the reporter is done, the message may not look very much like the one the organization hoped to get across. To make sure that at least their side of the story is conveyed accurately, organizations might want to write the story themselves and issue it in the form of a news release. News releases (and increasingly news videos) can be hand delivered to papers or television stations or presented at press conferences, where reporters can ask follow-up questions and take pictures.

If a community or social action organization has real hard news to release, it can hold a press conference. In planning a press conference, first inform the local papers and television and the wire services of the time of the conference. Have the PIOs phone their friends at the local stations and papers, send personalized letters, and then follow up with a reminder. Organization members should show up at the press conference; their fervor will communicate the importance of the issue to the reporters.

If the organization is releasing statistical data, take the time to prepare attractive graphics, using computer software that is now readily available. Explain the meaning of the data using dramatic personal illustrations. A child with a disease caused by toxic waste can be present at the news conference to humanize the facts and figures about how much pollution factories are releasing.

If the news conference has been called to publicize a project or demonstration, the organization can provide copies of a video for TV, or, for newspapers, 8-by-10 glossy photographs. If the pictures and film portray action, not just people talking, reporters may incorporate the materials directly into their stories.

All the reporters who attend the conference should receive the media package with the press release, graphics, and photos and videotapes. Leftover packets should be sent to media people who were not there. Besides the news editor, the editor of the Homes page might be interested in the plight of a displaced family, while real estate or business editors pay attention to campaigns to pressure banks and businesses to reinvest in poor communities. Business editors are also interested in community-based housing and commercial projects.

If preparing a video, leave time for editing and retakes. A certain homemade quality adds credibility, but the video has to be good enough to broadcast. Press releases should look professional, be neat, with correct grammar and spelling, and with space between lines so they can be edited. Sentences and paragraphs should be short. The closer the news release comes to a style that newspapers and broadcasters use, the more likely the release is to be quoted.

Press releases should answer the questions: Who? What? When? Where? Why? and How? In Figure 14.1 we have included a press release on a direct-action campaign that was circulated on the Internet *(http://www.ainfos.ca)*.

Note the funnel writing style. The core event, the hook for the story, is reported first. More details are given later. The hope is the press will use the story as written, but if it has to be cut, the earlier parts alone present a coherent message. While reporters will sometimes dig for a story, if they are approaching deadline, they may use the news release without much change. In case reporters want more details, make sure the release has the name and phone number of a contact person who they can reach easily and who can provide additional information.

Alternative Forms of Publicity

Neighborhood organizations can carry out low-cost publicity efforts without the aid of the mass media. Use bumper stickers, displays in public libraries, and wall posters; visit friends at homes, bars, and restaurants and talk about the organization. Printed T-shirts and badges with slogans are walking billboards for the organization.

Neighborhood organizations can set up displays in storefront offices, community centers or city hall. Pictures of deteriorated buildings that have been turned into decent housing or garbage-strewn lots that are now vest-pocket parks create a dramatic image. Take your own films with video cameras, and use software such as PowerPoint to automatically run vivid presentations that display the organization's accomplishments.

Newsletters can be easily set up on desktop computers and should be routinely sent out to community members. An effective newsletter realistically describes problems and progress. Newsletters explain to potential members and supporters what the organization is about, while enabling current members to feel they are part of the action even if only a few are actually involved in legal or lobbying efforts.

Increasingly, action organizations publicize their efforts electronically. *Alerts* that mobilize supporters to make phone calls or show up at city hall or at a rally are sent out by e-mail, while each day more organizations set up their own web pages, following advice given in books such as *NetActivism* (Schwartz, 1996). As an example, the web page maintained by the Kensington Welfare Rights Union provides a neat and pleasant display, describing the background of the group, detailing its campaigns, presenting a diary of individuals who work closely with the group, providing links to press releases, books, and films about the organization, and including an online radio interview with leaders of the organization. Several cities sponsor web pages that allow community groups and activists to share information and electronic services such as the Twin-Cities

FIGURE 14.1   Press Release on a Direct-action Campaign

Activists Arrested for Demanding Housing at San Diego, CA, Military Base

FOR IMMEDIATE RELEASE - 5/17/98 3 A.M.

Shortly after midnight tonight, eleven activists walked into the grounds of Camp Nimitz, a deactivated military base, to claim the land for the use of San Diego's estimated 2,500 unsheltered homeless people. Six remained to be arrested and were charged with trespassing.

Under the 1988 McKinney Act, housing homeless people was to be the first priority use for deactivated military bases. In 1994, Mayor Susan Goding sent a lobbyist to Washington to subvert the plain intent of the law, so that it was revised to allow for free use by local redevelopment agencies, so long as "representatives of the homeless were consulted and plans made to house the homeless population elsewhere." Four years later, the City is using the base for police and fire training, and over a hundred homeless people are camping together in public places to protest San Diego's callous neglect of housing needs.

The consensus of the group is that we could not continue to accept this blatant misuse of the law to further enrich the powerful at the expense of the poorest of us, that this was an injustice that had been crying for rectification for too many years already. After attempting to hold a small rally in the Naval Training Center and finding the gate (normally open to the public) locked, the group deployed signs along Harbor Blvd for the passing traffic until nightfall. Finding no access to any of the numerous barracks visible through the fence, the group decided to march in through the gate to claim the entire facility. Bewildered security guards called the police, while the activists settled down quietly and waited at a picnic table just past the guardhouse. Five have been cited for trespassing and released; one remains in custody for an unexpected warrant from the 1996 Concourse protest.

For info Contact: Shawnie Meade at the Street Light Office 338-9081, 935 E. Street, San Diego, CA 92101, or Forrest Curo at 283-5582.

Free Net in the Minneapolis–St. Paul area (*http://tcfreenet.org*) and maintain discussion groups on community issues.

Bringing a Campaign to an End through Bargaining and Negotiations

The purpose of direct-action campaigns is to force the opponents to accept the legitimacy of the demands of the action organization and to promise to implement them. Through direct actions, mass mobilizations, and favorable press coverage, social change organizations communicate to the opponents that "we won't go away so you might as well sit down and talk with us." Still, most targets usually don't just concede to demands. Instead, concessions are obtained only after sustained face-to-face negotiations (Goodpaster, 1997; Susskind & Cruikshank, 1987).

To get such talks started, the action organization has to communicate that opponents will be better off if they negotiate rather than continuing the confrontations. Simply forcing people to show up by the threat of continued force, however, can create a wall of hostility. Instead, action organizations must indicate that the opponents, too, can benefit from discussions. Police who have been targeted because of disproportionately stopping and frisking minorities can be told that negotiations might lead to residents forming neighborhood watches that help in crime control. Banks that are being picketed, more readily show up for negotiations once they have been informed that working with community groups in neighborhood reinvestment programs not only is required by the CRA but also is financially profitable.

While negotiations are vital, they can be a trap for the unwary. An inexperienced bargainer might accept unenforceable agreements, or so much posturing occurs that no one is able to make necessary concessions. Or, opponents may take a slice and divide approach in which minor concessions are made while the larger problem remains unresolved.

Preparing for Negotiations

Successful negotiators work out in advance what tactics they might use and what the overall goals are for the final agreement. Four general principles should be kept in mind in preparing for negotiations:

Negotiations Are about Power and the Perceptions of Power. Successful negotiations occur because the organization has demonstrated that it has power, even if only the power to disrupt. Research has shown that both sides do better when each understands that the other has some power. As one report indicates,

> . . . the greater the total amount of power in a relationship, the greater the use of conciliatory tactics . . . an unequal power relationship fosters more use of hostile tactics and less use of conciliatory tactics than an equal power relationship. (Lawler, 1992, p. 17)

In Planning Negotiations Think beyond the Immediate Problem at Hand. Solving the issue at hand is important, but negotiators should not lose track of the underlying social and economic structures that create the problems. Convincing a university not to allow its logo to be used on clothing made with sweat labor is important. More is achieved, however, if the action organization persuades the university to set up a permanent panel that makes sure purchases are not made from any firm that has a history of treating its employees badly. Forcing the city to preserve an affordable apartment building that commercial developers want to demolish is a victory, but it would be even better to extract from the bargaining the right of community groups to plan the land-use decisions that affect their neighborhoods.

Negotiators Speak for Constituencies not Simply Themselves. Individuals who meet frequently develop a rapport that increases trust and allows each to better comprehend the others' arguments so that usually only a small number are involved in the actual negotiation sessions (Susskind & Cruikshank, 1987). Negotiators, however, must keep in mind that even if they ultimately agree with one another, they are merely representing a larger group and later on must convince people for whom they speak that the settlement is just and fair.

Negotiations Often Involve Multiple Players on Each Side.   A coalition of housing groups, community development corporations (CDCs), neighborhood organizations, and advocates for the homeless might be on one side, trying to pressure government to provide more housing subsidies. Multiparty negotiations bring up questions beyond those of dealing with the opponent (Cormick, 1989; Pruitt & Carnevale, 1993). Should the coalition stick together at all costs? Can separate deals be made that benefit individual members of the coalition at little harm to others? Will opponents offer concessions to selected members of the coalition hoping to break up the alliance? Leaders of action organizations should spend time talking with each other to figure out what they will do if they receive separate offers. In addition, they need to agree on their demands and on at what point they will consider the negotiations completed or impossible.

With these rules in mind and before negotiations, activists plan an overall strategy. How has the action campaign affected the opponent? If the actions have delayed completing financial deals, businesses might be more amenable to financial pressures, while public figures want to reduce the embarrassment in the press. As part of this strategizing, figure out how the opponents might behave during bargaining, perhaps by talking to others who have negotiated with them. Constituents might expect public officials to make some concessions when issues of social justice are on the table, while the actions of a branch of a large company might be curtailed by a stubborn home office.

In picking the negotiating team, choose people with complementary skills. Who is quickest on his or her feet? Who can tactfully sum up a situation, appear conciliatory to the opposition, yet not concede on fundamental issues? Who has the facts and figures at his or her fingertips and can catch the opponents' deceptions? Is there someone whom the opponents trust? If the negotiations drag on for a while, who has the patience and humor to help everyone keep their cool and stay at the bargaining table?

Before a negotiating session, the bargainers should simulate—game out—the negotiations. Divide the team into two and have one group pretend to be the opponents who think out the strategies that the other side might follow. Use these sessions to try to imagine what the opponents might offer and under what constraints they may be operating. Perhaps during these simulations, your side will figure out a concession of little import to your members, but of real value to the opponent, that will move the discussions to a successful conclusion.

Make sure your negotiators have mastered the facts. If the problem is lack of expenditures in poor neighborhoods, double check that the negotiators know the size of the city's infrastructure budget and where funds have been spent in the past. In efforts to end gender or ethnic discrimination, make sure the team knows how many men and women of which ethnic groups work at different levels in the opponent's organization. If public officials argue that new resources are not needed for the poor because welfare rolls have dropped and more people are working, have the figures at hand to show that those getting off welfare are employed at minimum wage, are the first to lose their jobs during cutbacks, and lack medical insurance.

Most important, those on the negotiating team must plan how much they can concede and still gain a victory. Most activist organizations do have room to maneuver.

Any progress beyond mere tokenism that improves gender or ethnic equality is a step to the good. An organization arguing for a fairer allocation of government contracts to minority groups might initially demand that contracts be let in rough proportion to the population of the various groups. If African Americans constitute 13 percent of the local population, the group might demand 13 percent of the contracts go to African American owned firms. In fact, negotiators might be willing to accept an allocation of contracts in proportion to the number of minority firms; negotiators can back off the original demand and still bring about improvement.

Concessions extracted during bargaining should be expressed in specific and verifiable terms so that the organization does not accept a vague, unenforceable promise. If a neighborhood group is agitating for street repairs, negotiators should work out exact terms of what will be done, by whom, and when:

> The City Department of Streets and Roads will replace both storm and sanitary sewers under Maple Avenue from Main to Alpine and then resurface the street. The contracts for the work are to be let no later than February 1, 2003 for work to be completed no later than October 1, 2003.

Because most cities have to let bids in public, the group can determine if the contract was issued in time, and community members can observe the physical construction to make sure agreed upon plans are carried out.

The Mechanics of Negotiating Sessions.   Especially when the two sides in negotiations have a history of mistrust, preliminary agreements are needed on the mechanics of the negotiating sessions (Cormick, 1989). On whose turf will the sessions be held, or is a neutral setting required? How many from each side can show up for the sessions? Will there be neutral third parties, and, if so, how will they be chosen? Will recordings be allowed? Will the press be kept informed, and, if so, how often and by whom? Will negotiators be required to keep all discussions confidential, even from their own organization members, to permit the participants to try out off-the-wall ideas without fear of embarrassment? How long will the meetings last?

One activist described how neighborhood groups created a set of such procedures that helped them in negotiations with bankers.

> We met with those guys and we all, our poor community people, and they had their guys and we set the agenda: Does it mean that there will be no smoking or no breaks every five minutes (chuckles) because we are all organized. . . . So we set the agenda. There is only one break during the morning. Only one lunch break, only thirty minutes, you know, if anybody wants to call a break to chat about a piece of the agreement, they're only allowed five minutes. No smoking. We knew all the executives there smoke. . . . We met actually for about two days at one of the richest law firms in the loop of Chicago, which I consider is history. You know a bunch of poor community people got together . . . they were getting upset because they were used to having their secretary bring them coffee and all of that. We said, none of that. Only persons allowed in this room are the people invited to this meeting. No phone calls, no phones in the

room. . . . We met from like eight-thirty in the morning to five-thirty, six in the evening. So that was a long meeting for those top, number one executives. (Chicago activist interviewed by Herbert Rubin)

The negotiations ended with the community groups receiving a written guarantee for tens of millions of dollars of affordable housing.

Tactics During the Negotiating Sessions

Activists who follow the Alinsky model frequently target an individual as a symbol of the problem, but the same approach can be harmful once negotiations begin. Negotiations must focus on issues, not people. Little will be accomplished if either side is responding to personal animosities (Pruitt & Carnevale, 1993, p. 151).

To bypass personal animosities, each side might appoint as principal negotiator an individual who was not a central figure in the campaign leading up to the negotiations. The mayor and the president of the community group might not be speaking to one another, but the chosen negotiators begin with no personal animosities. To improve relations further, skillful negotiators chat with each other during breaks and try to discover the common interests that will help them bridge gaps. Just because people like one another doesn't mean they will reach agreement, but if bargainers think opponents are incarnations of evil they won't be able to listen to each other and respond in good faith.

Negotiations can run on, be fatiguing, and appear to be accomplishing little. To keep the negotiations going, each side must see some short-term progress, even if that progress is more symbolic than real. Professional negotiators advise making some minor concessions to keep discussions alive. For instance, if bargaining among environmentalists, public officials, and developers on how much land to reserve for park space has stalled, environmentalists might concede that open space next to a mall is not required. Both sides recognize that little is really being granted, as the land near the mall is too expensive for public authorities to buy for a park, but the willingness to make the concessions communicates that the environmentalist are willing to talk and encourages the other side to be less stubborn.

Sometimes negotiations are not real but merely a ploy by the opponent to make an action organization cease its pressure tactics. Opponents may posture and make speeches without really listening to the action organization's proposals. If this is occurring, it is probably time to leave. Sometimes, though, both sides are delaying because they don't know how to reach a resolution. If this seems to be the case, set a firm deadline by which time the negotiations must be concluded. As such deadlines approach, people tend to be more willing to make concessions.

Negotiating tactics involve a delicate balance between having a fixed goal in mind, being able to concede some points without giving up crucial issues, and being flexible enough to respond to unanticipated ideas from the opponent. Research suggests that firmness usually pays off.

> [H]igh initial demands, slow concession making and positional commitments are useful for eliciting unilateral concessions. This is especially true when the other [side] is under high time pressure. (Pruitt, 1981, p. 74)

Recognize, however, that community organizations have to concede something, even if just to preserve the face of the opponent. If concessions are made too quickly, your side may be seen as weak, but if they are made too slowly, the opponent may also get stubborn (Pruitt, 1981, p. 20).

If opponents bring in an unanticipated offer, take a break and regroup to think it over. For instance,

> Let's say that we're members of a tenants' organization negotiating with the landlord over a rent increase. The landlord has announced a 20 percent increase. In our planning sessions . . . we agreed that we would accept no increase but that we would actually be willing to accept 7½ percent. . . . The landlord comes up with a totally different sort of suggestion . . . he will agree to no rent increase but that instead of a month-by-month rental, there should be year-long leases with a one-month security deposit for damages. This is a possibility that we had not thought of. Rather than trying to think this through in front of the landlord, the thing to do is to call for a "caucus." This means we take a break to discuss the new offer. (Kahn, 1982, pp. 164–165)

Opponents who fear the resumption of direct actions do have an incentive to come up with mutually acceptable agreements, so examine their proposals carefully and do not automatically reject them.

Numerous ways can be found to structure offers that encourage opponents to work toward what your side wants (Goodpaster, 1997, pp. 33–50). One is to split the difference, finding a position half way between the initial stance of the community organization and the counteroffer of the target. With "salami" tactics, an issue is broken into parts to enable the opponent to make smaller (and less threatening) concessions, until, piece by piece, the entire issue is resolved. A quite different approach is to link issues together into one package that has something in it for everyone.

Some tactics can inadvertently terminate the discussion and so should be used with care. One approach to use when concessions are not forthcoming is to escalate demands rather than seek a compromise (and then hope that the initial position is listened to with the respect that it deserved). Another approach when the talks are deadlocked is to threaten to walk out.

Negotiators worry about how honest to be with the opponent. Lying might help in the short run, but if the lies are discovered, the organization loses the credibility it needs for subsequent negotiations. Short of outright prevarication, there are a variety of forms of mild deception that are common in bargaining, for example, asking for more than the group really needs or understating the amount of flexibility that the negotiator actually has. Gambits such as shifting attention, not fully answering questions, or avoiding questions by asking another question are accepted tactics (Goodpaster, 1997, pp. 51–61). Negotiators often bluff, threaten to do something that they don't really intend to do, as part of the bargaining.

The goal of negotiations is to reach an agreement that both sides accept as just. Skillful negotiators look for a *mutually prominent alternative* that

> . . . must stand out in both parties' thinking either because it embodies some standard of fairness or reasonableness or because it enjoys perceptual "uniqueness, simplicity,

precedent or some rationale that make [it] qualitatively different from the continuum of possible alternatives." (Schelling, 1960, p. 70)

Environmental activists who want to protect land that harbors an intact and rare ecosystem may get into seemingly irresolvable disputes with developers who don't want to give up the property. One possible solution might involve a land swap, in which the developer gets to keep the original land, but donates a large tract with similar characteristics farther from the city. The apparent fairness of the deal and the fact that both sides get most of what they want sets up a mutually prominent alternative.

Mediation and Third-Party Intervention

On occasion, negotiators find face-to-face discussions nonproductive but still want to reach a resolution. In these situations, organizations call in a professional mediator who can help facilitate the discussion or suggest ideas to solve the problem.

Mediators are people whom all contenders accept as being neutral and concerned about achieving a successful resolution. The facts gathered by the mediator are considered less slanted than those provided directly by either side. Further, the presence of a mediator during discussions compels people to act with enough civility that they are more likely to hear each other's arguments.

A skilled mediator allows people to talk but when tensions seem out of control calls a break until calm returns. A mediator can meet separately with each side and try to make opponents understand each other's perspective. Mediators can carry ideas back and forth between the two sides, focusing attention on the issues and ideas rather than on personalities and confrontations. A good mediator performs shuttle diplomacy, probing and advising both sides, figuring out ways of linking or separating out issues that those caught up in the heat of the moment might miss. Further, it is often easier to agree with ideas presented by a mediator (even if they are only warmed-over versions of the opponent's ideas) than with the ideas presented by the opponent.

Mediation, though, has a downside. Most professional mediators are part of the established political and social structure and may tilt away from the more radical goals of social change. The essence of mediation is to tone down the edge of conflict but doing so might dull "the fighting edge of some participants" (Amy, 1987, p. 114). Their goal might be getting people to momentarily agree rather than address fundamental concerns with social or economic inequality. Care is advised in the choice of a mediator.

The purpose of social action campaigns is to pressure an opponent, either through confrontations, the law, or political means to grant the demands of the social-change organization. Opponents may be forced to capitulate by the power of the action organization. Such power can be achieved through building coalitions that increase the numbers and expertise on which community groups can call; it can also be achieved through skillful use of the media to frame an issue consistent with the perspectives of the action organization. To bring the matter to a successful close, however, requires the action organization to negotiate an enforceable agreement. In doing so, the negotiating team must cast issues in ways that allow or even encourage opponents to concede. The goal is to end a long campaign with an agreement that enables the organization to implement its core goals.

PART SIX

The Social Production Model

Social production organizations provide needed community services, build homes, or recreate businesses in poor neighborhoods. Chapter 15 describes the wide variety of social production activities in which community groups engage. The chapter examines the values that underlie community control of social production and presents the variety of organizational forms through which social production is accomplished, paying particular attention to community development corporations. Chapter 16 introduces the technical tools that enable social production organizations to accomplish their goals including how to plan projects, obtain financing, and carry out construction or service delivery.

Accomplishing social production tasks (and developing the knowledge for much of direct action work) requires expertise. Chapter 17 describes the expertise and funding assistance that smaller organizations can get from a wide variety of support organizations that offer aid to those involved in community empowerment efforts.

15 The Social Production Model

Social production organizations make goods and services available to those in need in ways that empower the recipients and the communities in which they live. Community-based organizations offer shelter to battered women, comfort the dying and their families in hospices, partner with the police to combat neighborhood crime, and build quality housing at reasonable cost. Social production organizations help stimulate the neighborhood economy through job training and financing start-up companies; they provide customized social services for immigrants. Community development corporations (CDCs) enable families to own their own homes or be housed in quality, affordable apartments.

Social production organizations not only help individuals but in doing so work to recreate the fabric of community. Social production organizations are concerned about the impact of their actions on neighborhoods and communities, not just on the bottom line. They try to do no damage to the community through pollution or tearing down housing without replacement. Following a *community building model,* developmental activists combine efforts to physically renew housing, stores, schools, and parks with social services and direct-action organizing (Traynor, 1995, p. 12). Those involved in social production understand that physical redevelopment, social services, and direct action each support one another as parts of broader efforts of community empowerment. Building new apartments is important, but without day-care services, job training, and placement people cannot afford even modest rents.

The projects of social production organizations not only provide needed goods and services but also rekindle hope that the community can be rejuvenated. For instance, after a community development organization built a mall in the impoverished Liberty City area of Miami, participants explained:

> "There is a real sense of pride in what has happened here," says Otis Pitts, the ex-cop who is Tacolcy's executive director. "It's not like people just coming to shop in a store. It's like they're coming to something that is a vital part of the community." Says a local merchant . . . "We don't just look good, we are good. Now everybody is committed to staying in the neighborhood. Why leave now? We sweated out the worst. Ain't nothing to do but look forward now." (Peirce & Steinbach, 1987, p. 37)

Projects done by CDCs symbolize the way for future improvement. The actions of social production organizations in enhancing the appearance of the community and making visible investments in blocks that commercial businesses have abandoned counter the image of defeat. One developmental activist explained that a small mall built in a community that lacked shopping was as much about creating pride as it was about providing stores.

> I had to put down a big enough footprint to influence the community. And I just refused to do little bitty things because I know you are just pissing money down a rat hole that way. And, [you see] the psychological implications of putting a lot of glass back in the neighborhood [the mall being described was built with large glass windows] would have on people's appreciation of what you did. (Interview with Herbert Rubin)

The community development activist explained that the mall became a focus of pride because it was controlled by African Americans. People have something that they can say, "This is ours."

Social production creates pride in the possibility of community members taking charge and providing their own needs. Those who work with social production organizations gain skills, confidence, and new knowledge and feel empowered. Social production organizations, however, have to carefully balance the effort spent in providing goods and services with that spent in working to empower individuals. Often, CDCs that establish businesses and build affordable housing do so by using their own professional staff rather than engaging community members in the project. In such circumstances there is a need to ensure that community members affected by the projects are intimately involved in determining what is done and for whom.

Community-based social production organizations provide jobs, housing, services, and commodities in ways that benefit the poor and poor communities. Social production organizations are concerned with providing a material product but want to do so in ways that increase *social equity* and help those most in need. Projects are about increasing *personal empowerment* through helping individuals gain dignity and pride. Dignity comes from holding a productive job that has a future, doing skilled work, and creating useful and healthful products. Pride is obtained as people gain ownership in their own homes through "sweat equity" contributions, putting their own labor into building the place in which they will dwell.

For social production organizations, the *process* of bringing about change is as important as the outcome. Goods should be produced, but decisions on what to make and how should involve workers and residents. A capitalist-owned business might appear to be efficient, but social production organizations tend to favor worker-owned firms, where people not only earn a living but also feel empowered, more competent, and more committed to the collective task (Wetzel & Gallagher, 1990).

Even the best of social production organizations cannot escape the pressures of the marketplace. Projects have to make sense both economically and socially. A food cooperative will not survive if chain supermarkets sell fresher foods more cheaply. Still community-controlled supermarkets can be more sensitive to local needs than are the chains, for instance, by establishing neighborhood groups that monitor the quality of the food and service and assure the cultural appropriateness of what is being sold.

The Variety of Community-Based Social Production Organizations

What social production organizations provide in terms of social services, housing, and economic development can serve many people or a few, be done informally, or can take legal business forms. At one extreme, neighbors informally provide services by watching each others' homes and children at no cost; at the other extreme, CDCs spend millions of dollars to build new homes or businesses and are run as fully incorporated businesses. A handful of friends might maintain a community garden, an informal social production task, while one of the nation's largest social production organizations, the Newark-based New Communities Corporation, owns and manages several thousand apartments, provides day care, job training, nursing, and food services, and is a partner in a large supermarket.

In extremely poor communities, such as those found in the delta region of Mississippi, social production organizations concentrate on expanding the economic pie. To accomplish this goal, the Delta Foundation helped set up factories to manufacture blue jeans, electrical components, and attic stairs and provided seed capital to others through its venture capital subsidiaries. The Delta Foundation also helps train entrepreneurs (Task Force on Community-Based Development, 1987, p. 35).

Some social production organizations concentrate their efforts on specialized clientele. The Women's Self Employment Projects helps low-income, usually minority, women, obtain capital, peer-group counseling, and economic mentoring, and guides them in setting up their own microenterprises. Other social production groups act as community-controlled extensions of government. When public assistance programs changed, forcing many on welfare to obtain employment, social production organizations sought and received contracts from local governments to help former welfare recipients learn new skills and find jobs (Harrison & Weiss, 1998).

Social production organizations often engage in several tasks at once because the needs of community members are often interdependent. For instance, the Comprehensive Community Revitalization Program (CCRP), a social production project in the Bronx, has helped other community groups build homes and set up a meals program for poor people, that in turn created a community catering business. CCRP established community crime patrols, improved parks, and pressured the city to provide social amenities. CCRP encouraged another local organization to do the preliminary planning that eventually resulted in a supermarket in this poor neighborhood (Walsh, 1997).

To give a sense of the range of social production activities we have grouped them according to four major criteria: (1) the type of service or product provided, (2) the intended client, (3) the tactical approach followed in providing the service, and (4) the legal structure of the organization providing the goods or services.

Types of Services or Products Provided

Social production organizations offer a variety of services that vary from individual social services to economic projects that affect the broader community.

Self-Help Alternatives to Therapy.   People who share a problem—chemical addiction, bereavement, divorce, or illness—come together to talk over their difficulties and teach one another how to recover. These self-help services replace professional counseling. Such activities empower because the people who receive help develop sufficient skills and confidence to later help others. No one dictates solutions to participants, they work them out on their own.

Social Services.   Social production organizations offer a variety of social services. Hospices ease the physical and emotional pain of dying, providing support for terminally ill people, their friends, and their families, often in a home or homelike setting. Home health-care programs, in which community members are the providers, create jobs, and enable the elderly to live with dignity outside of institutional settings. In New York City, for instance, community members who had been on welfare formed a cooperatively owned home health-care service that provided poor people with needed health care, while enabling the workers to earn fair wages plus benefits (McKay et al., 1997, p. 29).

Other social production organizations provide day-care facilities to accommodate to the special needs of the communities. For instance,

> Inquilinois Boricuas En Accion in Boston developed a bilingual/bicultural child care center at the request of community mothers, with the idea of promoting self-esteem and respect for Puerto Rican culture and heritage and at the same time providing a badly needed service that would enable mothers to enter the workforce. (McKay, 1997, p. 42)

In another approach, Bethel New Life, in Chicago, has formed family day-care programs in the apartment buildings that this CDC constructed. Such community care programs provide assistance to the elderly, who, while needing no particular medical care, are too frail to be left alone while their children work.

Community-based social services combat spouse abuse by establishing centers that provide counseling, legal advice, and a place to stay for victims. Members of community organizations reach out to locate those suffering from AIDS and work with teenagers to instruct them in AIDS prevention (Orians et al., 1995). Such human service programs become job training efforts as the volunteers develop skills that later qualify them as counselors who can be employed by the very organizations that trained them (McKay et al., 1997).

Education.   Social production organizations educate community members in a wide variety of ways. Some housing cooperatives have set up home educational efforts in the afternoons or during the summers for at-risk youth. Other social production groups form their own charter schools, which receive public money but whose agenda is determined by the community groups.

The advocacy organization Associations of Community Organizations for Reform Now (ACORN) had been working with the Hmong community to pressure school officials in St. Paul to show more concern for students from this minority group. When changes weren't forthcoming, ACORN joined with the Hmong community and established a charter school that would be more sensitive to cultural and linguistic needs.

Once underway, ACORN withdrew to enable the parents and teachers to run the school themselves (Finkel, 1998).

Community Identity and Integration.   Many neighborhood associations, such as Baltimoreans United in Leadership Development (BUILD) in Baltimore (McDougall, 1993), were founded to help community members develop a sense of shared identity and neighborhood loyalty. Such organizations run neighborhood fairs and sponsor festivities and public events at which different ethnic groups discover each others' foods, dances, and cultural heritages (Goode & Schneider, 1994).

Protective Services.   Some social production organizations focus on combating crime. Their mission might include interrupting the distribution of drugs or forcing public authorities to respond more quickly to calls for help. Community organizations set up neighborhood watches in which community members observe their neighborhoods, looking for suspicious people and events, and work out systems for making quick contact with the police. They hope the presence of a neighborhood watch will deter crime, and the ongoing relationship with the police will encourage officers to intensify their efforts to keep the neighborhood safe.

Neighborhood Appearance and Maintenance.   Some social production organizations routinely survey community conditions for deterioration in streets, sidewalks, and housing. This information is reported to government authorities and to community development corporations. CDCs and local governments may make low-interest loans to property owners to fix up store facades or repair porches, window casements, and external stairs. Many cities have grant programs to help fix sidewalks, repair neighborhood parks, and plant parkways with trees and grasses. Such funding can be especially helpful if neighbors do the cleanup and feel a sense of pride in creating new and usable open space.

Consumer Services.   Social production organizations try to help those in poor communities obtain the consumer services that wealthier neighborhoods routinely receive. One way this is done is for the social production organization to encourage privately owned businesses to open stores in the neighborhood. Developmental activists provide the data that convinces entrepreneurs that there are unmet needs and that profits are possible even in poor communities. Social production organizations may try to get government to help the new firms, maybe by providing some new street lighting, parking facilities, or additional police patrols.

In another approach, community organizations establish their own businesses. For example, people form consumer cooperatives that sell food and other goods and keep costs down through the use of voluntary labor (Cox, 1994). Some food cooperatives form direct linkages with producing farms, cutting out wholesaler profits. Cooperatively owned neighborhood restaurants provide wholesome food and a place for community members to congregate, helping to establish a foundation for subsequent efforts at organizing.

Many consumer services operate within a market model, in which cash is exchanged for goods. Cash can be scarce, however, especially in poor communities. As a result, some consumer services are provided through barter systems, in which an electrician, for example, might trade wiring work for meat from a butcher. In some communities, the arrangement has been formalized through the creation of barter currency. Businesses that sell goods receive instead of money an I.O.U. worth so many hours of labor. That I.O.U. can be spent by the business owner to buy something else, until ultimately someone presents the person who initially paid for goods with the I.O.U. with the request to pay with hours of work.

Housing.   In many neighborhoods, the most visible signs of community renewal are new or repaired apartments or homes. In poor neighborhoods, many of these newly constructed buildings have been built by community-based organizations. By the late-1990s nonprofit community groups had built over 550,000 units of affordable housing (National Congress for Community Economic Development [NCCED], 1999).

Church affiliated groups, such as Habitat for Humanity, coordinate community members and volunteers to build homes, while CDCs put together government grants and conventional mortgages to fund affordable housing, with rents made affordable through government subsidies such as Section 8 housing certificates. Some community groups establish temporary housing for the homeless until they can get a more permanent apartment. Others focus on building apartment buildings for special needs populations, for example, by providing rooms for caregivers in housing specially constructed for the physically disabled.

In many neighborhoods, social production organizations obtain free vacant lots from the city, seek out grants and loans to lower construction costs, and then build single family homes that are sold to working class people whose return to the neighborhood increases the available social capital. Community organizations also sponsor limited equity housing cooperatives that provide quality apartments to poor people, made affordable in part, by the grants the community group receives. Those who take up residence in the cooperative own the building and have a say over decisions about maintenance and improvements.

In another type of affordable housing program, future owners help build their own homes and apartments, often supervised by trained contractors who teach community workers new skills. The labor of the new owners is considered sweat-equity, allowing the poor to substitute this physical work for the cash down payment. For instance, in Boston, new owners of affordable cooperative apartments contributed 300 hours of sweat-equity, as their down payment (Medoff & Sklar, 1994, p. 161).

Still another housing arrangement is lease-purchase. In this type of program, poor people rent homes owned by the social production organization. Each month, however, a share of their rent is counted toward the purchase price of the home until the tenants have put aside enough to become owners.

Economic and Job Creation Projects.   Social production organizations seek to rectify the failures of the conventional economy through a series of economic development and job creation activities.

Some social production organizations work with successful private sector entrepreneurs who grew up in the neighborhood, to encourage them to invest in the neighborhood, to make a profit and provide jobs for community members. Such firms might supply ethnically appropriate goods and services, such as Hispanic or Asian groceries or specialized cuts of meat that different ethnic groups prefer. For-profit companies owned by coethnics help create a cultural focus and identity for a neighborhood and provide opportunities for youngsters to enter the labor force. Social production organizations may ask these business owners to mentor new entrepreneurs, to help them through some of the rough spots in starting a business.

In another approach, social production organizations partner with traditional entrepreneurs to build shopping centers, restaurants, and malls. Private companies provide skills and know-how and some cash, while the community group obtains grants to repair the lots on which the stores are built. The nation's best known community-controlled mall was built by a CDC in Kansas City on property that was so derelict that it was used as a filming site for a TV movie about the day after a nuclear war.

Social production organizations might set up "incubators" that offer inexpensive space for start-up firms. The organizations first acquire and refurbish an abandoned commercial or industrial building that is then rented out at affordable rates. Many incubators have common facilities such as photocopying, faxes, and secretarial, legal, or accounting support that new firms need but might not be able to afford individually. As an example, the Sam Adams beer company got started in a community-built incubator in the Roxbury section of Boston. On the south side of Chicago, another community incubator provides affordable working space for local artists.

Another way social production organizations encourage local businesses is by providing capital to local entrepreneurs from revolving loan funds. Start-up firms, especially those owned by minorities or women, often lack sufficient funds to see them through the first critical years of operation. Banks, however, are unwilling to provide capital at reasonable interest rates, in part, because they perceive the loans as risky, and, in part, because the costs of handling numerous small loans is too high. Instead, government agencies, foundations, and, sometimes even banks, make available a lump sum loan or grant to a community group, that in turn lends the money to the new firms at below market rates. Community-based organizations know those applying for the loans and can figure out which people are most likely to succeed, reducing the risk. As old loans are paid back, the development organizations reuse the money to make new loans.

Microenterprises take this process one step further. In setting up a microenterprise, the social production organization works with very-low-income people, usually women, providing them with a few hundred to several thousand dollars to help them with their small start-up businesses, such as selling music, beauty products, or special types of shoes or other niche enterprises (Counts, 1996). The participants meet together as a group that helps its members work out business plans, and once the individual enterprises are under way, group members continue to provide advice. Often successful entrepreneurs volunteer to act as mentors to help these start-up firms. Many microenterprise firms fail, but the process of just starting a business is empowering and helps even those whose businesses fail gain skills that help them improve their economic lot.

Recently, community development corporations have been active in helping people get off welfare. Unlike the one-size-fits-all approach common in government training programs, successful community organizations customize their efforts. In the most effective models, community groups first contact potential employers and receive promises (even guarantees) of job placement for graduates who have mastered specified skills. The community groups then teach people the specified skills, while helping participants compensate for any educational deficiencies they might have. The success rate for such employment programs is high (Harrison & Weiss, 1998).

Many projects run by community-based economic development organizations become part of the *alternative economy,* in which efforts to maximize bottom-line profits are less important than promoting social and economic equity. *Producer cooperatives,* in which the workers are also the owners and managers of a firm, exemplify this approach. The best-known case of this alternative to capitalistic ownership is found in the Basque region of Spain where the Mondragon cooperatives employ thousands of people, manufacture numerous products, and own and control their own banks (Whyte, 1988). Such cooperative business projects are less common in the United States, but there have been some successful ones. The Hoedad cooperative in Eugene, Oregon has employed over 300 members (Jackall, 1984) while in San Francisco, much of the scavenger business was run as a cooperative, though eventually the cooperative owners employed regular workers.

Primary Beneficiary

Another way of understanding what social production organizations do is to see how their efforts sometimes benefit individuals, other times firms, and, on occasion, help the community as a whole.

Individuals.   Community-based social service programs work with individuals, for instance, training people for new jobs, providing inhome health care or helpers for elderly people living alone, or sheltering victims from abusive relationships. The goal is not just to help individuals but also to help alleviate structurally caused problems that continue to disempower those in need.

Poor people often stay poor because they have so little money to meet emergencies, lack time for schooling, or capital to start a business. One approach to overcoming these problems is to set up *individual development accounts.* For example, as part of a job preparedness program, or as an incentive to stay in school, teens or individuals who are leaving welfare participate in training programs, for which they are paid. Each week they receive some cash, but part of each check is also placed in an escrow bank account, as an individual development account (IDA) that slowly accumulates into a modest sum (Sherraden, 1991). At the end of the training program, participants can access the entire IDA so long as they spend the money either for further job-related education or as an investment in a business endeavor.

Lending circles, such as those set up by Chicago's Women's Self Employment Project, help individuals expand both social and economic capital. In lending circles, people join with others, often friends, who want to start small businesses but lack the moderate amounts of capital needed. To apply for a loan, each individual in the lending circle works out a business plan. Members of the group and outside mentors make suggestions about the plans and then the group collectively recommends who should receive the first loan.

Group members meet at fixed intervals and provide advice to each other on how to run the businesses. No new money is made available to group members unless those who have already borrowed are repaying their loans. In practice, the women in the lending circles provide help to each other with social and management problems (Counts, 1996).

Firms and Business Enterprises. Social production organizations recognize that neighborhoods without job opportunities and commercial businesses are not going to survive. In response, many groups, especially CDCs, help start new industries and commercial endeavors in neighborhoods. Community organizations may establish businesses like recycling firms that clean up the local environment while teaching people the technical skills needed to make a profit from the wastes found in older industrial areas. Similarly, health-care and social service businesses do double duty providing urgently needed services and training and employing residents from the community. CDCs that build apartments offer jobs in maintenance and management to community members.

Another approach involves pressuring established businesses to help community members. For instance, when businesses receive special considerations from government to locate in a poor community, neighborhood organizations might demand *first source hiring agreements* that guarantee that the firms will hire from the neighborhood, often the people recommended (and trained) by the community organization itself. In one case, the social production organization lent money to stores that were opening in a local mall but did so only after taking a share in the ownership. Those businesses that showed concern for the community by selling needed goods and hiring community members were allowed to buy back the shares from the community group, while the others were encouraged to sell out to more responsible owners.

The Neighborhood as a Whole. Social production organizations can undertake activities that for-profit organizations do not, because activists in community organizations believe in the importance of helping a community, not simply in increasing the organization's bottom line. For instance, some social production organizations intentionally choose projects, such as repairing derelict buildings, on which they might not make money, as a first step in improving the community enough so that for-profit firms will be willing to make subsequent investments. One person described that her group has "taken the worst properties in the neighborhood because of private individuals not being able to do much with totally gutted buildings." Another activist explained that her non-profit organization repaired derelict buildings that were located in strategic places to

> . . . act as a catalyst and as sort of a leader and as a mobilizer of resources in the community to bring attention to the area and do something about the area, and maybe put it in a position so that it can be redeveloped.

Neighborhood watch programs, antidrug crusades, and efforts to clean up abandoned lots and parks improve the neighborhood as a whole. In addition, anticrime programs encourage community members to participate in other collective activities and by doing so increase community social capital (Skogan, 1990, p. 134).

Social production organizations build affordable housing, with the idea that it will help regenerate the community and make it better for the present residents, but do so in ways that help those most in need. Community groups fear that those who are initially helped to buy a home might want to sell the properties at a profit to gentrifiers, and by doing so make homes too expensive for current neighborhood residents. To prevent this from occurring, housing organizations set up *land trusts,* in which the nonprofit organization keeps ownership of the land underneath the affordable homes. So long as the original owners (and their heirs) live in the homes they have full ownership rights, but because they cannot sell the homes without the land, the community group is able to stop people from selling to the rich. Land trusts can keep homes affordable even if property values go up in the rest of the neighborhood.

Other projects, such as efforts to clean up parks, chase away dope dealers, or repair streets and sidewalks, directly benefit the community as a whole, as does providing needed business services. For example, low-income neighborhoods often lack banks, so the poor have to use expensive currency exchanges. Community organizations can create credit unions, technically a cooperative banking institution, to provide financial services to the neighborhood and assure that the money saved by people in the community is expended on local projects.

The Legal Structure of Social Production Organizations

Social production groups take on numerous different organizational forms with important implications for how they get funds, what they legally can do, and the degree of participation clients, tenants, or workers have in decision making. Such structures vary from informal unincorporated groups to formal, incorporated ones; from nonprofit to profit making entities; and from accountability to members to reporting to elected officials or even stockholders.

Informal groups rarely incorporate. Such groups might try a variety of tasks such as cleaning up a park, counseling members, patrolling the neighborhood, or running fairs, but the groups themselves have no legal status. Individual members (rather than the group) can be sued if things go wrong. Foundations rarely give money to informal groups, while people who make donations cannot get a tax deduction. Such groups depend on volunteer labor and donations without tax benefits. There is typically no money to hire staff to perform ongoing tasks.

Most social production organizations incorporate as nonprofit companies, usually under section 501(c)3 of the federal tax code. Doing so is easy, requiring a nominal fee, registering with the state's secretary of state, and indicating the purpose of the organization and the names of its chief officers. Once incorporated, the organization, rather than individuals holds legal responsibility for the group's activities. To obtain a nonprofit designation, an organization must provide a public, charitable, or educational service, but almost any group set up to help a neighborhood or a community does precisely these activities.

Nonprofit means that there are no stockholders or owners who benefit from the organization's activities. If the nonprofit takes in more money (say in rents) than it costs to maintain housing and pay the mortgage, such extra money must be used for a social purpose, for instance, staffing a day-care facility. Because nonprofits provide a public good and no one makes a profit, foundations are allowed to contribute money and individuals who donate funds receive a tax deduction. Many federal grants can be allocated to nonprofits; in fact, some legislation mandates a certain percent of federal grant money must go to community nonprofits.

Social production organizations that provide professional services, such as nonprofit day care or health care, are staffed by paid employees. The boards of directors of most nonprofits, the people who set the overall policy of organizations, are volunteers. Some neighborhood nonprofits might have only one or a few paid employees with all the other work done by community members. Nonprofits try to have typical community members on their boards, as well as experts, such as lawyers, who can provide free services.

Though most community organizations are nonprofit, many are structured in ways that take on some characteristics of for-profit organizations. Because of the federal tax code, nonprofit community groups are required to do some of their business through for-profit subsidiaries. A nonprofit CDC might partner with a commercial business and together build and manage a for-profit store in the poor community. Because the nonprofit is a partial owner, foundations are willing to help pay for land clearance, while the for-profit provides its expertise in running the store (and keeps its share of any profit). Profits made by the community group might be used to pay for related community services, for instance, to provide a free bus to help the elderly shop.

Some social production organizations are set up as cooperatives that have characteristics of both for-profit and nonprofit organizations. In housing cooperatives, the tenants are the owners. In producer and consumer cooperatives the workers control the business, rather than absentee stockholders. In most cooperatives, policy is set by an elected board. While workers in consumer cooperatives can accumulate ownership shares, depending on their work efforts and seniority, they receive the cash value of these shares only when they retire or leave the cooperative. They are not allowed to sell their shares to nonworkers. Further, each worker or tenant has only one vote, regardless of the number of shares he or she owns. In cooperatives, human effort is the crucial investment; capital is a means for accomplishing collective goals, not the controlling element.

Some states allow the formation of *limited equity cooperatives* to help house poor people. Lower-income people become members of the housing cooperative by investing a nominal down payment and then pay monthly charges that are enough to cover the mortgage and operating expenses. The rest of the money for the down payment for the building comes from charitable sources, church investments, or government. The interest rate on the mortgage is often subsidized. When people leave the cooperative, they get back their down payment (plus interest) but do not make a profit, even if the value of the building has increased. That way the building remains affordable for others.

Mutual housing associations (MHA) are legal entities composed of individuals who are owners of an organization that in turn owns housing, in which the individuals often live. A cooperative is a form of MHA, but MHAs can be larger scale corporations that build cooperatives or other forms of affordable housing. MHAs encourage democratic participation in both establishing and managing affordable housing.

Community Development Corporations (CDC) are another kind of hybrid organization, spanning both the for-profit and nonprofit worlds. CDCs harness the power and skills of capitalist firms to make investments that benefit people and communities in need. At the end of this chapter, we shall describe the CDC model in more detail; here we shall just sketch its organizational form.

CDCs' charters specify that they are to develop housing and community businesses and provide economic opportunities within the neighborhoods they serve. As nonprofit companies that are incorporated as 501(c)3s, CDCs are eligible to obtain grants from foundations and government and receive free land donated by government. The boards of CDCs are usually composed of community members, and if the CDC wants to receive certain federal housing funds, the boards must be primarily made up of lower-income community members.

Unlike most nonprofits that provide a direct social service, CDCs focus on capital intensive, physical development projects, such as housing, incubators, or commercial strips. Unlike most 501(c)3s, CDCs are allowed to make capital investments in property, become stock holders or partners in commercial ventures, invest capital in projects, acquire debt, and maintain earnings from profits, as long as the earnings are used for community betterment, including investments in other neighborhood projects. For-profit firms are willing to partner with CDCs because in doing so they receive significant tax advantages. CDCs act like for-profit firms seeking investments that pay off but in doing so seek profitable investments that serve social purposes.

Nonprofits can go bankrupt if their income and savings are less than expenses. Many social service organizations stay afloat from the fees they receive, whether directly from their clients or from government. As long as fees match expenses, these social production groups keep out of financial trouble. In contrast, CDCs borrow large amounts of money in anticipation of income from housing or commercial projects that might never materialize. CDCs are at financial risk if the project does not pay off so projects have to be chosen to have a social purpose (or else the CDC cannot receive charitable contributions) and also to be economically viable.

Development banks are capitalist firms that, like other banks, can be fully federally insured, receive deposits, and issue mortgages and commercial loans. But unlike conventional banks, the mission of a development bank is to rebuild poor communities, by making loans to economically viable projects in ways that benefit the people already living there. The best known development bank is the South Shore Bank, which helped renew parts of south Chicago, provides advice to development banks throughout the nation, and now has branches in Ohio, Michigan, and Arkansas.

Finally, most *community building initiatives* are coordinated by *network organizations* that bring together the efforts of a wide variety of advocacy, social production, neighborhood and identity organizations, and government agencies, working within one community. In some locales, coordination is handled by neighborhood associations; in others, a special group is set up, while in several places, a CDC acts as the lead organization in consultation with volunteer community groups (Wright, 1998, p. 60; Stone, 1996).

Tactics and Philosophies of Doing Projects and Providing Services

Many social production organizations follow a self-help philosophy that argues that people should provide needed services or goods by themselves. Such organizations encourage people to establish roof-top gardening or swap labor on needed projects. Their goal is as much about making people feel empowered as it is about accomplishing the immediate tasks.

By helping people help themselves, social production organizations *build community and individual capacity.* For instance, community-controlled shelters for abused women or neighborhood health-care centers not only provide vital services but try to encourage the people they help to learn how to provide the services themselves. Former residents of a spouse abuse shelter become peer counselors; people who have had heart attacks may counsel others on how to live with heart disease. A director of a project to teach women how to run their own businesses reported that "you pay as much attention to developing the business owner as you are paying to developing the business," for example, by teaching people how to maintain checking accounts. As such "our biggest success has been that we have been able to change peoples' attitude about themselves. . . . Our biggest measure of success is how have we empowered people so they can take control" (Interview with Herbert Rubin).

While self-help and capacity building emphasize a go-it-alone strategy, other social production organizations recognize the need to work with government. A city might fund community groups to administer its housing redevelopment plan or state agencies might fund job training efforts that are administered by community groups (Harrison & Weiss, 1998).

If all the production organization is doing is implementing government contracts, it can become dependent on government and lose its freedom to pursue what it thinks best for the community. To maintain its independence, social production groups try to diversify their sources of funding. For instance, when Chicago's progressive Mayor Washington was in office, the city contracted with 350 community organizations to provide economic development, housing, and social services for the city. These community organizations, however, were able to follow much of their own agenda by making sure they had other sources of funding besides these contracts (Wiewel & Clavel, 1991, p. 278).

Social production organizations differ in the extent to which they can accept and work within the capitalist economy or feel they have to reject capitalist values. Some social production organizations reject many capitalist values. These groups redefine what ownership means and the privileges it entails and question whether capital is more important than labor. They argue that social costs and social benefits should be included in economic decisions. A new job or better housing in a poor community is worth more than one in a wealthier area, because the former helps alleviate a social problem.

In addition, social production organizations that manage affordable housing assume responsibilities that capitalist owners avoid. As a proponent of this approach described:

> We don't see the point in developing affordable housing and then evicting somebody the first day they're past due on rent because they become unemployed. I mean we want to work with them to get a job and get their family back together. . . . We don't see the point of doing affordable housing and then letting the gangs paint graffiti all over. . . . We want to rent to large families. It's more expensive to rent to large families. The kids tear the place up but that's why large families can't get apartments in this neighborhood so, because they can't, we are going to. (Interview with Herbert Rubin)

Projects might not make a profit because they are also accomplishing a social mission.

Contentious Issues

The social production model represents a different approach to community work than does the direct-action model. With social production, government can be a partner; with direct action, government is often the target. As a result, tensions occur between those who support each approach. People involved in direct action challenge those who support the social production model to work out answers to three difficult questions:

1. To what extent does social production work distract from advocacy?
2. Does hiring professional staff to run social production organizations disempower other community members?
3. To what extent does the need to obtain resources from government or the private sector disempower the social production organization?

Does Social Production Work Distract from Advocacy?

With limited hours in a day, is it better for community groups to try to pressure government to preserve the multibillion dollar affordable housing programs or to spend their time building a limited number of affordable houses? Does the effort required in managing a small hospice distract from the direct-action campaigns and lobbying needed to pressure government to form an equitable national health service?

When neighborhood organizations start to work on social production projects they may lose some of their militant edge. In one study, after a neighborhood advocacy organization started development work its "identity began to shift toward convergence with the conservative community" while "transformative populism within [the organization] ebbed" (Stoecker, 1995, p. 121). Critics argue that CDC directors choose a "bottom-line business pragmatism" rather than working to promote "neighborhood controlled social change," and in doing so CDCs brush aside an "advocacy agenda"

(Lenz, 1988). Others fear that the consensus organizing model, meant to coordinate government, business, and community members in housing and economic development projects, reduces the possibility for protest actions (Gittell & Vidal, 1998). Observers of foundation-sponsored community building initiatives worry that these social production projects are about fixing buildings and not about changing the broader social structure (Yeoman, 1998).

Certainly social production is distinct from advocacy; a person cannot manage an apartment complex and simultaneously march on the streets. Even so, there is some evidence that social production is compatible with direct action. Housing production organizations have joined with housing advocacy groups to pressure cities to set up housing trust funds, to attack banks that ignore the Community Reinvestment Act (CRA), and to pressure Uncle Sam to expand the money for affordable housing (Rubin, 2000b; Goetz, 1993, 1996).

Social production organizations are cautious about joining advocacy efforts for fear of losing government money, but they do join, albeit indirectly. For instance, in Chicago, the REHAB Network, a coalition of housing developers, pressured city government to redirect hundreds of millions of dollars into community-based projects. The coalition contracted with an Alinsky-style organizer to coordinate a nonviolent, direct-action campaign (Ervin, 1994).

Both the Industrial Areas Foundation (IAF) and ACORN, two of the nation's leading advocacy organizations now work to build homes, yet do so without forgetting their histories as protest organizations. ACORN still will conduct a sit-in at abandoned homes to demand that the homes be repaired. When IAF worked with South Bronx Churches to build affordable homes, they relied on direct-action tactics to persuade the city to cooperate (Rooney, 1995).

Advocacy can lead to social and economic production efforts, which in turn empowers and helps mobilize those who receive services. A few years ago in Chicago, Voice of the People (VOP), a community-based advocacy organization for affordable housing, started doing housing rehabilitation to "maintain Uptown as a decent neighborhood for low-income families" (Vidal, Howitt, & Foster, 1986, pp. iii–5). Through using pressure tactics, VOP was able to gain resources for the rehabilitation projects and at the same time organized those housed to set up empowered tenants councils (Vidal, Howitt, & Foster, 1986, pp. iii–8).

In general, individuals who benefit from social production projects tend to be more active in other activities that empower neighborhoods. For instance, people who live in housing cooperatives are more likely than most in the neighborhood to be involved in advocacy work (Briggs et al., 1997). Members of worker cooperatives are also more likely to be active in the community. As one observer pointed out,

> . . . much of the energy of the co-op members goes not into building the co-op, but into developing the community where most members live. Community projects have included a food co-op and building a free school and a combined community center, health clinic, and co-op office. Members have a reputation for being ardent environmentalists who strongly oppose the use of herbicide and are willing to take direct action against their use. (Gunn, 1984, p. 85)

Social production work helps help build community integration.

Further, those who do social production work and those who undertake advocacy have begun to cooperate more extensively.

> It appears that the development and advocacy factions have begun to move closer together . . . although tensions remain. "We now see that groups can fail by putting too much emphasis on one or the another end of the spectrum" said Andrew Baker of the Institute for Community Economics. . . . "You've got to have both tree shakers and jam makers to make community development work." The bricks and mortar organizations require the additional resources that advocacy groups have been able to pressure financial institutions and local and state government to provide. At the same time, advocacy groups need development organizations to use the concessions they have won and translate them into real housing and jobs. (Peirce & Steinbach, 1990, p. 22)

Empowerment and Professional Staffing

Running social production organizations requires expert knowledge. Keeping a spouse abuse center alive takes fund raising skills and background in psychology and law; providing affordable housing requires understanding of finance, tax credits, and sometimes property or business management. Government often requires organizations that receive grants to employ professional staff; however, if an organization is dominated by professionals who have the expertise and other community members do not participate, capacity building does not take place.

Shelters for battered women were initially run by former victims who taught themselves how to help others. Over time, however, a variety of pressures resulted in an increasing professionalism on the staff. As counseling professionals established "family violence" as a speciality area, they began to discredit and put down the volunteers who had been running the shelters.

> Shelters had to lay their claim to expertise in order to ward off competition from more traditional agencies and obtain funding . . . adding more difficulties, funding agencies, boards, and some staff advocated or demanded the hiring of professional directors or counseling staff in order to acquire the expertise needed to survive and help battered women. (Schecter, 1982, pp. 107–108)

Histories of CDCs show that many began with volunteer boards and staffs. After a short time, however, most of the volunteers could no longer afford the time required to master the technical details and the organizations became more dependent on trained, professional staff (Rubin, 2000b). As

> . . . CDCs make projects more affordable, the CDCs and the projects become more complex, time consuming, costly and hard to manage. . . . This increasing complexity redirects ever more control to staff, who often live outside of the community and are more likely to emphasize the technical details of development over community empowerment. (Stoecker, 1996, p. 14)

There are no simple solutions to the problems caused by the need for professional skills. For ongoing social production projects, pure volunteerism simply won't work. Volunteers don't have the time to spend months negotiating over complicated financial deals, and parttime inexperienced people should not be handling the finances of a community credit union.

One solution is to accept the need for permanent, professional staff, but then assure that a strong supervisory board is composed of community members. Experts on the staff thus become the hired laborers whose job it is to achieve what the members of the organization want to do. For instance, the Dudley Street Neighborhood Initiative (DSNI) accomplished many technical tasks that required both professional staff and consultants. To maintain community control, the organization formed numerous subcommittees of community members that worked with the professionals while requiring all major decisions to be approved by an informed community board.

The DSNI succeeded because of the great care taken in choosing executive directors, the belief among the professionals hired that empowerment was important, and the insistence on community participation in hiring technical consultants. The volunteers on the DSNI board made sure those they hired not only had the requisite technical skills but also were able to work with elected community boards (Medoff & Sklar, 1994).

A second kind of accommodation occurs when the professionals running the social production group make sure that the product provided by the organization empowers community members. Social service organizations that help people with problems end up empowering their clients when they establish support networks among those served. Similarly, a vast array of literature shows that homeowners feel more empowered than do tenants, as do people who serve on tenants' boards or cooperative boards, so that CDCs, even when dominating the construction efforts, can empower community members by setting up homeowners or tenants' groups (Rohe & Stegman, 1994).

Resource Dependence

Community-based social production organizations need money, from government, foundations, and perhaps from the private sector. Funders, however, have their own priorities and grants come with strings, conditions placed on spending that may go against the preferences of the members of the community organizations. Can groups that are financially dependent on others make independent decisions?

A study done in Pittsburgh suggests that when partnering with the city to obtain funds, neighborhood groups lose their community focus (Jezierski, 1990). Developmental activists report "mission drift," the propensity of nonprofits to follow the priorities of the granting agency. A director of one community-based economic development organization reflected:

> Housing seems to be the hot topic and sometimes we get accused and maybe I accuse myself, of chasing grants. Don't look at your neighborhood to see what is important but find out what is hot and see how you can fit that into your neighborhood. (Interview with Herbert Rubin)

Other developmental activists worried if their shift to building apartments for the homeless and then later emphasizing housing for the disabled reflected more than compliance with the agendas of the funders. To what extent is the desire for social transformation compromised to get the material resources?

Organizations comply with the funders because if they fail to do so, they will die. In Chicago, VOP lost funding and eventually went out of business because it wanted to spend more time on social programs and less on housing than funders wished. In Minneapolis, the Whittier Alliance died, in part, because it was far more aggressive in trying to provide housing for poor people of color than was acceptable in that city (Rubin, 2000b).

What can a community group do? The simplest solution is to try to avoid dependence on outside funders. Consumer cooperatives sell products; as long as they provide what their members want, they do not need outside funding. Other groups engage in a variety of projects with the hope that some of them will make enough funds to cover costs on projects that the group members really want to accomplish. In Arizona, Chicanos Por La Causa, a CDC that began as a Chicano activist organization, has as

> . . . a major goal . . . to become a self-sufficient CDC, not dependent on outside funding sources. It is working toward this goal by creating for-profit subsidiaries that generate both revenue for nonprofit social services and economic growth for the community. (NCCED, 1995, p. 15)

In Spain, the Mondragon cooperatives own their own banks and use profits from one progressive organization as seed money for other cooperatives (Whyte & Whyte, 1988). The effort in the United States to establish community development finance institutions to fund neighborhood projects might enable the community groups to control both capital and programs.

Community groups themselves, however, cannot earn enough money to pay for major housing and redevelopment projects that serve the poorest neighborhoods; government grants are required. Rather than simply do the projects government suggests, however, numerous small social production groups form coalitions to pressure public officials to adopt the ideas from community groups. Coalitions of social production organizations directly lobby city government and the foundations to establish the housing and redevelopment programs that carry out the demands from the neighborhoods (Rubin, 2000b).

The Community Development Corporation Model
(from Rubin 2000b)

What do production organizations accomplish? How can they conceivably do enough to be of any real use with all the problems poor neighborhoods face? A few houses here, a new start-up firm there, a drug rehab facility in a third place, how much does it add up to? Can this type of community-based organization really solve social problems?

An examination of CDCs shows that when the separate projects are added up they do make a difference.

CDCs perform a range of tasks, including building affordable housing, financing neighborhood shopping malls, and loaning start-up capital for small businesses. CDCs help create jobs, do job training and some even provide social services. CDCs have discovered that they must undertake tasks that complement one another. Building affordable homes is not reasonable if the new owners don't know how to maintain the property and don't have jobs to pay the mortgages. A new supermarket won't get the traffic to survive if people are afraid to walk the streets. CDCs not only might help fund the store and also be involved in crime reduction efforts.

Overall, CDCs have been successful. As developers of affordable housing, by 1999, CDCs had constructed or repaired 550,000 units. CDCs do more:

> . . . 18 percent of CDCs reported completing commercial or industrial development. Some 23 percent of the groups reported having done business lending, equity investing or owning/operating a business enterprise. More mature CDCs tend to venture into this complex arena in order to meet the comprehensive needs of their communities. (NCCED, 1995, p. 11)

Cumulatively, CDCs have developed 71 million square feet of commercial and industrial space, lent $1.9 billion to business enterprises, and, without counting temporary construction work, created 247,000 full-time jobs (NCCED, 1999, p. 5).

CDCs have set up industrial or commercial incubators that provide affordable space for start-up industrial and commercial enterprises. In the Roxbury section of Boston, a CDC converted an old brewery into an incubator that now includes the offices of the Sam Adams beer company and a Hispanic food distributor. In Milwaukee, a CDC took out a master lease on large empty warehouses, subletting over a 149,000 square feet of space to help over sixty businesses locate in a declining neighborhood. The CDC of Kansas City opened a mall on an abandoned hospital site that now provides over 175 community jobs and maintains $35 million of business in a poor community (NCCED, 1995, p. 17). In Oakland economic and social development are brought together in work done by the East Bay Local Development Corporation that

> . . . developed the 47,000 square foot Asian Resource Center on the site of a vandalized warehouse . . . the Center provides the local Asian community with health and mental health clinics, English classes and offices for assistance with employment and housing for the disabled. The Center's commercial tenants include a bank, variety store, furniture store, snack shop, pharmacy, two doctor's offices and a medical laboratory. The center employs 228 people, mostly local residents and generates $632,000 a year in gross rents. The $230,000 of net income provides operating support to EBALDC and is used to support other EBALDC projects. (NCCED, 1995, p. 13)

By administering revolving loan funds, CDCs provide the capital to community members to start up small businesses (Parzen & Kieschnick, 1992). CDCs pressure city hall to provide services such as repairing potholes or more frequent garbage pickups that help community businesses. CDCs sometimes recycle closed neighborhood schools into medical care facilities for the poor or elderly. In partnership with chain supermarkets, CDCs develop stores to provide affordable, quality food and household goods in neighborhoods that have no supermarkets. In one case, doing so caused community members' grocery bills to drop 38 percent (Sullivan, 1993, p. 125).

CDCs are also involved in social services. The Urban Institute reports that about half of the CDCs provide homeowners' or tenants' counseling; two-thirds of CDCs do community organizing; 28 percent do job training while only 10 percent are exclusively physical developers. A third of CDCs do advocacy to support the CRA, the law that pressures banks to reinvest in poor communities (Center for Public Finance and Housing, 1994, pp. 55–56).

CDCs have accomplished this huge variety of activities, while generally remaining financially viable and independent enough to be able to work on a community agenda. To obtain funds, CDCs solicit contributions from foundations, government, and social service agencies. To complete the package of funding, CDCs set up partnerships with private investors and take out mortgages from conventional bankers. To fund an inner-city shopping area, for example, a CDC may have to obtain land from the city and start-up capital from contributions from local churches, and leverage these sources with equity provided by a federal grant. That sum is then used as a down payment that enables financial institutions to provide conventional mortgages. To make sure the projects work, CDCs find funding from foundations to help train those it serves.

CDCs also are about empowering people. While they have not always involved community members in every aspect of their decision making, they have facilitated the empowerment that comes about as lower income people become property owners (Rubin, 1994, 1997). The founder of the Christian Community Development Association wrote

> The motto of community development in the 1960s could have been this: "Give people a fish and they'll eat for a day." The 1970s motto could have been: "Teach people to fish and they'll eat for a lifetime."
>   . . . The 1990s (and beyond) approach to development needs to ask the question: "Who owns the pond?" (Perkins, 1993, p. 119)

The answer given by CDCs is that it should either be the poor themselves or organizations responsive to the communities. People who own their own homes and control their own businesses are empowered.

CDCs have also empowered people through providing job training and increasing employment possibilities. Bethel, a CDC in Chicago, set up social service agencies in apartments it built and then taught community members to become service providers (Barry, 1989). The New Communities Corporation in Newark constructed day-care centers for the children of those enrolled in job training programs many of whom had been homeless and now live in apartments owned by the CDC. In an ethnically mixed neighborhood, a CDC turned an abandoned supermarket into a *mercado,* providing space for low income people to set up stalls and sell needed goods. An abandoned facility for repairing railroad cars was transformed by a CDC into a factory in which the formerly unemployed repair industrial pallets and resell them. People with new job skills that match market demand feel confidence in themselves and see possibilities for improving their economic status.

Most CDCs work hard to ensure the participation of community members, if not in the original investment and financing decisions, then in the running of projects. Some CDCs establish tenants' organizations to run the housing, while others set up community-based committees to determine who will get into the homes. CDCs encourage the establishment of community-owned businesses in the buildings they refurbish.

The fourth and perhaps most important measure of CDC success is that they set up reinforcing cycles of improvement within lower income communities. CDCs catalyze economic development by owning or investing in businesses in poor communities. One of the best known examples is the Path Mark Supermarket built in the devastated first ward of Newark. Together the CDC and the private grocery company developed a 43,000 square foot $12 million shopping center including a supermarket, a restaurant emporium, and a donut shop in an area of the city without food shopping except for expensive minimarts.

CDCs focus on projects that keep money earned by community members within the neighborhood, rather than allowing it to be exported to wealthier areas, in part by creating locally controlled businesses that hire community members. One developmental activist reported:

> What we have is a community that exports more money than it imports. Part of what we are trying to do is to change that balance of payments. . . . Over 53% of the community is rental despite being mostly single family. On Friday people export rent checks. . . . And, when people have to go outside of the community to buy goods and services which are no longer here that's gone in terms of exporting. What we really are trying to do over time is to change the balance of payments, to try to create wealth here in this community by importing dollars not exporting them. (Rubin, 2000b)

A study in Miami showed that "it has been estimated that each $1,000 of goods or services sold . . . in the Cuban community generates $1,630 in total community earnings; the comparative figure in the Black community is only $1,140" (Bendick & Egan, 1989). In poor communities, wealth evaporates as people go outside the community to shop or pay rent because there are no stores or locally owned buildings in the neighborhoods.

In addition, CDCs focus on the community benefit in a second way, as they act as turnaround managers. CDCs demonstrate what can be done in communities from which others have disinvested, where there is little economic life and the costs and risks of doing business seem very high. In Kansas City, the Linwood Shopping Center, built by a CDC, became the first inner city mall replacing what had been a totally destroyed block; in Chicago, the Carroll-Fullerton incubator keeps jobs in a community that businesses had fled; in Newark, clean apartments, day-care centers, a new supermarket, and restaurants built by the New Communities Corporation provide a contrast to the surrounding decay and indicate that it need not last. By taking on the higher risks of the initial projects, CDCs make it easier for private businesses to follow at lower costs and with lower risks. CDCs generate hope and momentum.

Why have CDCs succeeded in communities that the capitalistic sector has abandoned? The National Congress for Community Economic Development (NCCED) suggests several reasons:

> As grassroots organizations, [CDCs] understand their communities—the needs, opportunities, resources.
> They operate with a clear mission and a comprehensive, strategic approach to community revitalization; they are involved in a long-term process, with each project building on the last and toward the next.
> They form partnerships with local developers, lenders, businesses, foundations, religious institutions, other nonprofit organizations and government at all levels. They have the political and technical skills and tenacity needed to pull together a complex array of resources needed to get projects done. (NCCED, 1989, pp. 3–4)

CDCs achieve success because they use technical skills to solve community problems.

CDCs keep their community focus by continually monitoring themselves against a set of premises developmental activists have worked out (Rubin, 1994, 1997).

- Development activists have a moral obligation through their work to symbolize hope for those in poor communities
- Redevelopment is done to create empowerment for poor people. Such empowerment occurs as individuals gain material ownership in property and through such ownership develop a sense of communal responsibility
- Renewal involves building an economically more self-reliant community in which businesses and wealth that are created work to generate more wealth in poor communities
- To provide hope, empowerment, and build economic autarchy requires a holistic strategy, uniting development with social services, while not shunning advocacy
- To bring about a holistic strategy, CDCs act as niche organizations that stimulate and coordinate others in redevelopment work

The ownership that CDCs bring about empowers people, giving them a material stake in society. Such empowerment is the end product of a variety of linked programs and projects aimed at community uplift. For instance, successful projects might involve linking an employment training program for community residents to a day-care service that the CDC had set up to provide social and medical services to the frail elderly. Part of CDCs' success, then comes from leveraging one success into another and viewing both problems and solutions as interdependent.

In Support of Community-Based Social Production

Community-based social production organizations provide services, jobs, and housing to those in need, while encouraging democratic involvement in the efforts. Social production organizations represent a hope that people can reempower themselves. Through participating in social production efforts, people gain skills and capacity that are inherently empowering. Social production organizations play a bridging role joining market forces and government services to help poor communities.

The social production model is not antagonistic to direct action or advocacy. Direct actions are necessary to assure that resources are available from government and that the public is receptive to empowerment strategies. In turn, through social production work, community members are able to control, guide, and direct the gains that advocates are able to bring about.

Successful social production simply doesn't happen. To develop ideas for projects, to package the financing, and to accomplish the tasks over the long run requires managerial and administrative skill, the topic of the next chapter.

16 Accomplishing the Social Production Project

The social production projects that community groups attempt are difficult to accomplish. Resources are scarce, while the problems faced are those that have already baffled the broader society. To increase the chance of successfully carrying out such challenging work, activists in social production projects have to master a variety of technical skills. In this chapter, we introduce five families of needed skills: planning, funding, implementation, management, and evaluation.

Planning	Deciding what projects should be undertaken and what steps need to be accomplished when
Funding	Obtaining the money, especially when banks and conventional businesses are reluctant to invest
Implementation	Taking the steps to build a project or provide a service
Management	Sustaining the project over time in ways that make sense financially yet achieve the community mission
Evaluation	Measuring whether the project accomplished its intended goals

Project Planning

Planning means anticipating what will happen and how to respond. Planning involves exploring a range of problems and alternative solutions to prevent mistaken actions and oversights. Organization members might see a crack house in a deteriorated building and quickly determine that the group should shut down the building. Doing so is fine, but planning forces the organization members to think about the more fundamental causes of the problem—why has crack invaded the neighborhood—suggesting longer-lasting actions that might prevent the problem from reoccurring.

Planning highlights the interdependence of tasks. For instance, if the goal is to keep a neighborhood economically viable, should the organization try to repair homes and build new and affordable housing first or concentrate on rebuilding the commercial strips? Without the homes, the stores won't make it economically, but without stores, why would people move back into that neighborhood? Planning forces people to examine alternative paths of how to get from the present circumstances to a new better situation.

If the problem is unemployment of young men, a number of approaches might be considered, including funding start-up businesses, training programs to give young men marketable skills, or transportation programs, to get eager workers to where the jobs are.

Technical planning can be guided by professional staff, but the organization members must play the central role in choosing community goals and the projects to achieve these goals. In the Dudley Street Neighborhood Initiative (DSNI), for example, planning efforts began "at a community-wide meeting attended by 150 DSNI members" where consultants encouraged "members to think about the neighborhood in new ways" (Medoff & Sklar, 1994, p. 101). Later, community members worked with technical people on the details of the plans, but the process was led by the membership not by hired experts.

Thinking about Overall Goals

The first stage of planning involves reaching agreement on the goals the membership wants to achieve. Is it the elimination of one crack house? Or does the group want to address safety in the community more broadly? Was the original problem that bothered people drugs or abandoned housing? Is the goal of a jobs-creation program to find employment for community members, even if the jobs are located in other communities, or is it to bring back jobs to the neighborhood?

To what extent is the project intended to accomplish a broader social agenda? Is building cooperative housing just a way of providing a shelter, or is it about teaching the owner–tenants managerial skills? Is the cooperative part of the broader effort to help poor people own the community in which they live?

Once people agree about the overall goal of a project—reduce crime, improve housing, provide support systems for Asian American women—they must consider the necessary steps to achieve these goals. In this stage of planning people link their goals to more precisely defined *objectives* and then determine measurable *tasks* that accomplish these objectives.

In efforts to reduce crime (the planning goal), one objective might be to improve lighting, a task that involves counting the number of functioning street lights and replacing incandescent lights with bright sodium–vapor lamps. To reduce fear of crime (another goal), an objective might be to increase the police presence on the street. One task might be to prepare a report explaining the need for extra police presence and then presenting this report to the city council. If the goal is to increase neighborhood security, one task might be setting up a community watch program; another might be midnight basketball to provide restless young people with constructive activities; a third might be installing more call boxes for residents to use to reach the police quickly. In planning efforts, people determine how particular tasks relate to a broader goal and work out ways to judge if the tasks are accomplishing their objectives.

Choosing Projects

During the planning phase, people choose which of hundreds of social service, physical construction, economic development, or community building projects to attempt. There are no hard and fast rules on which projects to pick, but some overall principles apply.

The idea is to pick projects that accomplish broad goals, that are doable, provide the most community benefit, help those in need, and have a realistic chance of breaking even financially. Projects should be done in ways that participants take pride in their work and feel empowered.

To begin, choose a project that accomplishes a broader goal. A community-based housing organization might build affordable apartments with a substantial government subsidy to house the very poorest, or it might build quality, single-family homes to encourage working-class people—police officers, fire workers, carpenters, plumbers—to remain in the neighborhood as a community resource. What will the project accomplish over the long run? Housing the poorest gets people off of the streets and provides poor families with a permanent address from which to seek jobs. Housing slightly better-off people more rapidly increases social capital.

Projects should have a lot of impact beyond the immediate effort. Projects that make the renewal of a neighborhood seem possible and in which residents can take pride have disproportionately large impact. Projects that create visible change and improvement create this sense of the possibility for continued progress. By helping stores owned by community business people purchase neat appearing facades, community organizations have changed the look of an entire street and encouraged others to invest. By taking on the hardest tasks, social production organizations can stimulate others to work on less difficult but needed improvements. For instance, a community-based development organization bought a badly deteriorated apartment building that had been used for drug distribution and repaired it, even though doing so was expensive, because

> . . . we recognize that the whole adjacent block was so much of a threat that nobody in the world was going to want to buy a house knowing that they are next to a crime-infested building.

Another reason to choose a project is to convince local officials and foundation staff that the organization has the ability to accomplish work successfully. Turning a small, abandoned school into housing for the elderly, shows the funders that the community organization can get the job done and encourages future support. Projects should showcase the organization.

There are also reasons not to do certain projects. Some projects require more skills than the organization has or more effort than the small number of volunteers can contribute. Projects can be too ambitious. The ideal is to choose work that will help the organization expand its capacity without at the same time being overwhelmed with a seemingly impossible task. It may make sense to try a neighborhood watch on a couple of blocks before extending it to the whole neighborhood. The organization should build toward capacity for the larger projects. Overall, successful social production organizations seem to choose projects using the following seven principles.

Capitalize on Niches and Filling Economic Gaps.

Work on projects that provide goods and services that are lacking and fill an economic niche in the community. Social production organizations train poor women to provide in-home day care in their neighborhoods, helping the community with a needed service and the women with a job

(Community Information Exchange [CIE], 1995). Efforts to improve the environment through metal recycling or waste removal from abandoned lots benefit poor neighborhoods, provide community jobs, and take on economically profitable tasks that those outside the neighborhood might not know are possible (CIE, 1998).

Think Catalytically.   At least initially, most projects that community organizations have the capacity to try are small. To increase their impact, projects should be thought out in ways that one small success can make subsequent actions easier. A community organization might set up an incubator that provides mentoring and inexpensive rental space to help small businesses get started. As those businesses grow, they will hire more local residents. Tearing down a crack house or refurbishing a dilapidated building can encourage private investors to build homes or open up their own businesses because the eyesore has been removed.

Think Symbolically.   Social production projects are meant to show the possibility of success. Efforts in which the young join with community artists and put up wall murals, especially those that assert ethnic and community pride, symbolize hope and the potential for the future. Community development corporations (CDCs) often convert abandoned old schools to new functions to show that the community is still alive. A new shopping area with lots of glass symbolizes the confidence of the community just as shattered windows and burned out apartments symbolize despair.

Think Holistically.   There is nothing wrong with planning a project that accomplishes a single important goal, especially as the organization's first major endeavor. But as organizations grow in capacity, they should take on more complex projects that accomplish social and economic goals simultaneously. Build homes, but why not use home building as a way to teach young people carpentry skills? Set up a day-care facility, but also train community people as certified day-care providers, giving them meaningful jobs, while assuring that most of the day care will be provided for children of community members who in turn are now able to find their own jobs.

Recycle Resources within the Community.   Poor communities export money because people need food, medical care, clothes, and other necessities, but they have to buy them elsewhere because there are no local suppliers. Establishing supermarkets, clothing stores, and clinics that employ people from the community helps keep money in the neighborhood. Any business formed by community members that attracts outside money is a plus.

Bootstrap Successes.   Success in one project motivates the next. If dope pushers have been chased from a park, for the next project increase the target area. A shelter for the homeless can provide a base for providing social services, job training and employment, and eventually homes for those served. Use construction projects to train community members in new skills. For instance, refurbishing old homes often requires removing asbestos. Rather than hiring an outside firm, some creative community-based development organizations have trained their own employees in asbestos removal, simultaneously fixing up the houses and providing community members with their own business (Rubin, 2000b).

Plan for Empowerment. Projects should not simply accomplish a material end, but should also empower participants. CDCs that enable people to become home owners also encourage political participation, because homeowners are more likely to be involved than others. Microenterprise programs provide people with technical skills that make them feel more competent and confident of their earning capacity, even if the initial businesses don't work. Spouse–abuse shelters house the victims and work to rebuild shattered self-confidence.

Planning about Benefits and Costs

During the planning stage, questions about benefits and costs of the projects should be asked.

1. Is the project worth the effort? Even if the organization has the money and personnel, it might not be worthwhile to set up its own day-care center if the neighborhood already has good quality day care at affordable prices.
2. Do alternative solutions produce more benefits at lower cost? Should a community group try to own a store, with all the management hassles that might entail? Or is it better to try to attract private businesses, by providing parking, increasing safety, and providing job training for potential employees?
3. Who gets the benefits and who pays the costs? Programs to build new homes may improve the appearance for the neighborhood but force out the poor as wealthier people purchase the homes.

In comparing costs and benefits don't just include the dollars spent; examine the value of opportunities foregone, the social costs of working with politicians, and the broader impact on community members.

Begin with monetary costs and benefits. The dollar costs of setting up and running a community day-care center should include rent, personnel, insurance, and supplies. Monetary costs should also include the value of lost opportunities, in this case, what was not accomplished because the group was working on the day-care center. The costs can then be compared to the monetary value produced, for instance, the income people can now earn because they have a safe place to leave their children. Other monetary benefits include the tax payments that parents who are now employed can make, instead of drawing welfare payments, and the income earned by community members who work at the center.

Less tangible benefits and costs need to be included in the calculation. For example, a project might win the attention and approval of the mayor that can later be turned into contracts, grants, or future work. A project that angers politicians might not be worth doing even if its financial benefits are substantial. Efforts that make an organization appear to be a legitimate actor, a player in the social production game, might have more value than a purely dollar-and-cents calculation might imply. The first successful housing project lets banks and government know that the organization has arrived and makes getting resources for future work easier. Another intangible benefit is the symbolic value of new homes or a small shopping center built in neighborhoods that people felt could never be repaired.

When deciding between possible projects, be sure to examine social consequences that are difficult to measure in purely economic terms. How does one estimate the value of the increased efficacy that community members feel when, through their efforts, local crime rates drop? What about the value to the elderly and their friends when a housing project for those with special needs enables the elderly to stay in a familiar community? What about the pride an individual feels when he or she finally gets a real job?

Potential projects need to be examined carefully to see who benefits and who pays. A new stadium might benefit shop owners, souvenir sellers, restauranteurs, and ballpark food vendors, but the stadium might bring a massive invasion of automobiles into residential neighborhoods or attract vandals. Subsidies to attract businesses may leave local workers without jobs unless there are provisions for job training or requirements to hire locally. Proposals to increase the intensity of police patrol might be oriented to making shop owners feel more secure rather than residents, or they might result in increasing humiliating stop-and-search routines of minority youths. Changing some features of a program can help distribute the benefits more fairly or reduce the costs to poor people.

Sequencing the Steps of Doing a Project

Project planning also involves figuring out how to order tasks. A plan indicates when concrete has to be poured before the weather gets too cold, when resources will be needed, and where bottlenecks can occur if there is insufficient personnel or money. Plans highlight when a particular step is crucial and if not taken will destroy the entire project. An environmental organization might start work to acquire ownership of a nesting site for migratory birds, but unless the area around the proposed sanctuary is reasonably undisturbed, with natural water flow allowed, the project would be unsuccessful. In Illinois, the government was planning to build a maximum security prison near the site of a proposed sanctuary. The environmental organization had to switch the order of tasks, fighting off the prison construction first before engaging in land acquisition.

Project Funding

Though much can be accomplished through voluntary effort—people on neighborhood watches work for free, and hospices rely on contributed labor—cash is needed to pay bills, buy property, and support staff. Even a community fair put together by volunteers requires funding for advertising, city permits, stringing electric wires, insurance, and Port-A-Potties. Rehabilitating inner-city housing necessitates large amounts of capital.

Further, projects done by community groups have costs that for-profit organizations avoid. Building a home costs the same no matter whether it is to be sold to gentrifying yuppies or to poor people in lease–purchase programs. With a lease–purchase program, however, community groups have to find additional money to teach new homeowners about maintenance, taxes, insurance, and fire prevention. For conventional builders to get a mortgage is fairly straightforward, as long as the banks feel the project will make a profit. For CDCs, building affordable homes requires special funding, through grants or tax credits, that often require community groups to hire lawyers, at substantial cost, to make sure everything is done right.

For the most part, community-based social production organizations are dependent for funding on government, foundations, and community contributions. To piece together money takes time and skill while requiring community groups to deal with richer organizations that have their own ideas about what should be done, sometimes creating problems in ensuring that community goals are being accomplished (Rubin, 1995). Further, the funding environment for nonprofit organizations is turbulent (Groenbjerg, 1993), that is, it rapidly and unpredictably changes. Banks invest in affordable housing because they are required by law to make investments in poor communities, but the willingness of government to enforce the law varies while government and foundation grant programs can quickly disappear.

To complicate matters, community projects involve some expenses that funders are less willing to pick up than others. Getting money for the physical development costs of a conventional, charitable project, such as the construction of a soup kitchen that feeds the unemployed homeless, is comparatively simple, as the funders get to brag about the accomplishment. Community groups, however, also need to pay for staff that hunts for the site and plans the project and for ordinary office expenses. Few foundations are willing to pay for these routine expenses because there is no glory in doing so.

Before a project is undertaken, work must be done that costs time and money, yet this money might never be recouped if the project fails. Such *predevelopment expenses* include costs for market research to see if certain services or products are needed, architects to design potential projects, lawyers to check on who owns what land, land purchase, and tests for environmental hazards. Cash is required to pay interest on the purchase of the property or the fees to contractors who construct the building; this money is required long before the project produces any income. Similarly a community fair might have to pay electricians to install lines before the fair is run. Such risk capital is hard to obtain, especially for a community organization.

One other substantial cost is insurance. No matter what the activity, projects require fire and theft insurance and liability coverage against accidents. If the community organization plans to take the elderly shopping, vehicle insurance and driver liability coverage are essential. Organizations providing health or any form of counseling services should carry malpractice insurance. What if a counselor advised a woman to return to her husband after he had beaten her, and she followed the advice, only to be beaten again and hospitalized? Presumably the woman could sue for having been given bad advice. The organization needs to be protected against such costs.

Especially in doing large projects, substantial capital funds might be involved. In this case, organizations obtain a form of insurance called bonding that guarantees that if someone runs off with the project's money, the insurance company will make up the loss. Before someone is bonded, he or she must be approved by the insurance company, so that a person with a record for embezzlement is not likely to be bonded.

In planning project financing, social production organizations negotiate with their funders which expenses should be charged to a specific project and which to the organization's general overhead. Obtaining money for general overhead is hard, because there is little glory associated with paying for lights and heat. For smaller organizations, money to pay the overhead is derived mostly from gifts and the small profits that the organization makes from bake or rummage sales, book fairs, or fish fries. CDCs are often eligible to receive money for overhead from the Community Development Block Grant, while some specialized funders such as the Local Initiatives Support Corporation (LISC) sometimes supply funds for overhead expenses.

Fund Raising

A few social production organizations receive all their funds from government contracts. More often, funds are pieced together from a variety of sources. Doing so requires skill in *leveraging* in which a small, initial contribution acts as a seed to convince government, foundations, and eventually banks to provide additional money. A $10,000 grant from a foundation to assess the feasibility of converting a small abandoned factory to a day-care center can be leveraged into a $100,000 grant from the city to buy the building, and then, with this investment already in hand, a bank might be willing to loan money for the costs of rehabbing the building.

Funds come from many places. One study (Pogge, 1991, p. 12) showed overhead money for housing organizations in Chicago were obtained from the following sources:

Sales and income	32.5%
Local support	15.5%
United Way	0.7%
Government	20.8%
Foundations	13.3%
Corporations	9.7%
LISC	7.5%

An Urban Institute report (Center for Public Finance and Housing, 1994) noted that to fund affordable housing, community groups routinely work with seven major federal programs and solicit state, local, and private sector contributions. Another study that focused on apartment housing projects run by neighborhood organizations concluded that the nonprofits "averaged 7.8 sources [of funding] per development" (Hebert, 1993, p. ES-15).

A developmental activist described in an interview how he leveraged LISC's support for a project into the large amount of capital he needed:

> You gotta go to all of these entities and sell your project. . . . Usually LISC is the first group because they're the ones who give you the predevelopment money. So once you've

got LISC money then you can go out and say, "LISC believes in this project, we want you in on this project."

They've already put up some money so you sell that to the city, you sell it to HUD [Department of Housing and Urban Development], you sell it to whomever. And as people begin to buy in then you've got more clout when you go to the next person so when you get a LISC grant, then you get a nationally competitive grant, then people begin to listen again. You see 'em saying, "well geez, these guys got a grant that's nationally competitive, it must be a good project."

And then you go to the next group and say "ok I've got LISC, I've got [a federal grant] I need the city," and the city kicked in $200,000. Then you say "I got LISC, OCS, and the city, I go to the banks and say, hey I've got tax credits." (Rubin, 2000b)

Many smaller projects are paid for by fund–raising events, such as bake sales, raffles, or community dinners. Part of the costs for community groups doing social service activities is paid for by those using the services, while much of the operating costs for affordable housing comes from the rents paid by tenants, that, in turn, might come from Section 8 subsidies. In addition, social production organizations receive contracts from cities to provide services or to manage subsidized housing projects.

Some social production organizations generate a part of their overhead funding from profits they make on a few projects. A community group may serve as the manager of an incubator, earning a little money that can be put into newer projects. A few community groups that own affordable apartments actually make some money from the rents, but this is rare. Social production organizations that build homes or commercial developments take out of the deal their own developers' fees, money paid for coordinating the project, that can be used to support other activities. In practice, these developers' fees are small, and much of the money is spent on providing social services for clients or is put back into the project to keep rents low.

For small projects, corporations are often willing to donate goods or provide services. For example, a car dealer might donate a van to a group transporting the elderly (Flanagan, 1982, pp. 79–80), while larger industrial companies or banks might spring for the overhead for community fairs and other noncontroversial projects. Companies can be asked for furniture or equipment they no longer need. With the rapid change in computer technology, many companies are quite willing to give usable but slightly dated equipment to nonprofits.

Corporations and unions can also help in a more substantial way. CDCs partner with for-profit businesses, having worked out a fair allocation of the capital investments and the distribution of profits. The community group gets a grant from government or the foundations to prepare the land or repaint the building, while the commercial firm provides the funds to set up a business on the site. Labor unions sometimes invest money from their retirement funds in community housing and commercial projects, especially if the community organizations hire unionized workers to do the construction.

Some corporations are nervous about directly investing in nonprofit projects, so they do so through intermediaries such as LISC. Intermediaries act as brokers between for-profit firms and community organizations, interpreting each to the other, and providing the technical help needed by nonprofits. In 1993 alone, LISC provided CDCs with $12.6 million in grants, $37.4 million in low-interest loans, and $158 million in equity investments (Local Initiatives Support Corporation, 1994, p. 15). Most important, LISC and other intermediaries have helped community-based development organizations raise money from corporations for tax credit projects. We discuss this type of support in Chapter 17.

The most important funders are government and the foundations. Governmental funds can run into the billions and are crucial to the work done by community groups. Still many of the most innovative projects are funded by foundations that can try riskier projects than public-sector organizations are willing to fund.

One of the first steps in getting grants is to figure out who actually controls the dollars. As the federal government has gotten smaller and less concerned with accomplishing a social agenda, many programs once run by the federal government are run by the states. To find out about federal grant programs, the *Catalogue of Federal Domestic Assistance* is helpful, or click on to the home pages of the relevant federal agencies. These web sites often include information on grants available (Notices of Fund Availability or NOFAs). Organizations can ask to be put on a list to be notified of NOFAs. To find out what money is available from foundations, look in sources such as the *Grassroots Fundraising Journal.*

Local governments sometimes help fund the projects of nonprofits. Many localities actively partner with nonprofits in projects to build homes (Suchman, 1990), while others have set up *linkage programs* that require downtown builders to provide money for nonprofits to build homes in poor neighborhoods.

Through extensive lobbying efforts, and sometimes after direct-action campaigns, community groups have persuaded state and local governments to set up Housing Trust Funds (Brooks, 1989, 1992, 1994). These funds provide the subsidies needed to make housing affordable to the very poor. What makes this source of money significant is that a mechanism is usually in place that automatically replenishes the trust funds. So in some states, a small tax is levied every time property is sold and this money is placed in the housing trust fund.

Foundations are an important source of funds for community projects. Foundations vary in size from the giant Ford, Pew, and McArthur Foundations that are worth billions down to small community foundations that number in the hundreds and collectively control billions in cash. Major projects almost always have the imprint of some foundation. For instance, when the DSNI acquired eminent domain powers to force owners to sell land, DSNI still needed cash to make the purchase; the Ford Foundation provided a no-interest $2 million loan (Medoff & Sklar, 1994, p. 149). Still, the DSNI would not have succeeded if the small Riley Foundation had not patiently paid for its operating expenses, as DSNI worked with community members to plan what projects to undertake.

Foundations usually carve out a niche in terms of the type of program or project they will fund, and sometimes restrict funding to particular geographic areas. The Aspen Foundation has been very active in funding microenterprise projects, while the Annie Casey Foundation concentrates more on social service programs that help families and children. Foundations such as the Joyce Foundation have been receptive to innovative ideas that come from the community groups, such as helping start up businesses that employ the poor. Some foundations establish programs to which community groups apply. For instance, Ford, Surdna, and Annie Casey Foundations each have set up different community building initiatives for which community groups are eligible.

To learn about foundation funding, consult the web pages of the individual foundations and explore the publications of the Foundation Center in New York which lists foundations, their location, their objective, how much money they have, and how to make contact with them. The Grantsmanship Center publishes the *Grantsmanship Center News,* which provides information on deadlines, how to manage grants, and ways of applying.

Foundations don't want to bother with irrelevant applications, so they are forthright in their descriptions of what they will fund. If a community organization has questions about whether it is worth applying, answers can usually be obtained by phone or by writing a brief letter of inquiry.

Preparing a Proposal.   Leaders of community organizations have to convince government, foundations, or corporations to fund their projects. The organization prepares a formal, written proposal explaining the problem faced, how the project will solve the problem, how much it will cost, and precisely the ways in which the money will be spent. In addition, proposals indicate the capacity of the organization to handle a project by describing its previous experiences, staffing, and its financial strength. Prior success in getting grants and carrying out projects is one way of demonstrating capacity. Sometimes proposals succeed because of lobbying efforts in which appeals are made to elected officials. Most grant requests, though, are judged on their own merits.

Some government grants are distributed according to formulas. If an organization is designated the official recipient, money is allocated according to objective criteria, such as the number of families in the neighborhood with incomes less than the poverty level or the number of unemployed people who are looking for work.

There is no sure fire way of writing a proposal that will be funded; however, some of the following advice should help:

1. Preface the proposal with a brief overview of the project's goals, its budget, and procedures for evaluation. Board members who make the final decisions appreciate a concise summary.

2. Early in the proposal, clearly discuss the objectives and the plans for achieving these objectives. Funders look for innovative plans. Don't go off the wall with some flight of imagination, but do have a clever twist that will gain attention. A utopian housing scheme in the inner city might be discarded immediately, but proposals that house poor people who have physical handicaps in apartments that have an additional room for their care givers might be treated more seriously, because it is new, appropriate, and feasible. Especially with innovative proposals, be prepared to resubmit after getting feedback from the funding agency.

3. Provide evidence documenting the problem, but make sure that the evidence speaks to the immediate issues at hand. Funders get bored reading endless statistics showing certain neighborhoods are poor. Much of this background material belongs in a technical appendix.

4. Funders are looking for evidence that the organization can actually accomplish what it proposes, so the application has to include a description of the staff and membership, what the organization has achieved, and who has benefited. Take a few sentences to show how prior experiences relate to the present proposal. Having picketed city hall is not appropriate experience for managing a large housing rehabilitation grant, but rehabbing several small buildings might be.

5. Be precise in the project budget, carefully justifying how resources will be spent and indicating whether the requested grant funds will be combined with money from other sources. If the foundation or governmental agency accepts the ideas and believes that the organization has the capacity to implement them, the budget becomes the central focus of their evaluation. Too big a budget will make them nervous about the percentage of their funds going to one organization. Too small a budget and they will worry about whether those proposing the activity understand the realities of doing the work.

6. Describe the contributions of equipment, labor, and cash that the community and members of the organization will provide. Where appropriate, show that work is already underway and has been somewhat successful. *Sweat equity*—the voluntary contribution of community members' labor—is an important indicator to funders that people are serious about the project. Also, because most funding organizations like to leverage their money, a proposal has a better chance of getting funded if some costs are being covered by other agencies. Describe how the organization will evaluate the project, as evaluations reflect good management and show a determination to improve.

7. Finally, and especially for innovative projects, indicate how what is learned will be shared with other community groups. With standard projects—a rehabbed house or a day-care center—funders know what to expect and are satisfied if so many people are housed per dollar, or so many children are cared for at a reasonable price. Innovative ideas, however, may be complicated and costly and are more easily justified as demonstrations, to work out the kinks, and then teach others how to do them. To assure funders they will get this additional advantage, it is useful to build in a dissemination plan that may include sending out reports to other organizations doing similar work, presentations at conferences, or special workshops.

On occasion, a proposal is presented orally to a panel or the board of a foundation or corporation. In such personal presentations, describe the idea briefly. Even if the organization has submitted a written proposal, assume that the panel has not yet had the time to read it. Make sure to describe the importance of the project for the community and how it fits within the mission of the foundation or agency. If board or panel members are interested in the proposal, they will ask questions that will help them justify funding it.

Don't get discouraged. Few organizations get funded every time. Fortunately, foundations and government agencies usually provide feedback on grant requests. Pay attention to these comments when rewriting the proposal. Program officers who write such commentaries are experienced, and a sharp rejection might really mean you should rethink the idea before asking for funds from someone else.

Still, there are many agencies and foundations to which to apply, so if the idea is sound, just keep rewriting it and sending it out again. Chances are good that with persistence the organization will win a grant. Sometimes funders will negotiate about a plan and may be willing to pay for a jointly agreed on demonstration proposal. Remember, after an initial grant has been won and carried out, it is usually easier to get subsequent funding.

Project Implementation

Project implementation refers to how the work is carried out, though what is involved can differ from case to case. To manage a housing construction project, social production activists have to work with building contractors, check out the site and monitor progress, and trouble shoot, that is, solve problems as they emerge on a day-to-day basis. To carry out a training program for would-be entrepreneurs, organizational members have to contact those who want the training and lure them into the program, hire instructors, and examine the curriculum to make sure that it is pitched at the right level, is sufficiently informative, and is respectful of the clientele.

While each project is a little different, there are some common concerns. Carrying out community-based social production projects is difficult; all kinds of strange problems crop up for which the activist must be prepared. In addition, projects done by nonprofits are often undertaken in partnerships with others, which requires efforts to make sure that partners live up to their promises.

Implementing Community Projects is Difficult

Community-based social production organizations do projects in neighborhoods that others have abandoned, working with the poor who lack experience, the elderly, unemployed, the handicapped, and people with little formal education. In these neighborhoods, crime rates may be high and infrastructure poor.

Further, community organizations are small and lack the staffing and funding to finish all the projects they attempt. For example, Bethel New Life, an exemplary community-based CDC, set up a home health-care service but eventually had to withdraw from the effort because

> Bethel New Life is a community-based organization and not a medical institution, it was difficult and more costly than they anticipated to build the infrastructure to deliver health care services. Specifically, the start-up costs associated with the program prior to the delivery of services, were not covered. In addition, administering such a complex and large program required Bethel New Life to establish procedures and hire staff for a much different program than had previously existed within the organization. (Community Information Exchange, 1995, p. 14)

Luring new businesses into the neighborhood is difficult because of the neighborhood problems. A developmental activist described the problems his organization faced in recruiting businesses for an incubator.

> When we go to talk to tenants [and say]—"would you like to relocate to the [incubator]?"
> What are we telling them? We are telling them wouldn't you like to move into a high
> crime area in the inner city, in an old building with a developer who doesn't have enough
> capital to do all the repairs in an efficient way? (Rubin, 2000b)

When working in neglected neighborhoods, the physical construction can become
a real nightmare. A community group described the problems that occurred in assembling
a site for a community shopping center:

> Before the site was cleared, one Saturday night some winos were in the basement of
> one building. Torched it, burnt it, they pulled out a body Monday morning. So that there
> were so many things that went wrong. During construction people stole wood, they stole
> bricks, they harassed people. I was down there every night. Finally, we got the damn
> thing built.

Persuading neighborhoods that a home for AIDS victims or work-release prisoners
or transitional housing for people with mental illnesses will not destroy property values
or threaten their personal security can prove daunting.

Scheduling and Adaptation Rather than Fire Fighting

Scheduling means laying out the necessary steps in order, in advance, in ways that
anticipate problems. *Adaptation* implies midcourse correction and is necessary when
unanticipated difficulties emerge. Community-based employment training programs
have to respond to changes in the job market; plans for construction projects are often
interrupted or delayed when contractors don't show up, or, as in one case we studied,
when storage tanks of toxic material are found on the property and have to be removed.

In every project, groups must respond to emergencies and unanticipated problems.
Organizations have to respond quickly if a crack house opens up in a block being
renovated or a cold wave wipes out the fuel budget of an affordable housing complex.
With sufficient planning, however, *fire fighting,* responding piecemeal to problems as
they occur, can often be minimized. For instance, a contingency fund can be set up
with the idea that cold waves will occur and require extra expenses. Then, when a cold
wave does occur, it does not have to be treated as an emergency. If the organization is
fighting fires because it is engaged in too many projects and something is always going
wrong, maybe the group needs to concentrate on fewer activities.

Scheduling tasks is partly a matter of logic and partly a matter of experience. For
example, land acquisition has to occur before construction can begin or a vehicle must
be purchased and delivered before a program to transport the elderly to doctors can
commence. Experience helps in figuring out where bottlenecks can occur, what is likely
to go wrong, and how long it is likely to take to recover from those problems. If group
members have not done similar projects before, they should talk to other people who have.

Once you know what the tasks are, and roughly in what order they should be
done, it is often helpful to draw flowcharts that show when each task is supposed to
start and how long it is supposed to last. Some tasks have to be done more or less at
the same time, but before other sets of tasks. Table 16.1 provides an abbreviated version

TABLE 16.1   Steps in Building an Affordable Housing Project

Property Development	Financing	Tenants
1. Finding an appropriate property and having architectural and environmental assessment made	1. Obtaining funding to pay for preliminary site and property inspection	1. Determining the types of tenants wanted—families, homeless, special need populations
2. Acquiring the site, including doing title searches	2. Securing an initial subsidy from the local government, an intermediary or a foundation to lower mortgage costs	2. Gain neighborhood support for the project, perhaps by offering to house those in the community most in need
3. Assuring zoning compliance	3. Investigate special incentives such as historic tax credits that could encourage corporations to invest in the project	3. Try to locate tenants that have rent subsidies, for instance as owners of Section 8 certificates
4. Contracting for construction and rehabilitation, supervising the construction (this then breaks down into hundreds of smaller steps; each requiring inspection and repetition, if not done satisfactorily)	4. Structure the deal in ways that enable banks and corporations to obtain the benefits of the Low Income Housing Tax Credit so they invest equity money	4. Check out the background of potential tenants to make sure they are suitable for the development. What is their credit history? Is there a history of crime? Are the people poor enough so that the building is eligible for the Low Income Housing Tax Credit?
5. Getting hookups for water, sewer, electricity from the appropriate agencies	5. Apply for Low Income Housing Tax Credit that the city or the state can allocate	5. Helping organize the tenants into a tenant's association
6. Gaining occupancy permits from government after the property is checked for safety, building codes, etc.	6. Look for banks that are usually helpful in affordable housing deals or those amenable to community reinvestment pressures to invest in the main mortgage for the property	
7. Setting up a management team to collect rents, clean and maintain the building, and handle tenant problems	7. Calculate the costs for heat, light, general maintenance, insurance, and taxes for operating the property	
	8. Calculate the total costs of running the property including the operating expenses and the repayment schedule for the mortgage	
	9. Calculate the rents needed to maintain the property and compare with the rents that can be reasonably expected. If the rents are not adequate, other subsidies have to be found to keep the property affordable. Perhaps churches can be approached	

of the hundreds of steps involved in putting together an affordable housing project. It shows how the physical development work, the financing, and the leasing have to coincide in timing.

Each of the steps listed can involve dozens of smaller tasks, from hiring carpenters and electricians to checking out the chances of getting subsidies from foundations. Later steps depend on the outcomes of earlier ones. If the *pro formas*—the business sheets on which costs and revenues are estimated—show that the rents will not cover the mortgage and operating costs, either rents have to be increased, making the property less affordable for the poor, or more work is required to find additional subsidies. Discoveries made when doing the physical construction, such as a defective sewer line or evidence of vandalism, can increase costs. Communities might object when poor families are housed nearby, and then the organization has to decide whether to try to persuade neighbors or to change the project to one that houses the poor elderly.

Project planning examines the overall sequential interdependence of tasks, determining which ones affect the others and what to do if failures occur anywhere along the line. Knowledge garnered from other organizations might be sufficient to estimate how many people will show up at a spouse abuse center. Whether or not construction companies are willing to work for nonprofits can depend upon how well the economy is doing. Planning about funding, especially from government, permits few guarantees, while physical construction, especially with older, deteriorated properties, always takes longer than planned. If a particular grant comes through, the purchase date for equipment may be pushed up, or if the grant fails to come through on time, the purchase may be delayed.

To plan for such contingencies think about a project in the following way:

1. Divide up tasks into *separable action steps.* For example, break up a program to hold a community fair into the distinct steps of gaining permission to use a park, hiring security, arranging for cleanup, talking with other neighborhood associations on what they want to present, and printing tickets.
2. Examine tasks to see if together their completion will accomplish the overall goal. Is anything missing that should be added?
3. Examine the length of time to complete each task. It is especially important to know which tasks can be speeded up with more effort and which take a relatively fixed amount of time. A grant will or will not arrive on a given date—a task that cannot be hurried with more effort—whereas fifty people can clean up a park more quickly than can ten.
4. Note the *interdependence* among tasks. Legal title must be obtained to property before any physical work is done on it. If it might be difficult to obtain legal title, then the start date of physical work needs to be flexible.
5. Prepare a *chart,* sometimes known as a program evaluation and review technique (PERT) chart, in which the timing and relationship among the tasks are laid out. The bottom line of the chart is marked with a calendar. Each task is represented by a line starting at its beginning date and continuing to when its conclusion is anticipated. The chart shows the interdependence of the tasks and points out potential bottlenecks.

6. The schedules for different tasks are worked out to isolate those tasks that can be done almost any time from those that provide a vital step in the project completion.
7. The chart is examined for *critical events,* that is tasks that must be performed or the goal cannot be reached. Not getting a permit for the park makes the fair illegal, while if the city tears down housing before it can be repaired, the plans for the organization's sweat-equity program will have to be terminated.
8. When roadblocks and delays are noted, resources are shifted to the extent possible to reduce the delays.

Implementing Joint Efforts

To successfully complete social production projects, community organizations require cooperation from others. At times, the community organization hires someone else to accomplish a task. On other occasions, community organizations partner with government or for-profits. The most complicated arrangement is participation in a community service network.

Contracting for Services.   Social production organizations often contract for particular services. For instance, few people in community groups have the expertise needed to write up a federal grant proposal so the group might hire a consultant. There are also technical tasks, such as auditing, that have to be done by outsiders to be credible. Before hiring someone, it's best to ask other community organizations which contractors they found satisfactory.

Many technical firms can be found that provide services for nonprofits and community groups in ways that carry out an empowerment agenda; usually people in these firms have experience with working in community groups. Several universities, especially those located in inner-city areas, maintain technical centers to work with community groups, while some professionals, including lawyers and architects, work for free or at nominal costs for nonprofits.

When hiring consultants, managerial firms, builders, or others, it is vital to carefully spell out obligations in a legally binding contract. *Put everything in writing* and make sure to specify:

1. The scope, quantity, and quality of work expected.
2. The balance of responsibility between the contractor and the community organization. The community organization writes the first draft of the grant proposal, then the contractor turns the ideas into governmental prose. Or, the members of the group will clean out the debris before the electricians and carpenters begin their work.
3. The time when the contract is to begin and when the contractor is to complete the work and submit the results.
4. An exact description of what the results are to be, including how the results are to be delivered to the organization.

5. The standards that must be followed in completing the contract. Spell out who judges whether these standards have been met and what happens when they are not met. Work out in advance who will reconcile disputes between the two parties.

6. The amount and timing of the payment. Some contractors want a down payment for materials. If moderate, such requests are reasonable. More often, the first payment may be made on the submission of the first *deliverable*—that is the first product done by the contractor—and the remainder may be paid as each step of the work is completed.

7. The conditions under which one or both parties can back out of the contract.

Care is needed in wording the contract because alterations can be expensive. Remember that contractors have schedules and other obligations and cannot always adjust if your organization changes its mind.

Partnering with Commercial Firms. Partnering with commercial firms, especially in economic development and housing projects, can be a mixed bag. At one extreme, there are unethical, for-profit firms that will try to use community social production organizations to get money from government programs. Many government programs to help poor neighborhoods insist that the money be spent by firms owned by the poor, women, or minorities. Unscrupulous for-profits pretend to partner with less experienced community groups but really are just using the nonprofit as a front. Such situations should be avoided.

Sophisticated CDCs, such as the New Community's Corporation in Newark, enter into true partnerships with commercial firms, such as Path Mark Supermarkets or Dunkin' Donuts. In these partnerships, profit is fairly shared, stores are opened that benefit the poor community, the CDC is actively involved in management, and the commercial firm provides technical expertise.

An approach that might be more suitable for less experienced community-based social production organizations is to locate and work with a responsible, successful business person who cares for the community. These people are often born and raised in the neighborhood, have made it on their own financially, but maintain ties to the community, often through religious affiliations. Such people want to help community groups succeed.

For instance, an African American organization wanted to build a small office complex to rejuvenate a neighborhood, had access to grant money, but lacked the know-how. The developmental activist knew many business people including a well-known commercial developer who had religious ties to the neighborhood.

> We told him we don't want you to develop this building for us and you walk away and it is a good deed and we don't benefit from the experience of having learned. What we want you to do is . . . assist us, so that we learn [emphasis], because we are doing this so that we can learn and we want to be in a position what we learn can be shared with the broader African-American community.
>
> And, this is what this guy said. "We'll do it." He said "The reason we'll do it is I don't feel that there is enough African-American participation in this city's development.

And, we are not going to do it for you. We're going to do it with you and to the extent
that you learn from us, then hopefully you will be in a position to do this your own self
one day and help some other folk." (Rubin, 2000b)

That is a mutually empowering partnership.

Partnering with the Public Sector.   Each time a community group receives a grant
from a public agency, a partnership of sorts evolves. Much of the government role is
monitoring to see that the money has been spent in a legal fashion. Compliance with
HUD programs might involve obeying sixty or seventy pages of regulations. Even more
complicated partnerships evolve when social production organizations partner with
government in development projects. Government might give land to a nonprofit for
its project or might use eminent domain to force slumlords to sell the land. Local
governments provide permits or may donate water and sewer hookups. In a partnership
relationship, the government agency might try to do so much of the scheduling that it
ends up taking over the project from the community group.

Dealing with government can be a nightmare, as in the following case that a
development activist described in which a community group partnered with a city to
acquire and upgrade a deteriorated block of buildings. First, the city incorrectly con-
demned the existing buildings. Then the community group had to lobby the city's legal
department to make sure the case did not slip into the nether land of unfinished public
business. During this time, the city administration changed, creating further delays as
all neighborhood projects were once again reviewed. To further complicate matters,
some of the money was to be borrowed, but with the delays, the supportive lender
backed out. Then government became reluctant to buy the land because it thought the
price was too high. Cooperation was only obtained after the community group "threatened to embarrass people" through direct-action tactics.

While partnering can be difficult, it can work out to the community group's
advantage. In Boston, the city granted eminent domain powers to the DSNI, and adopted
the community group's development plan as its own. In other places, partnerships have
helped fund affordable housing programs whose goals are determined in large part by
community members.

One complication that occurs in partnering with government is that elected officials
need credit for what they do. In taking credit for joint projects, they might inadvertently
minimize the successes of the community organizations, reducing the sense of empowerment felt by members of the community organization. Fortunately, credit is stretchable,
so that politicians can receive publicity while the community group looks successful.
Encourage the politicians to show up for ribbon cuttings publicized on citywide media,
but make sure the community group circulates flyers about its successes and has its
name and address prominently displayed on the large poster boards that are planted in
front of new projects.

Still, there are no simple ways of assuring that projects done in partnership with
government will increase community empowerment. When dealing with government,
enter the relationship gradually, and if a little bit works, try some more. Successful
public–nonprofit partnerships emerge over time as city department heads realize that

community groups can be quite efficient. If the relationship works, the community organization and the public sector partner will work out clear boundaries on who is responsible for what.

Networked Partnerships.   Another approach to partnerships occurs when several community-based social production organizations join together to provide a service so that each helps the other to succeed. A wide variety of such networks have come into being, some uniting community groups with traditional social service providers. Social service providers and community-based agencies work together to help the homeless (Johnson & Castengera 1994), victims of environmental problems (Schopler, 1994), and AIDS victims (Mancoske & Hunzeker, 1994). In many cities, community-based housing and economic development organizations combine their efforts (Metzger, 1998; Rubin, 2000b), while community-based organizations join with each other, social service agencies, and conventional businesses to provide employment training, especially as part of welfare-to-work programs (Giloth, 1998; Harrison & Weiss, 1998).

When set up appropriately, such networks enable community-based organizations to remain small, focused, and participatory, yet garner the needed expertise for project implementation. Several distinct models are followed:

In *mentoring models,* an established community group partners with novice organizations. For instance, a neighborhood group might refurbish apartments to house community members only to discover it doesn't have any idea how to manage the complex. It then contracts with a CDC that has such skills, that manages the project for a fee, but teaches the newer group how to do the work itself.

Service networks are set up to help community organizations aid people with a variety of personal problems that go beyond the individual organization's speciality. A community member who is alcoholic, for instance, might approach one organization that focuses on such concerns. Alcoholics, however, might have problems retaining a job or finding housing or need medical help. The initial organization is networked with other social service organizations, for instance specializing in job training, to whom it refers the person.

In *bridging models,* a community group links together diverse people and organizations needed to accomplish a task. For instance, a community organization that provides job training must locate the people who need the training, teach them the technical skills, and make sure they have the attitudes necessary to succeed in the world of work. When the bridging organization discovers the person it is helping has gaps in his or her education, it refers the person to a school program set up for adult learners. Meanwhile, the organization maintains direct linkages to employers who are readily willing to hire those trained by the group, especially because the community organization knows the skills that this particular employer needs.

Sometimes bridging entails helping community members set up their own networks. A developmental activist explained how such bridging is done.

> The place I go to lunch . . . He's got a Mexican restaurant, he is starting to catch on. . . . we . . . loan him a $1,000 to buy a new refrigeration system. And, he begins to pay us back and . . . we expand it to $5,000 so he can do some remodeling. . . . All

the while what we are doing is helping him build a credit history. And, then we are working with a bank that . . . has agreed to buy any loan that is performing out of our portfolio. . . . The idea here is not to make [the community entrepreneur] a permanent client of [the community organization] but to serve as the bridge to get into a banking relationship. (Rubin, 2000b)

In *centralized task networks* a different approach is followed. Community organizations that are working on similar tasks together set up another, specialized organization that hires staff with the technical skills that all the community groups in the network need. The separate community organizations don't have to hire these experts, whose skills they only need some of the time. For example, in Cleveland, community-based housing organizations set up the Cleveland Housing Network. The centralized network organization hires specialists in handling tax credits, in making sure the refurbished homes meet building code standards, and in teaching new homeowners and tenants skills. The individual neighborhood organizations choose which homes are to be refurbished and work with community members to determine who is to be housed. Expertise and community control are both achieved.

Networked social production organizations also gain power through their connections with advocacy groups. For example, the Center for Employment Training (CET), a bridging organization, is considered the nation's most effective community-based training program, having obtained jobs for over 75 percent of the people it serves (Harrison & Weiss, 1998, pp. 51–53). The model works, in part, because of the close relationships CET maintains with future employers. But in addition,

> . . . the second aspect of CET's success . . . has to do with empowerment and respect derived from the organization's long-standing relation to (embeddedness within) West Coast Hispanic politics and culture. Simply stated, CET derives great strength from its association with a powerful social movement. Many of the same forces and actors who created or sustained the modern farm workers organizing activities and eventually the United Farmworkers of America (UFW), played a role in the formation and sustenance of CET. (Harrison & Weiss, 1998, p. 57)

Project Management

Once a project is under way—apartments built, a day-care center opened, a community garden planted, an incubator up and running—it has to be managed. Someone from the social production organization has to make sure that there is money to pay the bills, do the hiring, and, assure that the work is being done appropriately. New problems need to be handled, while routine services are provided. Running a home for abused women requires provision for security, for food, laundry, phone service, legal support, medical backup, emotional support, job counseling, and child care, in addition to the maintenance of the building itself. Added to those tasks are those of gaining funding and paying bills. At any time, problems can erupt, maybe a crisis in staffing or a resident who becomes catatonic or a boyfriend who tracks down his victim.

Project development can provide a sense of the possible that then is celebrated. A ribbon is cut for a day-care center that now enables dozens of parents to work; or a clean, affordable apartment building for families replaces a run-down, vermin-invested hideaway for substance abusers. Someone has to make sure the furnace works, the rents are collected, and the halls kept clear, or that only certified day-care teachers are hired and the milk for the children arrives every day. As one development activist reported, "development is exciting, but property management is forever" (Sullivan, 1993, p. 44).

More social production projects probably fail from lack of good management than from choosing a bad project or not obtaining grants. Developmental activists need to acquire managerial skills. Some can be learned on the job or through internships; other skills are best picked up through course work at school or by seeking help from mentors or support organizations.

Management of social production projects is difficult. Expenses are often greater in affordable rental property than for-profit projects, because the property often has more problems and people are less experienced in maintaining their own places. Further, income streams to pay for regular expenses may not be stable. Only three of a dozen housing developments in one study had been able to put aside the recommended reserves from the rent (Bratt et al., 1994, p. 110) and many organizations had no reserves whatsoever (Bratt et al., 1994, p. 105). Many community-based development organizations do not cost out services such as snow removal against the monthly income received, forcing them later to scrounge for money to provide such essentials (Bratt et al., 1994, p. 6).

Those managing properties set up by community groups confront a "double bottom line" between their social missions and their need for economic survival (Bratt et al., 1994, p. 3). Developmental activists recognize the problems the people they house face:

> We have to collect the rent. We're not a social service agency, per se, but in dealing with people [we] realize that there are a lot of folks who live in our units that have multiple problems. We've got babies having babies. . . . We've got people with very low education levels, people who are getting AFDC and towards the end of the month the food stamps run out. (Rubin 2000b)

Further, as landlords, developmental activists recognize that if they do not provide close supervision undesirables enter the building and destroy property (Bratt et al., 1994). One activist explained what happened before management tightened up tenant screening in a community apartment building, where people were paying rents with Section 8 certificates:

> We started getting an average of 20 police calls a week to it. The management company was explicitly told to tighten screening like crazy, err on the side of being too conservative. . . . They screened like 200 people to get 11 units filled . . . 20 cop calls a week. We got like 4 units that were averaging 5 domestic abuse calls to them a week.

Intense screening, however, means that some people who desperately need the housing will be rejected, and the community organization may be seen as authoritarian and rule bound.

The goal is not simply to manage well, minimizing financial problems and emergencies, but to do so in ways consistent with the empowerment ideals of the community movement. Three principles may help in developing a management orientation that balances effectiveness and empowerment.

1. *Grow your own managers.* Find people from colleges and from the community who accept an empowerment ideology and have them learn the technical skills from the support organizations.
2. *Segregate functions.* Set up separate divisions in the organization in which those who make final policy and those who choose what projects to undertake are separate from the technicians who do the management.
3. *Choose Community Members for the Board.* The more technical the management problems and the more extensive the need for experts, the more important it is to make sure the board of the organization, the people who set policy and monitor what is happening, are community members, including those who are receiving the services. Make sure that the board and the managerial staff interact frequently. The board needs to understand managerial problems—rents have to be collected or bills cannot be paid. The technical staff may need to be reminded that the bottom line is caring for people and improving the community, not simply running in the black.

Project and Program Evaluation

Evaluations monitor how a program is being conducted and what its impact might be. To use a medical analogy, *monitoring* is the daily measurement of vital signs, while *impact analysis* shows if a treatment is effective. The purpose of an evaluation is to get information to improve services and programs.

Evaluations that show a program is working should be widely shared so that community members know the value of the organization's effort and can praise those who brought about the success. For instance, one study evaluated the effects of community-based housing on a neighborhood and found that neighborhoods where community groups had built affordable housing were seen as better than otherwise economically similar neighborhoods. In addition, people felt safer in neighborhoods that had cooperative housing and were more willing to participate in community activities (Briggs et al., 1997). An evaluation of housing in New York City reinforced these findings, noting that people who lived in cooperatives were more likely to volunteer for collective efforts than those in regular apartments (Saegert & Winkel, 1998). These evaluations not only showed that affordable housing programs can work but that certain ones had positive effects on the community.

Evaluation can also be useful if it zeros in on the reasons why some programs are not working. Accepting negative findings is easier if the organization performs its own evaluations. If technical help is needed (especially if a funder insists that an outside agency do the work), there are numerous support organizations that can do the mandated evaluation. In Minneapolis, the private Rainbow Research evaluated neighborhood crime watch programs, while in Chicago, the University of Illinois Center for Urban Economic Development works with community groups to help plan and evaluate projects.

Program Monitoring

Program monitoring allows those who have set up a project to learn what is being accomplished.

1. *How much service is being produced?* How much money has the community credit union lent out with what return rate? How many women have been housed in the spouse abuse center, and of those, how many were able to restart their lives? How many children are taken care of in the day-care center, and how much more income are parents able to earn because of the availability of this care?
2. *How many people are served and who are they?* How many people come to the homeless shelter each night? Are they families or individuals? What is the income level of the people who participate in the lease-purchase program?
3. *How do people in the social production organization spend their time and re-sources?* Are workers in the housing organization responding to tenants' complaints, or are they able to find time to plan new projects? How much money is spent on serving clients and how much on general organizational overhead?

Program monitoring helps a group identify and shore up weakness. If those who are relatively better off are buying the new homes being built, perhaps the organization should try harder to reach out to the very poor. If women return again and again to the shelter, maybe different services are needed to bolster their confidence.

As part of program monitoring, the organization prepares *efficiency measures,* which determine how much of an activity is being accomplished for how much cost. Community employment training is evaluated in terms of the money spent to train new employees for each permanent job. With further refinements, one might measure the quality of a job obtained per dollar spent. Efficiency measures help a group decide on important tradeoffs such as whether to house two working poor families or to use the same money to house one extremely poor family.

Careful program monitoring distinguishes between effort and outcome. *Effort* measures the energy or money spent by the organization to accomplish its goals: dollars put into rehabilitation; number of hours a day that an emergency hot line is available. *Outcome* measures the changes brought about by the program: How much did the quality of housing improve as a result of the rehabilitation? Did the rate of illegal dope transactions decline in the area served by the hotline? Were fewer people cold in winter?

People work hard on projects and want to be praised for their efforts. Hard work at activities that are poorly conceived or implemented, however, is of little benefit to the community. Evaluations must measure both outcome and effort, with outcome being the more important.

Impact Evaluation

Program monitoring provides descriptions of the actions that are taking place. Impact evaluation measures the overall consequences of the project or program. Have the overall goals been accomplished, especially those promised to the funders?

If the goal of improving housing is to give people a secure base from which to find jobs, to give children the opportunity to attend the same school with the same classmates, and to stabilize the neighborhood, is the plan working? If the goal of a neighborhood watch program is to make people feel more secure, is it working? Are they out on the street after dark more than before; do they shop in their own neighborhoods without fear their groceries or handbags will be stolen or that they will be pushed down or knifed?

Many measures of program success are learned from reports people give of whether they are satisfied or not. The question "Do you feel more secure in the neighborhood?" is a satisfaction measure for a community crime watch program. Does the neighborhood look more attractive? This might be a relevant question in evaluating a program to plant trees and flowers on the parkways and remove grafitti from buildings. Satisfaction measures may not coincide with other ways of measuring outcomes. For example, community crime patrols may make people feel more secure without reducing crime rates.

Impact evaluation asks, what were the goals of the program and were they achieved? It also asks who benefited from the program or project; it is almost always easier to run a successful project for the elderly than for families, to get jobs for experienced and educated workers rather than inexperienced and uneducated workers, or to help successful rather than marginal businesses. Programs need to not only look good but also help the intended beneficiaries.

Toward Empowering Social Production Work

Community-based social production organizations carry out projects that provide services while enabling people to develop the skills and confidence to help themselves. Social production projects build capacity, provide resources for the community as a whole and work to help those who have been left behind by a changing economy. Social production projects offer a way for people to take control of declining economies and to overcome the disempowering consequences of personal problems. Such projects are part of the can-do spirit of community action and a reassertion of human dignity.

The skills of knocking on doors, motivating people to act, and leading direct actions differ from those needed to build homes or run community services. To do social production work, traditional community organizers must master new skills, encourage other community members to learn them, or lure developmental activists into the community.

The work of developmental activists shows that mastering skills in social administration—in budgeting, in personnel management, in negotiations, in coordinating the work of multiple organizations, or in preparing a spread sheet—need not imply withdrawal from a social-change agenda. It is through learning these technical matters that social production organizations are able to do the projects that renew hope and empower those in poor communities.

17 The Support Sector

Smaller community and social-change organizations often lack the technical knowledge and economic resources needed to battle big business and government. Fortunately, help is available from an array of larger, established organizations that include coalitions, technical assistance providers, action networks, consultants, foundations, and financial intermediaries that collectively provide advice and financing and help plan strategies. These *support organizations* help community groups build their own capacity and become better able to accomplish the agendas that their membership chooses.

The World of Support Organizations

Support organizations can be loosely grouped into three clusters. In the first are the organizations maintained by the activists themselves, including direct-action and development coalitions, networks, and trade associations. The agendas of these support groups are decided directly by their membership of community organizations, while the boards of directors are composed of people experienced in protest or social production work.

The next cluster includes research shops, some national political-action organizations, and technical assistance groups, along with many consultants who specialize in problems facing nonprofit community groups. These organizations are usually founded by experienced activists but may hire those with less experience in community work.

The third cluster of support organizations, includes large, technically sophisticated, and often rich organizations whose funding is supplied by banks, foundations, and government. Within this cluster are the socially responsible foundations, developmental intermediaries, and housing partnerships. The staff and boards of these organizations are sympathetic to the work of community groups but may not have activist experience themselves. At times, the agendas of these larger organizations are limited by what public agencies, businesses, or rich donors permit.

Activist Coalitions

Activist coalitions are set up when organizers talk with one another and discover that they face common problems and that some have discovered solutions that could help other groups. Neighborhood organizers might meet at lunch to discuss how to persuade the new alderperson to pay attention to community members; over coffee and donuts, developmental activists puzzle out the newest vagaries of federal financing. Eventually, those attending the informal discussions decide to set up coalitions and networks whose missions it is to keep track of the political, social, or economic environment that affects community groups. Some coalitions are local, focusing on problems in one place, such as finding jobs for the unemployed in the Chicago area, while others, for instance, the National Organizers Alliance, encompass a national membership.

Coalition organizations garner information from government, foundations, and technical assistance providers and distribute it to their membership. While individual activists might be too busy to deal with government on a daily basis, the coalition monitors core agencies and lobbies officials for its membership. Through such ongoing lobbying efforts, the coalitions make those in public office aware that they are dealing with a movement, not simply an array of isolated groups. As one developmental activist described,

> It is helpful for [my organization] to be part of a larger movement because the state won't create programs to fund [my organization] but the state will create a program to fund community economic development. . . . I mean it doesn't do any good for [CBDO] to be terrific and on its own. You know if it is not part of a larger movement there aren't going to be resources to support it. (Rubin, 2000b)

Organizing Networks

Many organizing networks—IAF, DART, or ACORN—came about after individual activists who had learned their skills through experience decided to share their knowledge with others through training programs. To pass along the insights her group learned in combating redlining in Chicago, Gale Cincotta, for instance, helped set up the National Peoples' Action, a national network that coordinates community action and sponsors a training academy in protest techniques.

These organizing networks teach the network's own model of social action, work with communities that want to set up organizations that carry out these models, and then offer technical support to their affiliates. For example, the IAF provides formalized training in the Alinsky model. In addition, the networks help their members keep abreast of the changing political climate and newer organizing techniques. The following list describes several active networks (Gamaliel, 2000; Mott, 1997; O'Brien, 1994).

IAF	The Industrial Areas Foundation, with over three dozen affiliates is the oldest of the networks. It offers training to individual organizers and when invited into communities by churches and local organizations, will do the initial mobilizing and organizational building work.
ACORN	The Association of Community Organizing for Reform Now began as part of the welfare rights movement and has expanded to include chapters in five hundred neighborhoods in thirty cities. It offers continuing training

	in confrontational, political approaches, organizes communities from scratch, and provides technical assistance in areas such as housing renewal.
DART	Direct Action and Research Training is a southern–United States–based network with most of its affiliates in Florida but also includes organizations in the Midwest. It offers training and technical assistance.
GAMALIEL	Gamaliel emerged out of attempts in the late sixties to combat redlining in African American communities. Today Gamaliel trains and provides advice to forty grass-root organizations, mostly faith-based groups, in the Midwest.
PICO	The Pacific Institute for Community Organizations is a West-Coast and Midwest network of twenty-two affiliated organizations.
NPA	National Peoples' Action began as a national coalition of neighborhood groups battling redlining. Today, through a loose network of self-selected affiliates, it works to link local issues affecting neighborhoods to national policies.
NCLR	National Council of La Raza, a constituency-based Hispanic organization, provides technical assistance to its two-hundred affiliates while trying to build a consensus on what policy recommendations to make to government to benefit its membership.

Networks differ in their structure and what they seek to accomplish. NPA is primarily an umbrella group for like-minded organizations that while offering training is more concerned about building a national policy for change that is argued at an annual meeting during which "304 neighborhood organizations from 38 states participate" (Mayer, 1996, p. 22). Other networks work directly with neighborhoods who want to set up their own action groups. For instance,

> PICO goes into an area only after being asked by local pastors or congregations. It helps people form a sponsoring committee, raise seed money from local sources and go through the legal process of becoming incorporated. The network also assists the congregations in selecting and hiring a PICO-trained organizer. . . . PICO helps to train the pastors, staff and congregation members in organizing techniques. (O'Brien, 1994, p. 33)

IAF follows a model of *institution-based organizing*. Paid, professional IAF organizers are invited into a community by local churches, neighborhood associations, and unions. IAF provides technical help to established community groups on setting up the boards of umbrella organizations, fund raising, and canvassing. In contrast to

IAF, ACORN organizers themselves do the canvassing, sign up people one by one while talking about problems of economic justice. Recently,

> . . . several networks have moved from a primarily consulting role to actually staffing their local affiliates. They see this as the way to maximize professionalism of locally based staff . . . the initial organizers are usually experienced members of the network's ongoing staff; their successors are often recruited locally and trained by senior organizers until they are ready to take on more responsibilities. (Mott, 1997, p. 27)

Networks coordinate action among their affiliates, emphasizing selected issues on which coordinated campaigns are conducted. For instance, Texas IAF has helped local affiliates bring about educational reform and improve health care while enabling the dirt-poor colonias in southern Texas to obtain clean water. Texas IAF turns a local issue into a statewide one by encouraging its separate affiliates to pressure their individual representatives on an issue that initially was faced in only one locale (Wilson, 1997).

The Washington-based Center for Community Change (CCC) provides a wide array of support services to organizations throughout the country (Rubin, 2000b; on-line information from CCC [*www.communitychange.org*]). The CCC summarizes changes in economic and social policy, circulates technical publications on a wide variety of action tactics and distributes action alerts to organizations throughout the country, especially on issues dealing with poverty. Its publications have explored topics including fund raising, economic development tools, media relationships, federal housing programs, and philosophies of direct action. The Washington staff of CCC monitors government programs on poverty and housing, and when lobbying is needed, the CCC electronically circulates alerts to those in its network.

In addition, the CCC has helped set up numerous local direct-action and social production organizations. The CCC obtains the grants so that it is able to provide technical assistance to start-up organizations for free. The CCC, however, is careful in choosing those whom it helps. As a CCC organizer told us,

> . . . we're particularly focused on very low income organizations mostly led by people of color. . . . 'Cause it really is an organization that believes in grass roots empowerment and skills transformation.

The CCC works only with groups that mandate meaningful involvement of community members on their boards (Center for Community Change, 1991, p. 15). Recently, the CCC has worked with local groups that are trying to help people getting off welfare obtain the training needed to find jobs.

In addition, at both the state and federal level, the CCC's staff advocates for programs to support low-income housing, has worked in antihunger efforts, and in general advocates for programs to alleviate poverty. The CCC has been at the forefront of efforts to maintain and expand the Community Reinvestment Act. As a result of its lobbying, the CCC has established many state and local housing trust funds that provide a dedicated, albeit often small, income stream to help subsidize affordable housing.

Today these trust funds generate about $300 million a year for housing programs (Center for Community Change, 1994, p. 2).

Training Academies

Many *training academies* are sponsored by support networks and consequently follow their underlying approaches. Training varies from a few days to several months duration.

The training not only emphasizes practical issues, such as fund raising and research on targets, but also communicates the broader philosophical orientation of the sponsor. Participants at sessions offered by the Center for Third World Organizing reflect on issues about intergroup relations. The Midwest Academy supplements its skills training with sessions that discuss the political context in which organizing occurs, while IAF training emphasizes theories on how to reconstruct the social fabric through faith-based organizing. The Consensus Organizing Institute instructs its attendees on the importance of building bridges between neighborhoods and business rather than setting up confrontations.

Universities also offer course work in community-based economic development. The Pratt Institute and the Management and Community Development Institute hold training programs and provide academic classes on developmental issues, set up to match the requests made by practitioners. Some universities, such as Spertus College in Chicago, New Hampshire University, and North Park University, offer master's level training in community economic development.

Many development activists learned their craft at the Development Training Institute (DTI) (Rubin 2000b). DTI's formal curriculum instructs participants in the philosophy of community economic development, while providing an introduction to accounting, economic development procedures, real estate development, and organizational effectiveness. The curriculum also includes specialized seminars in housing and commercial real estate and business development (Development Training Institute, 1992). The program is intense, as one of its graduates described:

> Basically DTI has a year long training program. . . . The first meeting of your training is for two weeks, so you leave your place and are in DTI for two weeks, 10–11 days of training, maybe one of those days you might have a break but it is pretty intense. Then you come back home. And, then you actually have to work on a housing project and a commercial project. . . . And, so you have homework between that first meeting and the next meeting . . . and reading materials. Then you go back once each quarter for one week of that intensive training and come back. So you get maybe about 5 weeks of training over that year's period of time. And, they cover all aspects of development. Strategic planning, accounting, cost accounting, projections, rehabbing, recruiting, and community development. . . . So its quite extensive. And intensive. (Rubin 2000b)

Citywide and statewide development coalitions also sponsor abbreviated versions of DTI's training, and even DTI itself offers less intensive programs on topics such as building developmental leadership.

Training also takes place during conferences sponsored by coalitions and trade associations. At conferences, participants teach others how to deal with a changing environment. Community groups learn how to integrate neighborhood development with anticrime efforts; developmental activists learn the ins and outs of supermarket development in poor communities. Attendees at the annual meetings of the National Peoples' Action discover new approaches to direct action; those who go to meetings of the National Organizers' Alliance discuss philosophies of mobilization; people who attend meetings of the National Low Income Housing Coalition explore the technicalities of new housing legislation and discuss what actions can be taken to influence housing policies.

Workshops and panels at conferences sponsored by trade associations, such as the National Congress for Community Economic Development (NCCED), continue the training of experienced developmental activists, while introducing newcomers to needed information. A typical NCCED conference might include several plenary sessions about the overall direction of the movement and about three dozen panels on specific topics, such as how to finance commercial real estate or form microenterprises. Some workshops focus on emerging tools of the trade—electronic communications or techniques for applying for an Office of Community Services grant—the major source of federal money for community economic development. Representatives of funders and technical assistance providers teach how to package funds or explain the intricacies of reselling loans. At breakfast round tables, conferees chat informally about their experiences with these techniques (Rubin, 2000a).

Trade Associations

For activists involved in social production, *trade associations* provide backup support, often quite similar to that made available by coalitions. The trade associations circulate newsletters that teach about current trends, publicize successful projects that other community groups can emulate, and sponsor training programs on housing development, organizational management, or grantsmanship. Like the coalitions, and often in concert with them, trade associations lobby government for their respective movements. In addition to lobbying for specific legislation, trade associations maintain a continuing, political presence that shapes how public officials view community and social change organizations.

At their conferences, trade associations run training sessions that teach technical skills but that also communicate to the newcomers the possibilities of success. At NCCED conferences, for example, organizers offer tours of effective projects, exposing newcomers to what can be done and helping old-timers learn the technical details that can spell the difference between failure and success. Finally, meetings sponsored by trade associations (and coalitions) provide the time and place during which people get to form relationships that later become the networks along which help is provided (Rubin, 2000a).

Technical Assistance Providers and Consultants

Technical assistance (often called TA) refers to the support that organizations and consultants provide to individual community groups to solve the immediate, specific problems they face. Coalitions and trade associations provide technical assistance with their own staff, and there is a whole small industry of consultants who specialize in helping the community movement.

Numerous technical assistance organizations help social production organizations especially with their work in building homes or restoring local economies. Community Builders in Boston works with community development corporations (CDCs), helping them prepare cost estimates, hire contractors, or supervise physical construction. South Shore Advisory Services provides advice on establishing incubators and running community businesses and has helped CDCs that face financial problems find ways of getting out of trouble. Chicago Association of Neighborhood Development Organizations (CANDO), a coalition of community economic development groups in Chicago, helps its members with the paper work needed to obtain Small Business Administration loans while working to link its members with problems with others in the coalition that have already resolved similar issues.

Even direct action groups need technical assistance. Dudley Street Neighborhood Initiative required technical assistance to bridge the tensions in its politically and ethnically diverse community and hired Community Training and Assistance Center (CTAC) to help. Direct-action groups need help to assure that gains made from action campaigns are properly implemented. For example, having negotiated funds for a land trust, a community organization still may require considerable legal advice on how to structure the trust in ways that benefit poor people. Or a community group might have concluded a campaign to keep a factory open by agreeing to buy the company and make it worker owned. If so, the group may need advice on management from specialized technical assistance organizations.

There are literally hundreds of technical assistance organizations. The Center for Urban Economic Development at University of Illinois Chicago researches the economics of community projects, while the Property Management Research Center helps teach groups how to manage property. The Consortium for Housing and Assets Management assists organizations in handling the capital assets involved in affordable housing. In a single year, the CTAC worked on tasks including designing action campaigns for public school reform, neighborhood beautification efforts, and establishing entrepreneurship training programs (Betzold, 1998).

Activists who have learned a particular skill sometimes become consultants in that area. For instance, to battle the problems of toxic waste at Love Canal, Lois Gibbs, a homemaker turned agitator, successfully fought a recalcitrant government and a deceptive chemical company. To make her case, she had to master information about toxic chemicals. After leading her neighborhood to victory, she discovered that many other communities faced similar problems to her own. Gibbs moved to Washington, DC and set up the Citizens Clearinghouse for Hazardous Waste that teaches working-class women how to fight government and chemical companies (Krauss, 1998).

Individual consultants help with a huge variety of tasks. Some work with community groups to teach their board members the difference between supervision and micromanagement. Others help set up bookkeeping systems. Consultants accomplish one-time tasks, such as working with start-up groups as they prepare bylaws, perform specific technical tasks, such as writing a grant proposal, teach group members how to remove asbestos, or provide instructions on how to how to get and use Community

Reinvestment Act (CRA) data as a tool to pressure banks. Because consultants work with many groups, they disseminate information and experiences from one end of the field to the other.

In working with a consultant, the trick is to ensure that the consultant helps empower the group rather than assumes its responsibilities. A grant writer has the expertise to structure the budget of a proposal in a way that increases the chance of a project being funded. Little in the way of empowerment is lost if a budgeted item is put under category A rather than B or if the consultant writes up the proposal using jargon that appeals to the funders. Much may be lost, however, if the consultant chooses the idea for the proposal (because the funders will like it) and by default determines the agenda for the community group.

Leading consultants understand the need to help build the capacity of community groups and not dictate their agendas. As one consultant described,

> We did [name's] . . . proposals . . . but those are [name's] ideas. Those are all his, we don't force anything else . . . the CDC has to be able to generate the idea. We can tell them what makes more sense as far as funding goes and then we work with them. . . . We work with their staff in generating it and we have to be sure that the CDC can follow on and deliver. Because if they can't, the money is lost. If the money is lost, it works against us. I mean you get a reputation of turning in those great proposals but no delivery. (Interview with Herbert Rubin)

There are several things a community organization can do to assure that a consultant will not take too much control. First, most consultants will have worked on other projects with other groups. Make a few phone calls to make sure the group was satisfied and find out how willing the consultant was to follow the directions of the group. Second, be as clear as you can up front in telling consultants what their roles are to be and what the group members will do. Put all that in writing as part of a contract.

When choosing a consultant keep in mind that few activities can be carried out in a cookie-cutter manner, that is, by simply applying what was learned elsewhere to the current situation. A good consultant needs to spend time learning about the immediate project and the goals of each group with whom he or she works. If a consultant comes in with a model that he or she wants to immediately impose without being aware of the local contingencies, you might want to steer clear of this person. Even something that sounds as routine as setting up an accounting system must be tailored to the organization's needs. If one size fit all, the group could learn simply by copying others and would not need a consultant.

Consultants usually are paid; however, the money need not come out of the organization's core budget. Foundations provide grants to coalitions, trade associations, or intermediaries to hire the consultants that community groups use; the CCC seeks out its own grants to fund itself as a consultant to the community movement. Similarly, Local Initiatives Support Corporation (LISC) and Enterprise fund consultants to help neighborhood development groups.

Consultants may charge a fixed fee to do a specific task, or they may charge per hour when they are not sure how much time they will need. Fees are often negotiable and might be less if the consultant is aware that the community group is paying out of its own limited funds; the consultant might charge more if a foundation or bank is paying the bill. Some consultants write grants on a contingency basis, that is, they only get paid if the grant is funded. At first glance this would seem to be a good arrangement because it prevents the community group from spending cash it doesn't have; however, at least in the housing field, the most successful and reputable grant writers only work for a fixed fee, so the contingency arrangement may actually lower the chance of getting the grant.

Support Organizations that Monitor and Diffuse Information

Both direct-action and social production organizations require a lot of backup information that its members don't have the time to find. Federal programs can change dramatically, shifting the functions of community organizations; grant programs change the rules for eligibility and application procedures regularly. Such changes have to be monitored continuously by someone who knows the implications for community groups.

Trade associations and coalitions compile such information, and other support organizations prepare technical analyses of the changing environment that community groups can purchase, often at nominal costs, or obtain free from the Internet. Handsnet, for instance, electronically circulates an array of news, events, project descriptions, and action alerts to many nonprofits. For a nominal fee, participants can have customized clippings sent to an e-mail address daily. Support groups such as the Welfare Law Center maintain web pages on which information on welfare reform, including court cases, can be accessed easily. Similar web pages exist on a wide variety of other topics. Tenant activists in New York set up an array of web pages suggesting how action organizations can cope with the changing housing code in New York City. The National Low Income Housing Coalition puts out a weekly bulletin on housing, government housing programs, and innovative community responses to housing needs. The Center for Neighborhood Technology prepares reports on recycling abandoned industrial sites, tying together environmental cleanup techniques with job creation in the inner city.

The Center for Budget and Policy Priorities issues detailed analyses of how changes in the federal budget affect the poor. The Center monitors changing laws, such as welfare reforms, posting its reports on the Internet. Its reports strip away the numeric gobbledygook with which politicians try to obscure reductions in funding for social programs. The Center's reports explain where the problem areas are, where the cuts are, what their effects will be.

Many monitoring organizations issue alerts to their members when key issues come up. Such reports and warnings are widely disseminated through mailing lists of activists and through the Internet. In addition, trade associations and coalitions, activist research centers such as the National Housing Institute and the National Low Income Housing Center (NLIHC), and electronic news services for activists such as Handsnet, publicize the availability of these reports. These reports become part of the process through which support organizations help frame the action agenda.

Foundations and Other Funders

Social change and neighborhood organizations find they have to pay for consultants, national mailings, trips to the capital, project costs, and routine expenses. They often need more cash than is easily raised from community members. To maintain a small office, pay for heat, light, phone, and one organizer with a part time secretary or clerk adds up in most cities to over $80,000. Far larger sums are required for groups doing social production work, especially property development. Fortunately, many support organizations, including religious groups and foundations, provide financial help.

Churches, synagogues, and mosques often allow community groups the use of their facilities and sometimes encourage their religious leaders to spend time working on community issues. Religious networks have frequently helped activist organizations. The Catholic Campaign for Human Development and similar quasifoundations sponsored by the Presbyterian and Methodist churches provide funds for projects and operating support to numerous community groups, especially those involved in missions to the poor. Today the IAF, the descendant of the Alinsky movement, receives much aid from the Campaign for Human Development. Overall, the Campaign for Human Development provides about $6 million dollars a year for activist causes (Dreier, 1998, p. 125).

For large sums of money, community organizations seek grants from foundations. Foundations are nonprofit organizations set up to accomplish a charitable purpose, as defined by the Internal Revenue code. Foundations may be set up by wealthy families, by contributions from smaller contributors, or by banks and banking support organizations. They usually focus on a specific cause, such as helping poor children or improving health care, or a specific geographic area. Foundation policies are usually specified in a charter that is interpreted by a board of directors and carried out by hired, professional program officers. Regional and local foundations tend to be more accessible to community groups and more responsive to innovative ideas than are the larger national organizations.

By law, foundations cannot directly engage in political activity. Most foundation funds are allocated for mainstream, nonpolitical causes, such as to find a cure for particular diseases or to support an opera company. Within those safe broad topics, however, there can be a consciousness of race, class, and the environment. For example, medical research can focus on poor children with lead poisoning from eating paint chips, the rise in asthma deaths of children in inner city neighborhoods, or the differential death rate between Black men and White men. The border between neutral policy research and action research easily blurs.

Less than a quarter of a percent of foundation spending directly supports social movement organizations (Dreier, 1998, p. 110). While many of the largest foundations spend most of their money on mainstream causes, some foundations focus on community and social-change activities. Among the larger foundations, Ford has provided start-up funds for social change organizations in many areas, such as poverty, environmental preservation, ethnic social justice, and community-controlled renewal. Annie Casey focuses on issues that impact children. Though very much part of the mainstream, the Lily Foundation has funded religious groups involved in social-change work. The Pew Foundation and the Mott Foundation have programs to support microenterprises. Among its numerous program areas, McArthur funds community groups who research government policies. Another McArthur program provides money for religious leaders who set up organizations meant to rebuild social capital in devastated neighborhoods. A number of foundations contribute to Comprehensive Community Building Initiatives.

Recently, banks and gigantic federally chartered agencies that purchase mortgages have spun off their own foundations, often matching in size the larger national foundations. These foundations provide funds to help the affordable housing movement by subsidizing home purchases by the poor, funding Community-based Development Organizations (CBDOs), or sponsoring the conferences or training sessions at which developmental activists learn more about their craft.

An array of small foundations set up by the children and grandchildren of the wealthy also support progressive social causes. The Haymarket Foundation in Boston funds groups involved in direct action and includes community activists on its boards. Many progressive foundations, like Haymarket, are small, but not all of them are strapped for funds. MacArthur, the largest of the foundations that routinely helps those involved in the community movement, is worth about $4 billion; the Mott foundation about $2 billion, the Chicago Community Trust almost a billion dollars, and the Northwest Area Foundation $400 million (Shuman, 1998).

Many progressive foundations are part of the National Network of Grantmakers whose purpose is to

> . . . increase financial and other resources to groups committed to social and economic justice . . . eliminate discrimination and oppression based on age, class, disability, ethnicity, gender, race, religion, and sexual orientation . . . promote the significance and vitality of the grassroots community in the broader movement for systemic progressive social change. (Shuman, 1998)

Background on such foundations can be found on-line through the Progressive Foundations Database *(http://www.progressivepubs.com/foundations/).*

While it is possible to come in cold to these foundations and convince them to fund a creative idea, most grants are given out in program areas that describe projects the foundations are willing to support and for which community groups specifically apply. Community organizations that receive grant funds from these program areas are evaluated on whether or not they have accomplished foundation objectives. By contrast, some foundations encourage experimentation.

Before applying for a foundation grant, find out what types of projects a particular foundation is willing to fund. Much information can be found from the Foundation Center whose web page is *http://www.fdncenter.org/.* In addition, foundations publish lists of what they have funded recently. For example, the MacArthur Foundation presents descriptions on its web page (*http://www.macfdn.org/*) of its recent grants. The list runs twenty-one pages. Recent grants have gone to the activist 9 to 5 Working Women Education Fund (in an educational effort) and the Center on Budget and Policy Priorities (to monitor the changing welfare environment). A similar list put out by the Fannie Mae Foundation emphasized support for organizations involved in physical redevelopment projects. Some foundations periodically publish pamphlets in which they reflect on what they fund and why, such as the Northwest Area Foundation pamphlet *Building Communities of Opportunity,* which summarizes the foundation's holistic approaches to renewal. Wise applicants pay close attention to such documents in formulating the wording of their proposals.

In writing a proposal, try to take the perspective of the program officers who review proposals and then have to convince the boards of the foundations to fund particular projects. Program officers generally want to encourage innovative ideas and are usually not afraid of efforts to bring about community change. They have to sell their ideas to a board, however, often consisting of upper status people, who are more conservative than they. If the idea can be framed in such a way that it makes the program officer's job easier, it is more likely to be funded.

To increase the chances of obtaining money, some activists have set up their own fund-raising entities that collect money and distribute it to social change groups. There are almost two hundred such alternative funds that distribute several hundred million dollars to progressive causes. Seventeen Black united funds collect and distribute money to nonprofits that help minority groups.

Financial Intermediaries

Financial intermediaries play several roles in facilitating funding for projects. They package money from mainstream banks, corporations, and foundations and disburse it to community groups (Rubin, 2000b; Liou & Stroh, 1998). They combine projects proposed by community groups in ways that make them more appealing to investors. They also spin off subsidiaries that repurchase loans made by community groups so that the money can be recycled into further efforts.

Two examples of intermediaries are Enterprise and LISC. Enterprise, set up initially by a socially concerned private developer, works in poor communities to link housing with social service efforts, while LISC, created by the Ford Foundation, coordinates residential with commercial development in a variety of cities. LISC has worked with a thousand CDCs while Enterprise has helped over seven-hundred community groups, producing over a hundred thousand affordable homes (Liou & Stroh, 1998). Intermediaries reassure foundations and corporate funders about the legitimacy and feasibility of proposed community projects. An intermediary can assess the economic viability of proposed low-income housing tax credit projects and then package the projects so that the riskier ones are offset by less risky ones, creating a bundle that investors are willing to purchase.

Sometimes intermediaries represent activist organizations to the banking and financial community to soften the radical images of the community groups. Conventional bankers might worry about organizations that previously engaged in direct actions that now are involved in housing programs. Why should a bank loan money to a group that recently picketed the bank?

Intermediaries argue that the group can deliver what it promises, despite its history of direct action. One intermediary told the bankers,

> "Look. I know these [old radical] people. And, I know that they are kind of wild. I know they do activism; I know they march in the streets. But I also know, they should be able to do what they say they are going to do which is build some houses." (Rubin, 2000b)

Intermediaries also provide community organizations money that has very few strings attached. For example, they provide risk capital to explore innovative renewal ideas, sometimes by issuing forgivable loans, funds that are repaid only if the project succeeds. LISC and Enterprise persuaded the Department of Housing and Urban Development (HUD) and a group of thirteen foundations to establish the National Community Development Initiative to help CBDOs develop the technical capacity to undertake high-risk renewal work. In addition, LISC worked with the Consensus Organizing Institute to set up community development organizations in locales that did not have a history of community-based work (Gittell & Vidal, 1998). Finally, in several cities LISC or Enterprise affiliates partner with community groups on projects, with the intermediary providing funds and technical assistance.

Intermediaries such as Enterprise circulate technical books and provide training on the nuts and bolts of refurbishing old homes; LISC pays for consultants who help community groups plan commercial renewal projects. Intermediaries disseminate information on changes in government funding policies. Local affiliates of LISC and Enterprise help fund training programs for developmental activists and sometimes receive pass-through money from foundations to help pay for the operating expenses of community development organizations.

Partnerships with Support Organizations

Partnership projects occur when community or social-change organizations work as coequals with their support organizations on a project. LISC and Enterprise or their local affiliates might partner with a community group to build a shopping mall or housing complex. Coalitions sometimes form partnerships on technical work with their members. The community group determines the overall goals while the coalition hires the needed expertise.

Even direct-action groups enter into partnerships with their support organizations. In Chicago, a campaign to pressure city hall to fairly distribute funds for infrastructure projects worked, in part, because direct-action community groups gained needed information from a partnership that provided back-up data. The CCC frequently works with local welfare justice organizations to pressure city governments to help those who have been affected by the changes in welfare laws. For example, the CCC has helped community groups as they pressure city officials to establish the public transit necessary to connect poor neighborhoods to areas that have jobs (Dingerson, 1998).

Because the partner from the support sector often has more resources and experiences than the community group, it can be difficult to manage this relationship as one of equals. Do not enter into these partnerships unless you are fairly certain the community group will gain the capacity to do similar work by itself later on. Avoid working with funders as partners because funding and partnership relations differ dramatically. With a partner, the community group is open and frank, as it wants to make clear the help it needs, while with funders the goal is to appear to be on top of the matter. When partnerships are run by supervisory boards, make sure the community group has a substantial voice and is not simply a pawn for the larger organizations represented on the boards.

Support organizations, too, must be careful about partnering with individual community groups lest they spend so much time with one organization that others feel neglected. Still, support organizations can learn a lot through such partnerships, as a director of one coalition explained to us.

> [Working as partners with the community group] has really been very valuable in terms of keeping us grounded in the day to day experiences of our member organizations. . . . I was reminded of it again just a couple of days ago in a tragedy, one of the youth leaders of the Youth Venture Clubs that we sponsor at [name] High School was shot in the chest and died in a drug deal thing up there. So you don't get that downtown. Downtown you read it in the paper and there are a hundred of these murders in a month. And, so you know it washes over you. But you don't lose that community perspective.

Support Organizations as a Social System

Support organizations help individual community and social-change organizations. In addition, support organizations themselves play an active role in social-change activities. They lobby and pressure government for changes and help frame the public's understanding of community efforts.

Linkages among Support Organizations

In part, support organizations are effective in influencing government and the public because they help one another. The boards of support groups are tightly connected and communication is frequent between their staff. Employees of support groups meet each other at conferences and phone one another for advice.

Intermediaries and technical assistance providers depend on foundations for their financial support. In turn, foundations want to help community groups, but they lack the staff to pay close attention to what each group is attempting. So instead of providing hundreds of small grants, the foundations allocate large chunks of money to intermediaries, coalitions, or technical assistance providers that, in turn, make the decisions on which smaller groups to fund.

Recently the progressive Mott Foundation funded what it calls "intermediate support organizations" that include the CCC, the Community Training and Assistance

Center, Mississippi Action for Community Education, the National Council of La Raza, the National Training and Information Center, and the Seventh Generation Fund for Indian Development. In turn, each of these support organizations provides technical assistance to community groups that lack the capacity to carry out campaigns by themselves. For instance, the Community Training and Assistance Center has worked with tenants' groups in public housing to help them build the capacity to take back the community from disruptive elements, while the national Council of La Raza helped set up a CDC in neglected neighborhoods near San Juan (Betzold, 1998).

Helping Shape and Frame the Image of Community Action

Activists want to frame an action agenda in a way that government and the public will accept. To do so, some consensus is required among those in the community movement, but building a consensus among dispersed groups can be problematic. The support sector provides the forum for building a shared culture of change and helps communicate this framing to the world outside.

Coalitions and trade associations provide a place where activists can meet, share knowledge, argue out alternative approaches to community change, and work out what they have in common. Through training programs and a constant barrage of newsletters and reports, organizations in the support sector help foster and disseminate a common framing of what community organizing and development are about.

Much of the internal dialogue about broader issues takes place at conferences organized by support organizations. Historically, at such conferences, those in the Women's Movement fought over how inclusive and militant to be (Ryan, 1992); civil rights activists argued over the tactics and direction of their movement (Payne, 1995); and at Port Huron, students worked out an ideology for an indigenous American left (Anderson, 1995).

At conferences sponsored by support groups, activists argue about the values that guide their work and come to some shared understanding about the goals of the field (Rubin, 2000a). That shared understanding then becomes part of the message presented to funders and legislators. Representatives from government and funding agencies attend panels and plenary sessions where speakers discuss the dilemmas of community organizing and the values that animate and divide them. They talk about the need to provide social services to occupants of new affordable housing; they talk about the tensions between development and advocacy work; they talk about what they mean when they say community empowerment. They are not only talking to themselves but also to the supporting organizations, funders, and representatives of government. Funders and intermediaries hear these discussions of what the movement is about and absorb a shared image which they implement in funding decisions.

Support organizations also implement the movement's values through their lobbying. Organizations such as NLIHC or NCCED communicate to those in Congress that giving community groups access to loans is a way to support those poor individuals who are willing to work, save, and pull themselves up through their own efforts. Support groups for environmental organizations work hard to get across the idea that environmentalists do not destroy jobs to preserve some small creatures few of us have heard of but are working to maintain breathable air and drinkable water that both the small creatures and human beings need.

Another approach to shaping and communicating the values of community work is to publicize successful projects. The support organizations use newsletters, on-line computer services, and meetings attended by activists, funders, and government officials to publicize the successful projects. In addition, support organizations get out the message of successful projects by granting awards for the best ones, such as the Maxwell award that the Fannie Mae Foundation provides for outstanding community-based development projects. By advertising exemplary projects, the support sector documents that what the community organizations are doing works and that continued support will help community groups solve deep-rooted social and economic problems. These awards not only call attention to the successes of the movement, but they also help frame the goals of redevelopment by holding up some projects as exciting and successful, suggesting that other community organizations try similar projects and that foundations support these efforts.

Support Organizations as Political Activists

Support organizations carefully monitor the political and social environment, pointing out to the community groups changes that can affect their work. In addition, many support organizations themselves are active players in the political game, lobbying, and, at times, conducting or instigating direct actions in support of needed changes.

Sometimes the coalitions themselves orchestrate direct actions against those in office. For instance, citywide housing coalitions lobby local government on such issues as support for affordable housing (Goetz, 1993), the rights of the disabled, and social justice for minorities and gays. In Chicago, coalitions such as the Rehab Network and CANDO have quietly worked with the city to change technical requirements on how community groups can spend housing or economic development funds. On other occasions, these coalitions have been part of direct-action meta-coalitions that have orchestrated demonstrations at city hall demanding (and obtaining) substantial increases in money for neighborhood reinvestment.

Nationally, coalitions such as the NLIHC or the National Community Reinvestment Coalition lobby to preserve and enhance housing programs; leaders at LISC and Enterprise work to persuade government officials, businesses, and foundations of the value of funding community-based urban renewal. In Washington, DC, the National Community Reinvestment Coalition spends much of its time advocating for the CRA.

These organizations testify at congressional hearings and lobby representatives, suggesting necessary changes in enforcement of housing legislation and vigorously battling whenever opponents try to gut CRA. When such lobbying proves insufficient, the CCC and the National Community Reinvestment Coalition notify other support organizations, such as the NLIHC, and collectively the support organizations contact their own membership who in turn individually lobby representatives and senators.

Support organizations are part of a new approach to direct action, a *new advocacy,* in which support groups themselves carry on the direct actions and by doing so buffer smaller community groups, especially those dependent on government for funds for social production, from retaliation (Rubin, 2000b). The new advocacy unites a diverse array of organizations that because of ideological disagreements might otherwise find it difficult to work together. For example, a coalition representing sometimes contending constituencies forced the First National Bank in Chicago to reinvest in poor neighborhoods. The three constituencies were led by three individuals with very different perspectives.

> . . . Gale Cincotta was a leader of the original redlining fight . . . who had become the single most prominent national leader on reinvestment issues. Mary Nelson was executive director of Bethel New Life, one of the most productive community development corporations in Chicago struggling to develop low-income housing in . . . one of Chicago's poorest communities. Jim Capraro, executive director of Greater Southwest Development Corporation, was a national pioneer in commercial and industrial revitalization. The combination of perspectives that included community organizing, low-income housing development, and commercial and industrial revitalization was key to shaping an agreement. (Pogge, 1992, p. 137)

Support groups sometimes unite to bring their different constituencies together to form a coalition of coalitions. Such meta-coalitions bring together direct action and social production groups in a single, powerful campaign. For instance, as part of a successful effort to increase funding for affordable housing, the Chicago Rehab Network, a coalition that primarily speaks for housing production groups, joined with the activist Neighborhood Peoples' Action. In such campaigns

> . . . the combined strategy of different actors in the housing movement seems to be a (perhaps unplanned) version of "good cop, bad cop" in which one or more groups engage in highly visible acts of protest to publicize housing problems, while other groups work in a more cooperative mode with local officials to exact and implement policy changes. (Goetz, 1993, p. 71)

On the national level, virtually all those in support of affordable housing, including financial intermediaries such as LISC, trade associations such as NCCED, and direct-action organizations such as the CCC, joined to convince Congress to mitigate the problems caused by a twenty-year-old law that would have allowed owners who had been subsidized by HUD to convert affordable housing to full market value. A similar coalition of coalitions succeeded in convincing government to make permanent the low-income housing tax credit.

Conclusions and Concerns

Support organizations are of immense help to community groups. They enhance the efforts of community organizations to empower and bring about social change while helping smaller organizations gain the skills and resources needed to turn ideas and dedication into effective action (Chavis, Florin, & Felix, 1993). Support groups provide a setting in which activists can communicate with one another and circulate publications that provide needed information. Collectively, support organizations help frame common understandings of what community organizing and development is about and help disseminate that idea within and outside the movement.

Working with support groups, however, can be time consuming. The full-time director of a coalition expressed his concern:

> I'm worried about competition for the time and energy and interest of our members. That's by far the most scarce of resources. . . . And the plain truth is that somebody can't be on the board of NCBG and on the board of CANDO and on the board of the REHAB NETWORK and be on the board of CWED at the same time. They can't do it. They physically can't do it. They shouldn't do it. If they do that they become professional meeting goers and aren't actually doing anything in their community.

Sometimes the support organizations, because of their bigger size and disproportionate control of resources, unduly influence the agenda of community groups (Rubin, 1995). At times, support organizations have funded their own image of what community action should be about, as with LISC's support for consensus organizing (Gittell & Vidal, 1998).

Still, intermediaries and many funders are on the side of community activists and many staffers have direct experience in community and social-change movements. Support organizations enable those at the grassroots to obtain needed expertise, without losing their independence, and, as such, are vital to the continued success of those involved in social-change work.

EPILOGUE

Toward an Empowered Future

In the body of this book we have presented a model of organizing and development. To repeat our core premises, community organizing involves bringing people together to combat shared problems and increase their say about decisions that affect their lives. Community development occurs when people strengthen the bonds within their neighborhoods, build social networks, and form their own organizations that provide a long-term capacity for problem solving. When many people and many organizations join together to combat injustice and inequality they create a social movement.

Through involvement in community organizations and in social movements, people control their own futures by doing tasks themselves and by compelling those in political office to carry out agendas that have been decided in a democratic manner. Organizing empowers by providing an alternative approach to conventional politics for bringing about social change.

Change involves solving individual problems while combating the social structures that allow the problems to persist. Helping individuals is important, yet, as Harry Boyte warned, organizers must battle the tendency to concentrate too narrowly on the immediate and personal.

> Activists have not often asked what their work "means" in a larger sense. . . . much of grass-roots activism has spoken a thin, sometimes cynical language of narrow interests and protest detached from any enlarged political vision. (Boyte, 1989a, p. 12)

Activism is about battling the bigger issues, fighting for racial, sexual, and gender justice and working to reduce the extremes of economic and political inequality.

We have spent much time discussing our approach, still no model for organizing and development is ever complete. Situations change, new strategies are required, and emerging groups face new problems. To discover where future work is needed and how present work can be improved, organizers must pause and reflect about their work. Such reflections point out past problems and tensions and suggest possible resolutions. In addition, such reflection points out where organizing is heading and how to prepare for the future.

Self-Reflective Organizing

Community and social-change organizations are the means to get from a troubled present to an empowered future. But measuring success is not always easy. Is a victory in one battle a success, or might one narrow victory distract from the larger goal? Activists need time for reflection, noting what is still wrong, what efforts seem effective, which approaches should be discarded, where innovations are needed, and, most important, to reinforce in their minds the basic goals to be achieved.

Organizers think about individual campaigns to determine whether these efforts are steps in the right direction. After an action campaign or on the completion of a social production project, activists should pause and ask themselves what has been accomplished, what went right, and what went wrong. Why did the county board ignore our picketing? Do we now owe a favor to the council person who offered the amendment we wanted? Did the commercial partners in the supermarket project take too large a share of the profits? These postcampaign and project discussions shape future actions.

Detailed project-by-project, campaign-by-campaign postmortems are vital for improving future work. Developmental activists describe that when projects are complete their

. . . organizations rethink their missions, often at extended retreats or workshops. CBDOs wrestle with moving from programs of renting homes to those of selling them and in doing so ended up with internal discussions "on what constitutes the behavioral manifestations of empowerment. How do you measure empowerment and so forth and so on." Staff and board ask each other: Are renters truly empowered? (Rubin, 2000b)

Asking whether immediate efforts are accomplishing longer-term goals is vital. Providing shelter for people is important, as is maintaining clean apartments. But if activist groups act as managers and owners, without working with and teaching tenants, the organization has become just another landlord and has forgotten the importance of building community and individual capacity. A self-evaluation might remind those running a spouse abuse shelter that their goal is to empower women and not simply to protect them from physical harm.

Activists must pause to reflect whether or not their organization's efforts are helping to bring about a more democratic future. Such periods of reflection occur, for instance, at membership retreats, during which, as a developmental activist explained:

We focus a lot on whether or not what we do is truly progressive. . . . Are we just dividing up the pie a little different? Or, are we participating in some way, to some measure, in a fundamental change . . . [that] really calls into question the ways that decisions are made, the way control is exercised, the way resources are allocated. We look carefully at what we do to see if we are doing the latter or not. And, because if we are just doing the former, maybe we are just helping this lousy system work a little bit easier, to get by a little better. We often ask ourselves if we are not just the pimp for downtown. (Rubin, 2000b)

During periods of reflection people reconsider the values of the organization, about where it is going, why, and if the actions being taken at present are getting them there. How militant should the organization be? How oriented to short-term improvements versus long-term gains? To what extent does the organization wish to work within the capitalist economy and to what extent in the alternative economy? Does the organization group need to reframe its issues so society can understand and sympathize with its needs and demands? Is now the time to make a push for major structural changes or concentrate on gaining small improvements? Self-reflection is about assuring that campaigns and projects are carried out consistent with the organization's longer-term goals while at the same time questioning underlying values. During periods of reflection, activists work out theories that reconcile their experiences with the goals they hope to achieve.

Reconciliations

In our own reflections we have noted five areas in which activists appear to be forced to choose between possibly incompatible goals:

1. *Interdependent Problems.* Need a determined effort to solve one problem inadvertently make others worse?
2. *Individual or the Collective.* People fight back because of individual concerns. Is it possible to reconcile the sense of individualism that mobilizes people with the communal spirit on which longer-term organizing depends?
3. *Expertise and Involvement.* Successful organizing and development requires technical knowledge. Can such knowledge be obtained in ways that empower people, rather than make them dependent on experts?
4. *Autonomy or Dependent Partnerships.* Is it possible for activists to work with those in the mainstream, or does doing so create a subservient dependency?
5. *Social Production, Social Services, or Direct Action.* Is the grassroots, direct-action model for community change fundamentally incompatible with the social production or social services approach?

Ways can and must be found for reconciling these tensions. One approach is for people to recognize that each path can bring about needed gains. Supporters of direct action must keep in mind that consensus organizing works in less radical communities, while consensus organizers must not forget that without the potential of direct action much of their work would be ignored by those in positions of power. Another reconciliation is to look for the underlying structural problems that create the tensions in the first place. That solving one problem seems to make another problem worse is less aggravating when the common source of both problems is understood and a campaign designed to deal with both issues. A third approach to dealing with these tensions is to carry out projects in a way that minimizes the negative consequences for the group. Experts can be hired without letting them dominate the group.

Interdependent Problems

Organizing efforts can bog down when solutions to one problem seem to worsen another problem. To earn a living, native Alaskans, among the poorest people in the country, engage in extractive industries that are harmful to the environment (Egan, 1990). Affirmative action programs to undo past discriminations against women and minorities are seen as disempowering by dominant-group men. In multiethnic communities, when one group organizes it is seen as a threat by others.

Initially, choices seem harsh, but the options as presented may be misleadingly narrow. Either the polar bear's habitat should be preserved and Native Alaskans relocated to cities, or the Native Alaskans stay and polar bears starve. Either a job goes to a woman or minority person or to a white male.

Framing the choices in a different way, however, can sometimes lead to a solution that is not "zero sum," win or lose. To reach such solutions often requires searching for the broader structural causes of problems and then designing campaigns that confront these deeper causes. Anger against immigrants, for example, is often the result of a belief that immigrants take away jobs from those already living here. The gain of one group is seen as a loss to another. But that tension may be based on a misunderstanding about what types of jobs each group is taking. Many immigrant groups are working in jobs that citizens are not interested in because the pay is too low and the working conditions too harsh. An education campaign can help resolve this antagonism.

There are times, however, when the situation seems to be in fact zero sum; when a woman is hired at a plant, a man is not, and if fifty men applied for the job, each one thinks he didn't get the job because a woman did. The real problem though is not that one woman got the job, but that jobs have been reduced at the plant, the plant is old and has not been modernized, and the company is planning to close it. The solution may revolve around ways of making the plant more economically viable, with new equipment or production processes, or it may involve workers buying the company to control the investment process, or it may involve worker retraining for new jobs in growing sectors. In any case, however, the problem has to be recast so structural solutions are possible rather than allowing interpersonal resentments to fester preventing unity and empowerment.

The Individual or the Collective

Organizing is about enabling people to help themselves, while discovering that others face similar difficulties. Getting people to band together to solve personal problems, however, is far easier than creating a sense of responsibility for the collective. Why should someone who now has a new job or house stick with the effort until others are likewise benefited? Organizers recognize this problem and understand that mobilizing people based solely on promises of individual gain is not an effective strategy for building long-run gains.

In working with individuals, organizers try to communicate that those who do gain a material good or service have obligated themselves to help others. People who are provided affordable housing should be asked to serve on tenants' boards or apartment committees. A person receiving job training should become a volunteer and pass on to others what he or she learned.

People, though, may still reject the idea of collective responsibility because our society values individualism. People have difficulty seeing what they owe to the group. Today a young woman moving up the organizational hierarchy assumes her advancement has occurred because of her individual skills and contributions, forgetting that feminist activists had to campaign vigorously to make possible that women be promoted. To bridge this gap between individual and collective success, activists must teach about the work of earlier feminists and point out that because of their efforts a woman of ability now can move up in the organization, but that more work is still required.

Thinking individualistically, people feel the constraints imposed by the collective as unfair burdens. If a tenants' council restricts renters by limiting the number of people who can live in one unit, those renters feel their autonomy has been violated; however, the council may only be trying to comply with the law and prevent the property from deteriorating, protecting those in other units of the building. Given this overwhelming assumption of individuality, representatives of the collectivity must explain to everyone where the rules come from and involve those who must obey the rules in helping set them up.

In short, publicizing the history of social change and how recently gains have been made is one approach to giving people a sense of obligation to the group. A second approach is to make sure individuals participate in the rule making especially in situations that might result in a curtailment of individual autonomy.

Expertise and Involvement

Increasingly technical expertise is required to run action campaigns and social production efforts. Mobilizing people electronically, handling the new forms of media, and keeping on top of a changing policy environment requires computer skills. Obtaining funds can be complicated, and learning how to manage apartments, run a business, or administer a social service agency can take years.

Organizations want to get many members involved in the tasks but also need to finish an activity in an efficient way. Professional carpenters can build better and more quickly than less experienced people, but should a housing group contract out all the work? Sometimes hiring an activist lawyer to bring suit can win a campaign more quickly than having hundreds of community members lobby. A consumer cooperative that relies on community volunteers risks having no one show up to open the store, but hiring full-time workers can contradict the goal of creating a participatory organization.

The tension between participation and effectiveness can be avoided. Experts may not be needed for every task. The goal might be to have organization members learn how to accomplish something. For example, the members of the Kensington Welfare Rights Union, experientially learned how to conduct a national campaign. Most of the founders of Community Development Corporations (CDCs) began with little or no knowledge of housing finance or property management; they taught themselves these technical matters. When experts have to be hired, find those with whom sister organizations are satisfied. Gain assistance from support organizations, especially those whose staff understands that their job is to empower group members by teaching them skills. For them, expertise is about getting things done by building capacity in others. Finally, try to assure that key policy decisions are made by the membership as a whole.

Autonomy or Dependent Partnerships

Partnering with government or the support sector can create a dependency that weakens the social-change organization. Accepting funds from investors and government agencies might require following their conditions for the expenditure of those funds. Similarly, working in coalitions risks that other groups' agendas or values may determine what the individual organizations undertake.

Groups follow an array of tactics to minimize becoming dependent on others. Organizations that contract to provide one government service should make sure they have other sources of funding so that if officials demand too much control, the community group can drop the contract and still survive. In coalition work, the trick is to assure that the coalition's board is structured democratically so each participating group has an effective say.

A more difficult situation occurs when social production organizations accept capital funds from government or intermediaries. In these circumstances, small community groups would seem to have little choice in the short run but to comply with the demands of the funders. Community work, however, is not about the short run. Over time, activists can persuade funders and government to fund the projects that community groups want, by showing them that these projects are the most effective ones (Rubin, 2000b).

Social Production, Social Services, or Direct Action

At times, advocates of housing, economic development, social service provision, and direct-action protests have squabbled with each other instead of working cooperatively. These approaches are so different that they appear not to be easily reconciled.

Activists in community-based economic development recognize that they operate with different priorities from social action organizations. As one activist offered,

> Organizing, well if I don't go out and talk to these people, today, I
> can talk to them next week. But, if I don't get this [financial] stuff in
> line for the development, it's not going to happen.

Polemicists warn community developers, however, that "ignoring their roots in political protest and organizing . . . puts them on a collision course with their poor constituents" (Lenz, 1988, 24).

Further, providing a social service or housing to those most in need is expensive, and resources are often in short supply. Even progressive community groups face a "'double bottom line'—the simultaneous need for *financial accountability* and attention to the nonprofit organization's *social goals*. . . . many nonprofit housing sponsors have had to struggle mightily with this duality, given the inexorable logic of 'the numbers'" (Bratt, Keyes, Schwartz, & Vidal, 1994, p. 3).

Direct-action and social production may not be easily combined, but they do complement each other. Community activists need to row the boat with the two oars of direct action and social production by "increasingly using these two strategies, and their related tactics, in complementary ways" (Callahan, Mayer, Palmer, & Ferlazzo, 1999) and recognizing that pressures from direct-action groups are needed to persuade (or coerce) local governments to provide the funds needed for housing, while social production groups can make gains permanent.

Such reconciliations are now occurring. Two of the leading periodicals on community activism, *Third Force* and *The Neighborhood Works,* published a joint issue containing numerous examples of how organizations can and should do both production and advocacy. The Urban Institute reports that two-thirds of community-based development organizations do community organizing and a third advocate in support of the Community Reinvestment Act (Center for Public Finance and Housing, 1994). Herbert Rubin's research shows that while some community-based development organizations neglect empowerment concerns, many also work in coalitions that include protest groups (Rubin, 2000b).

The rhetoric that emphasizes the antagonisms and differences between different paths to community organizing and development should be toned down. The approaches are in fact complementary, whether they are pursued by the same organization or by different and specialized ones.

Next Steps

Community organizing will continue as it has for generations, solving immediate problems and helping to resolve the bigger issues of inequality, injustice, and the environment. Activism has created a vocabulary of responses, an understanding that a range of choices are available other than those permitted by top-down, authoritarian models. Each victory reduces the feeling of helplessness, empowers those involved, and builds capacity for future community efforts. Successful organizing efforts reinforce a culture of collective responsibility and make people aware of the possibility of change. Community organizations will continue to work at creating an atmosphere in which members with varied backgrounds and abilities feel comfortable with each other and with the opportunities presented.

New issues will appear and old ones will come back in different forms. Racism and sexism persist, but they take on more subtle forms than those that existed a generation ago, and must be combated in increasingly sophisticated ways. Today's crisis in health care may stimulate community organizing to create insurance pools, provide alternative health delivery in poor neighborhoods, or pressure existing pools to provide better and more responsive services. Globalization continues to export many industrial jobs abroad, so job training and the creation of new jobs will become even more important. Changes in welfare programs have shifted attention to concerns of the working poor.

The incidence of violent crime has dropped as the population ages, but the problems of aging will present new opportunities for organizing. In-home assistance and improvements in transportation services for the elderly will become more urgent. Builders may have to be pressured to construct accessible homes and offices, and laws may have to be strengthened to prevent job discrimination against the elderly. More hospice facilities will be required.

Problems of the environment are also likely to become more acute, in part because of the effects of global warming. Suburbanization continues to eat up and pave over wetlands, water tables are being polluted by pesticides and herbicides, and larger vehicles have been spewing out smog-producing chemicals at an increased rate. Genetically altered food presents unknowable risks. The need for collective action on all areas of the environment is likely to be keen over the next few decades.

Social-change organizations must continue or even accelerate their rear guard actions to protect past gains. Change has been dramatic for women and minorities during the last generation. The economy has been strong for many years, but when it turns around and slows down, when traditional elites find themselves out of jobs, the tendency to blame women and minorities for their losses will be great and will undoubtedly be fed by unscrupulous politicians. Gay bashing, antiabortion campaigns, and antiaffirmative action referenda suggest widespread dissatisfaction with recent gains.

As the issues change, techniques of organizing will evolve. Multiissue organizing will increase as more activists recognize that problems are linked to one another. Rather than just fighting crime, building homes, or improving schools, activists are likely to combine housing, anticrime efforts, and programs to upgrade schools. Those pushing for new jobs will also work on improved transportation and education or job training and day care. Such holistic approaches will encourage activist groups to work together. Because of the increased recognition that development work is holistic, and because coalitions can exert much more political power than individual groups, organizers are going to need to use networking skills more than in the past.

Networking will also be more important because it allows small groups to maintain their democratic decision making while providing the power that comes from large numbers of coordinated groups. The problems social change organizations face are rarely solvable by only a handful of people. Whether working in regional alliances to find jobs for the poor, seeking advice on how to fund affordable housing, or joining with sister organizations to pressure government, organizers increasingly need networking skills. Activists must learn how to reach out to others for help and use information networks, especially electronic ones, to spread their message.

New approaches will have to be worked out to build multiethnic coalitions and bridge the gaps between old-timers and new immigrants, and between ethnic and racial groups already here. In the past, one approach to multiethnic organizing was to concentrate on generic issues, such as traffic or crime, that all ethnic groups could support. Another approach was to let each group go it alone.

In the future, other techniques for building multicultural alliances will be needed, because the tension that occurs between cultural and ethnic groups is likely to become more disruptive and more serious. Even now, groups fight over jobs, the slant of education, and the ownership of housing and stores. When one ethnic group obtains political access the others feel excluded or threatened. These problems will get worse as more people feel threatened by the influx of immigrants and the export of manufacturing jobs.

Underlying the building of multiethnic and multicultural coalitions should be the understanding that separate groups share the same economic and social problems. Intergroup tensions should not be ignored but dealt with and resolved. Activists may need to examine the experiences and techniques of organizations such as the Dudley Street Neighborhood Initiative that have made progress in bridging interethnic gaps.

Another element in the new organizing paradigm is the ability to lobby collectively. In generations past, some activists simply gave up on government and assumed whatever progress was made would be achieved by their organizations alone. Few today believe that social change can occur without support from those in public office (even if that support has to be forced). Pressuring government, partnering with government agencies, and, at times, working to place supporters in office are now standard parts of the organizer's repertoire. Although the need to reach government and frame issues is becoming more important, some conservative politicians have been eager to silence activist organizations; they have tried to require that any nonprofit that has accepted federal funds be forbidden to lobby. In the face of such pressures, it makes sense to lobby collectively rather than individually.

Most activists do not have the time to do much lobbying, so they will have to learn how to work effectively through coalitions. The first step is to join these coalitions and work on their boards to help set the collective agendas. The second step is to phone or write legislators when the coalitions send out action alerts. Coalitions garner publicity with special "Days," as in Earth Day or Community Economic Development Day, and individual groups should join in. On that day, each local organization has a chance to show its community what it has accomplished; collectively all those organizations can show elected officials and the broader public how widespread participation in the movement is.

Though the problems addressed and techniques used will continue to evolve, the energy and determination of community groups to address those problems is growing. Lit by past successes, the path ahead is clear, though much remains to be done. Victories have built on each other, providing hope for future progress. When people work together they develop a mutual respect that goes beyond the issue at hand. Community organizing promotes equality and dignity and creates the power to sustain the fight.

Activism is about creating social change, action by action, project by project. This sense of progress gives people the energy to keep going. As an activist organization declared on winning a crucial battle:

VICTORY
One Step Forward, One Mile to Go

BIBLIOGRAPHY

Ahlbrandt, Roger S., Jr., and James Cunningham. *A New Public Policy for Neighborhood Preservation.* New York: Praeger, 1979.

Alderson, George, and Everett Sentman. *How You Can Influence Congress: The Complete Handbook for the Citizen Lobbyist.* New York: E.P. Dutton, 1979.

Alexander, Ernest R. *How Organizations Act Together: Interorganizational Coordination in Theory and Practice.* Luxembourg: Gordan and Breach, 1995.

Alinsky, Saul D. *Reveille for Radicals.* New York: Random House, 1969.

Alinsky, Saul D. *Rules for Radicals.* New York: Random House, 1971.

Amy, Douglas. *The Politics of Environmental Mediation.* New York: Columbia University Press, 1987.

Anderson, Terry. *The Movement and the Sixties: Protest in America from Greensboro to Wounded Knee.* New York: Oxford, 1995.

Anner, John. "Having the Tools at Hand: Building Successful Multicultural Social Justice Organizations." In *Beyond Identify Politics: Emerging Social Justice Movements in Communities of Color,* edited by John Anner, 163–166. Boston: South End Press, 1996.

Anner, John, and Carl Vogel. "Getting It Together." *The Neighborhood Works* 20 (March/April 1997):3.

Anner, John, and Carl Vogel. "New Directions in Economic Development and Grassroots Organizing." Special Issue Jointly Sponsored by Third Force and The Neighborhood Works. *Third Force* 5 (March/April 1997).

Anon. "Community Group Sues Over Information Withheld by Police." *The Illinois Brief* 55 (Winter 1998–1999):1–2.

Ashkenaz, Judy. "Grassroots Organizing and the Democracy Party—the Vermont Rainbow Experience." *Monthly Review,* May 1986, 8–21.

Avery, Michel, Brian Auvine, Barbara Streibel, and Lonnie Weiss. *Building United Judgment: A Handbook for Consensus Decision Making.* Madison, WI: The Center for Conflict Resolution, 1981.

Bachrach, Peter, and Aryeh Botwinick. *Power and Empowerment: A Radical Theory of Participatory Democracy.* Philadelphia: Temple University Press, 1992.

Bachrach, Peter, and Morton Baratz. "Decisions and Non-decisions: An Analytical Framework." *American Political Science Review,* 57(3), (1963):632–642.

Bacon, David. "Contesting the Price of Mexican Labor: Immigrant Workers Fight for Justice." In *Beyond Identity Politics: Emerging Social Movements in Communities of Color,* edited by John Anner, 97–110. Boston: South End Press, 1996.

Bailis, Lawrence. *Bread or Justice: Grassroots Organizing in the Welfare Rights Movement.* Lexington, MA: Lexington, 1974.

Barkan, Steven E. "Legal Control of the Southern Civil Rights Movement." In *Social Movements: Readings on Their Emergence, Mobilization and Dynamics,* edited by Doug McAdam and David Snow, 384–396. Los Angeles, CA: Roxbury Publishing, 1997.

Barry, Patrick. *Rebuilding the Walls: A Nuts and Bolts Guide to the Community Development Methods of Bethel New Life, Inc. in Chicago.* Chicago: Bethel New Life, 1989.

Bass, Gary. "Lessons Learned from Proposition 226: Preparing the Nonprofit Sector." *OMB Watch www.ombwatch.orgl/ombwatch.html* (1998).

Baylor, Tim. "Media Faming of Movement Protest: The Case of American Indian Protest." *Social Science Journal* 33, no. 3 (1996):241–255.

Bays, Sharon. "Work, Politics, and Coalition Building: Hmong Women's Activism in a Central California Town." In *Community Activism and Feminist Politics: Organizing Across Race, Class, and Gender,* edited by Nancy A. Naples, 301–326. New York: Routledge, 1998.

Beckwith, Dave. "Organizing Today: Ten Reasons to Cheer!" *Shelterforce,* no. 101 (September/October 1998):8,37.

Bellah, Robert N., Richard Madsen, William M. Sullivan, Ann Swidler, and Steven Tipton. *Habits of the Heart: Individualism and Commitment in American Life.* New York: Harper and Row, 1985.

Bendick, Marc Jr., and Mary Lou Egan. "Linking Business Development and Community Development: Lessons from Four Cities." Prepared for Presentation at the Community Development Research Center. Washington, DC: 1989.

Bennett, Larry. *Neighborhood Politics: Chicago and Sheffield.* New York: Garland, 1997.

Bernstein, Mary. "Celebration and Suppression: The Strategic Uses of Identity by the Lesbian and Gay Movement." *American Journal of Sociology* 103 (November 1997):531–565.

Berry, Jeffrey M., Kent E. Portney, and Ken Thomson. *The Rebirth of Urban Democracy.* Washington, DC: Brookings Institution, 1993.

Best, Joel. "Typifications and Social Problems Construction." In *Images of Issues: Typifying Contemporary Social Problems,* Second Edition, edited by Joel Best, 1–10. New York: Aldine de Gruyter, 1995.

Betten, Neil, and Michael J. Austin, eds. *The Roots of Community Organizing, 1917–1939.* Philadelphia: Temple University Press, 1990.

Betzold, Michael. *Community the Vital Link: Intermediary Support Organizations: Connecting Communities with Resources for Improvement.* Midland, MI: The Mott Foundation, 1998.

Bingham, Mary Beth. "Stopping the Bulldozers: What Difference Did It Make." In *Fighting Back in Appalachia: Traditions of Resistance and Change,* edited by Stephen Fisher, 17–30. Philadelphia: Temple University Press, 1993.

Blakely, Edward J., and Mary Gail Snyder. *Fortress America: Gated Communities in the United States.* Washington, DC and Cambridge, MA: The Brookings Institution and the Lincoln Institute of Land Policy, 1997.

Bobo, Kim, Jacki Kendall, and Steve Max. *Organizing for Social Change: A Manual for Activists in the 1990s.* Washington: Seven Locks Press, 1991.

Booth, Heather. "Victories & Lessons." *The Neighborhood Works* 16 (December 1993/January 1994):8–12.

Boyte, Harry C. *The Backyard Revolution: Understanding the New Citizen Movement.* Philadelphia: Temple University Press, 1980.

Boyte, Harry C. *Commonwealth: A Return to Citizen Politics.* New York: The Free Press, 1989.

Bradshaw, Catherine, Steven Soifer, and Lorraine Guttierrez. "Toward a Hybrid Model for Effective Organizing in Communities of Color." *Journal of Community Practice* 1, no. 1 (1994):25–42.

Branch, Taylor. *Parting the Waters: America in the King Years 1954–1963.* New York: Simon and Schuster, 1988.

Branch, Taylor. *Pillar of Fire: America in the King Years 1963–65.* New York: Simon & Schuster, 1998.

Bratt, Rachel G., Lanley C. Keyes, Alex Schwartz, and Avis C. Vidal. *Confronting the Management Challenge: Affordable Housing in the Nonprofit Sector.* New York: Community Development Research Center; Graduate School of Management and Urban Policy; New School for Social Research, 1994.

Brauner, Sarah, and Pamela Lopest. "Where Are They Now? What States' Studies of People Who Left Welfare Tell Us." *Series A, No. A-32* (1999). Washington, DC: The Urban Institute.

Briggs, Xavier de Souza, Elizabeth J. Mueller, and Mercer Sullivan. *From Neighborhood to Community: Evidence on the Social Effects of Community Development.* New York: Community Development Research Center, New School for Social Research, 1997.

Brooks, Mary. "Housing Trust Funds." In *The Affordable City: Toward a Third Sector Housing Policy,* edited by John E. Davis, 245–264. Philadelphia: Temple University Press, 1994.

Brooks, Mary E. *A Citizen's Guide to Creating a Housing Trust Fund.* Washington, DC: Center for Community Change, 1989.

Brooks, Mary E. "Housing Trust Funds: What Makes Them Work." *Shelterforce* XIV (May/June 1992):6–10.

Brown, Prudence. "Comprehensive Neighborhood-based Initiatives." *Cityscape* 2 (May 1996): 161–176.

Browning, Rufus, Dale Rogers, and David Marshall Tabb. *Racial Politics in American Cities, Second Edition.* New York: Longman, 1997.

Buechler, Steven M. "New Social Movements Theories." *The Sociological Quarterly* 36, no. 3 (1995):441–464.

Burghardt, Steve. *Organizing for Community Action.* Beverly Hills: Sage, 1982a.

Burghardt, Steve. *The Other Side of Organizing: Resolving the Personal Dilemmas and Political Demands of Daily Practice.* Cambridge, MA: Schenkman Publishing, 1982b.

Cable, Sherry. "Women's Social Movement Involvement: The Role of Structural Availability in Recruitment and Participation Processes." *The Sociological Quarterly* 33 (Spring 1992): 35–50.

Callahan, Steve, Neil Mayer, Kris Palmer, and Larry Ferlazzo. "Rowing the Boat with Two Oars." Working papers for comm-org; *http://uac.rdp.utoledo.edu/comm-org/papers99/callahan.htm* (1999).

Carroll, William K., and R. S. Ratner. "Master Framing and Cross-Movement Networking in Contemporary Social Movements." *The Sociological Quarterly* 37, no. 4 (1996):601–626.

Cassidy, Robert. *Livable Cities: A Grassroots Guide to Rebuilding Urban America.* New York: Holt, Rinehart and Winston, 1980.

Castells, Manuel. *The City and the Grassroots: A Cross-Cultural Theory of Urban Social Movement.* Berkeley: University of California Press, 1983.

Center for Community Change. *Annual Report 1990.* Washington, DC 1991.

Center for Community Change. *How and Why to Influence Public Policy: An Action Guide for Community Organizations.* Washington, DC: Center for Community Change, 1996.

Center for Community Change. *How to Tell and Sell Your Story: Part 2.* Washington, DC: Center for Community Change, 1997a.

Center for Community Change. *How to Tell and Sell Your Story: Part 1.* Washington, DC: Center for Community Change, 1997b.

Center for Community Change. "State and Local Governments: A New Frontier for Housing Dollars." *Community Change* 16 (summer 1994):1–3.

Center for Public Finance and Housing. *Status and Prospects of the Nonprofit Housing Sector.* Report to the U.S. Department of Housing and Urban Development Office of Policy Development and Research. Washington, DC: Community and Economic Development Program, Urban Institute, 1994.

Center of Budget and Policy Priorities. *Without Reductions in Discretionary Programs, There Would Be Little Budget Surplus Outside Social Security. http://www.cbpp.org/3-23-99bud.htm,* 1999.

Center on Budget and Policy Priorities. *http://www.chpp.org/615house.htm* (1998). *In Search of Shelter: The Growing Shortage of Affordable Rental Housing.* Washington, DC: Center on Budget and Policy Priorities.

Chavez, Cesar. "La Causa and La Huegla." In *Community Organizers,* edited by Joan Ecklein, 15–27. New York: John Wiley & Sons, 1984.

Chavez, John R. *Eastside Landmark: A History of the East Los Angeles Community Union, 1968–1993.* Stanford, CA: Stanford University Press, 1998.

Chavis, David M., Paul Florin, and R. J. Michael Felix. "Nurturing Grassroots Initiatives for Community Development: The Role of Enabling Systems." In *Community Organization and Social Administration: Advances, Trends, and Emerging Principles,* edited by Terry Mizrahi and John D. Morrison, 41–68. New York: The Haworth Press, 1993.

Checkoway, Barry, and Annette Norsman. "Empowering Citizens with Disabilities." *Community Development Journal,* October 1986, 270–277.

Churchill, Ward, and Jim Vander Wall. *Agents of Repression: The FBI's Secret Wars against the Black Panther Party and the American Indian Movement.* Boston: South End Press, 1988.

Clavel, Pierre. *The Progressive City: Planning and Participation, 1969–1984.* New Brunswick, NJ: Rutgers University Press, 1986.

Clavel, Pierre, and Wim Wiewell, eds. *Harold Washington and the Neighborhoods: Progressive City Government in Chicago, 1983–1987.* New Brunswick, NJ: Rugers University Press, 1991.

Cnaan, Ram A. "Neighborhood-Representing Organizations: How Democratic Are They." *Social Services Review,* December 1991, 614–634.

Committee for Economic Development. *Rebuilding Inner-City Communities: A New Approach to the Nation's Urban Crisis.* New York: Committee for Economic Development, 1995.

Community Information Exchange. *Economic Revitalization and Health Care.* Washington, DC: Community Information Exchange, 1995.

Community Information Exchange. "Green Communities, Green Jobs." *Strategy Alert,* no. 50 (Winter 1998).

Community News Project of the Community Media Workshop. "National Issues: The Chicago Experience." Chicago, 1996.

Cormick, Gerald W. "Strategic Issues in Structuring Multi-Party Public Policy Negotiations." *Negotiation Journal* (1989):125–132.

Cortes, Ernesto. "Community Organizing and Social Capital." *National Civic Review* 85:3. Fall (1996):49–53.

Cortes, Ernesto, Jr. "Reweaving the Social Fabric." *http://my.voyager.net/ttresser/cortes.htm* (1996).

Counts, Alex. *Give Us Credit.* New York: Times Books, 1996.

Cox, Craig. *Storefront Revolution: Food Co-ops and the Counterculture.* New Brunswick, NJ: Rutgers University Press, 1994.

Crenshaw, Edward, and Craig St. John. "The Organizationally Dependent Community." *Urban Affairs Quarterly* 24 (March 1989):412–434.

Crenson, Matthew. *Neighborhood Politics.* Cambridge, MA: Harvard University Press, 1983.

Crenson, Matthew. "Social Networks and Political Processes in Urban Neighborhoods." *Journal of Political Science* 22 (1980):578–594.

Cronin, Thomas E. *Direct Democracy: The Politics of Initiative, Referendum, and Recall.* Cambridge, MA: Harvard University Press, 1989.

Crosby, Ned, Janet M. Kelly, and Paul Schaefer. "Citizen Panels: A New Approach to Citizen Participation." *Public Administration Review* (March/April 1986):170–178.

Crozat, Michael. "Are the Times A-Changing? Assessing the Acceptance of Protest in Western Democracies." In *The Social Movement Society,* edited by David Meyer and Sidney Tarrow, 59–82. New York: Rowman & Littlefield, 1998.

Cunningham, James V., and Milton Kotler. *Building Neighborhood Organizations: A Guidebook Sponsored by the National Association of Neighborhoods.* Notre Dame, IN: University of Notre Dame Press, 1983.

Cutler, Ira. "The Working Poor: Sittin' Here Thinkin'" *Http://www.handsnet.org/index_show .htm?doc_id=15531&frme_id=1331,* June 1999. Handnet.

Daley, John Michael, and Julio Angulo. "Understanding the Dynamics of Diversity within Non-profit Boards." *Journal of the Community Development Society* 25, no. 2 (1994):172–188.

Danielson, Michael. *The Politics of Exclusion.* New York: Columbia University Press, 1976.

Deckard, Barbara. *The Women's Movement: Political, Socioeconomic and Psychological Issues.* New York: Harper and Row, 1983.

del Castillo, Richard Griswold, and Richard A. Garcia. *Cesar Chavez: A Triumph of Spirit.* Norman, OK: University of Oklahoma Press, 1995.

Delbecq, Andre, Andrew H. Van de Ven, and David Gustafson. *Group Techniques for Program Planning: A Guide to Nominal Group and Delphi Procedures.* Glenview, IL: Scott, Foresman and Company, 1975.

Delgado, Gary. *Beyond the Politics of Place: New Directions in Community Organizing in the 1990s.* Oakland, CA: Applied Research Center, 1994.

Delgado, Gary. *Organizing the Movement: The Roots and Growth of ACORN.* Philadelphia: Temple University Press, 1986.

Delgado, Gary. "Building Multiracial Alliances: The Case of People United for a Better Oakland." In *Mobilizing the Community: Local Politics in the Eras of the Global City,* edited by Robert Fisher and Joseph Kling, 103–127. Newbury Park, CA: Sage, 1993.

DeParle, Jason. "Rash, Rude and Effective, Act-Up Helps Change AIDS Policy." *New York Times* (1990):11.

Department of Housing and Urban Development. *Waiting in Vain; an Update on America's Rental Housing Crisis.* Washington, DC: Department of Housing and Urban Development, 1999.

Department of Housing and Urban Development. *The State of the Cities 1999.* Washington, DC: Department of Housing and Urban Development, 1999.

Deutschman, Iva Ellen. "Feminist Theory and the Politics of Empowerment." Prepared for Delivery at the 1988 Annual Meeting of the American Political Science Association. Washington, DC, 1988.

Development Technical Institute. *Training Plan for the National Internship in Community Economic Development: Class of 1992.* Baltimore: DTI, 1992.

Diani, Mario. "Social Movements and Social Capital: A Network Perspective on Movement Outcomes." *Mobilization* 2, no. 2 (1997):129–148.

Dill, Bonnie Thornton. "'Making Your Job Good Yourself': Domestic Service and the Construction of Personal Dignity." In *Women and the Politics of Empowerment,* edited by Sandra Morgan and Ann Bookman, 33–52. Philadelphia: Temple University Press, 1988.

DiMaggio, Paul J., and Walter W. Powell. "Institutional Isomorphism and Collective Rationality." In *The New Institutionalism in Organizational Analysis,* edited by Walter W. Powell and Paul DiMaggio, 63–82. Chicago: University of Chicago Press, 1991.

Dingerson, Leigh. "Pulling Together to Fight for Jobs." *Shelterforce* XX, no. 2 (1998):18–19, 20.

Dittmer, John. *Local People: The Struggle for Civil Rights in Mississippi.* Urbana, IL: University of Illinois Press, 1994.

Dreier, Peter. "Philanthropy and the Housing Crisis: Dilemmas of Private Charity and Public Policy in the United States." In *Shelter and Society: Theory, Research, and Policy for Nonprofit Housing,* edited by C. Theodore Koebel, 91–138. Albany, NY: State University of New York Press, 1998.

Dresang, Dennis L., and James J. Gosling. *Politics, Policy & Management in the American States.* New York: Longman, 1989.

Ducharme, Donna. "Planned Manufacturing Districts: How a Community Initiative Became City Policy." In *Harold Washington and the Neighborhoods: Progressive City Government in Chicago, 1983–1987,* edited by Pierre Clavel and Wim Wiewel, 221–237. New Brunswick, NJ: Rutgers University Press, 1991.

Ecklein, Joan. *Community Organizers.* New York: John Wiley & Sons, 1984.

Edelman, Murray. *Constructing the Political Spectacle.* Chicago: University of Chicago Press, 1988.

Edin, Kathryn, and Laura Lein. *Making Ends Meet: How Single Mothers Survive Low-wage Work.* New York: Russell Sage Foundation, 1997.

Egan, Timothy. "Mired in Poverty, Alaska Natives Ponder How Much Land to Spend." *The New York Times,* 1 June 1990, 1, 11.

Ehrenreich, John H. *The Altruistic Imagination: A History of Social Work and Social Policy in the United States.* Ithaca, NY: Cornell University Press, 1985.

Eisinger, Peter. "City Politics in an Era of Federal Devolution." *Urban Affairs Review* 33 (January 1998):308–325.

Enchautegui, Maria E. "Latino Neighborhoods and Latino Neighborhood Poverty." *Journal of Urban Affairs* 19, no. 4 (1997):445–467.

Ervin, Mike. "Building Blocks: A Step-by-Step Organizing Campaign Leads to New Funding for Housing." *The Neighborhood Works* 17 (February/March 1994):7–10.

Fainstein, Susan, Norman Fainstein, Richard Child Hill, Dennis Judd, Michael Peter Smith, and Jeffrey Armistead, with Marlene Keller. *Restructuring the City.* New York: Longman, 1982.

Faludi, Susan. *Backlash: The Undeclared War Against Women.* New York: Anchor Books/Doubleday, 1992.

Fantasia, Rick. *Cultures of Solidarity: Consciousness, Action, and Contemporary American Workers.* Berkeley: University of California Press, 1988.

Fellner, Kim. "Hearts and Crafts: Powering the Movement." *Shelterforce* XX (Sept/Oct 1998): 20–22.

Ferraro, Kathleen. "Policing Woman Battering." *Social Problems* 36 (February 1989):61–74.

Ferree, Myra Marx, and Patricia Martin Yancey, eds. *Feminist Organizations: Harvest of the New Women's Movement.* Philadelphia: Temple University Press, 1995.

Finkel, Ed. "A School of Their Own." *The Neighborhood Works* 21 (January/February 1998):15, 28.

Fisher, Robert. *Let the People Decide: Neighborhood Organizing in America,* Updated Edition. New York: Twayne, 1994.

Fisher, Robert. *Let the People Decide: Neighborhood Organizing in America.* Boston: Twayne, 1984.

Fisher, Robert, and Joe Kling. "Community Organization and New Social Movement Theory." *Journal of Progressive Human Services* 5, no. 2 (1994):5–23.

Flanagan, Joan. *The Grass Roots Fund Raising Book: How to Raise Money in Your Community.* Chicago: Contemporary Books, 1982.

Foley, Michael W., and Bob Edwards. "Escape from Politics? Social Theory and the Social Capital Debate." *American Behavioral Scientists* 40 (March/April 1997):550–561.

Fordham, Christopher C., III. "Shanty-Town Protests: Symbolic Dissent." *The Atlantic Community Quarterly* (1986):244–247.

Foreman, Christopher H., Jr. "Grassroots Victim Organizations: Mobilizing for Personal and Public Health." In *Interest Group Politics,* 4th edition, edited by Allen J. Cigler and Burdett A. Loomis, 33–54. Washington, DC: CQ Press, 1995.

Frankfort-Nachmias, Chava, and J. John Palen. "Neighborhood Revitalization and the Community Question." *Journal of the Community Development Society* 24, no. 1 (1993):1–14.

Freire, Paulo. *Pedagogy of the Oppressed.* Translated by Myra Bergman Ramos. New York: Seabury Press, Continuum, 1970.

Freudenberg, Nicholas. *Not in Our Backyards! Community Action for Health and the Environment.* New York: Monthly Review Press, 1984.

Friedman, Monroe. "Grassroots Groups Confront the Corporation: Contemporary Strategies in Historical Perspective." *Journal of Social Issues* 52, no. 1 (1996):153–167.

Galaskiewicz, Joseph, and Deborah Stein. "Leadership and Networking Among Neighborhood Human Service Organizations." *Administrative Science Quarterly* 26, no. 3 (1981):434–448.

Gamaliel Foundation. "Gamaliel Foundation." *Http://www.gamaliel.org.*

Gamson, William. "Constructing Social Protest." In *Social Movements: Perspectives and Issues,* edited by Steven M. Buechler and Cylke, F. Kurt, 228–244. Toronto: Mayfield Publishing, 1997a.

Gamson, William A. "The Success of the Unruly." In *Social Movements: Readings on Their Emergence, Mobilization and Dynamics,* edited by Doug McAdam and David A. Snow, 357–364. Los Angeles: Roxbury Publishing, 1997b.

Gans, Herbert J. *The War Against the Poor: The Underclass and Antipoverty Policy.* New York: Basic, 1995.

Gans, Herbert J. *Middle American Individualism: The Future of Liberal Democracy.* New York: The Free Press, 1988.

Garland, Anne Witte. *Women Activists: Challenging the Abuse of Power.* New York: The Feminist Press at the City University of New York, 1988.

Gaventa, John, Barbara Ellen Smith, and Alex Willingham, eds. *Communities in Economic Crisis: Appalachia and the South.* Philadelphia: Temple University Press, 1990.

Giloth, Robert, ed. *Jobs and Economic Development: Strategies and Practices.* Thousand Oaks, CA: Sage, 1998.

Giloth, Robert. "Social Investments in Jobs: Foundation Perspectives on Targeted Economic Development During the 1990s." *Economic Development Quarterly* 9 (August 1995):279–289.

Gitlin, Todd. *The Sixties: Years of Hope, Days of Rage.* New York: Bantam, 1989.

Gittell, Marilyn, Kathe Newman, Janice Bockmeyer, and Robert Lindsay. "Expanding Civic Opportunity: Urban Empowerment Zones." *Urban Affairs Review* 33 (March 1998):530–558.

Gittell, Ross, and Avis Vidal. *Community Organizing: Building Social Capital as a Development Strategy.* Thousand Oaks, CA: Sage, 1998.

Goetz, Edward G. "The Community-Based Housing Movement and Progressive Local Politics." In *Revitalizing Urban Neighborhoods,* edited by W. Dennis Keating, Norman Krumholz, and Philip Star, 164–178. Lawrence, KS: University Press of Kansas, 1996.

Goetz, Edward G. *Shelter Burden: Local Politics and Progressive Housing Policy.* Philadelphia: Temple University Press, 1993.

Goetz, Edward G., and Mara S. Sidney. *The Impact of the Minneapolis Neighborhood Revitalization Program on Neighborhood Organizations.* Minneapolis: Center for Urban and Regional Affairs, Hubert Humphrey Center, 1994a.

Goetz, Edward, and Mara Sidney. "Revenge of the Property Owners: Community Development and the Politics of Property." *Journal of Urban Affairs* 16 (November 1994b): 319–334.

Goffman, Erving. *Frame Analysis.* Cambridge, MA.: Harvard University Press, 1974.

Goode, Judith, and Jo Anne Schneider. *Reshaping Ethnic and Racial Relations in Philadelphia: Immigrants in a Divided City.* Philadelphia: Temple University Press, 1994.

Goodpaster, Gary. *A Guide to Negotiation and Mediation.* Irvington-on-Hudson, NY: Transaction, 1997.

Gottlieb, Robert. *Forcing the Spring: The Transformation of the American Environmental Movement.* Washington, DC: Island Press, 1993.

Gramsci, Antonio. *Letters from Prison,* edited and translated by Lynn Lawler New York: Harper & Row, 1973.

Granovetter, Mark. "The Strength of Weak Ties." *American Journal of Sociology* 78, no. 6 (1973):1360–1374.

Green, Paul M. "SON/SOC: Organizing in White Ethnic Neighborhoods." *Illinois Issues* 14 (May 1988):24–28.

Greenbaum, Thomas L. *The Handbook for Focus Group Research,* Second Edition. Thousand Oaks, CA: Sage, 1998.

Greenberg, Edward S. *Workplace Democracy: The Political Effects of Participation.* Ithaca, NY: Cornell University Press, 1986.

Greenburg, Jan Crawford. "States Begin Pushing Limits on Heels of High Court Ruling." *Chicago Tribune,* July 25, 1999, Section 1, p. 6.

Griffin, Kelley. *Ralph Nader Presents More Action for a Change.* New York: Dembner Books, 1987.

Groenbjerg, Kirsten A. *Understanding Nonprofit Funding: Managing Revenues in Social Services and Community Development Organizations.* San Francisco: Jossey-Bass, 1993.

Gunn, Christopher Eaton. *Workers' Self-Management in the United States.* Ithaca, NY: Cornell University Press, 1984.

Gutierrez, Lorraine, Ann Rosegrant Alvares, Howard Nemon, and Edith Lewis. "Multicultural Community Organizing: A Strategy for Change." *Social Work* 41, no. 5 (1996):501–508.

Hammerback, John C., Richard J. Jensen, and Jose Angel Gutierrez. *A War of Words: Chicano Protest in the 1960s and 1970s.* Westport, CN: Greenwood Press, 1985.

Hanna, Mark G., and Buddy Robinson. *Strategies for Community Empowerment: Direct-action and Transformative Approaches to Social Change Practice.* Lewiston, Maine: Edwin Mellen Press, 1994.

Hardy-Fanta, Carol. *Latina Politics, Latino Politics: Gender, Culture, and Political Participation in Boston.* Philadelphia: Temple University Press, 1993.

Harrison, Bennett, and Marcus Weiss. *Workforce Development Networks: Community-based Organizations and Regional Alliances.* Newbury Park, CA: Sage, 1998.

Hartman, Chester. "Debating the Low-income Housing Tax Credit: Feeding the Sparrows by Feeding the Horses." *Shelterforce* XIV (January/February 1992):12, 15.

Hartman, Susan M. *From Margin to Mainstream: American Women and Politics Since 1960.* Philadelphia: Temple University Press, 1989.

Haymes, Stephen Nathan. *Race, Culture, and the City: A Pedagogy for Black Urban Struggle.* Albany, NY: State University of New York Press, 1995.

Hebert, Scott, Kathleen Baron Heintz, Chris, Nancy Kay, and James E. Wallace. *Non Profit Housing: Costs and Funding Final Report Volume I—Findings.* Prepared for U.S. Department of Housing and Urban Development Office of Policy Development and Research. Abt Associates with Aspen Systems. Washington, DC, 1993.

Henig, Jeffrey. *Neighborhood Mobilization: Redevelopment and Response.* New Brunswick, NJ: Rutgers University Press, 1982.

Hirsch, Eric L. "The Creation of Political Solidarity in Social Movement Organizations." *The Sociological Quarterly* 27, no. 3 (1986):373–387.

hooks, bell. *Talking Back: Thinking Feminist, Thinking Black.* Boston: South End Press, 1989.

Horton, John, with the assistance of Jose Calderon, Mary Pardo, Leland Saita, Linda Shaw, and Yen-Fen Tseng. *The Politics of Diversity: Immigration, Resistance, and Change in Monterey Park, California.* Philadelphia: Temple University Press, 1995.

Horwitt, Sanford D. *Let Them Call Me Rebel: Saul Alinksy—His Life and Legacy.* New York: Alfred A. Knopf, 1989.

Houle, Cyril O. *Governing Boards: Their Nature and Nurture.* San Francisco: Jossey-Bass, 1989.

Hula, Kevin. "Rounding up the Usual Suspects: Forging Interest Group Coalitions in Washington." In *Interest Group Politics,* 4th Ed., edited by Allan J. Cigler and Burdett A. Loomis, 239–257. Washington, DC: Congressional Quarterly Press, 1995.

Hummon, David. *Commonplaces: Community Ideology and Identify in American Culture.* Albany, NY: State University of New York Press, 1990.

Hyde, Cheryl. "A Feminist Response to Rothman's 'The Interweaving of Community Intervention Approaches.'" *Journal of Community Practice* 3, no. 3/4 (1996):127–146.

Iannello, Kathleen. "A Feminist Framework for Organizations." Prepared for Delivery at the Annual Meeting of the American Political Science Association. Washington, DC, 1988.

Imbroscio, David L. *Reconstructing City Politics: Alternative Economic Development and Urban Regimes.* Thousand Oaks, CA: Sage, 1997.

Issac, Jeffrey C. *Power and Marxist Theory: A Realist View.* Ithaca, NY: Cornell University Press, 1987.

Jackall, Robert. "Work in America and the Cooperative Movement." In *Worker Cooperatives in America,* edited by Robert Jackall and Henry Levin, 277–290. Berkeley: University of California Press, 1984.

Janis, Irving. *Groupthink: Psychological Studies of Policy Decisions and Fiascoes.* Boston: Houghton Mifflin Company, 1982.

Jargowsky, Paul A. *Poverty and Place: Ghettos, Barrios, and the American City.* New York: Russell Sage Foundation, 1997.

Jencks, Christopher. *The Homeless: Rethinking Social Policy.* Cambridge, MA.: Harvard University Press, 1994.

Jenkins, J. Craig. *The Politics of Insurgency: The Farm Worker Movement in the 1960s.* New York: Columbia University Press, 1985.

Jenkins, J. Craig, and Charles Perrow. "Insurgency of the Powerless: Farm Worker Movements 1946–1972." *American Sociological Review* 42, no. 2 (1977):249–268.

Jennings, James. "The Politics of Black Empowerment in Urban America: Reflections on Race, Class, and Community." In *Dilemmas of Activism; Class, Community, and the Politics of Local Mobilization,* edited by Joseph M. Kling and Prudence S. Posner, 113–133. Philadelphia: Temple University Press, 1990.

Jennings, M. Kent, and Ellen Ann Andersen. "Support for Confrontional Tactics Among AIDS Activists: A Study of Intra-Movement Divisions." *American Journal of Political Science* 40 (May 1996):311–334.

Jezierski, Louise. "Neighborhoods and Public-Private Partnerships in Pittsburgh." *Urban Affairs Quarterly* 26 (December 1990):217–249.

Johnson, Alice, and Alice Rollins Castengera. "Integrated Program Development: A Model for Meeting the Complex Needs of Homeless Persons." *Journal of Community Practice* 1, no. 3 (1994):29–48.

Johnston, David Cay. "Gap Between Rich and Poor Found Substantially Wider." *New York Times,* September 5, 1999, 14.

Johnston, Hank, Enrique Laraña, and Joseph R. Gusfield. "Identities, Grievances and New Social Movements." In *New Social Movements: From Ideology to Identity,* edited by Enrique Laraña, Hank Johnston, and Joseph R. Gusfield, 3–35. Philadelphia: Temple University Press, 1994.

Jones, Bryan, Lynn Bachelor, and Carter Wilson. *The Sustaining Hand: Community Leadership and Community Power.* Lawrence, KS: University of Kansas Press, 1986.

Jones, Stanley E., Dean C. Barnlund, and Franklyn S. Haiman. *The Dynamics of Discussion: Communication in Small Groups.* New York: Harper & Row, 1980.

Jones, Van. "Operation Harriet Tubman: Student Solidarity with Haitian Refugees." In *Beyond Identity Politics: Emerging Social Justice Movements in Communities of Color,* edited by John Anner, 65–77. Boston: South End Press, 1996.

Kahn, Si. *Organizing: A Guide for Grassroots Leaders.* New York: McGraw-Hill, 1982.

Kaner, Sam, with Linny Lind, Catherine Toldi, Sarah Fisk, and Duane Berger. *Facilitator's Guide to Participatory Decision-Making.* Gabriola Island, BC: New Society Publishers, 1996.

Katzenstein, Mary Fainsod. "Comparing the Feminist Movements of the United States and Western Europe: An Overview." In *The Women's Movements of the United States and Western Europe,* edited by Mary Fainsod Katzenstein and Carol McClug Mueller, 3–20. Philadelphia: Temple University Press, 1987.

Katzenstein, Mary Fainsod. "Discursive Politics and Feminist Activism in the Catholic Church." In *Feminist Organizations: Harvest of the New Women's Movement,* edited by Myra Marx Ferree and Patricia Yancey Martin, 35–52. Philadelphia: Temple University Press, 1995.

Kelly, Caroline, and John Kelly. "Who Gets Involved in Collective Action? Social Psychological Determinants of Individual Participation in Trade Unions." *Human Relations* 47, no. 1 (1994):63–88.

Kendrick, Karen. "Producing the Battered Woman." In *Community Activism and Feminist Politics: Organizing Across Race, Class, and Gender,* edited by Nancy Naples, 151–174. New York: Routledge, 1998.

Klandermans, Bert, and Dirk Oegema. "Potentials, Networks, Motivations, and Barriers: Steps Towards Participation in Social Movements." *American Sociological Review* 52 (August 1987):519–531.

Klein, Kim. *Fundraising for Social Change.* Third Edition. Berkeley, CA: Chardon Press, 1996.

Kleyman, Paul. *Senior Power: Growing Old Rebelliously.* San Francisco: Glide Publications, 1974.

Knoke, David, and James Wood. *Organized for Action: Commitment in Voluntary Organizations.* New Brunswick, NJ: Rutgers University Press, 1981.

Kornblum, William. *Blue Collar Community.* Chicago: University of Chicago Press, 1974.

Kornblum, William, Joseph Julian, and Carolyn D. Smith. *Social Problems,* Ninth Edition. Upper Saddle River, NJ: Prentice Hall, 1998.

Kowitz, Albert, and Thomas Knutson. *Decision Making in Small Groups: The Search for Alternatives.* Boston: Allyn and Bacon, 1980.

Krauss, Celene. "Grass-roots consumer protest and toxic wastes: Developing a critical political view." *Community Development Journal* 48 (1988):258–265.

Krauss, Celene. "Challenging Power: Toxic Waste Protests and the Politicization of White, Working-Class Women." In *Community Activism and Feminist Politics: Organizing Across Race, Class, and Gender,* edited by Nancy A. Naples, 129–150. New York: Routledge, 1998.

Kretzman, John P., and John L. McKnight. *Building Communities from the Inside Out: A Path Toward Finding and Mobilizing a Community's Assets.* Chicago, IL: Center for Urban Affairs and Policy Research, Neighborhood Innovations Network, Northwestern University, 1993.

Kubisch, Anne C. "Comprehensive Community Initiatives." *Shelterforce* XVIII (January/February 1996):8–11.

Kweit, Mary Grisez, and Robert Kweit. *Implementing Citizen Participation in a Bureaucratic Society: A Contingency Approach.* New York: Praeger, 1981.

Lang, Robert E., and Steven P. Hornburg. "What is Social Capital and Why It is Important to Public Policy." *Housing Policy Debate* 9, no. 1 (1998):1–16.

Laraña, Enrique, Hank Johnston, and Joseph Gusfield, eds. *New Social Movements: From Ideology to Identity.* Philadelphia: Temple University Press, 1994.

Latting, Jean Kantambu, and Angela Blanchard. "Empowering Staff in a 'Poverty Agency': An Organizational Development Intervention." *Journal of Community Practice* 4, no. 3 (1997):59–76.

Lauer, Robert. *Social Problems and the Quality of Life,* 7th Edition. Boston: McGraw-Hill, 1998.

Lavine, Richard. "School Finance Reform in Texas, 1983–1995." In *Public Policy and Community: Activism and Governance in Texas,* edited by Robert H. Wilson, 119–165. Austin, TX: University of Texas Press, 1997.

Lawler, Edward J. "Power Processes in Bargaining." *The Sociological Quarterly* 33 (Spring 1992):17–34.

Lawson, Ronald, with the assistance of Reuben B. Johnson, III. "Tenant Response to the Urban Housing Crisis, 1970–1984." In *The Tenant Movement in New York City, 1904–1984,* edited by Ronald Lawson, with the assistance of Mark Naison, 209–278. New Brunswick, NJ: Rutgers University Press, 1986.

Lee, Hoon. "Building Class Solidarity Across Racial Lines: Korean American Workers in Los Angeles." In *Beyond Identity Politics: Emerging Social Justice Movements in Communities of Color,* edited by John Anner, 47–61. Boston, MA: South End Press, 1996.

Lee, N'Tanya, Don Murphy, Lisa North, and Juliet Ucell. "Bridging Race, Class and Sexuality for School Reform." In *Beyond Identity Politics: Emerging Social Justice Movements in Communities of Color,* edited by John Anner, 31–43. Boston, MA: South End Press, 1996.

Lenz, Thomas J. "Neighborhood Development: Issues and Models." *Social Policy* 19 (Spring 1988):24–30.

Levine, Adeline. *Love Canal: Science, Politics, and People.* Lexington, MA: Lexington, 1982.

Levine, Hillel, and Lawrence Harmon. *The Death of an American Jewish Community: A Tragedy of Good Intensions.* New York: The Free Press, 1992.

Levitan, Sar A., Frank Gallo, and Isaac Shapiro. *Working but Poor: American's Contradiction,* Revised Edition. Baltimore: John Hopkins Press, 1993.

Levy, Jacques E. *Cesar Chavez: Autobiography of La Causa.* New York: W.W. Norton, 1975.

Lewis, George H. "Style in Revolt: Music, Social Protest, and the Hawaiian Cultural Renaissance." *International Social Science Journal* 66 (December 1987):168–177.

Liou, Y. Thomas, and Robert C. Stroh. "Community Development Intermediary Systems in the United States: Origins, Evolution, and Functions." *Housing Policy Debate* 9, no. 3 (1998):575–594.

Lipsitz, George. *A Life in the Struggle: Ivory Perry and the Culture of Opposition.* Philadelphia: Temple University Press, 1988.

Lipsitz, George. *A Life in the Struggle: Ivory Perry and the Culture of Opposition,* revised edition. Philadelphia: Temple University Press, 1995.

Local Initiatives Support Corporation. *1993 Annual Report.* New York: Local Initiative Support Corporation, 1994.

Lopez, Daniel. "Language: Diversity and Assimilation." In *Ethnic Los Angeles,* edited by Roger Waldinger, 139–164. New York: Russell Sage Foundation, 1996.

Lyman, Rick. "Got a Cause and a Computer? You Can Fight City Hall." *New York Times,* Oct 3, 1998, A12.

Majka, Theo J., and Patrick G. Donnelly. "Cohesiveness Within a Heterogeneous Urban Neighborhood; Implications for Community in a Diverse Setting." *Journal of Urban Affairs* 10, no. 2 (1988):141–160.

MacLeod, Jay. *Ain't No Makin' It: Aspirations & Attainment in a Low-income Neighborhood.* Denver: Westview Press, 1995.

Mancoske, Ronald J., and Jeanne Hunzeker. "Advocating for Community Services Coordination: An Empowerment Perspective for Planning AIDs Services." *Journal of Community Practice* 1, no. 3 (1994):29–48.

Mansbridge, Jane J. *Beyond Adversary Democracy.* New York: Basic Books, 1980.

Mansbridge, Jane J. *Why We Lost the ERA.* Chicago: University of Chicago Press, 1986.

Marciniak, Ed. *Reversing Urban Decline: The Winthrop-Kenmore Corridor in the Edgewater and Uptown Communities of Chicago.* Washington, DC: National Center for Urban Ethnic Affairs, 1981.

Marcuse, Peter. "Neighborhood Policy and the Distribution of Power: New York City's Community Boards." *Policy Studies Journal* 16 (Winter 1987–1988):277–289.

Massey, Douglas S., and Nancy A. Denton. *American Apartheid: Segregation and the Making of the Underclass.* Cambridge, MA: Harvard University Press, 1993.

Mayer, Gordon. "Is This Any Way to Get a Meeting?" *Shelterforce* XVIII (May/June 1996):22–23.

Mayer, Martin. *The Builders.* New York: Norton, 1978.

McAdam, Doug. "Tactical Innovation and the Pace of Insurgency." In *Social Movements: Readings on Their Emergence, Mobilization, and Dynamics,* edited by Doug McAdam, and David A. Snow, 340–356. Los Angeles: Roxbury Publishing, 1997.

McAdam, Doug, and Ronnelle Paulsen. "Specifying the Relationship Between Social Ties and Activism." *American Journal of Sociology* 99 (1993):640–667.

McAdam, Douglas. "Culture and Social Movements." In *New Social Movements: From Ideology to Identity,* edited by Enrique Laraña, Hank Johnston, and Joseph R. Gusfield, 36–57. Philadelphia: Temple University Press, 1994.

McCann, Michael W. *Rights at Work: Pay Equity Reform and the Politics of Legal Mobilization.* Chicago: University of Chicago Press, 1994.

McCarthy, John D., and Clark McPhail. "The Institutionalization of Protest in the United States." In *The Social Movement Society,* edited by David S. Meyer and Sidney Tarrow, 83–110. Lanham, MD: Rowman & Littlefield Publishers, 1998.

McCarthy, John, and Mayer Zald (eds.). *Social Movements in an Organizational Society: Collected Essays.* New Brunswick, NJ: Transaction Books, 1987.

McCreight, Mac. "Lawsuits for Leverage." In *Roots to Power: A Manual for Grassroots Organizing,* edited by Lee Staples, 181–187. New York: Praeger, 1984.

McDougall, Harold. *Black Baltimore: A New Theory of Community.* Philadelphia: Temple University Press, 1993.

McKay, Emily Gantz, and Cristina Kanter with Lynn Rothman, Iris Mott, Andrew Saasta, and Timothy Lopez. *Linking Human Services and Economic Development.* Washington, DC: Center for Community Change, 1997.

Medoff, Peter, and Holly Sklar. *Streets of Hope: The Fall and Rise of an Urban Neighborhood.* Boston: South End Press, 1994.

Mesch, Gustavo S., and Kent P. Schwirian. "The Effectivenes of Neighborhood Collective Action." *Social Problems* 43, no. 4 (1996):467–483.

Metzger, John T. "Remaking the Growth Coalition: The Pittsburgh Partnership for Neighborhood Development." *Economic Development Quarterly* 28 (February 1998):12–29.

Meyer, David S., and Nancy Whittier. "Social Movement Spillover." *Social Problems* 41 (May 1994):277–298.

Meyer, John W., and Brian Rowan. "Institutionalized Organizations: Formal Structure as Myth and Ceremony." In *The New Institutionalism in Organizational Analysis,* edited by Walter W. Powell and Paul J. DiMaggio, 41–62. Chicago: University of Chicago Press, 1991.

Midwest Academy. *Midwest Academy Organizing Manual.* Chicago: Midwest Academy, various dates.

Milbrath, Lester. *Political Participation.* Chicago: Rand McNally, 1977.

Miller, James. *"Democracy is in the Streets": From Port Huron to the Siege of Chicago.* New York: Simon and Schuster, 1987.

Milofsky, Carl. "Structure and Process in Community Self-Help Organizations." In *Community Organizations: Studies in Resource Mobilization and Exchange,* edited by Carl Milofsky, 183–215. Yale Studies on Nonprofit Organizations. New York: Oxford, 1988.

Mondros, Jacqueline B., and Scott M. Wilson. *Organizing for Power and Empowerment.* New York: Columbia University Press, 1994.

Moore, Carl M. *Group Techniques for Idea Building.* Applied Social Research Methods Series. Newbury Park, CA: Sage, 1987.

Morgan, David L. *Focus Groups as Qualitative Research.* Qualitative Research Methods Series. Newbury Park, CA: Sage, 1988.

Morgen, Sandra. "It's the whole power of the city against us: The Development of Political Consciousness in a Women's Health Care Coalition." In *Women and the Politics of Empowerment,* edited by Ann Bookman and Sandra Morgen, 97–115. Philadelphia: Temple University Press, 1988.

Morgen, Sandra, and Ann Bookman. "Rethinking Women and Politics: An Introductory Essay." In *Women and the Politics of Empowerment,* edited by Ann Bookman and Sandra Morgen, 3–29. Philadelphia: Temple University Press, 1988.

Morris, Aldon. *The Origins of the Civil Rights Movement: Black Communities Organizing for Change.* New York: Free Press, 1984.

Mott, Andrew H. *Building Systems of Support for Neighborhood Change.* Washington, DC: Center for Community Change, 1997.

Moyer, Bill. *The Movement Action Plan: A Strategic Framework Describing the Eight Stages of Successful Social Movements.* San Francisco: Social Movement Empowerment Project, 1987.

Mueller, Carol M. "Conflict Networks and the Origins of Women's Liberation." In *New Social Movements: From Ideology to Identity,* edited by Enrique Larana, Hank Johnson, and Joseph R. Gusfield, 234–263. Philadelphia: Temple University Press, 1994.

Nagel, Joane. *American Indian Ethnic Renewal: Red Power and the Resurgence of Identity and Culture.* New York: Oxford, 1996.

Naples, Nancy A. "Women's Political Activism: Exploring the Dynamics of Politicization and Diversity." In *Community Activism and Feminist Politics: Organizing Across Race, Class, and Gender,* edited by Nancy A. Naples, 327–349. New York: Routledge, 1998.

Nash, Fred. "Church-Based Organizing as Participatory Research: The Northwest Community Organization and the Pilson Resurrection Project." *The American Sociologist,* Spring 1993, 38–55.

Nathan, Richard. "The Newest New Federalism for Welfare." *Rockefeller Institute Bulletin* (1998):4–11.

National Congress for Community Economic Development. *Against All Odds: The Achievements of Community-Based Development Organizations.* Washington, DC: National Congress for Community Economic Development, 1989.

National Congress for Community Economic Development. *Tying It All Together: The Comprehensive Achievements of Community-Based Development Organizations.* Washington, DC: Author, 1995.

National Congress for Community Economic Development. "Washington Policy Conference." Washington, DC 1999.

National Congress for Community Economic Development. *Coming of Age: Trends and Achievements of Community-Based Development Organizations.* Washington, DC: National Congress for Community Economic Development, 1999.

Needleman, Ruth. "Building Relalationships for the Long Haul: Union and Community-Based Groups Working Together to Organize Low-Wage Workers." In *Organizing to Win: New Research on Union Stratgegies,* edited by Kate Bronfenbrener, Sheldon Freidman, Sirchard W. Hurd, Rudolph A. Oswald, and Ronald L. Seeber, 71–86. Ithaca, NY: ILR Press, 1998.

Nes, Janet, and Peter Iadicola. "Toward a Definition of Feminist Social Work: A Comparison of Liberal, Radical, and Socialist Models." *Social Work* 34 (January 1989):12–21.

Newman, Katherine. *No Shame in My Game: The Working Poor in the Inner City.* New York: Alfred A. Knopf and The Russell Sage Foundation, 1999.

Nickel, Denise R. "The Progressive City? Urban Redevelopment in Minneapolis." *Urban Affairs Review* 30 (January 1995):355–377.

NLIHC, *www.NLHIC.org.*

Nissen, Bruce. *Fighting for Jobs: Case Studies of Labor-Community Coalitions Confronting Plant Closings.* Albany, NY: State University of New York Press, 1995.

Nyden, Philip, and Joanne Adams. *Saving Our Homes: The Lessons of Community Struggles to Preserve Affordable Housing in Chicago's Uptown.* A Report Completed by Researchers at Loyola University of Chicago in Collaboration with Organization of the Northeast. Chicago: Loyola University Department of Sociology, 1996.

Nyden, Philip, Anne Figer, Mark Shibley, and Darryl Burrows. *Building Community: Social Science in Action.* Thousand Oaks, CA: Pine Forge Press, 1997.

O'Brien, William. "Network Effect: Door to Door, City by City, PICO Helps Communities Organize." *The Neighborhood Works* 16 (December 1993/January 1994):32–34.

O'Donnell, Sandra M. "Is Community Organizing 'the Greatest Job' One Could Have? Findings from a Survey of Chicago Organizers." *Journal of Community Practice* 2, no. 1 (1995a):1–20.

O'Donnell, Sandra M. "Urban African American Community Development in the Progressive Era." *Journal of Community Practice* 2, no. 4 (1995b):7–26.

Oegema, Dirk, and Bert Klanderman. "Why Social Movement Sympathizers Don't Participate: Erosion and Nonconversion of Support." *American Sociological Review* 59 (1994):703–722.

OMB Watch. "Speaking up in the Internet Age: Use and Value of Constituent E-Mail and Congressional Web Sites." Washington, DC: OMB Watch, Nonprofits' Policy & Technology Project. 1998.

Orfield, Myron. "Regional Coalition Building." *Shelterforce* XIX (January/February 1998):18–20, 28.

Orians, Carlyn E., Liebow Edward B., and Kristi M. Branch. "Community-Based Organization and HIV Prevention Among Seattle's Inner-City Teens." *Urban Anthropology and Studies of Cultural Systems and World Economic Development* 24 (Spring 1995):36–59.

Orland, Chris. "Economic Human Rights Tribunal." Typescript Report. DeKalb, IL. 1998.

Padilla, Felix M. *Puerto Rican Chicago.* Notre Dame, IN: University of Notre Dame Press, 1987.

Parzen, Julia Ann, and Michael Hall Kieschnick. *Credit Where It's Due: Development Banking for Communities.* Philadelphia: Temple University Press, 1992.

Payne, Charles M. *I've Got the Light of Freedom: The Organizing Tradition and the Mississippi Freedom Struggle.* Berkeley: University of California Press, 1995.

Peirce, Neal R., and Carol F. Steinbach. *Corrective Capitalism: The Rise of America's Community Development Corporations.* New York: Ford Foundation, 1987.

Peirce, Neal R., and Carol F. Steinbach. *Enterprising Communities: Community-Based Development in America, 1990.* 80. Washington, DC: Council for Community Based Development, 1990.

Perez-Pena, Richard. "New York's Income Gap Largest in Nation." *New York Times,* December 17, 1997, A14.

Perkins, Douglas D. "Speaking Truth to Power: Empowerment Ideology as Social Intervention and Policy." *American Journal of Community Psychology* 23, no. 5 (1995):765–794.

Perkins, John M. *Beyond Charity: The Call to Christian Community Development.* Grand Rapids, MI: Baker Books, 1993.

Perlman, Janice E. "Grassrooting the System." In *Strategies of Community Organization,* edited by Fred W. Cox, John L. Erlich, Jack Rothman, and John E. Tropman, 403–425. Itasca, IL. F.E. Peacock Publishers, 1979.

Perrucci, Carolyn C., Robert Perrucci, Dena B. Targ, and Harry R. Targ. *Plant Closings: International Context and Social Costs.* New York: Aldine De Gruyter, 1988.

Piven, Frances, F., and Richard Cloward. *Poor Peoples' Movements: Why They Succeed, How They Fail.* New York: Pantheon, 1977.

Piven, Frances, F., and Richard Cloward. "Social Movements and Societal Conditions: A Response to Roach and Roach." *Social Problems* 26, no. 2 (1978):172–178.

Podolefsky, Aaron, and Fredric DuBow. *Strategies for Community Crime Prevention: Collective Responses to Crime in Urban America.* Springfield, IL: Charles C Thomas, 1981.

Pogge, Jean. "Reinvestment in Chicago's Neighborhoods: A Twenty Year Struggle." In *From Redlining to Reinvestment: Community Responses to Urban Disinvestment,* edited by Gregory D. Squires, 133–148. Philadelphia: Temple University Press, 1992.

Portney, Kent, and Jeffrey M. Berry. "Mobilizing Minority Communities: Social Capital and Participation in Urban Neighborhoods." *American Behavioral Scientists* 40 (March/April 1997):632–644.

Pruitt, Dean. *Negotiation Behavior.* New York: Academic Press, 1981.

Pruitt, Dean G., and Peter J. Carnevale. *Negotiation in Social Conflict.* Pacific Groves, CA: Brooks Cole, 1993.

Putnam, Robert D. *Making Democracy Work: Civic Traditions in Modern Italy.* Princeton, NJ: Princeton University Press, 1993.

Rappaport, Julian. "The Power of Empowerment Language." *Social Policy,* Fall 1985, 15–21.

Rappaport, Julian. "Empowerment Meets Narrative: Listening to Stories and Creating Settings." *American Journal of Community Psychology* 23, no. 5 (1995):795–807.

Rast, Joel. *Remaking Chicago: The Political Origins of Industrial Change.* DeKalb, IL.: Northern Illinois University Press, 1999.

Reitzes, Donald C., and Dietrich C. Reitzes. *The Alinsky Legacy: Alive and Kicking.* Greenwich, CN: JAI Press, 1987.

Rich, Michael J. *Federal Policymaking and the Poor: National Goals, Local Choices, and Distributional Outcomes.* Princeton, NJ: Princeton University Press, 1993.

Rivera, Felix G., and John L. Erlich, eds. *Community Organizing in a Diverse Society,* second edition. Boston: Allyn & Bacon, 1995.

Robert, Henry M., and William J. Evans, eds. *Robert's Rules of Order: Newly Revised, ninth* edition. New York: Harper Collins, 1991.

Roberts-DeGennaro, Maria. "Conceptual Framework of Coalitions in an Organizational Context." In *Community Practice: Models in Action,* edited by Marie Weil, 91–108. New York: Haworth Press, 1997.

Rochefort, David A., and Roger W. Cobb. "Problem Definition: An Emerging Perspective." In *The Politics of Problem Definition,* edited by David A. Rochefort and Roger W. Cobb, 1–31. Lawrence, KS: University of Kansas Press, 1994.

Rogers, David, David Whetten, and Associates. *Interorganizational Coordination: Theory, Research and Implementation.* Ames, IA: Iowa State University, 1982.

Rogers, Mary Beth. *Cold Anger: A Story of Faith and Power Politics.* Denton, TX: University of North Texas Press, 1990.

Rohe, William M., and Michael A. Stegman. "The Effects of Homeownership on the Self-Esteem, Perceived Control and Life Satisfaction of Low-Income People." *Journal of the American Planning Association* 60 (Spring 1994):173–184.

Rooney, Jim. *Organizing the South Bronx.* Albany, NY: State University of New York Press, 1995.

Rosenthal, Donald B. "Gay and Lesbian Political Mobilization and Regime Responsiveness in Four New York Cities." *Urban Affairs Review* 32 (September 1996):45–70.

Ross, Timothy, and David Olson. "The Impact of Industrial Areas Foundation Community Organizing on Voting in Eastern Brooklyn, 1982–1990: A Comparative Study of 12 Elections." A Paper Prepared for the Annual Meeting of the Urban Affairs Association. New York City, 1996.

Rossi, Peter, and James Wright. "The Urban Homeless: A Portrait of Urban Dislocation." *The Annals of the American Academy of Political and Social Science* 501 (January 1989):132–142.

Rossides, Daniel W. *Social Stratification: The Interplay of Class, Race, and Gender,* second edition. Upper Saddle River, NJ: Prentice Hall, 1997.

Rothschild, Joyce, and J. Allen Whitt. *The Cooperative Workplace: Potentials and Dilemmas of Organizational Democracy and Participation.* Cambridge, England: Cambridge University Press, 1986.

Rothschild, Joyce. "Do Collectivist-Democratic Forms of Organization Presuppose Feminism? Cooperative Work Structures and Women's Values." Paper Presented at the Annual Meetings of the American Sociological Association. Chicago, 1987.

Rubin, Herbert J. "What Conferences Accomplish for Social Change Organizations: Illustrations from the Community Based Development Movement." *Journal of Community Practice* (2000a): 35–55.

Rubin, Herbert J. *Renewing Hope Within Neighborhoods of Depair: The Community-based Development Model.* Albany, NY: SUNY Press, 2000b.

Rubin, Herbert J. *Applied Social Research.* Columbus, OH: Charles E. Merrill, 1983.

Rubin, Herbert J. "Being a Conscience and a Carpenter: Interpretations of the Community Based Development Model." *Journal of Community Practice* 4, no. 1 (1997):57–90.

Rubin, Herbert J. "Renewing Hope in the Inner City: Conversations with Community-Based Development Practitioners." *Administration and Society* 27 (May 1995):127–160.

Rubin, Herbert J., "There Aren't Going to Be Any Bakeries Here If There is No Money to Afford Jellyrolls: The Organic Theory of Community Based Development." *Social Problems* 41 (August 1994):401–424.

Rubin, Herbert J., and Irene S. Rubin. *Qualitative Interviewing: The Art of Hearing Data.* Thousand Oaks, CA: Sage, 1995.

Rubin, Irene S., and Herbert J. Rubin. "Economic Development Incentives: The Poor (cities) Pay More." *Urban Affairs Quarterly* 23 (September 1987):37–62.

Rucht, Dieter. "The Structure and Culture of Collective Protest in Germany Since 1950." In *The Social Movement Society,* edited by David Meyer and Sidney Tarrow, 29–58. New York: Rowman & Littlefield, 1998.

Russell, Daniel. *Political Organizing in Grassroots Politics.* Lanham, MD: University Press of America, 1990.

Russell, Dick. "The Monkeywrenchers." *The Amicus Journal,* Fall 1987, 28–42.

Ryan, Barbara. *Feminism and the Women's Movement: Dynamics of Change in Social Movement, Ideology, and Activism.* New York: Routledge, 1992.

Ryan, Charlotte. *Prime Time Activism: Media Strategies for Grassroots Organizing.* Boston: South End Press, 1991.

Sabagh, Georges, and Mehdi Bozorgmeh. "Population Change: Immigration and Ethnic Transformation." In *Ethnic Los Angeles,* edited by Roger Waldindger and Mehdi Bozorgmehr. New York: Russell Sage Foundation, 1996.

Sabatier, Paul A., and Hank C. Jenkins-Smith. "The Advocacy-Coalition Framework: Assessment, Revisions, and Implications for Scholars and Practitioners." In *Policy Change and Learning: An Advocacy Coalition Approach,* edited by Paul A. Sabatier and Hank C. Jenkins-Smith, 211–236. Boulder, CO: Westview, 1993.

Saegert, Susan, and Gary Winkel. "Paths to Community Empowerment: Organizing at Home." *American Journal of Community Psychology* 24, no. 4 (1996):517–550.

Saegert, Susan, and Gary Winkel. "Social Capital and the Revitalization of New York City's Distressed Inner-City Housing." *Housing Policy Debate* 9, no. 1 (1998):17–60.

Salomon, Larry. "Sweatshops in the Spotlight." *Third Force* 4 (September/October 1996):10–13.

Sampson, Robert, Stephen W. Raudenbusch, and Felton Earls. "Neighborhoods and Violent Crime: A Multilevel Study of Collective Efficacy." *Science* 277 (August 1997):918–924.

Sanders, Heywood T. "Communities Organized for Public Service and Neighborhood Revitalization in San Antonio." In *Public Policy and Community: Activism and Governance in Texas,* edited by Robert H. Wilson, 36–68. Austin, Tex.: University of Texas Press, 1997.

"Santa Monica seeking a return to on-line civic forum of Yore," *New York Times* 9/18/98, A17.

Savage, J. A. "Radical Environmentalists: Sabotage in the Name of Ecology." *Business and Society Review* 58 (Summer 1986):35–37.

Schecter, Susan. *Women and Male Violence: The Visions and Struggles of the Battered Women's Movement.* Boston: South End Press, 1982.

Scheiber, Matthew Schuck. "Home Equity Plan Put Before Local Voters." *The Neighborhood Works* 10 (April 1987):6–7.

Schein, Edgar H. *Organizational Culture and Leadership.* San Francisco: Jossey-Bass, 1985.

Scheisl, Martin J. *The Politics of Efficiency: Municipal Administration and Reform in America, 1800–1920.* Berkeley, CA: University of California Press, 1977.

Schelling, Thomas. *The Strategy of Conflict.* Oxford, England: Oxford University Press, 1960.

Schillinger, Elisabeth. "Dependency, Control, and Isolation: Battered Women and the Welfare System." *Journal of Contemporary Ethnography* 16 (January 1988):469–490.

Schoenberg, Sandra Perlman. *Neighborhoods That Work.* New Brunswick, NJ: Rutgers: The State University of New Jersey, 1980.

Schmidt, David D. *Citizen Lawmakers: The Ballot Initiative Revolution.* Philadelphia: Temple University Press, 1989.

Schmitz, Joseph, Evertt M. Rogers, Ken Phillips, and Donald Paschal. "The Public Electronic Network (PEN) and the Homeless in Santa Monica." *Journal of Applied Communication Research* 23 (1995):26–43.

Schneider, Cathy. "Framing Puerto Rican Identity: Political Opportunity Structures and Neighborhood Organizing in New York City." *Mobilization* 2 (September 1997):227–245.

Schopler, Janice H. "Interorganizational Groups in Human Services: Environmental and Interpersonal Relationships." *Journal of Community Practice* 1, no. 3 (1994):2–28.

Schwartz, Alex. "The Limits of Community Reinvestment: The Implementation of Community Reinvestment Agreements in Chicago, Cleveland, New Jersey, and Pittsburgh." Presented at the 1998 Annual Meeting of the Urban Affairs Association. Fort Worth, TX, 1998.

Schwartz, Ed. *NetActivism: How Citizens Use the Internet.* Sebastopol, CA: Songline Studies, 1996.

Scotch, Richard K. "Disability as the Basis for a Social Movement: Advocacy and the Politics of Definition." *Journal of Social Issues* 44 (1988):159–172.

Seitz, Virginia Rinaldo. *Women, Development, and Communities for Empowerment in Appalachia.* Albany, NY: State University of New York Press, 1995.

Sekul, Joseph D. "Communities Organized for Public Service: Citizen Power and Public Policy in San Antonio." In *The Politics of San Antonio: Community, Progress & Power,* edited by David R. Johnson, 175–190. Lincoln, NE: University of Nebraska Press, 1983.

Servon, Lisa J. "Credit and Social Capital: The Community Development Potential of U.S. Microenterprise Programs." *Housing Policy Debate* 9, no. 1 (1998):115–150.

Shapiro, Joseph P. *No Pity: People with Disabilities Forging a New Civil Rights Movement.* New York: Times Books, 1993.

Sharp, Elaine. "Organizations, Their Environments and Goal Definition: An Approach to the Study of Neighborhood Associations in Urban Politics." *Urban Life* 9, no. 4 (1981):415–439.

Sharp, Gene. *The Politics of Non-Violent Action.* Boston: Porter Sargent Publisher, 1973.

Sheets, Karen. "A Welfare Reform Primer." *The Neighborhood Works,* 20 (September/October 1997):8–9.

Sherkat, Darren E., and T. Jean Block. "Explaining the Political and Personal Consequences of Protest." *Social Forces* 75 (March 1997):1049–1076.

Sherraden, Michael. *Assets and the Poor: A New American Welfare Policy.* Armonk, NY: ME Sharpe, 1991.

Shuman, Michael. "Why Do Progressive Foundations Give Too Little to Too Many?" *The Nation,* January 12/19, 1998.

Simmons, Louise B. *Organizing in Hard Times: Labor and Neighborhoods in Hartford.* Philadelphia: Temple University Press, 1994.

Skogan, Wesley G. *Disorder and Decline: Crime and the Spiral of Decay in American Neighborhoods.* Berkeley: University of California Press, 1990.

Slayton, Robert A. *Back of the Yards: The Making of a Local Democracy.* Chicago: University of Chicago Press, 1986.

Smith, Christian. *The Emergence of Liberation Theology: Radical Religion and Social Movement Theory.* Chicago: University of Chicago Press, 1991.

Smith, David Horton, Richard Reddy, and Burt Baldwin. *Voluntary Active Research.* Lexington, MA: Lexington, 1972.

Smith, David Horton, Richard Reddy, and Burt Baldwin, eds. *Participation in Social and Political Activities.* San Francisco: Jossey-Bass, 1980.

Smith, Michael Peter, and Joe R. Feagin, eds. *The Bubbling Cauldron: Race, Ethnicity, and the Urban Crisis.* Minneapolis: University of Minnesota Press, 1995.

Smith, Steven Rathgeb, and Michael Lipsky. *Nonprofits for Hire: The Welfare State in the Age of Contracting.* Cambridge, MA: Harvard University Press, 1993.

Smock, Kristina. "Comprehensive Community Initiatives: A New Generation of Urban Revitalization Strategies." on-line paper from *http://commorg.utoledo.edu/1997*

Snow, David A., E. Burke Rochford Jr., Steven K. Worden, and Robert D. Benford. "Frame Alignment Processes, Micromobilization, and Movement Participation." *American Sociological Review* 51 (August 1986):464–481.

Snow, David A., and Robert Benford. "Master Frames Amid Cycles of Protest." In *Frontiers in Social Movement Theory*, edited by Aldon D. Morris and Carol McClurg Mueller, 133–155. New Haven: Yale University Press, 1992.

Sonnenshein, Raphael J. "The Battle Over Liquor Stores in South Central Los Angeles." *Urban Affairs Review* 31, no. 6 (1996):710–727.

Specht, Harry, and Mark E. Courtney. *Unfaithful Angels: How Social Work Has Abandoned Its Mission.* New York: The Free Press, 1994.

Speer, Paul W. "Organizing for Power: A Comparative Case Study." *Journal of Community Psychology* 23 (January 1995):57–73.

Speer, Paul W., and Joseph Hughey. "Community Organizing: An Ecological Route to Empowerment and Power." *American Journal of Community Psychology* 23, no. 5 (1995):729–748.

Speer, Paul W., and Joseph Hughey. "Mechanisms of Empowerment: Psychological Processes for Members of Power-Based Community Organizations." *Journal of Community & Applied Social Psychology* 6, no. 3 (1996):177–187.

Squires, Gregory, ed. *From Redlining to Reinvestment: Community Response to Urban Disinvestment.* Philadelphia: Temple University Press, 1992.

Staggenborg, Suzanne. "Social Movement Communities and Cycles of Protest: The Emergence and Maintenance of a Local Women's Movement." *Social Problems* 45 (May 1998):180–204.

Staples, Lee. *Roots to Power: A Manual for Grassroots Organizing.* New York: Praeger, 1984.

Steggert, Frank. *Community Action Groups and City Government.* Cambridge, MA: Ballinger, 1975.

Stern, Susan Parkison. "Conversation, Research, and Struggle Over Schooling in an African American Community." In *Community Activism and Feminist Politics: Organizing Across Race, Class, and Gender*, edited by Nancy A. Naples. New York: Routledge, 1998:107–127.

Stoecker, Randy. "Are Academics Irrelevant? Roles for Scholars in Participatory Research." *http://uac.rdp.utoledo.edu/comm-org/papers98* (1998).

Stoecker, Randy. "The CDC Model of Urban Redevelopment: A Critique and an Alternative." *Journal of Urban Affairs* 19, no. 1 (1997):1–22.

Stoecker, Randy. "Community, Movement, Organization: The Problem of Identity Convergence in Collective Action." *The Sociological Quarterly* 36 (Winter 1995):111–130.

Stoecker, Randy. *Defending Community: The Struggle for Alternative Redevelopment in Cedar Riverside.* Philadelphia: Temple University Press, 1994.

Stoecker, Randy. "Empowering Redevelopment: Toward a Different CDC." *Shelterforce*, no. 87 (May/June 1996):12–16, 27.

Stone, Clarence. *Economic Growth and Neighborhood Discontent: System Bias in the Urban Renewal Program of Atlanta.* Chapel Hill, NC: The University of North Carolina Press, 1976.

Stone, Clarence. *Regime Politics.* Lawrence, KS: University of Kansas Press, 1989.

Stone, Melissa Middleton. "Competing Contexts: The Evolution of a Nonprofit Organization's Governance System in Multiple Environments." *Administration and Society* 28 (May 1996):61–89.

Stone, Rebecca, ed. *Core Issues in Comprehensive Community-Building Initiatives.* Chicago: Chapin Hall Center for Children at the University of Chicago, 1996.

Struyk, Raymond J., Margery A. Turner, and Makiko Ueno. *Future U.S. Housing Policy: Meeting the Demographic Challenge.* Urban Institute Report 88-2. Washington, DC: The Urban Institute Press, 1988.

Suchman, Diane R., D. Scott Middleton, and Susan L. Giles. *Public/Private Housing Partnerships.* Washington, DC: Urban Land Institute, 1990.

Sullivan, Mercer L. *More Than Housing: How Community Development Corporations Go About Changing Lives and Neighborhoods.* New York: Community Development Research Center Graduate School of Management and Urban Policy New School for Social Research, 1993.

Suro, Roberto. *Strangers Among Us: How Latino Immigration is Transforming America.* New York: Alfred A. Knopf, 1998.

Susskind, Lawrence, and Jeffrey Cruikshank. *Breaking the Impasse: Consensual Approaches to Resolving Public Disputes.* New York: Basic Books, 1987.

Tarrow, Sidney. *Power in Movement: Social Movements, Collective Action and Politics.* New York: Cambridge University Press, 1994.

Task Force on Community-Based Development. *Community Based Development: Investing in Renewal.* Washington, DC: Task Force on Community-Based Development, 1987.

Taylor, Verta. "Social Movement Continuity: The Women's Movement in Abeyance." In *Social Movements: Perspectives and Issues,* edited by Steven Buechler and F. Kurt Cylke, 423–440. Toronto: Mayfield Publishing, 1997.

Teaford, Jon C. *Post-Suburbia: Government and Politics in the Edge Cities.* Baltimore: John Hopkins University Press, 1997.

Temkin, Kenneth, and William Rohe. "Social Capital and Neighborhood Stability: An Empirical Investigation." *Housing Policy Debate* 9, no. 1 (1998):61–88.

Thomas, John Clayton. *Between Citizen and City: Neighborhood Organizations and Urban Politics in Cincinnati.* Lawrence, KS: University of Kansas Press, 1986.

Tigges, Leann, M., Irene Browne, and Gary Green. "Social Isolation of the Urban Poor: Race, Class and Neighborhood Effects on Social Resources." *The Sociological Quarterly* 39, no. 1 (1998):53–77.

Tom, Allison. "Children of Our Culture? Class, Power, and Learning in a Feminist Bank." In *Feminist Organizations: Harvest of the New Women's Movement,* edited by Myra Marx Ferree and Patricia Yancey Martin, 165–179. Philadelphia: Temple University Press, 1995.

Torres, Andres. *Between Melting Pot and Mosaic: African Americans and Puerto Ricans in the New York Political Economy.* Philadelphia: Temple University Press, 1995.

Traynor, William. "Community Building: Hope and Caution." *Shelterforce,* no. 83 (September/ October 1995):12–16.

Trister, Michael B. "The Lobbying Disclosure Act of 1995." Alliance for Justice. *Alliance for Justice Web Pages, http://www.afj.org/fai/ida.html.*

Tulloss, Janice K. "Transforming Urban Regimes—a Grassroots Approach to Comprehensive Community Development: The Dudley Street Neighborhood Initiative." on-line paper from *http://com-org.utoledo.edu.* (1998).

United for a Fair Economy. *The Activist Cookbook: Creative Actions for a Fair Economy.* Boston: United for a Fair Economy, 1997.

United for a Fair Economy. "Dow Breaks 10,000 But Typical Household Wealth Down Since 1983." *http://www.stw.org/html/shifting_fortunes_ press.html,* April 1999.

U.S. Conference of Mayors. *Rebuilding America's Cities.* Cambridge, MA: Ballinger Publishing, 1986.

Van der Werf, Martin. "'Sweatshop' Protests Raise Ethical and Practical Issues." *The Chronicle of Higher Education,* March 5, 1999, A38–A39.

Van Ryzin, Gregg G. "Residents' Sense of Control and Ownership in a Mutual Housing Association." *Journal of Urban Affairs* 16, no. 3 (1994):241–253.

Verhovek, Sam Howe. "Growing Popularity of Ballot Initiatives Leads to Questions." *New York Times,* Nov. 1, 1998, A1, A20.

Vidal, Avis C., Arnold M. Howitt, and Kathleen P. Foster. *Stimulating Community Development: An Assessment of the Local Initiatives Support Corporation.* A Report Submitted to the Local Initiatives Support Corporation, June 1986. Cambridge, MA: The State, Local and Intergovernmental Center, John F. Kennedy School of Government, Harvard University, 1986.

Waldinger, Roger, and Mehdi Bozorgmehr. "The Making of a Multicultural Metropolis." In *Ethnic Los Angeles,* edited by Roger Waldinger and Mehdi Bozorgmehr. New York: Russell Sage Foundation, 1996.

Wagner, David. "Radical Movements in the Social Services: A Theoretical Perspective." *Social Service Review* 63 (June 1989):264–284.

Walsh, Edward J., Rex Warland, and D. Clayton Smith. *Don't Burn It Here: Grassroots Challenges to Trash Incinerators.* University Park, PA: University of Pennsylvania Press, 1997.

Walsh, Joan. *Stories of Renewal: Community Building and the Future of Urban America.* A Report from the Rockefeller Foundation. New York: Rockefeller Foundation, 1997.

Wandersman, Abraham. "A Framework of Participation in Community Organizations." *The Journal of Applied Behavioral Science* 17, no. 1 (1981):27–58.

Warcquant, Lois, J. D., and William Julius Wilson. "The Cost of Racial and Class Exclusion in the Inner City." *The Annals of the American Academy of Political and Social Science* 501 (January 1989):8–25.

Warren, Mark R. "Connecting People to Politics: The Role of Religious Insitutions in the Texas Industrial Areas Foundation Network." on-line paper from *http://com-org.utoledo.edu.* (1998).

Wei, William. *The Asian American Movement.* Philadelphia: Temple University Press, 1993.

Weicher, John. *Maintaining the Safety Net: Income Redistribution Programs in the Reagan Aministration.* Washington, DC: American Enterprise Institute for Public Policy Research, 1984.

Weil, Marie. "Model Development in Community Practice: An Historical Perspective." *Journal of Community Practice* 3, no. 3/4 (1996):5–68.

Wellman, Barry, and Barry Leighton. "Networks, Neighborhoods, and Communities: Approaches to the Study of the Community Question." *Urban Affairs Quarterly* 14, no. 3 (1979):363–390.

Wenocur, Stanley, and Michael Reisch. *From Charity to Enterprise: The Development of American Social Work in a Market Economy.* Urbana, IL: University of Illinois Press, 1989.

West, Guida. *The National Welfare Rights Movement: The Social Protest of Poor Women.* New York: Praeger, 1981.

West, Heather L. "Community Organizing in Ohio: A Need for Networking, Assistance, and Support." *http://uac.rdp.utoledo.edu/comm-org/paper98,* 1998.

Wetzel, Kurt W., and Daniel G. Gallagher. "A Comparative Analysis of Organizational Commitment Among Workers in the Cooperative and Private Sector." *Economic and Industrial Democracy* 11 (February 1990):93–109.

Whelan, Robert K., Alma H. Young, and Mickey Lauria. "Urban Regimes and Racial Policies in New Orleans." *Journal of Urban Affairs* 16, no. 1 (1994):1–22.

Whittier, Nancy. "Political Generations, Micro-Cohorts, and the Transformation of Social Movements." *American Sociological Review* 62 (October 1997):760–778.

Whyte, William Foote, and Kathleen King Whyte. *Making Mondragon: The Growth and Dynamics of the Worker Cooperative Complex.* Ithaca, NY: ILR Press, 1988.

Wiewel, Wim, and Pierre Clavel. "Conclusion." In *Harold Washington and the Neigbhborhoods: Progressive City Government in Chicago, 1983–1987,* edited by Pierre Clavel and Wim Wiewel, 270–293. New Brunswick, NJ: Rutgers University Press, 1991.

Wilcox, Clyde. "The Dynamics of Lobbying the Hill." In *The Interest Group Connection: Electioneering, Lobbying, and Policymaking in Washington,* edited by Paul S. Herrnson, G. Shaiko, and Clyde Wilcox, 89–99. Chatham, NJ: Chatham, 1998.

Wilson, Robert, ed. *Public Policy and Community: Activism and Governance in Texas.* Austin, TX: University of Texas Press, 1997.

Wilson, Robert H., and Susan G. Hadden. "The Changing Role of Communities in Policymaking." In *Public Policy and Community: Activism and Governance in Texas,* edited by Robert Wilson, 275–288. Austin, TX: University of Texas Press, 1997.

Wilson, William Julius. *The Truly Disadvantaged: The Inner City, the Underclass, and Public Policy.* Chicago: University of Chicago Press, 1987.

Woliver, Laura R. *From Outrage to Action: The Politics of Grass-Roots Dissent.* Urbana, IL: University of Illinois Press, 1993.

Woliver, Laura R. "Mobilizing and Sustaining Grassroots Dissent." *Social Issues* 52 (Spring 1996):139–152.

Wolman, Harold, and David Spitzley. "The Politics of Local Economic Development." *Economic Development Quarterly* 10 (May 1996):115–150.

Wong, Pat. "The Indigent Health Care Package." In *Public Policy and Community: Activism and Governance in Texas,* edited by Robert Wilson, 95–118. Austin, TX: University of Texas Press, 1997.

Wood, Richard. "Faith and Power." on-line paper from *http://comm-org.utoledo.edu,* 1998.

Wright, David J. "Comprehensive Strategies for Community Renewal." *Rockefeller Institute Bulletin* (1998):48–66.

Wright, Talmdage. *Out of Place: Homeless Mobilizations, Subcities, and Contested Landscapes.* Albany, NY: State University of New York Press, 1997.

Yeich, Susan, and Ralph Levine. "Political Efficacy: Enhancing the Construct and Its Relationship to the Mobilization of People." *Journal of Community Psychology* 22 (July 1994):259–269.

Yeoman, Barry. "Left Behind in Sandtown: The Enterprise Foundation Led a $60 Effort to Repair a Broken Baltimore Neighborhood. All It Fixed Was the Buildings." *City Limits* xxiii (January 1998):25–29.

Yukl, Gary A. *Leadership in Organizations.* Englewood Cliffs, NJ: Prentice Hall, 1989.

Zald, Mayer, and John McCarthy, eds. *The Dynamics of Social Movements: Resource Mobilization, Social Control and Tactics.* Cambridge, MA: Winthrop, 1979.

Zisk, Betty H. "Coalitions Among Peace and Environmental Groups: A Comparative Study of the Impact of Local Political Culture." Paper Presented at the Annual Meeting of the American Political Science Association. Atlanta, 1989a.

Zisk, Betty H. "Green Agenda-Setting and the Consensus Process: A Comparative Study of Local and National Green Organizing Efforts in America." Paper Presented at the Annual Meeting of the American Political Science Association. Atlanta, 1989b.

Zisk, Betty H. *The Politics of Transformation: Local Activism in the Peace and Environmental Movements.* Westport, CN: Praeger, 1992.

INDEX